W9-CUF-681

Popular Science

HOMEOWNER'S ENCYCLOPEDIA

FULLER & DEES

TIMES MIRROR

New York • Los Angeles • Montgomery

© Fuller & Dees MCMLXXIV
3734 Atlanta Highway, Montgomery, Alabama 36109

Library of Congress Cataloging in Publication Data
Main entry under title: Popular Science Homeowner's Encyclopedia

1. Dwellings — Maintenance and repair — Amateurs' manuals. 2. Repairing —
Amateurs' manuals. 3. Do-it-yourself work. I. Title: Homeowner's encyclopedia.
TH4817.3.P66   643'.7'03   74-19190
Complete Set ISBN 0-87197-070-8
Volume V ISBN 0-87197-075-9

Popular Science

HOMEOWNER'S
ENCYCLOPEDIA

Roof Types

There are a variety of roof types which can add to the decorative style or period of a building. Roofs come in basic styles plus a large number of combinations and variations. Some of the basic types of roofs are described below.

A *gable roof* is a double-sloping roof which forms a gable on each end. Since it has a simple design and is relatively low in cost, this roof is used widely for construction in residential areas. Similar to the gable roof are the *low slope* and the *saddle roofs*. A low slope roof, which is almost as popular as the gable, looks much like a gable roof except it has less pitch. A saddle roof is a small gable type roof having two gables and one ridge. Sometimes it is placed behind a chimney on a pitched roof to shed water.

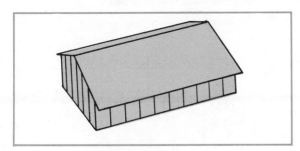

Gable Roof

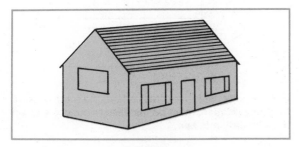

Saddle Roof

A *flat roof,* or single plane roof, is a roof which does not have a slope or pitch; it may have a slight pitch to provide for drainage. Frequently this kind of roof is used in comtemporary styled houses which have carports, patios and courts. It does not provide space for an attic.

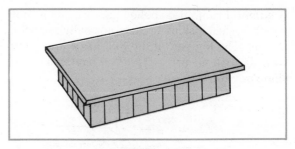

Flat Roof

A *shed roof,* another single plane roof, is also called a *lean-to roof;* it has one slope. This roof can be put above ground level rooms, garages and porches in association with multi-level buildings and is often used in contemporary designs where the ceiling and the roof framing are attached directly.

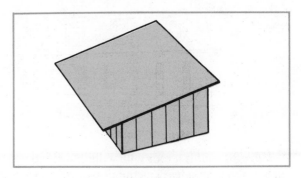

Shed Roof

A *hip roof* is a roof of four planes which rise from the sides of a building. French Provincial styled houses often have hip roofs which have a high slope. Ranch houses and contemporary houses frequently have hip roofs which have a low pitch to cover a large area of rooms. The main advantage of this roof is the protective overhang on the end and side walls.

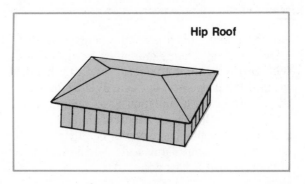

Hip Roof

A *gambrel roof,* also spelled gambriel, is a roof which has each slope broken, normally near the middle. The top part of the roof has a low pitch with the bottom part of the roof having a steep slope down to the eaves.

Gambrel Roof

Mansard Roof

A *mansard roof* is a roof with a double slope on each of the four sides. The upper part of the roof is usually flat with the lower pitch being almost vertical. The main advantage of this roof, like the gambrel roof, is the large amount of additional space for use in two-story construction and in attics. It is a French style roof. *SEE ALSO ROOF CONSTRUCTION.*

Room Additions

Adding a new room to a home is a major undertaking that most home craftsmen have to share with professional craftsmen. They can handle most of the carpentry, but usually have to leave the laying of the foundation to a concrete contractor. Furthermore electric, heating and plumbing installations should be done by licensed professionals unless the home craftsman is experienced in this area.

Most municipalities have codes that govern the building of structures, especially electric, heating and plumbing work. If a building code exists, a building permit from the town is usually needed before construction can begin. Attaching a room to an existing structure without first securing a permit may subject you to a fine.

Before beginning construction, get in touch with the building inspector to determine your legal obligations. You will probably have to submit a blueprint to show what you are proposing to do. Once you have established your legal responsibilities and have made a plan, get in touch with a reputable concrete contractor. Show him the plan and walk him around the construction site, which should be marked off with stakes.

When the foundation is poured, the contractor should install anchor bolts in the concrete that will hold the mud sill. The mud sill is the wooden base that lies on the foundation. It supports the floor and wall frames.

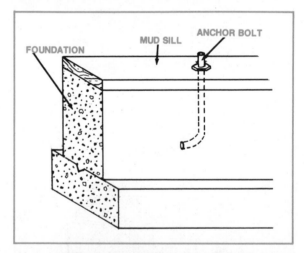

Anchor bolts, which in effect attach the room's frame to the foundation, must be installed in concrete when the foundation is laid.

Mud sill anchor bolts should be at least 8 inches long. They should extend into the concrete about $5\frac{1}{2}$ inches and above the concrete about $2\frac{1}{2}$ inches. Anchor bolts should be placed in the concrete so that when the mud sill is put into position there will be a 1 inch clearance between the mud sill and the edge of the foundation. This 1 inch is left to be filled later by the thickness of the exterior sheathing.

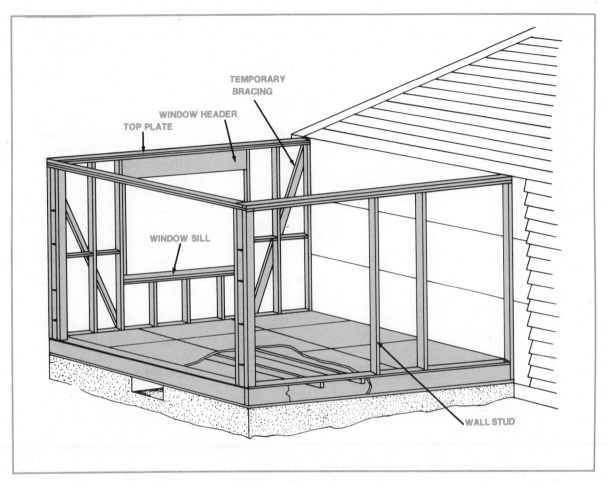

A room addition is composed of a number of individual parts. Use this drawing to become acquainted with parts. A crawlspace foundation is depicted.

The concrete contractor will excavate footing trenches if they are needed to support foundation walls of crawlspace or basement construction. The footing is an enlargement at the base of the foundation that permits even distribution of the load.

The contractor will then build the wooden form and pour the concrete. A foundation may be laid out in one of several ways. You can have a crawl space. If you do, a polyurethane membrane should be laid over the earth to prevent moisture from seeping up from the ground and damaging wooden parts of the structure.

If you install a crawl space (or full basement) beneath your new room, you will need concrete pier blocks to support girders and posts. The concrete contractor can advise you about this.

Another type of foundation is a simple concrete slab. The site of the room is excavated and concrete is poured to fill the entire area. No girders or posts are needed to support flooring. Flooring is laid right on the concrete.

Once the foundation has been laid, you can start to build the frame. This is where you as a do-it-yourself carpenter can get physically involved.

FRAMING OUT YOUR NEW ROOM

First, buy lumber for the mud sill (usually redwood or cypress). Get lengths that limit the num-

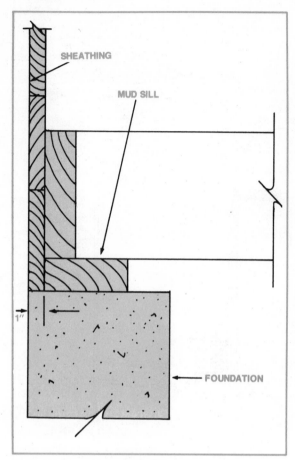

The mud sill is usually offset 1 inch to provide clearance for exterior sheathing.

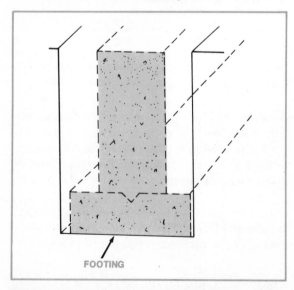

The base of a crawlspace (and basement) foundation is given a footing so the load on the foundation is distributed.

ber of joints. To install the mud sill, follow this procedure: See to it that each anchor bolt is straight (plumb). To straighten a bolt, tap it lightly with a hammer, but be careful not to bugger threads.

Lay the sill lumber right against the bolts. With a carpenter's square, mark off the center of each bolt on the face of the sill lumber. Bore holes into sill lumber where the anchor bolts will go. Holes should be in the exact center.

Place the sill on bolts and push down so bolts project through the holes. This is a fitting to allow you to make adjustments for bolt holes if necessary. Remove the sill and brush creosote on both sides. Creosote protects the lumber from termites and moisture.

Mix a cement grout consisting of equal parts of screened sand and cement. Grout should not be too thick or too thin. Hose down the top of the concrete slab with water where the sill is to be placed and spread grout along the slab. Lay in the sills. Check their level. They must be straight and true. Press down high spots.

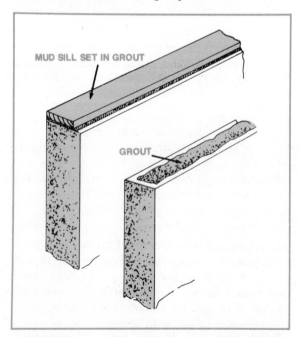

The primary purpose of setting a mud sill in grout is to allow leveling of the sill in spots where the concrete foundation is not level. Grout fills voids beneath the wood sill.

Place washers and nuts on anchor bolts; tighten them down with a wrench. Double check level, and remove excess grout that squeezes out from around sill edges with a small pointing trowel.

Join sill lumber together at corners by toenailing them securely with 8d nails (d = pennyweight).

BUILDING THE SUBFLOOR

You have two options with a concrete slab foundation. You can lay down underlayment grade hardboard on the concrete and install floor tile. Or, you can build a subfloor on which to lay a finished hardwood floor or tile.

These instructions deal with the latter, which is somewhat more complicated, but which provides more solid construction. Essentially, to construct a subfloor, you lay flooring joists across the *shortest* dimension of the room.

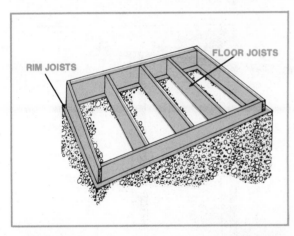

Flooring joists are laid across the shortest dimension of the foundation. Be sure joists are level and solidly installed.

Joist lumber may be 2 x 8 inch, 2 x 10 inch or 2 x 12 inch in size. The size you select depends upon the span to be crossed. Pieces that are 2 x 8 inch and 2 x 10 inch serve most installations. If the span is very wide (in excess of 20 feet), use 2 x 12 inch.

Space floor joists 16 inches apart on center — that is, 16 inches from the center of one joist to the center of the ones next to it. This spacing allows the edges of subflooring, which is nor-

mally 4 x 8 feet in size, to fall properly on joists for nailing.

Lay in a subfloor in the following manner: First cut the rim (header) joists. Rim joists go around the perimeter of the foundation to *box in* the area. Place the rim joists on mud sills. Make sure they are straight and true before toenailing them in place with 8d common nails. Space nails 24 inches apart. Drive in 16d common nails to hold joists solidly where they butt together at corners.

Next mark off the position for each floor joist. Measure carefully and cut the joist lumber so each member will fit snugly between the two facing rim joists.

Put joists in place. Be sure each is straight and level before toenailing it to the mud sill with 8d common nails. Drive 16d common nails through the joists into the end of floor joists. Floor joists must be solid.

When floor joists have been installed, check their level. Look for high and low spots. A joist that is higher than its neighbors can be brought down to level by shaving it with a wood plane. A joist that is lower than the others can be raised by nailing shim stock to the joist. (Shim stock, available in a lumber yard, are thin pieces of wood.)

Complete the subfloor by nailing panels to joists. Use exterior grade plywood, which is available in 4 x 8 foot sheets, and 8d common nails that are spaced 12 inches apart.

With the subfloor down, put in sole plates. Sole plates are pieces of 2 x 4 inch lumber nailed to the subfloor around the perimeter of the room. They are the base on which 2 x 4 inch studs that form the wall frame are nailed. Use 10d common nails to fasten sole plates to the subfloor.

Clean off all sawdust and dirt, and prepare to frame out the walls.

BUILDING THE WALL FRAME

Start by installing corner posts. Corner posts for the two corners that are up against the house can be single 2 x 4 inch pieces. Nail them to the house with 10d common nails, and toenail them to the sole plate with 10d common nails.

Corner posts for the outside corners can be made by nailing three 2 x 4 inch pieces together with 10d common nails. Set studs so flats are provided on each side of the corner. Toenail posts securely to the sole plate with 10d common nails.

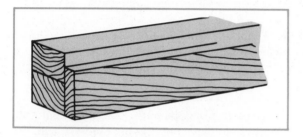

This illustration shows the way to position the three 2 x 4 inch pieces of lumber that make the corner post.

Now, install the top plate. The top plate is composed of two 2 x 4 inch pieces, nailed one on top of the other with 10d common nails to provide maximum rigidity. Nail the top plate to the corner posts.

Mark off the position of doors and windows, and install wall studs. Cut 2 x 4 inch pieces to fit snugly between the sole plate and top plate. Space studs 16 inches apart, on center, and toenail each of their four sides to the sole plate and top plate with 8d common nails. Make sure that studs are installed straight and level.

Provide the wall with maximum support by nailing permanent bracing pieces between studs. These are lengths of 2 x 4 inch lumber installed horizontally between the vertical studs. You can add one, two or even three — whatever it takes to hold the studs solid.

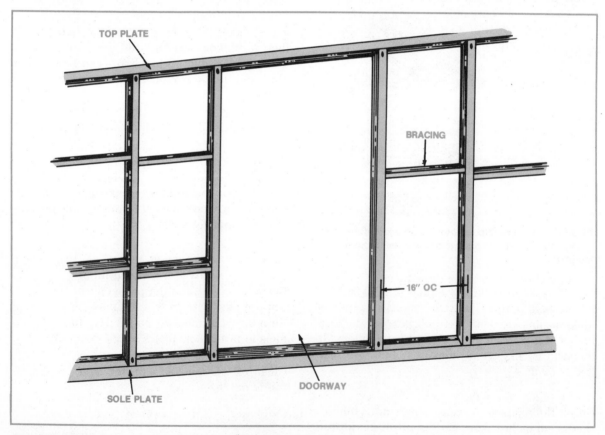

This illustration shows the frame of a wall. Before the door is completed, the sole plate in the doorway has to be cut away.

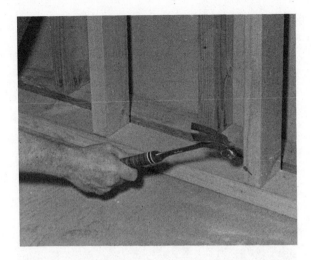

Studs are toenailed to the sole plate and top plate on all four sides, if possible. Make sure studs are straight and nailed tightly in place.

In addition, install temporary bracing pieces diagonally across wide expanses. These will be knocked out when you nail up exterior sheathing, but for the time being they keep the frame from being knocked out of kilter.

With studs up, frame out doorways. Measure the width of the entrance and cut out the sole plate. Measure the height of the door you are going to use (usually 6 feet 8 inches or 7 feet). Add 1 inch for the height needed for the frame and 1 inch if you are installing a threshold.

Cut two studs to this dimension and nail them to the studs framing the doorway. Cut a stud to fit across the frame and nail it to the top of the two short studs. This is the header. Measure the space between the header and top plate, and cut another short stud. Nail this in place. It is called the cripple. Other doorways and window frames are formed in the same way. This completes the wall frame.

ADDING THE ROOF

The roof discussed here is the gable roof, which is the simplest one to install. First, mathematically calculate the layout of the roof. Such things as pitch and overhang have to be carefully considered.

Once you have made the plan for the roof, the first thing to do is nail ceiling joists from one top plate to another across the shortest span of the room. This is similar to the way in which you installed floor joists. Ceiling joists are usually 2 x 6 inch pieces of lumber. They are spaced 16 inches on center and are nailed down with 10d common nails.

With joists in place, raise roof rafters. This is done by selecting two rafters for one of the peaks (end) and nailing them to one end of a ridge board that runs the length of the roof. Have an assistant hold the ridge board level at the other end as you nail the rafters securely to the top plate. Use 10d nails.

Now, nail rafters to the ridge board and top plate at the other peak. This procedure is followed by nailing intermediate rafters into place between peaks. As with floor joists, roof rafters are placed 16 inches apart on center.

With the roof frame installed and securely braced, sheathing panels are nailed to the rafters with 10d roofing nails. Sheathing panels are to a roof what subflooring is to a floor. Sheathing panels for the roof may be 4 x 8 foot panels of exterior plywood.

Sheathing panels are then covered with roofing paper, which is a specially treated material that prevents water from penetrating through to the wood sheathing. Overlap roofing paper so no joints through which water can seep are formed. Roofing shingles are installed over the roofing paper.

The exterior walls of your additional room are completed in much the same manner as the roof.

Sheathing panels are nailed to studs. A building paper is tacked to sheathing, and then siding is installed. Choices include clapboard, board-and-batten, cedar shakes, redwood siding, aluminum siding, PVC siding and masonry.

Next, move inside. Position and install electric fixtures, heating and air conditioning ducts and plumbing. Call in contractors to perform that work which is foreign to you.

FINISHING THE INTERIOR

Wallboard panels come in ³/₈ inch thicknesses, and in 4 x 8 foot, 4 x 10 foot, 4 x 12 foot and 4 x 14 foot sizes. Order the largest size paneling you can use. Larger panels cover larger areas, thus requiring less total effort on your part and reducing the number of joints that have to be taped and cemented.

For instance, if your new room is 21 feet long, plan on using 4 x 14 foot panels and 4 x 8 foot panels to cover the 21 feet long walls. You will, of course, have to trim 1 foot from a panel. This is assuming you will install panels horizontally, which you should do.

As for thickness, the ¹/₂ inch panel has greater strength to resist knocks and bumps. It is worth the small extra cost.

Before installing wallboard, place a good quality insulation between wall and ceiling studs. Now, close up the room. First nail wallboard panels to ceiling studs. You should always start at the top and work down.

Set several planks on horses or some other type of support so your head just touches the ceiling when you stand on the planks. The idea is to brace the wallboard panel against the ceiling with your head as you nail it to the joists. You will need an assistant working on the other end.

As you hammer wallboard nails into the ceiling, use a backhand motion and hit the head of the nail with the crown of the hammer. Use a hammer designed for installing drywall.

There are two ways to install panels to wall studs. You can nail them in place, or you can use nails and drywall adhesive. The latter method is preferred. It cuts down on the amount of nailing that is required.

Lay a bead of wallboard adhesive down each stud. Nails are used around edges.

Start by applying adhesive to the studs. Before you install the panel, drive drywall nails part way into the top edge of the panel. Remember that studs are 16 inches apart, on center, so nails will have to be spaced to hit studs.

Lift the panel into place (if it is the top panel, butt it right against the ceiling) and drive the nails home. Press the panel firmly against the studs as you do. Finish nailing by driving nails along the bottom border and along the left and right edge.

Panels may be installed vertically or horizontally — that is, with the length going across the room or up and down. Installing panels horizontally cuts down on work and joints.

Use your head when installing ceiling panels. The panel is head-braced by two people as it is nailed in place. Ceiling studs should not be attached with adhesive. Use nails only.

Drive nails into plate. The combination of adhesive and nails will hold wall panels firmly in place.

The professional way of making a window or door cutout is to nail the panel right over the opening and cut it with a saw using the window or door frame as a guide.

When you come to doors and windows, do not take time to cut the panel before installing it. Apply the panel right over the opening. Then make cutouts with a saw, using the door or window frame as a guide.

When you panel a wall on which there is electric fixtures, or heating or air conditioning ducts, place the panel against the wall in the exact position it will be installed and press it firmly against the object. Pressure will dent the panel, outlining it. When the panel is nailed in place, all you have to do is knock a hole in the panel where the dent is. Insert a keyhole saw and make the cutout.

When all panels have been put up, nail corner bead to outside corners. These metal strips protect the edges against chipping.

The final stage of installing wall paneling is to tape and cement joints and fill nailheads. Buy ready-mix joint cement. Using a broad knife, cement joints formed by panels butting together. Overlap the edges of the joint with cement about 3 inches.

This creates a bed for perforated wallboard tape. Cover the joint with the tape, pressing it down into the joint cement with a broad knife. Excess joint cement will seep through the holes in the tape. Remove excess, but leave a thin, even coat over the tape. Allow the cement to dry.

Then apply a second, third and fourth layer of cement, overlapping each previous layer and allowing each layer to dry thoroughly before applying the next. Furthermore, sand each dry layer lightly until it is smooth before applying the next.

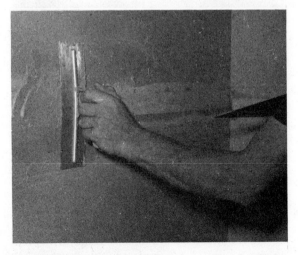

Succeeding layers of cement are applied until the joint disappears.

Nailheads are covered with joint cement in a similar manner; that is, fill the dimpled area made by your hammer with cement, let dry, sand and fill again. Apply three layers.

Corner bead is covered with a heavy topping of cement. Non-perforated drywall tape is then creased in half and laid over the corner bead. Another layer of compound is applied, covering the tape. This is allowed to dry before it is sanded smooth.

Cover nailheads by applying cement to the dimpled area around the nail that should have been left when nails were driven home.

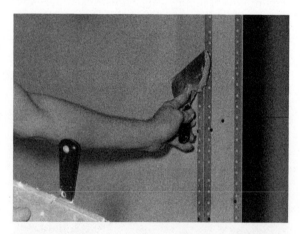

Cover corner beads with cement and nonperforated wallboard tape.

Cut 1 x 4 inch clear pine for the jamb. Nail it loosely to the side studs and lintel with 10d finishing nails. Check the level of the jamb on all sides. If necessary, insert thin shims of wood be-

tween jamb pieces and studs to level the jamb. If you want a threshold, nail it into place. Set nails on both shoulders of the threshold piece — never in the center. You may split the lumber. Place the door in the jamb for a fitting. There should be no more than $1/8$ inch clearance between the jamb and door. If you have to narrow the gap, insert shim stock behind the jamb piece on the latch side. Nail all jamb pieces securely in place.

Nail casing pieces (trim) around the frame. You should now hang the door. Position the top hinge on the jamb seven inches down from the top of the frame. Outline the hinge leaf on the jamb. See to it that the leaf edge falls on the edge of the jamb so the leaf slots for the hinge pin extend beyond the edge.

Cut the mortise into the jamb for the jamb hinge pin. Use a very sharp chisel. (*Important*: all mortises, whether on the jamb or on the door, should be cut to a depth that is equal to the thickness of the hinge leaf.)

Screw the hinge leaf to the jamb and line the door up in the frame to mark off the location of the corresponding hinge leaf on the door. Cut the mortise in the door and screw the door top hinge into place.

Attach the door to the jamb by means of the top hinge. Set the door so the gap between it and the jamb is equal all around. Now, mark off the location of the bottom hinge on both the door and jamb. Place the bottom of the lowest hinge 11 inches above the floor. Remove the door. Cut mortises for the bottom hinge, screw the hinge into place and hang the door. Set the door squarely in the frame and mark off the position for the door stop. Nail door stop pieces to the jamb. Install the door lock set, following the instructions and using the template provided with the lock set.

The last part of the operation in finishing off your new room is to lay the floor, whether it is tile or hardwood. Then, paint the room or cover walls with a wall covering. Your new room is ready for use.

Room Dividers

Room dividers are designed to separate rooms or different areas of one room. Room dividers may be constructed of many different materials including fabric, wood, fiberglass and pegboard and may be built in the form of a bookcase, storage unit, display area, screen, panel or a combination of any of these ideas. Before buying or building a divider, consider how much of the area is to be screened, how large the divider should be in proportion with the rest of the room, if the divider is to also serve the purpose of a storage unit or bookcase, if lighting will need to be added where the divider will block present light, how much weight the post and beam construction can carry, if the divider is to be mobile and if the divider design will blend with that of the room or rooms.

FOLDING PANELS & SCREENS

Folding panels and screens are probably the simplest and most conventional method of dividing rooms. Screens and panels need little floor space and allow both light and air to penetrate through the screened off area. Folding panels add to a room's versatility and are easily installed. Screens can be one or more panels of matching or different heights hinged together and covered with painted canvas or other fabrics, wall hangings, rice paper or have strands of beads tightly strung inside the frame between the top and bottom rails. Screens may also be carved wood or cork board with rocks glued on each surface. Screens may rest on legs or sit exclusively on the bottom rails. Panels are basically the same as screens except that they generally run from the floor to the ceiling. A folding or accordion door is another form of panel divider. These doors are available in wood, fabric or synthetic panels that run on a track attached to a threshold or wooden strip placed along the ceiling.

BOOKCASE & STORAGE UNIT DIVIDERS

The most practical form of room divider is one that can act as a storage unit, bookcase, display area or all three. These dividers can complement a room if the right materials and design are chosen. Brick, wood, fiberglass and other artificial building products may be combined to create a unit that is both useful and decorative. Modules of different sizes may be left open or equipped with doors for storing linens, records, toys and other items. Open modules are a showcase for antiques, floral arrangements and plants, ceramics and crafts.

In building a bookcase or storage unit divider, it is important to have sufficient support under the shelves to prevent sagging or breaking. This may be achieved by keeping the modules relatively short or by placing supports under long shelves. On those dividers which will house only books or heavy objects such as a stereo or television, use extra sturdy material or have additional braces installed to hold the shelves.

PEGBOARD DIVIDERS

Pegboard is perforated sheets of masonite or hardboard into which hooks may be inserted. Because of its coarse texture and unfinished appearance, pegboard is better used in areas like the kitchen, utility room, children's bedroom or playroom or in a workshop. With proper reinforcement, pegboard can hold over five pounds on one hook. This makes it helpful for hanging pots, pans, tools, toys and other small items. In a student's room, pegboard can be used similarly to the idea previously mentioned for closet, drawer and bookcase fronts.

SPINDLE DIVIDERS

Large spindles extending from floor to ceiling are more decorative than useful in dividing rooms. Unfinished wood spindles in different lengths and patterns can be purchased from many building suppliers and either stained or painted to match room decors. Spindles of the same length or two or three lengths may be set in a pattern to form a unique design across the room.

Room Wiring
[SEE ELECTRICAL WIRING.]

Ropes & Knots

Most rope is made from strong jute fibers twined together for strength. However, other materials have been used for ropemaking to give it strength and flexibility. Some of these materials are nylon thread, spun steel for reinforcement cable, fiberglass and plastic. The type of rope selected will depend on the job it has to do.

The traditional way to fasten rope is to knot it. There are several useful knots that adapt well to anything. A good knot holds fast under stress and unties without much difficulty.

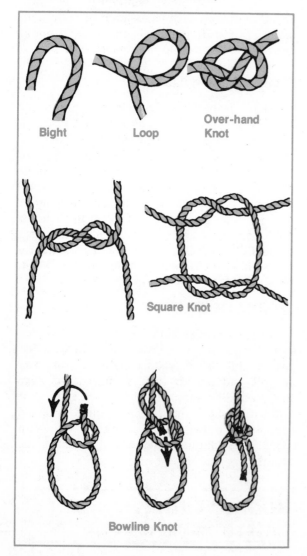

Bight   Loop   Over-hand Knot

Square Knot

Bowline Knot

Two Half Hitches

To tie knots, three main combinations are used: loops, bights, and overhand knots. *Loops* are made by crossing one section of the same rope over another section. A *bight* is a U-shaped rope that has both ends pointing in the same direction and running parallel to each other. An *overhand knot* is made by pushing one end of the rope through a loop. If these three methods are learned, then it is easy to put all the combinations together.

Rotary Cut

The rotary cut is a method of slicing a veneer off a log in a continuous sheet. The log is steamed to make it soft and pliable and then mounted on a lathe which rotates it toward a knife. The knife peels off a sheet of veneer and after each full turn the knife is automatically moved closer to the center of the log so that the peeling is continuous.

Rotary cutting produces large veneers and reveals the beauty of inexpensive as well as expensive wood. It is also the basis of the plywood industry, since plywood is made of glued sheets of veneer.

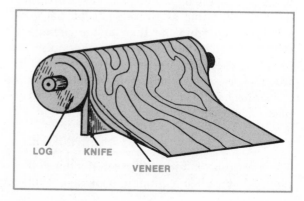

LOG   KNIFE   VENEER

Rotary Lawnmower
[SEE LAWNMOWERS.]

Rotor

Rotors convert the potential of electrical energy into usable mechanical energy. The armature is made to turn by the attraction-repulsion principles of an electromagnetic field. The rotor is attached to the armature in such a way as to force them to rotate simultaneously with each other. *SEE ALSO ELECTRIC MOTORS.*

Rottenstone

Rottenstone is an abrasive powder, made of decomposed siliceous limestone, used in producing hand-rubbed, high gloss finishes on wood. Rottenstone is finer than pumice and is usually used after it to achieve a higher gloss. *SEE ALSO ABRASIVES.*

Rough Floor

The rough floor, or subfloor, consists of the boards or panels laid over the floor joists and sills or the concrete foundation. The finish floor is laid over the rough floor. *SEE ALSO FLOOR CONSTRUCTION.*

Roughing-In

Roughing-in is the installation of all pipes in the drainage system, all water pipes to places where they connect with fixtures and also the installation of fixture supports and vents. Roughing-in also applies to electrical wiring which is partially completed and other mechanical aspects of the building structure.

Rough Lumber

Rough lumber is lumber as it comes from the saw. It has been cut to rough size but has not been planed or dressed. *SEE ALSO LUMBER.*

Rough Measuring

Rough measuring is the use of your hands, feet and arms for judging widths and lengths. The average breadth of a man's hand is three inches and the breadth of the hand with the thumb extended is seven inches. The span of the hand can be used to determine the width of a board. Outstretched arms are a ready means of measuring length. If a natural stride is adjusted, a person can pace off distances of two- and three-foot intervals with good accuracy. Of course, if any of these forms of rough measuring are not in even feet and inches, the measurements are less precise. *SEE ALSO HAND TOOLS.*

Rough Opening

A rough opening, R.O., is an opening left in the house framing for window and door frames, stairs, chimneys and other passages. Provisions for rough openings are usually made in the architectural plans, and the size of the openings are calculated from the size of the window or door to be placed in the opening. *SEE ALSO WALL & CEILING CONSTRUCTION.*

Rough Plane

A rough plane is used when more than $1/4''$ of waste is to be removed from a board. Also referred to as a scrub plane, its rounded cutting edge removes heavy stock fast. Prior to doing a finish job with either the jack or smoothing plane, the rough plane cleans up rough, dirty timber and trues up large pieces of wood to approximate size. Two sizes of this type plane are available, 9½ and 10½ inches long. *SEE ALSO HAND TOOLS.*

Round File

Round files, also called rattail files, are tapered at one end to a blunt tip. Because they are completely round, these files are used by metal and woodworkers to shape and smooth small, round recesses and for enlarging holes. *SEE ALSO HAND TOOLS.*

Round File

Round-Nose Chisel

The round-nose chisel is one of the four kinds of cold chisels and is characterized by the shape of its point. It is used to cut through shaped grooves, chip rounded corners, scrape cuts and move drill holes that were improperly started. A ball peen hammer should be used to drive this chisel. Goggles should always be worn when doing this type of work. *SEE ALSO HAND TOOLS.*

Router
[SEE PORTABLE POWER TOOLS.]

R.P.M.

R.P.M. is the abbreviation for revolutions per minute and refers to the number of times per minute an object, such as an armature, crank shaft or propeller, rotates.

Rubbed Finish

A rubbed finish on wood provides smoothness and a dulled lustre to a naturally glossy varnish, lacquer or enamel surface by means of abrasion. The finished surface is carefully rubbed or ground down with pumice, rottenstone, or a very fine grade of sandpaper or steel wool. The grade of the abrasive paper used will determine the degree of dullness produced. The sandpaper should be wrapped around a small wood block for best results, and only light pressure should be applied. Steel wool may be rubbed over the surface as forcefully as desired. The abrasive should be stroked with the grain of the wood. The final step in this polished finish is a good waxing, to wet the powdery surface. The waxed surface should be buffed after it has dried. *SEE ALSO WOOD FINISHING.*

Rubber Base Adhesive
[SEE ADHESIVES.]

Rubber Base Paints

Rubber-base paints are coatings that have synthetic rubber solids added. Rubber-base paints are resistant to alkali, abrasion, wear, moisture and oil. They can be used on concrete floors of cellars and garages, asbestos cement siding and shingles, swimming pools, patios, steps, walks and porch floors whether the surface is old or new. *SEE ALSO PAINTS & PAINTING.*

Rubber Tape

Rubber tape, often used in wet areas, makes a seal impenetrable by water when it is wrapped around a wire splice so that the sides overlap. This type of insulation is necessary, especially for homes built in wet climates; however, the home craftsman in a dry climate will find it almost essential for basement wiring. *SEE ALSO ELECTRICIAN'S TOOLS & EQUIPMENT.*

Rubbing Varnish

Rubbing varnish is a type of varnish used on wood to achieve what is called a piano finish. Alkyd or urethane varnishes are particularly good for rubbing. Rubbing varnishes are applied and sanded with a sanding block several times. After the varnish has been rubbed down several times, oil and pumice are spread over the surface to complete the finishing process. This effort will produce a luxuriously rich finish such as on a piano. *SEE ALSO WOOD FINISHING.*

Rubblestone

Rubblestone, or rubble, is rough, irregular stone as it comes from the field or quarry. Rubblestones are used in masonry construction, called rubblework, for walls or fireplaces. *SEE ALSO BRICK & STONEWORK.*

Run

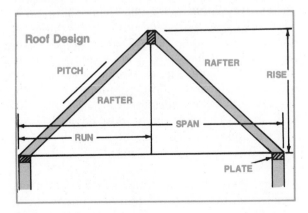

In roofing layout terms, a run is the horizontal distance from the ridge's center, where sloped surfaces of the roof meet, to the outside of the plate, or horizontal girder that supports the rafter. In an equally pitched roof, this is half the span. *SEE ALSO ROOF CONSTRUCTION.*

Runner

A runner is a grooved or concave wooden strip attached to the side or bottom of a drawer which fits on the guide bar. The runner and guide bar support the drawer and permit a smooth sliding action when the drawer is moved. The runner and guide bar principle is also used on sliding doors.

Running Bond

Running bond is the simplest pattern of brick bonding. All bricks are laid as stretchers (bricks laid end to end) except corners and ends. The corners are headers, bricks laid crosswise, and ends are half- and three quarter-bats, portions of

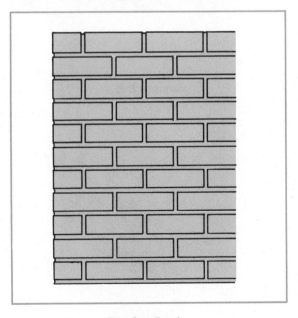

Running Bond

a brick. A stopped end uses a $1/2$ bat whereas, a junction wall (a wall joining another wall at a right angle) uses a $3/4$ bat at the junction. A running bond is strong longitudinally but is very weak transversely. *SEE ALSO BRICK & STONEWORK.*

Corner

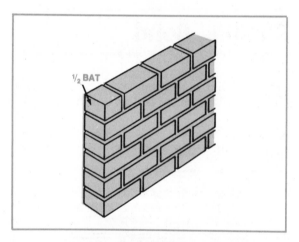

Stopped End

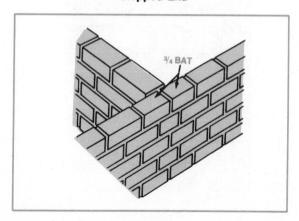

Junction Wall

Running Foot

Running foot is a term used to denote continuous length.

Rust & Corrosion

Rust and corrosion is a gradual wearing away of a metallic surface by a chemical action. Rust is an oxidizing process producing a brittle reddish-brown deposit. Corrosion, whether it is rust, a white powder, green discoloration or some other chemical substance, is the wearing away of a metal surface. Rust and corrosion form when moisture and oxygen are present.

A car's cooling system should be protected from rust. Each year the system should be drained, flushed and refilled with antifreeze or a coolant.

In the workshop, humidity and condensation can be real problems. If the conditions are severe enough, installation of a dehumidifying unit may help in rust control and also eliminate the need of a cooling unit in the workshop during muggy summer months. In especially humid weather, some type of dust cover should be placed over power tools. Silica gel bags can be placed in drawers, cabinets and other confined areas to absorb moisture. A low watt bulb left burning in a small area will help keep moisture down.

Silocone sprays and penetrating oils replace moisture and prevent rusting. Metal objects such as tables can be coated with paste wax or paraffin. Tools that are more likely to rust such as planes and handsaws can be wiped with a lightly oiled cloth. The chrome on a car can be protected with an application of linseed oil with a soft rag to a clean surface. The strip along and behind the chrome can be cleaned and filled with a liquid wax to prevent rust and the accumulation of foreign materials.

Before any painting of a new or rusted surface begins, all the corrosion must be removed. A

wire brush, scraper, sanding disc or metal file can be used to remove the major portions to achieve a smooth, uniformly rusted surface. Any grease or oil should be washed away with a strong detergent. The surface should be dry, smooth and free of grease and oil. It is the trappings of oxygen and moisture that causes corrosion.

A rust penetrating protective coating is compounded to eat through the rust and displace any oxygen and moisture until it reaches the metal. A primer forms a corrosion resistant, tightly adhering film on galvanized surfaces, copper, aluminum, unrusted steel and other metals. A primer should be covered with a finishing coat for maximum service.

There are various methods of preventing rust and corrosion. Fuel-oil tanks should be painted with a rust-resistant paint. And, roof gutters need a coat of anti-rust primer. Free of rust, steel and iron objects should be primed with a red-lead paint or a new latex metal primer that allows the application of a top coat in thirty minutes. ,

Galvanized iron as found in gutter and down spouts can take a latex paint without a primer. If the object is new, remove the oil left by the manufacturer's processing method and check to see if the manufacturer suggests a primer.

Rusted galvanized iron is, in reality, no longer galvanized and is to be treated as steel. After brushing away the rust, apply two coats of a fast-drying latex primer and a top coat.

Although aluminum does not rust, corrosion is found in the form of a white powder substance. A latex can be applied and some manufacturers recommend a zinc-chloride primer.

Copper turns green when it corrodes. After it is sandpapered, a fast-drying latex primer must be applied.

Whenever a rust-preventing primer is applied, do not brush it too thin. Use at least two coats for good protection and apply a finishing coat quickly for best rust and corrosion protection.

Sabre Saw

Small and easy to handle, the sabre saw is actually a variety of cutting tools in one when used with the proper blades. It will crosscut a 2 x 4 rafter or even a 4 x 4 using a 6'' blade. It will cut curves or scroll work in plywood, metal, composition or plastic panels. Because of its compact size and light weight, it can easily be used for cutouts in finished walls or ceilings for electrical outlets or fixtures or openings for pipes and basins in bathrooms or kitchen tops.

To select the proper sabre saw, first determine its probable use. The higher horsepower units should be chosen for heavy-duty or continuous use. Other options to consider are two speed switches, variable speed switches and tilting shoe models.

Tilting shoe models produce straight or curved bevel cuts with accuracy, and allow compound miter cuts which are often impossible to match with hand saws. Speed control switches allow the user to select the speed to suit the job and the material. This affords the greatest cutting efficiency and prolongs saw-blade life. Two-speed saws let you choose low or high speeds. Variable speed sabre saws let you vary the speed from zero to top cutting speed or preset the switch at any speed selected. The variable speed sabre saw, in addition to letting you select the proper speed for each job, also has the advantage of letting you slow the saw down on tight corners and then speed up on straight cuts. The speed can be adjusted while cutting. High speeds are used for cutting wood and compositions, low speeds for metal and plastics. Thus, the harder the material the slower the speed used.

Speed control switches can be the slide type, normally located on top of the handle; or the trigger type located under the handle. The farther forward you push the slide switch, the faster the speed; with the trigger switch, the farther back you pull it, the faster the speed.

Locking buttons permit you to lock the trigger at full, low, or intermediate speeds, depending upon the model sabre saw you select. This eliminates having to hold the trigger while cutting. *SEE ALSO PORTABLE POWER TOOLS.*

Saddle

Saddle, or threshold, is the raised board that fits under a door between the jambs. Saddle also refers to a curved fitting between the chimney and roof to support flashing or deflect water and debris. *SEE ALSO MOLDING & TRIM; ROOF CONSTRUCTION.*

Safes

Although expensive jewelry, documents and other valuables may be insured, some are irreplaceable at any price. For this reason, a concealed, lockable fire resistant safe or vault is a

The most common type of fire-resistive, combination-lock wall vault looks like this. A closet vault is similar in appearance but lacks the rim at the front that would prevent it from sitting properly on a shelf; and in place of the twin flanges at front has one at rear top.

logical part of any home. A safe is thought of as a freestanding box; one that is big and heavy enough to baffle a pair of determined burglars is probably too big and unwieldy (and expensive) for use in most homes. Vaults are considered more practical. A vault goes in a wall, or occasionally a floor, and derives its security in part from being firmly attached and perhaps well-concealed.

Vaults for home use come in three principal types. Easiest to install, but obviously less effective, are *stud-wall strong boxes*. These are ones so shallow they fit within a wall 3¹/₂ inches thick, are lockable with a key, will hold a modest collection of papers and small valuables and obviously can offer no more fire protection than any other single-layer steel box. The other two types are called *closet vaults* and *wall vaults*. Both have heavy walls and fire ratings, are likely to be about a one foot cube in outside size, weigh about 50 to 80 pounds and cost roughly $1.50 a pound. They differ mainly in that the closet vault has a flange at the back that enables you to fasten it to the wall while it sits on the floor or, more conveniently, a closet shelf. The wall vault has two flanges (one on each side) at the front, making it easy for you to attach it to wall framing. To find space for it, you will ordinarily need a wall that has a closet or cupboard behind it or perhaps surrounds a fireplace chimney.

Flanges are drilled for screws on 16″ centers. Fasten securely into the joists with screws and grout into place.

When installed, entire unit including combination lock is flush with wall and may be concealed by picture or mirror.

Making opening between joists large enough to insert unit.

There are several reasons for owning a home vault. If fire struck your home today or tonight are your irreplaceable documents protected from fire loss? This vault will provide security and convenience for these documents. The contents are always available. You are not regulated by banking hours and trips back and forth to the bank are unnecessary. There is no legal red tape in the event of death. Your initial cost is the only cost. It is like insurance but you pay the premium only once.

Records that need protection include insurance policies, bills of sale, bonds, notes, deeds, contracts, birth certificates, discharge papers, certificates and mementos.

All metal boxes or asbestos lined boxes with locks are not fire-resistive. Fire-resistive boxes or containers must have insulated walls and doors. Steel boxes offer less than 3 minutes protection. An asbestos lined box will protect its contents for approximately 5 to 10 minutes. A metal door, drawer or box may stop the flames of a fire, but the heat that does the damage goes right through. Paper chars at about 350° F. even though untouched by flame. To keep papers and documents safe in the event of a fire it is best to purchase a safe or vault that has been tested to withstand high temperatures. Many units today are constructed to withstand temperatures up to 1700° F. for one hour with ample protection for the contents (the interior temperature is kept below 350° F).

A professional burglar given the time and tools can open any safe. To protect yourself from the amateur burglar select a vault that is equipped with a paracentric key lock, or if you prefer, a three-tumbler combination lock.

Safety

Safety is a matter of planning and vigilance, planning to eliminate hazards and vigilance against carelessness. This is especially true of safety procedures for the home craftsman. Planning to eliminate hazards requires first planning a project to know what is to be done, what special clothing or protective equipment is needed, what tools and materials are needed and how to use them safely.

Most accidents are caused by carelessness, due to either ignorance and fatigue. The two funda-

mental rules for the home craftsman should be these: (1) know what you are doing and (2) quit before you become tired.

SPOT THE HAZARDS

Learn what can cause accidents in connection with home projects. Falls are the most common cause of home inury, and the handyman is a prime target for a fall. Ladders, tools and supplies, all necessary to the job, can be hazards to both footing and balance.

Using Ladders

Some simple precautions will protect against falls from ladders. Before using any ladder, check it for defects. Make sure all of the rungs and the side rails are sound.

Brace the top of a ladder if necessary. If a window is in the way, bore holes near the top of the side rails just large enough to hold a rung-sized dowel or pipe that will span the window. To brace a ladder against a corner of a tree, use the same holes to hold a hose-covered chain.

When putting up a ladder, place it on firm ground. Make sure the feet will not slide or sink in. Use rubber caps on the feet; place them on planks to ensure a firm footing. Make sure that the hinge of a stepladder is locked or braced before climbing. Do not set a straight ladder too close to a wall. The base of the ladder should be one foot from the wall for every four feet of its length. When climbing up or coming down a ladder, always face it and take one step at a time. Always make sure that shoe soles are clean before starting to climb. Do not carry anything that will prevent the using of both hands in climbing. For example, wear a tool belt to carry hand tools, carry paint buckets over an arm and use a rope to raise awkward objects after climbing.

If a project will require extensive work from a ladder, arrange to use a scaffold instead of just a ladder. Standing on a ladder is extremely tiring. A satisfactory low scaffold can be made by suspending a straight ladder between two stepladders and laying a plank over the rungs. Keep tools, equipment and supplies at the ends of the scaffold to avoid tripping or falling over them.

Keeping the Floor Clear

Wood chips, nails, small and large tools, spilled liquids, sawdust on smooth floors and any number of objects and substances can unbalance the home craftsman. Electrical cords, hoses, wires and pieces of lumber can easily trip him as he moves around the work site. A fall becomes a double threat when someone is holding tools or other objects.

Handling Tools

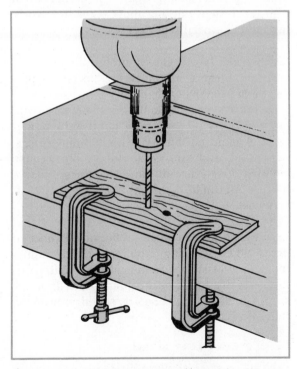

Clamp down thin pieces of metal when you are drilling them. The drill bit can bind and spin the piece just before finishing the cut.

Edged or pointed tools are particularly dangerous, and power tools, even though they may have guards and safety switches, demand special attention. Inspect all tools before use to be sure that they are in good condition. Never work by bringing edged or pointed tools toward one's hands or body. Carry them with edges and points down or away from the body. Don't try to carry too many tools at once, and keep sharp tools out of pockets.

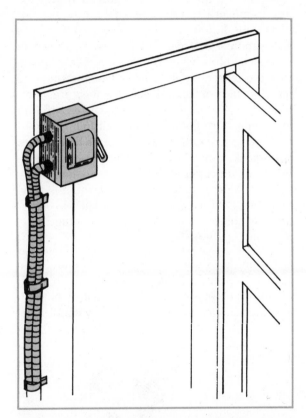

The best protection against unauthorized use of power tools is a separate circuit that allows you to shut off power to the workshop. Place the switch high up, near the door to keep it out of the reach of children.

Using Flame and Heat

In working with torches and heating elements, such as those in electrical paint burners, be aware of the possibility of igniting combustible materials.

Keep the work area clear of litter and flammable substances. Sawdust and paint-soaked or solvent-soaked rags are great fire hazards. Dry paint also ignites fairly easily, so do not work with a welding torch or soldering iron near painted surfaces. If flame or heat is used to remove old paint, work on a small area at a time. If the paint ignites, smother the flame immediately with a damp towel.

Using Flammable and Dangerous Liquids

The basic rule for using any finishes, solvents or fuels is *Read the label thoroughly.* Virtually every home craftsman will use flammable or dangerous liquids in some projects. The fumes and vapors from many of the solvents used in oil-based paints, wood finishes and related products are extremely dangerous because they are harmful to breathe and because they are flammable. Use such products in well-ventilated areas and store them only in their tightly-closed original containers, if you must store them. Store paint-soaked and solvent-soaked rags in airtight metal containers after they have been thoroughly dried outside. If they cannot be stored this way, then burn the rags. They are subject to spontaneous combustion if stored in any other way, and they ignite easily.

Gasoline, kerosene and other fuels should be stored — if they *must* be stored — only in small quantities and only in approved, clearly marked, airtight metal containers. Under any conditions,

Gasoline can be ignited even by the static electricity created by pouring it from one metal container to another. To prevent spark ignition, you can bond the two containers by keeping them in contact through a metal spout or funnel or by connecting them with wire.

it is never entirely safe to store and use gasoline in the house.

Acids, alkalies, and other chemicals should also be used according to package directions and stored safely.

PROTECT YOURSELF

Safe work procedures are a major part of the battle against hazard and injury, but working in safety often means that the home craftsman must take additional precautions, such as wearing special clothing or protective masks.

With Clothing

Almost any protective devices needed by a home craftsman are on the market because skilled professional craftsmen need them. Hard hats and hard-toed shoes are obvious examples of protective equipment, but few home craftsmen would consider these worthwhile investments for only occasional use. However, when working on a cooperative project such as garage construction, a person should wear a hard hat when someone else is working above — or stop working until overhead work ceases.

Lightweight fabric gloves protect hands from splinters, blisters, and heat. Rubber gloves protect them from many chemicals. However, never wear gloves around tools or machinery with moving parts — including hand-held power tools. Around machinery, always remove rings, bracelets, and similar jewelry. Ties, loose clothing, long hair and long sleeves are also a hazard. All can be caught by a moving belt, shaft or wheel.

It is a good idea to wear rubber-soled shoes or boots when working around electrical equipment, or at least be certain to stand on a dry surface — a dry board or a rubber mat will do. Be sure, too, that electrical cords stay dry. Suspend them if necessary.

With Proper Equipment

Modern power tools are usually adequately grounded, but the grounding can be undone by some very common mistakes. If a tool has a metal case, it will be ground wired, but it will not be grounded in use if plugged into an outlet that does not have grounding connection. The grounding can be undone even when using the proper outlet by wearing a metal ring on the hand holding the tool or holding the tool in one hand. The body becomes the path for the ground current rather than the ground wire. A rule that many electricians heed is to keep one hand in a pocket when working around "live" equipment.

With Proper Lifting and Carrying Techniques

Back injuries are common among home craftsmen. A bit of study will often tell when help is needed to lift a very heavy object. If an object must be lifted alone, do not "put your back into it." Lift with the legs and arms. First check the path to follow in moving the object. Clear the floor and make sure the object will be able to pass through the doorways and narrow spots. When ready to lift, squat close to the load with one foot beside it and one foot behind it. Grasp it with both palms *and* fingers, keeping both arms close to the body. Lift by straightening both legs. If the object is large enough to keep the body weight from being centered over the feet, then certainly help is needed.

To set a load down, reverse the lifting procedure. Let one side of the load touch down first so that hands are not trapped underneath. If positions or grips have to be shifted, set the burden down or rest it on a sturdy support. *SEE ALSO HOME SAFETY; WORKSHOP SAFETY.*

Sailboat, Family

One of a series of 12 to 21 foot trailerable sailboats can provide both boatbuilding and sailing experience for the entire family. Designed by Richard Hartley, the Trailer Sailer Family Sailboat can be built by even the inexperienced home craftsman.

For the average family, the 16 foot Trailer Sailer Family Sailboat offers space to take groups sail-

ing during the day, yet provides the family with adequate sleeping room during the night.

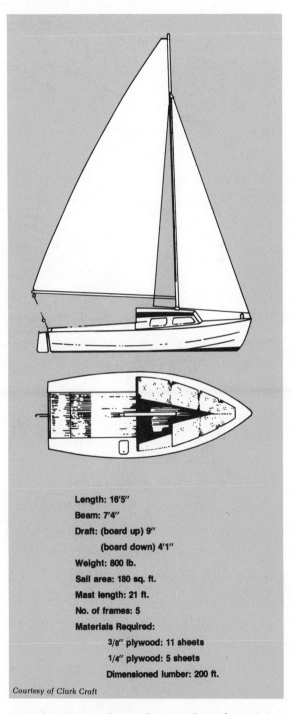

Length: 16'5"

Beam: 7'4"

Draft: (board up) 9"

(board down) 4'1"

Weight: 800 lb.

Sail area: 180 sq. ft.

Mast length: 21 ft.

No. of frames: 5

Materials Required:

3/8" plywood: 11 sheets

1/4" plywood: 5 sheets

Dimensioned lumber: 200 ft.

Courtesy of Clark Craft

A multi-chine plywood centerboard cruising sailboat. Accommodates 8 for day sailing; sleeps 4. Space for portable galley and head. Accepts outboards from 2½ to 10 horsepower.

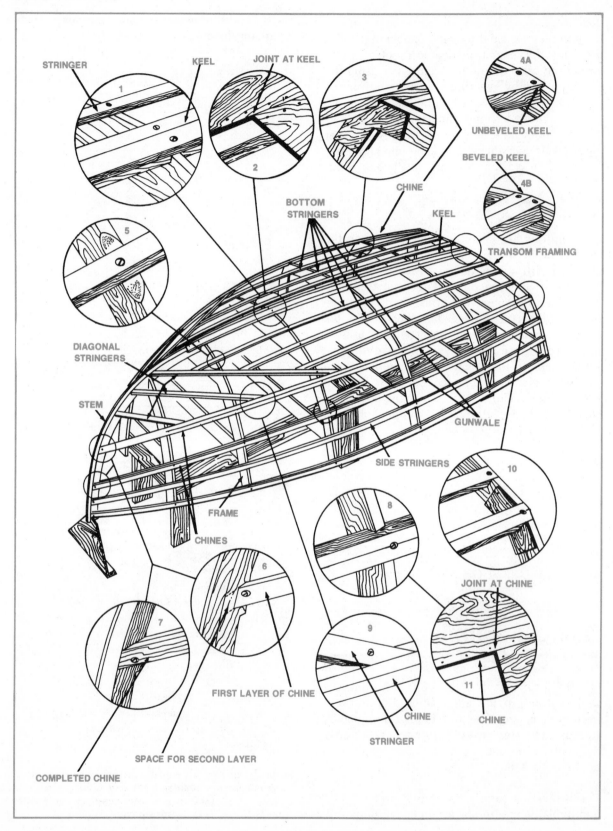

STRINGER
KEEL
JOINT AT KEEL
1
2
3
4A
UNBEVELED KEEL
BEVELED KEEL
4B
CHINE
KEEL
TRANSOM FRAMING
BOTTOM
STRINGERS
5
DIAGONAL
STRINGERS
STEM
GUNWALE
SIDE STRINGERS
10
FRAME
CHINES
8
JOINT AT CHINE
6
7
9
11
CHINE
CHINE
FIRST LAYER OF CHINE
STRINGER
SPACE FOR SECOND LAYER
COMPLETED CHINE

CONSTRUCTION OF FAMILY SAILBOAT

If the frame kit is not purchased from the manufacturer, the stem, frames, and transom must be laid out, cut and assembled from full-size plans.

When the stem, frames, and transom are complete, a building jig must be constructed. This jig is a platform of rough lumber that holds the frames in alignment until the hull is planked. The jig also raises the hull to a convenient working height.

Hull Framing

Set up the frames on the building jig. Each frame must be individually plumbed and squared to the boat center line. When in alignment, temporarily fasten the frames to the jig, and run battens between the frames to hold them in complete alignment.

When the frames are locked in alignment, set the beveled stem in place in the frame notches. Glue and screw in place. Once the stem is fitted, fasten the keel to the cutout in the stem, and bend and clamp it in place over the frames. Bevel the keel to the frames until fair.

◊

Fully framed hull of Trailer Sailer Family Sailboat. Inset 1: Stringer and keel fastened to frame. Note keel is inset in frame, and beveled for attachment of planking. Stringer is laid on top of frame. Inset 2: Planked keel. Planking is butt jointed at keel. Bevel of keel creates V-bottom. Inset 3: Properly fitted chine fastened in notch in frame. Note plywood gusset strengthening joint in frame. Inset 4: Joining of keel and transom. A) before beveling; B) after beveling. Inset 5: Trimming a frame to fasten a stringer. The frame has been planed away to allow the stringer to assume a fair curve. Inset 6: First layer of a chine screwed to the stem. Inset 7: Completed chine flush with stem bevel. Inset 8: Chine properly beveled for bottom and lower side planking. Inset 9: Diagonal stringer correctly fastened to chine. Inset 10: Proper fastening of stringer and chine in notches in transom. Note how chine is beveled to match transom shape. Inset 11: Butt joint of planking on chine.

After the frames, stem, transom, and keel have been assembled and aligned, the chines and stringers are fitted to the hull frames. (The temporary battens are removed as they are replaced by stringers) The chines fit into notches provided in the frames; the stringers are laid over the frames. The stringers must be clamped temporarily to each frame while that frame is trimmed to permit each stringer to both lie flat against the frame and form a fair continuous curve. Each frame must be trimmed or shimmed until each stringer does lie in a fair, continuous curve. Once fitted, both the chines and the stringers are permanently glued and screwed to the frames.

Diagonal stringers are fastened from the lower stem to the chine. These stringers must either be straight or slightly bowed out. They *must not* sag toward the middle of the boat. The chines must be beveled before planking. A straight line extended from the end of a diagonal stringer provides the correct bevel angle.

Planking The Hull

The planking is laid in three sections: from the keel to the lower chine, between the chines, and from the upper chine to the gunwale. Begin planking at the bow and complete each section before beginning another.

The plywood is butt jointed down the center of the stem and keel. To establish a tight butt joint at the chine, the first plank should have at least a 1/4" overhang at the chine bevel. The easiest way to mark the plywood for cutting is to lay the sheets directly on the hull and mark from the frames. Install butt straps (pieces of plywood fastened between stringers to strengthen planking joints) at the ends of planking sheets. Glue and fasten planking to butt strap and continue new sheet of planking to stern. Be generous in application of the glue. It is easier to sand down a glue run then calk a leaking joint. If nailing rather than screwing the planking to the hull, back the nailing area with a heavy weight to damp any spring in the framework.

Inverting and Leveling Hull

When the hull is completely planked, it should be removed from the framing jig and inverted into a fitting-out cradle. The cradle may be built from scrap lumber or sandbags, or the transporting trailer may be set on blocks and pressed into service.

Use a carpenters level to make sure that the hull is perfectly level, both fore and aft and gunwale to gunwale. This leveling is extremely important for all future construction. If it is not done properly at this time, there will be no way to establish an accurate vertical dimension.

Fitting The Centerboard Case

The centerboard case is constructed of two sheets of plywood, dimensioned lumber end-piece spacers, and the case logs (two heavy timbers that fasten to the keel and support the case and the centerboard). Assemble the case with bronze screws, then bore holes for the mounting bolts in the case logs.

Fit the case to the keel by trial and error. A fit tolerance of $1/16$ of an inch is necessary. Plane the case to fit the keel, not the keel to fit the case. When the case fits the keel, use the already drilled holes in the case logs to drill the mounting holes in the keel. Spread a coat of sealant on the bottom of the case logs and mount the case.

Building The Mast Step

The mast is set into a fitting on the cabin top. A pipe support is run from the cabin top to a mast step on the keel. This step is a hollow box built of dimensioned lumber and plywood and fitted between the centerboard case and the next frame forward. The plywood sides of the box are drilled to permit drainage of possible bilge water.

Setting Foredeck Beams & King Plank

Lay out the foredeck beams on either a wide piece of solid lumber or a laminated timber. Cut the beams, then fit, glue and screw them to the tops of the frames. The beam tops should be level with the frame tops, so that the deck and gunwale will meet neatly.

A king plank, of either timber or plywood, is fit-

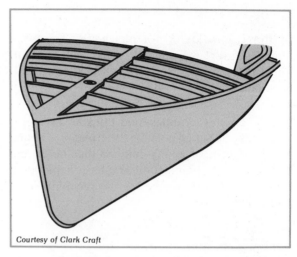

Courtesy of Clark Craft

Deck beams and king plank installed in planked hull.

ted into notches along the centerline of the deck beams.

To prevent warping or distortion of the deck beams before the deck is laid, temporarily brace or shore the deck beams with scrap lumber.

Setting Side Deck Beams

The short beams that will support the side decks should next be fastened in place. These beams become somewhat longer in the cockpit area where the deck is used as seating.

Decking and Cabin Framing.

Fit the cabin bulkheads and sides at this time. Do not fasten permanently in place. Glue and screw the foredeck and the side decks in place. Fasten the bulkhead in place, then fit the cabin sides. Do not cut the side windows until the cabin side has been fitted and fastened in place. The cabin roof beams are now cut and fitted in place.

Framing Summary for Amateur Builder

The building sequence recommended for the amateur builder by the designer, following the inverting of the hull, is as follows: 1) install deck beams; 2) plank deck; 3) fit centerboard case; 4) install cabin sides and bulkheads; 5) install cabin beams, king plank (to support joint of cabintop plywood), cabin front base piece, cabin corner posts, and 6) install mast fitting.

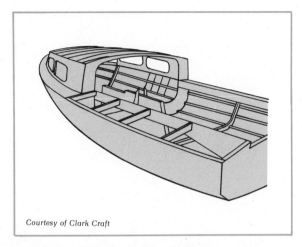

Courtesy of Clark Craft

Partially completed Family Sailboat. Foreground framing will support side decks that serve as cockpits seats. The cabin roof kingplank and the self-bailing well for the transom-mount outboard are not yet installed.

Interior accomodations such as length of bunks, location of galley sinks, etc., may be varied to suit the individual boat builder.

Construction and Installation of Rudder

The Trailer Sailer Family Sailboat has a kick-up rudder arrangement.

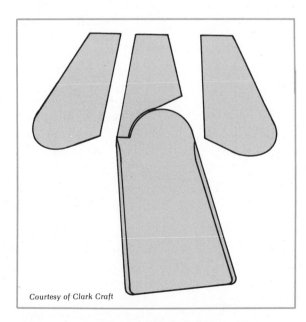

Courtesy of Clark Craft

The kick-up rudder is composed of the rudder blade and spacing pivot, plus the two cheek pieces.

The rudder is mounted with a standard pintle and gudgeon arrangement.

Note: Detailed information about plans, framing kits, and rigging kits available for all Hartley Trailer Sailers is available in a catalogue available for $1.00 from Clark Craft, Tonawonda, New York.

Courtesy of Clark Craft

Sailing Pram

Easily available tools and materials are used in the construction of this 8-foot sailing pram. The boat is constructed of readily available exterior grade AC plywood and clear white pine. Hand tools are sufficient for construction, although a table saw, sabre saw, and portable electric drill would save time.

Note: Other woods and materials may be used if available and desired. For example, marine plywood may be used instead of exterior, spruce or white oak may be used for chines and clamps; redwood, spruce or 2 inch diameter aluminum tubing may be used for the mast; and mahogany may be used for the rudder and daggerboard.

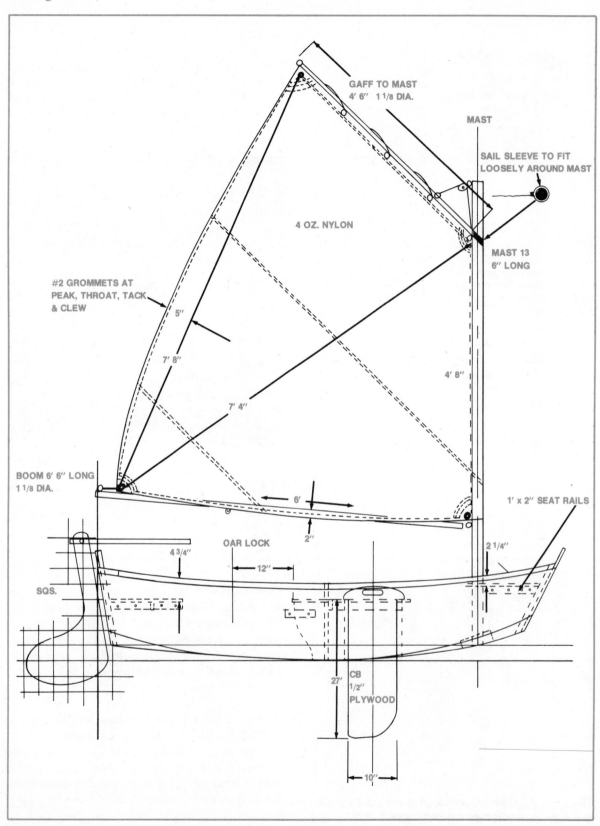

GAFF TO MAST
4' 6" 1 1/8 DIA.

MAST

SAIL SLEEVE TO FIT
LOOSELY AROUND MAST

4 OZ. NYLON

MAST 13
6" LONG

#2 GROMMETS AT
PEAK, THROAT, TACK
& CLEW

5"

7' 8"

7' 4"

4' 8"

BOOM 6' 6" LONG
1 1/8 DIA.

6'

1' x 2" SEAT RAILS

2"

4 3/4"

OAR LOCK

2 1/4"

12"

SQS.

CB
1/2"
PLYWOOD

27'

10"

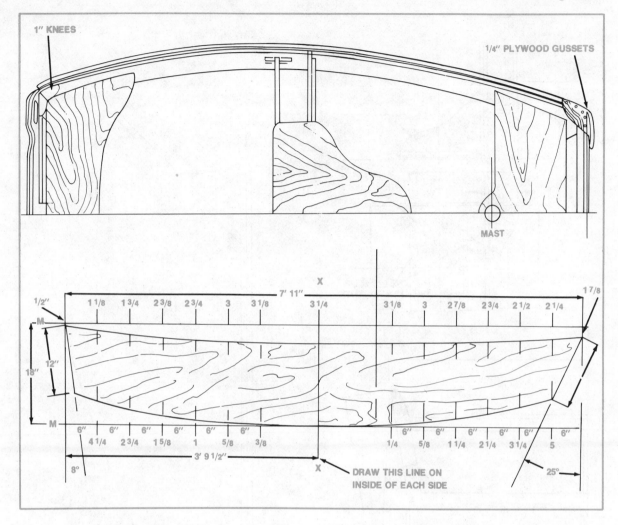

These substitutions will increase costs, and they may not be as readily available as exterior plywood and clear pine. *SEE ALSO PROJECTS.*

CONSTRUCTION STEPS

Make Sides and Chines.

Working from the long edge of a 4 x 8 sheet of plywood, lay out the dimension points for one side. Join these points by springing a piece of light wooden lath along the points, and penciling in the cutting line. If a dimension point does not seem to be in the right place, remeasure it. The lines should be fair, that is all points should fall in a smooth curve or line.

After the lines are drawn, cut out the first side with a hand saw or sabre saw. When the first side is cut out, flip it over and trace it on the sheet of plywood. Make sure enough stock plywood remains to lay out the centerboard sides later. In addition, make sure both boat sides are the same size and shape after cutting.

Next, make and attach the chines. Cut $2^5/_8$ x $1^1/_4$ x 8 foot pieces of white pine. Cut a 10° bevel from end to end of each piece, leaving a 1 inch thickness as the narrow side. Glue and nail the chines to the bottoms of the plywood sides, the 1 inch sides against the plywood. Glue with any waterproof glue, and nail with $^3/_4$ inch No. 15 boat nails spaced 3 inches apart.

Build Centerboard Trunk and Main Frames.

Lay out and cut the centerboard trunk from the

Sailing Pram

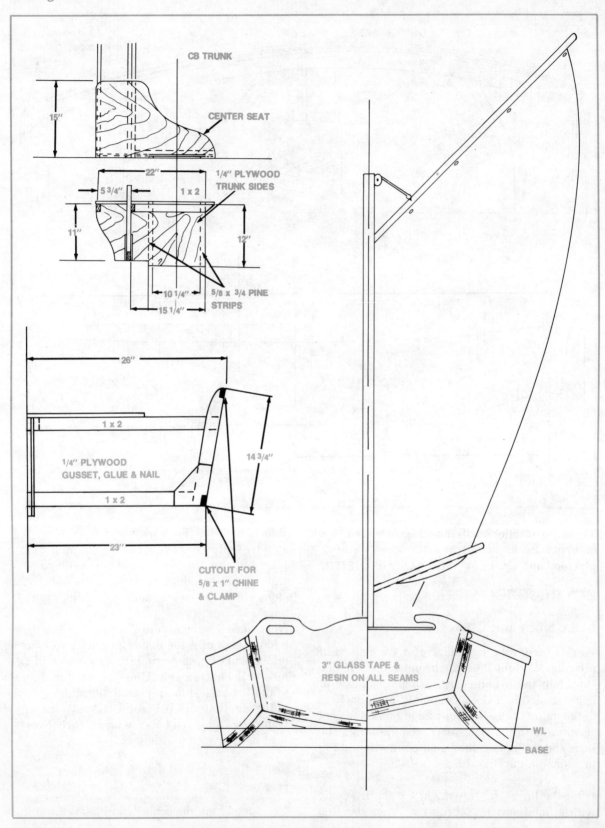

CB TRUNK

CENTER SEAT

15"

22"

5 3/4"

1 x 2

1/4" PLYWOOD
TRUNK SIDES

11"

12"

10 1/4"

15 1/4"

5/8 x 3/4 PINE
STRIPS

26"

1 x 2

1/4" PLYWOOD
GUSSET, GLUE & NAIL

1 x 2

14 3/4"

23"

CUTOUT FOR
5/8 x 1" CHINE
& CLAMP

3" GLASS TAPE &
RESIN ON ALL SEAMS

WL

BASE

remaining ¹/₄ inch plywood. The center main frame is cut from 1 x 2 pine or fir; the seat is cut from ¹/₂ inch plywood. Assemble as indicated in the plans.

Build Bow and Transom.

Lay out and cut bow and transom from ¹/₂ inch plywood; frame as shown in the plans. Note the angled sides of the frames. These angles are so that the boat sides will fit flush when attached to the bow and transom.

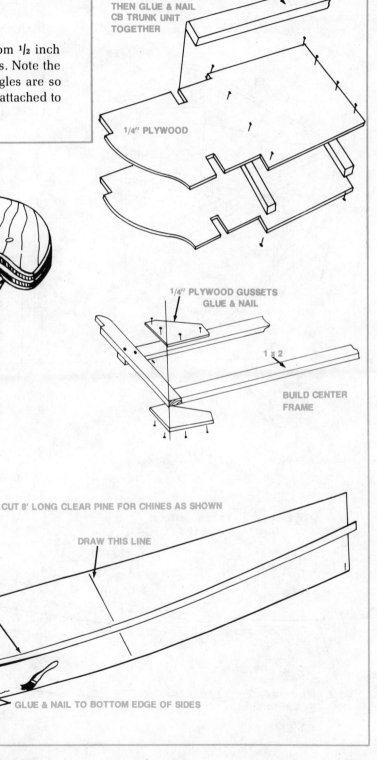

CENTER SEAT

1 x 2 PINE STRIPS

COAT INSIDE WITH EPOXY THEN GLUE & NAIL CB TRUNK UNIT TOGETHER

1/4" PLYWOOD

1/4" PLYWOOD GUSSETS GLUE & NAIL

1 x 2

BUILD CENTER FRAME

CB TRUNK

5/8"

THIS SIDE TO PLYWOOD

1"

10°

CHINE

CUT 8' LONG CLEAR PINE FOR CHINES AS SHOWN

DRAW THIS LINE

GLUE & NAIL TO BOTTOM EDGE OF SIDES

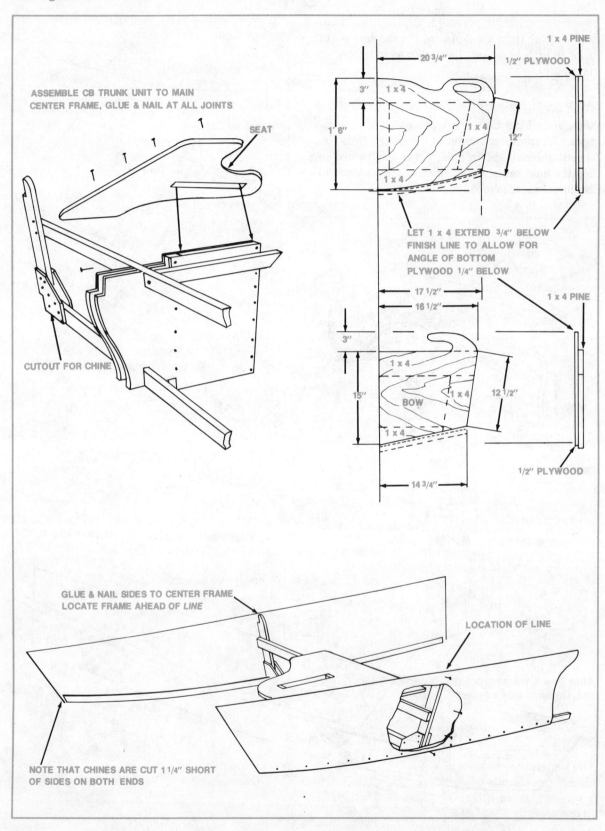

ASSEMBLE CB TRUNK UNIT TO MAIN
CENTER FRAME, GLUE & NAIL AT ALL JOINTS

SEAT

CUTOUT FOR CHINE

1 x 4 PINE

20 3/4"

1/2" PLYWOOD

3"

1 x 4

1 x 4

1' 6"

12"

1 x 4

LET 1 x 4 EXTEND 3/4" BELOW
FINISH LINE TO ALLOW FOR
ANGLE OF BOTTOM
PLYWOOD 1/4" BELOW

17 1/2"

16 1/2"

1 x 4 PINE

3"

1 x 4

15"

1 x 4

12 1/2"

BOW

1 x 4

14 3/4"

1/2" PLYWOOD

GLUE & NAIL SIDES TO CENTER FRAME
LOCATE FRAME AHEAD OF *LINE*

LOCATION OF LINE

NOTE THAT CHINES ARE CUT 1 1/4" SHORT
OF SIDES ON BOTH ENDS

Assemble Basic Framework of Boat

Glue and nail each side to the center frame. The frame is positioned to the front of the line indicated on each side (see plan drawing).

Glue and nail the transom and the bow to one side. Tie a length of rope around each end of the boat. Wrap a broomstick or similar piece of wood in each rope to form a Spanish windlass. Slowly tighten the rope until the other side can be glued and nailed to the transom and bow. Do not hurry this bending. Allow the plywood time to assume its new curve.

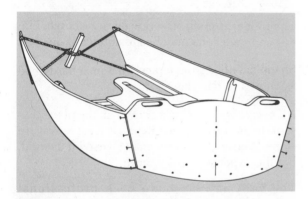

Pull front & back together. At the same time, glue & nail transom in place first, then slowly pull bow in to bow piece, glue & nail it in place.

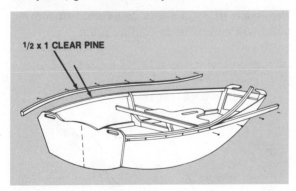

After bow & transom are dry, fit & install clamp & rub rail. Do both sides evenly & together.

Build the Gunwales

The gunwale is formed of two pieces, an inside clamp and an outside rubrail, both formed of 1/2 x 1 clear pine. Spring the clamps into place, then fit the rubrails. Glue and nail both in place, using 1 1/4 inch nails driven through the rubrail and plywood into the clamp strips.

Fasten Hull Bottom in Place.

Place the hull upside down on a pair of sawhorses. Using a straight stick laid across the sides as a guide, plane the edges of the sides, and the bottom of the bow and transom to fit the curve of the bottom. On the centerline of a 4 x 8 sheet of plywood, mark the location of the centerboard trunk. Cut the opening for a snug fit, then glue and nail the sheet of plywood to the edges and center frame of the pram. Trim off the excess plywood, sand all edges smooth, and round off all corners. Apply ·3 inch wide fiberglass tape to all seams, using a suitable resin.

Install Gussets, Knees and Seats.

Nail the 1/4 inch plywood gussets and 1 inch knees in place at the corners. Position rails for rear seat, then glue in place. For additional

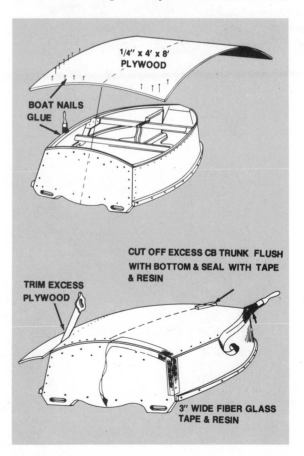

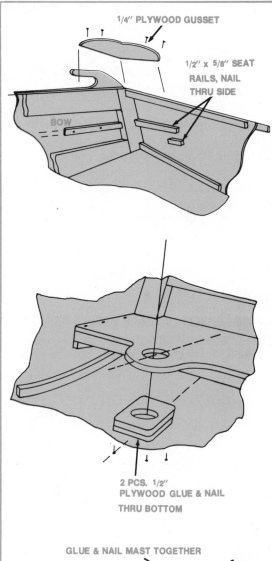

1/4" PLYWOOD GUSSET

1/2" x 5/8" SEAT RAILS, NAIL THRU SIDE

BOW

2 PCS. 1/2" PLYWOOD GLUE & NAIL THRU BOTTOM

strength, nail seat rails from outside of boat. Cut out the front seat (which also serves as the mast partner) and fasten in place. Making sure that the mast hole is centered on it, locate, glue and nail the mast step in place beneath the seat.

Constructing the Mast.

The mast may be built up from four pieces of 1/2 x 1 1/2 x 8 foot clear pine glued and planed to shape, or it may be formed from either a 2 inch solid pine pole or 2 inch diameter aluminum tube. The gaff and boom are made of 1 1/8 inch closet poles.

Fitting Out.

The rudder is hung on screw eyes as shown. Pintles and gudgeons may be substituted if desired.

Shape the tiller from a piece of 1 inch hardwood as shown in the plans.

All necessary hardware shown on the plans (except the oarlocks) is available at most hardware stores. Marine hardware may be used if desired, but the expense will be more.

The sail may be made by a professional sailmaker, using the dimensions shown on the plan. Sailcloth may be purchased and the sail made at home if desired.

Two coats of a good quality exterior or marine paint will complete the sailing pram.

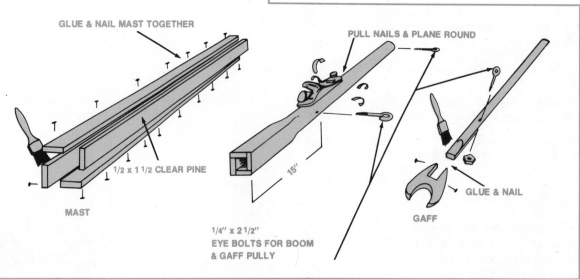

GLUE & NAIL MAST TOGETHER

PULL NAILS & PLANE ROUND

1/2 x 1 1/2 CLEAR PINE

MAST

15"

1/4" x 2 1/2" EYE BOLTS FOR BOOM & GAFF PULLY

GLUE & NAIL

GAFF

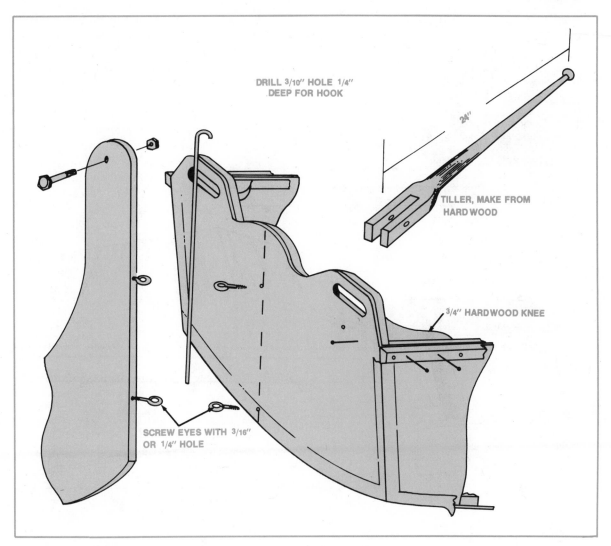

DRILL 3/10" HOLE 1/4"
DEEP FOR HOOK

24"

TILLER, MAKE FROM
HARDWOOD

3/4" HARDWOOD KNEE

SCREW EYES WITH 3/16"
OR 1/4" HOLE

Sand Box

Only the simplest tools are necessary to build this generous sized sand box. It can be completed, including the first coat of paint or stain, in less than a day. The unique cover will protect the contents from rain, leaves and debris.

Dimensions given can be altered to make a larger or smaller box. Sides of the sand box are cut from 2 x 8's with two sides 51¼" long and two sides 44½". The shorter sides are nailed six inches in from the ends of the longer sides providing support for the inside edge of the seat.

The seats, 7½" wide x 47¾" long, are nailed to the sides. Two 2" x 51¼" strips are then ripped from the same 1 x 10 from which the seats are cut. These strips are nailed along the sides of the sand box and serve as a ledge upon which the cover rests when closed.

Nine pieces of 1 x 6 tongue-and-groove boards serve as the bottom of the box, supported by three 2" x 4" skids each 46" long, with diagonally-cut ends.

The tapered sides of the cover are cut from one six-foot piece of 1 x 8. Eleven pieces of 1 x 6 tongue-and-groove boards, each 49¾" long, serve as the top of the cover.

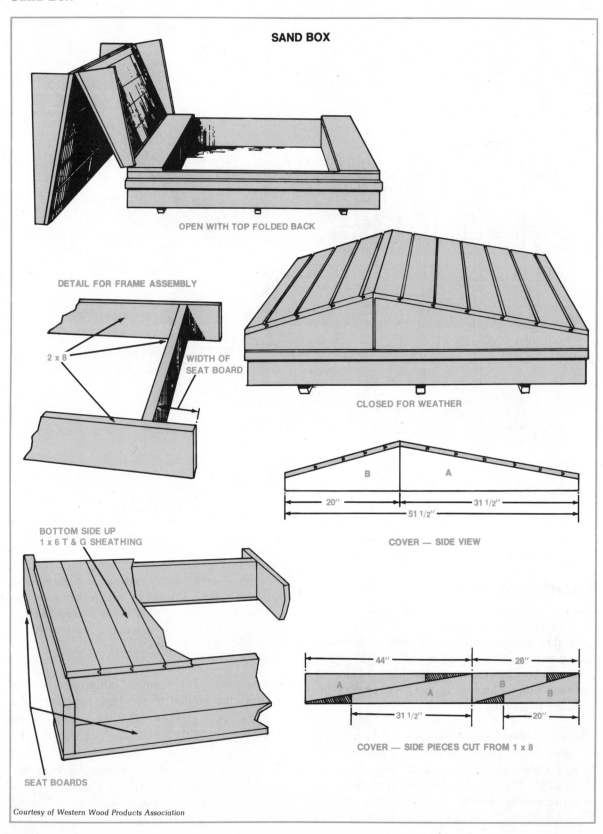

SAND BOX

OPEN WITH TOP FOLDED BACK

DETAIL FOR FRAME ASSEMBLY

2 x 8

WIDTH OF
SEAT BOARD

CLOSED FOR WEATHER

B   A

20''   31 1/2''

51 1/2''

COVER — SIDE VIEW

BOTTOM SIDE UP
1 x 6 T & G SHEATHING

44''   28''

A   A   B   B

31 1/2''   20''

COVER — SIDE PIECES CUT FROM 1 x 8

SEAT BOARDS

Courtesy of Western Wood Products Association

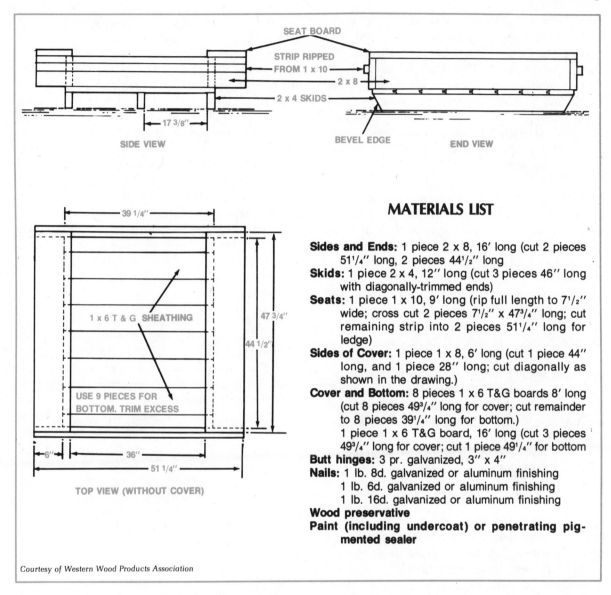

SEAT BOARD

STRIP RIPPED FROM 1 x 10

2 x 8

2 x 4 SKIDS

17 3/8"

SIDE VIEW

BEVEL EDGE

END VIEW

39 1/4"

1 x 6 T & G SHEATHING

47 3/4"

44 1/2"

USE 9 PIECES FOR BOTTOM. TRIM EXCESS

6"

36"

51 1/4"

TOP VIEW (WITHOUT COVER)

MATERIALS LIST

Sides and Ends: 1 piece 2 x 8, 16' long (cut 2 pieces 51 1/4" long, 2 pieces 44 1/2" long

Skids: 1 piece 2 x 4, 12" long (cut 3 pieces 46" long with diagonally-trimmed ends)

Seats: 1 piece 1 x 10, 9' long (rip full length to 7 1/2" wide; cross cut 2 pieces 7 1/2" x 47 3/4" long; cut remaining strip into 2 pieces 51 1/4" long for ledge)

Sides of Cover: 1 piece 1 x 8, 6' long (cut 1 piece 44" long, and 1 piece 28" long; cut diagonally as shown in the drawing.)

Cover and Bottom: 8 pieces 1 x 6 T&G boards 8' long (cut 8 pieces 49 3/4" long for cover; cut remainder to 8 pieces 39 1/4" long for bottom.)
1 piece 1 x 6 T&G board, 16' long (cut 3 pieces 49 3/4" long for cover; cut 1 piece 49 1/4" for bottom

Butt hinges: 3 pr. galvanized, 3" x 4"

Nails: 1 lb. 8d. galvanized or aluminum finishing
1 lb. 6d. galvanized or aluminum finishing
1 lb. 16d. galvanized or aluminum finishing

Wood preservative

Paint (including undercoat) or penetrating pigmented sealer

Courtesy of Western Wood Products Association

The three supporting skids of the sand box should be treated with a wood preservative since they come in contact with the ground. The rest of the sand box needs only an undercoat or sealer before being painted or stained.

The finished sand box is sturdy enough to accommodate several rough-and-tumble children. Folded back, the top serves as a windbreak and seat backrest. Used as a protective cover, the lid is strong enough for the children to climb and sit on. *SEE ALSO PROJECTS.*

Sander
[SEE PORTABLE POWER TOOLS; STATIONARY BELT & DISC SANDER.]

Sanding

Sanding is a process of cleaning or smoothing a surface by rubbing it with an abrasive material.

Sanding may be done by hand or by machine, and precedes the final finish on wooden furniture or floors. The project should be thoroughly cleansed of all gums, waxes and dirt before sanding, to assure a satisfactory final finish and to make the sanding process easier. This cleaning is best accomplished with lacquer thinner, turpentine or a commercial wood-cleaning fluid, for sanding to clean may remove too much of the wood.

Mechanical sanding machines are popular tools because they reduce the work involved in the sanding process. There are several types of these sanders. The electric motor in a vibrating sander operates a vibrating pad, which moves either in a straightlined or a quick-speed circular motion. The orbital type of sander is not well-suited to wood finishing work, because half of the circular strokes of the pad move across the grain of the wood, and the swirl marks produced by the motion must be removed by a final with-the-grain sanding. One type of sander in this group, however, provides both the quick-speed orbital movements and the smoothing straightlined movements in the same machine. The movements of the pad may be quickly switched by the use of a lever on the machine. Regular sheet sandpaper is used in these types of sanders, cut to fit the machine.

Belt sanders offer great cutting speed with a straightline motion. This quick cutting must be carefully watched, however, as it can take away more than the desired amount of wood in refinishing projects, especially antiques. Belts are not available in as big a variety of grits as are abrasive sheets, and are rather expensive. However, they are long-lasting if protected against clogging.

Disc sanders are composed of a circular piece of paper attached to a rubber disk. The motor moves the disc in a spinning motion. Disc sanders are used more for buffing or polishing than for wood sanding because of the swirl marks produced.

Drum sanders are for use on floors only, and a smaller disc-type sander is usually required to sand the floor edges and corners, where the large drum cannot reach.

Machine sanding is suitable for doing rough work, but most furniture projects call for a final fine finish hand sanding to produce the desired smoothness. The effort involved in hand sanding can be reduced by choosing the coated abrasive that is best suited for the job, or the one that cuts the fastest and the sharpest. Three types of sandpaper grit are used on wood: flint, garnet and aluminum oxide. These abrasives come backed with paper or cloth. Emery cloth is good for removing small amounts of rust from a surface, and crocus cloth polishes metal surfaces. An aluminum oxide based cloth is good to use on metal that is to be finished with a coat of paint or lacquer.

To begin the sanding process after cleanup, go over the whole piece with medium grit paper on a sanding block, sanding as uniformly as possible. The entire project is then re-sanded with a finer grade paper. If a clear or enamel finish is desired, or if a water stain is to be applied, the next step is dampening the wood with warm water. This will cause swelling of the surface wood fibers, preventing swelling later on and eliminating the chance of a rough, uneven surface after sanding. Dampening also raises the tiny fiber ends so that they may be easily sanded off. The final step after the water has dried is another sanding with the fine grade paper. Additional smoothness is provided by the use of a sanding sealer. Sealer hardens the tiny end fibers and gives the wood surface a plastic-like quality, allowing repeated sanding. Sealers may be purchased at paint stores or made at home from shellac diluted with three to four parts alcohol.

A sanding block is a must in smoothing and planing a surface. Sanding blocks are generally hand-made wooden blocks, four and one-half inches by slightly under two inches. A thickness of ordinary felt should be placed on the block under the sandpaper to prevent the passage of friction from the wood to the paper. This causes the paper to clog and fill with greater speed. Blocks of rubber or metal or other materials may be purchased but are not as flexible as the wooden blocks. Sanding blocks may also be made round or curved, to follow the shape of the piece being worked on. When using a sanding block near the edges of a flat surface, the pressure should be kept on the back part of the block to prevent the block from slipping over the edge and cutting deep.

Abrasive cord, in ribbons, tapes or strips is used on turnings and other oddly shaped furniture parts. A sandpaper strip is handy for smoothing out dents or other blemishes in the wood. Place the strip over the blemish and press a finger over the paper. Slowly pull the paper out from under your finger with the other hand, repeating until the marred spot is removed. A sandpaper pad, for use on convex curves, may be made by folding and interleafing two sheets of sandpaper. A small piece of abrasive paper may be folded twice for sanding in corners and crevices, changing the fold as it wears. Sandpaper is never torn, for the ragged edges cause scratching. Use an awl to mark the back of the paper, then pull to separate the pieces. *SEE ALSO ABRASIVES.*

Sandpaper

Sandpaper is a paper, cloth or fiber backing coated with various minerals. The abrasive particles may be applied *closed* or *open*. If closed, there is no space left between the particles, and if open, the space remaining allows dust or other materials to fall, preventing clogging.

Flint sandpaper is inexpensive and dulls rapidly. It is used on minor sanding jobs. Garnet is harder than flint and is best for wood sanding. Emery, aluminum oxide and silicon carbide sandpapers are the best for use on metal. Silicon carbide is the hardest substance known. It works best on brass, copper and aluminum. Emery cuts slowly and wears out quickly. It is usually used to remove rust and dirt from metal. Aluminum oxide sandpaper works on glass, leather, wood, metal, enamel, lacquer and marble. It is durable and fast-cutting. The work to be done will determine the type of sandpaper needed and the degree of abrasiveness. This ranges from very coarse to very fine. *SEE ALSO ABRASIVES.*

Sanitary Tee

A sanitary tee is a cast-iron soil pipe fitting. It connects a branch entering at a right angle to a straight run pipe. The inlet for the branch has a curved arm. *SEE ALSO PIPE FITTINGS.*

Sapwood

Sapwood is the outer, newer layers of wood close to the bark. It carries sap, and the life processes of the tree take place within its layers. In some species, the sapwood is lighter in color than the core, or heartwood, of the tree. Sapwood is usually softer, less resistant to decay and not quite as strong as heartwood. *SEE ALSO LUMBER.*

Sash

A sash includes the members which hold the glass in place as well as the wooden framework in which panes are mounted in a window or door. The sash which fits into the framework may be in a fixed or sliding position, or it may be mounted by pivots or hinges. *SEE ALSO WINDOWS & WINDOW HARDWARE.*

Sashcord Replacement

Sashcord replacement is necessary when the sash cord becomes worn or broken. To repair it, remove the wooden or metal access near the bottom of the channel in which the sash rides. Pull out the sash weight and remove the window so that both ends of the sashcord are available. Remove the cord and cut a new one the same length as the old sashcord. Slip one end of the cord over the top window pulley, feed it into the frame and work with it until it falls near the bottom. It may be necessary to tie a piece of weighted string to the cord in order to feed it through the top opening. If so, pull out the weight and the string will bring the sashcord with it. Tie the weight to the end of the sash cord, slip it back into the slot and replace the window. *SEE ALSO WINDOWS & WINDOW HARDWARE.*

Satin-Finish Varnish

Satin-finish varnish is made with either alkyd or possibly urethane resins. It becomes smooth and satiny as it dries and is almost as luxurious as a rubbed finish. Satin-finish varnish penetrates into the wood and seals the pores.

After the final coat of satin, rub with pumice and oil or number 400 wet sandpaper. Then wax the surface, and the finish will be almost identical to a rubbed finish which requires much more work. *SEE ALSO WOOD FINISHING.*

Saunas

The sauna is basically a thermal bath, making use of very high dry heat, 175 to 200 degrees Farenheit — quite the opposite of the familiar Turkish steam bath, which relies on high humidity and relatively low heat. Sauna humidity is kept to below 20 percent. Because the human body tolerates heat in inverse ratio to humidity, it is possible to be quite comfortable enjoying sauna bathing at around 200 degrees or more. People in Finland have learned to tolerate 250 degrees.

There are saunas for do-it yourselfers, prefab saunas, mobile saunas. Cost will be determined by whether you do the work yourself, whether you hire an architect to design it, whether you custom design it in a special shape or for a particular spot, or whether its an integral part of a small cabin.

WHY HAVE A SAUNA?

Stress, tension, stiffness from too much athletic activity, or discomfort after being out in the cold are all good reasons for building a sauna. Sauna is by no means a cure for any illness, nor is it a way of reducing one's weight. The Food and Drug Administration carefully monitors sauna advertising and at this time has not given approval to any curative claims. Weight loss there will be, but only very temporarily, just as it is with athletes who lose several pounds during a game of tennis or football through perspiration. Essentially sauna cleanses your body through perspiration, but as soon as you replace the water by drinking liquids the pounds come right back on. It is possible, though, that the stresses which lead people to overeat could be lessened by the kind of relaxation which comes from the use of a sauna.

Dr. Donald Snyder, in a report to the convention of the American Society for Artificial Organs, has reported favorable results in kidney patients who apparently get rid of accumulated poisonous fluid products in their bodies by daily sauna periods. Sauna won't cure a cold or get rid of adolescent acne, but there's no doubt that it cleanses the body through perspiration. Whatever the reasons, a large number of people are beginning to consider a house is not a home without some kind of sauna.

SAUNA IN A PACKAGE

For the amateur, the best sauna might be the one that comes in a package. You can buy one of the one-to-two person units or get one large enough to hold 12 of your friends and put it up in less than a day. Pre-built package units come with insulated walls and ceiling, floor, carpet, heater, sauna stones, electrical controls, door, light and benches.

One of the companies has a pre-built which goes up in about an hour. It is designed with a patented locking device so you don't have to bother with nails, screws or bolts. Just one turn with the special wrench lock, which is provided, sets the panels in place.

Complete portability is the big advantage with this unit. You can move it from one house to another, or from one area to another within the same house. Taking it apart, relocating it, and putting it back in use can be done in as little as two hours. The exterior is unfinished mahogany or prefinished walnut grain wood. Interior is kiln-dried redwood which will not warp or splinter and has excellent resistance to high and rapidly changing temperatures.

SAUNA FOR ONE

If you're living in an apartment or condominium where space is at a premium you might be able to spare a small closet for a sauna. There is one called Solo Sauna. It will fit into a space 31$\frac{1}{2}$ inches x 48 inches wide, 34$\frac{1}{2}$ to 36 inches front to back. Ceiling height should be 74 to 84 inches. These are all inside dimensions. You take off the existing door and you're ready to go to work.

The sauna unit is contained in a 2 x 6 foot redwood door which has a heating unit, control, window and light fixture. It comes with hinges and catches, is ready to connect to any ordinary 20-amp outlet.

Start the job by insulating walls and ceiling with mineral wool. To fit the door the floor should be $\frac{3}{4}$ inch plywood over 2 x 4 sleepers. Carpet with indoor-outdoor material. The recommended lining material is kiln-dried redwood tongue and groove boards. V-groove 1 x 6 is excellent, and the less-expensive "A" grade will do as well as the clear all-heart if you want to economize.

To conform to traditional sauna seating, build a bench about 15$\frac{3}{4}$ inches wide and 32 inches high across the back of the closet. Provide a step 8 inches high. Make these of 2 x 2 and 2 x 4 redwood.

When it is complete your solo sauna will heat up in about 25 minutes rather than the hour needed by a large sauna. If possible, try to locate your sauna in an area reasonably close to a shower so there will be less dripping between the two places. Because of its small size, the solo does not have a stove, rocks and steam as do the large models. Without them, you get the dry heat, but you will have to forego that moment when the water is tossed on the rocks and your body responds with a tingling sensation.

Courtesy of Viking Sauna Co.

CUSTOM SAUNAS — DESIGN YOUR OWN

If money doesn't matter, you can hire an architect to build your sauna. If it does matter, several companies have a custom design service as well as advisers who will work with you.

Some designers require that you send only a rough floor plan of where you would like to put the sauna, room dimensions, door location and information on the existing walls, if any. In a few days you will get your plan accurately worked out on paper. You, of course, order any necessary equipment from the company in exchange for this service. Should you have trouble during the building process you can get additional consultation.

SAUNA SPECIFICATIONS

What Kind of Wood to Use

Redwood is the favorite, although sometimes aspen, red cedar, spruce and some of the pines are also used. Occasionally redwood will blacken in a very steamy sauna, but since it contains no resins or oils as do most of the light-colored woods, the surface will never become tacky from the extremely high temperatures. Sauna wood is never painted, sealed, or stained, since it must breath and absorb moisture. There is not much difference between the various woods in their heat-resistant qualities.

Size

Minimum square footage per occupant should be not less than 3.5, and 6 square feet is best. Normally, when you buy a pre-built, or custom design a sauna you specify the number of people you expect to use the unit at any one time. Ceiling height in the sauna should never be less than six feet and usually not over seven.

Interior

The surface temperature gets so high it is important that no metallic or plastic products be used. Metal items such as staples, nails and screws must be countersunk or blind to prevent burns on occupants. Redwood is a good choice because the surface remains comfortable to bare skin even at 200 degrees.

Hardware

Wood is the only material used. Locks are not permitted to prevent the possibility of someone being contained in the unit and unable to get out. A friction or roller latch is permitted.

Windows

Insulating glass or twin glazing should be used for any window larger than 6 x 9 inches.

Heating Unit

Most saunas are heated by a gravity convention-flow model with no fan. A sauna using 1800 watts or less can be plugged directly into an ordinary wall outlet; a high-capacity unit should have a 220-volt line. It is also possible to heat a sauna with a couple of radiant glassheat panels, not unlike the smaller one you may use as a hot tray to keep your buffet dinner warm throughout a meal. The tempered glass in a heater of this type is fused with aluminum heating elements. A glassheat panel is slow, but doesn't take up much room in a small sauna. A couple of them could bring the heat up to nearly 170 degrees in an hour or so.

The typical sauna stove has a pile of special igneous rocks within and above the stove. Special ventilation leading under the stove causes fresh air to pass through the hot rock called *kanna-*

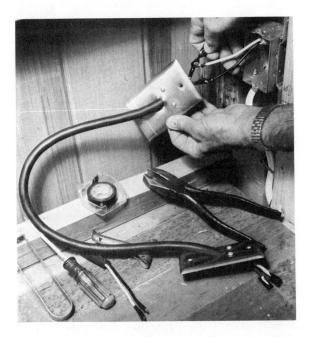

stone. The rock is black peridodite, a type which doesn't disintegrate or explode, a danger which you might run using field-stone or river stone.

Gas heaters are available for saunas but have the disadvantage of needing fuel system ducted to the outdoors. The traditional Scandinavian wood-fired sauna is not feasible.

Accessories

A heat-control thermostat and an automatic timer-control are almost essential for safety. A hygrometer to indicate humidity, a wooden bucket and a dipper, pine oil and specially scented soap, back and headrests of redwood, and a stereo-music system are a few of the extras available. You might even be able to buy a genuine birch-whisk as used by the Finns to invigorate the skin after water is thrown on the rocks. There is also a special towel with coarse texture which does about the same job as the whisk.

Cost

The heating unit will cost around $200 and plan for another $200 for insulation and wood lining. Lumber costs may require careful shopping to find high quality redwood, or other suitable softwood. Labor is about half the cost of building a sauna. A deluxe model installed by a contractor could run close to $10,000, or the price of a good swimming pool.

Maintenance

There is almost no maintenance cost. Redwood benches can be stained by perspiration. Although stains can be removed with a solution of oxalic acid and water, it is better to keep stains from forming by supplying towels for the bathers to sit and lie upon.

HOW TO USE A SAUNA

Start by taking a hot lathering shower. Rinse off all the soap thoroughly to keep from bringing soap stains to the fresh redwood benches. Go into the sauna while you are still damp.

The temperature of the sauna should be about 175 degrees for a first-time user. Later it can be increased to nearly 200 degrees. Ten minutes is long enough for a novice. Soon you can work up to 20 or 30 minutes. Set the timer. It will wake you up should you doze off. Then go out for a tepid shower, a dip in a cool pool or a brief swim in a lake.

Go back for a second 10 minute session. Finns top off the bath by throwing a ladle of water on the hot rocks (not all saunas have these). Customarily this is followed by whisking with the birch branches. A coarse towel or a special Finnish sauna towel will create the same stimulation to the skin. Take another cool shower or dip. Relax 15 minutes and then dress. Drink to restore fluids. Finns usually eat heartily too.

PRECAUTIONS

Don't eat before taking a sauna. Your body can not handle the digestive process and high heat at the same time. Wait at least an hour after a meal before going into the heat.

Don't smoke or exercise in a sauna.

Remove metal ornaments—earrings, watch, bracelet. You could be burned since these items heat up rapidly.

No pets in the sauna. An animal's cooling system is different from yours.

No one who has a respiratory ailment, heart condition, or high blood pressure should use a sauna without specific permission from a doctor. Elderly people may not be able to stand the high heat.

Children can enjoy a sauna, but it is best to keep the temperature around 175 degrees or a little lower.

Noise, chatter, moving about, and even music have no place in a sauna.

Saw Sharpening

Sharpening the teeth of a saw is necessary to keep them in proper cutting condition. This is done with files and a vise which holds the saw during filing. Place the saw blade in the vise, teeth up, and tighten the vise until it is clinched firmly around the blade. If a saw vise is not used, place boards in the vise to prevent damage to the blade. Holding a flat file evenly across the teeth tops, slide it so that small, flat areas are formed. These will act as sharpening guides. A small,

triangular file is used for sharpening both crosscut and rip teeth with the procedure beginning at the blade tip. Set the file at a 60 degree angle in the first gullet to the left of the first tooth bent toward you. When working with a crosscut saw, adjust the file so that it sits against the bevel of the teeth and begin filing until half of the adjacent flat tops are cut away. Moving the file to the right, skip the next tooth and repeat the process on the next gullet. Continue skipping and filing until the end of the blade is reached. Reverse the saw in the vise and start filing at the tip again. File the other half of the flats down completely.

Rip saw filing is done the same way as crosscut filing except that the file is run at a 90 degree angle across the teeth. This same method applies to utility and keyhole saws.

Pruning and timber saws have both crosscut and raker teeth on the same blade. Use a flat file to level the tops, filing the raker teeth shorter than the cutter teeth, keeping each type all the same height. Cutter teeth are filed with a mill or triangular file held at a 45 degree angle, using the same motion as when sharpening a crosscut saw. Occasionally, a round-edge mill file may be used to deepen a gullet and file the outer bevel at the same time.

To file the raker teeth, clamp the blade in the vise in a vertical position and use a square-edged mill file along the inside edges. If a cantsaw file is used, both tooth edges are sharpened at once. No matter which file is used, hold it perfectly level and file straight across.

Bucksaw blades should be removed from the frame and clamped in a saw vise before sharpening. File bucksaw teeth like crosscut teeth and mount the blade back in the frame. *SEE ALSO TOOL SHARPENING.*

Saws & Saw Blades

There are different types of saws for cutting wood, plastic and metal. In woodwork, one can achieve a coarse, medium or fine cut, depending on the saw's teeth. Those saws used most in wood and metalwork are the crosscut saw, hacksaw, coping saw and miter box saw. *SEE ALSO HAND TOOLS.*

Scaffolds & Ladders

Scaffolds and ladders are used by carpenters, painters and sign men to reach high work areas. The homeowner will probably use either of these devices more for painting or repairing gutters and chimneys, patching a roof, replacing outdoor lights or pruning trees. Choose a scaffold or ladder for its practicality around the house. Each homeowner's needs usually differ somewhat, so there is no particular scaffold or ladder that can be considered ideal for everbody. Most scaffolds are made of steel or aluminum while ladders are built of wood or aluminum.

LADDERS

Aluminum and wooden ladders can be used in similar ways to scaffolds except that they do not have as much working room. However, a ladder will probably be more practical for the homeowner. Before purchasing a ladder, keep in mind that aluminum resists age and moisture deterioration, aluminum channel rails are much stronger than wood rails and aluminum ladders weigh 30 per cent less than wooden varieties. Two ladders may be necessary around a home; an extension or sectional ladder to lean against the house when roof or chimney repairs are needed and a step ladder for inside work like changing light bulbs or painting ceilings. Ladders may have either cylindrical or flat, rectangular rungs. The flat style should be reinforced to prevent sagging or breaking. Rubber pads called safety shoes should be attached to the four ladder legs. Some ladders are equipped with a shelf on the top or preceding rung to hold buckets or tools. Consider how a ladder will be used before purchasing one.

SCAFFOLDS

Scaffolds provide more support than ladders for working in high areas but are harder to manipulate. A single scaffold with one small to medium sized platform is good for repair work requiring at least two people. Twin scaffolds run longer than singles and are useful in painting the full length of gutters or the second story on a house. Scaffolds today require little or no tools in assembling and automatically lock into position when set up. Of all the scaffold styles available, probably one of the most convenient to use is the one-man type. This unit adjusts to different heights, folds down for storage and makes work safer with a waist high cage at the top of the scaffold. *SEE ALSO LADDER SAFETY.*

Courtesy of Up-Right Scaffolds

Scarf Joint

A scarf joint is an end joint made by notching, grooving or cutting the ends of two pieces of wood and fastening them so that they join firmly into one continuous piece. A scarf joint is usually glued, in which case the angle-cut faces should be cut and planed with accuracy. To achieve full wood strength the slant of the scarf should be eight to one or greater. With modern resin glues, screws are not needed for extra strength. It is important, however, that the joint be clamped while the glue is setting.

If the plane is not continuous, a step or hook may be machined into the scarf. This is known as a stepped or hooked scarf joint. *SEE ALSO WOOD JOINTS.*

Scarf Joint

Scissors

Scissors are cutting instruments which have two blades with cutting edges that slide past each other. Blade length is generally from 3¹/₂'' to 6.'' By bowing the blades against each other to maintain pressure at their contact point as they open or close, scissors cut material by shearing it between the two fairly obtuse-angled edges. The blunt point at the end of some scissor blades is to prevent snagging.

Because excessive grinding reduces contact pressure, cutting effectiveness is maintained by not sharpening scissors until definitely needed. When wear is slight, there will be a narrow bright line along the top of the blade face. *SEE ALSO HAND TOOLS.*

Scissors

Scooters
[SEE MOTORCYCLES, MINIBIKES & TRAILBIKES.]

Scorched Finish

A scorched finish is used most commonly on pine. A flame, usually from a propane torch, blackens the wood surface to varying degrees. The charcoal is then removed with a wire brush and varnish or lacquer may be applied. *SEE ALSO WOOD FINISHING.*

Scrapers

Scrapers are tools with thin, sharp, straight edges used for removing wood, paint, varnish and other finishes. Some scrapers have a frame and a handle and others do not. The cabinet scraper resembles a small spokeshave and its blade is sharpened to a 45° angle for removing small amounts of wood. Hand scrapers are a piece of rectangular steel with no frame or handle which permit easy scraping in corners. To take off large quantities of wood or thick finishes, a pull scraper can be used effectively because pressure can be applied to its handle, thus enabling the operator to "pull" off large amounts of material. The pull scraper is a strip of square steel with a handle fastened to the center at a 90° angle. *SEE ALSO HAND TOOLS.*

Scratch Awl

The scratch awl has two primary uses. Its sharp pointed tip makes precision holes for starting screws and marking hole locations. It is also used to mark lines on lumber and metal. *SEE ALSO HAND TOOLS.*

Scratch Awl

Scratch Repairs

There are simple solutions to repairing scratches and scrapes on most tiles and wood surfaces. Many common household goods, such as shoe polish, turpentine and iodine, may be used for these repairs.

Scratches on tiles may be repaired by scraping some of the same material from a scrap piece and grinding it into a powder. Mix the powder with clear lacquer or varnish into paste form, then trowel it onto the scratched surface. When it has dried, buff it with steel wool.

Shallow scratches, or those which haven't penetrated the finish on wood surfaces, may be colored to match the surrounding area. Rubbing the meat of a walnut, Brazil nut or butternut will match walnut. Iodine will usually color mahogany properly. Care should be taken, however, not to drip any on the surface around the scratch. Iodine which has darkened with age is good for brown or cherry mahogany. Dilute iodine about 50 percent with denatured alcohol for maple. Follow up this application by waxing and buffing.

Shoe polish matches some wood finishes: tan for light finishes, brown for walnut, black for black lacquered wood and cordovan shades for mahogany. There are commercial liquid colors available also. Shoe polish or any other liquid used in repairing scratches should be tested first on an inconspicuous portion of the furniture.

Another way to fill minor scratches is with padding lacquer. This is a special lacquer, used with blending stains, which are manufactured in a variety of colors. Apply the lacquer and stain together over a scratch.

For wood surface abrasions on varnish, turpentine is brushed around the damaged area to liquify the varnish. The liquid then oozes into the scratches or cracks and hardens.

Tiny surface cracks on varnished wood should be scrubbed with a stiff brush and mild detergent. When the surface dries, apply a solution of two parts turpentine, three parts varnish and four parts boiled linseed oil. Rub the mixture into the surface cracks, repeating the process until all have disappeared.

Stick shellac is used to repair deep scratches and scrapes on finished wood. It is available in a variety of colors, which may be blended by heating the sticks over a gas or alcohol flame until the shellac flows. The smoky heat of matches or lighters might turn the shellac off-color.

After the color or mixture of colors is chosen, heat the hardened shellac with a soldering iron. Let it flow into the cracked surface using a heated spatula to smooth it. Scrape away the excess shellac and rub steel wool over it for leveling.

The techniques described above for repairing heavy scratches are basically the same for veneer-finished furniture. However, veneer is thin material which splits easily so working with it requires precautions. To make the material more flexible, add moisture to it by applying a hot iron over a damp cloth onto the working surface. Light scratches on veneer disappear when rubbed with a cloth dampened with furniture polish containing a few drops of alcohol.

Natural scratches or blemishes, which appear on unfinished wood are best repaired by blending them into the surrounding wood. Use a sharp knife to scrape and smooth the edges of the marred surface, making the most level indention possible. Use a rasp and sandpaper to smooth out the edges. SEE ALSO WOOD FINISHING.

Screen Repairs

Screen repairs usually involve either patching or replacement. For a small hole ($1/4$ inch to $1/2$ inch), clear nail polish may be used. Put several coats on the hole, letting each coat dry in between until the hole is completely covered.

A large hole may be repaired by using a patch of screening. The first step in repairing a hole is to cut off any uneven edges of the hole with tin snips or household shears. The patch should be a piece of screening cut a little larger than the hole. On all four edges, strip off several strands of wire. Then bend all four edges 90 degrees downward. Place the patch over the hole, forcing the bent edges through the screen. The edges may then be bent to secure the patch.

Sometimes the entire screen must be replaced. Buy a piece of screening larger than the opening so that edges can be held tightly while assembling the frame. Remove the molding and screening by using a chisel to pull tacks out. Staple or tack the new screen on one end only. Bow the frame by clamping it at the center and placing the ends on 2 x 4 blocks. Draw the screening taut and tack down the opposite end. The sides may be fastened after the clamps are removed. Then trim off excess screen and replace molding.

Screw Bit

The screw bit, also known as a combination screw bit, *screw-sink,* or *screw-mate,* is a newer type of drill which combines three jobs: drilling holes the correct screw size and depth, countersinking and counter-boring. It is used with an electric drill and comes in a variety of sizes. Screw bits may be purchased separately or in sets. *SEE ALSO HAND TOOLS.*

Screw Countersinking

Screw countersinking is a technique used by a workman who desires to make an especially nice piece of cabinet work. To perform this process, the woodworker drills a hole slightly deeper than the screw he plans to use, and with a countersink drill bit, forms a recess large enough so that the head of the screw will fit flush or slightly below the surface. He then fills the depression with wood putty and totally hides the screw to make a more attractive surface. If a countersink is unavailable, a twist drill slightly larger than

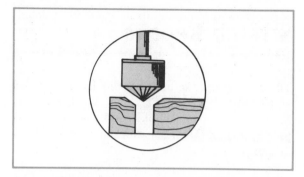

Use a countersink bit to form a countersink above the screw shank hole.

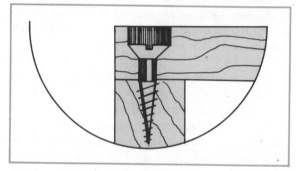

Fit the screw into the hole and fill the depression with wood putty.

the screw hole can form the space for the screw head.

Screwdriver Brace & Bit

A screwdriver brace and bit is a screwdriver with a ratchet operation which has blades to fit most of the ordinary screw sizes and types. It is most suited to jobs requiring maximum turning force and, as such, is somewhat slower working than a spiral ratchet screwdriver. *SEE ALSO HAND TOOLS.*

Screwdrivers

Screwdrivers are used for driving screws into wood, metal, concrete and brick. Among the more common are the Phillips, standard, ratchet and spiral-ratchet screwdrivers in sizes of six and eight inches. *SEE ALSO HAND TOOLS.*

Screw-Holding Screwdrivers

The screw-holding screwdriver grips the head of the screw with spring steel jaws and holds it on the blade tip. This is useful in starting screws where fingers cannot reach. After the screw has been started, pull up on the screwdriver handle and the jaws will retract so the screwdriver can be used to tighten the screw. Screw-holding screwdrivers are available in both standard and Phillips styles. *SEE ALSO HAND TOOLS.*

Screws

A screw is a threaded, solid cylinder that generally has a head and is used to hold wood and metal objects together. The ones most commonly used are the flathead, Phillips and roundhead. *SEE ALSO FASTENERS.*

Scribers

Scribers used in metal work are steel instruments that have one sharp point extending from the round body and another point extending at a right angle from the other end. The bent point is useful in marking lines that are out of reach of the straight point, which is used for marking guidelines before cutting.

Another style of scriber has a flat, rectangular body with a slot in the middle that runs nearly the body's entire length. This permits the sharp point underneath the scriber to be adjusted to various lengths for marking; the point is locked in position with a screw that sits on the top side

of the scriber. This scriber is especially helpful in fitting linoleum around door facings and irregularly shaped walls. *SEE ALSO HAND TOOLS.*

Scroll Saw

The scroll saw is a thin handsaw used for cutting curves or irregular designs. Easily distinguished by its frame depth of 8 to 12 inches, this tool is often referred to as a deep-throated coping saw. Since the blades are mounted with teeth slanting toward the handle, the cut is made on the pull stroke, reducing the chance of blade spring-out.

A small hand-held jig is also known as a scroll saw. Able to cut ¾" stock, plastic and light metals, it is especially suited to sawing intricate scrollwork in very thin material. Those that do not have a motor work by magnetic impulse like a doorbell. *SEE ALSO HAND TOOLS.*

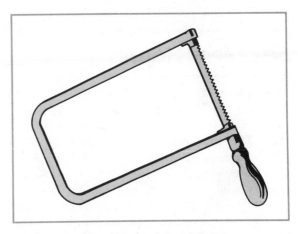

Deep-Throated Scroll Saw

Scrub Plane

Although sized comparably to the smooth plane, the scrub plane or rough plane has a narrower blade (1¼") that is rounded. When the material to be removed is not quite enough to be ripsawed off, but too much for ordinary planing in reasonable time, the scrub plane is used. It is designed to take heavy slices to reduce the width of a board quickly. Choose it to create a hand-hewn appearance on exposed beams. *SEE ALSO HAND TOOLS.*

Sealants

A sealant is a substance used to adhere two surfaces and form a protective barrier. Silicone sealants are generally used around joints in sinks, basins, bathtubs or showers. The sealants, whether they are silicone or a combination of silicone and rubber, form barriers that resist penetration of liquids, dust, air or any number of other elements that might seep from around the plumbing fixture and cause damage. A butyl rubber sealant is used to form joints between different types of materials such as metal, glass, wood or masonry. It is used as an adhesive to seal the building juncture against air, dirt and water.

Seamless Floors

Simply by strewing colorful flakes and adding a plastic coating, you can have a seamless plastic floor. This three-dimensional coating suspends plastic chips in a clear acrylic or urethane plastic over an opaque base coat. The process works equally well with a disreputable old floor or with a new one, and all the tools that are needed are a brush or a roller. It's an easy do-it-yourself type project which produces a durable, low-maintenance floor surface.

The glossy plastic topping resists wear from heels, furniture, play, or heavy traffic. Ordinary household spills and stains wipe off quickly. The lack of dirt-catching seams and cracks makes for a hygienic floor, especially important in kitchen and bath areas. It can be poured into cracks around fixtures and cabinets, even into odd-shaped corners, where other types of flooring might require difficult fitting.

Courtesy of Flecto Company, Inc.

Outdoor deck or porch can also be renewed with seamless flooring. Subfloor must be firm and free of cracks.

Although the system was developed primarily for use on floors, other uses were soon discovered. Seamless flooring materials are now used for shelves, counters, bar surfaces, indoor and outdoor table tops, decks, walkways around a pool, diving boards, coating an entire shower room, making a cast-in-place tub, soap dish and towel bar, and patio chairs.

Courtesy of Flecto Company, Inc.

Special types of flake-plastic materials can be used on metal or tile. An old metal shower, for example, needn't be removed, merely prepared properly, and then renewed with flooring plastic. All the soil laden cracks and crevices disappear with the job. On surfaces which tend to be slippery, such as outdoor steps or diving board, a little sand can be added to the final coat to provide a skidproof surface.

Seamless plastic has one other asset. It is light in weight compared to terrazo or tile, materials normally used for surfaces which often get flooded with water, and it does not add dangerous weight to structural supports, when it is used to recover old fixtures.

DIFFERENCES IN SEAMLESS FLOORING MATERIALS

Some types of seamless floors are not suited for metals or tile, while others will not take a lot of ultra-violet rays or the surface will turn yellow. Some do not stand up to extremely hard wear unless special techniques are used and still others cannot be used outdoors or where water will be excessive.

Check the manufacturer's label to see if the type you plan to use is suitable for your project. Some flooring systems are urethane, some are acrylic, and there are two-part epoxy materials which are especially durable.

Acrylic plastic is less likely to delaminate than is a urethane-based plastic. A urethane type works best when all coats of plastic finish are applied 4 to 6 hours apart. With the acrylic system a homeowner can wait 24 hours, or until the next weekend, to finish the job and there will be no adverse effect on the bonding durability of the coats.

Directions with the various kinds list the types of projects for which the material is adapted.

Almost any sound surface can be covered. Plywood, hardwood, asphalt tile, vinyl, asbestos, linoleum, sheet and tile vinyl are all suitable but most manufacturers do not recommend it over cork or rubber tile. Before starting on a large area, do a sample test. This will give you an indication of appearance results, but, of course, will not prove durability.

COLORS

Basic white or a neutral beige are easiest to keep looking attractive and make a good background for area rugs. However, one company lists 27 colors, plus gold, silver, bronze and nutmeg metallics. These last four have an iridescent effect, are more colorful for outdoor use and are highly resistant to cigarette burns and hot dishes. You can even invent your own combination by mixing flakes of different colors since they, not the plastic, determine the final effect. As with other types of flooring, remember that dark colors show dust and footprints more easily.

LAYING A SEAMLESS FLOOR

Although you must follow instructions for the type of seamless material you have chosen, there are some procedures basic to all flooring jobs. The surface to be covered must be clean, free of wax, grease, or paint. The floor should be firm and dry. A rough subfloor in new construction should be smoothed and cracks filled. Paint on an older surface can be removed by sanding (a rented professional machine will do the job more effectively than you can by hand). If you are covering a tile or sheet surface material, any loose edges or broken pieces should be glued down or nailed flat. Countersink nails or they may work their way up through the new flooring. A concrete surface with pits and cracks should be patched and smoothed.

If yours is a new house with a concrete slab, allow the concrete to age 45 days before laying the flooring. If it's a slab in an existing garage, workshop, or basement, place a rubber or plastic mat on the concrete overnight. If you find the mat is damp, seamless will not adhere properly. You'll get a better bonding job on a concrete floor if you sand the surface with a medium of coarse grit sandpaper.

Underlayment

If the floor is in poor condition, it should be covered with underlayment. Badly worn sheet or tile material and old wood strip flooring or parquet are easier to cover than repair. An experienced professional on seamless floors recommends particleboard for underlayment.

Stagger underlayment panels to avoid four corners meeting at a common joint and stagger all joints with respect to subfloor joints. Use galvanized nails to avoid rusty spots when the seamless waterbase coat is applied. Nail the sheets with a slight (one-eighth inch) gap between panels. Fill all joints with a crack filler, including the one between underlayment and wall, unless a molding will be used there.

Some manufacturers make a sealer to be used over a subfloor that might produce asphalt or color bleeding. Test for colorfastness by painting a small sample of your floor with the base coat. If in doubt, use the sealer.

Precautions Before Starting

Provide adequate ventilation to remove solvent vapors. Wear a mask if you are sensitive to chemicals. Do not smoke and extinguish pilot lights or possible spark sources in nearby rooms as well as the one you are working in.

Use masking tape to mask off moldings, baseboards, or appliances. Tape should be removed before the first coat of clear plastic is applied over the color flakes.

Have on hand some lacquer thinner and aluminum foil. Roller or brush can be kept soft and re-usable between coats if wet with the thinner and tightly wrapped in foil.

Vertical surfaces should be completed first, and be sure you are working toward an exit.

Base Coat

For the base coat, a roller works easily. One with a long handle will be more comfortable to use. A small paint brush (pure bristles) will get into tight corners. You may need two coats. If so, apply the first coat in one direction, the second at a right angle to the first coat. Three or four hours drying time are needed between coats. You need not be a perfectionist as the flakes will almost entirely conceal the base coat.

Applying the Plastic

Room temperature should not be below 50 degrees nor above 85; humidity a comfortable fifty percent. In a desert area with humidity 25 percent or less, curing may be somewhat slow.

Apply a full, wet coat of plastic with a short nap mohair roller or pure bristle brush. Make sure

Plywood subfloor shown was smooth enough for seamless flooring without further repair. Water-soluble base coat goes on with either roller or brush.

First coat of clear laminating plastic goes on over base coat. The worker is using a thin metal paint edger to level and smooth the plastic. A long-handled mohair roller would be easier on his back and would speed up the job.

that no lint has accumulated on the floor. Colored threads may bleed into the plastic. Work only a small area at a time, about 10 square feet, so the colored flakes can be scattered while the plastic is still wet.

Adding Flakes

Sprinkle or toss color flakes over the wet area from either a crouching or standing position, letting chips fall like seeds or snowflakes. Do not let them build up excessively. Just let them cover the surface evenly. If a spot looks bare and the flakes will not stick, spread more plastic and add chips. If you are using more than one color of flakes, or several containers of the same color, it is advisable to mix colors together in a large container to ensure an even color effect. Handle flakes gently to avoid crushing them into powder. Apply chips a little beyond the edge of the wet plastic to avoid lap marks. Excess chips can be swept up and re-used.

Next, use a clean dry roller and roll firmly over the just sown flakes to embed them in the plastic. Complete each section of the floor to this stage. Roller will pick up bits of flake, but deposit most of them again with no harm done.

Allow the floor to dry at least two hours (check the instructions for type you are using). Sweep with a clean broom, or vacuum, all loose flakes. Bare spots can be touched up. Apply final coat or coats of laminating plastic over entire floor. Drying time will vary depending upon weather and product you are using.

The more coats you add the greater the durability and depth appearance you will get. Be sure each coat is thoroughly dry before adding another.

Final Step

Allow about an 18 hour drying period. The floor will stand light traffic after 12 hours. Protect it, however, with plastic sheeting. Even when the floor seems dry, lint and fibers can adhere to the plastic and be difficult or impossible to remove. Wait 24 hours or more before moving in furniture. Use glass cups under legs of heavy items.

In some future year, when the surface has lost gloss or shows wear, clean the floor with a detergent, rinse and give it a light sanding. You can spread on another coat of plastic only, or add plastic and flakes with a final plastic glaze to areas that have had hard wear. Patches blend in with the original floor. You won't need to renew seamless flooring under the heavy furniture and

you won't need to move it out to do touchups elsewhere in the room.

CLEANING SEAMLESS PLASTIC

Don't wax seamless plastic, as the gloss is built in, and future touchups will be easier if you do not have to worry about wax. A little vinegar in the mop water helps retain the new look of seamless.

Seat Cut

The seat cut is a cut near the end of the rafter which permits the rafter to rest on and be fastened to the top plate of the building framework. The seat cut combined with the plumb cut form a notch, called a bird's mouth, which rests on the top plate. When the rafter does not overhang the top plate, the bottom of the rafter is seat cut and the end of the rafter is cut plumb. *SEE ALSO ROOF CONSTRUCTION.*

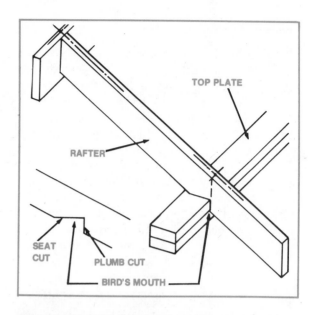

Seepage Pits

Seepage pits are holes in the ground, lined with stone, bricks or concrete blocks, made to collect

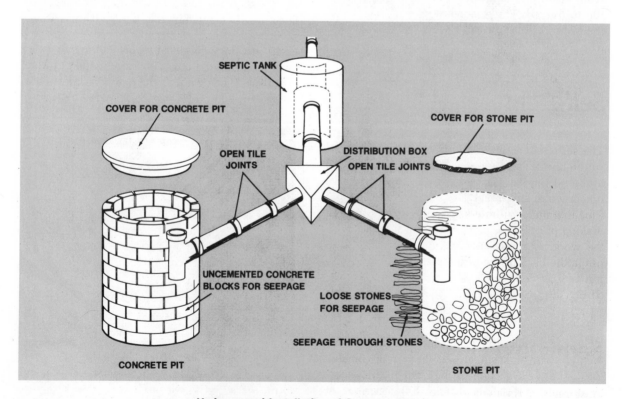

Underground Installation of Seepage Pits

household drainage before it is absorbed into the ground. They are used on steep slopes or hilly land where disposal fields are not practical.

There are two main kinds of seepage pits: the stone pit and the concrete pit. A hole dug in the ground and filled with loose stones is called a stone pit. When built near trees, it has tree roots to help absorb the effluence. A concrete pit, which is concrete block laid with uncemented joints, may also be filled with stones if they are needed to support weak walls.

Although most seepage pits are cylindrical, they are not all round; they may be any size. A large pit may be dug with a bulldozer, filled with loose stones and thinly covered with backfill. However, since most seepage goes through the walls, smaller pits are more efficient than the larger ones. In order for the large pits to work sufficiently, they must be extended over a larger area than the smaller ones.

A distribution box sends the flowing material from the septic tank through open-joint lines of tile to the pit. The absorbing process occurs in the ground bottoms and porous sides of the pit. *SEE ALSO DRAINAGE SYSTEMS.*

Self-Centering Punch

The self-centering punch centers screw holes in countersunk hardware so the screw head can be hidden or makes pilot holes for screws and drill bits in wood and metal. It is also useful in setting finishing nails without scarring the wood. When making pilot holes, place the tip of the punch on the wood or metal surface and strike the loose pin in the back of the punch with a hammer. The pin will drive forward and form the pilot hole. *SEE ALSO HAND TOOLS.*

Semigloss Finish

A semigloss finish is a varnish or lacquer or enamel which contains de-glossing chemicals to break up a surface shine. Semigloss is more shiny than a satin finish in a gloss-to-flat progression of glossy, semiglossy, satin, flat.

The modern semigloss varnishes lose their gloss due to chemicals which do not impede durability. Two coats may be applied without harming the finish. Semigloss varnishes basically provide a satiny look without the work of sanding and waxing down the final coat.

The quality and make-up of lacquered finishes overlap varnish in some ways. Their ability to withstand abuse is good, and they intensify the grain and color of wood without changing its hue.

Semigloss enamels are rarely packaged in dark colors as are glossies which come in dark blues, greens, browns and reds. The reason for this is because the semigloss enamels are generally intended to be used as trim colors to match wall paint. However, both dark and light semiglosses can be obtained from most paint stores which carry custom-color systems. In the very dark shades, semigloss enamels are more expensive because of the additional pigment used to make them. Another disadvantage of highly-pigmented semiglosses is their low resistance to abrasion, water and other damages. Dark semigloss enamels are often less durable than lighter-colored semiglosses and may take a week or more to dry and harden. *SEE ALSO PAINTS & PAINTING; WOOD FINISHING.*

Septic Systems

The bacteria found in a septic tank flourish in the absence of oxygen. This process of decomposing without oxygen is known as *septic*, which is how the tank got its name.

Septic systems are needed in rural and in some suburban residential areas where there is no city sewer to dispose of household wastes. To serve a home efficiently, the septic system must be planned, installed and maintained properly. The

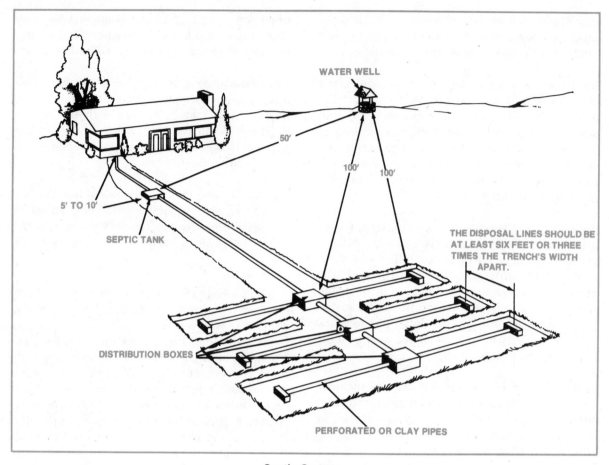

WATER WELL

50'

100' 100'

5' TO 10'

SEPTIC TANK

THE DISPOSAL LINES SHOULD BE
AT LEAST SIX FEET OR THREE
TIMES THE TRENCH'S WIDTH
APART.

DISTRIBUTION BOXES

PERFORATED OR CLAY PIPES

Septic System

system includes a sewer line, septic tank and disposal field.

The local or state code should be consulted before installing a septic system and it should be used as a guide to meet requirements for distances from houses, wells and property lines. If no local code is available, the state health department should have a list of regulations.

Before installing a septic system, a percolation test must be made to check the absorbency of the ground in order to determine the amount of land necessary for the drainage area. The square footage needed for a drainage area is determined by the number of bedrooms in the home. The percolation test involves digging several post holes about 18 to 36 inches deep, or as deep as the proposed trenches. After these holes are filled with six inches of water, note how many

minutes it takes for the water to be absorbed into the ground. The absorbency time will help determine how much square footage to allow for the disposal area. When this area has been figured, the trenches may be dug and the pipes installed. Because a large amount of digging is involved for trench work, the best tool for this job is the backhoe. The first trench to dig connects the house sewer line to the septic tank; it should range from five to ten feet in length. At least four inch diameter pipes of cast iron, clay tile, plastic, fiber or cement-asbestos are laid in this trench, sloping from $1/_8$ inch to $1/_4$ inch per foot from the house. These pipes must be watertight to keep the sewage in and the roots out. Sewer lines should be laid on the trench bottom for best performance, but if the trench is dug too deeply, crushed gravel or stone may be put in it and leveled. The next trench leads from the septic tank to the distribution box and should be just deep enough to connect the two areas with sealed-joint pipe. Radiating from the distribution box is a network of pipe lines known as the drainage field. These pipes should be laid on about six inches of gravel, either leveled or sloping away from the box not more than six inches for every 100 feet. Made of concrete or clay tiles or plastic fiber pipes, these pipes should be four inches in diameter. Perforated pipes, normally in lengths of ten feet, or one-foot long pipes, with $1/4$ inch to $1/2$ inch gaps in between, are laid to permit seepage. These lines should not be longer than 100 feet and at least six feet or three times the trench's width apart. The ends of these disposal lines may be closed with a masonry block or filled in about six inches with gravel to prevent large amounts of end seepage. After settling the drainage tiles, cover them with two inches of gravel or crushed stone. Then put down a layer of newspaper or straw, preventing the earth which is shoveled in, from getting into the gravel. After inspection, the system may be spread with soil and graded. The field's location should not be in an area where cars and trucks will pass over. A few small perennial flowers can be planted at the pumpout opening and distribution box area to help designate their locations and reduce the amount of exploratory digging when repairs are needed or the tank is pumped out.

If a city water supply system is not available, water will be obtained from a well. The well should be located on the higher part of the property and should be at least 50 feet from the septic tank and 100 feet from the disposal field. Depending on the area, either a shallow or a deep well may be dug. The water supply for the well should be both separated and upslope from the disposal field to avoid contamination.

The homeowner must have a general knowledge of how the system works to get satisfactory service. The septic system begins operation with the wastes from the house entering the septic tank, which is a large watertight structure made of metal or concrete. When the sewage enters the tank, solids settle to the bottom and separate from the liquids. A bacterial process decomposes the waste into three forms: liquid, which

flows to the disposal field; gas, which drifts back to the house, escaping up through the vent and sludge, the decomposed solids, which remain on the tank's floor. To keep sewage from flowing straight through the tank or backing up in the sewer line, the outlet is placed lower than the inlet of the tank. Both openings have sanitary T's pointing downward. The drainage field enables the liquid effluent to be absorbed by the ground.

If there is limited land space or the land is too hilly or steep, dry wells or seepage pits may be used in place of a disposal field. If trees or wooded areas are near, a stone pit or a well filled with crushed rocks will be best so that the tree roots can assist in disposing the water.

A good system can become both a nuisance and an expense if it does not have adequate care. The septic tanks should be checked every 12 to 18 months and cleaned every two to four years to prevent sludge build-up from clogging the disposal or sewer lines. Using appliances which economize on water helps prevent effluent overflow in the drainage field. Grease traps may be installed to collect grease which comes mainly from kitchen sinks and dishwashers and clogs disposal fields. *SEE ALSO DRAINAGE SYSTEMS.*

Septic Tanks & Drainage Fields

A septic tank is a large, watertight settling tank, usually made of masonry or steel, which decomposes solids and treats sewage by bacterial action. A drainage field is composed of a group of disposal lines made of large clay pipes. These pipes are either perforated or laid with small gaps in between them to allow seepage.

When laying out a septic tank and drainage field, be sure to use the local or state code as a guide in meeting requirements for distances to houses, wells and property lines. The state health department should have a copy of the regulations, if there is no local code. Normally a minimum distance of five feet is recommended between the house and septic tank, 50 feet between the tank and water well, 100 feet between the drainage field and water well and ten feet between the drainage field's circumference and any property line.

Before installation, the ground's absorbency must be checked by performing a percolation test, which will help determine how much square footage is necessary for the drainage area. The number of square feet needed for the absorption area is based on total bedrooms in the home. To test the ground, dig several post holes to the proposed depth of the drainage trenches, normally from 18 to 36 inches. Fill the hole with water six inches deep and begin clocking how many minutes it takes for the water to be absorbed completely. See the chart for the minimum square feet of drainage area per bedroom.

At least 150 feet should be allowed for the drainage area. Once the required area is figured, the system may be installed.

Septic tanks should be checked every 12 to 18 months and cleaned every two to four years to prevent sludge build-up. Sludge settles to the floor of the tank while the liquid flows to the distribution box or boxes and continues to the drainage field. *SEE ALSO TRENCH DETAILS IN SEPTIC TANK INSTALLATION.*

Time required for water to fall 1 inch (in minutes).	Absorption area in sq. ft. per bedroom
2 or less	85
3	100
4	115
5	125
10	165
15	190
30	250
60	330
Over 60	Special design using seepage pits.

Service Panel

The service panel is a component of the service entrance of a house wiring system. As the panel is also the fuse box or circuit breaker panel, all house circuits originate and terminate at the service panel. The main switch is also located at this point.

Although most power companies prefer to connect the service panel through the service entrance to the utility pole, the home owner is usually left with the actual house wiring. Whether he does this wiring himself or hires a professional for the job, the location of the service panel is of primary concern. Therefore, he should consult the power company as to the location of the nearest utility pole when he is drawing up the plans for the new wiring installation. *SEE ALSO ELECTRICAL WIRING.*

Setscrew Connector

The setscrew connector is used to make wire splices without solder. There are two compo-

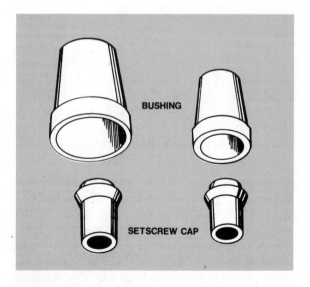

BUSHING

SETSCREW CAP

The size of the setscrew connector depends upon the size of the wires being spliced.

nents to a setscrew connector: the bushing and the setscrew cap. To use such a connector, push the bare wire ends through the hole at the bottom of the bushing and screw the cap onto the bushing, making the wire splice. *SEE ALSO ELECTRICAL WIRING.*

Setscrew Wrench

The setscrew wrench is the same tool as the Allen or key wrench, which is used for headless setscrews found in power tools, door locks, lighting fixtures, etc. There are various sizes of setscrews, consequently, setscrew wrenches are available in sets contained in boxes or plastic pouches. Setscrew heads are also available for socket-wrench sets. *SEE ALSO HAND TOOLS.*

Setting Saws

Setting is a sharpening process used with saws. When a saw is set, the alternating bends in the saw's teeth are restored to the correct angle. When the teeth are set correctly, the resulting kerf is the right width. If the teeth are bent at an excessive angle, the kerf will be too wide; when it is set at a perpendicular angle, the resulting kerf is not wide enough. Observe kerf width and it will indicate when the saw needs to be set. *SEE ALSO SAW SHARPENING.*

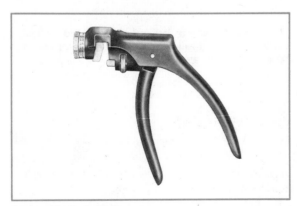

Courtesy of the Stanley Works
Saw Set

Sewage Disposal

A sewage disposal system is needed in rural and in many city homes, where city sewer systems are not built to handle household wastes. Either a septic tank or a cesspool may be installed.

Septic tanks break down solid materials and treat the sewage by a bacterial action before it is absorbed into the ground. The tank, built of masonry or steel, is constructed to stay watertight. When sewage enters the tank, solids are separated from the liquid and fall to the bottom. Then bacterial action begins decomposing the matter. The bottom of the tank retains the insoluable material while the liquid flows to the distribution box or boxes where it branches out into various disposal lines. These disposal lines, known as the drainage field, are made of large clay pipes which have gaps between them to permit seepage. The septic tank's size and the type of drainage field may vary, depending on the number of household occupants and the soil condition.

These tanks must be cleaned out regularly to keep the decomposed solids or sludge on the tank's floor from building up enough to clog disposal or sewer lines. The level of sludge should be checked every 12 to 18 months and cleaned usually every two to four years.

Cesspools are similar to septic tanks except a cesspool does not decompose and treat sewage. It collects raw sewage, disposing of the liquid part by seeping or leaching into the ground. The solids fall to the bottom and remain inside the pit.

Since raw sewage is allowed to seep directly into the ground, cesspools should be located only in porous or sandy soils. They should be placed 150 feet or more from wells and 15 to 20 feet from building groundworks.

Cesspools located near an underground water source can pollute the water slowly, making it unusable and harmful for drinking. When this water reaches the ground surface, it can also expel foul odors.

Should a cesspool become clogged, it will start filling up and overflowing. To clean the tank, it may be pumped or emptied, but this is no guarantee that it will be completely unclogged. If not, the cesspool will refill quickly. At this point, a new cesspool must be built or another cesspool attached to the old one. Because cesspools can become an unsanitary menace to health, many communities have outlawed them. *SEE ALSO SEPTIC SYSTEMS.*

Sewer

As the drain leading from the house enters the ground outside the foundation, it becomes the house sewer. This sewer may lead out through the wall or floor of the basement. If there is no basement, it can lead through the slab of the first floor or the crawl area beneath the first floor.

The kind of sewage disposal required will depend upon the house sewer's level beneath the lawn. A house sewer, which is assembled to a city sewer under the street, will be quite deep, normally slanting downward from the basement level to the street sewer. The house sewer connected to a septic tank will usually be nearer to the surface of the lawn, since septic systems do not operate as well when too deep below the ground.

The procedure to follow when laying a house sewer is included in local regulations. To insure full compliance of the local code, a copy of it should be obtained at the city building department or county courthouse before any work begins. Any questions about installation details may be referred to the sanitary inspector. Running a sewer line to a septic tank rather than a city sewer usually involves easy planning, since most of the septic system is under the homeowner's control and a little shifting may be done if necessary. However, the city sewer is fixed under the street, so before the plumbing job

begins, all information concerning depth and location of the sewer is needed.

Basic procedures in laying the house sewer are common, even though local code details may vary. If possible, the pipe to be used should have at least a four inch diameter and run straight to the sewer from the house. Any changes of direction in it should be gradual; for example, a 90-degree turn should be changed to two 45-degree ones. A clean-out fitting is required in the house, beginning at the outgoing run of the sewer, and continuing every 50 feet along the run and at each 45- or more degree bend. Required clean-outs found underground are normally sanitary T's, which have a capped, threaded clean-out plug and fitting. These are attached to the pipe leading directly up to the surface of the lawn. When a clean-out tape is pushed down the pipe, the curve of the sanitary T guides the tape curving it toward the street sewer. A house sewer should slope downward from at least $1/8''$ to $1/4''$ per foot. *SEE ALSO DRAINAGE SYSTEMS.*

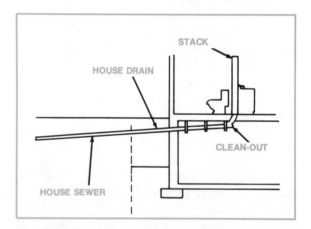

This house sewer is led out through the wall of a basement and is near the lawn surface for connection to a septic tank.

Sewer Gas

Sewer gas is an explosive vapor produced when waste matter is decomposed. If pressure is allowed to build up in the drainage system, this vapor will rise to all the plumbing fixtures in the house. To prevent the gas from drifting through the drains and entering the house, there are pipe traps, which act as seals, and also vents, which allow the gas to escape. *SEE ALSO DRAINAGE SYSTEMS.*

Shakes & Shingles

A shingle is a building material that is usually rectangular, square or hexagonal in shape and may be used to cover roofs or exterior walls. Asphalt, wood and mineral fiber are the more common types of shingles.

Shakes are also used to cover roofs and exterior walls and are available in many different dimensions to match the size of the home. Unlike shingles, shakes are primarily made of wood.

Courtesy of Western Red Cedar & Hand Split Shake Assn.

Shingle and shake installation may vary somewhat according to the roof pitch, the type wall and the effect desired. The following methods of applying shakes and shingles to wall and roof are only basic and can be altered for different materials.

APPLYING ROOF SHINGLES

After the sheathing and underlayment have been laid, use a chalkline to insure a straight application. Then, space the first row of shingles 1/4 inch apart to allow for expansion and align them with the roof edge. Only two nails are used on each shingle and their placement should be two inches up from the area that is to be exposed. If one half of the length of the shingle is to lay open, add two inches to one half of the length of the shingle, measure that far up the shingle from the edge and drive in the nails. The nails should be no more than 3/4 inch from the shingle edge so

it will lie flat. Double or triple the first course. Nail the second layer of shingles over the first so the course joints are no less than 1½ inches apart. Shingles may be cut to a miter around a valley. In those areas, the shingles should be laid from the valley first.

When installing wood shingles, allow them to extend ½ inch to ¾ inch over the eave edge. Longer nails are required with wood shingles than with other types because of their extra thickness. Use 5d zinc-coated or rust-resistant box nails for 16 inch and 18 inch shingles and 6d nails for 24 inch shingles. Wood shingles may be purchased in panels to make installation easier.

To form tight hips and ridges, alternately overlap two rows of shingles or cut the last course even with the roof ridge. Then, place a hip and ridge unit over the ridge.

APPLYING ROOF SHAKES

A roof must have enough slope to provide proper drainage before wood shakes may be applied. Begin shake application by running a 35 inch strip of 30 pound roofing felt along the eaves. As with shingles, the first course is doubled. If 32 inch shakes are used, leave no more than 13 inches exposed, 10 inches for 24 inch shakes and 8½ for 18 inch shakes. Apply an 18 inch strip of felt over the upper portion of the shakes and onto the sheathing after each course. Place the bottom edge of the felt above the butt a distance twice that of the desired exposure. Space the shakes ¼ inch to ⅜ inch apart and offset the joints no less than 1½ inches in adjacent courses.

When nailing the shakes, use hot-dipped zinc coated nails; 6d should be sufficient size. Drive the nails one to two inches above the butt line of the following course and one or more inches in from the edge. Avoid driving the nailheads into the shakes. Select shakes the same size for the final course at the ridge line. Place roofing felt along the hips and ridges and then apply the shakes. Nail them in place and top with a hip and ridge unit.

APPLYING WALL SHINGLES

Basically, wall shingles are applied the same as

roofing shingles. However, both vertical and horizontal chalklines should be used for perfectly aligned work. Metal corner beads are applied at outside corners and a flashing strip 12 inches wide of asphalt-saturated felt is installed at every inside corner. Around wall openings where the trim is even with the backer board, a metal stop or narrow wood molding should be installed one inch from the edge of the outside trim. Use asphalt plastic cement under joints between shingles and trim.

APPLYING WALL SHAKES

To reduce installation time, wood shakes for side walls are available in panel form. Metal corners come with the shakes to provide a water tight surface and the same procedure for wood shake installation may be followed for panels. *SEE ALSO ROOFING MATERIALS.*

Shallow Well Pump

A shallow well pump is a motorized adaptation of the lift pump. Although no adhesives are used, a shallow well's inner surface is lined with stones. Rain and other surface resources provide water for the shallow well that is normally located 15 to 30 feet below ground-level.

Because it is sealed, pressure builds in the water-storage tank. The bubbling air along the pipe, also, helps to maintain the pressure. Even though the automatic pressure switch for the pump may be off, a steady pressure is maintained in the water-supply system by the rising water in the tank compressing the air above it.

The pressure switch which is about the size of an orange, is attached to the pump by a slim copper tube. This switch is turned on and off by the water pressure in the tube which pushes a flexible diaphragm in the switch outward until it shuts off. As the pressure decreases, the diaphragm moves back in until the switch comes on again. *SEE ALSO PUMPS.*

Shaper

In most home shops, shaping operations are usually done on a drill press, radial arm saw or table saw with a molding head. Quite often, homecraftsmen use a router mounted under a table setup or work with a hand-held router. Such applications can result in very acceptable shaping jobs.

The individual shaping machine is a tool specifically designed to provide optimum shaping results. All basic shaping techniques are constant regardless of the tool being used.

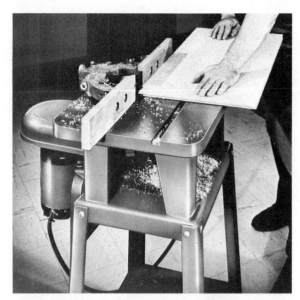

The individual shaper has its mechanism mounted under the table. It has adequate speed for the job, the right power and a control that permits changing the direction of cutter rotation.

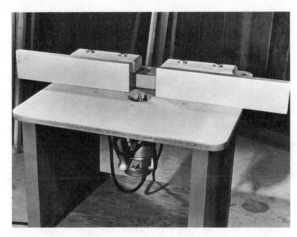

Many craftsmen mount a portable router as shown for use as a shaper. The fence in the drill press entry for use with shaper work can be used as part of a router-shaper design.

General Features

Cutter mounting on the shaper is by means of a vertical spindle, but it differs from the drill press in that it is mounted under the work table and is designed to withstand considerable side thrust and speed. Since the drive mechanism is below, there are no top side obstructions (such as a drill-press column) to interfere with work size and work handling.

A good shaper will have a hollow spindle so designed that it will accept auxiliary spindles such as a "stub" for doing cope-type cuts. Built-in adjustments permit raising or lowering the

spindle so you can position the cutter; positive locks let you secure it at the desired height.

The usual spindle diameter is $1/2''$, and this goes along with the common $1/2''$ hole size of popular three-lip shaper cutters. Other spindle diameters

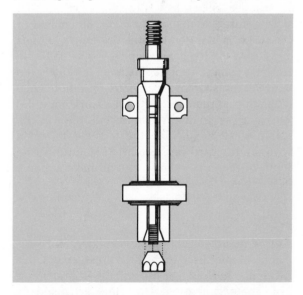

Spindles thread onto one end of a stud or "tierod" that slips through the hollow main spindle and is secured with a lock nut at the opposite end. This arrangement permits the use of different spindle designs.

Shaper

can be $5/16''$ or $3/4''$, but the latter is a commercial concept for constant, superduty functions. The spindles are fitted with a tie-rod or stud that passes through the main, hollow spindle and is secured at the free end with a nut.

A good home-size shaper — one that will handle three-lip shaper cutters with a $1/2''$ hole efficiently — can be driven with a $1/2$ HP motor. If you plan to expand the use of the tool by using some of the other types of cutters, then a $3/4$ or 1 HP motor will not be out of line.

It is important to be able to reverse the motor's direction of rotation. Being able to work in two directions is part and parcel of shaper technique. Sometimes a switch, in addition to the on-off switch, is provided for motor direction changes. Other times a lever is provided as part of the main switch to accomplish the same thing.

Motor speed and pulley relationship should be organized for a spindle speed of about 10,000 rpm's. Some shapers might be designed for more speed, some for less, so be sure to read the owner's manual that comes with the tool you buy and obey the speed recommendations.

The shaper fence is basically a two-part deal that locks securely to the shaper table. Either half of the fence is adjustable, and the entire unit is removable for freehand shaping against fulcrum pins and collars. Fence adjustment is exactly the same as for shaping operations on other tools. When the cut removes part of the work edge, the fences are set in line. When the cut removes the entire work edge, then the outfeed fence is brought forward an amount that equals the depth of the cut so the work will have support after it has passed the cutter.

Cutters

Cutters mount on the spindle as they do on a shaper adapter used in the drill press. Again, the difference here is that the spindle is under the table instead of over it. Collars are used in freehand work to control the depth of the cut, but they are also used when working with a fence to take up spindle length that is not occupied by the cutter.

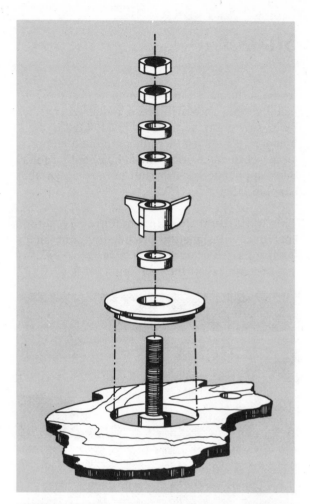

Three-lip shaper cutters mount on the spindle as they do on a shaper adapter that is used with the drill press. Collars are used for freehand work, but also to take up unused spindle length when working against a fence.

Collars made for the shaper are available in thicknesses ranging from $1/8''$ up to $1/2''$ and in various diameters. Many shaper craftsmen will make up special collars to suit a particular application. You can even buy ball-bearing collars. The advantage of this feature is that the collar will not turn with the spindle, thus eliminating scoring and burning that can occur with solid collars. The most you can do with solid collars is to keep them clean and polished.

You can buy cutters, such as the *glue joint* or the *tongue-and-groove*, that are designed to do a specific job; or you can buy combination cutters, such as the *bead and quarter round*. The latter

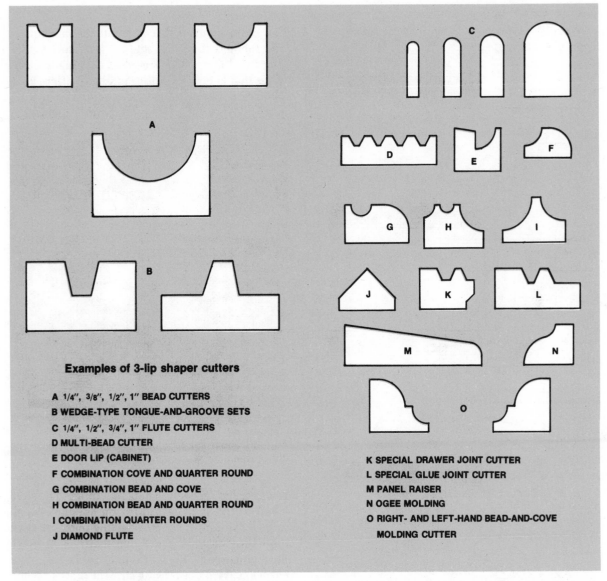

Examples of 3-lip shaper cutters

A 1/4", 3/8", 1/2", 1" BEAD CUTTERS

B WEDGE-TYPE TONGUE-AND-GROOVE SETS

C 1/4", 1/2", 3/4", 1" FLUTE CUTTERS

D MULTI-BEAD CUTTER

E DOOR LIP (CABINET)

F COMBINATION COVE AND QUARTER ROUND

G COMBINATION BEAD AND COVE

H COMBINATION BEAD AND QUARTER ROUND

I COMBINATION QUARTER ROUNDS

J DIAMOND FLUTE

K SPECIAL DRAWER JOINT CUTTER

L SPECIAL GLUE JOINT CUTTER

M PANEL RAISER

N OGEE MOLDING

O RIGHT- AND LEFT-HAND BEAD-AND-COVE
   MOLDING CUTTER

types are designed for partial cuts; you use that portion of the profile that suits a particular job. The others are designed for full profile cuts.

A three-knife cutterhead is often used on a shaper. This is like a small-size table-saw molding head, and there are a variety of ready-shaped knives that can be used with it. Since they come with a ³/₄" center hole, they are a heavy-duty tool. But they can be used on a ¹/₂" spindle by mounting them with a bushing.

Another type of cutter consists of open-face knives that are locked between slotted collars.

They have an advantage in that you can buy blank knives and grind them to any shape. You can grind a different shape at each end of the knife. You must be extremely careful when mounting such knives. If the collars do not bear equally and tightly on both knives, the less secure one could fly out when you flick the switch. This can happen because you have done a poor job of securing the knives to begin with or because you have installed knives of unequal width. This would cause one knife to be gripped, the other to be loose. Should you check out this type of cutter, be sure to read carefully the accompanying instructions.

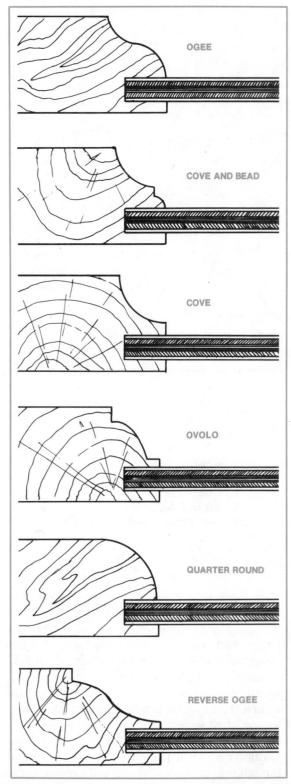

OGEE

COVE AND BEAD

COVE

OVOLO

QUARTER ROUND

REVERSE OGEE

Examples of classic molding forms, shown with inserted panel sections.

Safety

Use all the guards that come with the machine or buy them if they are sold as accessories. The guard that is used for freehand shaping is a ring affair that is held over the spindle. It offers good protection and even does some hold-down work if you set it so it rests on the work's surface.

The ring above the table is a guard that is used when doing freehand work against collars.

Never try to freehand shape anything that is too small or too narrow to provide adequate hand room. If you must shape a narrow piece, do it on the end of a wide board and then slice off the part you need. This practice holds for even curves, varying curves or straight pieces. When feeding, keep fingers hooked over work edges. This will guard against your hands slipping where they should not be. When working against collars, be sure that there is sufficient bearing surface against the collar. As stated before, keep the collars clean and polished. Soiled or scarred collars will not only harm the work, they will make it harder to feed.

Whenever possible, set up so that the cutter is under the work. This positioning will put the work between you and the cutters and eliminate the possibility of damaging the work should you accidentally lift it during a pass.

Operational Techniques

Regardless of which way the cutter turns, the work must always be fed against the direction of rotation. When the cutter is turning in counterclockwise fashion, the work is fed from the right to the left. When the cutter turns clockwise, work is fed from left to right. This method applies whether you are working against a fence or doing freehand feeding against collars.

Work may be placed flat on the table or on the edge. Since there is nothing above the cutter (like the drill-press spindle), you can handle any work width when doing an on-edge pass.

Try to feed so you are cutting with the grain, which will always produce the smoothest cuts. When conditions demand otherwise, slow up on the pass. Many times in such circumstances, it's wise to do the job in repeat passes; simply increase depth of cut after each pass until you have the shape you want.

Cross-grain cuts will usually result in some slight imperfections at the end of the pass. You can minimize these by being very cautious at the end and finishing with minimum feed speed. You can eliminate them by shaping a piece that is oversized and then doing a jointer cut or a slight rip cut with a hollowground blade on the edges after the shaping operation. The idea is to remove any imperfections by making a second cut.

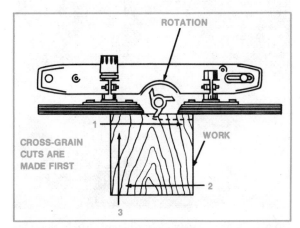

When cutting crossgrain, do it slowly. On multi-edge work, do the crossgrain passes first. The last passes should be on with-the-grain edges.

When you must shape all edges or adjacent edges of a workpiece, do the cross-grain cuts first. The final with-the-grain cuts will remove the imperfections left by the previous passes.

Most shapers provide for the use of a miter gauge. It's a good idea to use it on all cross-grain work, but it's very important to use it when you are shaping an end on narrow stock. If you don't have a miter gauge, make a right-angle backup block to use in its place. Such precautions will keep the work square to the cutter and will prevent rocking of the work.

When you are doing a full cut, the outfeed fence must be advanced to support the work after it has passed the cutter. The best way to do this is to start with the outfeed fence retracted. Then adjust the infeed fence for the depth of cut you wish. Make a partial pass — that is, hold the work against the infeed fence and feed until an inch or so of the work edge has passed the cutter. Turn off the machine and then adjust the outfeed fence until it bears lightly against the shaped edge.

Feed speed, regardless of the power and rpm's of your machine, should always be slow and steady. Make wise judgments in relation to the results you are getting and in tune with how the machine is reacting. It's never wise to cut so deep or so fast that there is an obvious decrease in rpm's or a noticeable objection in terms of motor sound. The harder the wood, the deeper the bite, the more cautious you must be. You will find when you force the cut that you will get obvious burn marks. Some of these will be difficult to remove, so it makes sense not to create them at all by working with sharp tools, sensible feed and reasonable depth-of-cut settings.

Special Fences

Almost any type of fence can be secured to the shaper table in place of the regular fence by organizing the item to use the same hardware employed with the standard fence or simply by using clamps.

A long fence can be handy for work that requires more support than you can get from the regular

To use this fence, brace one end of the work against the stop pin and then move the work direcly forward into the cuter. Pull the work back, re-position the pin and repeat.

shaper table. It's also good to have when you wish to use stop blocks to control the length of a cut. Regular shaper fences are seldom long enough to permit much flexibility in this area. This type of fence is usable for many jobs such as shaping, narrowing and precutting strips. Cut a work-size rabbet in a block that you then clamp or nail over the cutter. The narrow work can then be fed through the block in complete safety.

Since the regular shaper fence is quite low, you can provide more support for wide work that must be shaped with on-edge passes simply by making an extra-high auxiliary fence. Be sure that the vertical member is square to the table and that it is adequately braced to provide rigidity.

A miter fence, when used with blank knives, will do bevel-type operations on the shaper. It will also do shaping cuts on edges that are already beveled, as well as form tongue-and-groove joints on miters. You can make the jig adjustable simply by using hinges to attach the table to the fence. An assortment of angle braces that you use under the table will let you organize for different bevel settings. Attach the angle braces with screws driven through the top of the table. Thus, you can change quickly from one set of braces to another. The braces you make, at least to start, should include 45°, 30° and maybe 15° settings.

You can do some fairly decorative edge work by making a special fence that permits you to move work directly into the cutter without any normal feed action. The fence is a straight board with a series of equally spaced holes drilled along the bottom edge. A pin in the holes acts as a stop for the work. To do the job, you brace one edge of the work against the pin and then move directly forward to make the cut. Pull the work back, set the pin in the next hole and then make the next cut. Just keep repeating the same procedure. Spacing of the cuts will depend on how you place the stop pin. Be sure to use at least 3/4" stock for the fence. Quarter-inch holes, spaced an inch apart, will do to start. You can always add more holes. Use a short length of 1/4" drill rod as the stop pin.

Pivot Work

You can do pivot work by using a hardwood bar in the miter-gauge slot. A nail driven through the end of the bar serves as a pivot point. This operation should not be approached carelessly. Place the work over the pin and leave the hardwood bar loose as you hand feed to get the depth of cut you want. Then, turn off the machine and use a clamp to secure the bar position. Hold the work firmly, turn on the machine and rotate the stock against the direction of rotation of the cutter. If you neglect to use a positive grip, the cutter can take over and spin the work out of control. Keep the depth of cut light and feed slowly.

Do pivot work by using a hardwood strip in the table slot. Here, the pivot pin is extra long just so it can be seen; best to keep it as short as possible. Read the text before trying this technique.

Segment Jigs

The examples of segment jigs are much the same as those for shaping operations on other tools. The jigs can be organized for inside or outside cuts. It is important for the bearing edge of both the jig and the work to be true and smooth.

These jigs are designed for mass production use. When you have a few pieces to do, it's probably faster to handle them as freehand cuts against collars. An advantage of a segment jig is that it provides a little more safety than a similar freehand operation on narrow work.

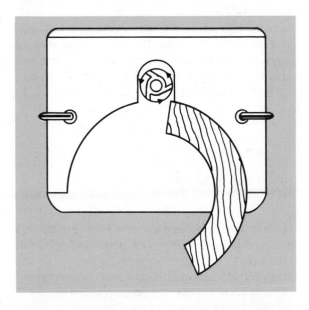

Segment jig for outside curves. When working like this, be sure that the curve of the jig and of the work are perfect matches. Both the jig-edge and the work-edge must be even and smooth.

If you check the shaping sections of the radial-arm-saw and the drill-press entries, you'll find a V-jig that is recommended for shaping the edge of circular stock. The same thing can be done on the shaper. The advantage of the V-jig lies in its being able to handle any diameter work within its capacity. *SEE ALSO BAND SAW; BENCH GRINDER; DRILL PRESS; JIGSAW; LATHE; JOINTER; RADIAL ARM SAW; STATIONARY BELT & DISC SANDER; TABLE SAW.*

Shaping Saws

Shaping saws are a group of saws used for making forms like circles, semi-circles and ovals. Coping, keyhole and compass saws fall into this category.

Shaping saws also defines the process of shaping a saw with a file. "Shaping" a saw restores its teeth to their original contour and size. This is necessary when teeth are too small and misshapen due to continuous filing, jointing or hand use. *SEE ALSO HAND TOOLS.*

Sharpening Stones

Sharpening stones are inexpensive and produce very sharp edges. The stones may be natural or synthetic. Good natural stones are more costly and include Hard Arkansas and Soft Arkansas stones. Synthetic stones are often made by bonding together aluminum-oxide grains or silicon-carbide grains.

There are different forms of abrasive stones. Files, used for fine work, are stones in stick form. Bench stones are rectangular-shaped and used mainly for sharpening small cutting tools. Slipstones are for sharpening straight-edge tools or concave tools because of the stones' flat surfaces and rounded edges. There are also oval and diamond shaped stones designated for specific purposes.

Some stones are oil-filled by the manufacturer, but if they were not, the stones must soak in oil overnight. The best oil for this is highly refined mineral oil or medicinal mineral oil. Sewing machine oil or kerosene may also be used.

A lubricant should be used with even the oil-filled stones. This prevents dust and metal from becoming embedded in the stone and making it eventually useless. The oil should be wiped off after using the stone. Apply a small amount of fresh oil before storing it. Kerosene and a fiber brush can be used occasionally for cleaning. Always soak the stones in oil after cleaning.

Store a bench stone in a wooden box. This will protect it from dirt and dust, and the box can hold the stone in place during sharpening. To save the flat surface of a stone, use all areas of it, not only the center. *SEE ALSO TOOL SHARPENING.*

Shear Cut Bit

There are two types of shear cut router bits. The down-cutting variety produces very fine edges and is an excellent tool to use in grooving veneered surfaces. The up-cutting type is useful for making deep cuts as the bit helps to lift the chips out of the groove. *SEE ALSO ROUTER.*

Shears

Shears are identical to a pair of scissors except typically larger. Blade lengths average 6″ or more. Blade shapes are straight, curved or hooked, depending on the work to be done. Grass shears are straight-bladed, whereas the pruning shears are hooked for greater leverage. The blades may be attached either horizontally or diagonally for better maneuvering and comfort for the user.

The two basic types of blade surfaces are smooth and triangular. The triangular surface provides a

ravel-resistant edge as well as a decorative finish. Types of shears include dressmaking, animal grooming, grass clipping, gardening, pruning, light-weight metal cutting and paper cutting. *SEE ALSO HAND TOOLS.*

Sheathing

Sheathing is the covering applied to the outside of studs and rafters to make the framework rigid and strong. This covering usually consists of plywood, rough boards or fiberboard panels used as a base for the roof and wall finish materials. Application may be horizontal, vertical or diagonal depending on the material used and the ease of application. Sheathing may be anywhere from $1/2$ to $3/4$ inches thick and come in sheets from 4 x 8 feet to as large as 8 x 14 feet. *SEE ALSO WALL & CEILING CONSTRUCTION.*

Shed Roof

A shed roof, also known as a lean-to roof, is a simple kind of pitched roof which is frequently connected to a larger structure, especially in contemporary designs. This roof may be used above ground level rooms, garages and porches. *SEE ALSO ROOF CONSTRUCTION.*

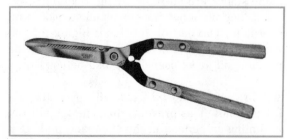

Courtesy of The Stanley Works

Gardening Shears

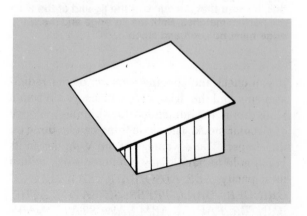

Shed Roof

Sheet Metal

The sheet metal category includes brass, copper, aluminum, iron, galvanized iron, tinplate, zinc, and perforated steel. The sheets are no more than $3/16$ inch in thickness. Welded wire mesh, used for decorative purposes, animal cages and screens for windows and related purposes, is also considered a sheet metal. In the area of building construction, downspouts and gutters are made of galvanized iron in sheet metal form. Sheet metal is also used for sidewalls, window heads and sills, door heads and flashing for roofs. Sheet metal projects are easily worked with and assembled, including cutting, bending and hammering, in a home workshop.

Sheet Vinyl

Sheet vinyl is a sheet flooring available in 6, 9 and 12 foot widths. Years ago tile was the flooring most handymen tackled because it was relatively simple. Because of the 12 foot widths, sheet vinyl has become practical for the handyman to use. Its design is covered by a resilient layer of clear vinyl, and it needs little maintenance and is quite durable.

The back of sheet vinyl is made of moisture proof asbestos. This backing makes it suitable for sheet vinyl to be placed in damp areas such as basements and porches. The backing provides stability to eliminate creeping and buckling.

INSTALLATION

Installation of sheet vinyl is simple and requires only nine steps.

1. Check the old flooring. Smooth out roughness and pound down high places and nail heads. Sweeping the old floor will remove debris that will cause lumps in the new flooring.

2. Remove the base of the quarter round molding. This is done by placing the edge of a claw

hammer or wrecking bar under it and raising it carefully to loosen the nails.

3. Measure the room to find the maximum length and width. Several measurements are needed on irregular or odd shaped rooms. Roll the vinyl out in another area and allow it to reach room temperature. After the vinyl is rolled out, transfer the measurements on it allowing three inches longer and wider than the measurements indicate. Snap a chalk line along one side of the vinyl for a true edge. At this time make as many cut-outs as possible for pipes, radiators and other protrusions.

4. Use a linoleum knife or heavy shears to cut along the measurement lines. Cut the flooring face up for a cleaner, more even edge.

5. Place the true edge of the vinyl along the straightest, longest wall. Allow the vinyl to curve up on the other walls.

6. Press the sheet vinyl gently, but firmly, in place and trim off excess. Leave an additional 1/8 inch clearance along all vertical surfaces.

7. Seaming is only needed for rooms wider than 12 feet. If seaming is necessary, overlap the two pieces and match the pattern. Make certain there is enough sheet vinyl lengthwise and widthwise to match the pattern. Then, tape the matched edges so that they do not shift. Cut the vinyl to fit along the walls allowing $1/8$ inch clearance. Place a straight edge along the overlap as a cutting guide and cut completely through both sheets using a sharp knife. Be sure to keep the knife vertical, not leaning any to the right or left. After the cutting is complete, remove both cut-off pieces.

Lay back one side of the sheet vinyl and draw a pencil or chalk line along the edge of the second piece. Now, fold back the second piece and apply a six inch band of adhesive on the floor under the seam area. For a sounder bond, lightly sand the portion of the underside of the sheet vinyl that will come in contact with the adhesive. Replace the pieces of vinyl onto the wet adhesive and wipe firmly with a damp cloth.

8. Doorways are finished with a metal threshold. The screws should be fastened to the floor and not through the vinyl. At doorways where vinyl meets with hardwood, trim the vinyl flush and cement or cap the threshold.

9. The last step is replacing the quarter round. Slip a piece of cardboard or scrap piece of vinyl under the molding to allow clearance for wall and floor movement. Nail the molding into the base but definitely not into the floor. After the nailing is complete, remove the cardboard or scraps of vinyl. The sheet vinyl is now completely installed. Most flooring jobs take only three to four hours. *SEE ALSO FLOOR CONSTRUCTION.*

Shellac

Shellac is one of the more common surface finishes. The natural resin obtained from an insect is dissolved in alcohol to produce shellac. Shellac has a low resistance to water damage and usually softens in contact with alcohol or other chemicals, but it does give a good sheen, waxes well and is economical. Shellac is flexible, and if applied correctly, it will not craze or check.

Shellac flows on the surface easily. When applied, the brush should be full of shellac and pulled evenly and slowly so that lap marks will not show. Because shellac is not a one coat finish, the application of two or more coats allows the handyman to repair mistakes and smooth out spots caused by dust. One of the added features of shellac is that successive coats fuse. Although shellac dries in a half hour, recoating should be done three to four hours later.

When buying shellac, remember to purchase an equal amount of alcohol. Thinned shellac is necessary for a smooth, no lap mark finish, proper application and a good drying time. When purchasing shellac, the handyman will find the term *cut* used, such as a five pound cut. Cut simply refers to the amount of resin to one gallon of alcohol. A five pound cut is five pounds of resin to one gallon of alcohol. A three pound cut can be used on floors without adding alcohol, but all other cuts for any other use need to be thinned. The two basic types of shellac are orange and white. White shellac becomes a clear finish while orange shellac has an amber cast.

To achieve maximum results, sand between applications with flint or an open-coat abrasive. After the desired thickness of shellac is achieved, use steel wool to rub grainwise. Waxing, if desired, can be done 24 hours after the last coating of shellac. Applications of wax adds a water-resistance to the finish that shellac, in itself does not provide. While steel wool gives a flat finish, waxing and buffing provides a satin finish. Although wax is applied with steel wool, buffing should be accomplished with lamb's wool, a rotary sander pad or a soft pad made of rags. If an additional coating is desired, do not use urethane finish. The adhesion between urethane finish and shellac is poor.

French polishing requires a mixture of shellac and a few drops of linseed oil to achieve a luxurious, deep shine. *SEE ALSO WOOD FINISHING.*

Shelves & Shelf Construction

Shelf storage is planned storage. Shelves must fit the items now needing storage and allow for future acquisitions.

The items to be stored should determine the length, shape, strength and placement of shelves. Shelves of uniform length and identical separation boxed across a wall are seldom the most efficient or effective way to store or display items.

An area's use influences the location and design of shelves. A narrow hallway is no place for open shelves of delicate china. Similarly, projecting display items should not be placed on shelves next to high-traffic areas.

a

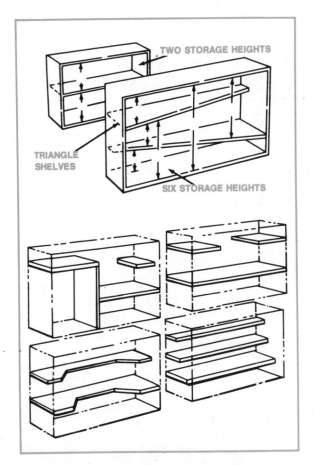

Each of these shelf arrangements provides storage for tall and short items. Notice that tall items are stored to the front where they may be easily removed.

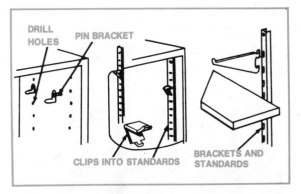

Three means of adjusting shelf height are shown. They may be built in or added to walls or case units.

Step shelves, balcony shelves, triangular shelves, and other specially shaped shelves provide attractive ways to precisely plan storage. Triangular shelves, for example, can provide six storage heights in the space normally used by two. Narrow balcony shelves along the sides of cabinets or built-ins are efficient ways to store small items.

Fixed shelves limit the homeowner to one set pattern of storage. Often this means fitting the items to be stored to the shelves. Adjustable shelves, on the other hand, provide the homeowner with greater flexibility.

Most adjustable shelves are supported by some form of a pin or bracket system. The pins or brackets are easily shifted to raise or lower the shelves. Such changes enable the shelves to accommodate different sized times.

Adjustable shelves may be used in most any room. Adjustable shelving in a child's room may be moved up the wall to accommodate for the child's growth. Bookshelves may be repositioned to accommodate changes in a collection of books, or curio or display items.

A wide variety of supports are available for adjustable shelves. In addition to the various commercial supports, the home craftsman can form his own. For example, purchased metal pin brackets may be fitted into a series of blind holes (holes drilled partway through a support or bookcase side). Nails or screws may be used in the same way. Some brands of paneling contain a support system for wall brackets.

Adjustable wall shelves may not solve all of the homeowner's storage problems. Case pieces (bookcases, china cabinets, etc.) provide additional space for storage. Unfinished furniture often may have adjustable shelving added easily.

Freestanding shelves provide another alternative to wall shelves. Probably most familiar as metal shop shelves, freestanding shelves are now available in wood and metal and in a variety of furniture styles.

A particular type of freestanding shelf that is gaining in popularity is the furniture component system. With this system, the homeowner buys the parts that he needs to build the storage unit

Commercial shelf units come in a wide variety of possible design combinations. Spindles are available in several popular furniture styles. This type shelving may be added to or changed to meet changing storage or decorating needs.

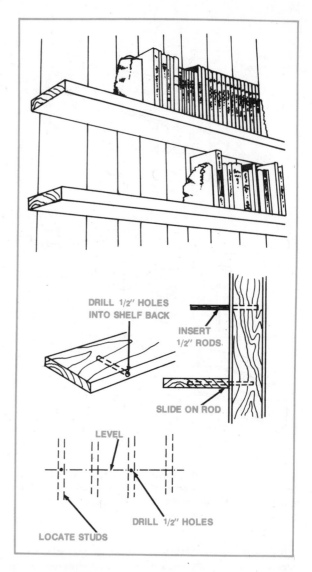

he wishes. Most systems now available provide both the basic parts — shelves, feet, caps, spacers or spindles (the "legs") — plus a variety of special use parts: quarter-round shelves, bookcase units, desk units and storage units with or without doors. A variety of furniture styles, usually including Early American, Mediterranian, Scandivanian or Modern, can be found in the component systems.

Wall shelving also offers the homeowner a wide choice. With the careful combination of commercial shelving and homeowner-designed units, attractive and useful storage can be built. Wood, metal rods and metal straps can all be used to support wall shelves. Rods may be driven into wall studs to support "floating" shelves.

Wall brackets are fastened to the wall in two general ways: by nails or screws driven into wall studs, or by toggle or expansion bolts that grip the plaster or gypsum board of the wall between the studs. The total weight of the shelves and the stored items should be carefully estimated when deciding whether to fasten the supports with ex-

pansion bolts or to the studs. For example, one book may weigh less than a pound; 600 books will weigh more than 500 pounds. That weight, plus the weight of the shelves themselves, might place a severe strain on the plaster or wallboard if just expansion bolts were used to hold the shelves to the wall. To avoid the possible collapse of the shelves and the wall, such a heavy load should be fastened to the wall studs.

A wide variety of supports can be built by the home craftsman. In addition to the commercially available brackets and pins mentioned earlier, the home craftsman may also make shelf brackets or supports out of material usually available in the home workshop. For example,

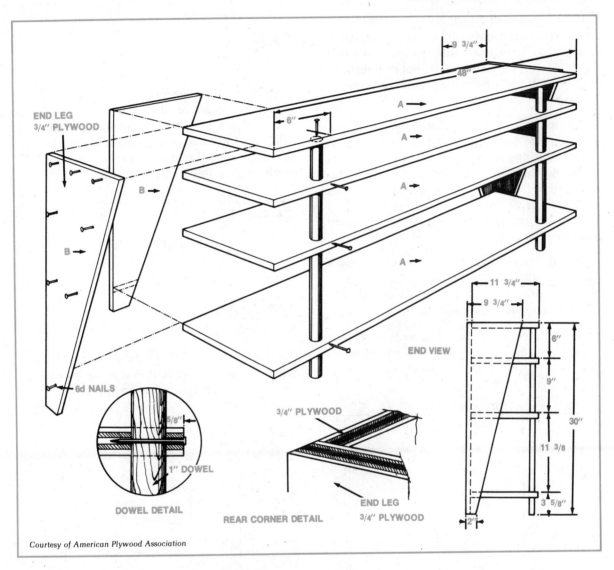

END LEG
3/4" PLYWOOD

6d NAILS

5/8"

1" DOWEL

DOWEL DETAIL

REAR CORNER DETAIL

3/4" PLYWOOD

END LEG
3/4" PLYWOOD

END VIEW

9 3/4"

48"

6"

11 3/4"

9 3/4"

6"

9"

30"

11 3/8

3 5/8"

2"

Courtesy of American Plywood Association

short lengths of scrap dowel may be converted into shelf supports when inserted in a series of blind holes. Most of these supports may be made with either hand or power tools.

Some shelf supports provide the homemaker with a multiple use capability. For example, some shelf supports are hinged, so that the shelf may fold out of the way if not in use. If a plastic laminate or enamel paint is applied to the top of the shelf, a necessary bar, buffet or desk also becomes part of the room decor. Some metal shelf supports also have provision for a clothes pole. This hanger may be used to support a rod for a curtain that conceals storage below the pole. *SEE ALSO BUILT-INS.*

HOW TO BUILD A SET OF UTILITY SHELVES.

The utility shelves described below may be used in a laundry room, a craft area, a potting shed, or other areas around the house. They may be built from 4' x 7' sheet of plywood.

1. Allowing for saw kerfs, lay out all parts on the plywood, following the cutting diagram.

2. Cut out all parts using either a hand saw (10- to 15-point crosscut) or a table saw (plywood or combination blade). Sand mating edges as necessary, and check for fit.

3. Mark location of 1-inch holes for dowel legs, using measurements shown on plan. Drill through the three lower shelves, using a brace and bit to avoid splintering. Do not drill through the top shelf; drill holes ³/₈ deep as sockets for the dowels.

4. Assemble the shelves. Butt joints are used throughout to simplify construction. Using glue and 6d finishing nails as shown, attach "B" legs to shelves. Cut dowels for front legs to length. Insert through holes in lower shelves into top shelf, then drive finishing nail through top shelf to anchor. Nail through shelves as shown on plan to anchor remaining shelves to dowels.

5. Set all nails. All holes and exposed edges should be filled with spackle or wood paste before painting. Sand edges and ease corners with 3-0 sandpaper on a soft block.

6. Use a flat enamel for an undercoat on all surfaces. Finish the shelves with two coats of semi-gloss enamel. Sand lightly between coats.

Courtesy of American Plywood Association

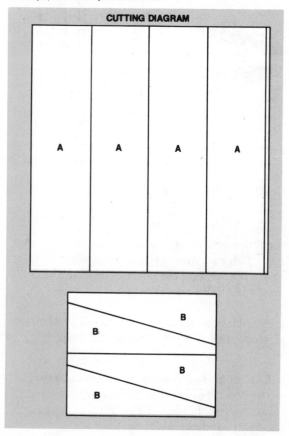

CUTTING DIAGRAM

Shim

A shim is a thin piece of material, either wood, cardboard, metal or stone, positioned between two surfaces for leveling purposes. Shims are often used when door or window frames are set. A shim is placed under the hinge leaves in door jambs so that the door hangs better.

Shingles

[SEE SHAKES & SHINGLES.]

Shiplap

Shiplap is a kind of bevel sheathing or siding in which the boards are rabbeted in the lower edge so that each board overlaps the upper edge of the board below it.

Shiplap

Shoe Molding

Shoe molding is a quarter round concealing the joint made by the baseboard and the floor. Shoe molding is made by quartering a round dowel. *SEE ALSO MOLDING & TRIM.*

Shoring

Shoring is the heavy timber support used to prevent a dirt slide or cave-in at an excavation or in a trench. It is also the temporary support against a wall or under a platform.

Shoring

Short Brace

A short brace is the smallest bit brace made. It has no crank and the chuck spindle is directly below the cap. This brace has a ratchet box which is joined to the handle. The drilling action is produced as the handle is turned alternately from one side to the other.

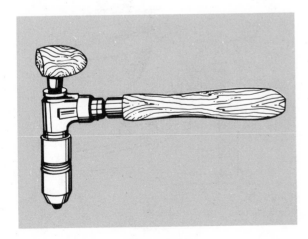

Short Brace

Shower

A shower is a space for bathing in a standing position. Normally associated with indoor plumbing, a shower may also be an outdoor fixture.

An outdoor shower is usually found in vacation areas or by recreation facilities such as swimming pools. Those used by swimmers rinsing off sand or chlorine consist of a pipe, handle and shower head with a floor surface and a drain located on the ground or in the immediate area. These showers usually have no siding. Vacation areas having outdoor showers for bathing privacy have wooden screens built around the floor. The screens begin one or two feet from ground level and extend only five or six feet above the ground. Usually, there is no ceiling.

Indoor showers are either a showering cubicle or stall or a shower head over the tub. The tub model is the most inexpensive of the two. In

Courtesy of Eljer.

The prefabricated shower with curtain gives the bathroom extra space.

either case, the shower head should be at least six feet two inches from the floor. More modern showers have two shower heads, one located beneath the other. While the lower one is usually used by shorter people to prevent unnecessary dampening of the hair, one or both may be used. The shower must be enclosed to prevent water from splashing into the room. Either a door or a curtain may be used. Both are available in different shapes, colors and designs. If using a curtain, the rod needs to be at least six feet six inches high to prevent splashing.

A cubicle or stall is prefabricated or made from masonry or tile. Prefabricated cubicles are made from either porcelain enameled steel or fiber glass. Cubicles are available in rectangular or circular shapes. A variety of faucet fixtures are available including a telephone shower head, swivel head, adjustable spray head and adjustable arm. *SEE ALSO PLUMBING FIXTURES.*

Shower Head

A shower head is attached to the end of a shower arm by a flange. The shower arm extends at a 90 degree angle from the water supply line to the bath area. Located at, or slightly above, head level, the shower head is funnel-shaped with the smaller opening attached to the pipe line and the larger end having a covering containing small holes. These holes permit water to flow from the shower head in many small streams of water rather than gushing from the pipe.

As water travels to the bathtub supply line, it may either flow through the faucet or the shower head. By manipulating the diverter spout or handle in one direction or another, water will flow through either the faucet or the shower head.

A clogged shower head is easily fixed. After unscrewing the shower head for removal, scrub it with a stiff brush to remove grit and rust. A small wire, such as a paper clip, can clean the holes in the head. Completely rinse the shower head prior to replacing it. *SEE ALSO PLUMBING FIXTURES.*

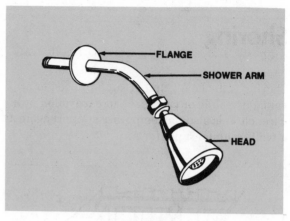

Shower Head

Shut-Off Valve

A shut-off valve on a pipe fitting is necessary in home plumbing works to control water flow in the supply system. Shut-off valves should be located in places where a water line branches off from a main line coming in from the street; in places where an alternate line branches off to service a nearby appliance; in places where water enters or leaves and in the pipe attached to fixtures or home appliances.

Hot and cold water pipes connected to sinks and lavatories have separate shut-off valves, while

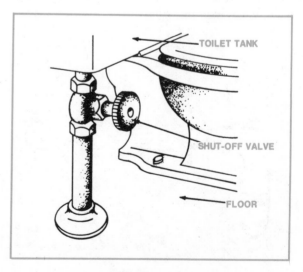

Shut-off Valve to Fixture

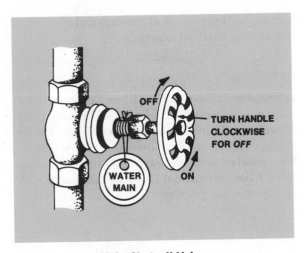

Main Shut-off Valve

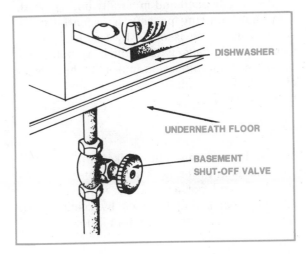

Shut-off Valve to Appliance

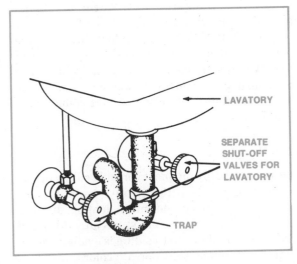

Shut-off Valves to Fixture

toilet connections have only one. The main shut-off valve for the hot water supply can be found at the hot water heater. Most water-control shutoffs can be found underneath fixtures. They may be located in a basement, utility room or open area close by the fixture. If there are not shut-off valves for each of the fixtures, one control valve can be found at the water meter. Extra shut-off valves for a water main, placed near a sidewalk or lawn under the ground, can be reached by way of a lined hole.

A shut-off valve is located inside a wall where an outdoor faucet or sill cock is attached. In winter, these are turned to let water drain out and prevent the faucet from freezing.

The first step in making plumbing repairs is to turn the water off at the shut-off valve. This is done by turning its handle clockwise. Shut-off valves are helpful in plumbing emergencies such as overflowing toilets, also. *SEE ALSO PLUMBING.*

Shutters

A shutter is an assembly of wood rails and stiles that forms a frame that is placed vertically next to a window or door. Shutters were originally designed to protect windows during a storm or safeguard a home against burglars. However, today shutters are used more as decoration, particularly on large homes. Shutter heights vary but widths are from 14 to 20 inches. Few shutters are hinged anymore but are attached with screws that usually come with the shutter set.

Most people think of shutters as wood, but they are available in artificial materials, like polystyrene, that require no painting or preservatives. This reduces the cost of repair or replacement due to chipping, splitting or breaking. If painting the shutters is necessary for them to match the house, use a quality exterior latex enamel. Because each shutter manufacturer may have varying installation directions, consult the package or hardware distributor before placing the shutters.

Side-Cutting Pliers

Side-cutting pliers are fixed pivot pliers that are useful for cutting wire. Although made for electrical work, they may also be used for stripping insulation from wire without damaging the wire itself. Edges of side-cutting pliers can be kept sharp with the aid of an oilstone. *SEE ALSO HAND TOOLS.*

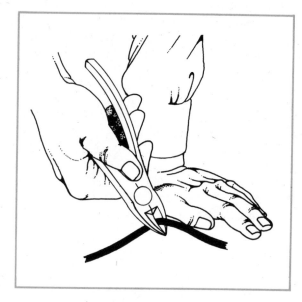

Side-Cutting Pliers

Siding

There are six basic materials used as exterior sidings: aluminum, wood, insulated, asbestos, steel and vinyl. Each has its own advantages in durability, choice, price and installation.

ASBESTOS SIDING

Soft, flexible asbestos siding is made from mineral fibers so it resists acids, burning, alkalies and other chemicals, denting, scratching and is not affected by termites. Asbestos was the first alternative to wood siding and became extremely popular. It is still found on some older homes, but because of aluminum and vinyl siding, is now used infrequently.

ALUMINUM SIDING

Aluminum is rust, fire and termite proof, light weight and reduces cooling and heating costs because of its insulating qualities. This type of siding may be applied over existing siding in horizontal or vertical patterns. Aluminum siding has a baked-on enamel finish that is coated with epoxy or other plastics.

INSULATED SIDING

Even though there are two basic kinds of insulated siding, asphalt and minerally impregnated, the manufacturing process is essentially the same. This siding is made by coating asphalt-saturated felt pads with a thick asphalt compound made of mineral granules that have been crushed. The result is a weather and shatter proof material.

STEEL SIDING

Steel siding is manufactured like aluminum siding. The main differences are that steel is more expensive and not as flexible, so its uses are limited. Steel siding is made by coating steel sheets with zinc and then with plastics.

WOOD SIDING

Wood was once the only form of siding available. However, unless wood siding is treated, and, to a certain extent, after having been treated it contributes to the spreading of fire. Wood is affected by termites, weather, is a poor insulant, dents easily, requires much care and maintenance, all of which means that wood siding is quite costly.

VINYL SIDING

Vinyl is probably the most versatile siding on the market. It needs little, if any, maintenance, resists fire, corrosion, termites, denting, dirt, is a good insulant, sheds moisture and does not flake, peel or chip. Vinyl siding is available in an almost unlimited selection of colors, textures, sizes and shapes to please most homeowners.

Sill

The sill rests on the foundation of a building and is the basis for metal or wood framing. If the exterior wall is to be brick or concrete, a sill is not needed.

The main types of sills are balloon frame, braced frame, box and T sill. All sills should be termite-resistant. Most are chemically treated or a metal termite shield is embedded. A sill should also resist crushing across the grain of the wood.

Wooden sills, usually of oak or pine, consist of a header and a bed member. They are built up at the construction site. Steel sills are one-piece and are also assembled at the site. *SEE ALSO FLOOR CONSTRUCTION; WALL & CEILING CONSTRUCTION.*

Sill Faucet

A sill faucet, also called an outdoor faucet, is mounted on the wooden sill of the house structure. It is used primarily for the garden hose.

Adding an extra outdoor faucet is a simple job. Either rigid copper tube or galvanized pipe should be used, depending upon which best matches the rest of the plumbing system. The pipe should be slanted down toward the outside to allow for easy drainage.

In cold areas, the sill-cock supply pipe outside the house may have an extra valve, called the stop-and-waste valve, attached to it. This valve shuts off the water to the outside faucet. It also provides a vent which admits air to the intervening section of pipe to drain it and the outside faucet. The waste cap should be mounted on the side of the valve so that it is toward the outside or non-pressure side. This small brass cap must be removed to open the vent.

A regular sill faucet may be prevented from freezing in winter. (Freezeproof faucets may

only be installed outside basement walls.) A stop-and-waste valve must be used in the pipe inside the wall in this process if, for structural reasons, the pipe to the outside faucet is level or slanted upward toward the outside.

Regardless of which way the pipe slants, the water will drain out with the valve closed, the waste cap removed and the faucet left open. If the pipe slants toward the outside, water will run out of the faucet opening while air comes in through the waste opening. If the faucet pipe slants toward the inside, water will drain through the open waste cap into the cellar. The waste cap should be replaced on the valve when draining is complete. *SEE ALSO FAUCET.*

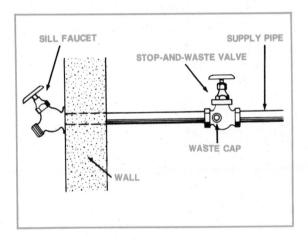

Sill Faucet Structure

Singing Toilet

A singing toilet is one which continues to run after it is flushed, resulting in a low whistling noise.

This noise occurs when the tank is not filling properly after being flushed. A stopper ball, which is a soft rubber ball valve, fits into the flush valve at the bottom of the toilet tank. If the stopper ball does not fall into place, water will continue to rush through the flush valve. This problem can be spotted by simply lifting the tank cover and looking inside.

Sometimes jiggling the handle will make the stopper ball go into the right position. If not, a new part or readjustment may be needed.

Should a singing noise occur when the tank is filled and water is going through the overflow pipe, usually, the float valve has failed to cut off the water coming in. In this case, the float has probably become disconnected from the float arm. It can be easily replaced. *SEE ALSO PLUMBING NOISES.*

Single Coursing Side Walls

Single coursing of side walls is a method of applying shingles so that the shingles overlap slightly more than half of their respective surfaces. *SEE ALSO SHAKES & SHINGLES.*

Single-Cut File

A single-cut file is any file that has only one set of straight-edged ridges running diagonally across it in parallel lines. These files are used for sharpening knives, shears, saws and other cutting edges that require a smooth, sharp surface. *SEE ALSO HAND TOOLS.*

Single End Bit

A single end bit is a cutter attachment for a router and is used on a flat surface for thin-line decorative work. *SEE ALSO ROUTER.*

Single-Fluted Router Bit

The single-fluted router bit is designed for removal of general stock and forming grooves, dadoes and rabbets. *SEE ALSO ROUTER.*

Sink

A sink is a plumbing fixture which supplies water for preparing foods and washing. Normally having one or two bowls, the more modern sinks may have three bowls. Sinks are available as wall-hung or cabinet models. Color choice is wide so that the sink will color coordinate with other appliances and room decor.

Equipped with a hot-and-cold water system, faucets come in a variety of styles for individual need and preference. Conveniences such as a sprayer attachment, swing-away nozzle, lotion-soap dispenser and instant hot water for coffee and tea are now available. Be sure to check the local dealer for the latest innovations before installation.

Garbage disposals are easily attached to a one bowl sink. When installing a garbage disposal on the two bowl sink, each drain will need a separate trap and waste connection. *SEE ALSO PLUMBING FIXTURES.*

Skewbacked Saw

The skewbacked saw is any saw whose top edge slopes from the center of the blade toward the tip end. The skewback, like the straightback, has no bearing on the performance of the saw. *SEE ALSO HAND TOOLS.*

Skew Chisel

A skew chisel is one of the five basic kinds of turning chisels used for lathe work. The blade size is usually $1/2''$, but is available in $3/4''$ and $1''$. It is best suited for a kind of notching called chip carving. Other uses include cylinder smoothing and shoulder cutting. *SEE ALSO HAND TOOLS.*

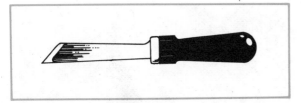

Skew Chisel

Ski House

[SEE VACATION HOMES.]

Skylights

Today's skylight is an attractive and valuable working part of the cheerful daylit house, in which natural lighting plays a featured role as an element of design. Both in new building and in remodeling, it is a way to gain light and cheer without loss of privacy or protection. Properly insulated where necessary, it can be an energy saver that absorbs heat and replaces daytime artificial lighting in poorly windowed, or windowless interior regions of the house.

Courtesy of Ventarama Skylight Corporation

Many gable roofs have windows only in the end walls. Skylights offer an alternative way to provide natural light in the attic area.

The most usual home skylight is square or oblong and consists primarily of a metal frame, usually aluminum, and usually hinged to allow ventilation, which holds twin domes made of acrylic plastic. The domes are separated by an air space to provide insulation. With a typical unit, the outer is clear plastic and the inner dome either clear or translucent white. With the clear, you have a full view of the sky, while the translucent permits diffused light. Many modern skylights are self-washing to a considerable degree, thanks both to the dome shape and to the ultrasmooth surface of the Plexiglas used.

Also part of a typical dome skylight is an operating crank for opening the skylight to the air and an inner insect screen. Since the crank is not easily reached, except with the occasional unit installed in a low sloping roof, a hooked stick with which to reach and turn the crank is a necessary part included with the skylight unit. This problem can be avoided, although at substantial extra cost, by choosing a motor-operated skylight, wired to a wall switch. With this arrangement, a skylight becomes a superior ventilating device. It makes no noise, requires no fan, produces minimum sensation of draft and, because of its location, is very effective at exhausting heat, smoke and odors from a kitchen or steam from a bathroom.

One traditional problem with skylights is moisture condensation and dripping. The insulating effect of a double dome reduces this problem and it is further handled by what some makers call a "condensation and weepage gutter."

Both condensation and heat-loss problems in the homemade skylight can be reduced by placing a second layer of plastic at ceiling level. Where the outer part of the skylight will ordinarily be made of a heavy-duty translucent fiberglass-reinforced plastic, the inner sheet can be of lighter weight. This lower sheet should rest loosely on molding so that it can be removed at intervals for cleaning.

A skylight built as described is ready to become a lighting fixture as well, at very little additional effort or expense. It is only necessary to install a fluorescent tube along each side (or a porcelain socket for an incandescent bulb, perhaps at each end) with a connection to a power source and a wall switch. When a skylight has been designed to give ideal daylighting, it will then function equally well at night, duplicating daytime illumination closely.

Although any double-layer arrangement reduces heat intake, this still remains probably the major problem that must be considered before installation of a skylight is decided upon. In cool climates, as along some of the West Coast, the problem may not arise at all. In general, areas in which air conditioning is not considered important are ones in which skylight heat intake need not be a matter of concern.

Heat intake may be sharply reduced by placing the skylight so that the sun of summer strikes its surface at a sharp angle and is largely reflected away. If this angle is also one (as in a sloping south wall) such that winter sun will reach the skylight nearly head-on, so much the better for winter comfort and fuel bills.

If heat will be a frequent problem, translucent plastic is a better material to use than fully transparent. A glass skylight or a plastic one may be obtained with heat-absorbing material used. With some trouble, even more effect of the same type may be obtained by painting the skylight for summer, removing the paint in the winter. In Western climates where rain is seasonal, a washable paint can be used to last through the summer, then washed off as winter approaches. A more permanent solution is to build a miniature lath house using slanted slats or louvers pitched to keep direct sun off at midsummer yet expose the skylight to almost full sunshine as winter comes. The louvers should be above the skylight and also to east and west, but will not be needed north and south.

If you design your own skylight, keep in mind safety demands. One common building code provision is the simple one that a skylight must be strong enough to support the weight of a man.

In the common situation where the skylight is put into a roof with a ceiling intervening be-

Courtesy of Ventarama Skylight Corporation

In many attic situations, the simplest and most economical way to get natural light into an area is by the installation of a skylight. Such skylights often provide imaginative solutions to difficult lighting problems.

tween it and the room to be lighted, it is usual to build a light shaft or well. Common construction is with $1/_2$ inch plywood or plasterboard, painted white to reflect light. If at least one wall of the shaft is splayed or angled, appearance, light reflection and ease of operation of the skylight, if it is a type that opens manually, will be improved.

Slate Floors

Slate is an attractive and very practical floor covering for home areas exposed to mud, snow and water. It is a good choice for a hearth in front of a fireplace, for an entryway, for a porch floor or walkway as well as the dining room and kitchen. As a natural material, slate is well suited for rooms done in rough textures and where lots of glass is used to bring in the outdoors. A natural material is costlier than other floor coverings yet advantageous in the long run because of its durability. Slate comes in gray-green and blue-gray colors, in geometric designs and in flagstone- or ashlar-patterned tiles. It seldom needs polishing; damp mopping is adequate for maintenance.

Slate tiles are sold loose or packed in 1/4 to 1/2 inch thicknesses by masonry dealers. One carton usually covers 10 square feet. When tiles are broken, they can be simply fitted back together since their natural fissures hide the break.

Before laying slate tiles, make a dry run in an area adjacent and close in size to the proposed floor or walk. Place the tiles in a pleasant pattern with the smooth side down. The fissured side is the walking surface.

Slate may be laid over any sound concrete, wood or composition flooring. A concrete base at least four inches thick is required for outdoor slate surfaces. Indoors, slate may be laid in a bed of cement mortar about 3/4 inch thick. Slate goes down well in mastic also, especially over a wood or plywood floor where having less thickness is important. However, it takes more mastic to get a level floor where slate is irregular in thickness.

Sledge Hammer

A sledge hammer, which can weigh between two and 20 pounds, is used for rock breaking, masonry work, log splitting, demolition work and heavy hammering jobs. These hammers are double-faced and are available in various head lengths and face sizes. The heavier sizes are usually used with both hands. Choose a sledge hammer that can be swung with ease. *SEE ALSO HAND TOOLS.*

Courtesy of The Stanley Works

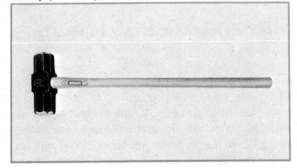

Sleeper

A sleeper is a piece of timber, stone or steel laid horizontally, as on the ground, to support a structure above, such as floor joists. Small timbers set in or on a concrete subfloor to serve as a basis for finish flooring are also known as sleepers. *SEE ALSO FLOOR CONSTRUCTION.*

Sliding Doors

Sliding doors are used in an opening where a swinging door would take up too much space. Because they need no clearance, sliding doors are often used on wardrobe closets or cabinets and as entrances to patios or gardens.

Sliding doors used on closets or cabinets are usually made of wood and finished to match the walls or trim in a room or cabinet. Patio sliding doors are usually glass which should be tempered in case of impact. The frames may be wood or aluminum.

Courtesy of the Andersen Corp. (Perma-Shield Gliding Doors)

Sliding glass doors offer an entrance to the house from a patio.

Sliding glass doors may come in two, three or four-panel groups, with one or more panels fixed, or not movable. The fixed panel is usually on the outside. Most sliding glass doors come in kits which include the hardware and instructions for installation.

Sliding doors move on tracks with or without rollers or wheels. Hangers with fitted rollers, either nylon or stainless steel, may be adjusted when the doors are hung, and a floor guide keeps the doors from rubbing. Read manufacturer's instructions carefully before attempting to install sliding doors.

Sliding T-Bevel

The sliding T-bevel is used for marking and checking angles during beveling. It has a blade with two separate slots extending to each of its ends. The blade fits into the slotted end of a steel handle and is centered or adjusted to different angles with a wing nut. By using a protractor, the sliding T-bevel can be set at any angle, or it can be adjusted to an existing angle or bevel so others can be duplicated from it. *SEE ALSO HAND TOOLS.*

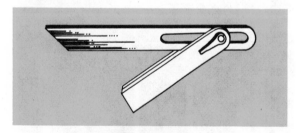

Sliding T-Bevel

Slip Coupling

A slip coupling, which has one end that slips on the pipe and another that is flared for a larger sized pipe, is a copper pipe fitting. *SEE ALSO PIPE FITTINGS.*

Slip-Joint Pliers

Slip-joint pliers have a pivot rivet that will slip into two or more positions, making grasping of large or small objects easy. The pliers have as many as a four-position joint and can apply pressure ten times as great as the pressure being exerted by the user. Some slip-joint pliers have doubled-curved jaws that can grip an item from $3/16''$ to $1''$ with equal force. These slip-joints (the 8-shaped hole) work smoothly but not sloppily. If the joint is sloppy, the wire cutting process becomes impossible. *SEE ALSO HAND TOOLS.*

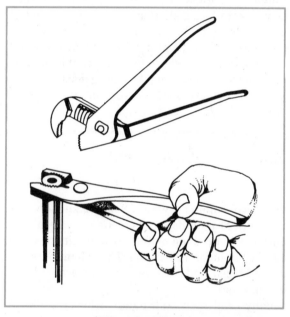

Slip-Joint Pliers

Slip-and-Lock Wrench

The slip-and-lock wrench is also known as the adjustable spud wrench and it is used for all large hex fittings, such as toilet tanks and sink traps. It, along with the hex wrench, is one of the best tools to use in getting a strong, fixed grip on multisided fittings, and its smooth jaws will not

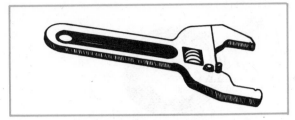

Slip-and-Lock Wrench

scrape a chromed part. *SEE ALSO HAND TOOLS.*

Slipstones

Slipstones are a type of sharpening stone. They have both flat surfaces and rounded edges making them useful for sharpening straight and concave edges of tools. Slipstones are especially good for use on molding knives and gouges. *SEE ALSO SHARPENING STONES.*

Small Shank Bit

A small shank bit is one which permits a drill with a 1/4 inch chuck to utilize larger bit sizes. There are small shank bits available for drilling both wood and metal. Drill bits such as the brad point bit and the spade bit can be purchased with a small shank. *SEE ALSO HAND TOOLS.*

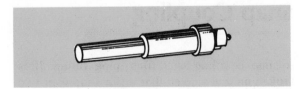

Small Shank Bit

Smoke Chamber

A smoke chamber is the part of the fireplace that is directly below the flue and just above the

throat. The flue widens into the smoke chamber where the smoke accumulates. The throat and smoke chamber are divided by the damper. *SEE ALSO FIREPLACES.*

Smooth Plane

The shortest of the bench planes, the smooth plane ranges from 7″ to 10″ in length and has a blade width of about 1³/₄″. A "plane iron cap" mounted on top of the blade close to the cutting edge provides sharp bends and greater breaking effects on the shavings. This also minimizes surface roughening when the plane is used to smooth irregular grain areas. Good for light to moderate general use, the smooth plane is convenient when only small areas are to be leveled off, as its short length makes it simple to locate and remedy these uneven spots. *SEE ALSO HAND TOOLS.*

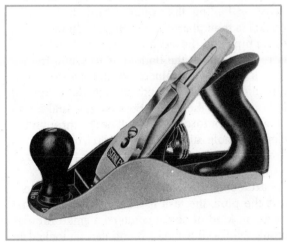

Courtesy of The Stanley Works

Snake, Plumber's

A tool used when the force cup fails to clear clogged drains is commonly called a plumber's snake or auger. There are various kinds of augers, such as the closet auger, the hook-end or corkscrew-tipped augers, power augers and the clean-out auger.

A closet auger, which is normally 5¹/₂″ long with a protective rubber guard, is used for clogged toilets. The hook-end or corkscrew-tipped augers, which range from 15 feet to 50 feet in length, may be used for clearing drains and pipes. The 15 foot auger is good to buy for average jobs. Power augers, fitting ¹/₄″ or ³/₈″ electric drills, are available in lengths of 6 feet and 12 feet. They are made to use in the home. Drills with variable speeds and a forward-reverse switch are best suited for these electric snakes. The clean-out auger or snake, which comes in lengths up to 25 feet, is a flexible tool made of metal. It has a central spine of steel which is wrapped with a finer steel wire.

To operate these tools, push the auger into the nearest convenient opening of the clogged drain. The shorter augers may be flexible enough to be pushed down the drain opening in the sink, through the U-trap and on to the pipe.

If it is a long drain pipe, a longer snake which is stiffer will be needed. Initially, this procedure involves bailing the water out of the sink. A bucket is then placed under the trap in the sink's drain pipe and the clean-out plug, if there is one, is removed from the bottom of it. When the remaining water is drained into the bucket, see if the snake can be worked through the clean-out hole and into the drain. Because the snake will tangle, do not force it. If it will not go through the clean-out hole, disconnect the trap from the sink, drain pipe and continue the regular procedure.

Regardless of the manner in which the snake enters the pipe, the task is an easy one. The most common kind of snake contains a small tubular crank which slides over it and can be locked in place anywhere on the snake with a thumbscrew. This crank should be kept tightly on the snake several inches out from the entry point into the pipe and turned slowly as it is pushed. Loosen the crank as the snake is moved farther into the pipe, slide it back several inches and tighten it again. To help get past snags and stubborn blockages, the snake may be rotated as it is pushed back into the pipe. The blockage can usually be felt when it is hit. If the snake becomes hard to turn, withdraw it an inch or until it will turn freely. Then crank it back into the

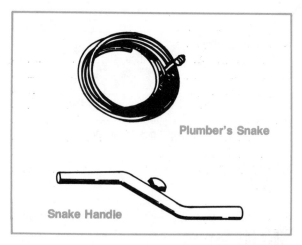

Plumber's Snake

Snake Handle

blockage. When the snake can be easily moved beyond the blockage, slide it back and forth to be sure the solid material has been broken. As soon as possible, run hot water through the pipe to wash away the remaining waste. *SEE ALSO PLUMBER'S TOOLS & EQUIPMENT.*

Snakewood

Snakewood is a type of wood that comes from East India. Its name is derived from the appearance of the root and stem systems which twist and twine to resemble snakes. It is a rare wood that must be veneered to be used in furniture making. *SEE ALSO WOOD IDENTIFICATION.*

Snap Coupling

A snap coupling is a fiber pipe fitting. It is broken on one side so that it can *snap* over two lengths of pipe. *SEE ALSO PIPE FITTINGS.*

Snips

Snips are shears which require no more than hand pressure for cutting thin sheets of metal.

Aluminum, copper, or galvanized steel sheets can be cut by aviation snips. Compound-power snips come in three varieties: those that cut to the right, to the left and to the right or left. Straight-cut snips demand more muscle power on the part of the user.

A beginning point for the snips can be made by piercing the metal with a punch or chisel. To insure a smoother cut, use the full length of the blade. Use the tips of the blade to avoid overrunning a cut. *SEE ALSO HAND TOOLS.*

Courtesy of The Stanley Works

Snips

Snow-Thrower

A snow-thrower is a handy power tool that is used to remove snow from driveways, walks, porches, etc. Available in sizes to suit the property area that must be cleared and the amount of snowfall that can be anticipated in a locale, snow-throwers save people hours of hard work every snowy season.

Two basic kinds of snow-throwers are sold today: the *single-stage paddle-type* and the larger, heavier *two-stage auger-type.* The light-weight paddle-types are usually powered by a one or two horsepower two-cycle gas engine. This is just the right size for city dwellers or suburban residents with only modest snow removal problems. The machine is like a scoop on wheels. As the snow is pushed into a snow pile, a chain-driven rotating drum with two attached paddles cuts off a section 20 inches or wider and carries it backwards about the scoop, literally flinging it out at the top. Here, the snow is deflected by a series of vanes that can be angled to left or right, so that a steady stream of snow is thrown far to the side of the path that is being cleared. Paddle-type throwers work best on powdery snow.

Ice-encrusted or heavy, wet snow is hard to remove with a paddle-type thrower. If an area is buried under heavy snows every other day or so, if the property is large or if an area is subject to rapidly changing freeze-melt cycles, a heavyweight, two-stage thrower will probably be needed. These come in push and self-propelled types, the largest weighing about 250 pounds with eight-horsepower four-cycle engines. Their action stems from a heavy, steel rotating auger which cuts into the snow and continuously forces sections to the center from either side. Since this type's average bite is 26 inches, an appreciable amount of snow can be removed each minute. At the auger center, a rotating paddle forces the snow backward, into an impeller blade. The spinning blade of the impeller whips the snow upward, expelling it with great force through a chute that directs the snow stream to the side.

TIPS FOR BETTER, SAFER OPERATION OF SNOW-THROWER

A   Never allow children to operate a snow-thrower or adults to operate it without proper instruction.

B   Know the controls and how to stop quickly. READ THE OWNER'S MANUAL! Keep it handy for brush-up reading before the season begins.

C   Handle gasoline with care since it is highly flammable; do not smoke anywhere near it.

D   Use only an approved metal gasoline container. Do not store gas for long periods. Keep it in a cool place.

E   Fill gas tank outdoors, *never* while engine is running. Wipe up spilled gasoline. Dispose of rags safely.

F   Replace gasoline cap securely.

G   Open doors if the engine is run in a garage. Exhaust gases are extremely dangerous.

H   Keep children and pets a safe distance away at *all* times.

I   Stay in the safety zone behind handles. *Never* leave this position without shutting engine down.

J   Give complete and undivided attention to the job at hand.

K   Personal injury or property damage can result from debris thrown by the machine. Therefore, never direct discharge toward bystanders or windows nor allow anyone in front of or near the machine while operating it.

L   Adjust skid height to clear gravel or crushed rock surface.

M   Maintain solid and secure footing at all times. Wear proper shoes, or boots.

N   Never look into the discharge chute while engine is running. Do not put your hand in the discharge chute.

O   Stop engine before cleaning discharge, removing obstacles, making adjustments or when leaving operating position.

P   Never place hands or feet under rotating parts or into concealed areas. Keep hands and feet clearly away from auger, belts, pulleys, gears, etc., while engine is running.

Q   If snow-thrower should vibrate or strike a foreign object, stop engine immediately, disconnect spark plug lead wire and check for damage or loose parts. Repair damage *at once.*

R   Do not use machine when temperature is below 30°F.

S   Follow maintenance instructions outlined in the machine's manual. Data given in this article is general, only.

T   Keep machine in good operating condition and keep safety device in place.

U   If the machine needs repair, get replacements that the machine's manufacturer specifies and install with care.

Socket Chisel

The tang and socket are two main kinds of chisels and gouges. Because the socket chisel is more durable, it is preferred for general use and for working on wood, such as smoothing and finishing. This chisel has been designed for heavier duty than the tang chisel and, on rough work, should be driven with a wooden mallet. A cone-shaped socket, which fits over the narrowed end of a wood or plastic handle, forms the chisel's steel blade end. The handle removes easily and can be replaced. *SEE ALSO HAND TOOLS.*

Socket Chisel

Socket Wrenches

Socket wrenches, used for loosening and tightening nuts, are usually purchased in a set comprised of as few as six to as many as 200 different types of handles, adapters, sockets and other pieces, making the socket wrench a very versatile tool.

Socket wrench drive handles come in four sizes determined by the peg on the working end of the handle. The $1/4''$ drive should be used for light-duty work, the $3/8''$ drive for average jobs, the $1/2''$, $3/4''$ and the $1''$ for various other heavy-duty jobs.

There are many types of handles available, also. With the regular spinner handle (nonratcheting), the socket must be lifted off of the nut at each turn of the handle. A reversible ratchet handle, because it never has to be lifted off the nut as it works, speeds the job, and either loosens or tightens the nut with a flip of a lever. Other handles multiply the use of the wrench. The flex, or hinged offset handle swings at right angles to the socket, giving tremendous leverage to the tool. After the nut is loosened, the handle can be placed vertically to the socket and turned to remove the nut. A speed handle, which works and looks like a brace, makes nut removal easy and fast. When used with a universal joint, it can be placed at any angle to the socket. This is the answer in close quarters and odd situations. Straight extension handles are another useful addition to the set.

Because automobile work is one of the most popular uses of socket wrenches, torque-limiting handles are also available, but these have little other use in the home shop, and are of greatest value to expert car enthusiasts.

Corresponding wrench socket sizes are available for every type drive handle. They can be purchased for nuts from $3/8''$ to $1/4''$ in diameter. A full range of metric-sized wrench sockets may also be obtained.

Other handy additions to your drive handle and socket wrench set include spark plug sockets, drive handle adapter sockets and screwdriver sockets for regular, hollow and Phillips head screws.

Quality socket wrenches are heat treated for durability and strength and chromium plated to prevent rust. *SEE ALSO HAND TOOLS.*

Sod

Sod is the upper layer of soil that is filled with grass roots or the roots of other plants. Sodding is transported and used to establish a new lawn over a prepared soil bed. This method is superior to the seeding method of beginning a lawn in terms of ease, quickness and probable success. Sodding can be purchased from a nursery in strips that are generally 16 inches wide, six feet long and approximately one inch thick. Good quality sod is heavily rooted, uniformly thick, has a rich green color and few weeds. The edges should not be ragged and the sodding should hold together well when held up by one end. A new lawn started with sodding can be begun from spring to late fall. The sod is fitted together tightly, with the ends in a staggered formation. Voids or gaps should be patched immediately. If the sodding is being laid on an incline, small stakes may be required to hold the pieces in place. The lawn should be heavily watered from shortly after placement of the first sod piece until root penetration into the subsoil. Light rolling of the new lawn a few days after work completion will aid in firming the sod to the soil. *SEE ALSO LAWNS & GARDENS.*

Soffit

Soffit is the name for the underside of a structure, such as an eave's overhang, staircase or arch. In roof construction, soffit refers to the panel that encloses the eaves overhang. *SEE ALSO ROOF CONSTRUCTION.*

SOFFIT

Softwood

Softwood is a designation given to lumber from evergreen or needle-bearing trees such as pine, fir, cedar, redwood and spruce. The term softwood, however, is misleading since some hardwoods are softer than some softwoods. Softwoods are easier to work and finish than hardwoods and are used more in general construction for exterior trim, framing, siding, subflooring or fencing. *SEE ALSO LUMBER.*

Soil P-Trap

A soil p-trap is a cast-iron soil pipe fitting. Designed to stop escaping pipe odors, a soil p-trap has a liquid barrier in the U-shaped portion of the pipe fitting. Its purpose is to eliminate the backward passage of air. An added feature of the soil p-trap is that it catches objects that are accidentally dropped into drains. *SEE ALSO PIPE FITTINGS.*

Soil Stack

The soil stack, which runs vertically from the top of the roof vent down through the house to the

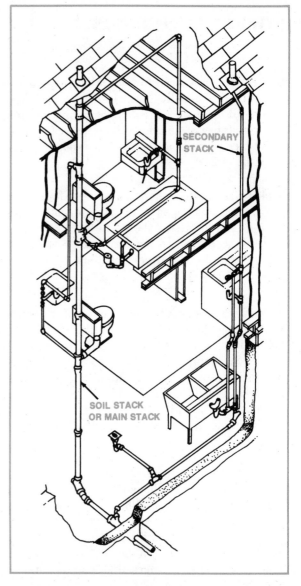

SECONDARY STACK

SOIL STACK OR MAIN STACK

sewer, is the major pipe in a drainage system. It can be made of copper, cast-iron or plastic. Although most soil stacks are four inch cast-iron pipes, three inch copper tubes are sometimes permitted by the local code.

There are main and secondary soil stacks. Both are connected to the house drain. The main stack is the larger one into which a toilet's waste is emptied. A smaller pipe, the secondary stack removes the waste from other fixtures, such as sinks and appliances. Most homes have at least one main soil stack and, if there is an additional toilet to serve, they may have more. All waste from plumbing fixtures near a stack will drain into it.

Stacks remain open at the top for three main reasons. Air must be able to be admitted to prevent a partial vacuum that would slow the drainage downflow. To make sure that pressure does not build up in the drainage system, sewer gas must be released. In addition, air in the stacks keeps drainage downflow from sucking air through the pipes.

If additional plumbing fixtures, such as sinks or lavatories, are needed in the house, they should be placed near the main soil stack for draining and venting. This same stack should be used, if possible, to prevent having to install a completely new one. Connections to a cast-iron soil stack can be made by cutting the stack and adding a connecting fitting or it may be possible to fasten the stack onto a clean-out fitting. A sanitary T-Y fitting or Y branch may be used. For a copper soil stack, a new T can be inserted with special slip couplings. Instead of cutting the plastic stacks apart, an opening is cut and a saddle, which is solvent-welded, can be installed. *SEE ALSO DRAINAGE SYSTEMS.*

Soldering

Soldering is the act of joining two or more surfaces or objects together with a metal or a metallic alloy by using a blowtorch, soldering gun or soldering iron.

Sole Plate

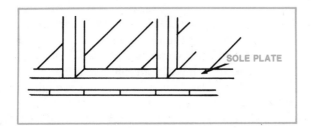

The sole plate, or wall plate, is a horizontal timber onto which the wall studs are nailed. *SEE ALSO FLOOR CONSTRUCTION; WALL & CEILING CONSTRUCTION.*

Solid Doors

Solid doors are doors which have a one-piece core that is made by laying lumber side by side in horizontal or vertical patterns. This style door weighs approximately 30 pounds more than hollow core varieties, so they are used more as exterior doors than inside the home.

Solvents

Solvents are used in cleaning paint brushes and rollers because of their dissolving powers. Always use a solvent intended for the type of paint that was used. If the paint job was done with latex paints, warm water will clean the brushes. If the paint was alkyd or oil-base, use turpentine followed by paint thinner. For alcohol-base stains or shellac, use alcohol or lacquer thinner.

Solvent Welding

Solvent welding is the process of joining two plexiglass surfaces or joints with a special solvent or cement. This is done by taping the plexiglass structure together on the outside, always keeping the pieces perpendicular to each other, and then applying the solvent around the inside so that when dry, it is a solid object. Some solvents or cements come in a tube that has a special nozzle for even application. If an applicator is needed, purchase one to insure proper distribution of the welding material.

Solvent welding also applies to the joining of plastic pipe by a solvent or cement. In this type of welding, one pipe end is coated with the solvent and pushed and turned into the fitting so that the solvent is spread evenly. Follow the manufacturer's specifications for materials and drying time.

Soss Hinges

Soss hinges are invisible hinges which fit into holes drilled in the edge of doors and the side of cases. These hinges permit the door to open completely and are invisible when the door is closed. They are available in many sizes for various door thicknesses. *SEE ALSO HINGES.*

Sound Control
[SEE ACOUSTICS & SOUND CONTROL.]

Space Heaters

Space heaters are units which may be separate from or added to an existing central heating system. They operate on electricity, gas, coal or wood and are generally used to heat workshops, small rooms or large room areas. The space heater chosen depends on the heat required, flue availability (if a flue is needed), fuel or power cost and the local code, as some types of heaters may be banned in certain areas.

ELECTRIC SPACE HEATERS

Space heaters operated by electrical power are the cleanest and easiest to operate, but supply a limited amount of heat at a high cost. These rectangular, square and bowl shaped heaters are generally limited in power to 1,250 watts so that a heater, lamp or other small appliance may be operated on the same circuit without blowing a fuse.

GAS SPACE HEATERS

Gas space heaters are manufactured in both vented and unvented models and may also come

in the form of a floor furnace or logs that are set in an existing fireplace. The floor furnace is a good selection for heating large areas because its BTU output can range from 30,000 to 85,000 per hour. The furnance has a grille that is set into the floor from which heat rises, so it must remain unobstructed. Gas logs are considered a form of space heater and emit fumes which must be expelled through a flue. Through-the-wall direct vented gas heaters work well in areas where a flue is necessary but not present. These devices burn air outside and release combustible products outside, too.

WOOD & COAL SPACE HEATERS

The Franklin and pot belly stoves are two of the most common wood and coal burning heaters. Both are still widely used today and require only a flue for dispersing fumes. The amount of heat put out by one of these stoves depends on what kind and how much material is used. Dry fire can produce approximately 5,000 BTU per pound and coal, 19,000 BTU. *SEE ALSO HEATING SYSTEMS.*

Spacer Strip

A spacer strip is normally a ³/₈ inch wooden strip which is placed between tile flooring to maintain uniform spacing. *SEE ALSO FLOOR CONSTRUCTION.*

Spackle

Spackle, or spackling compound, is a plaster-like filler used to patch holes and cracks in painted wood, plasterboard and plaster walls and ceilings. It differs from plaster in that it is slow drying and remains workable for several hours. Spackle is available in two forms: a dry powder that is mixed with water and a premixed vinyl paste. The dry powder should be mixed to a smooth, lump-free consistency stiff enough to hold shape but flexible enough for easy spreading. *SEE ALSO PLASTER & PLASTER REPAIR.*

Spade Bit

Spade bits are wood bits which drill holes that range in size from 1/4″ to 1 1/2″. Spade bits may be purchased individually or in sets. Some sets come with only one shank and a variety of cutter sizes. Cutters are replaceable, which eliminates the need for an entire new drill bit each time the cutter is damaged. As the spade bit has a point rather than a screw, the handyman must exert pressure to push it through the wood. In order to form a clean break-through, back up the work with a piece of scrap wood or remove the bit from the hole just before it breaks through and drill the remaining part from the opposite side. Spade bits can be used in hand as well as power drills. *SEE ALSO HAND TOOLS; PORTABLE POWER DRILL.*

Courtesy of The Stanley Works

Spade Bit

Span

Span is the horizontal distance between structural supports such as walls or columns, or the distance spanned by roofs, girders, beams, joists or arches. *SEE ALSO ROOF CONSTRUCTION.*

Spar Varnish

Spar varnish is made from phenolic-resin varnish. The word spar means good quality. Spar varnish provides a tough, durable finish. Because it can be subjected to changes in temperature and humidity, spar varnish can be used on both the exterior and interior. Spar varnish was intended for outdoor use and contains additives for resistance to salt water.

Spar varnish can be used on copper surfaces, galvanized surfaces and natural wood siding and trim. Although thinning is not usually required, thinning can be done using only pure turpentine. Spar varnish should be applied with long, flowing brush strokes. Be sure to brush out any air bubbles. *SEE ALSO WOOD FINISHING.*

Sparkplugs

Sparkplugs are fitted into the cylinder of an internal-combustion engine to ignite the fuel mixture. A sparkplug contains two electrodes separated by an air gap. Current from the distributor discharges across this gap forming a spark that ignites the air-fuel mixture.

Sparkplugs are offered today in a variety of heat ranges. Different makes of cars operate with different engine heat ranges and therefore use varying types of sparkplugs. A cold plug has a short insulator while a hot plug has a longer insulator.

The driving pattern of a car is the most important factor in the life of sparkplugs. Stop-and-go driving causes faster wear on them. In new automobiles, sparkplugs should be checked after

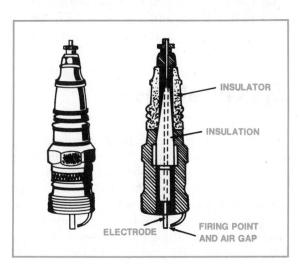

1000 miles of driving. Afterwards, they should be checked every 5000 miles.

Sparkplugs with cracked or broken insulators should not be used. Plugs should be kept clean since a crack or coating of dirt or grease can allow high voltage to escape into the engine block without firing them. This also leads to hard starting, poor engine efficency and excessive fuel consumption. *SEE ALSO SYSTEMS, AUTOMOTIVE.*

Spatter Finish

Spatter finishing is used in producing an antique appearance on furniture. Initially it was used to simulate wormwood or worm holes. It is made by using a dark opaque shellac or a thin black enamel which is shaken out of a worn brush. The paint will spatter, giving it a speckled look. Apply it between the sealant and the final coat of finish. *SEE ALSO PAINTS & PAINTING.*

Spear-Point Chisel

One of the five basic kinds of turning chisels used for lathe work and for scraping jobs is called a spear-point or diamond-point chisel. This tool is best used to clean out sharp corners and to cut V-shaped grooves. *SEE ALSO LATHE.*

Specifications

Specifications are written as the supplementary information to blueprints. There are at least fifteen categories such as general requirements, excavating and grading, sheet metal work, rough carpentry and roofing, tile work, electrical work, plumbing, insulation, landscaping, heat and air conditioning, painting, plaster work, masonry and concrete work and a schedule for room

completion. Other specifications may include building permits, insurance, contract payment schedule and provisions for changes in the building plans.

Before work is begun, the builder should carefully check the specifications as these standards of quality protect the builder and the buyer. By defining what is required in each category, quality and safety are maintained. If specifications are followed, the FHA Minimum Construction Requirements as well as local requirements will be met. If there is a conflict, the highest specification requirement should be satisfied. Each item should have equal or better quality than described in the specifications. *SEE ALSO BLUEPRINTS.*

Spiral Ratchet Screwdriver

The spiral-ratchet screwdriver drives screws quickly and many have interchangeable blades to fit different screw heads. When the screwdriver handle is pushed, the spiral ratchet turns the screw two-and-one-half times, then the spring forces the handle up for the next push. As with the ratchet screwdriver, the direction of the spiral ratchet can be reversed or locked so that it only turns one way. Some spiral-ratchet screwdrivers have kits that contain socket bits to tighten or remove nuts and bolts, standard, cabinet and Phillips heads and a countersink, which add to their adaptability. *SEE ALSO HAND TOOLS.*

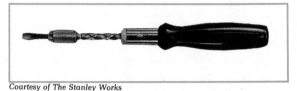

Courtesy of The Stanley Works

Spiral-Ratchet Screwdriver

Splash Block
[SEE GUTTERS & DOWNSPOUTS.]

Spline

A spline is a tongue of wood that is fitted into grooves made in the facing edges of two pieces of wood to form a joint. Boards that are connected by a spline joint are used to form a large surface. Longer splines are used in window construction to secure the edges of the screen in grooves made in the screen frame. *SEE ALSO WOOD JOINTS.*

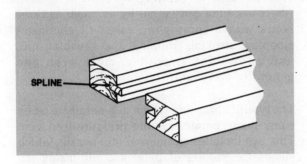

Split Circuits

A split circuit is a wiring technique in which three wires are used to carry two circuits. One white wire acts as a ground for the two "hot" wires of different circuits. In this way, a three-wire cable may be used instead of running a set of two-wire cables where two circuits are desired. To install a split circuit, connect one of the hot wires of a three-wire cable to the brass terminal screws on an outlet. Connect the second

hot wire to another set of terminal screws on the same outlet. Connect the white wire to both sets of chrome ground terminals.

There are two types of outlet receptacles used in this type of wiring, the interchangeable device and the duplex outlet receptacle. The interchangeable device locks into a plate which is attached to the box instead of the duplex outlet. This device has a single outlet receptacle. The locking plate has three holes for any combination of outlets, switches, pilot lights, or night lights. Such a device is handy if, for instance, the home owner would like to place a switch, a night light for a young child, and a plug receptacle close together on the same circuit.

A popular receptacle in kitchens is the duplex outlet receptacle. This receptacle is equipped with a *break out* that connects the circuitry between the terminals on each side. If the hot side break-out is slipped out of the device, the circuit is broken and the outlet receptacle becomes ideal for split-circuit wiring. One half of the receptacle is wired to one circuit while the other half is wired to another circuit. For this reason, when there are many outlets, the lower receptacle plates should belong to one circuit and the upper plates belong to another making the process easier. *SEE ALSO ELECTRICAL WIRING.*

Split-Phase Motors

Washing machines and many easy-starting, low-voltage devices are run on split-phase motors. A complex version of the induction motor, the split-phase differs in method of starting. Two windings set on either side of the shaft create a force field that sets the rotor into action. A centrifugal switch cuts the starting windings off after the rotor reaches a predetermined speed and no longer needs the magnetic boost, hence, the split-phase theory. The voltage required to start a split-phase motor is approximately five times greater than that to run it. For this reason, split-phase motors are easily overloaded. *SEE ALSO ELECTRIC MOTORS.*

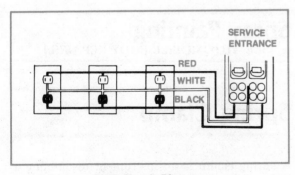

Split-Circuit Diagram.

Split Receptacles

Split receptacles or two-circuit duplex outlet receptacles have each outlet wired to a different circuit. This arrangement permits one of the two outlets in each receptacle to be permanently live for clocks or radios and the other to be controlled by a wall switch for lamps and similar devices. With the ordinary duplex outlet receptacle both outlets are either on or off at the same time.

Split receptacles look like ordinary duplex outlets except that each of their outlets has separate terminals. Split receptacles have a break-out section between the paired terminal screws on each side. This break-out can be snapped out with a screwdriver, removing all electrical contact between the two terminal screws on that side. With the break-outs removed, the terminals are separate and can then be wired to two different circuits. *SEE ALSO SWITCHES & OUTLETS.*

Spokeshave

A kind of plane which was originally designed to shape the wooden spokes of wagon wheels, the spokeshave is excellent for smoothing and shaping curved edges, concave or convex. Its short frame consists of handles extending from both sides and a cutting blade in the center. Since this tool must cut in the uphill direction of the grain, it is usually pushed, rather than pulled, along one section. The cutting depth of the blade is set by hand or by screw adjustment, depending upon the model. Remember that the cutter must be kept sharp to do its job well. *SEE ALSO HAND TOOLS.*

Courtesy of The Stanley Works

Spray Gun

A spray gun is a painting tool which includes a compressor, nozzle, hose, and in most cases, an adjustable screw device for controlling the spread and flow of the paint as it sprays from the nozzle. A spray gun is ideal for use on large surfaces or objects that can be worked on in an open space, such as large wall areas, fences or furniture. When compared to the brush and/or roller method of painting, spraying is quicker (the work time can be cut by as much as three hours with a spray gun), easier (it eliminates stooping, stroking, dipping and brushing out) and allows for smoother, more even and generally more uniform results.

The type of spray gun which is generally used by many home painters is the pressure-feed gun. This gun includes an internal mix nozzle, which allows for mixing of paint and air inside the nozzle, and an external mix nozzle, which allows the paint and air to flow separately and mix just as they leave the gun. The internal nozzle gun is most efficient for spraying heavy-bodied paint, while the external mix nozzle type is best for quick-drying paint. When spraying a surface, the paint flow from the gun determines how fast the nozzle should be moved over the surface. It is generally best to use a fast flow setting on the spreader control screw, which calls for a rapid stroke to provide coverage free of runs and sags. Continuity of motion over the entire surface is important, from the time the gun is turned on until it is triggered off and the painting is completed.

Spray Painting
[SEE AUTOMOBILE BODY REPAIRS.]

Spring Clamp

A spring clamp is an instrument resembling a large clothes pin that is used when heavy pressure is not required. The spring clamp is the simplest type of gripping device and is excellently suited for fast-drying glue work or temporarily holding objects. Although most spring clamps open by one hand squeezing the handles together, some larger models require two hands.

Opening from $1/2''$ to $4''$, some spring clamp jaws are covered with plastic or vinyl to prevent marring. The length of the spring clamp ranges from $4''$ to $81/4.''$ Since spring clamps come in three sizes, most people find it convenient to have several of each. *SEE ALSO HAND TOOLS.*

Sprinklers

A sprinkler system is composed of pipes and nozzles for carrying water to all parts of a lawn, greenhouse or garden. Some available conveniences for sprinklers are rain watchers, which turn off the sprinkler system whenever it rains, and water timers, which shut the system off when watering is done.

Usually the pipe and fittings of a sprinkler unit are plastic with the exception of metal sprinkler heads. Modern sprinklers have pop-up heads which help the system to maintain an excellent spray pattern and effectively water heavy-bladed as well as shortly cropped grasses. Some stationary rotary sprinklers on the market today have control arms which adjust from 0 to 90 degree angles to cover a 5 foot to 50 foot diameter of lawn.

Plastic polyethylene tubing is black, comes in 100-foot coils, and is very suitable for use in underground systems. It should never be used with hot water, however. This tubing is lightweight and easy to use. Few joints are required in an installation because of the length, so the tubing presents minimum resistance to the water flowing through it.

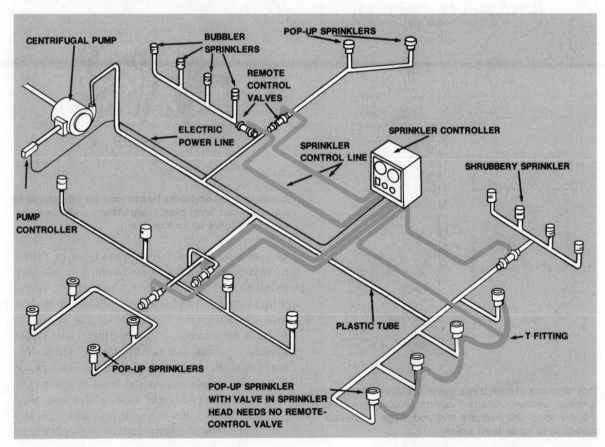

CENTRIFUGAL PUMP

BUBBLER SPRINKLERS

POP-UP SPRINKLERS

REMOTE CONTROL VALVES

ELECTRIC POWER LINE

SPRINKLER CONTROL LINE

SPRINKLER CONTROLLER

SHRUBBERY SPRINKLER

PUMP CONTROLLER

PLASTIC TUBE

T FITTING

POP-UP SPRINKLERS

POP-UP SPRINKLER WITH VALVE IN SPRINKLER HEAD NEEDS NO REMOTE-CONTROL VALVE

Sprinklers

Perforated hose-type sprinklers of plastic are often good buys. Another fairly simple sprinkler system available attaches to a T-fitting in an outdoor faucet line. It has about six pop-up sprinkler heads and can water up to 900 square feet of lawn.

The more complex systems have built-in pumps which pressure-feed water to more than a dozen sprinkler heads. These systems include programmers operated by timers to regulate different lawn zones by a preset plan.

An antisiphon valve in a more complex system prevents contaminated water held in sprinkler heads from getting into the house water supply. A vacuum breaker installed a foot or more above the highest sprinkler outlet will also prevent interference with the house water supply.

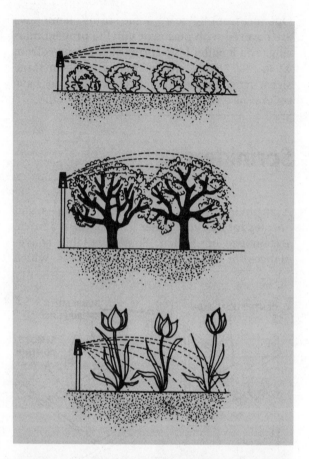

Above-ground sprinkler heads may be adjustable to water ground level plants, shrubbery and flowers of various heights up to four feet.

An underground sprinkler system can be rather inexpensive when the homeowner does his own installation. The first step in installing a sprinkling system is to check local plumbing regulations. If requirements are met for the system to be built, determine the waterflow rate. Water flowing 9 gallons per minute takes 5 sprinkling heads in a full circle; 4 heads in 2 circles; 3 heads in 3 circles or one sprinkling head in one circle. These sprinklers should first be located on a graphed plan of the area. Spray coverage will vary in sections of a lawn for adequate coverage.

KEY

STAGE 1 —·—·—
STAGE 2 — — —
STAGE 3 ————

DRIVE

GARAGE

This drawing shows three coverage areas for lawn sprinkler systems. Stage 1 covers 2700 square feet, stage 2 about 2800 square feet and stage 3 extends coverage to outer lawn areas.

When a plan has been decided upon, have the equipment ordered through a dealer. Upon arrival, the plastic pipe should be uncoiled and left in the sun to soften which makes it easier to install.

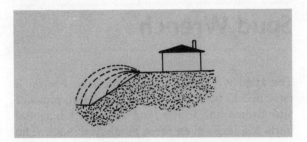

A hillside should be watered with even sprinkling to avoid puddling which causes erosion.

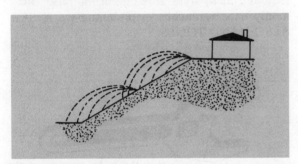

Parallel rows of sprinklers may be used to water a long and deep hillside.

A circular pattern of sprinkling is effective at the face of a hill to hit surrounding areas.

Before testing materials, turn off the water at the main valve. Then attach the control valve kit to the outlet pipe. Connect the sprinkler pipe to the valve, making sure an antisiphon is included. Locate correct spots for sprinkler heads and connect all the heads of one group together with pipe. Test the entire system before putting pipe into the ground.

Dig V-shaped trenches for the pipe about 6 inches deep, taking care with sod so that it may be replaced when the pipe is underground. A small trencher may be rented to aid in digging the required passages.

Dig trenches about 6 inches deep.

A branch-tee pipe fitting allows for side branch connections in the sprinkler systems. Use ³/₄ inch nipples to fasten the hose valve into the tee. Use a ³/₄ by ¹/₂ inch reducer bushing for the connection if the valve is ¹/₂ inch. Use a 90 degree plastic sprinkler elbow at ends of lines.

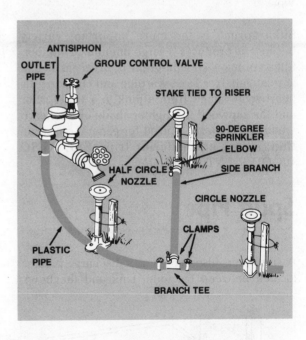

Install sprinkler heads at ground level. They will pop up above grass level when the water pressure is turned on. Let the connection set for two weeks so the ground will settle before inspecting heads again to see if they are too high.

1633

Post-summer check-ups of sprinklers include the removal of nozzle tips and the inspection and replacement of worn washers. Parts should be dried and bushings and bearings oiled with waterproof grease. Metal surfaces should also be covered with oil. *SEE ALSO OUTDOOR PLUMBING.*

Spruce

Spruce is a softwood. There are many varieties of spruce but the ones of most interest to the handyman are the white and red eastern spruce and the Sitka spruce.

The red eastern spruce is exceptionally strong in relation to its weight. Its heartwood is nearly white with a slight red tint. Red spruce is used in light construction and carpentry. White eastern spruce has a light yellow heartwood and a nearly white sapwood. Red and white spruce are used for general building construction and in mill-work.

Sitka spruce is the more important variety because it produces a large amount of lumber. Sitka spruce is straight-grained, dries easily and is relatively free from warping and checking. Its heartwood ranges from a pink to a straw color and the sapwood is a lighter shade of the heartwood. Sitka spruce is used for general construction, siding and exterior trim. *SEE ALSO WOOD IDENTIFICATION.*

Spud Pipe

A spud pipe, also known as a discharge pipe, is located between the toilet tank and the bowl.

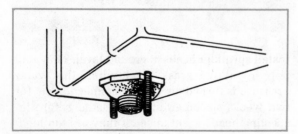

Each end is connected with rubber-sealed slip joints. When the toilet has been flushed, this pipe is empty. *SEE ALSO DRAINAGE SYSTEMS.*

Spud Wrench

The spud wrench is a very wide-jawed wrench designed to fit the "spud," or discharge pipes of sink drains and toilets, and all other hexagonal parts too large even for a monkey wrench. The spud wrench is made in both a solid style, to fit only standard spud sizes, and an adjustable (slip-and-lock) style. It is one of the most commonly used wrenches in plumbing work. *SEE ALSO HAND TOOLS.*

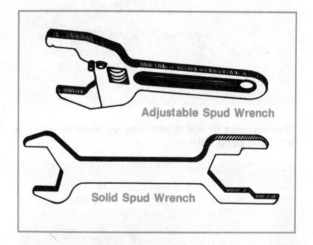

Adjustable Spud Wrench

Solid Spud Wrench

Square File

The square file is a good tool for filing flat surfaces, slots and keyways because its tapered

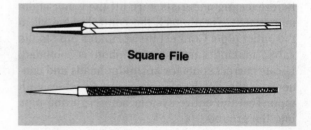

Square File

body and square end make smoothing the inside of square, flat holes easy. *SEE ALSO HAND TOOLS.*

Stab Saw

The stab saw, sometimes called a hacksaw blade holder, is a tool useful in working in tight areas. It will hold a blade, or the broken end of one, to permit cutting flush with a surface, and requires only enough clearance for the blade to reach the work. *SEE ALSO HAND TOOLS.*

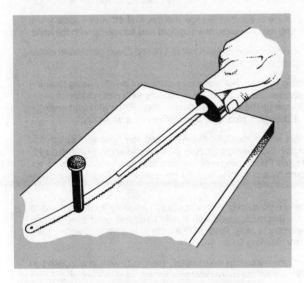

Stab saw holding blade for close cutting.

Stack Control

A stack control is one of the most familiar automatic shut-off switches for an oil burner. Located in the chimney or stack, a stack control consists of two bimetallic strips.

A bimetallic strip is a thin metal strip made of two layers of different metals. They have a wide difference in expansion and contraction rates so that when one metal is heated, it arches toward the other metal. And when it cools, the process is reversed.

A stack control uses two bimetals to determine if an oil burner has properly ignited. A small electric heater is switched on next to one of the bimetallic strips when the burner starts. Upon warming, the bimetallic strip arches and opens a switch that turns off the burner. If the burner lights, then the second bimetallic strip is exposed to the heat flowing through the stack so that the strip arches in such a way to prevent the first strip from switching off the burner.

If for some reason the burner does not light, then the second strip does not arch and can not interfere with the first strip in shutting off the burner. These two strips act as a safety measure for the oil burner so that in case the burner does not light, the oil will not continue to spray into the tank. *SEE ALSO HOME HEATING SYSTEMS.*

Stain Removal

When fabrics become stained, begin trying to remove it as soon as possible. A fresh stain can be removed easier than an older stain which has set in the fabric. The right treatment will depend on the type of stain and the type of fabric. Before using a stain remover, always test it on a hidden section of the fabric.

Some of the chemicals which help in removing stains include: water (the most widely used), carbon tetrachloride, denatured alcohol, vaseline, turpentine, gasoline, kerosene, absorbents (such as cornstarch, chalk, cornmeal or white talcum powder), salt, acetic acid, vinegar, ammonia, bleaches (such as hydrogen peroxide or chlorine) and pepsin.

The following list gives some household stains and methods for removing them.

Alcoholic Beverages: Immediately soak fresh stains with cold water and glycerine and if the stain stays, rinse briefly with vinegar. Often these stains will turn brown with age. Another method for removing fresh liquor stains on carpeting or upholstery is to pour some effervescent club soda on the spot and cover with a cloth,

HOW TO REMOVE STAINS

TYPE OF STAIN	CLEANING AGENTS	PROCEDURE
Milk	Hand soap, water, baking soda, cleaning fluid	First clean with cloth and cold water. Then wash with soap and warm water. Take out rancid smell with one teaspoon baking soda in a cup of warm water. Soak, then rinse with cold water. Try naphtha on any remaining stain.
Blood	Cold water, ammonia, corn starch	Clean with a cloth and Cold water. Hot water sets the stain. Pour household ammonia on any remaining stain and rub with a wet cloth. Any bloodstain remaining should come off by spreading on a thick corn starch paste made with cold water. Let it dry. Lift it off and brush away what is left. Repeat until the stain has gone.
Grease, Oil	Cleaning fluid	Remove the excess with a table knife, then use cleaning fluid and blot.
Gum, tar	Cleaning fluid	Harden with an ice cube, then scrape the material off with a table knife. Soften remaining material with cleaning fluid and scrape up with the knife.
Chocolate	Water, cleaning fluid	Rub with a cloth dampened in warm water. Let dry. Clean gently with cleaning fluid and blot up the stain.
Candy	Hot water, cleaning fluid, soap, detergent	Start by rubbing with very hot water on a cloth. Let dry. Try using cleaning fluid. Filled candies usually come off by rubbing with cloth dipped in warm soapsuds. Scrape up the stain immediately after. Rinse with cold water on a cloth. Try a detergent cleaner if the spot remains when dry.
Fruit and liquor	Hot water, cleaning fluid	Soap and water will set the stain. Avoid dry heat, too. Start with a cloth dipped in hot water. Scrape off fruit pulp with a table knife. Rub thoroughly with the wet cloth. Pour boiling water on as a final effort, followed by scraping and rubbing. Watch that the fabric is not discolored. Finally, try a cleaning fluid.
Ice Cream	Hot water, soap, cleaning fluid	Clean up ice cream quickly before it dries, removing it like fruit stains (above). Warm soapsuds, made with a mild soap and used after the first hot-water treatment is okay. Rinse with a cloth soaked in cold water. If any stain is left, try cleaning fluid.
Catsup	Cold water, detergent	Clean with cloth soaked in cold water, then rub with one soaked in detergent. Rinse, then use more detergent if the spot is still showing. Rinse again.
Water Spots	Cold water, detergent	Rub with a cold-water-dampened cloth. Follow that by rubbing lightly with a detergent-dampened cloth. No need to rinse.
Battery acid	Ammonia	The danger in battery acid is fabric damage. Act as quickly as possible. Pour household ammonia right onto the spot. After a minute, rinse well with cold water to get all the neutralizing ammonia out.
Urine	Hand soap, cold water, ammonia	Start by rubbing with warm soapsuds. Rinse with a cloth soaked in cold water. Dilute household ammonia in five parts water and sponge that onto the fabric. Leave it for a minute; rinse with a cloth wetted in water.
Ball point pen	Petroleum jelly, carbon tetrachloride	Spread petroleum jelly on the stain to lubricate it, then flush it through by applying carbon tetrachloride. Take care not to breathe fumes. Scrape gently with a table knife to loosen the stain. Keep repeating these steps until the stain disappears. Ball point ink stains are hard to remove. Try asking a shirt launderer to do it for you. They have special chemicals for getting ball-point ink out of shirts.
Lipstick	Detergent	Pour some detergent directly onto the spot, then press a clean white blotter over it to pick up both lipstick and detergent. Keep repeating these two steps, using a fresh area of the blotter until the stain is gone.

pressing it to help absorb the moisture. Leave the cloth on the spot several hours to absorb the stain. If neither of these methods removes a wine stain, scrub with a concentrated detergent and if necessary repeat this procedure.

Blood: Soak in cold or warm water until stain becomes lighter. If the stain remains, soak it in warm water with three tablespoons of ammonia added per gallon, and then rinse. To bleach, dampen the fabric with the ammonia water and set it in the sun or dampen with hydrogen peroxide.

Candle Wax: Using a dull knife, scrape off wax or crumble it off. Put fabric between two blotters and press with a warm iron. If necessary, dampen with carbon tetrachloride.

Chewing Gum: Hold ice to the area until gum is frozen and then scrape off with dull knife. It can be softened in kerosene or carbon tetrachloride. If gum remains, sponge with alcohol.

Chocolate & Cocoa: Soak in warm or cold water and sponge with carbon tetrachloride. Grease stains can be removed with an absorbent. If stain remains, sponge with hydrogen peroxide.

Coffee: Soak in cold water or pour boiling water through the stain from the opposite side. If stain remains, cover with glycerine and then soak again.

Crayon: Scrape off as much as possible with dull blade. Launder with detergent with one or two cups of baking soda added.

Deodorants: Sponge stain with white vinegar and if persistant, soak with alcohol.

Dyes: Wash in cold water or lukewarm water for about ten minutes. Wash in very soapy water and dry in sun. For white material, use a bleach or color remover.

Eggs: Scrape off extra egg. Soak in warm or cold water with pepsin about 30 minutes. If stain remains, sponge with carbon tetrachloride or dry cleaning solvent.

Fruit & Fruit Juices: Dampen with cold water; then soak in cold or warm water with pepsin for about 30 minutes. If stain remains, rub a few drops of glycerine into it or dampen with vinegar or oxalic acid and rinse with water.

Glue: Soak in warm water or sponge with vinegar.

Grass: Soak in cold or warm water with pepsin for about 30 minutes or sponge with alcohol.

Grease, Oil, Tar: Apply absorbent, removing as much grease as possible; rub with detergent, dry cleaning solvent or shampoo and wash in hot water. Another method is to apply lard or vaseline to the stain and sponge with carbon tetrachloride.

Ink: For ball-point pin ink pour alcohol through the stain and then rub with vaseline. Next sponge with dry cleaning solvent and soak in detergent. For fountain pin ink, run cold water through stain, then put an absorbent on the stain. If the stain remains, put oxalic acid solution on spot and apply some ammonia.

Iodine: If still damp, rub with soap and water or use ammonia.

Lipstick: Apply a dry cleaning solvent or vaseline and then scrub with detergent until stain is removed. Hydrogen peroxide and sodium perborate or alcohol may also be applied.

Mercurochrome: Dampen with part water and part alcohol. If stain remains, apply glycerine, wash in detergent and rinse with ammonia and water.

Meat Juices: Scrape off as much as possible with a dull blade. Soak in cold or warm water and pepsin for about 30 minutes.

Mildew: Wash it off with detergent or put oxalic acid and Javelle water on it. If stain persists, sponge it with lemon juice and salt.

Milk, Cream, Ice Cream: Soak in warm water with pepsin for about 30 minutes and then launder. Any grease spots should be sponged with dry cleaning solvent.

Nail Polish: Sponge with polish remover, banana oil, peroxide, alcohol or laquer thinner; then rinse. If stain stays, sponge it with alcohol which has a few drops of ammonia in it.

Paint: For oil-base paints, sponge or soak the stain in turpentine, cleaning fluid or paint remover. Old stains should be sponged with banana oil and then with a dry cleaning solvent. For water base paints, scrape off as much as possible with a dull blade and launder with detergent in hot water.

Perspiration: For a fresh stain, sponge with ammonia and for an old stain sponge with vinegar. Then soak in cold or warm water with pepsin for about 30 minutes. Launder and use bleach if the fabric is yellow.

Rust: Soak in lemon juice or an oxalic acid solution which has three tablespoons oxalic acid per pint.

Scorch: Launder and bleach in sun. For heavier scorches, cover the spot with a cloth dampened with hydrogen peroxide. Place a dry cloth on top and press with a hot iron. Rinse well.

Soft Drinks: Sponge as soon as possible with cold water and alcohol.

Tea: Sponge or soak in cold water immediately.

Urine: Soak in warm, soapy water which has ammonia added and then rinse; or soak in warm water, then soak in hot water and rinse.

Stains & Staining

Stains and staining accentuate wood grain and color by penetrating and giving clarity to it. Types include penetrating wiping stain, water, nongrain-raising, oil, spirit, chemical, padding and varnish stains.

Penetrating wiping stains leave the pigment in the pores to greatly accent the wood. This type of stain works best on softwoods.

Water stains are actually more of a true stain than the rest. This type actually dyes the fibers of the wood. Water stains can not be used on a surface that has been finished before, even if the old surface has been removed.

Nongrain-raising stains are made from petroleum industry chemical by-products. One feature of this stain is that it dries in a few hours. As its name implies, this stain does not accent the grain as much as it produces desired coloring.

Oil stain has an oil base in which oil-soluble dyes are dissolved. This stain takes about 24 hours to dry.

Spirit or alcohol stain is a touch-up stain. Most often used to cover small defects, large surfaces can be stained although a good result may be difficult to obtain.

Chemical stains are permanent, fadeproof and dangerous. The stain is either an acid or an alkaline and is used to discolor the wood.

Padding stains are used for touch-ups and old finishes. Applied with cheesecloth or a rag dampened with diluted lacquer or thinned shellac, the stain which is in powder form is rubbed over the surface. This stain requires a topcoat of varnish or another protective coating.

Varnish stains do not give good penetration and clarity, which is the real purpose of a stain. It does, however, stain and gives a protective coating in one operation.

STAINING

Individual techniques can be found in manufacturer's instructions, paint store directions or in this encyclopedia under the particular name of the stain. However, there are a few general recommendations for all types of stains. Artificial light is not suggested when staining nor is direct sunlight since it tends to darken the finish.

Try to use a room with plenty of natural light. Always test the stain on a scrap of the same wood or in an obscure place where the test results are not likely to be seen. The surface should be flooded with the stain so that the wood can absorb as much stain as possible. After the stain has had ample time to saturate the wood, wipe the surface with soft rags to remove excess stain so that the wood grain is not obscured.

If a varnish stain is used, the handyman should use the normal varnish application method. There should be no flooding and no wiping. *SEE ALSO WOOD FINISHING.*

Stair Construction

All things considered, a gentle incline, or ramp, is probably the safest and easiest way to change altitude, but the shallow angle of such a slope makes it impractical except for some outdoor settings.

While a 15 degree angle is about right for a ramp, this won't work indoors. The slope must be broken into steps and this permits the angle to be increased to 30 or 35 degrees. This angle is an almost ideal situation, considering the tread-riser relationship, and this seldom happens. We most often must figure angles between 20 and 50 degrees. Below 20 degrees you might just as well build a ramp. Above 50 degrees you can plan on a ladder or elevator.

The relationship between riser and tread is as important as the stair angle. The normal total of riser height and tread depth should be about 17 or 18 inches. This means that the risers should be 7 inches or less; in some cases you may create treads that are so wide they require more than one stride.

In constructing a stairway there are two factors to work with, the *total rise* and the *total run*. Measure the height between the bottom and top floors and this is the total rise. Divide that figure by the ideal *unit* rise, seven inches, and the

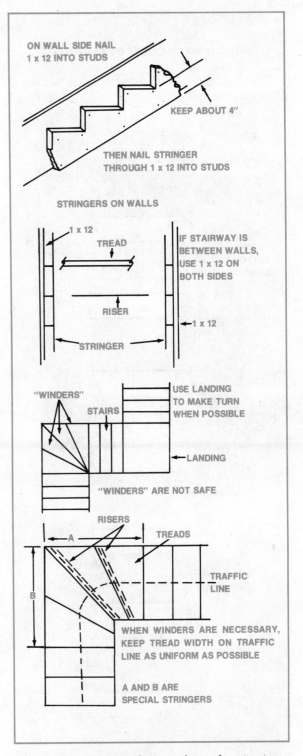

result will indicate the number of unit risers needed. Forget any fraction, and use that figure to divide into the total rise and this will give you the *actual* unit rise.

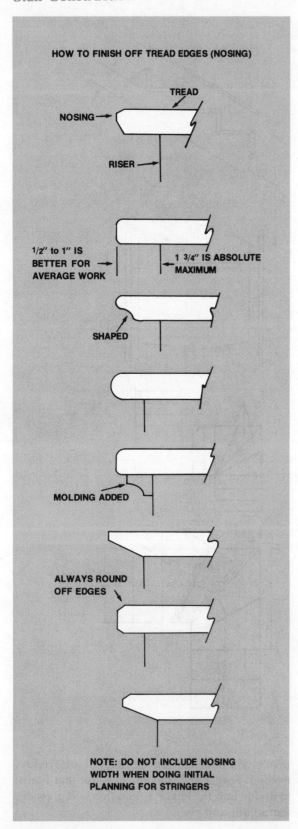

HOW TO FINISH OFF TREAD EDGES (NOSING)

NOSING →

TREAD

RISER →

1/2" to 1" IS BETTER FOR AVERAGE WORK →

1 3/4" IS ABSOLUTE MAXIMUM

SHAPED

MOLDING ADDED

ALWAYS ROUND OFF EDGES

NOTE: DO NOT INCLUDE NOSING WIDTH WHEN DOING INITIAL PLANNING FOR STRINGERS

To establish a starting point for the tread depth or *unit run*, subtract the unit rise from 18 inches. Now, multiply the result by the number of risers, minus one, to set the total run. Under good conditions this arithmetic will work out all right, but should the answer prove impractical for the available space, a compromise must be made. Achieve a solution by changing the riser-tread relationship — subtracting from one to add to the other — so long as you remain within the boundaries of good, safe design. It may be easier to draw a scaled layout of the situation. You might even bend up a piece of stiff cardboard to make a scale model. The more preplanning you do, the easier construction will be.

Remember that head room is important. The width of a stairway is determined by the use it will receive. For one-way traffic a width of 24 inches is sufficient. For two people walking together, or for the passage of furniture, figure on a minimum of 36 inches. The 24 inch width is not recommended for indoor stairs, and a local building code will probably dictate a greater width. If you have any doubt, check the local code.

Those components to which the treads and risers are attached are called *stringers*. They have sawtooth cuts for the step parts and are set at the angle of the stairs. Their job is to provide parallel-to-the-floor bearing surfaces for the treads. Once you have established the tread-riser relationship, the lay-out on the stringer is quite simple.

The drawing indicates how to make a simple template that you can just trace around. A carpenter's square also can be used; just mark the unit rise on the tongue, the unit run on the blade. When these two points are adjusted to the edge of the stock, you mark around the corner of the square for the cutout pattern. By measuring between the legs of the notch on a straight line, then multipling this distance by the number of risers, you can determine the length required for the stringers. Add a few inches to play it safe.

Clamp the two stringers together and cut the notches with a handsaw, or portable electric saw and finish with a handsaw.

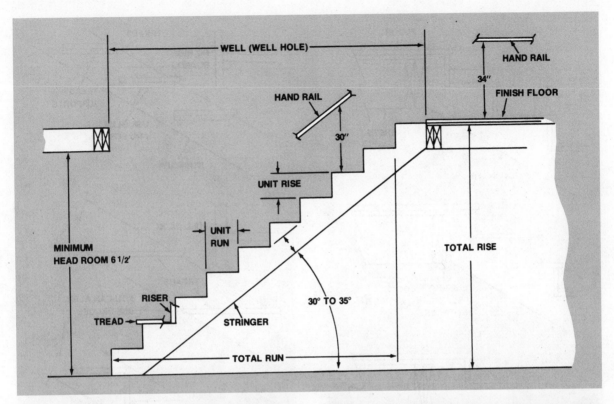

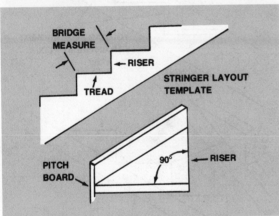

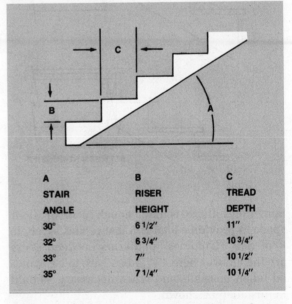

A STAIR ANGLE	B RISER HEIGHT	C TREAD DEPTH
30°	6 1/2″	11″
32°	6 3/4″	10 3/4″
33°	7″	10 1/2″
35°	7 1/4″	10 1/4″

You can avoid the sawtooth cuts by going along with one of the other ideas shown. A number of these designs are used on "utility" stairs, where riser boards are not used. One of the sketches shows how you can include vertical as well as horizontal cleats to provide nailing surfaces for risers. Another method is the "carriage" stringer. The advantage here is that you can cut the riser-tread blocks on a table saw.

Shown in another drawing are methods of attaching the upper ends of the stringers.

When attaching stringers to walls, first nail a 1 x 12 against the wall, driving the spikes into the studs. The stringer then is nailed to the 1 x 12 plate. A number of ways of finishing tread "nosings" are shown. Remember that this nosing dimension is *not* included in planning the tread depth.

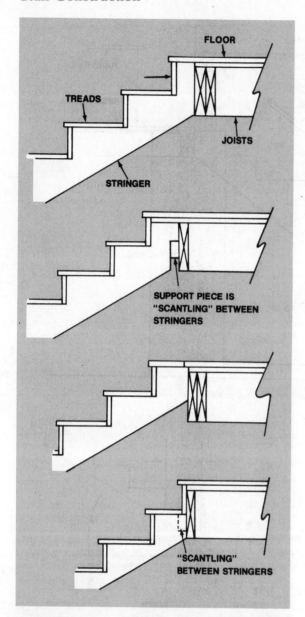

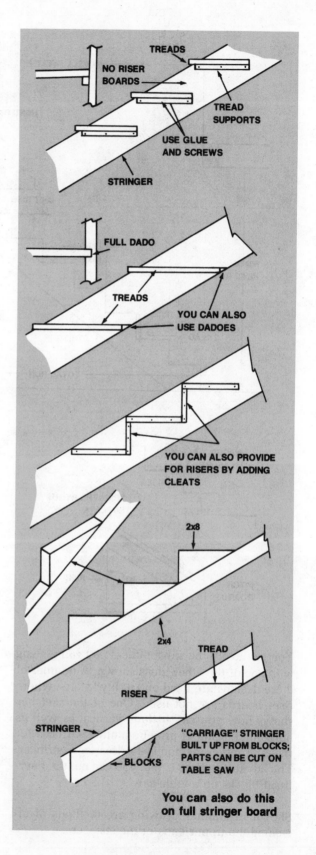

Sometimes there is not enough wall or floor space to provide a total run that relates safely to total rise. "Landings" platforms between stairs are the answer here. "Winders" are to be avoided when possible, and when necessary, should be installed as shown.

Circular stairways sometimes are the only solution, but all safety organizations advise against them. Where they must be used, we suggest you contact companies that provide units in kit form. These stairs are of steel for maximum strength, and designed to fit the minimum space.

Stairs, Stone
[SEE BRICK & STONE WORK.]

Stairway, Disappearing

A disappearing stairway, also called a folding or extension attic stairway, is used frequently for access to an attic when there is plenty of space; it can also be installed in the ceiling of halls, garages and storage rooms. The main advantage of disappearing stairways is that the floor space below the stair device is not occupied which allows freer planning. One type of disappearing

stairway has two bottom treads which fold under and the next part folds up to fit in the ceiling opening. Another kind of disappearing stairway has the ladder pushed up to clear the hinged panel; when the ladder is lowered, the doweled frame is swung up and over to bring the top of the ladder to the edge of the opening. In many houses the folding stairway is installed as standard equipment with frame opening which has trim around it. Springs or counterbalances compensate for the weight of the folding stairway and coil springs provide the necessary amount of lateral balance.

A type of disappearing stairway which is pushed up into the ceiling opening.

Standard Sill

A standard sill supports both live and dead loads of the structural frame except for interior loads which are supported by interior girder posts. Standard sills are placed on the foundation and can be made of wood or steel. The width of a sill varies with the local code but generally consists of 2 x 6 inch lumber. A sill sealer, a waterproof material, may be placed under the sill before it is bolted. When the exterior walls are concrete or brick, sills are not needed. However, brick veneer does need a sill. *SEE ALSO FLOOR CONSTRUCTION.*

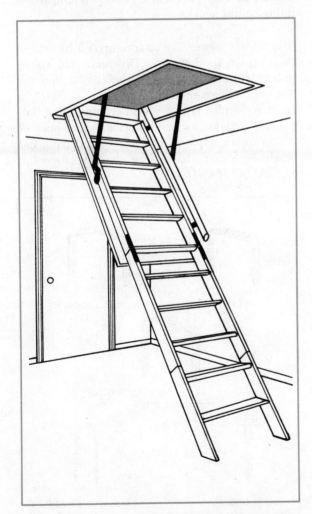

A disappearing stairway which folds for flat storage.

Staple Guns

Staple guns have taken the place of nails and tacks in many aspects of home repair. The right staple gun and staples can be used for practically everything from tacking webbing to installing wire and cable.

Lightweight staple guns usually weigh a little over a pound and are good for securing screening, plastic storm windows, insulation and upholstery. These staple guns generally take only one size of staple, but some can take two or three sizes for varied work.

Heavy-duty staple guns can accommodate five or six staple sizes which makes them useful for installing ceiling tile, gypsum board, cables and wire. These guns usually weigh over two pounds and some models have variable spring power to adjust the firing strength to the work. When stapling cable or wire on a surface, use a staple gun that can be adapted to different sizes and has a channeled base to prevent stapling through wire or holding it too tightly against insulation.

Stapling with either a light or heavy weight gun is done much the same way. Place the flat surface of the staple gun on the surface to be fastened.

Grasp the hand hole with the fingertips and place the thumb to one side of the gun lever so that the finger tips and thumb tip are facing each other. By squeezing with the fingers and pushing the lever down with the thumb, the staple is fired from the gun.

There are some models of staple guns, however, in which the lever is pulled up rather than pushed down. This makes it easier to hold while doing ceiling work.

Staples are generally characterized by either their crown or their tips. Divergent and chisel point staples may appear to be similar, but the tips in the divergent branch off when fired into a surface. Staples with a round crown do not flatten and are good for fastening cable. The head of a high crown staple will flatten when driven, and single leg staples have only one beveled point. *SEE ALSO HAND TOOLS.*

Correct Way to Hold a Staple Gun

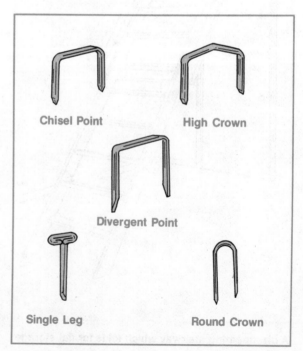

Chisel Point

High Crown

Divergent Point

Single Leg

Round Crown

Stapling Tools

Stapling tools are used to drive staples into various materials to hold them together. Depending on the tool, its uses can range from securing webbing to a chair frame or fastening roofing felt to a house in construction work.

Stapling hammers derive their power from arm strength rather than a spring as in staple guns. These tools are not designed for accurate work such as installing ceiling tile, but make work faster in tacking down roofing felt, insulation and tar paper.

Mallet-driven staplers get their power from a mallet swing and are capable of driving staples over one inch long for underlayment and sheathing.

The most common stapling tools are the manually and air-powered staple guns. They have become increasingly popular for performing the jobs once accomplished with tacks and nails. Upholstery, screening, installing ceiling tile and insulation and building furniture are a few of the many purposes of staple guns. *SEE ALSO HAND TOOLS.*

Starter Punch

The starter punch is used to drive rivets from wood or metal when the head of the rivet has been cut off. To use the starter punch, center the small flat head at one end of the punch over the rivet and using a hammer, drive the rivet out of

Courtesy of The Stanley Works
Starter Punch

the object by hammering the opposite end of the punch. *SEE ALSO HAND TOOLS.*

Starter Strip

A starter strip is a narrow piece of mineral surfaced roofing used as a backing for the first row of shingles. Usually nine inches or wider, the starter strip should be of approximately the same weight and color as the shingles. The strip should be applied so that it slightly overhangs the drip edge and is secured with nails three to four inches from the edge. An inverted row of shingles can substitute for a starter strip.

Stationary Belt and Disc Sander

Belt and disc sanders on stands have become standard finishing tools in the home woodworking shop. Often, the enterprising craftsman will rig up his own disc sander by mounting a suitable plate directly to the shaft of a properly powered motor and then adding a table for work support.

In concept, the disc sander is a fairly simple tool. The belt sander is a bit more complicated since it requires two drums and built-in adjustments so the belt may be positioned correctly.

The tools may be purchased individually or as a combination. The combination unit is perhaps the better choice for the homecraftsman. It provides both items mounted on a single stand and powered by one motor. So mounted, they do not impose any operational restrictions. Anything you can do on either as individual tools may be accomplished when they are combined.

If a choice had to be made between the individual tools, it would probably be wise to decide in favor of the belt sander because you can improvise on other tools for disc sander chores.

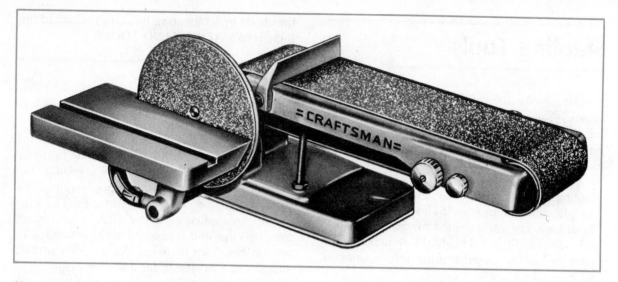

You can spend a lot of money for a combination unit, especially if you are attracted by a heavy-duty model that's powered by a plus 1 HP motor and runs on 220V. But good homecraftsman designs are also available. You can even buy a belt sander in kit form or an unadorned type that

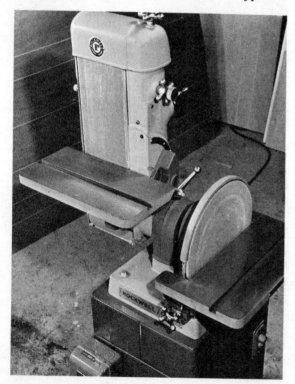

Heavy-duty belt-disc combination is driven by a plus 1 HP motor and sits on a totally enclosed stand. The belt is 6″ x 48″ and the disc is 12″ in diameter. Note that each unit has its own separate tilting table.

provides function without frills. Whichever model you choose, remember that sanding operations, especially when you are trying to remove a lot of material, require considerable power. Generally, a 1/2 HP to 3/4 HP motor is not out of line. When you shop, check the motor size recommended by the manufacturer. Never use less.

Disc sizes can range from 6″ up to 12″, belt widths from 4″ to 6″. Two common belt sizes for home shops are 4″ x 36″ and 6″ x 48″. The latter dimension in each size (36″, 48″) indicates the full length of the belt; the larger the belt (or the disc), the more abrasive surface you have to work with.

These abrasive tools are among the best finishing aids you can have in the shop. They do not replace portable versions, but they will substantially reduce the amount of postconstruction finishing that remains to be done. You can finish project components as you go so they are fairly well organized for final coats before you even assemble them. Also, many sanding jobs are much easier to do when you can apply the work to the tool, such as a final touch on the end of a 2x4 or the precise finished sanding of a picture-frame miter.

In addition, keep a few general safety rules in mind when using belt and disc sanders. Whenever possible, feed work so your fingers are hooked over the edge of the stock to guard against sanding your fingers instead of the work. Don't, without special precautions, work pieces so small that they can be drawn in between the abrasive surface and the edge of the table. Remember that metal sanding causes sparks which might contact an accumulation of wood dust and easily cause a fire. When you change from wood to metal sanding, be sure that you first clean the tools.

The Belt Sander

This tool uses an endless abrasive belt that rotates over two drums. The bottom drum is powered; the other is an idler. Since the abrasive moves in a straight line, the belt sander is an especially good tool for doing sanding that is parallel to the wood grain.

The width of the belt does not indicate a limit on the width of the stock you can sand. By making repeat passes and adjusting the work position after each, you can sand boards that are wider than the belt itself.

Cross-grain work is also permissible but done mostly when you wish to remove a lot of material quickly. It should always be followed by with-the-grain sanding to remove scratches that remain after the cross-grain work.

All belt sanders can be used in either a vertical or horizontal position. This is possible because they tilt back from the bottom end. In general, use the vertical position for any kind of end sanding; use the horizontal position for surfacing and sanding of edges on long pieces.

Adjustments

The back of the belt is marked with an arrow to indicate the correct direction of rotation. When you view the drums, you'll note that they turn down or in a clockwise direction. Point the arrow on the belt so it will follow the same route.

To mount a belt, lower the upper drum. This decreases the distance between the drums and permits the belt to slide into place easily. Then, raise the drum until there is no visible slackness in the belt. Don't overdo this *tensioning* adjust-

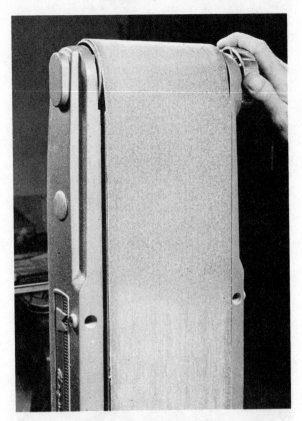

Belts are marked with an arrow. When placing the belt over the drums, be sure the arrow points in the direction of rotation of the drums. Tensioning of the belt is done by raising or lowering the upper drum. Tracking is done by tilting the upper drum.

ment. The second adjustment is *tracking*, which is centering the belt over the drums and keeping it moving in the same line. Tracking is accomplished with a tilt action in the upper drum. Tilt one way and the belt will move to the left; tilt the other way and the belt will move to the right. The idea is to adjust so the belt does neither. Your best bet is to sight the upper drum and make an as-close-as-possible arbitrary adjustment. Then turn the motor switch quickly on and off. If the belt moves one way or the other, make an adjustment to compensate.

When the belt is tracking correctly, you may use the machine. After a short period of work, increase the tension a slight amount. You may find that slight tracking readjustments may become necessary as you work. At such times, you may work the adjustment knob as the belt is turning.

The methods of accomplishing tensioning and tracking may vary from machine to machine, so read your owner's manual carefully for specifics in relation to the tool you own.

Edge sanding

Use the machine in the vertical position with the table adjusted to form a right angle with the abrasive surface. Rest the work solidly on the table and advance it slowly to make contact. When the work is curved, make the pass in a sweeping motion; remember that the belt cuts quickly, so allowing the work to sit too long in one position will produce too flat a surface.

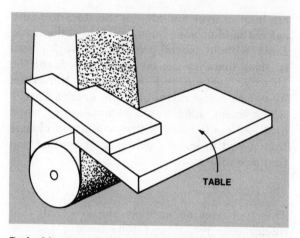

Do inside corners this way. On some tools it may be necessary to remove an outboard guard. Be sure to track the belt so its edge is in line with the outboard edge of the back-up plate. Again, be careful of hand positions.

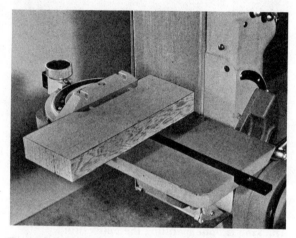

Do end sanding by moving directly forward into the belt. When possible, use a miter gauge as a guide. When removing a lot of material, move the work laterally as well as forward. Overworking one area of the belt can lead to clogging or even cause the belt to stretch.

If you are going from a flat edge to a round edge, approach the job with the flat edge parallel to the belt and swing gently into the curve. In essence, the surface of the belt should be tangent to the curve at point of contact at all times. Usually, you should do preliminary cutting with other tools so the amount of material to be removed by sanding will be minimal. In any case, excessive pressure against the abrasive is poor practice. Better to make two or three light-pressure passes than a single heavy one.

Try to work so you will be using the entire width of the belt. Keeping the work still will clog the

belt in one area and may very well stretch it out of shape.

For square ends, move the work directly forward into the belt. When possible, use a miter gauge to assure squareness. Here too, it's a good idea to move the work across the belt as you move it forward. This can be done whether you are working freehand or with a miter gauge. Another reason to keep the work moving is to avoid obvious striations that can result when you do nothing but feed directly ahead. This factor is more critical with coarse papers than with fine.

How you do inside corners will depend on the design of the machine. If there is an outboard guard, it must be removed. You must adjust tracking so the edge of the belt moves right on line with the outboard edge of the backup plate. Then the job becomes pretty straight-forward end sanding. Do one side of the corner; then flip the stock and do the other.

Angles

Simple bevels are done by tilting the table; the job is fairly much an end-sanding chore. You will be more accurate if you work with a guide. The guide can be the miter gauge or, lacking one, a piece of wood that you clamp in place after checking its position with a square. If the edge is compound, then you must set both the table and the miter gauge. The angles you use must be compatible with the miter-gauge and saw-blade settings you organized for the original cut. Remember that sanding removes material, so original cuts should be made a fraction oversize.

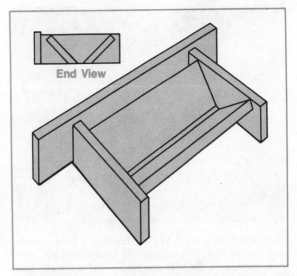

A trough jig does production work when the same chamfer is needed on many pieces. The angle of the side pieces determines the angle of the chamfer. This jig is used with the tool in horizontal position.

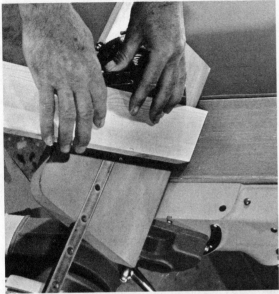

To do bevel work, tilt the table to the angle required. Here, both the miter gauge and the table are adjusted to match original sawing angles of a compound cut.

To do chamfers or to *break* edges (which simply means destroying a sharp corner), adjust the table to the angle you want and then move the stock directly forward. If you have a lot of chamfering to do on many similar pieces, it will pay to make a trough jig. The angle of the slanting pieces is organized to suit the chamfer you require. This jig is best used with the machine in its horizontal position.

When the bevel you are doing is on stock that is not longer than the belt is wide, then as previously mentioned, the operation is pretty much an end-sanding chore. For longer work, you will have to sweep across the belt and the results will depend on how skillfully you do it. Start close to an end, apply very light pressure and maintain it as constantly as possible as you feed across. Excessive pressure can cause the belt to dig in at one edge or the other.

You can, if you wish, clamp a straight piece of wood to the table parallel to the belt. Then you can pass the work between the guide and the abrasive. This procedure must be a light-touch operation.

Surface work

Surfacing, or sanding of long edges, is best done with the machine in a horizontal position and with a fence set up as a guide. How you organize

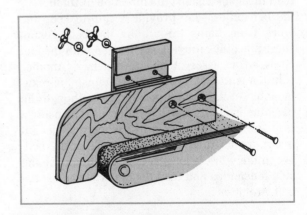

Even when using the table or a stop as a fence, it pays to make an auxiliary addition that will run the full length of the belt and curl over the top drum. Bolts go through holes in the table or stop. If necessary, drill them.

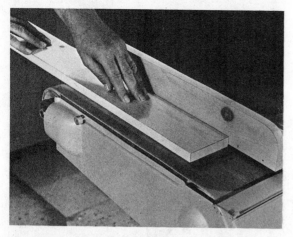

Don't work this way! We're showing a how-not-to-do-it photo simply because the mistake is so common. Action of the belt can throw out the work and leave nothing between your fingers and the abrasive. Always feed against the belt's rotation and hold the work firmly.

for the fence will depend on the design of your machine. In some cases, it's possible to use the one table in both its normal belt-upright position and as a fence when the tool is tilted horizontally. With other machines you can buy an accessory that is used as a fence. Many times you can make a simple L-shaped affair that you can bolt to the machine for fence use.

Don't feed the work in the same direction that the belt is traveling; you may well end up with no work between yourself and the belt. Always feed the stock against the direction of rotation of the belt unless you provide a stop to keep the work from being thrown by the belt. Again, some machines provide such a stop with the tool or as an accessory that you can buy. Another solution is to make your own or to use the regular table in its normal position even though the machine is horizontal. The latter idea or using a stop you make yourself works when stock length is not greater than the work surface of the belt. When the work is longer, then you must use the side fence idea and feed the material against the belt's rotation.

When you angle the fence to the belt, you can feed stock diagonally at times when you wish to remove a lot of material quickly. This results in cross-grain scratches, and the operation must al-

ways be followed by with-the-grain sanding in order to get an acceptable finish.

Inside curves

All machines permit the use of the top drum as a "drum sander." If there is a guard, it must be removed. The job can be done freehand, especially if you are smoothing something like a cabriole leg or doing irregular edge scalloping for an antique effect. When you want the sanded edge to be square to adjacent surfaces, then it's good practice to use a fence as a guide for the work.

Odd jobs

The belt sander is constructed so there is a back-up plate behind the belt only at the front of the machine. This feature allows you to use the backside of the belt for such jobs as sanding knobs, round edges and ball shapes. If you ease off on belt tension a bit, you'll get more slack in the belt which will help in these types of jobs. It's also possible to buy slashed belts for rounding-off operations although such items are not easily found in stores that deal mostly with the homecraftsman.

You can try slashing your own belt. Choose a fine-grit belt and use a sharp knife to cut slits on the back side of the belt that are about 5'' or 6'' long and from $3/16$'' to $1/4$'' apart. Do this across the width of the belt but leave about $1/2$'' of solid belt along each edge. Slit the length of the belt but leave about $1/2$'' of solid belt between groups of slits.

The Disc Sander
How to mount paper

There are many ways to mount paper on a disc sander, and everyone usually ends up with one method that he finds preferable. One older method is the use of a disc stick that is almost like a stick shellac wrapped in a cardboard tube. You peel back the paper and apply the exposed sticky material to the revolving disc until the disc is fairly evenly coated. Then you press the abrasive sheet against the disc. This method works best when you "warm" the disc by holding a block of wood against it while it is turning.

Another method involves the use of a special rubber cement that is applied with a brush to both the disc and the paper. When the cement dries enough to be tacky to the touch, you press the sheet and disc together.

You can also buy abrasive sheets with self-adhesive backings which work well. However, with long-period storage the paper backing that protects the adhesive sometimes sticks too well and comes off in pieces.

Another material that can be used is a spray mounting adhesive that is available in art supply stores. Even though it isn't made for the purpose, it seems to work well and is very easy to use. Simply spray the back of the sheet, and when the application is dry enough to be tacky, press the sheet onto the disc.

Whatever method you use, always be sure to clean the old adhesive from the disc before applying a new coating. If there are sticky areas, use a solvent to soften the adhesive and then rub off with fine steel wool. Always be sure to apply the adhesive evenly in order to get the sandpaper flat on the disc; any bumps will result in imperfections on the sanded surface.

Incidentally, when you are doing a job that can be accomplished best by working through two grits of paper, you can organize a double-sanding disc. This is simply a matter of cutting a circle from the center of the coarser paper and then cutting a disc from the finer paper to fit it. Both pieces of paper are mounted on the sanding disc so you can work on the outer portion for one grit and the inner portion for the second grit.

After mounting a new disc, run the machine freely for a minute or so and stand away from the edge. This procedure tests whether the bond between the disc and sheet of abrasive is good enough to be safe.

Direction of rotation

Most discs will turn in a counterclockwise direction, which means you should place the work on the table on the left so you will be using the "down" side. Using the "up" side will cause

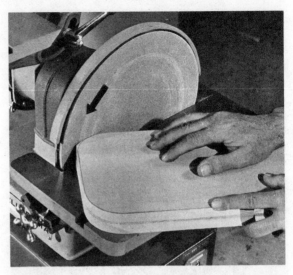

The disc rotates counter-clockwise (see arrow) so always place work on the left side of the table. This is the "down" side of the disc. Working on the right side will lift the work from the table and throw grit. Keep the work moving and try to feed laterally as well as forward. Staying too long in one position on curved work will create flats.

the disc to lift the work and will throw grit into your face. Even so, sometimes it's necessary to use the "up" side, such as in sanding a long edge freehand and sweeping across the full diameter of the disc. When you have to use the "up" side, keep a firm grip on the work, hold it snug to the table and wear goggles.

To some extent, you can choose the abrasive-surface speed at which you wish to work. The slowest speed is at the center of the disc; it increases as you approach the outer edge. Remember this is surface speed, not rpm's. Also, if you held a piece of wood directly against the midpoint of the disc, you would create circular marks, but do no sanding.

General operational procedures

Remember that the disc rotates. Therefore, it can't be used to do with-the-grain sanding. It is possible to surface cut by feeding with the stock on edge and its surface against the disc, but you will have arc marks that will have to be removed later by sanding with the grain. The depth of the arc marks will, of course, depend on the grit of the paper you are using.

It is always best to work with a light, smooth feed. Pressure should never be excessive even when you must remove a lot of material. A few light touches do a better job than a single heavy push. This approach is better for the work, and it will help prevent clogging the paper quickly. The no-force rule is especially true when you are working on material that is longer than the disc diameter. Forcing against the edge of the disc can cause gouging. Also, since disc speed is high, too much pressure can cause excessive heat which can burn the wood and the paper.

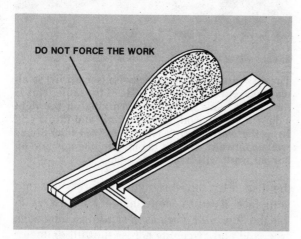

DO NOT FORCE THE WORK

Be very careful when sanding material that is longer than the disc diameter. For one thing, the "up" side of the disc will be used as well as the down. For another, it's easy for the edge of the disc to dig into the work and cause gouging.

Keep the work moving. If you hesitate in one spot when sanding a curve, you will create a flat surface in that area. If you are doing end sanding, move the work directly forward into the disc but add a lateral feed after you make contact. The length of the lateral stroke can be from the outer edge of the disc to somewhere close to the center.

Although the disc can't get completely inside the corner of a right-angle cut, you can get close enough so that only a little extra hand work will be required to complete the job. It is best to sand one leg of the work by moving it across the abrasive until the edge of the disc almost touches the adjacent side. Then, flip the stock and sand the second edge by moving directly forward. When both legs of the cut are long,

then it might be best to do each by moving across the face of the disc. In either case, don't force when you approach the inside corner. The exposed edge of the disc can mar the work.

Round off corners by using a gentle, sweeping motion. Start by holding the flat of the work parallel to the disc and then moving in to make light contact. Once you touch, start the sweeping motion. The plane of the disc must be tangent to the arc at all times.

Square ends and miters can be guided with a miter gauge. In either case, the work and the miter gauge may be moved laterally after the initial contact is made. When you have many similar jobs to do and the material to be removed by sanding is minimal, it's a good idea to clamp the miter gauge in position so all you have to do is move the stock directly forward. If you don't have a miter gauge, simply substitute a straight piece of wood for the gauge. The angle between the wood guide and the disc can be established with a protractor.

Chamfer jig

Chamfering can be done freehand; but when a groove is required on more than one edge of the stock or when it must be repeated on similar pieces, it's wise to make a simple jig as a guide. A chamfering jig is no more than a notched board that is clamped to the disc sander table.

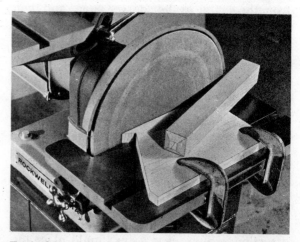

Typical jig setup for such jobs as chamfering. The short leg on the jig assures that exactly the right amount of wood will be removed from the work.

The long leg of the notch holds the work in position for the correct chamfer angle; the short leg limits the amount of material that can be removed. Thus, whether you are doing two pieces or a hundred pieces, you'll know that all the chamfers will be uniform.

Pivot sanding

This type of sanding is a fine way to sand perfect circles or arcs. The setup for the work doesn't have to be much more than a piece of plywood through which you have driven a nail for use as a pivot. When you clamp the plywood to the table, the nail should be about center on the down side of the disc, and the distance from the nail to the abrasive should equal the radius of the work.

An adjustable jig for pivot sanding is another possibility. The platform is a piece of ³/₄" plywood that is dadoed to receive a sliding, hardwood bar. If you make the sliding bar to fit tightly in the dado, you won't have to worry about clamping it in place for various radii settings. Drive a small roofing nail through one end of the bar. Make another bar to match the groove in the sander table and assemble the platform and the bar so there is about a ¹/₈" gap between the front edge of the platform and the disc. Clamp the platform to the table so the sliding bar

Then the work is rotated in a full circle. When there is much of this to do, reposition the platform frequently to avoid working on just one area of the disc.

is about centered on the down side of the disc. This position is variable. When you have many pieces to do, it makes sense to shift occasionally so you will be using the full width of the down side.

To use the jig, set the pivot point away from the disc a bit more than you actually need for the work. Place the work in position on the point and tap the sliding bar forward until the disc contacts the work line. Then, slowly rotate the disc to sand the full circle. It doesn't matter whether you turn the work left or right.

In pivot cutting, it's assumed that you have bandsawed, jigsawed or somehow prepared the work so that the bulk of the waste has been removed before you go to the final sanding.

Sanding to width

You can sand straight or curved edges to exact width if you clamp a guide to the sander table so you can pass the work between the guide and the abrasive.

For straight edges, use an offset fence as a guide. This fence can be a straight piece of wood clamped to the sander table so the distance from its inside edge to the down side of the disc is a bit

The adjustable jig for pivot sanding. The arrow indicates the pivot point which is only a short roofing nail driven through the end of the sliding bar. The center of the work is pressed down over the pivot point.

less than the width of the workpiece. The guide is angled just a bit so that when the pass is made, the work will contact the disc on the down side only.

To do the sanding, place the forward edge of the work on the up side of the table. Then move it forward in a steady, smooth manner. Don't take too deep a bite, and remember that since the abrasive does remove material, the original saw cut on the stock should be a bit oversize. Both this idea and the pivot circle-cutting technique can be used to do beveling simply by tilting the sander table.

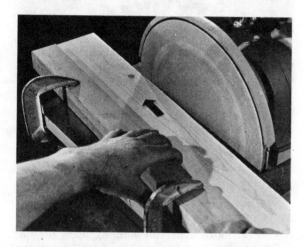

The sanding-to-width job can be accomplished by using a straight piece of wood as a guide. Feed is from right to left. The guide angle here is exaggerated just so it can be seen. In use, it should be minimal so as to use as much of the disc, from the outboard edge to the center, as possible.

There are two ways to sand curves to width. With one, you install a dowel guide in a platform that you clamp to the sander table. The distance between the dowel and the disc equals the thickness of the work. You pass the work between the dowel and the disc, turning the work as you go to maintain the point of tangency. Another way is simply to clamp a pointed stick to the sander table. The work is passed between the point on the stick and the disc.

In either case, it's assumed that the stock has been bandsawed or jigsawed so that a minimum of material remains to be removed. Also, the inside edge (the one that will ride the dowel guide

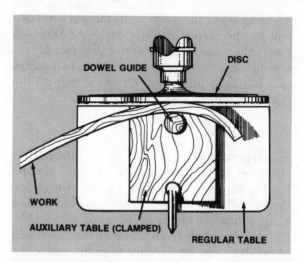

Sanding curved work to width using a dowel guide. The dowel is placed to allow just enough space to apply the work against the disc. The guide is clamped to the table.

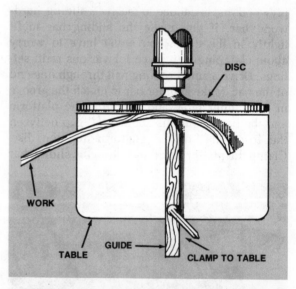

A pointed guide can also be used. In either case, the inside curve of the work must be sanded smooth to begin with. That can be done on a drum sander or by using the top drum of the belt sander.

or the point on the stick) must be sanded smooth before you do the outside edge. The inside surface can be done on a drum sander or by using the top drum of the belt sander.

Pattern sanding

Pattern sanding calls for an auxiliary table that is clamped to the regular table. A rigid, metal guide strip is attached with screws to the front edge of the auxiliary table. Size the guide strip so its length is a bit less than the radius of the disc and its width is ¹/₄'' or so more than the platform's thickness. The pattern, which is the shape of the work you want but undersized to compensate for the guide thickness and some clearance between the guide and the disc, rides the guide. The work, cut slightly oversize to begin with, is tack-nailed to the pattern. As you move the pattern while keeping it in contact with the guide, the work is sanded and matches the shape of the pattern. A simple way to secure work to the pattern instead of tack-nailing is to drive nails through the pattern so the points project on the top side. Then the work is simply pressed down on the points.

This method is not efficient when you need only one piece, but it is a very fine technique to use when you require many similar pieces.

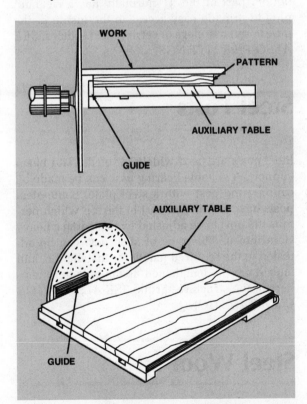

The setup for pattern sanding. The pattern is kept in contact with the guide strip. The work, tack-nailed to the pattern, gets sanded. The pattern must be smaller by the thickness of the guide strip plus the clearance between the guide strip and the disc.

Point dowels or other round stock

This process may be done freehand, but it's better to work with a guide. Simply drill a hole through a piece of wood with the size of the hole to match the size of the work. Clamp the guide block to the sander table at the required angle and then pass the work through the hole to make contact with the disc. Rotate the work to do either pointing or chamfering. To get a flat surface, move the work directly forward; don't allow it to rotate at all.

Metal work

Sanding metals (or plastics) doesn't differ too much from sanding wood materials on either the belt sander or the disc sander. Use the correct abrasive and when working with hard materials, use less feed pressure. It's important to wear goggles on all abrasive operations but especially critical when abrading metals. Remember what was said about the possibility of fire when changing from wood sanding to metal sanding.

You'll find that many of the ideas described for woodworking will do for metal. For example, if you needed a perfect circle in sheet metal, you could use the pivot sanding technique on the disc sander exactly as described for wood. When the metal is very thin and you have done the original cutting by supporting the sheet metal or scrap wood, do the pivot sanding with the sheet metal still on the scrap backup.

Metals do get hot. When doing work on small pieces, it's better to grip them with pliers instead of your fingers. *SEE ALSO BAND SAW; BENCH GRINDER; DRILL PRESS; JIGSAW; JOINTER; LATHE; RADIAL ARM SAW; SHAPER; TABLE SAW.*

Stationary Power Tools

[SEE BAND SAW; BENCH GRINDER; DRILL PRESS; JIGSAW; JOINTER; LATHE; RADIAL ARM SAW; SHAPER; STATIONARY BELT & DISC SANDER; TABLE SAW.]

Steel Pipe Adapter

A steel pipe adapter is a copper pipe fitting. Having a funnel appearance, it joins lengths of copper pipe to steel pipe. *SEE ALSO PIPE FITTINGS.*

Steel Pipe Drainage Fittings

Steel pipe drainage fittings are available in four major divisions: elbows, tee branch, Y's and p-trap.

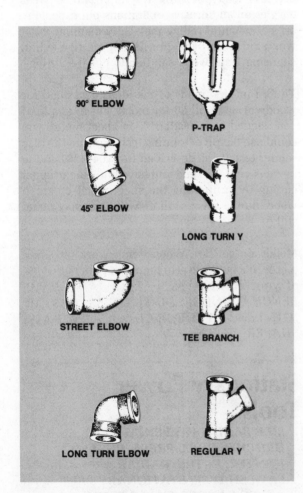

Steel Pipe Drainage Fittings

The elbows connect pipe entering at angles to one another. While most elbows have both ends with internal threading, the street elbow has one end with internal threading and the other end with external threading. The long turn elbow has more length between the ends of the fitting than the other elbows. The most common elbows are found with 45 degree and 90 degree angles.

While a tee branch connects a straight run and a branch entering at 90 degrees, the regular Y connects a straight run with a branch entering at an angle such as 45 degrees. Also connecting a straight run with a branch entering at an angle, the long turn Y has the inlet connecting the branch entering at an angle having an extended branch length.

A p-trap is a U-shaped pipe. Used to prevent drain pipe odor, the U-shaped area is a water lock to prevent back passage of sewer gas. The bottom part of the 'U' normally has a cleanout plug to provide easy access to the inside of the pipe to remove clogs or retrieve lost articles. *SEE ALSO PIPE FITTINGS.*

Steel Posts

Steel posts are used widely for girder and beam support. A suitable bearing base can be made by capping the post with a steel plate. Some steel posts have a threaded part in the top which permits the post to be adjusted by threading a heavy stem into it. This type of steel post can be adjusted to the required length for installation, and later it can be lengthened as the wooden members of the structure shrink. *SEE ALSO FLOOR CONSTRUCTION.*

Steel Wool

Steel wool is an abrasive having a scraping action which produces a very smooth surface. The three grades of steel wool are fine, medium and coarse. The finest grade is number 000 and is used for cleaning kitchen utensils. The medium grades give a gentle abrasion. The fine grade can be purchased in small pads with or without soap. All grades are purchasable in a roll so that when a section is rolled off and cut, it produces a small thin pad.

Steel wool can be used for rinsing. It holds the correct amount of water for wash-away removers. Steel wool is excellent for surfaces that are to be smoothed but are hard, or impossible, to reach with regular sandpaper. Steel wool can also be used for removing softened finishes on softer woods that a scraper might damage. *SEE ALSO ABRASIVES.*

Stepping Stones

Stepping stones can be made from concrete or ready mixed cement. These stones can be precast in forms of wood, or made of parts of concrete broken into any shape or geometrical form or poured straight into forms dug in the ground. Stepping stones should be about two or three inches thick. There are less chances of stepping stones cracking, but for added support a welded wire fabric can be placed in the concrete to spread the stresses. For stepping stones which are poured directly into the ground, dig about a three inch hole, add some rocks, fill the hole with concrete and trowel it smooth; these are about the easiest type of stepping stones to install. Some advantages of having stepping stones instead of sidewalks are that less concrete is needed (usually only about half as much), they do not have to be as thick as sidewalks and they can be made more decorative. *SEE ALSO BRICK & STONE WORK; CONCRETE.*

Stereo Systems

Stereo systems, or sterophonic sound reproduction systems, are available in two forms: manufacturer assembled unit systems or listener selected and assembled component systems.

Either system is an attempt to reproduce sound with both a high degree of fidelity and an impression of space or location. Stereo adds the dimension of depth to the high fidelity reproduction of sound.

TERMINOLOGY

In any discussion of stereo system components, certain technical terms are often used. Those terms should be defined before discussing any stereo component.

AM (Amplitude Modulation)

The traditional radio signal. Amplitude modulation is created by varying the strength of a signal being broadcast. Strong bursts of electrical energy (lightning, for example) can disrupt an AM signal.

dB (decibel)

A unit of measurement of relative loudness of sound.

Flutter and Wow

Wavering distortions of pitch caused by irregularities in the speed of the turntable or tape drive. If the fluctuation occurs 10 cycles or more a second, it is called flutter; below that point, it is called wow.

FM (Frequency Modulation)

The "static-free" radio signal. Frequency modulation is created by changing the frequency (vibrations per second) of the signal broadcast.

Hz (Hertz)

A measure of sound frequency indicating the number of cycles or vibrations per second of a sound. A sound of 50 vibrations a second has a frequency of 50 Hz.

Multiplex

A method of FM transmission in which both signals of a stereo broadcast are sent on one frequency as coded signals which a multiplex receiver can separate.

Rumble

Low frequency noise, generated by mechanical parts of the turntable or tape drive systems.

Sensitivity

Sensitivity is the minimum input signal required for a tuner or amplifier to generate a specified speaker signal.

SYSTEM COMPONENTS

In order to obtain the best sound fidelity, and the best stereo effect, quality components must form the system, whether manufacturer or listener assembled. The basic components of a stereo system are speakers, amplifier, tuner, turntable, and tape deck.

Speakers

The first item to consider in selecting a stereo system are the speakers, because the speakers must be matched to the room in which they will

Courtesy of Creative Environments, Inc.

be used. An over-large speaker system will create as much listener discomfort and system inefficiency as a too-small system.

In selecting a speaker system, one of the prime considerations is the resonant quality of the room. A highly resonant room is acoustically live; it has many surfaces which reflect a great deal of sound. A non-resonant room is acoustically dead; it absorbs most sounds. Sounds often seem muffled in a dead room.

The standard speaker system or enclosure will contain a large speaker for low frequencies (woofer), a mid-range speaker for the central frequencies (mid-range), and a small speaker for the upper frequencies (tweeter). A typical frequency range for these speakers would be 20-250Hz for the woofer, 250-7000Hz for the midrange, and 7000-20000 Hz for the tweeter.

In an acoustically balanced room, 10 to 12 foot speaker separation along one wall provides satisfactory stereophonic sound separation. Corner placement of the speakers will increase bass response as a result of additional reflection from the walls. (The corner walls become, in effect, part of the speaker projection system). High frequency sound is quite directional; for the best upper frequency sound, the listener should be relatively close to the centerline of the speakers.

Most speaker systems presently being manufactured are some variation of the acoustic suspension system. The important fact about speakers however is how pleasing to the listener's ear are the sounds produced.

Features to look for when examining speakers would include the following:

Frequency Response: The speaker should have a flat (non-distorting) frequency response over a wide range of frequencies (a 30-25,000 Hz range would be that of a good speaker system).

Power Rating: These ratings indicate the maximum power from the amplifier that the speaker can accept without distorting or overloading. Be sure that the speaker power rating matches or exceeds that of the amplifier. If not, be extremely careful of volume levels to prevent damage to the speaker enclosure.

Crossover Network

The basic speaker enclosure has three speakers, each of which has a range of frequencies it reproduces best. To insure that each speaker is driven only within its optimum frequencies, a switching device is necessary to channel high, middle, and low frequencies to the proper speaker. This switching device is the crossover network.

Amplifiers

Amplifiers are designed to amplify or strengthen electrical signals. The signals generated by microphones, pickup cartridges, and radio antenna systems are not strong enough to drive speaker systems. The amplifier increases that signal strength.

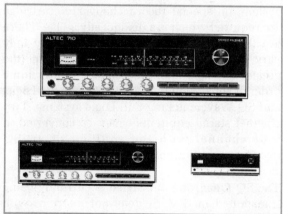

Courtesy of Altec

An amplifier consists of four basic systems: a power supply, a voltage amplifier, a phase inverter, and a power output stage. The power supply provides all the alternating and direct current needed by the other systems of the amplifier. The power supply contains transformers and rectifiers to provide the varied electrical needs of the amplifier. The voltage amplifier is designed to take the low voltages of the program source (microphone, tape head, or pickup cartridge) and increase the voltage on its path to the speaker system. The phase inverter is designed to provide two signals, equal in strength, but 180° out of phase for use by the

power output stage. The power output stage is designed to supply a large amount of distortion free power to the output transformer, which drives the loudspeaker.

The home listener should look for certain features in a good amplifier. Those features are as follows:

Frequency Response; Reproduction should be essentially flat from 30 to 15,000 Hz. (Flat response means minimum distortion of the input signal.) A fluctuation within the range of 3dB is considered excellent. Since frequency range and response are the important considerations, a unit rated 20-20,000 Hz ± 1 db is a superior quality amplifier.

Power Rating. This rating indicates the amount of undistorted power available to drive the speakers. Since electrical efficiency has been sacrificed for high fidelity in recent speaker designs, power is a prime factor. Also, regardless of volume setting, the "peaks" of some program material call for heavy output. If the power is not there, the sound is "clipped," and the total effect of the recorded sound is lost.

RMS indicates the continous power capability, operating with a single-frequency tone. *IHF* defines the complex wave form power capability (roughly 20 percent higher). If a 2 channel amplifier is rated 50 watts RMS, this means a power capability of 25 watts per channel (RMS). A good rating, but far from excellent.

Hum and Noise can come from many sources. A good amplifier will suppress most extraneous noise. A rating of -60db or more, is desirable.

Sensitivity is the amount of input power required to provide the rated output. The lower the figure, the better. Phono inputs of 2.5 and 4 mv, mike inputs of 4 to 9 mv, auxiliary and tape inputs of 250 and 500 mv are good.

The *distortion* figure of most importance is that of harmonic distortion at full rated power. One percent or less is desired.

Impedance is the electrical resistance measured in ohms offered by the speakers. Remember that the speaker is a part of the circuit; therefore, when output terminals call for a specified number of ohms resistance, use only a speaker with that value. (Variations are possible. Check the manufacturer's manual for speaker and microphone matching).

FM Tuners

Normally, the choice of a FM (or AM-FM) tuner is made after selecting an amplifier. There is good reason for this; the amplifier establishes the quality of the electronic components of a system. It follows that the characteristics of the tuner output should be as good or better than that of the amplifier.

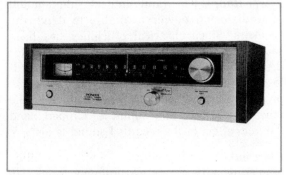

Courtesy of U. S. Pioneer Electronics Corp.

Currently, the ratings of a good tuner would be: a sensitivity of 1.7 mv or less, harmonic distortion at 100 percent modulation of .25 percent or less, selectivity of 50 dB or more, channel separation of 40 dB or more, signal to noise ratio at 100 percent modulation of 70 dB or more, image rejection of 70 dB or more. These ratings indicate the electronic capabilities of a unit. The ear of the listener is the final consideration when purchasing stereo equipment.

It is convenient to have tape output jacks on both the front and back of a tuner. While the amplifier should also have this feature, the tuner jacks offer flexibility in taping broadcast programs. Other desirable features in a tuner are the signal strength tuning meter, a multiplex high filter control, a FM mute switch to eliminate interchannel noise, and for very weak signals, a center scale tuning meter and Dolby circuit. (The Dolby Circuit is described under Tape Decks).

FM Programming

For stereo radio programming, FM multiplexing is now widely used. In multiplexing, the radio station electronically mixes and transmits both left and right channel of program material on one frequency band. In the receiver (tuner), the material is separated and a stereo signal reproduced.

Currently, 2 channel stereo is the most widely used, but 4 channel (quad) sound is increasing in popularity. The object of 4 channel sound is to increase the spatial quality of stereo by providing the listener with the reflected sound found at a live performance. To do this, two additional speaker systems are located across the room from their counterparts. Ideally the listener sits in the center of the room. There are three types of quadrophonic sound.

The *4 Channel SQ System* is employed in over 90 percent of present disc recordings. In this system, no special record changer or cartridge are required which is a distinct advantage. There are three types of SQ systems. Basically they vary in the degree of channel separation (the greater the separation, the better). In ascending order of separation they are the SQ-M, SQ Logic, and SQ Wavematching Full Logic systems. Two channel stereo equipment may be converted to four channel with the addition of an SQ decoder/amplifier and two speakers.

The SQ Quadrophonic signal is currently being transmitted on FM. It does not interfere with monaural or 2 channel reception of the same program material.

Discrete 4-Channel Systems are made for either tape or disc. The tape system (reel-to-reel or 8-track cartridge) requires special tape machines, playing into four channels of amplification and four speaker systems. In the CD-4 Disc System, a demodulator and special pickup cartridge are required. A standard 4 channel amplifier with auxiliary input may be used, plus four speaker systems.

Derived 4 Channel is simply a means of further separating 2 channel stereo. It provides a simulated quadrophonic sound through the addition of an adapter unit and two speakers.

Record Players

Record players fall into two groups; manual turntables and automatic changers. Common to both is the motor-driven turntable and the tone arm, equipped with a pickup device (cartridge). The stylus (or needle) of the cartridge rides in the grooves of the record.

Turntables

For the least wear of records and the greatest overall precision, a manual turntable is advised. Either a hysteresis/synchronous (h/s) motor coupled to a heavy turntable with belt drive, or a D.C. servo-motor similarly coupled will provide the most stable rotation. The heavy turntable provides mass, which once moving, tends to stabilize rotation much like an automobile flywheel. The h/s motor is an extremely stable source of power under varying loads. Belt drive is positive and quiet, eliminating gear trains and their attendant noise (rumble). The D.C. servo-motor is as dependable as its D.C. power source. Its advantage lies in a solid state, rather than mechanical, adjustment of speed. A good turntable will not vary in speed more than .5 percent. In addition, a turntable should have minimal values for flutter and wow.

Record Changers

Record changers are available in three or four speed ranges, the ranges being 16, 33$\frac{1}{3}$, 45, and 78 rpm. (16 rpm has limited use). Currently, most changers allow intermixing of 10″ and 12″ records of the same speed. Seven inch, 45 rpm records require a supplementary spindle, although record inserts are available which allow use on standard spindles.

As with the manual turntable, a hysteresis/synchronous motor and belt drive is desirable. A synchronous motor is better than an induction motor, and a 4 pole motor is preferable to a 2 pole.

To save wear, an automatic shutoff device is advisable.

Tone Arms

Low mass is desirable for a tone arm. Also, dynamically balanced (weighted, rather than springloaded) arms are preferable. Low mass and dynamic balance reduce disc wear. They also provide better tracking. (Most changers compromise between dynamic and spring balance).

Both automatic and manual arms should have cue and pause control. Cue control mechanically pinpoints the placing of the needle on the record. Pause control damps the descent of the arm to the record. Also desirable is an anti-skating feature, which aids in tracking. It is done most effectively with a counterweight chosen for the arm-and-cartridge combination.

For best tracking, a long arm is preferable to a short one, since it describes a flatter arc. (Less wear and better reproduction occurs if the angle of the needle to the groove is as uniform as possible, across the surface of the record). Finally, when matching a cartridge to an arm, a tracking pressure of 1 gram is now considered optimum.

Pickup Cartridges

Pickup cartridges are either magnetic or ceramic. A ceramic cartridge provides the highest output, while a magnetic offers the greatest range. Good amplifiers have provisions for either. Cartridge stylii (needles) are available in both conical or elliptical shape, the elliptical conforming best to present standards of reproduction.

Tape Decks

These components use magnetic tape to record and/or play back sound. Material can be taped from receivers (tuners, radio, TV), records, and microphones. Prerecorded tapes are now in serious competition with the disc record market. From the standpoint of optimum performance, reel-to-reel tape at 7$\frac{1}{2}$ ips (inches per second) is advised. Cassette and cartridge tapes, however, provide acceptable quality reproduction, and are steadily improving in quality.

As in the case of other equipment, tape deck quality should match or better the performance of the amplifier. A useful feature is the tape source monitor, which is most useful in checking the progress of a recording. This feature is possible with machines which have separate playback and recording heads. (A separate head is used for erasing). Other helpful features include the capabilities of recording both sound-on-sound and sound-with-sound. Circuit compensation for the use of either standard or high output tape is advisable.

Another desirable feature to look for is two synchronized drive motors rather than a single motor. Built-in reel locks are convenient, as is an automatic shutoff. Some units offer automatic cycling of all tracks on the tape, with an automatic cutoff at the end.

Cassette machines use a single head and offer sound-with-sound capability. Machines may be purchased which play stacked cassettes. Cassette recorders compare well with reel-to-reel types.

Cartridge machines use multiple heads and the current models record, as well as play back. Cartridges may be carousel-loaded or stacked. These features, coupled with 8 tracks, give the machine excellent long-play capabilities. Other features are similar to cassette machines.

Dolby Circuitry

The Dolby circuit is of particular value to tape machines and is an asset to other signal handling equipment. Essentially, this system changes the ratio of overall signal level to the noise level.

Program signals are fed into the preamp stage. The output of the preamp is fed into the Dolby circuit, where the signal is expanded. This signal is fed to the recording (or other) circuit. Any noise introduced during recording will lack expansion, thus the signal/noise ratio is greater. When the recorded signal is retrieved through the Dolby unit, it is compressed to the original signal level, but the high signal/noise ratio is maintained. Some machines and tuners have this circuit built-in, but the unit can be added to any machine with audio inputs and outputs.

Microphones

Popular types of microphones are the crystal, ceramic, ribbon, and dynamic. *Crystal* types have high output over a narrow range of audio frequencies. Generally, they are not recommended for stereo hi-fi recordings. *Ceramic* microphones are economical and superior to crystal microphones. They are excellent for outdoor use. Their main characteristics are high impedance, reasonable price, and good frequency response. *Ribbon* microphones have a uniform frequency response and are rugged, but they are intended for indoor use. Their impedance is adjustable. Ribbon mikes are recommended for music pickup from broadcasting and professional recording. *Dynamic* mikes are rugged and reliable. Frequency response is excellent and suitable for high quality home equipment.

The microphone should be selected for its intended use:

Unidirectional mikes pick up sound mainly from the front and suppress sound from the rear and sides. *Omnidirectional* mikes pick up sounds about the same from all directions. *Bidirectional* mikes pick up sound strongly from the front and back, while rejecting most sound from all other directions.

Headphones

Contemporary headphones are comfortable to wear for extended periods. They have a response of 10 to 20,000 Hz. They assure listening privacy and disturb no one. The greatest advantage to earphones is that there is complete channel separation. In effect, the listener is placed in the position of the recording mikes.

In matching impedance with equipment, follow the manual specifications. Also, headphones are manufactured for either 2 channel or 4 channel stereo, another factor in matching equipment.

TROUBLE SHOOTING

The great majority of equipment problems stem from carelessness, dust accumulation, and wear.

Simple checking will uncover a number of sources, easily remedied.

Electrical

Refer first to the manufacturer's equipment manual, then proceed as follows: If the machine will not come on, check the power supply plug, fuse and switch. Check all component leads for proper connection or shorts.

For low sound or random noise check all connections and look for open wires or shorts. Check the controls by moving them slightly. Check signal sources with a vol-ohm-meter for proper output. Tape heads may need demagnetization. Check the cartridge needle for dirt or wear also.

Mechanical

In all cases first refer to the equipment manual. If there is no or sluggish operation on phonographs and tape decks, check the amount of lubrication. Too little causes binding, while oil or grease in the wrong place causes slippage. Check the springs and linkages for positive connection. Look for and remove all dust or foreign particles. Test switches. For an inoperative changer, turn off the electric current and manually operate one full cycle, gently. Check tape clutch for proper tension, if it is accessible.

Noise may be caused by dust or foreign particles in drive train or controls of any kind. Again, check for positive mechanical connections. Check lubrication.

Much contemporary equipment carries the warning that the unit contains no home serviceable parts. This is largely true. Plastic parts are quite often heat-welded in place. Miniaturized circuit modules may be replaced (when obtainable), but individual parts are difficult to replace. Modules are quite often soldered and/or heat-welded in place. It is not unusual to find that mechanical parts were overlaid by circuit modules in manufacture. Anything which cannot be solved by the simple troubleshooting methods would be best left to a professional.

Stile

The stile is the vertical, outside framing member in a door, window sash or screen into which other parts are fitted.

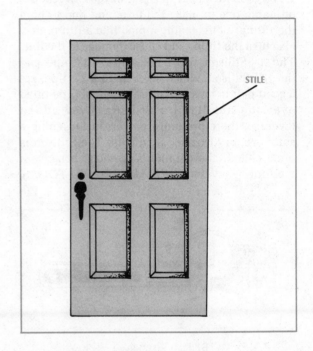

Stillson Wrench

One of the most familiar varieties of the pipe wrench is the Stillson wrench. It is used for turning round objects such as pipe, rods, or anything without flat sides. It can be used on hex and square-shaped nuts and fittings, but only if there is no other way, because the Stillson is likely to round off the edges of these. A Stillson should not be used on chrome, either, because the teeth grip so deeply that damage may result.

At first, the Stillson may seem very loose and wobbly, but when pressure is applied to the handle, the moveable upper jaw tightens automatically, giving one of the most powerful grips possible on pipe. When the pressure, or pull, on the handle is released, the jaw relaxes its grip.

The simple secret to adjusting a Stillson wrench is to set the jaws so that the pipe is jammed about halfway back. Then, when the handle is pulled, the jaws bite into the pipe as they should. If the jaws are too tight or too loose for their maximum grip, a few extra tries may be necessary.

It is a good idea to keep a pair of these wrenches on hand, one to make the turn, and one to hold the fitting, as tightening a pipe into a fitting may also turn the fitting and cause damage to the line. The 10″ Stillson, which takes up to a 1″ pipe, and the 18″ Stillson, which takes up to a 2″ pipe, are a good pair to have. An extra length of pipe fitted over the handle of a Stillson gives added leverage, therefore more power, in loosening a stubborn, or "frozen," pipe joint. The Stillson is often called "the plumber's wrench" because it is fit for heavy duty. *SEE ALSO HAND TOOLS.*

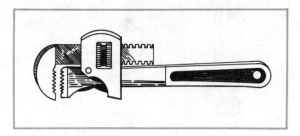

Stillson Wrench

Stirrup

A stirrup, or joist hanger, is a stirrup-shaped metal bracket that fits on a beam to fasten joists level with girders or headers. Using a stirrup eliminates the need for toenailing. *SEE ALSO FLOOR CONSTRUCTION; JOIST HANGER.*

Stoker

A stoker is a machine which automatically feeds coal into a furnace or boiler. Many stokers will also automatically remove ashes from the firebox and put them in covered ash cans. Various designs are available, but the two basic kinds are the hopper and the bin. Both kinds have a coal screw or auger which carries the stoker coal from the bin to the fire. The hopper type moves the coals from the bottom of the hopper and the bin type moves the coal from the bin. The hopper stoker must be filled daily; the refilling job is eliminated in the bin-type stoker.

Stokers should use coal which has a one inch or smaller diameter. Be sure that the motor is kept

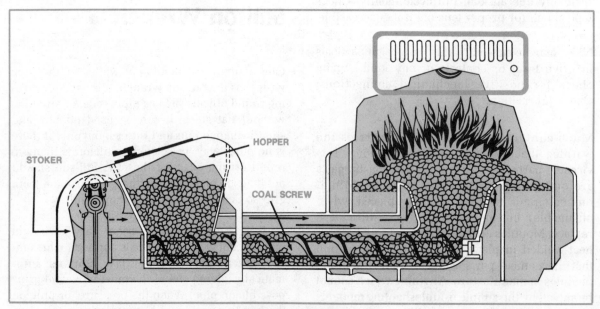

Hopper-Type Stoker

clean and is lubricated frequently. Before each heating season have a serviceman check the stoker and make any necessary repairs.

Stone Stairs
[SEE BRICK & STONE WORK.]

Stone Walls
[SEE BRICK & STONE WORK.]

Stool

The stool is the interior sill of the window frame. It is a flat, narrow shelf that can be either rabbeted or bevel-rabbeted to receive the exterior window frame sill. *SEE ALSO MOLDING & TRIM.*

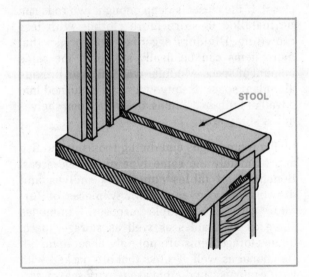

Stop-And-Waste Valve

A stop-and-waste valve is a copper tube fitting. Most often used in cold weather regions, this valve shuts off water to an outside faucet. Acting as an inlet for air into the pipe, it drains the pipe and the faucet completely. Ventilation is pro-

vided by a small cap on the side of the valve. *SEE ALSO PIPE FITTINGS.*

Stop-And-Waste Valve

Stopper Ball

Stopper ball is another name for ball valve, a device on a toilet which controls the flow of water from the flush tank into the toilet bowl. When the toilet is flushed by depressing the handle, the stopper ball is pulled off the flush-valve seat. This action allows water to flow into the toilet bowl. The stopper ball floats upward in the water until all has drained out. Then, the mechanism rests on its seat and closes the opening so that the tank can be filled again. *SEE ALSO TOILET.*

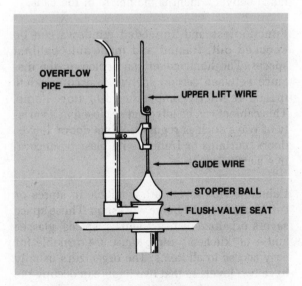

A portion of a toilet tank assembly.

Storage & Storage Areas

The problem of storage and suitable storage areas can be solved by the handyman. With a little imagination and planning, storage areas can be found in every room.

STORAGE TIPS

The kitchen is one room of the house that is always in need of extra space. Cubicles made by enclosing the side and front of the spaces above the cabinets with perforated hardwood can store those seldom used items. Large trays are often a nuisance to store. Angled shelves or vertical divisions in a cabinet can provide needed space for orderly storage. With angled shelves, a horizontal shelf at the bottom and top of that cabinet can utilize extra inches. Extra horizontal shelves can be placed in cabinets where the space above stored items is presently being wasted. The sides of a work counter, cabinet or refrigerator can be covered with perforated hardboard and used to hang objects such as pots and pans. The space behind a stove or an empty wall can also be used for this. An empty wall can provide an excellent space for storage of canned goods. A portion of the wall between studs can be removed and shelves placed in between the studding. Shelves can be built so that the distance between them is the height of the cans.

Functionless and unneeded windows can be knocked out, framed and made into cabinet spaces. The homemaker can decide on the distance between certain shelves to accommodate those irregularly-shaped, hard-to-store items. This cabinet can be left open or closed in a variety of ways such as regular cabinet doors, louver doors, curtains or frames with glass or decorative acrylic inserts.

Cabinet space savers are available in stores or can be made in the home workshop. These space savers organize dishes, utensils, spices, glasses and even kitchen wraps. Many are turnable for easy access to all items. The organizers usually have two levels so that two items can occupy the space previously occupied by one.

The bathroom is another room that needs quite a lot of convenient storage. If the lavatory is a wall-hung model, it can be enclosed in a cabinet to provide shelf and drawer space. Shelves or trays over the toilet tank can provide storage for towels as well as toiletries. In bathrooms with extra high ceilings and where the tub or shower is recessed, a storage area can be built by making a ceiling above the bathing area. Then, doors of some type are installed. This is a handy place to store seldom used items or extra supplies. Corners behind doors can be converted into shelves or a corner or wall cabinet.

Bedrooms also have storage problems. A bookcase headboard for the bed gives the individual the convenience of having personal articles close at hand but stored out of sight. Many closets waste valuable space above the rod and below the bottom of the clothes. Several shelves can be installed above the clothes rod. Partitions can be built so items can be separated. Shoe racks and storage bins can be installed in the bottom of the closet. If the closet is deep enough, two rods can be installed to store more clothes with less crowding. Dividers organize drawers so that more items can be neatly stored in the same amount of space. Modular wall units can provide abundant space. Empty walls can be turned into a wall of built-in cabinets, drawers, open shelves and a study area.

Living rooms, dens and dining rooms can utilize approximately the same type of storage areas. Benches and tables containing shelves and drawers are convenient. Many pieces of furniture can serve multiple purposes. Commodes serve as end tables as well as storage space. Some storage items are not only decorative, but functional as well. Trunks that are packed with various items can double as an extra seat or as a coffee table in the family room. Wicker shelves add a decorative touch while providing easy access to items otherwise stacked in a corner. Wicker suitcases can be painted and stacked to provide a unique touch to a room while the insides are used for additional storage.

Hallways often waste more space than any other portion of the house. Modular shelves, trunks, benches and tables with drawers and shelves can add a personal touch along with putting those items normally in the way in a convenient place. Closets can have shelves added above the rod and below clothes level or it is possible to remove the rod and shelve the entire closet.

Garages, attics and basements can utilize the open studs for shelves. Perforated hardboard can cover the studs and provide a way to hang tools and other items so that they are easily found but out of the way. Shelving placed in the attic among studs and rafters provides extra space for placing boxes and other stored articles. Basements can utilize studding, modular units, benches and trunks.

Houses containing stairs have an additional resource for storage. Under-stairwell space can be used in a variety of ways. This area can be constructed with rods for hanging out of season clothing, shelves for miscellaneous items or both. This space may serve as a study area by either buying or building a desk and installing shelves under the stairs.

Projecting windows such as bay windows are decorative and can be used for storage. They function as a sitting area with storage underneath.

Modular units can be used in many ways in any type of room. They can be made in the home workshop or purchased and are designed to be functional as well as decorative.

If room can not be found in the house, attic, basement or garage, many people find that outside storage houses provide the answer for them. In these storage houses, items can be stored permanently or temporarily. Perforated hardboard can be used to hang tools and modular units can be used to stack items.

Workshops often find themselves collecting unwanted articles from the house. The handyman now must store these along with his own things. Again modular shelves are helpful in stacking items. Metal or light-weight plastic storage cabinets keep small items such as small tools, nuts and bolts, nails and washers separated. For large quantities of nails, nuts and bolts and the

like, empty coffee cans that are labeled are neat and store easily. If the workshop has rafters and studs showing, these make excellent sources for storage. Shelves can be built in the studs and large flat objects such as lumber can be placed in the rafters.

Storm Doors

A storm door is an additional wood or metal door located outside the regular door. The storm door serves as an insulator by creating an air pocket. This helps keep the interior of the house warmer in the winter and, if air conditioned, cooler in the summer. Storm doors also help to eliminate drafts caused by poorly fitting regular doors.

Although a storm door opens outward, it is hung in the same manner as a regular house door. Storm doors are available in various designs and features. One of the more popular features is the moveable inside glass or acrylic panel. The panel can be removed and replaced with a screen during summer months. Other panels

Courtesy of Rohm and Haas Company, Manufacturers of Plexiglas Acrylic Sheet.

Glass or acrylic panels replace screen in cold weather.

have a screen already in place so that the panel can slide up and latch, and later moved down without any trouble.

Because they are exposed, storm doors take a lot of punishment from weather conditions as well as wear and tear. The majority of damage is located around the hinges. If the screws are not tight, they should be replaced. Screws on a wooden storm door can be tightened with plugs. However, screws on a metal door are to be replaced with stove bolts after holes have been drilled completely through the door.

For additional strength, washers should be used on both sides.

Cracks in a wooden door usually occur at the stile on the hinged side. A flat metal mending plate fastened over the crack can remedy the break. Storm door closers should be checked and oiled yearly. Tension can be tightened by turning a screw or nut at the end portion of the closer unit.

Storm Windows

Storm windows are an extra metal or wooden window used to form an air space between it and the regular window. This air space insulates and helps to reduce drafts. Both glass and acrylic are used for the panels.

Storm windows can be located outside double-hung windows or on the inside or outside of casement windows. In double-panel windows, they are not needed. The two major kinds of storm windows are permanent and removable. Originally designed for use in cold climates during the winter months, storm windows can be used year round to insulate the house not only against cold drafts but also hot, summer air. If cost prohibits all windows from having storm windows, then be sure the ones that are purchased are placed on the windows facing the prevailing winter winds or summer sun. Installation directions for the individual manufacturer accompany each type of storm window.

Straightbacked Saw

A straightbacked saw is any saw whose top edge slants at a straight angle from the handle to the tip. The straightback design, like the skewback, has no bearing on the performance of the saw, and the only advantage in a straightbacked saw is that its top edge can also act as a straightedge. *SEE ALSO HAND TOOLS.*

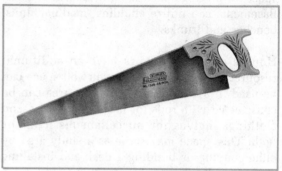

Courtesy of The Stanley Works.

Straightbacked Crosscut Saw

Straight-Blade Shears

Straight-blade shears or household shears are cutting instruments with blade lengths from 6″ to 8″. Straight-blade shears can be used for a variety of household or simple shop tasks. Most people refer to these shears as a large pair of scissors. *SEE ALSO HAND TOOLS.*

Straight Deep-Cutting Bit

A straight deep-cutting bit is one of the more common router bits. They are used in design work to form deep cuts. After the first cut is made, the shank of the bit is used as a guide for any following cuts.

Straightedge

A straightedge is a piece of steel or wood that is perfectly straight, commonly used for making straight lines in cutting and measuring. Squares and rulers are straightedges, but a few saws, such as the hacksaw, can double as a straightedge because of their even top edge. *SEE ALSO HAND TOOLS.*

Straight Ripping Bar

A straight ripping bar has a flat claw at one end enabling you to pull nails in close quarters where a hammer could not reach. Use it also for wrecking and prying where space does not permit you to use a gooseneck ripping bar. The average length of a straight ripping bar is thirty-six inches. *SEE ALSO HAND TOOLS.*

Stranded Wire

Wire that is twisted together or laid parallel for added strength or conductivity is known as stranded wire. Its size is the overall size of the group of strands, not the size of the individual strands. Stranded wire corresponds in diameter to solid wire of the same size. Wire sizes six and heavier are always stranded. *SEE ALSO WIRE SIZES & TYPES.*

Strap Wrench

A strap wrench resembles and works like a chain wrench, one difference being that a strap of very strong cloth takes the place of the chain. The advantage of the strap is that it will not chew up the surface of the pipe, as a chain wrench will do. The capacity of a 12-inch strap wrench is from 1/8″ to 2″, and like the chain wrench, it is

good for working on conduit, pipe and oddly shaped pieces, and in tight work spaces. *SEE ALSO HAND TOOLS.*

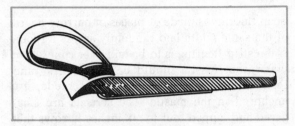

Strap Wrench

Street Elbow

A street elbow, a copper tube fitting, is used to join copper tubing at various angles to form curves or turns. Distinguishing characteristics of this type of pipe fitting are the two inlets. One inlet has external threads while the other has internal threads. *SEE ALSO PIPE FITTINGS.*

Strike Plate

A strike plate is the portion of a lock that is positioned on the door frame side jamb. The strike plate is made of metal and fits into a mortise so that it is flush with the jamb. The function of a strike plate is to receive the bolt or latch of the lock when the door is closed.

Stringer

A stringer, also called string or stringboard, is one of the side supports for the stair treads and risers. A stairway which has a stringer on each side is called closed-stringer stairway, while a stairway with a stringer on only one side is called an open string stairway. Most of the time, stringers are cut in a sawtooth pattern to make bearing surfaces which are parallel to the floor. *SEE ALSO STAIR CONSTRUCTION.*

Strip Flooring

Strip flooring is made of pieces of narrow board of the same width laid randomly across a room. If the strip flooring is to be laid over concrete, a waterproof mastic should be spread first, and then short pieces of 2 x 4s, or screeds, are anchored in the mastic. The screeds are staggered and lapped four to six inches in rows that are twelve inches apart. Laid at right angles to the screeds, the floor strips are nailed to the screeds. This ties the screeds together and gives strength to the floor.

If the strip flooring is to cover a subfloor other than concrete, then strips of a building paper

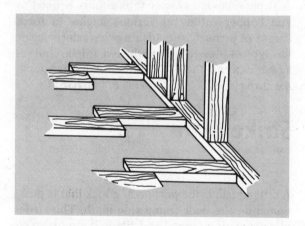

Screeds are staggered and lapped 4 to 6 inches in rows that are 12 inches apart.

Strip flooring is laid at right angles to screeds.

such as 15-pound asphalt-saturated felt should be placed in the same direction as the floor strips will run. All but the last two runs are toenailed through the tongue-edge to the subflooring to conceal the nail heads. *SEE ALSO FINISH FLOORING.*

Stripping Bar

A stripping bar is similar to a gooseneck bar. However, it has a more shallow hook, enabling it to get up close to vertical surfaces. Use it for lifting heavy objects, removing forms from poured concrete, and for prying or wrecking. The average overall length of a stripping bar is 36 inches. *SEE ALSO HAND TOOLS.*

Stub Tenon

A stub tenon is a variation of the tongue and groove tenon. Instead of the project having two right-angled edges as in the tongue and groove, the stub tenon has one edge rounded. *SEE ALSO WOOD JOINTS.*

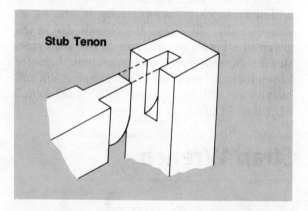

Stub Tenon

Stucco

Stucco is a rough plaster used for exterior walls. It can also be a fine plaster for decorating interior walls. Stucco is a mixture of portland cement, water, lime and sand.

Stucco can be applied in different textures over concrete block, masonry or wood frame walls. It is applied in three coats over wood sheathing, sheathing paper and metal lath reinforcement. The final coat can be lightly colored by adding mineral pigments to the portland cement mixture; for darker colors, finished stucco can be painted like concrete block.

Stud

A stud is an upright beam made of wood or metal in the frame of a building to which horizontal boards, laths and sheathing are attached. Studs come in nominal 2 x 4 inch and 2 x 6 inch sizes. The 2 x 4s are used for one and two story structures. The 2 x 6s are used in the bottom of three-story buildings. They may be spaced 24 inches on center in one-story buildings and not exceed 16 inches in spacing for three-story buildings. *SEE ALSO WALL & CEILING CONSTRUCTION.*

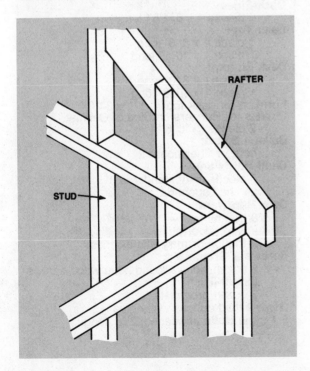

Stud Driver

A stud driver is a drive tool which helps provide control and support when hammering or fastening threaded studs or pins into metal, concrete or bricks. There are two types of stud drivers: the power-driven and the manual kind.

The power-driven stud drivers operate by pulling a trigger or by striking lightly with a hammer on an exposed stud or pin at the top. Gunpowder is used in special cartridges which powers the driver. Commercial or industrial stud drivers are power-driven. These kinds of drivers should be handled very carefully. Since many of the large, heavy-duty stud drivers are expensive, in most areas they can be rented from tool rental agencies.

The manual or hammer-in kind of stud driver is much lower priced and more popular. It is used by hammering on an anvil or head at the top. This type of stud driver, like the power-driven models, also holds the nail or pin in a tight-fitting tube. An anvil in the opposite end of the tube is projected at the top for the hammer to strike; it forces the pin or stud into the masonry when the bottom of the stud driver is held against the surface. Nails or pins no longer than two inches may

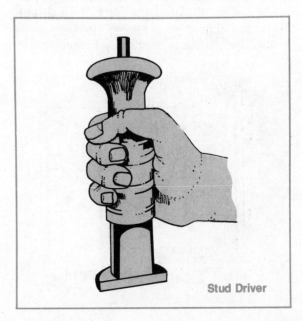

Stud Driver

be used. It is best to use a heavy hammer with a minimum weight of 2½ pounds. Lighter hammers do not deliver enough accurate power.

Student's Study Center

To create a handsome and sturdy backdrop for this study center, a paneled wall on which to hang the unit is recommended.

If a paneled wall is planned, but paneling is not yet installed, indicate on the ceiling or floor where the studs are located (use chalk to mark location of studs). The studs can then be easily found later when it's time to attach the furniture to the wall.

The study center has shelves enclosed with wood folding doors at one end, open shelves and a toy bin at the other end and a desk in the middle. A storage shelf underneath and a bulletin board above completes the desk section. A Formica desk top and a wall desk lamp are recommended to complete the unit, which is preassembled and then hung.

When attaching the unit to the wall, the following bottom-of-desk to floor clearances are recommended: children 5 to 12 years, 18″ to 24″; adults, 26″ to 28″. Attach the unit to the wall with No. 10 round head wood screws, spacing screws so that they bore into previously located studs.

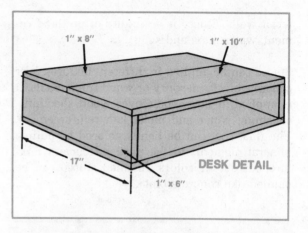

DESK DETAIL

MATERIALS LIST

Backboards:
    1 piece 1 x 10, 9′ long (top)
    1 piece 1 x 12, 9′ long (bottom)
Upright Dividers:
    4 pieces 1 x 12, 3′9″ long
Shelves:
    8 pieces 1 x 10, 2′10½″ long
Doors:
    2 pieces 1 x 10, 3′ long
    2 pieces 1 x 8, 3′ long
Bin Front:
    1 piece 1 x 8, 3′ long
Bin Bottom:
    1 piece 1 x 12, 34½″ long
Desk Sides:
    2 pieces 1 x 6, 1′5″ long
Desk Top:
    1 piece 1 x 8, 3′ long
    1 piece 1 x 10, 3′ long
Desk Bottom:
    1 piece 1 x 8, 3′ long
    1 piece 1 x 10, 3′ long
Formica for desk top — 17″ x 34½″
Dowels for Hangers on Side of Cabinet:
    2 pieces ¾″ x 6″
Bulletin Board:
    cork or fiber board 24″ x 36″
Shelf Hardware:
    8 pieces shelf standards 3′ long
    24 shelf supports
Door Hardware:
    8 butt hinges — 1½″ x ¾″
    2 wood door pulls
    2 friction or magnetic catches
Screws & Grommets:
    3 dozen No. 10 round head wood screws
    (bright finish)
    3 dozen grommets
Glue: 2 fluid ounces white glue
6 Toggle Bolts (if needed) 2½″ long

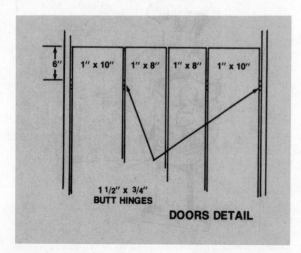

DOORS DETAIL

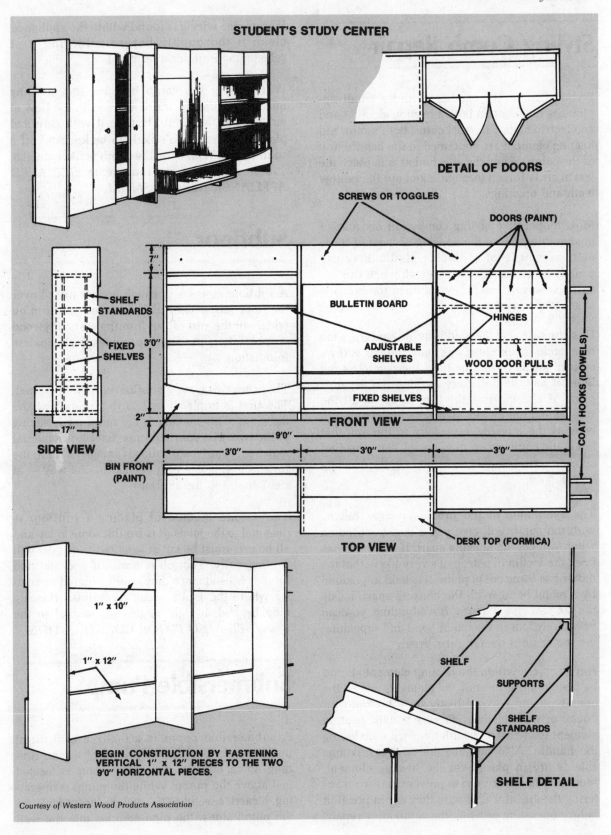

STUDENT'S STUDY CENTER

DETAIL OF DOORS

SCREWS OR TOGGLES

DOORS (PAINT)

SHELF STANDARDS

FIXED SHELVES

BULLETIN BOARD

HINGES

7"

3'0"

ADJUSTABLE SHELVES

WOOD DOOR PULLS

2"

FIXED SHELVES

FRONT VIEW

17"

SIDE VIEW

BIN FRONT (PAINT)

COAT HOOKS (DOWELS)

9'0"

3'0"   3'0"   3'0"

DESK TOP (FORMICA)

TOP VIEW

1" x 10"

1" x 12"

BEGIN CONSTRUCTION BY FASTENING VERTICAL 1" x 12" PIECES TO THE TWO 9'0" HORIZONTAL PIECES.

SHELF

SUPPORTS

SHELF STANDARDS

SHELF DETAIL

Courtesy of Western Wood Products Association

Styling Comb Repair

Styling combs are another of those small appliances that contain both a heating element and an electric motor. In most cases, both motor and heating element are contained in the handle unit of the comb. When the attachment is in place the warm air is forced through it and out the hollow teeth and openings.

Most inoperative styling combs fail because of mishandling. Since the housing of most of these units are made of a durable plastic, they can usually be repaired easily enough when this occurs. However, you'll have to open the housing to get to the works.

First, be sure that the cord is unplugged from the receptacle. Look closely for any hidden screws or trim strips on the body of the comb. Sometimes it may be necessary to remove a decal or piece of chrome metallic trim to get to all the screws that hold it together. Look closely at both ends of the housing, especially in the one that holds the comb when it is in use. You may find clips or screws in this area that hold the housing together.

The symptoms of the problem you're having with the comb will give you a clue to research when you get the housing apart. If the comb has been the victim of a drop, it's very likely that the motor has come out of place. It is held in position by a metal band. With the housing apart, locate the fan and give it a turn. If it's binding, you can very likely loosen the motor band and reposition the motor until the fan turns freely.

Any problem within the heating element should be visible since most of the elements are of the open-type and you can likely see a broken conductor or worn element. Be sure that the heating element is in correct position before reinstalling the handle. Also be sure that any insulations shields are in place over the heating element. Most combs use screens to prevent hair from entering the air intake. Be sure they are in position before operating or using the comb after repair.

If any loose wiring is found within the appliance, clean it thoroughly before soldering it or refastening it under a terminal.

When using the comb be sure that nothing lodges over the air intake and blocks the flow of air through the comb. Handle it with care and place it so that it isn't likely to be knocked off a counter top. With care, the comb is likely to give you service for many long years. *SEE ALSO APPLIANCE REPAIR, SMALL.*

Subfloor

A subfloor consists of rough boards nailed over the floor joists. The subfloor is the platform on which all the rest of the framing rests. Plywood is most often used and provides a squeakless foundation.

There are two ways a subflooring can be placed. The first is to place the boards squarely across the joists. This method is the more labor saving of the two. The subfloor must have end-material matched. The major disadvantage is that the finish flooring can only be laid in one way — at right angles to the subfloor.

The second method of placing a subfloor is diagonal to the joists. It is troublesome to lay and all boards must be cut at least twice so they will fit diagonally. The job is easier if end-matched lumber is used since they may be butted no matter where the joints occur. The finish flooring may be laid at right angles or parallel to the joists. *SEE ALSO FLOOR CONSTRUCTION.*

Submersible Pump

A submersible pump is actually a centrifugal pump attached to the lower end of a pipe running down into the well. The motor is located just above the pump. While the pump is operating, it carries water to the water-storage tank. As the pump stops, the pipe empties into the well and fills with air which is drawn from a special opening. When the pump is reactivated, the air is driven out of the pipe just ahead of the water traveling to the tank.

A submersible pump, excellent for use in deep wells, is not suitable in areas where the water is sandy. Although the initial price is high, it works more efficiently at greater depths than the jet pump. In addition, this type of pump requires only one pipe and cannot be heard when in operation.

The original submersible pump used only metal pipe. Today semi-flexible, light-weight plastic pipe is being approved widely since it can withstand the twist created by the starting of the pump, has the electrical cable to the pump in it and can be handled easily. *SEE ALSO PUMPS.*

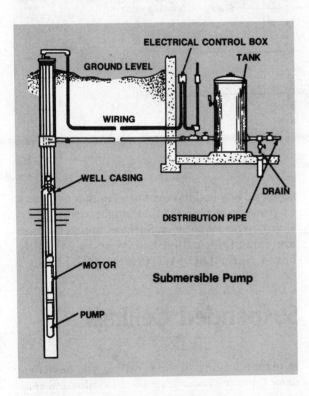

Submersible Pump

Suction Cup

A suction cup is used for fastening objects to walls, tile or woodwork. Rubbing the edges of

the suction cup with a wet bar of soap before application will prevent leaving an indelible ring on the wall when the cup is removed. Suction cups may be used to attach such items as towel racks in bathrooms and kitchens and a plumb bob when a threaded hole and bolt are connected to the cup.

Suction Pump

A suction pump relies on atmospheric pressure to bring water to the surface.

The atmosphere presses down on the earth with a constant pressure of about fifteen pounds per square inch at sea level. An example is a straw immersed in a glass of water. By sucking on the straw, a low pressure area is created. Since the pressure on the liquid in the glass is higher than that in the straw, the high pressure forces the liquid up and out of the straw.

The same principle is used in a suction pump. The pump lowers the pressure in the pipe while atmospheric pressure exerts force on the surrounding water in the well, thus pushing water up the pipe. The maximum height that atmospheric pressure can push water up a pipe is approximately 33 feet. The pressure can be lowered by means of a piston-cylinder pump or by narrowing the inside of a pipe to form a Venturi tube. *SEE ALSO WELL PUMP SYSTEMS.*

Sump Pump

A sump pump sucks rain or waste water from a sump pit which collects water from a foundation, basement floor drains or under the basement floor. A sump pump is needed only when drainage is located below the level of a sewage line.

A float on the sump pump indicates rising water. This float activates a stop that turns on a motor. As the water is pumped out, the water level falls

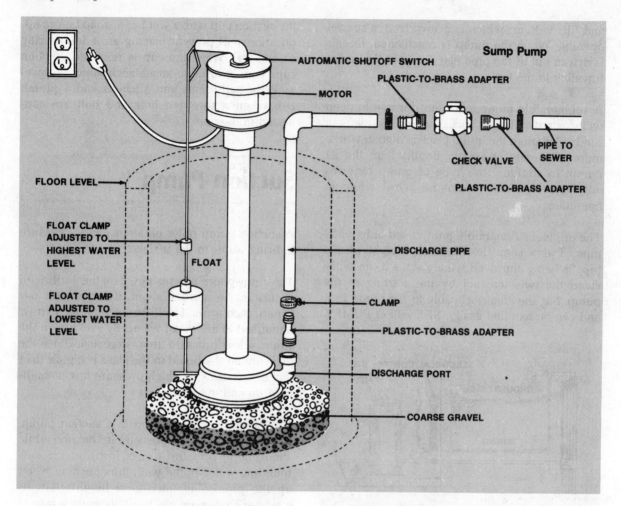

Sump Pump

AUTOMATIC SHUTOFF SWITCH
PLASTIC-TO-BRASS ADAPTER
MOTOR
PIPE TO SEWER
CHECK VALVE
PLASTIC-TO-BRASS ADAPTER
FLOOR LEVEL
DISCHARGE PIPE
FLOAT CLAMP ADJUSTED TO HIGHEST WATER LEVEL
FLOAT
FLOAT CLAMP ADJUSTED TO LOWEST WATER LEVEL
CLAMP
PLASTIC-TO-BRASS ADAPTER
DISCHARGE PORT
COARSE GRAVEL

and the float descends, triggering the stop which shuts off the pump. Since the stop is adjustable, the owner can adjust the pump to a desired water level.

The pump has a strainer to remove any solids that might clog it. Through a plastic pipe connected to the discharge outlet, the water can flow into a drain, sewer, seepage pit or the outside. *SEE ALSO PUMPS.*

Surface-Mounted Box

A surface-mounted box is an ordinary switch or outlet box (of metal or bakelite) mounted on the wall instead of recessed into it. Used for permanently exposed surface wiring, a surface-

mounted box and its cover have rounded corners to prevent accidents that might result from sharp, exposed corners. Surface-mounted boxes are sometimes called handy boxes or utility boxes. *SEE ALSO SWITCHES & OUTLETS.*

Suspended Ceilings

In planning to install a new ceiling, you have two basic types to choose from — glued tiles and suspended panels. The first of these is the more familiar; it is the kind that is fastened directly to the old surface with adhesive or staples. Suspended panels, usually larger than the 12-inch-square tiles, fit into a metal grid suspended from the ceiling or its framing. Many types of panels made for use in this suspended fashion may also

Courtesy of The Armstrong Cork Co.

be installed in the manner of the small tiles. The suspension method should be used in the common situation where there is no satisfactory attachment surface, where plumbing intrudes, or where a lowered ceiling is wanted.

Courtesy of The Armstrong Cork Co.

Factory-applied woodgrain finish is seen on this grid system. Lay-in panels, instantly removable, may be acoustical or not, depending upon whether noise-muffling or economy is the more important consideration.

A suspended ceiling consists of a metal gridwork, sometimes with a woodgrain finish, supporting panels of acoustical tile. The result can be attractive, however, one system now provides a ceiling with some overall texture but no distinct pattern of squares or oblongs.

In this system the tiles (usually 1 foot by 4 feet) butt together so that the metal suspension strips disappear within the joints and joint lines vanish.

There are three ways to install such an integrated suspension system. The choice of method is not so much a matter of taste as of the situation to be corrected.

Where a ceiling already exists and its height is satisfactory, lightweight steel furring channels are attached directly to the ceiling after molding has been nailed to all four walls 2 inches below the level of the existing ceiling. The furring channels are placed perpendicular to joists so that the nails can go through the ceiling and into the joists. Rigid enough to bridge off-level spots in the ceiling surface, the channels are self-leveling, eliminating the need for the braces, shims or wedges required with wood furring strips. The channels assure a permanently level ceiling.

After all furring channels are in place, the tile installation begins in a corner of the room. The first tile is laid on the molding, then a cross tee is snapped onto the furring channel and slid into a slot on the leading edge of the tile. The remaining tiles are installed in a similar way. The tiles butt tightly together, hiding all supporting metal and producing a smooth, monolithic appearance.

Courtesy of The Armstrong Cork Co.

Small, moderately strong pattern suits it to rooms of limited size and the design says kitchen. As might be expected, this one is manufactured so as to be highly effective acoustically.

Where joists for the floor above are exposed, there are two possible methods — clip or channel. Exposed joists exist most often in new construction, as when a house is being built or remodeled or when an unfinished basement is being completed.

The direct clip method calls for attaching small spring-metal clips to the exposed joists and snapping the cross tees to these clips rather than the furring channels. The clips can be attached snugly to the joist for a ceiling of maximum height. Or they can be adjusted downwards by as much as 3 inches to accommodate small pipes or wires extending below the lower edges of the joists.

The clips are being replaced by furring channels nailed to exposed joists. For wires or thin pipes, notching (where structurally permissible) may be necessary; or shims may be used to lower the channels — and the ceilings — sufficiently. In general, however, if the ceiling is to be suspended at a level appreciably below the undersides of the joists, the full-suspension method should be used.

The full suspension system is recommended where an existing ceiling is in too poor a condition or too uneven to use or where pipes, wires or framing members are in the way; or where the ceiling structure that exists is simply too high and a lower new ceiling is wanted. This system uses the same cross tees already described, that

Courtesy of The Armstrong Cork Co.

This effect is produced by use of very large—2 x 4 foot—lay-in ceiling panels in a visible-grid system.

disappear within the ceiling tiles. However, the cross tees are now held up by metal runners into which they snap. The runners, in turn, rest on the wall molding that is first nailed into place. The runners are supported at the desired height and kept perfectly level by wire ties that are attached through the old ceiling to the joists.

Until recently, acoustical tile had to expand or contract with changes in temperature and humidity making expansion space or edge-beveling necessary. One way to provide such space was by laying the tiles loosely within a visible metal grid.

This system is simple in installation, inexpensive and quick. It provides no difficulty in lowering the ceiling either to improve appearance or to avoid problems with plumbing and wiring. In many situations it is almost indispensable because it permits easy access at any time to wires, pipes or ductwork in the ceiling.

Sweat Soldering

Sweat soldering allows the solder alone to hold the pieces of metal together. With a fine abrasive cloth, clean the surfaces that will come in contact. Then spread soldering flux on the cleaned areas. Using a propane torch to heat the joint to a solder-flow temperature, lightly touch the flames along the joint. Touch the solder at regular spaces until it begins to melt. Capillary action will force the solder into the joint. Wipe excess solder off with a rag before it hardens. *SEE ALSO SOLDERING.*

Swimming Pools

The private swimming pool has seen a tremendous surge in popularity in recent years. New methods of construction, improved maintenance techniques, and better materials make even custom-designed pools available to just about anyone with a yard and a flexible budget.

Courtesy of Koppers

The home swimming pool has become a popular addition to many American homes.

Regardless of the type pool being considered, planning before installation will not only provide flexibility, but will also help the return on your investment.

PLANNING AND SITE SELECTION

The first step in planning a pool should be to check the building regulations in your area. Many localities have ordinances relating to outdoor pools, and these laws may limit or prohibit the project. Be sure that your property title is free of any restrictions on such improvements. In the case of a built-in, the real estate tax assessment will almost certainly be increased, and most localities also require a building permit.

Once a site has been chosen, check to be sure that excavation is feasible (in the case of below-grade pools): septic tanks, pipes, utility lines, and other obstructions will make digging difficult, or impossible. The responsibility for inquiring into these and other potential obstacles rests with the owner, *not* with the contractor, who will assume that the site is free of obstruction.

The finished pool of any size will require three or four feet of decking in walk areas, and this space should be a part of the pool design. In many cases pumps and filters will also demand ground space as well as poolside activities such as sunbathing and outdoor cooking. These features should be planned for during construction rather than modifying plans later. While you will want to plan the pool site for the maximum amount of sunshine, consider also taking advantage of any natural wind barriers, as well as making sure, for safety, it has the best possible view from the house.

Much of this concerns the built-in pool, but you may want to consider the advantages of an above-ground pool. Besides the savings in initial cost, above-ground models are portable, do not usually add to the tax value of the property, and have certain safety features not available in built-ins.

CONSTRUCTION METHODS

It is not a good idea to plan to design and build your own pool without professional help, unless you are a real expert. Savings in contractor fees are often used up by the costs of repairing a bad job, or even tearing out the pool and starting over. The *owner-buyer* plans are usually worth investigating. These are agreements in which the owner does the easier work himself and contracts out the excavation and shell construction. Also, some companies offer special package deals at reduced prices, supplying everything needed for the job. Whatever agreement is reached with the contractor, be sure the obligations of each party are fully understood, and in writing. A seemingly obscure point such as who is responsible for filling the pool can cause disagreements.

A good footing in solid earth is imperative. Loose or uneven footing could result in cracking or separation of joining walls. If natural footing is inadequate, it may be necessary to install pilings to guard against shifting. Here again, expert advice or supervision is mandatory.

Keep in mind that the excavation is *not* the pool; it is the receptacle which assures that the pool itself will not slide or shift in use. The pool itself may be of a variety of materials: concrete, metal, fiberglass, or vinyl. Concrete remains the most popular of pool construction materials. It is inexpensive, durable, and lends itself to many shapes and sizes. While several types of concrete construction are in use, they all employ a network of steel rods and mesh distributed over the entire surface of the excavation.

Once the interior of the pool has been completed, the finishing touches can be added. Coping, the edging of the pool, is an important feature, both functionally and esthetically. It furnishes a skid-free walking surface and a convenient hand-hold for the swimmer. It also defines the "frame" of the pool, setting it off from the surrounding landscape.

Pre-cut coping stones are available in standard lengths. Flagstone, natural rock and brick may also be used. In the case of fiberglass and vinyl pools, coping is often an integral part of the pool, and nothing more needs to be added, except for decoration.

Final installations include underwater markings, lights and heaters, ladders, grab rails, slides, diving board, and whatever other features that have been chosen for the pool.

POOL SAFETY

The rise in the number of private pools has been accompanied by a corresponding rise in the incidence of drownings and serious accidents around the home. These tragedies are compounded by the fact that the great majority of them involve very young children.

The homeowner must be aware of the responsibilities and obligations that a pool entails, and make every effort not only to protect himself against trespassers, but also to ensure the safety of his family and guests. In many areas, the law clearly outlines these responsibilities, and the individual pool owner should be sure he understands exactly how local ordinances apply to him.

A fenced-in pool area is the absolute first and minimum requirement for pool safety. The fence should be at least six feet high, with a locking gate for access. Chain link fences are popular for this purpose, especially since they do not restrict the view of the swimming area from the house or street; however, these fences are easy to scale since they provide easy hand and toe holds for little climbers. Chain link should thus be of a small enough mesh size to discourage climbing without restricting view. Outside supports and guywires should also be designed to prohibit climbing, or moved to the inside of the fence.

Many types of burglar alarms are available, and, although they may add to the cost of the pool, they should be considered. Alarms can be purchased (or designed) which operate by electric eye, pressure switches, circuit breakers, and even by detecting water movement. Water movement detectors, however, have the disadvantage of operating only *after* someone has already fallen into the pool.

Neighbors should be provided with a key to the gate, and asked to keep an eye open for unauthorized activity while you are away. They

should also have access to safety equipment and first-aid supplies, as well as a list of emergency phone numbers — police, doctor, ambulance, and so on. Basic safety equipment includes a well-stocked first-aid kit; a long, floatable pole or "shepherds crook" to assist swimmers in trouble; and a life preserver attached to a nylon rope. An outdoor phone extension is also a great convenience.

Covers must be inspected periodically for cracks, holes, and defective supports; a small child who climbs onto a large covered pool can easily slip through a torn cover, with tragic results. Solid enclosures should also be checked regularly for broken windows and defective locks; ventilation systems also require regular maintenance to be sure of efficient operation, especially during very warm weather.

When designing the pool, pay particular attention to coping and decking materials. Flagstone or natural rock coping must be free of sharp edges, and should be checked often for loose mortar. Wooden decking can be splintered with sufficient impact or if improperly maintained, leading to dangerous and painful slivers and cuts.

The decking and patio areas should be washed down every few days with a mild disinfectant solution to minimize the danger of athlete's foot and other contagious fungi. A shallow foot bath might also be provided for swimmers entering the pool (a 5 percent solution of chlorine or other commercial disinfectant will serve this purpose). Most important, swimmers with open cuts or infections should not be allowed into the pool: not only can swimming aggravate infection, but a pool is a perfect medium for the germs to spread to other swimmers.

Electrical accessories such as radios, TVs, lights, pump and filter must have waterproof connections, and be set well back from the swimming area. Cords and wires can not only be deadly shock hazards, but can result in falls, especially on slippery surfaces.

Depth perception through water can be misleading. Depth markings along the side should be accurate and clearly visible. Too-steep floor inclines can also result in misjudgment, especially in the case of tiled pool floors. A strong float line should be installed across the pool at a suitable depth, depending on the age of the swimmers. (If no small children will be using the pool, the float line can be attached at the four or five foot level).

There is no substitute for constant supervision by a responsible adult. Remember that children learn by example. If you are careful to observe all the principles of water safety, even the youngest toddler will quickly follow your lead.

Despite the most diligent precautions, of course, accidents can happen. Many insurance companies offer pool insurance, with comprehensive personal liability provisions. Check with your house insurance agent to see if he can arrange such a policy. (You may find out that you are already covered.) Chances are that it can be arranged easily and added to your present policy, at a modest increase in cost, or no cost at all.

Swirling

Swirling is a technique which forms an irregular pattern in a concrete surface. For less patterning, the swirling should be done after the slab has been prepared for final troweling. The steel trowel should be held flat on the surface and finished with swirling movements. For a more pronounced effect, begin the swirling while the concrete surface is too soft for final troweling. An aluminum or magnesium float can be used for a medium texture or a wood float for a coarser texture. *SEE ALSO CONCRETE.*

Switches & Outlets

The versatility of modern electrical wiring is due, in great measure, to the wide assortment of switches, outlets and wiring devices that are available for installation. This section describes the most common wiring products.

Wiring boxes: these steel (and occasionally plastic and ceramic) wiring devices protect *switches* and *receptacles,* and splices and connections between cables and conductors. Boxes shield the weak links of electrical wiring, the connections made to switches and receptacles. And, they provide mechanical strength to connections made between cables as the cable ends are secured to the box with clamps. Many different size and shape boxes are available; the standard box is the so-called *duplex* receptacle. Double-gang boxes hold two switches and so forth.

In use, the switch box (or other wiring box) is secured to the stud work (or, occasionally, directly to the wall), and then cables and/or conduit is joined to the box. Thus, all of the wires, conductors, and wiring devices are surrounded by metal (or, at least, insulating sheathing) when the installation is complete.

Clock hanger: a single *receptacle* (usually a two-wire nongrounding-type device) recessed into a plastic or metal *wallplate* that is designed to simultaneously support and provide power to an electric clock. A clock hanger should be installed in a single-gang wiring box. Clock hangers are special purpose devices and should not be used as general-purpose receptacles.

Combination wiring device: typically a *toggle switch* and single *receptacle,* a *toggle switch* and *indicator light* (pilot light), and, occasionally, two *toggle switches,* paired together much like a conventional *duplex receptacle* and designed to use the same *wallplate* as a duplex receptacle. Combination devices can be mounted in conventional wiring boxes and intermixed with conventional switches and receptacles. They are useful when space limitations force a single-gang wiring box to do double-duty or for specialized wiring installations.

Duplex receptacle: the correct name of the familiar "double wall outlet," duplex receptacles are perhaps the most common wiring device, with the possible exception of single-gang wiring boxes. Many types are available, including units with 15-amp or 20-amp ratings; units with and without grounding points and units in different colors. Prices can vary substantially because of wide variations in quality.

Interchangeable devices: physically smaller, full-capacity single *receptacles, toggle switches,* and indicator lights (pilot lights) that can be installed in mixed groups of two or three in single *wiring boxes,* and then covered with special *wallplates.* Interchangeable devices offer much the same custom wiring possibilities of *combination* devices, with somewhat greater flexibility since any group of three devices can quickly be assembled.

Light dimmers: electronic devices designed to control the brightness of electric lights. Two classes of light dimmers are available:

Two-stage dimmers (suitable for *incandescent* lights only) that are similar in appearance and operation to conventional *toggle switches.* These have two "on" switch positions: full brightness, and 30-percent brightness (equivalent to $1/2$ normal current flow through the bulb).

Full-range dimmers (different units are available to control incandescent and fluorescent lamps) equipped with rotating control knobs that operate much like the volume control on a radio. A full-range dimmer can vary lamp brightness from full-on to off.

In addition to permitting the adjustment of room illumination to any desired level, light dimmers can dramatically increase incandescent bulb life: the lifetime of a dimmed bulb may be twenty or more times longer than the life of a bulb operating at full brightness.

Most light dimmers are designed to replace toggle switches directly, as they fit into standard single-gang wiring boxes. However, commonly available dimmers are rated to control a maximum of 600-watts, compared to 1200-watts (or greater) for most switches.

Locking switch: a modified toggle switch in which the external switch lever is replaced with an internal mechanism operated by a simple metal key. A locking switch is intended for use in public areas where unauthorized control of an electrical light or fixed appliance must be prevented.

Mercury switch: a virtually silent toggle switch in which the switching element is a drop of liquid mercury. Flipping the switch to on tilts the mercury onto a pair of contacts closing the circuit.

Photoelectric switch: a toggle switch replacement that controls a lighting circuit in response to ambient light level. The device is equipped with a photocell electric eye that controls an electronic switching circuit. A photoelectric switch can be installed in a single-gang wiring box.

Pigtail: the short "power cord" (with a polarized plug) that connects to the terminal block inside an electric dryer or range. The use of a pigtail (and matching receptacle) is often more convenient than wiring a high-wattage appliance directly to a branch circuit; the appliance can be unplugged and moved easily.

Polarized receptacles and plugs: these are mating receptacles and plugs designed so that the plug can be inserted in only one orientation. At one time, polarized 120-volt devices were used in lieu of grounding-type equipment; today, polarized devices are generally restricted to 240-volt applications, specifically dryer and range connectors.

Solderless connectors: these simple-to-use devices, often called wire nuts, have virtually obsoleted conventional mechanical splices in electrical wiring. To join two (or three) conductors, the wire nut is simply screwed over the bared ends of the wires. The ends should not be twisted together first; they should simply be held close together.

Synthetic Fillers

Synthetic fillers are patching materials for wood. The greatest difficulty in their use is that when coated with clear finishes or stains, the patch of synthetic filler may not reveal the same color as the surrounding wood.

There are five major types of synthetic fillers. The first is plastic wood. It is hard and does not absorb stain well. It does not take water stain, but will color with oil stain.

Wood patch takes more of an oil stain since it is more absorbent.

Rock hard putty is a water-mix substance having a cement-like quality. It will take either oil or water stain. Since the putty dries to a whitish tint, rock hard putty colors best when analine dyes are mixed in the putty.

Vinyl patching materials have little penetration and are difficult to stain. Wiping stains can be used to blend them. Vinyl patching materials do offer easy water clean-ups, sandability and are pliable enough to be smoothed with the hand.

The last synthetic filler is homemade. It is stainable and can be blended until the coloring is nearly the same as the surrounding wood. Combine sawdust of the type wood to be patched and thinned plastic resin glue. Mix the ingredients together until they form a thick mash. After coating the hole with full-strength glue, place the mash in the hole and press firmly. Once the glue has dried, sand away the excess material.

Beware of synthetic fillers labeled *nonshrinking*. It is best to place a small amount of filler in the hole, allow it to dry and add more filler later, a little at a time, until the hole is completely filled. Allow the patch to be rounded above surface level so that it can be sanded level. Most synthetic fillers blend with the surrounding wood best when dyes are mixed into the filler before placing it into the area to be patched.

Systems, Auto Alarm

Cars can be effectively protected from intrusion and possible theft with an easily installed auto siren alarm. The operation is simple. The alarm is turned on by a key lock switch, usually mounted on the fender. When a door, hood or trunk lid is opened, the siren alarm sounds and continues until turned off by a key.

Contents of a typical auto alarm package includes a loud warning siren, six switches for protecting the doors, hood and trunk, a key lock switch with two keys, fifty feet of wiring and warning decals.

INSTALLING A SIREN ALARM

A typical alarm installation first involves mounting a siren or horn under the hood. The space between radiator and front grille or on a fender well is a suitable place, since neither location represents an obstruction to servicing the car's engine. There is also minimum interference with the wailing sound of the siren. In most cars, a cross-member will be found to which the siren can be attached with two or more screws.

Mount the key switch outside the car through a hole drilled into the fender cowl. The key switch turns the alarm on from the outside after you leave the car and disconnects it before you enter the car. The small pin switches are installed on the door jambs, hood, and trunk, even under a tape player, if desired.

Electrical interconnections are made through the firewall to the siren terminals (both wires are positive live leads and should be protected against grounding). One fused wire connects to one side of the key switch, the other is connected to the car's fuse block. The contact switches are of the *open circuit* type just like the car's domelight switches. That is, the contacts are open when the switch buttons are depressed (with the doors closed) and make contact when the switch button is not depressed. All switches are wired in parallel. One wire of this parallel circuit is connected to the second side of the central switch, the second wire to a good chassis ground. With the key switch on, closing of any one contactor in this circuit will sound the siren.

Systems, Automotive

HOW TO BUY A CAR

The most important considerations in buying a car, new or used, are: what kind of car you need; where to buy it; knowing that you are getting your money's worth; and getting the best deal on financing, if that is needed.

Most dealers are honest; but a few use questionable tactics. These few create a bad reputation for all car dealers. Try to select a local dealer with a good reputation. Ask friends and neighbors for their recommendations. There is no substitute for knowing someone who has been treated fairly.

Except for models with long waiting lists of customers, a new car's prices are negotiable. The manufacturer's suggested retail price (on the window sticker) is usually 18 to 25 percent more than the factory invoice cost to the dealer. Most new cars can be bought for less than $250.00 over the dealer's cost from the factory. This, of course, includes shipping and dealer preparation charges. But you must always figure more for sales tax, titling and licensing.

New cars are warranted against defects for a specific number of miles and a period of time, whichever comes first. Warranty work is best done by the dealer's service department where you purchased the car. If you are out of town; however, you can take it to any dealer of that make.

Depreciation

One car cost that you cannot actually put your finger on, nonetheless, a very real cost, is depreciation. Depreciation affects your car whether you drive it or not. The settlement for depreciation is made when you sell or trade the car. The difference between what you get for it and what you paid for it becomes the car's depreciation.

All cash is best for a car purchase. No finance costs are involved; the car is all yours from start.

Unless you pay cash for your new car, you will probably have to borrow money to buy it.

The best type of auto loan, and the one you should hold out for, charges interest only on the remaining unpaid balance.

A federal truth-in-lending law requires the lender to disclose the true annual percentage rate of interest. Insist on knowing this rate and make sure that it is on the final agreement that you sign.

Buying A Used Car

You will find three kinds of used car dealers, with a different set of built-in advantages and disadvantages for you: the private owner, the new-car dealer and the used-car dealer.

The private owner sells his car to you as is. A new-car dealer who is selling a used car offers a guarantee, has a service department and a reputation to uphold.

A used-car dealer gets most of his merchandise from new-car dealers (often getting second pick). Or he gets them at used-car dealer auctions.

Second Car

If there is more than one driver in the family, there is probably the need for a second car. What type of vehicle it should be depends on your needs, interests and preferences.

For commuting to work or for constant city driving, a compact or subcompact car can save money and can ease into parking spaces that a big car could not. Every year, more subcompacts are bought. For rugged off-road driving, a four-wheel-drive vehicle is the answer. Outdoor enthusiasts should consider a van, a jeep or other four-wheel-drive vehicles.

The pickup truck is no longer a hard-riding, bone-jarring work vehicle. Some modern pickups would make a limousine chauffer do a double-take. Almost all pickups offer a smooth ride along with hefty load-carrying capacity. For camping, hauling home-improvement materials, toting motorcycles, or just plain driving, a pickup truck is hard to beat.

Vans offer almost the same load space as a pickup, and can be locked. Their large interior space and carrying capacity make them excellent vehicles for camping. Vans have been fixed up with many different kinds of interiors: paneled, carpeted and with refrigerators and stoves.

How Long To Keep?

If you're trading for pure economy, never do it before a car is three years old because of depreciation. Many new-car owners trade at the end of three or four years, which seems a reasonable time. Those who wait to trade at four or five years probably spend less on their cars, overall. It depends on how much you drive, too. We are talking about 12,000 miles (19,000 K) a year.

By the time a car has gone some 60,000 miles (96,000 K), its costly maintenance-days are at hand. This mileage is 20,000 miles (32,000 K) less on compacts and subcompacts; that much more on luxury cars.

Renting and Leasing

Buying a car is not the only method that you should consider. If you use a car largely for business and can deduct much of its cost from income for tax purposes, it may well pay you to lease a car. No capital is tied up in a leased car. After the end of the three-year (most common) lease, you can walk away from the car. Some leases include maintenance and insurance. Car dealers who have lease plans and car-leasing agencies will be happy to explain the advantages of leasing to you.

WORKING ON YOUR OWN CAR

A recent survey found that two out of three car owners work on their own cars, at least to some extent. The third who do not, say it is chiefly because they lack the knowledge to do auto repairs and maintenance. This is a good reason for not opening the hood but not one for neglecting to learn what makes your car run properly.

Even if you know nothing about a car, you can tackle many basic repairs and maintenance yourself, which saves paying for someone else to do them. You do not need lots of expensive tools and equipment to do most jobs because you can start inexpensively with the basic ones and progress to more sophisticated tools as your knowledge and experience grow.

You can do simple jobs like tuning, lubricating and troubleshooting. Moreover, you can get into minor body repairs, perhaps doing brake relining, wheel balancing and installing accessories. Work you should not do until you are very experienced is wheel alignment, engine overhaul, and transmission repair. These jobs require highly specialized knowledge and equipment. On top of that, you should not get into any job for which you do not have either step-by-step instructions or the know-how.

Service Manual

The best set of how-to-fix-it instructions for your car comes in its service manual so if you are planning any work on your own car, get the service manual. Your dealer can tell you how. Some owner's manuals, the small booklets that come with the car, tell how to order the larger, more

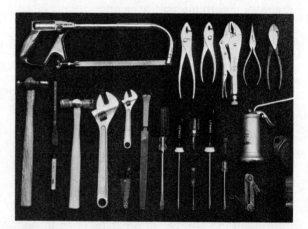

A good set of basic automotive tools includes (top row, left to right): hacksaw, 10" and 6" slip-joint pliers, 10" toggle-locking plier-wrench, long nose pliers and diagonal cutting pliers. (Bottom row): 12 oz. ball peen hammer, $1/2$" cold chisel, center punch, plastic-faced hammer, 12" and 6" adjustable open-end wrenches, thickness gauges, 8" mill file, assorted conventional and Phillips screwdrivers, oilcan, setscrew wrenches and 4" metalworking vise.

detailed service manuals by mail. Cost is usually about $5. It is worth it, because the manual applies specifically to your car. No other book can take its place.

Economics of Car Repair

Besides giving satisfaction in accomplishing something worthwhile, car repair is bound to save you money depending on how much of the work you do. The whole repair cost for one car beyond its dealer warranty is something like $250 a year. Part of this must go for parts; any car repair is about half labor and half parts. While you can provide the labor, you must buy the parts, so that leaves perhaps $125 per car per year savings from doing it yourself.

A good deal of auto repair is simply finding and replacing faulty parts. When you do it yourself, you have the choice of replacing with a new, a rebuilt or a used part, in descending order of cost. Which you should get depends on what part it is.

Routine parts that need relatively frequent replacement should be new. Spark plugs, distributor contact points, condensers, distributor caps and rotors, spark plug cables and drive belts all should be new. The same applies for any simply made, low-cost part. Some auto parts, like wheel bearings, must be purchased new, usually from the new car dealer because few other outlets carry them.

More complicated, higher-cost parts assemblies, such as carburetors, alternators, starting motors, water pumps, distributors and fuel pumps, are best purchased rebuilt. You can get rebuilt, tested assemblies from your car dealer's parts department, from independent auto parts dealers or through national retail chains. All are completely disassembled, rebuilt with some new parts and all new gaskets, then reassembled and tested.

Used parts cost about half what new ones would and some auto wrecking dealers will even give you a guarantee. Interchangeable parts from other makes or models of cars may be exact replacements for the ones you need. Your wrecking dealer can tell you what will fit. He always wants your old part in exchange for the new one, as with a rebuilt unit, or he will make a core charge.

Specifying Parts

When ordering parts, always specify the year, make and model of car. Some parts call for further descriptions, such as number of engine cylinders and displacement in cubic inches (CID) or cubic centimeters (cc). Ordering paint and body parts often requires the trim code number. Get it from the identification plate found under the hood or elsewhere on the car. Sometimes you may even have to bring in the old part to get the right replacement.

Professional Repairs

If you take your car in to a shop to have something fixed, get an estimate of the repair charges. Then, if the mechanic finds that repairs other than those estimated are needed, he should get your permission before going ahead with them. This is the foundation of the new consumer protective laws being set up across the country.

All repair costs are based on how long the repair will take, plus what parts are required. The shop owner applies his per-hour charge to the estimated time for doing the repair, adds in the parts cost and gives you a total estimate.

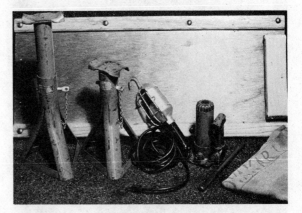

Garage tools you will want are a garage creeper for rolling underneath a jacked and blocked car to work on it; safety jack stands for blocking up a car; trouble light; 1½ ton hydraulic jack and protective fender cover.

Tools You Need

To do your own repairs, get a good, basic set of mechanic's tools. You can buy them as a complete set or separately. If you are starting from scratch, it usually pays to buy the set, as long as you will need every tool in it. Remember that metric tools are increasingly necessary both for repairing U.S.-made and imported cars. Since 1969, some domestic compact cars have been built partly with metric fasteners.

AUTOMOTIVE ACCESSORIES

Well chosen auto accessories can greatly improve the safety, convenience, economy and appearance of your car. Some accessories are available only by ordering them on a new car or by purchasing one with them already installed. Generally unavailable as aftermarket add-ons are power steering, power windows, concealed headlamps, power door locks and power seats.

Emergency Accessories

Few drivers have never had car trouble on the road. By being prepared for the most likely kinds of trouble including accidents, getting stuck, car breakdowns, or assisting other motorists in need, a driver has a head start in dealing with them.

Having a fire extinguisher in the car is recommended in case of fire. To make sure of getting the right kind, check the model's rating before buying it. A good auto fire extinguisher should be rated for grease, oil, gasoline, electrical and fabric fires. Most are the dry-powder type. A 5 pound one is a useful size.

A first-aid kit is a must. Get one containing antiseptic, strip bandages, gauze bandage material and tape.

It is also a good idea to carry safety flares. Several of the 9-inch-long, 15-minute types should suffice. Do not hold it upright or the drippings will fall on you and burn your wrist.

If you get stuck, equipment that can help includes a shovel, reinforced tire chains, tow chain, some sand and a pair of traction mats. A brush-scraper combination is useful in snowy climates for cleaning windshields, windows, headlights and outside mirrors before driving.

Mount a fire extinguisher in a convenient location on your car, one that is both accessible and out of the way. In case of fire, it will be ready to use quickly. Check periodically to see that the charge is still good.

To install tire chains, lay them behind the wheel and carefully back halfway onto them. Bring the two ends together on the top of the tire and secure the clamps. Installing kits that make the job easier are available where you buy the chains.

A basic tool kit with pliers, screwdriver, assorted wrenches, a hammer and a pocket knife could help you to make temporary roadside repairs. For unexpected breakdowns at night, a 12 volt plug-in worklight with a long cord is very handy.

Spare Tires

For tire changing, the manufacturer's lug wrench is rarely adequate. Invest in a heavy-duty cross lug wrench that will remove even hard-to-turn lug bolts quickly and easily.

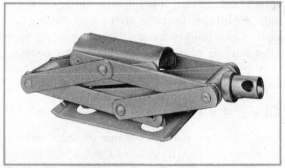

Courtesy of The Hein-Werner Corp.

Scissors jack lifts from under the car frame. When you rotate the worm (right) in one direction, the jack's base and top plate spread apart, lifting the car. Rotate in the other direction and the car is lowered.

A heavy-duty cross-type lug wrench gives you better leverage to loosen and remove lug nuts easily. After the nuts are loose, you can spin the wrench. Its momentum will thread the nut all the way off.

Jacks

Four kinds of aftermarket car jacks are offered: ratchet bumper, screw jacks, scissors jacks and hydraulic jacks. Ratchet bumper jacks, as standard equipment on most cars, fit under the bumper and lift the front or rear for tire-changing. You can buy much better and safer ones than the one that came with your car.

Screw jacks lift from underneath a frame member or jacking pad. Turning a long crank rod raises or lowers it.

Scissors jacks also operate with a long crank rod, the difference being that they lift by compressing the unattached ends of a hinged diamond.

Hydraulic jacks operate on oil pressure pumped from a small cylinder into a large cylinder. They are by far the most desirable jacks, because of their solid, easy lift and strong construction.

Radio and Tape Players

Most cars today come with an AM radio. If the one you have did not, you can get a radio to fit in the dash opening or to hang below the dash. Available are AM-FM (and FM multiplex stereo) radios and stereo tape decks. Stereo tape decks come in 4- and 8-track versions, the 8-track being more popular.

Gauges

If you are concerned with the way your car runs, a wise investment is a set of gauges, which are easily added. Engine coolant temperature, oil pressure and ammeter (battery charge) gauges are the most important. They let you know the condition of your car's cooling, lubrication and electrical systems.

If you tend to get lost, a windshield-mounted compass could help you find your directions again. The best ones are wired to the instrument-lighting circuit to be illuminated at night.

Protective Exterior Accessories

A parking lot is probably one of the poorest places to park your car. Car doors get opened into the side of your car; other drivers nudge your grille with their bumpers; grocery carts are rolled into your car while being unloaded. Vinyl side moldings, chrome strips and door edge guards can help to keep your car looking well after months of parking lot encounters because they prevent car doors and grocery carts from chipping the paint.

Gasoline Accessories

One of the best car investments you can make is a locking gas cap. It replaces the original to protect the gas tank from siphoning and contamination. If you do not want a locking cap, you might try an antisiphon coil. This fits into the tank's filler neck to keep a siphon hose from entering.

If you run out of gas, you may need to siphon gas from a helpful motorist's gas tank. Carrying a hand-pump siphon hose for this keeps you from having to swallow gasoline to get the siphon action going on a plain hose. Do not carry gasoline in the trunk of your car.

Static-Eliminators

If you have ever seen a car dragging a small strip from its body to the pavement, you have seen a static-eliminator. These prevent static buildup to keep you from getting shocked when you touch the car.

Starting Aids

A few mandatory items for cold, below-zero driving are battery jumper cables, a can of ether starting spray and an engine heater.

Carry booster or jumper cables in your trunk. Should your battery go dead, you can use another running car to start your own. See your owner's manual, to be sure of doing it right, as a wrong hookup can damage the electrical systems of both cars.

Ether spray is particularly useful in extremely cold weather when gasoline will not evaporate enough to ignite and start the car. Spray some ether into the carburetor with the air cleaner cover removed while someone tries to start the engine. Give up if it does not start within a few seconds as ether build-up in the engine can be dangerous.

Easy-to-install engine heater fits in the lower radiator hose. Simply cut one or two inches from the middle of the hose, slip the ends over this device and secure with the large hose clamps provided. Plugged into an electrical outlet it keeps your engine warm for fast, easy cold-weather starts.

An engine heater keeps your car's engine warm through the night, so that when you turn the key the next morning, it will start without delay.

Power Accessories

Some of the power accessories you might find on cars may seem somewhat frivolous, while others are very useful. It all depends on your own tastes and driving needs.

Power windows merely do the work of cranking windows up and down for you. With small children in the car they can be dangerous if used as playthings. They will not stop going up even if a child's hand or head is sticking out the window.

Power-operated door locks give you the convenience of safety-locking all the doors by pressing one button. With children in a four-door car, this is especially reassuring.

An automatic speed-control device is desirable for extensive freeway travel. For cross-country driving this feature lessens driver fatigue. A complex system of speed monitors and engine controls keeps the car moving at a steady, preset pace. Safety is assured by a mechanism that instantly kicks out the control when you touch the brake, clutch or accelerator pedal. Improved gas economy is an added benefit of steady-speed cruising.

For vacations you would probably appreciate having an automatic level control. Even with heavy loads, the rear end of the car will not sag.

Air shocks without automatic level control are manually filled with air to level the car. At a gas station you can pump air into them like filling a flat tire.

On some cars you will notice fine, parallel lines running across the rear window. These are electric window heaters. When switched on, they dispel fog on the inside and frost, ice or snow on the outside. Defoggers keep your rear vision safely clear.

In a new car, an electric rear-window defroster-defogger is a valuable safety device. It will keep the backlite free of fog, frost and snow. An aftermarket blower defroster-defogger can be added to the car you now own.

Car-Top Carriers

There may be times when you cannot fit enough luggage inside the car. This is when you need a car-top carrier, whether only a simple lugggage rack or a perch-on-top tent-like structure. On-top luggage should be covered with a waterproof tarp, if possible. Luggage racks can be ordered on most new cars or installed on others.

Transmission Cooler

A transmission cooler can do wonders for your car if you drive in a hot climate, pull heavy loads

or climb up steep grades. Any car originally equipped with a trailer-towing package usually has a transcooler as standard equipment. You can add one if your car does not have it. A transcooler can save you money in repairs, because too much heat is very damaging to the clutches and oil in a fluid transmission. The separate cooling unit with a tiny radiator core that is plumbed into the transmission is best.

BRAKING SYSTEMS

Automotive brakes are simply heat engines. When the driver steps on the brake pedal, the car's braking system converts the moving energy of the car's mass into heat energy, and the car comes to a smooth stop. But even with near-perfect brakes, at 50 mph it takes some 105 feet, which is five car lengths, to apply the brakes and stop. The fastest stopping comes when the brakes do not lock the wheels, but slow them almost to that point. How much force this takes depends on speed, road surface and the tires. During a stop, car weight is concentrated on the front wheels. Thus, the front wheels do from 60 to 75 percent of the braking.

The whole stopping process begins when the brake pedal pushes a piston inside the master cylinder, so called because other brake cylinders are controlled by it. The master cylinder is also the reservoir for holding a noncompressible, nonevaporating brake fluid. When the brake fluid is pressurized by the master cylinder piston, it has nowhere to go but travel along tiny steel tubes and rubber hoses called brake lines leading to the wheel cylinders. One wheel cylinder is located in each wheel. From a second master cylinder piston, the other brake lines lead to wheel cylinders in the rear. The force each wheel cylinder receives is regulated by its piston area. A large piston area receives more force than a small area. Thus, to put more braking in the front wheels, front wheel cylinders have larger pistons.

As it travels, each wheel cylinder piston pushes on two brake shoes containing friction linings that make contact with a rotating brake drum or disc which is attached to the wheel of the car. As

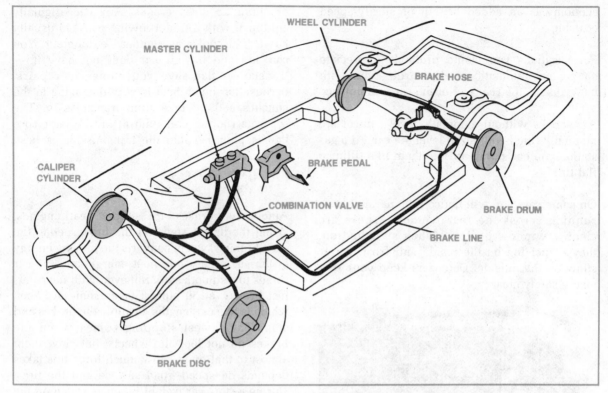

Disc/Drum Braking System

the brake lining rubs against the drum or disc, the drum slows down and heat is created.

This method of braking, called hydraulic braking, is used on all cars today. Since it sends fluid pressure to all four wheels at once, it far surpasses the lever-and-rod systems used on cars many years ago.

Drum Brakes

The wheel portion of braking systems varies more than any other part. Drum types make use of brake drums with friction linings mounted on curved brake shoes inside the rotating drums. As the shoes are forced outward against the inner drum braking surfaces, the car slows down. Years of development on the drum brake has made it highly efficient. Some of the drum's rotational action helps hold the brake linings in contact with the drum. This action is called self-energizing and it greatly lessens the amount of foot pressure needed to stop the car.

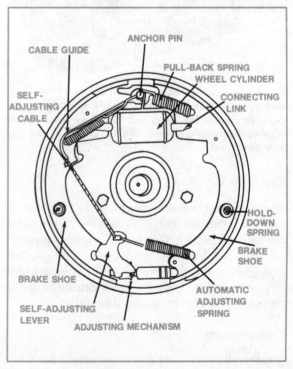

Self-Adjusting Brake Mechanism

The chief disadvantage of drum brakes is that all heat produced is concentrated inside a brake drum no larger than 11 inches in diameter. Since the drum has a pair of hot brake linings contacting most of its inner surface, heat finds little way to escape. Too much heat makes the brake linings lose some of their friction with the drum and causes what is called *brake fade.* To make the same stop with hot, fading brakes as with cold, efficient ones requires much more pedal pressure.

Moreover, drum brakes hold poorly when wet. If you drive through deep water, they may lose their stopping power for some time. Because of this, always try the brakes after a soaking to see that they work. If they don't, drive slowly for about 1/4 mile, holding light foot pressure on the brake pedal to heat up the linings and evaporate all moisture.

Disc Brakes

Developed to avoid the drawbacks of drum brakes, disc brakes are far superior. Most cars today come with discs on the front wheels, drums on the rear.

The operation of a disc brake is much like the caliper brake on a bicycle. A pair of brake blocks straddle a spinning rotor, pinching it between them. Wheel cylinder pistons are located on either side of the disc rotor in a U-shaped device called a caliper.

Disc brakes are not self-energizing. Instead, they require high hydraulic pressures in the range of 1200-1500 psi. Therefore, power-assist is often used, especially on heavy disc-braked cars. Disc brakes resist lockup. When brakes lock up and tires slide, stopping power diminishes.

Disc brakes also have their friction surfaces on the outside, exposed, where they can cool easily. Also they brake well when hot. This is because lining friction characteristics need not allow for self-energizing action and can be designed to prevent fade. Disc brakes with friction materials that are actuated by only one piston are called pads. Larger friction materials pushed by two pistons each are called linings.

Some light-duty disc brakes use single-piston calipers. In these, the piston is located on one side of the caliper. It works like the screw shaft of a C-clamp to squeeze the rotor between both pads. Most single-piston calipers, called floating calipers, are designed to be self-centering over the disc.

Water has little effect on disc brakes. The linings make light contact with the rotating disc at all times and water is squeezed or spun off as fast as it gets on.

The main problem with disc brakes has been in developing a simple, workable parking brake for use with them. According to automotive engineering standards, a car's parking brake must not only hold the car on a steep incline, it must bring the moving car to a stop. This makes it an emergency brake as well as a parking brake. Emergency braking rules out the use of a simple pawl-action parking brake. Combination emergency/parking brakes have been devised for disc systems, but so far none is easy or cheap to make.

With rear drum brakes, a simple cable-actuated emergency/parking brake works well. When you

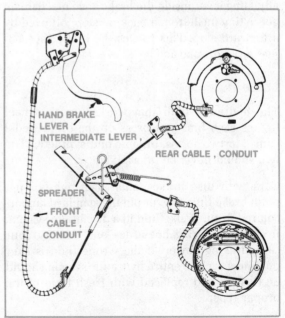

Courtesy of Pontiac Motor Div.

Parking Brake System

apply the parking brake, the tops of the drum-brake linings are levered apart mechanically. They contact the brake drum just as they do when activated hydraulically by the brake pedal.

Self-Adjusting Brakes

The more recent wheel-brake systems are designed to take up the gaps left as the brake linings wear thin from hundreds of uses. Disc brakes do it by their very nature. No springs are used to pull the linings back from the disc; none are needed because of no self-energization. Disc brake pads are always poised ready to stop as soon as the brake pedal is pushed.

Drum brake linings cannot be allowed to touch the drums when not applied because self-energization would make them drag too much. Sturdy brake-retracting springs pull the shoes back against metal stops as soon as the brake pedal is released. Some 0.007 inch or more clearance is kept between linings and drum.

But, as linings wear, the gap widens. Soon the brake pedal would have to be pushed to the floor to take up all the slack were it not for the self-adjusting feature. Whenever shoe-to-drum clearance becomes excessive, a ratcheting, self-adjusting lever inside the brake shoe mechanism gets a tiny push from a back-up stop followed by a forward stop. This rotates the brake shoe adjusting screw one notch.

Brake Fluid

The hydraulic fluid that works a car's wheel brakes each time you press on the brake pedal comes in two forms: organic and synthetic. The two should *never* be intermixed.

Cars with disc brakes *must* use high-boiling-point brake fluid. Never put the standard amber-colored drum-brake fluid in a disc brake system. It can boil during hot usage and destroy your car's braking power. If the wrong fluid is ever put into a car, the entire hydraulic system should be flushed and replaced with fresh fluid of the proper type.

Disc-brake fluid may be used in a flushed-out drum-brake system, *provided* there is a rubber

diaphragm underneath the master cylinder cover to keep out moisture. Disc fluid tends to take on moisture from the air. Moisture in brake fluid can cause boiling and loss of brakes or lock-up of wheels when hot.

Power Brakes

Many cars come with power brakes. When the brake pedal is pushed, a power booster unit uses stored-up vacuum from the engine's intake manifold to give the brake master cylinder piston a strong push. The push increases hydraulic pressure in the brake lines and saves the driver from having to push hard enough to do it alone. Sufficient vacuum for several stops is stored in a vacuum reservoir. A car can be stopped even without the vacuum-assist, but heavy pedal pressure is required.

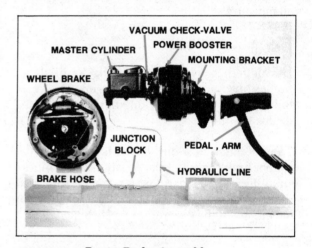

Power Brake Assembly

Brake Relining

After a car has traveled 10,000 to 40,000 miles its brake linings may need replacing or relining. How long a set of linings lasts depends on how hard and how often the brakes are used. Never ride the brake pedal, that is, let your foot rest on it while you drive. This practice holds the linings in tight contact with the discs and drums and wears out the linings prematurely. It also heats the brakes and wastes fuel. Also, don't jam on your brakes unless you have to. When going down long grades, shift to a lower gear to let the engine do some of the braking and save the brakes.

When riveted brake linings wear down to within 1/32 inch of the rivet heads, it is time for them to be relined. It is advisable to have the front and rear linings checked semiannually.

Relining Steps

Whether you should do your own brake relining depends on your experience as a mechanic and what information you have at hand. If you have the advice of a do-it-yourself garage mechanic, you can probably tackle a brake job. However, without a step-by-step guide on disassembly and reassembly, mistakes could result in either inoperative or poorly acting brakes.

Whether or not you do your own brake work, all of the following operations are recommended with every brake job: Turn drums and rotors on a brake lathe if the braking surfaces are faulty.

Install quality linings. Fit drum-brake shoes to the larger turned-out drums. Better yet, fixed-anchor grind them for good contact at the center of the shoe. Rebuild or replace all wheel and caliper cylinders. Check the master cylinder for leaks. Better yet, rebuild or replace it, too. Flush new hydraulic fluid through the system. Replace damaged drum brake shoe-retracting and hold-down springs, or simply replace all springs, damaged or not. Clean and lubricate the contact ledges on drum-brake backing plates (The backing plates support the shoes and wheel cylinder

assembly). Repack the front-wheel bearings with fresh wheel bearing grease of the specified type. Install new front and rear grease seals and new cotter pins on the front spindle nuts. Pull out and lubricate both parking brake cables. Replace them if frayed. Adjust the parking brake. Inspect all brake lines and hoses. Replace any that are damaged, cracked, worn or leaking.

A brake job like this can cost $100 or more. Cheap brake jobs often do not include wheel cylinder service. Within weeks the car may be back in the shop with one of its new brake linings soaked with brake fluid from a leaking wheel cylinder.

Once brake fluid or wheel bearing grease gets on a brake lining, it is ruined. That wheel and the one opposite it must be relined again. If you reline just one side, the car is sure to pull when braked, even though the new linings are the same kind as the old ones.

Brake Linings

The fade and friction characteristics of the linings you reline with must match the needs of your car. Since you can only rely on the brake lining manufacturer for this, choose a reliable brand of lining. You'll find three types of linings: low-cost, original-equipment, and premium, although they are not always called by those names. Use either original-equipment or premium linings, never low-cost ones. Whether linings are bonded or riveted types does not matter as both are good.

After a brake relining job, remember to brake gently for the first 300 miles to break in the new linings. They will work better and last longer.

Antiskid Braking

Antiskid braking is an excellent safety option which is available on some cars at extra cost. It prevents out-of-control, locked-wheel skids under all driving conditions.

With antiskid systems, controlled stops can be made on wet pavements or glare ice in as much as 20 percent less distance than without an antiskid system.

Hydraulic Switches, Valves

The hydraulic system contains a number of refinements, and a malfunction in any component requires its replacement. There are no repairs for them.

Proportioning Valve

Because of self-energizing, drum brakes need less hydraulic pressure than discs. For that reason, a proportioning valve is installed in the hydraulic line to the drum brakes to keep the rear wheels from locking up and sliding under heavy braking.

Metering Valve

Because they have no lining gaps and no hold-down springs, disc brakes take hold more quickly than drums. Sometimes a metering, or hold-off, valve is added to the front-disc system to delay the discs, giving the rear drums time to take up their slack.

Erratic Brakes

Normal braking stops the car straight ahead. Increasing pedal pressure results in increasing deceleration. Except for disc brakes, wheels can be made to lock up and slide on the pavement with heavy pedal pressure. Brakes rarely just fail. They usually signal for attention first. Give it to them before failure comes. Get brakes serviced if:

Brakes pull to one side.

Squeals or other noises come from the wheels when stopping. (A light wire-brush noise is normal with disc brakes, however.)

Brake pedal cannot be held down for 15 seconds without sinking under your foot. Excessive pedal pressure is required to stop quickly.

Pedal pulsates, indicating off-center or out of round drums or a rotor's roundout or lack of parallelism.

Brakes fade after several hard applications in a row.

Brakes drag.

Pedal feels spongy, indicating air in the system or leaks.

Brake pedal feels high and hard, indicating glazed, hard linings without proper friction characteristics.

Grease or brake fluid leaks from wheel brake, master cylinder or brake lines or hoses, or brake fluid must be added often to keep it topped off. (Note: low fluid in the front master-cylinder reservoir can be caused by front-disc lining wear.)

Brake pressure differential warning light comes on.

Brake pedal lacks ample reserve travel ($1\frac{1}{2}$ inches or 35mm) or must be pumped to hold. Pumping means low brake fluid or a faulty master cylinder.

Parking brake lacks ample reserve travel. Wheel brakes chatter or grab, or one wheel skids when others do not.

COOLING SYSTEMS

The automobile engine is only about 25 percent efficient. The unused energy becomes heat rather than motion and must be disposed of. One third of the heat passes out the exhaust pipe along with the products of combustion while one tenth is lost directly from the hot engine by radiation. Some 33 percent of the energy in each gallon of gasoline must be carried away by the engine's cooling system to keep its pistons and valves from melting.

In effect the automotive cooling system is also a heating system. For the engine must not run too cool. Cold oil flows poorly and cylinder walls below 140°F (60°C) collect residue. Combustion acids created inside the engine oil cannot be burned off. For these reasons a cold engine is warmed by the cooling system and a hot engine is cooled by it. With a properly functioning cooling system a car could drive 10,000 miles, stopping only for fuel, and never overheat.

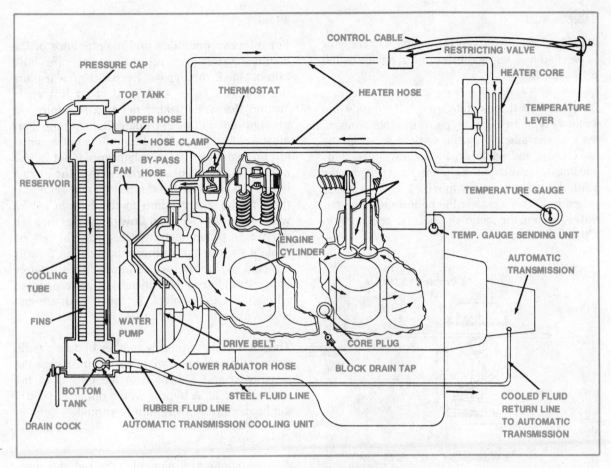

Sideview of an Engine Cooling System

Cooling System Parts

Autos use two kinds of cooling: liquid and air. Air cooling has the advantage of requiring no antifreeze or rust inhibitors to protect the system.

Liquid-cooling, which is much more popular, does a more uniform job of cooling the engine parts, plus it helps to keep engine noises from escaping. Therefore, a liquid-cooled engine runs much quieter than an air-cooled one.

Air Cooling

An air cooled engine is built with cooling fins cast into each of its cylinders and cylinder heads. These increase the surface area for heat exchange between metal and air. A blower driven by the engine forces air over the fins to remove heat. Often, a thermostatically controlled vent is built into the system to slow the flow of cooling air when the engine is too cool and open it up when too hot. Cowling and ducts around the engine and in the engine compartment direct the flow of air to where it is needed.

Liquid Cooling

A liquid-cooled engine contains a water jacket around its cylinders and cylinder heads. Liquid called *coolant* is driven by a water pump and flows around among the cylinders. Some cars before 1940 depended on thermosiphon action to circulate coolant. Hot coolant leaves the engine at the top and enters a radiator. The radiator contains small tubular passages for coolant to flow through. Fins attached to the passages help transfer their heat to air flowing through the radiator core. A fan helps draw air through the radiator core.

1697

Thermostat

The hot-coolant passage from engine to radiator is blocked by a temperature control device called a thermostat.

Two kinds of thermostats are used: pill type and bellows type. In the pill type, a small container of wax opens and closes the coolant valve as the wax heats and cools. In the bellows-type thermostat, an exact-boiling-point fluid inside the sealed bellows unit vaporizes and expands when hot. This spreads the bellows to open the valve. When the bellows cools, it contracts to close the valve.

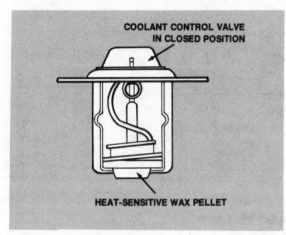

COOLANT CONTROL VALVE
IN CLOSED POSITION

HEAT-SENSITIVE WAX PELLET

Pill-Type Thermostat

When an engine is started cold, the thermostat is closed. No coolant can flow from engine to radiator. As the engine runs, the coolant bottled up in the water jacket soon heats. When it reaches operating temperature, the thermostat opens and coolant flows out of the engine into the radiator to be cooled.

When the engine is turned off, the thermostat opens wide, as what is called *heat-soak* takes place. The coolant, no longer being moved by the water pump, is static inside the water jacket. Hot engine parts still need cooling, but are not getting it, so the coolant becomes extra hot as it soaks up excess engine heat.

Thermostat operation is automatic, governed only by the temperature of the coolant flowing to it.

Bypass

For effective operation and maintenance of the cooling system, several refinements are built into it. One is the bypass. Even during warm up, the engine's valve seats and other hot spots around the water jacket need extra cooling to prevent spot boiling of coolant. But with the thermostat closed, stopping coolant flow to the radiator, no coolant would circulate were it not for the bypass. It takes coolant directly from the engine water jacket below the thermostat and returns it through the water pump to the bottom of the water jacket. A continual flow of coolant through the water jacket takes place, even though no coolant can escape to the radiator. The flow is directed by internal water jacket tubes directly onto critical hot spots. The metal tubes are cast in when the engine block is made and are not removable or replaceable.

The car's heater circuit is another bypass circuit, since it taps off hot coolant before it reaches the thermostat and returns it to the bottom of the cooling system. A bypass would not be needed if the heater's flow were uninterrupted.

Pressure cap

Another cooling refinement is the radiator pressure cap. Its purpose is to raise the coolant's boiling point. It is a physical principle that the more pressure a liquid is under, the higher its boiling point.

The pressure cap also has a vacuum valve that lets air enter the radiator tank as the coolant cools and contracts. It keeps the radiator hoses from being collapsed by external air pressure.

Antifreeze/Coolant

Cars with big engines and pollution controls and air conditioning emit so much heat that boiling can be a problem even with pressurized water. For that purpose, as well as to prevent freezing and corrosion in cooling system passages, plain water is no longer used for car cooling. Instead, a mixture of at least 33 percent antifreeze/coolant and water is used in cooling system. Antifreeze/coolant is a blend of ethylene glycol and corrosion inhibitors.

Straight antifreeze/coolant without water should never be used, even though its boiling point is some 330°F , it does not cool as well as antifreeze/coolant and water.

Never use alcohol-type antifreezes in recent-year cars. They *reduce* coolant boiling point. Be careful when buying glycol-type antifreeze/coolant also as off-brands have been found to contain one quarter water. Check the protection chart on the can. It should show freeze protection down to -34°F (-37°C) for a 50 percent mixture. If it doesn't go that low, too much water has been added in the can.

Antileak or Not

When you buy name-brand antifreeze/coolant, you will find two kinds: antileak and plain. Proponents of the antileak formula point out that it seals tiny leaks and thus protects your cooling system against loss of coolant. Opponents admit that this is true, but add that the antileak formula does nothing to seal leaks at hose connections, and that it may clog a partially restricted heater core. The best advice seems to be to keep your cooling system clean and free of restrictions. Then you can use either type you wish without worry.

"Cool" Additives

Should you add one of those "cool" additives to your car's radiator to help it run cool? At recent count there were some 30 brands flourishing. Ford-developed tests on sample cars have shown that cooling is often better without cool additives than with them. When a cool additive was used without an antifreeze/coolant, cooling system corrosion quickly developed despite the additive. No auto manufacturers recommend using any of the cool additiives. Most car makers plainly advise against them in service literature.

Closed Systems

Late model liquid-cooled automobile engines use closed cooling systems designed to keep air out and reduce corrosion. A plastic reservoir is mounted inside the engine compartment somewhere near the radiator. A small rubber hose leads from the radiator neck to it. A closed-system radiator uses a leave-on pressure cap on the radiator opening. Filling of the system is done at the reservoir. When the engine is cool, the reservoir is about half full. As the engine warms, a little expanding coolant is forced out of the radiator through the overflow tube and into the reservoir. Later, as the engine cools, the coolant flows by vacuum from the reservoir back into the radiator. Kits are available to let you convert your car's open cooling system to a closed one.

A few cars use a coolant recovery system that is open, but with a reservoir to catch overflow coolant and save it. Such a system has the usual pressure cap on the radiator. The overflow tube is routed to the reservoir catches outflowing liquid coolant and holds it. Trapped coolant is drawn back into the radiator whenever there is a vacuum in the system. The reservoir should run at about one-quarter full when cold. A coolant recovery system does not have the advantage of the closed system in keeping air out of the cooling system.

Drain Cock

To let the cooling system be drained and fresh coolant be added, most car radiators contain drain cocks at the bottom. These may be located either in the center or on one side. There may also be other drain cocks installed at the bottom of the engine block, one on inline engines and one on each side on V-8 engines.

Core Plugs

One of the engine's most misunderstood parts is its core plugs. These are almost always incorrectly termed *freeze plugs,* which they are not. They are steel discs about an inch in diameter or larger that have been pressed into circular recesses on the side of the engine block. If coolant in the engine should freeze, these, being the weakest spots in the water jacket walls, would be popped out by expanding ice, thus the misnomer. Core plugs do not protect the engine block from damage by freezing. By the time they pop out, the engine has surely cracked internally and is no longer usable. The real purpose of core plugs is to fill holes left when the engine block was cast. Leaking often occurs around core plugs because they are a weak spot for corrosion.

Head Gasket

Engine blocks and heads are cast separately and assembled later. This allows valves and pistons to be installed in them during assembly. Removable cylinder heads also give access to the combustion chambers for service. Since both the engine block and the cylinder head require cooling, their water jackets are joined through numerous passages around and between the cylinders. To prevent leaking of combustion chamber gases and water jacket liquids, what is called a head gasket is used between the head and block. It is about $1/16$ inch thick and effectively seals all openings as it is clamped between the two parts by heavy cylinder head bolts.

Water Pump

The water pump is a simple belt-driven centrifugal pump much like the one in a tropical fish tank, although larger. It turns as the engine runs to draw water from the cool side of the radiator, force it through the engine block and cylinder heads, and push it out past the thermostat to the hot side of the radiator. The water pump's only job is to improve circulation within

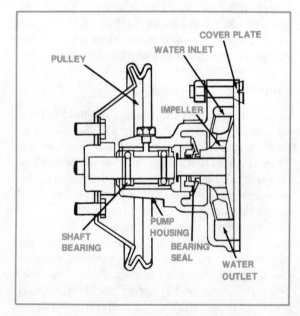

Centrifugal Water Pump Cutaway

the cooling system. Often, the fan is attached to its drive shaft.

Because the water pump shaft is both an internal and an external part, the pump must have a seal to keep coolant from leaking out along the shaft. Some of these seals consist of a pair of carbon blocks, one around the shaft and one around its housing. A spring holds them together and the contacting surfaces allow rotation yet keep coolant from leaking, even when under pressure. This seal is the weakest part of the water pump. When it wears out, the water will leak out past the shaft and the water pump must be removed and rebuilt. Water pump impellers also are subject to corrosion, which can eat them up and reduce their pumping power.

Fans provide positive air flow all the while it is needed. If there were no fan, both air- and liquid-cooled engines would overheat at low speeds and idling in traffic when not enough air is flowing through the radiator. Most fans are belt-driven from the engine. However, more and more imports are using motor driven fans. Electric, these are switched on and off thermostatically as needed to keep the coolant at the right temperature.

Because the need for fan cooling diminishes as car speed increases, and because fans draw lots of horsepower at highway speeds, some contain clutches. When cooling is needed, the fan turns; when not needed it merely free-wheels, drawing little power from the engine.

The chief wearing part of the whole cooling system is the fan/water pump or blower drive belt. It is a flexible V-type belt of the right length to fit over the engine's crankshaft and pulley. Often the same belt also drives other accessories, such as the alternator. Somewhere an adjustment slot is provided for setting tension on the belt.

Corrosion

The worst thing that can happen to a liquid-cooling system is corrosion and scaling of its inner passages. Hot water circulating among the cast iron, aluminum, copper, brass, and other metals that form parts of the cooling system sets up the problem. This either eats at some of the weaker metals or forms scale deposits on cooling passages. Scale, being a heat-retarder, gets in the way of heat transfer. The eventual result can be boil-over or even worse. Tiny leaks in the head gasket sometimes allow combustion chamber products to seep into the cooling system. These add oil, grease and acids to the coolant.

Every antifreeze/coolant contains acid- and corrosion-inhibitors to forestall these cooling system problems. That is one reason plain water should not be used as a summer coolant. In time, though, these inhibitors are depleted to the point where corrosion can take hold. Before that time, the coolant should be drained and flushed out and new antifreeze/coolant and water added to replenish the inhibitor protection.

Air Cooling

Air-cooling systems avoid most of these problems. They do not avoid overheating, however. In fact, overheating is much more serious in an air-cooled engine because it largely goes unnoticed. When grease and dirt build up on cylinder cooling surfaces, heat flow is impeded. Hot spots develop in the engine. The problem can reach the point where the engine would signal its problem by boiling long before it got that hot. For this reason, it is important to keep an air-cooled engine's cooling fins clean.

DRIVE TRAIN

Power from the engine to the wheels flows through the drive train. Its parts, in the order that power reaches them, are the following: clutch, transmission, driveshaft, differential and the axles. Front-wheel drive eliminates the driveshaft and combines transmission and differential into what is called a *transaxle*. So does rear-engine-rear-drive.

Clutch

The clutch is a means of disconnecting the engine from the wheels when meshing and shifting gears. A car clutch has two main parts: pressure plate and lined plate. The pressure plate is fixed to the engine's flywheel and revolves with it. The lined plate contains friction material and is tightly squeezed between machined surfaces of the pressure plate and flywheel. This makes the lined plate rotate at engine speed. When you depress the clutch pedal, clutch fingers (small levers) force the pressure plate away from the flywheel against heavy springs. This releases the lined plate from its squeeze-play so that it stops revolving. In between full down and full out, the clutch pedal lets the lined plate slip and pick up increasing amounts of engine power.

In time, clutch linings wear thin or become glazed. Then the clutch will either slip or grab. New linings are needed, which is a shop job.

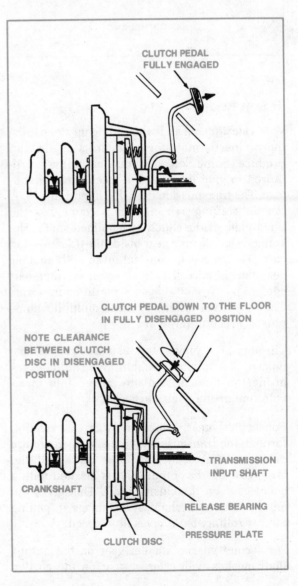

CLUTCH PEDAL FULLY ENGAGED

CLUTCH PEDAL DOWN TO THE FLOOR IN FULLY DISENGAGED POSITION

NOTE CLEARANCE BETWEEN CLUTCH DISC IN DISENGAGED POSITION

CRANKSHAFT

TRANSMISSION INPUT SHAFT

RELEASE BEARING

CLUTCH DISC

PRESSURE PLATE

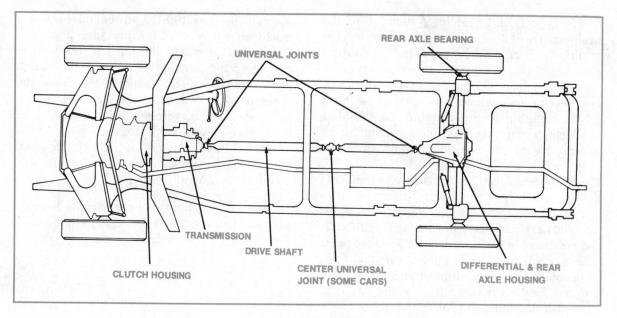

REAR AXLE BEARING

UNIVERSAL JOINTS

TRANSMISSION

DRIVE SHAFT

CLUTCH HOUSING

CENTER UNIVERSAL JOINT (SOME CARS)

DIFFERENTIAL & REAR AXLE HOUSING

The Drive Train

Transmission

When starting out and when going up steep hills, the car needs more torque than its engine can produce. Some sort of torque multiplier is required to give the engine a mechanical advantage. The transmission does this important job. A manual-shifting transmission is coupled to the lined plate of the clutch by a splined shaft. The splined shaft turns a gear inside the transmission case. The gear is in constant mesh with another gear that is part of a cluster-gear countershaft containing two other gears of differing sizes. They give two different torque multiplications, plus a direction-reversal.

Through a complex but usually trouble-free linkage to a column gearshift, two sliding gears inside the transmission are moved into mesh with one or the other cluster gears.

For neutral gear, which transfers no rotation through the transmission, both sliding gears are positioned free of meshing. For first speed, the large gear on the output shaft is meshed with a small gear on the cluster shaft. This gives the engine a large mechanical advantage in getting the car rolling, but it gives little speed.

For second gear, a smaller gear on the output shaft meshes with a larger gear on the cluster

shaft. This gives less mechanical advantage through the transmission along with more speed.

For third or top gear the cluster shaft simply turns free with neither sliding gear meshed. Instead, a broached portion of the smaller sliding gear is slipped over a splined portion of the input shaft. This makes both input and output shafts rotate at engine speed.

Reverse gear requires enmeshment of the large sliding gear with a counter-rotating idle gear.

The sliding gears usually contain *synchromesh* cones to bring the meshing gears to their speed before any teeth or splines meet.

Automatic Transmission

An automatic transmission does away with the friction clutch and manual shifting of gears. It uses a fluid clutch, called a torque converter, that is attached to the engine flywheel and works something like two fans aimed at each other, blade-to-blade. When one fan is started, its air flow makes the other fan run, even though both are not plugged into an electrical outlet. On cars it is done with fluid turbines.

Gear-shifting in the automatic transmission is done by a control mechanism that reacts to car speed and accelerator position. Instead of meshing gears, shifts are handled by premeshed planetary gears. Shifting among them involves pinching a friction-lined band around the drum of a planetary gear, combined with the functioning of hydraulically-operated multiplate clutches. Oil pressure from master shift valves controls this.

Manual transmissions run in heavy gear lubricant. Modern ones seldom need changing. Automatic transmissions run in transmission fluid, Type A or Type F (see your owner's manual). The fluid is filtered inside the transmission. Regular change intervals are specified. Fluid level is indicated by a dipstick and if it ever looks brown and smells burned, have it changed whether it is time or not. It should be clean and almost clear, or have a pinkish cast, like new oil.

Driveshaft

The driveshaft carries transmission rotation to the rear axle. One end of the driveshaft is splined to the transmission output shaft. Since the axle is at a different level than the transmission and is constantly moving in relation to it, a pair of universal joints is needed, one at each end of the driveshaft. These transmit rotation faithfully across a varying angle as the axle moves up and down. Driveshaft centering on its U-joints must be almost perfect, otherwise it would vibrate as it spins. Universal joints are the fastest-wearing parts of the whole drive train.

Rear-Axle Assembly

Three things happen inside the rear-axle housing.

Longitudinal rotation of engine, clutch, transmission, and driveshaft is changed to transverse rotation of the left and right axles.

Engine-speed driveshaft rotation in top gear is geared down to wheel-speed axle rotation.

Differing speeds of the rear wheels in rounding corners and running with different-diameter tires is accommodated.

The direction change and gearing down are done simultaneously by beveled ring-and-pinion gears. The small pinion gear drives the large ring gear some four times slower than it is rotating. And they turn the 90-degree corner in rotation.

The complicated function is the differential drive action. It is accomplished with half-axles with gears on their inner ends. These small gears mesh with pairs of tiny idler gears attached inside the large ring gear.

For equal wheel rotation the idler gears go around with the ring gear but do not rotate. In so doing, they pass ring-gear rotation equally to both half-axles. If one half-axle needs more rotation than the other, the idler gears rotate, giving power to both axles. But if one wheel rests on a slippery surface, the differential, by its gearing, sends all rotation to the easy-to-turn half-axle at double speed. No rotational power goes to the hard-to-turn axle with its wheel on pavement, and the car may be stuck.

Limited-slip differentials have been developed to avoid this. In them some of the power is

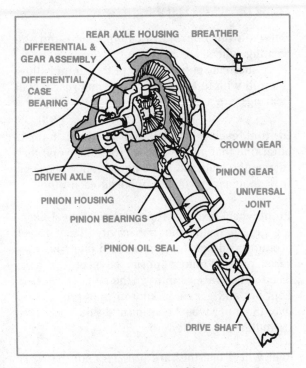

Rear Axle Assembly

transmitted to the hard-to-turn wheel by built-in clutches, letting the unstuck wheel help get the car moving. Limited-slip differentials are often available as extra-cost options.

Limited-slip differentials can be damaged with ordinary gear lubricants. Any noises coming from the differential signal that it needs attention, a definite shop job.

Axle Shafts

Half-axles run in the center in differential bearings; at their outer ends, they run in wheel bearings. This kind of axle design is called a semi-floating axle. The wheel is supported partially by the axle and partially by its own bearing. Heavier duty rear axles use three-quarter-floating design, in which each wheel is supported on its own bearing and the axle takes only cornering loads. If a semi- or three-quarter-floating axle should break, the wheel would come off.

Full-floating axle design which is used only on trucks, gives each wheel two bearings and takes no wheel loads. If it were to break, the wheel would not come off.

Hubs, Bearings, Bushings

Between the nonrotating suspension and the rotating wheel are heavy-duty wheel bearings. They share the entire weight of the car and allow it to roll with little friction. Front and rear wheel bearings are very different.

In front, each wheel has two bearings, a small outer one that guides and a large inner one that carries the load. All are tapered-roller bearings with their tapers facing opposite each other.

Front wheel bearings run in special wheel-bearing grease inside the hub cavity. They travel around inside of finely machined outer bearing races pressed into opposite ends of the hub. Their inner races slip over the spindle. Dust is kept out and grease is kept in by a grease seal over the inner wheel bearing and a dust cap over the outer end of the hub.

Rear wheel bearings are pressed onto the rear-axle shafts. These are permanently sealed and

lubricated roller bearings designed to take thrust as well as radial loads. Each bearing fits into a recess in the axle housing and is held there by a plate with bolts. A rear grease seal fits inside of the wheel bearing to keep rear-axle lubricant from escaping.

Front-Wheel Drive

In front-wheel drive, the transaxle usually mounts to the frame. This calls for articulated half-axles. Ordinary U-joints would whip the driven shaft when working through the sharp 30-degree angles that steered wheels turn .

Since whipping cannot be tolerated in steered wheels, a special kind of universal joint, a constant-velocity joint, is used at the outboard end of each front-drive half-axle. These U-joints get lots of wear and constitute the weakest links in front-wheel drive.

Four-Wheel Drive

Full-wheel traction for off-road use and better traction on the road are the advantages of four-wheel-drive cars and trucks. Both front and rear axles contain geared-alike differentials. The rear axle is standard; the front-axle contains half-axles with U-joints at their outer ends.

Power for both front and rear axles comes from a transfer case, a small gearcase after the transmissions with both a neutral position and a 2-to-1 reduction gear. The transfer case sends its output forward and backward via driveshafts to both axles.

ELECTRICAL SYSTEMS

A car's electrical system is not too different from a home electrical wiring system, except that a car has no convenience outlets where appliances are plugged in. Instead, each of the car's multitude of "appliances" is wired in and, instead of using 120-volt alternating current, the car electrical system handles 12-volt direct current (DC) (6-volt on pre-1956 cars). This current is created by an alternator (generator on pre-1965 cars) and is stored by a battery until needed.

Most automotive circuits consist of a wire (called the hot side of the circuit), similar to the black hot wire in house wiring. Hot wires feed from the battery's positive terminal. The white neutral wire in a house circuit is not needed in most automotive circuits because the car's metal body and frame parts complete the circuit from the load (light bulb, motor, etc.) back to the battery's negative terminal. Twelve volts is such a low electrical pressure that you are not in danger of shock from it. On a car, this nonwired half of the circuit is called the ground circuit, or just ground. Most metal parts of the engine, body and frame are grounded back to the battery's negative terminal. However, a few models of cars use positive-ground systems.

Circuit-Protection

The automobile electrical system consists of separate circuits, each to serve a purpose. Most are protected so that, should a hot wire become grounded against part of the car, the short circuit thus created would be broken before heavy current could make the wire hot enough to start a fire.

Fuses, Circuit Breakers

The circuit-protection job is done by fuses, circuit breakers and fusible links. The car's fuses are usually located together in a fuse panel. The fuse panel is accessible behind the instrument panel or elsewhere for replacement of burned-out fuses. Usually, the slot for each fuse is labeled for identification purposes. Fuse length often varies by fuse capacity, so that only the right-sized fuse will fit. If there is ever any doubt about what size of fuse to replace with, look in the owner's manual.

Circuit breakers interrupt an overload circuit without self-destructing like fuses. When a circuit breaker heats up, a bimetallic spring inside of it bends to break the circuit.

Fusible Links

A third type of circuit-protective device used on cars is called the *fusible link*. A fusible link looks like an insulated wire. It begins at the battery and protects any number of circuits served by it. A fusible link is designed to melt before any of the other wiring gets hot enough to be danger-

ous. After the short circuit is found and fixed, the fusible link must be replaced with a new one.

Circuits

The circuits in the modern car are: ignition, starting, charging, lighting and accessories. Switches and relays (remotely controlled electrical switches) indicator lights, guages, motors and solenoids (electrical push-pull devices) are all parts of these circuits.

Circuit wire sizes are engineered to carry the current for the job to be done. Lightly loaded circuits use thin stranded-copper wires no larger in diameter than a paper clip. More heavily loaded circuits use thick wires. The heavy-duty starting motor circuit has thick, stranded copper wire the size of a lead pencil. Hot wires are insulated to protect against short-circuiting to ground. Connections are made inside insulated terminals, tee-connectors, or complex bulkhead connectors between engine and passenger compartments.

Owner's manuals, and especially service manuals, show full circuit diagrams for the entire car's electrical circuits. While these use standard electrical symbols, they are not easy to understand.

Remember that the positions of electrical components on the diagram are not necessarily related to where you find them on the car. A wire that looks straight and direct on the electrical diagram may be long and circuitous. Also, circuit diagrams usually show accessories as standard equipment. The ground circuit is not drawn in.

Battery

An automotive battery is unlike a flashlight battery. Its job is to store electricity, not create it. The power in a car battery is not used, and then the battery thrown away for a new one. The car battery is supposed to last for several years. The only way it can do this is to receive as much electricity from the charging system as is called on to deliver to all the other systems.

The 12-volt auto battery contains six cells, each producing about 2 volts. The cells are connected by metal bars in *series*, negative side connected

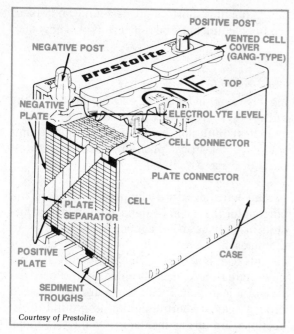

POSITIVE POST

NEGATIVE POST

VENTED CELL COVER (GANG-TYPE)

prestolite

ONE

TOP

NEGATIVE PLATE

ELECTROLYTE LEVEL

CELL CONNECTOR

PLATE CONNECTOR

PLATE SEPARATOR

CELL

POSITIVE PLATE

CASE

SEDIMENT TROUGHS

Courtesy of Prestolite

Battery Construction

to positive side, adding each cell's voltage to that of the next. Each cell has two sets of plates called electrodes that are submerged in a weak solution of sulfuric acid electrolyte. When the engine is started, the circuit between positive and negative terminals of the battery is closed so that electrons can flow. They flow through the circuit and back into the battery. As they do, a chemical reaction takes place inside the cells, changing some sulfuric acid to water. Current flow out of the battery is called discharge.

When the engine starts, the alternator begins producing electrons of its own and sending them backwards through the battery. The reverse flow current replenishes the battery. The process is called charge.

Discharge followed by charge is known as *cycling*. A battery that is cycled a great deal eventually goes dead and cannot be rejuvenated by charging.

When buying a battery, get one of both the right physical and the right electrical size to fit your car. Physical size, as well as shape, goes by group number. A Group 24 battery fits most U. S. cars. Your new battery should have at least as

much electrical storage capacity as the factory-original one.

Battery quality is important, too. A high quality battery will last longer than a poor quality one. The length of the battery warranty is not always a sign of quality, but it may be. Most are warranted for 12 to 36 months.

Batteries fail at an average life of about 30 months. Toward the end, a warranty is of little value. A new battery bought outright at a favorable price below list may be the better buy.

Clean iron-free drinking water is all you should ever put into a battery. Never pour in additives, even though they are supposed to help.

Most new batteries are stored in a dry-charged state. Just before delivery to you, the seller adds electrolyte to the cells.

Alternator/Generator

A car battery would run the car for only a few hours of night driving were it not replenished by the charging system. The heart of this is either an alternator which is short and fat, or a generator which is long and thin. Alternators make more electricity at lower speeds than generators, so most cars today have alternators. Since an alternator turns out alternating current, a series of solid-state, one-way electrical valves called *diodes* is necessary to convert AC to DC.

To keep a generator from "motoring" and using up battery current while the engine is not run-

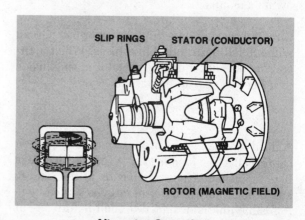

SLIP RINGS   STATOR (CONDUCTOR)

ROTOR (MAGNETIC FIELD)

Alternator Operation

ning, it needs a cut-out relay. The relay breaks the circuit as soon as the generator stops charging.Since the diodes of an alternator will not pass current backwards from the battery, it needs no cut-out relay. A generator also needs a current regulator to control its output.

Both alternators and generators have stators (called *fields* in generators) and rotors (called *armatures* in generators). Rotors turn; stators are what they turn inside of. Each contains many coils of wire, some to produce magnetic fields and others to slice through them or be passed over by them. As a wire moves through a magnetic field, an electric current is induced in it.

Both alternators and generators are belt-driven from the engine's crankshaft pulley. They are air-cooled with fans built into their drive pullies.

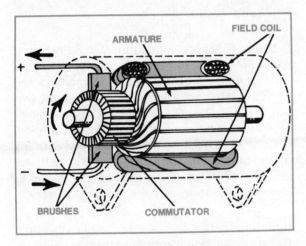

DC Generator Construction

Electrical Accessories

A good many accessories to a car function electrically. Electric windshield wipers, some power windows, self-leveling suspension systems, power seats and power convertible tops all use motors. Car clocks use an intermittent-running motor to rewind the clock's spring. Heater and air-conditioner blowers use electric motor power, too. Nonmotorized accessories are fog lights, driving lights, spotlights and trouble lights.

Electronic accessories, such as radios, tape players and citizen's band radio transmitters all work on the regulated 12 to 15 volt power source of an auto electrical system. These must be hooked up with correct polarity, however, because their tubes and transistors can be blown instantly by a backwards current flow.

Headlights

Among the largest regular power users are headlights. These come in sets of two or four. The four-light systems give a better view of the road at night.

Headlights are controlled by an on-off switch on the instrument panel. Both beams are contained in 7-inch diameter sealed-beam units in a two-lamp system. With four-lamp systems, the smaller 5-inch sealed beam units split the lighting job. On low beam, only the outer or upper lamps are lighted; on high beam, all four lamps are lighted.

Signals

The most complex circuitry on the car is found in the directional, or turn, signals. This is because the same filaments of the same bulbs are also operated in a different way by the hazard warning lighting system (if your car has one) and the rear filaments are controlled in a third way as stoplights.

In front, the turn signals share two-filament lamps with the parking lights. In the rear they share with the taillights.

Interior Lights

Lights inside your car let you see to get in and out and to drive. Brightest are the dome and courtesy lights, the better models coming on as the door is opened.

Instrument panel lamps are wired through a dimmer control, allowing for adjustments in the brilliance of the lamps. Bulbs are clustered behind the speedometer and other gauges, as well as in the radio and sometimes behind the cigarette lighter, ignition switch and ashtray.

Electric Motors

Driving some power accessories are small direct-current motors designed to run on 12 volts. Some are wired to run forward or backward, depending on which way the current is fed through them. These make power windows and seats move in two directions.

Switches

A switch is merely a set of electrical contacts that can be opened or closed to break or complete a circuit. Some are as simple as the push-button ones that control courtesy lights. Others are complex like the ignition switch. It has four or five positions and controls many functions.

Horn & Horn Relay

The car horn is simply an electrical vibrating coil controlled by a push-switch at the steering wheel. Because most horns draw quite a bit of current, many are controlled by relays. A little current passing through the horn button closes the relay contacts that turn on a heavier current to the horn.

Gauges

Most gauges on the dash of the car are either magnetic or thermal. Magnetic ones snap to a reading when the key is turned on. Thermal ones approach a reading more slowly. Both types consist of calibrated *registering units* mounted on the instrument panel and electrical *sending units* located near the source of what is registered.

Sending units vary in resistance, or ability to pass electricity, depending on conditions around them. The temperature gauge sending unit is immersed in engine coolant and passes more electricity when it is hot than when it is cold. The oil pressure sending unit is piped into an engine oil pressure line. It passes more electricity as oil pressure increases. The fuel gauge sending unit is located inside the fuel tank with its resistance-varying rheostat connected to a float arm. The float rides on top of the fuel level in the tank and passes more current as the fuel level increases.

Thermal guages contain tiny heating coils that get hotter as more sending-unit current flows. In turn, they heat up bimetallic arms that bend more the hotter they get. Bending moves the gauge needle to higher readings.

Magnetic units locate a gauge pointed between two magnetic poles. The poles pulling toward the low reading has a fixed pull, while the one pulling toward the high reading has a variable pull controlled by the amount of current coming from the sending unit.

Ammeter

An ammeter, if your car has one, shows whether the battery is being charged or discharged. The ammeter's needle swings to the charge side when current is flowing through it toward the battery. It swings to the discharge side when current is flowing away from the battery. All current, except that for the starting system and the horn, passes through the ammeter, making it an accurate indicator of what is happening in the car's electrical system.

Indicator Lights

Indicator lights for temperature and oil pressure use simple switches for sending units. When the sending units are receiving normal readings, the switch contacts are open and the indicator lights stay off. But when the oil pressure drops too low or the temperature gets too high (or, in some systems, too low), the contacts close and the dash lights comes on, indicating trouble. All are designed to be on when the engine is started to show that the lamps are working.

If the oil pressure indicator light comes on while you are driving, stop as fast as you safely can and switch off the engine. Drive no farther until you are sure that the engine has oil pressure, because if it does not, the engine can be ruined within seconds. If the temperature indicator light should come on to warn of overheating, stop and wait for the engine to cool before proceeding. Do not remove the radiator cap until the system cools enough that you can hold your hand on top of the radiator, or the liquid in the radiator can boil out and burn you.

If the charging system indicator comes on while you are driving, get the system checked before driving very far. However, the charging system indicator light may glow a little at slow idle, or when driving at night. This only indicates a heavy load on the charging circuit and is not an indication of trouble.

Starting Circuit

The starter circuit, like many horn circuits, is really two circuits: a light-current one and a heavy-current one. The 300-ampere starter draw is far too much to route through an ignition switch, as the necessary wiring would require hundreds of pounds of copper wire. Instead, small wires are carried to the ignition switch and to a heavy-current starter relay called a solenoid. When you turn the switch to the start position, a small amount of current flows through the ignition switch and to the starter solenoid. The solenoid's contacts close, switching the battery current through heavy cables to the starter. When the engine starts and the key is released from the start position, the solenoid's contacts open and cut off current to the starter motor.

Starting Motor

The starter is a small but powerful high-torque (high twisting force) DC electric motor. It takes a considerable effort to crank a cold auto engine, so the starter needs a great deal of mechanical advantage. It is geared to the engine by a small pinion gear that drives a large ring gear on the engine flywheel. The pinion gear turns many times to make the ring gear and the engine turn one time.

To keep the starter from spinning out of control once the engine starts, the pinion is designed with an in-out action. When you turn the ignition switch to the start position, the pinion meshes with the ring gear either by an inertia unit called a *Bendix drive* or by a strong push from a solenoid. After a start, the flywheel ring gear overruns the Bendix drive pinion and boots it out of the way on a spirally grooved shaft. After the solenoid engages, a spring pulls the pinion back out of the way when the ignition key is turned from the start position.

When starters and their solenoids go bad, they are removed from the car and replaced with new or rebuilt ones. Service of the defective units is too technical for most mechanics to bother with.

Ignition Circuits

The most complex of all electrical circuits on the car is the ignition system. It consists of an ignition switch, a coil, condenser, distributor, spark plugs and cables and the wires that connect them.

The ignition circuit takes 12-volt current from the battery, converts it to some 20,000 volts and delivers it to the right cylinder at the precise time it is needed to fire that cylinder.

The heart of the ignition system is a pair of electrical contact points, called simply *points*. The points are located inside of the distributor which sends sparks around to the right cylinders at the right time. One contact point is fixed while the other is movable. The movable contact opens and closes onto the fixed contact as lobes on the distributor cam pass beneath it. The cam has the same number of lobes as the engine has cylinders. It makes one revolution for every two revolutions of the engine.

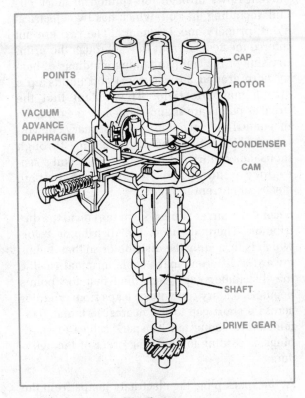

Distributor

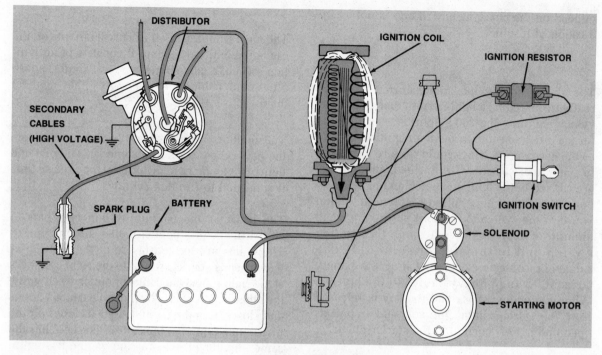

Automotive Ignition Circuit

Whenever the contact points are closed, electric current flows through the ignition primary circuit, including the coil, which has two electrical sides, primary and secondary. The two are not interconnected. Current flows through the *primary* side of the coil (containing windings of heavy wire around an iron core) and builds up a strong magnetic field. The instant that the breaker points are snapped open by the cam, the magnetic field surrounding the primary coil collapses. Magnetic lines of force slice through thousands of turns of tiny wire in the coil's *secondary* windings, inducing a high-voltage electrical current in them.

Secondary current flows out of the coil to the distributor. There it meets the distributor rotor, which is turned by the distributor so that it aims toward a different spark cable terminal (inside the distributor cap) each time that the points open. Secondary coil voltage leaps from the rotor across a short gap to the nearest terminal. Terminals are connected by spark cables to spark plugs, according to the firing order of the cylinders.

At the spark plug, the electricity jumps from the plug's center electrode to its grounded-side electrode. The spark ignites the air/fuel mixture, which has been compressed by the piston to be ready to explode and power the engine. The points close within milliseconds after opening to get ready for the next cylinder's spark. Some 10,000 sparks occur in every mile of driving, or 150 sparks per second at 55 mph.

Condenser

A small but important part of the ignition primary circuit is the condenser. It is a capacitor, a tiny can-like part containing slightly separated pieces of metal foil that stores a small amount of electricity. Its job is to intensify the spark caused by the collapsing magnetic field. Without a condenser in the primary circuit, very little spark would occur in the secondary circuit.

The high voltage of the secondary ignition, while it can give an uncomfortable shock, is no real cause for alarm.

Spark timing is carefully controlled by the distributor. Since a faster-running engine needs an earlier spark, most distributors have a speed, or centrifugal, advance built in.

Ballast Resistor

Cold spark plugs have a hard time firing cold air/fuel mixtures. Therefore, the ignition system needs a boost under most starting conditions. This is given by designing it to function normally as a 7-volt system and switching to 12 battery volts at start up. A full 12-volts hitting the coil-condenser makes a hotter spark and gets the cold engine going. Reduced voltage for running is achieved by routing the lead wire for the ignition circuit through an electrical resistance called a *ballast resistor.*

Electronic Ignition

A weak link in the mechanical ignition is its breaker points. The opening and closing and arcing of the contacts as they open causes their surfaces to deteriorate. If the points get bad enough, the engine will not start or may misfire.

Instead of a lobed cam, the typical electronic system uses a lobed *reluctor* located inside the distributor. Nearby is a pickup coil and permanent magnet. Ridges on the rotating reluctor react with a magnetic field created between the magnet and pickup coil. The pulses are sensed by a nearby electronic control module either on the distributor or some distance away. Each pulse tells a transistor (a solid-state electronic relay) to break the primary coil circuit and send a high-voltage secondary jolt on its way. Routing and distribution of the high-voltage is handled the same as in the conventional ignition, or else this is done electronically, too.

Spark Plugs

Spark plugs carry the high-voltage current to the inside of the combustion chambers and provide carefully spaced gaps between electrodes for the

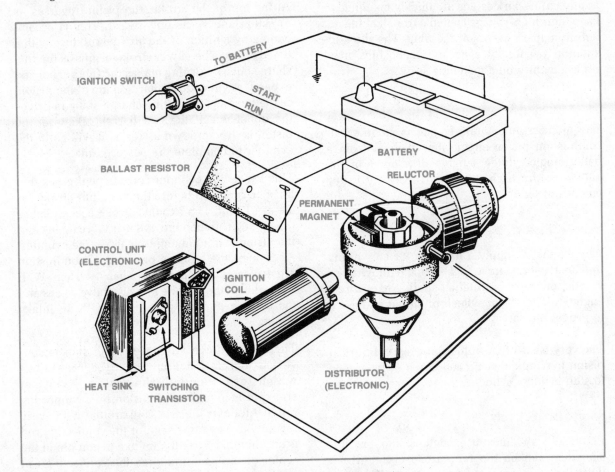

Electronic Ignition Circuit

spark to jump. Because they are subject to combustion chamber atmosphere, spark plugs age rapidly compared with other ignition system components. They need regular cleaning, regapping or replacement to keep an engine economical, easy-to-start and clean-running.

Spark plugs vary in their ability to keep cool. This is called *heat range,* and it goes by *normal, hot* and *cold.* Normal plugs are used unless there is some reason to use hot or cold heat-range plugs.

Resistance Cables

Resistance cables are a compromise between too much secondary resistance, which would keep the engine from getting enough spark to run, and too little resistance, which would upset nearby televisions.

In any case, spark cables are thickly insulated to keep their high-voltage contents from leaking out before a spark occurs at the plug. The thick insulation eventually ages and the cables need replacement with a matching set.

AUTOMOBILE ENGINES

The modern automobile engine is an internal-combustion piston engine that evolved from a balky single-cylinder engine developed in the 1800's to the highly refined multi-cylinder engines of today.

How A Piston Engine Works

Any engine is simply a machine for converting the heat energy in a fuel into the moving or kinetic, energy of a rotating shaft. Gears direct engine rotation to the wheels of the car and use it to propel the car.

The very basis of the auto engine is a cylindrical piston moving either up and down or from side to side inside a cylinder.

Four-Stroke Cycle

Practically all autos use engines that are designed to run on the four-stroke cycle, which defines the movement of the piston. The four

strokes are intake, compression, power, and exhaust.

The four-stroke cycle starts with the intake valve opening and the piston moving downward in the cylinder to draw a fresh air/fuel mixture into the cylinder. At the bottom of the intake stroke, the intake valve closes, sealing off the cylinder at the top and completing the intake stroke.

The compression stroke begins as the piston moves upward inside the cylinder, compressing the air/fuel mixture at the top. The degree of compression is controlled by how far down in the cylinder the piston reaches, how far up it travels and how much volume is left in the head above the cylinder. Degree of compression is called the compression ratio. Most modern cars have compression ratios between $8^1/_2$ to 1 and $9^1/_2$ to 1.

At the top of the stroke, the piston reverses its direction and starts downward. This is accompanied by ignition of the air/fuel mixture with a timed spark. The power stroke begins as the fuel charge burns. Burning makes the fuel get hot and expand, pushing down hard on top of the piston, as the burning, exploding charge of a gun drives the bullet out of the gun barrel. Likewise, the piston is driven down as far as it will go in the cylinder to complete the power stroke.

This leaves the cylinder full of spent gases that must be removed before the next four-stroke cycle can begin. The exhaust stroke accomplishes this. It begins when the exhaust valve opens and the piston starts moving upward in the cylinder. As it does, the gaseous products of combustion are driven out through the exhaust system. With the piston at the top, the exhaust valve closes and the cycle begins all over again with an intake stroke.

The up-and-down motion of the piston is converted to rotational motion by a crankshaft which turns beneath the piston. Its offset crankpin is joined to the piston by a connecting rod that follows the crankpin around with every revolution. The upper end of the connecting rod is attached in a swivel joint to a piston pin in the center of the piston, and so the connecting rod moves up and down with the piston.

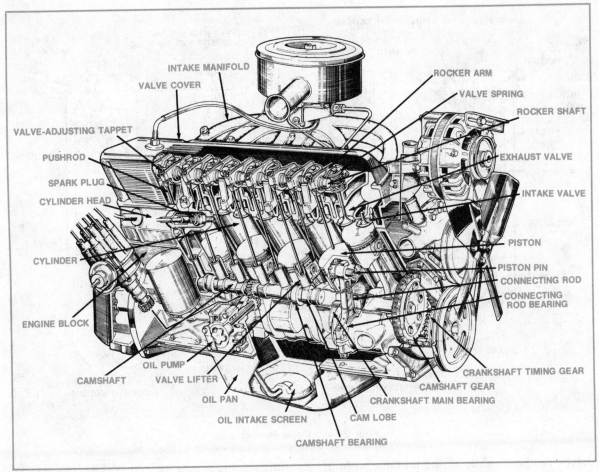

INTAKE MANIFOLD
VALVE COVER
ROCKER ARM
VALVE SPRING
ROCKER SHAFT
VALVE-ADJUSTING TAPPET
PUSHROD
SPARK PLUG
CYLINDER HEAD
EXHAUST VALVE
INTAKE VALVE
PISTON
PISTON PIN
CONNECTING ROD
CONNECTING ROD BEARING
CYLINDER
ENGINE BLOCK
OIL PUMP
CAMSHAFT
VALVE LIFTER
OIL PAN
CRANKSHAFT TIMING GEAR
CAMSHAFT GEAR
CRANKSHAFT MAIN BEARING
OIL INTAKE SCREEN
CAM LOBE
CAMSHAFT BEARING

Courtesy of The Chrysler Corp.

Inner Engine Parts

Only during the power stroke is the piston driving the crankshaft. During the other three strokes, the crankshaft must drive the piston. Thus a heavy flywheel is needed on the end of the crankshaft to store and release inertial power and to smooth out the drive-driven process inside the engine. The flywheel contains a large ring gear to mesh with the starting motor's pinion gear in getting the engine fired up.

Cylinders can be ganged together to produce more power, more smoothly than a single cylinder can. Multicylinder engines have their crankpins arranged to evenly divide the power strokes among the cylinders, making the engine run more smoothly.

The sequence in which the cylinders reach their power strokes is called the firing order. The common firing order for a four-cylinder engine is 1-3-4-2 or 1-2-4-3. For an eight-cylinder V type engine, a common firing order is 1-8-4-3-6-5-7-2. *V-type*, or V-8, refers to the compact way that eight cylinders are usually arranged: in two banks of four opposing cylinders in a "V" fashion. Some engines are V-6's. Cylinder banks may also be horizontally opposed, as those on air-cooled Volkswagens and Corvairs.

Valves

An automotive valve consists of a heat-resistant valve head and a slim, round valve stem. The valve head, located inside the combustion chamber, opens and closes on a valve seat. The seats lead to intake and exhaust passages called ports. Both valve head and valve seat are tapered so that, when closed, they form a gas-tight seal.

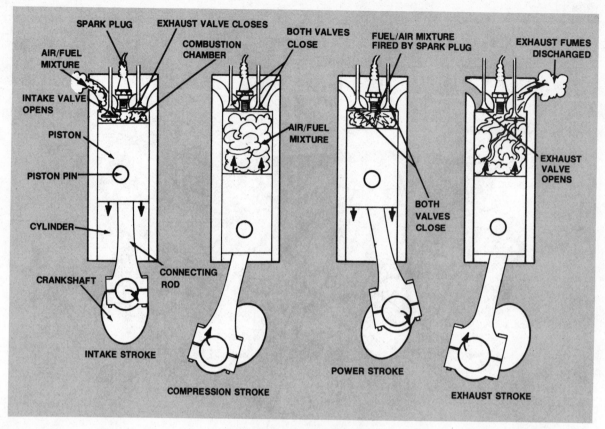

SPARK PLUG · EXHAUST VALVE CLOSES · BOTH VALVES CLOSE · FUEL/AIR MIXTURE FIRED BY SPARK PLUG · EXHAUST FUMES DISCHARGED · AIR/FUEL MIXTURE · COMBUSTION CHAMBER · INTAKE VALVE OPENS · AIR/FUEL MIXTURE · EXHAUST VALVE OPENS · PISTON · PISTON PIN · BOTH VALVES CLOSE · CYLINDER · CRANKSHAFT · CONNECTING ROD · INTAKE STROKE · COMPRESSION STROKE · POWER STROKE · EXHAUST STROKE

Four-Stroke Cycle Principle

Valves are held tightly closed on their seats by strong valve springs. To keep crankcase oil vapors and burned gases from getting past the valve stems, valve stem seals are provided to allow the stems to slide inside their guides, but to prevent anything from seeping out.

How Valves Work

The opening and closing of each valve must be timed according to the firing order of the engine. Instead of a crankshaft, the valves may use a simpler camshaft for their up-down movements. A little motion is sufficient to open and close them. The camshaft contains an intake cam and an exhaust cam for each cylinder.

Each cam is a rotating lobe shaped to control valve movement to best suit what is happening in the cylinder at the time. Valves are opened quickly to get their jobs done. The intake valve is opened even before the piston starts down on the intake stroke so it can be opened fully by the time the stroke gets underway. The intake valve does not close completely until after the piston has started upward on the compression stroke because the air/fuel mixture rushing into the cylinder possesses inertia that packs fuel into the cylinder if allowed to continue for a bit.

The exhaust valve stays open for an instant after the piston starts down on the intake stroke to utilize exhaust gas inertia in getting rid of burned gases. This also allows the exiting exhaust to help pull in the fresh air/fuel mixture and get the intake stroke off to a faster start. So, for a short time betwen the exhaust and intake strokes both valves are open. This is called *valve overlap* and is greater in high-performance engines than in street engines as faster engine speeds can use more valve overlap than slower ones. Therefore, the amount of overlap is a compromise between good fast speeds and smooth idling. Valve overlap also has an effect on engine emissions.

Cam Position

Engines are often identified by the location of their camshafts. The most desirable cam position for performance is above the cylinders. This puts the cam close to the valves and eliminates much valve linkage, called valve train. The more valve train the heavier, and the more the train tends to "float" (not follow cam action) at high engine speeds.

An engine with all intake and exhaust valves served by one overhead cam is called a single-overhead-cam (SOHC) engine. A pair of overhead cams can be used so that one cam serves only the intake valves and the other cam serves only the exhaust valves. This is called a double-overhead-cam (DOHC) engine. It is the ultimate in eliminating valve-train parts because each cam can be located exactly above the valves it serves.

Lower-cost engines use a single camshaft located beneath the cylinders that contains lobes for all valves. Riding on each lobe is a cam follower or *valve lifter* and fitted into a recess in each lifter is a *valve pushrod*. The pushrod extends lifter action up to above the cylinder. Since the cam lobe pushes upward from below and the valve must move downward to open, a *rocker arm* is used for direction change. One end of the rocker arm is pushed up by the pushrod, while its other end moves down, contacts the valve stem and pushes the valve open. As the cam lobe recedes beneath the lifter, the pushrod retracts and lets its end of the rocker arm down. The valve closes upward.

Valve timing is governed by how cam-lobe position is related to crankshaft position. Timing gears, chains or belts between crankshaft and camshaft are meshed to provide precise valve timing.

Valve Adjustment

Some clearance must be provided in the valve train parts to be sure that valves are fully closed after each opening. If a valve were held slightly open, combustion gases would push past it during each power stroke, lowering engine power and eventually burning off some metal from either the valve or its seat.

Any clearance in the valve train causes a clicking noise each time a valve opens and closes, so valve clearance is a compromise between best valve action and quiet running. Usually about 0.019 inch valve clearance (0.48mm) is provided when the engine is cold. This decreases as the engine warms and as valve-train parts expand. Adjustment is achieved through screws and locknuts on the rocker arms or cam followers. Valve adjusters are called *tappets*.

A number of engines use hydraulic valve lifters. These run without valve clearance but use oil pressure inside the lifter to take up play in the valve train while letting the valves close fully.

Piston Rings

The pistons face the combustion gases at one end and are open to the crankcase on the other. A seal between the two is provided by three or four piston rings. Piston rings are split circles of steel, some solid and some perforated. They match the diameter of the cylinder walls, with a small gap left between their split ends. Each piston ring fits into the ring grooves in its piston. Between the grooves are *lands*. Piston rings are designed to spring out so that they continually push on the cylinder wall to form a better seal between the two.

The top piston ring, called the compression ring, is solid and serves only as a seal. The middle ring (in sets of three) may contain a tiny groove around its lower edge and is called a scraper ring. Its purpose is to collect lubricating oil that has splashed onto the cylinder wall while the piston was at the top of a stroke and pull it down and out of the cylinder. If much oil is allowed to remain in the cylinder, it would burn along with the air/fuel mixture, producing a smoky exhaust and adding to carbon buildup inside the cylinder. The second ring also serves as a back-up compression ring.

The third and sometimes a fourth piston ring is an oil ring. Oil rings are perforated to let oil flow through from holes behind their grooves into the

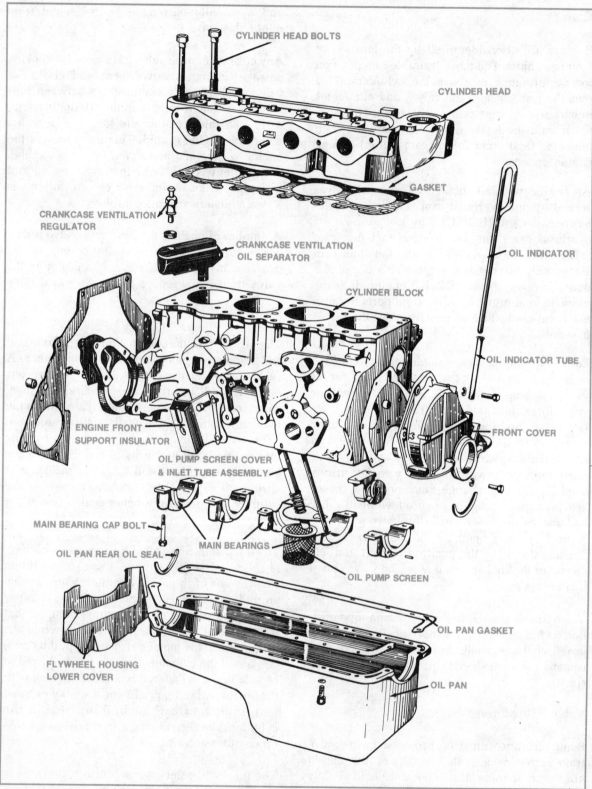

CYLINDER HEAD BOLTS

CYLINDER HEAD

GASKET

CRANKCASE VENTILATION
REGULATOR

CRANKCASE VENTILATION
OIL SEPARATOR

OIL INDICATOR

CYLINDER BLOCK

OIL INDICATOR TUBE

ENGINE FRONT
SUPPORT INSULATOR

FRONT COVER

OIL PUMP SCREEN COVER
& INLET TUBE ASSEMBLY

MAIN BEARING CAP BOLT

MAIN BEARINGS

OIL PAN REAR OIL SEAL

OIL PUMP SCREEN

OIL PAN GASKET

FLYWHEEL HOUSING
LOWER COVER

OIL PAN

Courtesy of Ford Customer Service Division

Engine Block Assembly

piston. This spreads a thin film of oil over the cylinder wall to reduce friction.

Piston rings can become lodged in their grooves by sludge, carbon and varnish deposits produced by the burning gases and oil. They can also wear out of full contact with the cylinder wall, allowing oil and exhaust gases to slip past them.

Engine Block

A description of the other parts in a typical piston engine will help in understanding how one works. The block is the largest part of the engine. It contains the cylinders and most other parts are fastened to it. Engine blocks are usually made of cast iron. They contain the water jacket (or fins) for cooling.

Cylinder Head

The cylinder head holds the valves in an overhead-valve engine. In older side-valve or L-head engines, the block contains the valves. The cylinder head bolts onto the block with a head gasket between them for a good seal. The cylinder head is usually made of the same material as the block. Removal of the cylinder head exposes the piston tops, cylinders, and combustion chambers.

Connecting Rod Bearings

Because tremendous forces are exerted on the piston and connecting rod during the power stroke, a sizable crankpin journal is needed, one that can wear and be replaced without replacing the whole crankshaft or connecting rods. Bearing inserts serve the purpose. Made of thin bearing material, they come in two pieces that fit together like the halves of an eggshell. Placed over the crankpin, the shell halves meet to fully surround the crank journal. The lower end of the connecting rod bolts snugly around the bearing inserts to hold them in place. They often contain grooves or holes for oil flow to the crankpin and always have a slight clearance to allow for an oil film and to prevent binding.

Crankshaft

The crankshaft, made of forged steel, contains all the crankpins for the cylinders, plus counter-weights to help balance the reciprocating motion of the pistons and connecting rods. At each end, and often in between cylinders, the crankshaft revolves in bearings of its own. These are called main bearings and run in bearing inserts larger than those the connecting rods have. The more main bearings there are, the better. The crankshaft contains internal oil passages that distribute lubricating oil under pressure to all main and crankpin bearings. At each end of the crankshaft, oil seals surround the end bearing journal to keep oil inside the crankcase. An oil pan bolts to the bottom of the crankcase to retain engine oil and seal off outside dirt. In its bottom is a threaded plug to allow the draining of old engine oil.

Intake and Exhaust Manifolds

To get an air/fuel mixture to each cylinder when necessary, an intake manifold is used. The carburetor fastens to one end of it. Individual intake ducts lead to the intake ports of each cylinder. The intake manifold is a part of the fuel system.

To conduct exhaust gases away from the engine, an exhaust manifold is used. It collects burned gases at the individual shared exhaust ports of cylinders and leads to a single connection with the exhaust pipe. The exhaust manifold is part of the exhaust system.

Oil Pump

Inside the crankcase and at the bottom of the oil pan is an oil pump. It sucks in oil, runs it thorough a porous paper filter to remove debris, then pushes it out through an oil gallery to all the engine parts that need pressurized lubrication.

Motor Mounts

Engine vibrations would be annoying if passed on to the driver, so the engine is mounted in rubber. Most engines have a three-point mounting. Two mounts are in the front and a single one is used at the transmission in the rear.

Overhaul vs. Rebuilding

An overhaul usually consists of removal of the cylinder heads, refacing of valves and seats, removal of the oil pan and removal of piston-connecting rod units from the cylinders. Ridges left at the cylinder tops where piston rings did not wear them are shaved off. Cylinder walls are honed to remove glaze. If left, it would keep the new piston rings from seating. Carbon is removed and all parts cleaned. The engine is reassembled with new piston rings, new connecting rod bearing inserts, new gaskets and any other new parts that are found necessary.

A rebuilt engine gets completely disassembled. Its cylinders are rebored and its crankshaft is reground for new oversize pistons and new undersized bearing inserts. Every part that might wear is either refitted like new or replaced with a new or rebuilt one. A rebuilt engine is the next thing to a new one and may be expected to last about half as long as the new engine did.

Wankel Engines

In production since 1964, the Wankel is a rotary-type internal-combustion engine. The Wankel has no pistons, no cylinders, no valves and few moving parts.

The Wankel, similar to the piston engine, uses a four-phase cycle, though it has no strokes. Its combustion chamber is shaped like a bulbous figure-eight. A triangular-shaped rotor turns inside the combustion chamber at one-third of shaft speed through an internal gear in the center of the rotor. This gear feeds power out through an output shaft.

As the rotor revolves inside its chamber, its three sides alternately take in the air/fuel mixture, compress it, explode it (with a pair of spark plugs) and exhaust the spent gases. Three power impulses come with each revolution of the rotor.

Tips of the rotor alternately exposing and closing off intake and exhaust ports in the side of the chamber serve as intake and exhaust valves without the need for valves or valve train. Most

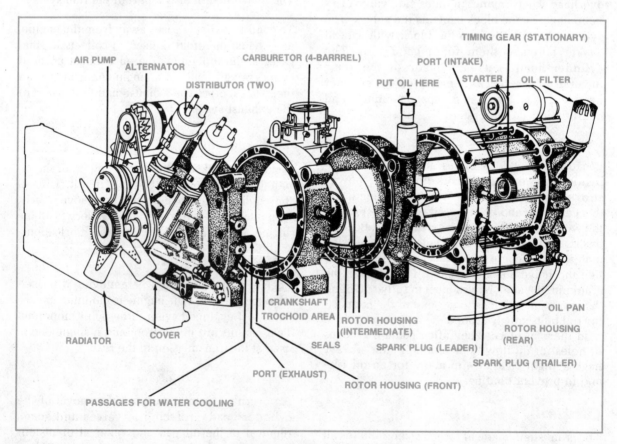

Multirotor Engine & Its Parts

Wankels are liquid-cooled and use carburetors to supply the air/fuel mixture to the chamber.

To get the desired power from a rotary engine, rotors can be ganged together like the cylinders in a piston engine. In multirotor engines, each rotor fires at a different time than the others to provide a smoother flow of power impulses. Gears and bearings in the shaft and rotor are lubricated from an oil pump beneath the engine. A fan, water pump, flywheel, starter, alternator and ignition system all are incorporated in practically the same way as those of a piston engine.

Diesel Engine

A diesel engine is a piston engine that uses no ignition system or carburetor. In place of a carburetor, the diesel has a fuel-injection system. The heat of a 12-to-1 compression ratio ignites the fuel. A diesel's fuel is diesel oil, a nonvolatile, slightly amber, petroleum product very similar to lamp oil, fuel oil and kerosene.

Diesel pollutants are low. Because of the greater heat content of diesel fuel over gasoline and its lower cost, a diesel engine is far more economical to run. Because it is built stronger, the diesel will run longer and with less maintenance than a gasoline engine. Its drawbacks are its weight (the diesel weighs much more than an equal-powered gasoline engine) its low torque and roughness. A diesel engine costs a great deal more than a gasoline engine, too.

Most diesel engines use the four-stroke cycle. Compression ratios reach as high as 22 to 1. Fuel injectors fit in openings to the combustion chambers. At the peak of the compression stroke, a measured amount of fuel is injected into the top from a fuel pump fed to its injector. At that time the air compressed inside the combustion chamber is hot enough to ignite the spray of fuel and so the power stroke begins. The other three strokes are the same as in a gasoline engine.

Other Engine Types

A number of other systems for automotive propulsion are being considered for automobiles. These are sought to reduce automotive pollution as well as to conserve the world's dwindling petroleum reserves.

One, the stratified-charge engine, is merely an improvement in the gasoline piston engine that more completely burns its fuel. A rich, easy-burning mixture of air and fuel is ignited to burn the rest of the charge, a very lean mixture.

Electric cars are not new. Nevertheless, the increasing need for them as short-range commuter vehicles is bringing about much research and development. The weak link, so far, has been the battery. Its size, weight and cost have proved prohibitive.

Steam power is another avenue of research. A steam engine is an external-combustion piston engine (or turbine). There is nothing new about steam power except the attempts to make it as light in weight, quick-warming and efficient as a gasoline engine of equal power. Progress is slow but tireless.

EXHAUST SYSTEMS

The auto exhaust system does two jobs: it conducts burned gases safely from the engine to the rear of the car and it quiets the explosive noises they make as they leave the engine. In front-engine cars the system is long and snake-like. In mid- and rear-engine cars, the exhaust system can be brief and direct. It consists of an exhaust manifold, exhaust pipe, muffler and tailpipe. Some cars include a resonator that looks like a miniature muffler.

Exhaust system parts join by flanges and gaskets or with a smaller pipe slipped into a larger one with both clamped tightly together. All parts from the muffler rearward are mounted in rubber hangers to keep vibrations from being transferred to the car body.

Exhaust Manifold

As the products of combustion leave the engine's exhaust ports, they enter a collector called the exhaust manifold. This accepts exhaust gas from individual cylinders and brings it to a single outlet. The manifold fastens to the cylinder head or engine block with flanges fitted over protruding studs. Burnproof metal-covered asbestos gaskets fit between the parts to prevent exhaust leaks.

V-type engines have two exhaust manifolds, one for each bank of cylinders. In-line engines have just one. Two manifolds are sometimes connected underneath the engine by a crossover pipe.

Heat-Riser Valve

Inside the exhaust manifold is a heat-riser valve. Its purpose is to restrict the exhaust passages while the engine is cold and force some of the hot exhaust to pass through the engine's intake manifold. There the hot gas helps to vaporize cold fuel and quickly get the engine running well.

Mufflers

An exhaust pipe conducts exhaust to the inlet end of the muffler. The muffler evens out explosive pulsations in the exhaust it receives and sends the gases out in a smooth, quiet flow without restricting them too much.

Because of their under-car location and because exhaust contains water vapor, mufflers are subject to considerable corrosion. Short trips that do not heat up the muffler leave water vapor in it to condense and react with other exhaust products to form acids. These quickly attack the metal from inside.

Single-Exhaust System

Most cars are fitted from the factory with single-exhaust systems including one exhaust pipe, one muffler and one tailpipe. Single-exhaust is the lowest-cost way of handling exhaust gases.

Dual-Exhaust System

A few big-engined cars come equipped with two separate exhaust systems called dual exhausts. The purpose of duals is quietness with a minimum of exhaust restriction, even at high speed when the largest volume of exhaust gases is flowing. Such a system has two manifolds, two exhaust pipes, two mufflers and two tailpipes.

The drawback of dual exhausts, beside higher initial cost, is higher maintenance cost.

Resonator

The purpose of the resonator is to provide one more chamber where the pulsating exhaust gases can be smoothed out, improving the sound of what comes out the tailpipe.

Carbon Monoxide

One of the dangers of driving a car is being overcome by tasteless, odorless, colorless carbon monoxide gas in the exhaust. You may not even know it is there, but it can put you to sleep or even kill you. Carbon monoxide can seep into the car through an open trunk lid or rusted-out spots in the body. Or it can enter through an open station wagon tailgate. Rust holes in exhaust system parts increase the chances of carbon monoxide poisoning. That is why maintaining a sound exhaust system is important.

If you notice any of the following signs, in ascending order of seriousness, stop the car, kill the engine, and open the windows: headache or throbbing head, nausea, impaired heartbeat, confusion, impaired vision, drowsiness or unconsciousness. (The next step is death.)

Once the symptoms disappear, drive to a shop with all the car windows open and get the exhaust system checked. If your symptoms do not disappear quickly, see a doctor right away. Breathing carbon monoxide for a very long can bring permanent injury to body and brain.

If you notice a rattling or hissing noise coming from underneath the car, it calls for a check of the exhaust system. Reach under and hit parts of the system with your fist to try to produce rattles. See what part is loose or out of position enough to cause the rattling noise.

AIR System

One commonly used emissions-control system is partially tied into the exhaust system. That is the air-injection reaction system (AIR). A belt-driven air pump on the engine sends a flow of fresh air through an air manifold next to the exhaust manifold. Air outlet tubes reach into each exhaust port behind each of the exhaust valves. Unburned gases left after incomplete combustion are afterburned by the added air. Carbon monoxide and other polluting emissions are thereby reduced.

Afterburning makes the exhaust system run hotter than normal. However, AIR is one of the better emissions-control systems because, except for a small power drain of the air pump, it has no effect on engine performance or economy.

FUEL SYSTEM

The automotive fuel system includes an air system as well as a fuel system, because air must be blended with fuel before it can burn and release heat to make the engine run.

The automotive fuel system begins where gasoline enters the filler opening of the gas tank. As needed, fuel is drawn from the tank through a fuel line by a fuel pump. It passes through the pump, is filtered and delivered to the carburetor float bowl, where it is stored briefly until needed

by the engine. Fuel flows through carburetor passages and is mixed with air inside the carburetor before it enters the intake manifold and flows to the engine cylinders.

This, of course, is oversimplified. Many refinements are necessary for smooth, economical running on reduced emissions.

Intake Manifold

The intake manifold is a tubed chamber located on the side of an in-line engine or between the cylinder banks of a V-type engine. Its purpose is to feed an air/fuel mixture to each cylinder. With the engine taking in fuel at one end and the carburetor blocking off full flow at its other end, the manifold runs under a vacuum much of the time. The vacuum ranges from almost zero at full throttle operation to some 25 inches or more while slowing down with a closed throttle. The intake manifold also handles the job of heating cold, hard-to-vaporize air/fuel mixtures immediately after a cold start. It accepts hot exhaust gases or engine coolant and uses them to improve vaporization.

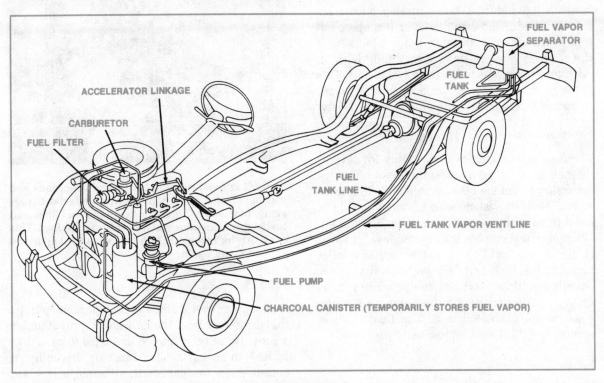

Fuel System

Leaks into the intake manifold let excess air into the air/fuel mix, making the air/fuel mixture to the engine lean and reducing engine smoothness and performance.

Carburetor

Bolted to the intake manifold is the carburetor. Its function is to mix the right amount of vaporized fuel with air entering the engine. To ensure the correct mixture under most engine operating conditions, five different systems are incorporated: float system, main metering system, power-enrichment system, accelerator-pump system, idle and choke system.

Carburetors are denoted by how many *venturis* or barrels they contain. A venturi is a wasp-waisted tube that speeds up air flow to create a slight vacuum. Carburetors come in single-barrel, two-barrel, and four-barrel. Four-and six-cylinder engines often use single-barrel carburetors. V-8's use two- and four-barrel ones. The bigger the engine the more barrels are needed for good breathing.

Each barrel has a throttle plate (a butterfly) beneath its venturi. When you step on the accelerator pedal, the throttle butterflies open, letting more air rush through the venturi. As it does, more fuel is drawn in along with it. Air/fuel proportions range from 11:1 to 15:1. This is the good-running range for an engine. A leaner or richer mixture makes the engine run poorly.

Float System

The float system creates a depository for several ounces of fuel at a constant level. This is necessary to get the other systems off to a level start. The float system works somewhat like a toilet flush tank. Gasoline comes in, lifts a float. When the float reaches the desired level, a valve closes to stop fuel flow. In action, unlike a toilet tank, the fuel level and flow stays steady, inflow equaling outflow. Accurate fuel level is vital to an efficient carburetor because the other systems are calibrated to it. The float bowl is vented to hold it near atmospheric pressure.

Carburetor Icing

Through no fault of the carburetor, ice can form

inside the venturis and restrict them to the point where the engine will not idle. The ice can also prevent the throttle plates from closing to the idling position. It normally occurs on a cold, but not necessarily freezing, morning when the air is quite damp. Air rushing through the cold venturis after start-up acts like an expanding refrigerant. Moisture collects and freezes. Gasoline is formulated to be nonicing, but sometimes icing still occurs. The best cure is to switch the engine off for a minute or two so that the ice will melt.

Vapor Lock

Another carburetor condition that can stall the engine is vapor lock: boiling of fuel in the carburetor float bowl and fuel lines. This happens when gasoline vaporizes before it is supposed to and the float bowl receives fuel vapor rather than liquid fuel. Sometimes a vapor-locked engine cannot be started until it cools off.

If your car quits running because of vapor lock and you have some rags, paper towels or facial tissues along, plus access to water, wrap the fuel lines and fuel pump, then pour water over the wrappings. This cools off the fuel enough to condense the vapor and get you going again.

Fuel Pump

Automotive fuel pumps are diaphragm pumps that draw fuel from the tank and supply it under a pressure of between $3\frac{1}{2}$ and 6 psi (0.25 to 0.42 kg/cm^2) to the carburetor. Most are driven by an eccentric on the camshaft, although a few are electric and should last the life of the engine. If the original fails, a new or rebuilt unit is installed.

Fuel Filters

To keep the inside of the carburetor free of sediment, one or more fuel filters are used. There may be a large spin-off cartridge fuel filter about half the size of a drinking glass used as part of the fuel pump. It is replaceable, like an oil-filter cartridge. Often an in-line fuel filter is used in the fuel line to the carburetor or mounted in side the carburetor's fuel inlet. It is a final filter designed to trap whatever might get through the main filter. Sometimes only one filter is used. Car maker, specify change intervals for fuel filters. Replacement is an easy do-it-yourself job.

Fuel Lines

Fuel lines, about ¼ inch in diameter inside, bring fuel from the tank to the fuel pump and from there to the carburetor. If they become pinched, the fuel supply to the engine may be restricted to the point where it will not pull a load. If fuel lines leak, your precious fuel may seep away, or else the fuel pump will draw in air bubbles with the fuel. Fuel line routing should avoid hot engine parts, such as the exhaust manifold, in the interests of preventing vapor lock.

Fuel Tank

The fuel tank is located in some unused space underneath the car or elsewhere. It is filled through a large ½-inch (40mm) or larger filler pipe beginning with a flange outside the car body. A fuel pickup inside the tank takes fuel off the low point of the tank and feeds it to the fuel line. The tank holds the fuel gauge sending unit. Baffles keep gasoline from sloshing excessively inside the tank.

Fuel tanks in pre-1970 cars (1970 in California) incorporate vents to let air in the top of the tank as fuel is used. Newer cars must provide for entrapment of evaporative fuel emissions, and so tank venting has been done away with. Instead, tank fumes are piped to a vapor separator, then to a canister of charcoal in the engine compartment where they are stored until the engine starts, when they are drawn in and burned.

Air Cleaners

Since an engine breathes 10,000 times as much air as it does gasoline, an air cleaner is vital to engine life. It removes particles of dust that might pollute engine oil or wear away bearing surfaces were they allowed into the engine. Chiefly, two types are used: dry paper-element and oil-wet plastic foam. The paper-element type is simple to replace when dirty. But it has more trouble handling oil-bearing crankcase vapors. That is why the polurethane fram filter is sometimes used. It accepts oil vapors without trouble, but is more trouble to clean.

Actually the air filtering elements are only part of the air cleaner. Another part serves as a heated-air system. A bimetallic valve moves a damper to let the air cleaner draw in warm air from the exhaust manifold when the engine is cold. When it warms, the damper starts drawing air from the engine compartment. A warmed-air system helps an engine to run on leaner, less polluting air/fuel mixture.

Gasoline

Buy the lowest grade of fuel your engine will burn without knocking. The knocking phenomenon, detected as a sharp metallic noise, occurs when the air/fuel mixture burns unevenly inside the engine. Besides causing a loss in power and fuel economy, knocking can damage the engine.

Figuring Gas Mileage

You can see how good your car is at squeezing the miles out of its gasoline through a little calculation. To do this, first fill the gas tank brim-full. Record only the mileage reading on the odometer. The next time you need gas, fill the tank brim full again. Record the number of gallons and tenths purchased, plus the odometer reading. Subtract the smaller odometer reading from the larger one to find out how far the fuel took you. Lastly, divide this miles figure by the number of gallons used. That is your car's miles per gallon.

Since one filling is too short a period to get a truly accurate picture of fuel mileage, your records can be continued over several fillings and the overall mileage figured by totaling the number of gallons purchased and dividing into the total miles traveled. Note that the first fill-up gallonage does not count. It is merely a starting point for your test.

Fuel Injection

The fuel-injection system is an automotive innovation usually associated with highly sophisticated racing engines. But this method of providing the proper mixture of air and fuel to the engine is available on an increasing number of standard models. It figures to play an increasing role in the auto industry's quest for cleaner-burning engines.

LP-Gas Setups

Gaining in popularity is the LP-gas conversion. Instead of running on gasoline, the engine is equipped to run on gaseous fuel, either liquefied petroleum gas (propane or LPG) or liquefied natural gas (LNG). These gases are stored as liquids under pressure so they cannot revert to gases before reaching special carburetors. A heavy pressure-type tank is fitted in the car trunk. A heat-exchanger is connected into the car's cooling system to warm the liquid fuel, helping it to vaporize. Usually a switch on the dash lets you burn either gas or gasoline. The octane rating of propane is 110-plus.

Gas-burning vehicles are practically pollution-free. At least one state, California, encourages them by allowing the motorist a fuel tax refund if his car is not equipped for gasoline burning, also.

Increase Your Mileage

Gadgets that are supposed to add to gasoline mileage have been marketed almost as long as automobiles have and many people are taken in by them every year. The truth is that not one has proved worthwhile. Fair tests always show them up.

The best way to increase your fuel mileage is to keep the engine well maintained and to follow good driving practices.

LUBRICATION SYSTEM

Friction is a constant factor in the moving parts of an engine. High-strength films of lubricating oil pressure-fed to and splashed onto these moving parts minimize the destructive effects of the metal-to-metal contact. Without oil to lubricate its moving parts, an engine would not run for more than a few minutes before locking up. With oil, it will run for 60,000 miles or more, needing only normal maintenance.

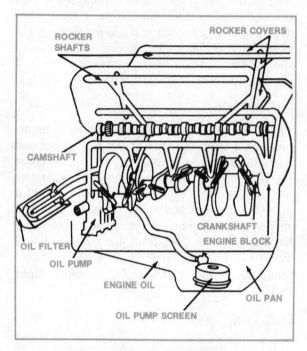

Engine Lubrication System

If lubricating the engine parts were all the engine oil had to do, it would seldom need changing. But, besides lubricating, oil helps to seal piston rings and to cool the engine. The oil pan beneath the engine serves as both a reservoir for oil and a broad surface for dissipating heat. Moreover, engine oil must keep the engine clean. It carries particles of carbon and dirt away and traps them in an oil filter. Oil also must hold in suspension such harmful waste products as water and acids.

As you drive, sooner or later the oil becomes saturated with contaminants and sludge begins to form. Sludge is a combination of oil, water, acid, carbon and dirt that builds up on the cooler surfaces inside the engine. Sludge also plugs up oil filters and the oil strainer screen. It even can seal off small lubricant passages, preventing full lubrication of the engine, which can have serious results.

So, to prevent damage to the engine, it is vital to follow the car manufacturer's recommendations on oil and oil-filter changes. Most recommendations specify a maximum interval for oil changes, usually in both months and miles. Often, it is 6000 miles or 4 months, whichever comes first. More frequent oil changes are recommended if the type of driving you do is hard on oil. Short trips, such as to the commuter station, store and school, do not permit the engine to heat enough to boil off oil pollutants. More frequent oil changes are called for, too, if you drive much on dusty roads. Driving at high speeds, with heavy loads or with lots of accessories going is hard use, also. The normal hard-use oil change is twice as often as normal: every 3000 miles or two months, whichever comes first. Usually the oil filter is changed every time the oil is.

Oil Circulation

The oil circulates inside the engine in a definite pattern. From the oil pan it is sucked up by a gear-type oil pump past a fine pickup screen on the end of the suction tube. The screen strains out sludge and large particles.

The oil then travels around with the teeth of the twin oil-pump gears and is squeezed out of the pump as the teeth mesh. Oil pump pressure reaches about 60 psi (4.2 kg/cm^2) with the oil warmed to 225° to 300° F. (107° to 149° C.) operating temperature.

Then the oil is routed through its second-stage filtration, the oil filter. The oil filter contains several square feet of folded-up porous filter paper that lets oil pass, but holds back grit, soot and unburnt residues from the combustion process.

However, when the filter paper becomes clogged with contaminants, not much oil can pass through it. Then a relief valve opens and lets unfiltered oil circulate to the engine. That is

why the oil filter cartridge should be replaced as often as specified by the car maker.

From the oil filter, oil flows through the engine's internal oil galleries to the parts that receive pressurized lubrication. These include the crankshaft bearings, connecting rod bearings (through holes inside the crankshaft), camshaft bearings and valve train.

Other engine parts are lubricated by splashing of oil inside the crankcase. The pistons, cylinder walls and parts of the valve train are receivers of splashed oil. Oil falls back into the oil pan where it is cooled and returned to circulation.

Lubrication system problems are indicated by low oil pressure, squeaks and knocks in the engine and some cases of overheating. Also the oil warning light coming on, and leaking oil are signs of trouble.

The Oil You Use

Oil comes in cans, most often quart-sized. The information needed in selecting an engine oil appears on the can. First to look at are the service standards, designated by the letters SC, SD, SE.

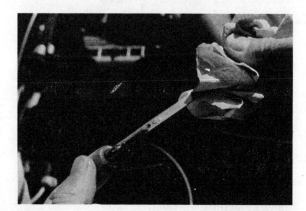

Even though dirty, oil on this dipstick still has lubrication qualities. But it would take laboratory tests to tell whether the oil's additives remain active. For this reason, oil should be changed by the odometer reading, not by appearance.

SC. This service oil was specified for use in engines up to 1967 models. It provides for control of high- and low-temperature deposits, wear, rust and corrosion.

SD. This service oil was specified for use in engines through 1970 and certain 1971 models (see the owner's manual). It provides greater amounts of protection than SC oil does.

SE. This service oil is specified for use in engines of 1972 and later models (and some 1971 models). It provides more protection against oxidation, more of all the other protections than SC and SD oils.

SE oil may be used when one of the lower classifications is called for. In fact, it is recommended for all cars, old and new. Because some oil manufacturers retain the old ML, MM, and MS oil-service designations, you may find both on the can.

Car manufacturers recommend the use of high-detergent oil for cleanliness. This designation appears as an *HD* on the can. It also stands for heavy duty. An old engine that has been run a long time on nondetergent (cheap) oil without the HD label may hold sludge buildups inside that could be loosened by switching to an HD oil. Once loose, globs of sludge can lodge in oil tubes resulting in a slow strangulation for oil. Therefore, such an engine probably should run out its life on nondetergent oils.

Oil Weight

The tops of the oil can usually contain a designation such as SAE 30W. This tells something about the viscosity or flowability of the oil inside. (Molasses has a high viscosity, water a low one.) *SAE* stands for Society of Automotive Engineers and shows that the viscosity of the oil conforms to the Society's standards. Oil viscosity and the expected temperatures in your area should correspond. A *W* after the number means that the oil is rated on its low-temperature viscosity. No *W* means that the oil is rated on its high-temperature viscosity.

Consult and follow the owner's manual as to what viscosity of oil to use each season. Multigrade oils can span several different viscosities. These are such as 5W-20, 10W-30, 10W-40, and 20W-40. A 5W-20 oil flows as well when cold as a 5W oil, yet retains the body of a 20-weight oil when hot. The use of a multigrade oil allows driving in temperature extremes. It combines the starting ability of a thin oil with the hot-lubricating ability of a heavier oil. It also costs more than single-viscosity oil.

SUSPENSION SYSTEM

The automotive suspension system has practically everything to do with car handling and ride. It has undergone more development than most other parts of the car so that, today, some four-door sedans handle as well as high-performance sports cars used to.

Every car has two suspension systems: a front one and a rear one, and often they are very different from each other. Front suspension carries the weight of the forward half of the car. In addition, it lets the front wheels pivot right and left for steering. Rear suspension carries the weight of the rear half of the car. Either front or rear wheels must let engine power through to the wheels.

Springs

Springs are elastic devices that hold the car up, yet yield to pressures, and return to their original position after the pressure is gone. Three kinds of springs are used on cars: leaf springs, coil springs and torsion bars.

Leaf springs come in single-and multi leaf construction, although most are multi-leaf because they support more weight. A spring leaf that extends the full length of the spring is called the main leaf. Leaf springs are most often used for rear suspensions. Modern ones are of the semi-elliptical design.

Coil springs are used in most front suspensions and in some rear suspensions. They are simply coiled-up torsion bars, in which deformation takes the form of twisting the bar.

Torsion bars are arranged fore-and-aft on the car. One end attaches to the suspension, and twists with deflection in it. The other end is anchored to the frame of the car and not permitted to turn. As the suspension swings, the bar winds and unwinds.

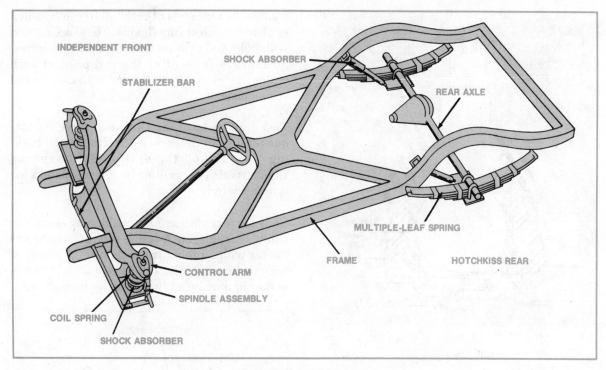

The Suspension System

Independent Front Suspension

Most cars and many light trucks built in recent times use what is called independent front suspension (IFS) systems. A few of the best-handling cars use independent rear suspension too. With IFS each wheel is free to move up and down without affecting the other wheel. No solid axle connects the pairs of wheels.

Ball-Joint IFS

Most-used is the ball-joint independent front suspension. It has replaced the older kingpin types since cars of the mid-50s. Two large A-frames or wishbones, also called control arms, hold the wheel's spindle assembly at the top and bottom so that it can move up and down and steer.

If the two A-frames were of equal length, wheel tread would move in and out with up-and-down suspension motion. This would strain the suspension parts and scrub the tires sidewise on the pavement. So, instead, the upper control arm is made shorter than the lower one. The long arc of the lower arm along with the short arc of the

upper arm causes the wheel to tilt out at the bottom as it moves upward. This maintains equal tread width in *jounce* (the engineering term for wheel moves up) and *rebound* (wheel moves down).

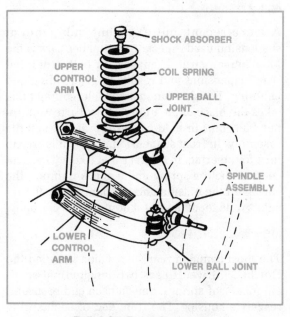

Ball-Joint Front Suspension

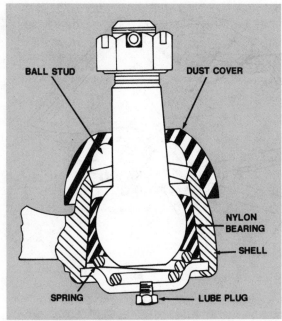

Courtesy of American Motors Corp.

Ball Joint

Rubbery ball joints in the upper and lower control arms hold the top and bottom of the spindle assembly. They cushion it, yet let it turn left and right and move up and down with the control arms. The spindle assembly is the axle, plus steering arm and ball joints.

MacPherson Strut

A more recent, but excellent independent suspension used especially in smaller cars is the MacPherson strut. It appears in both front and rear suspensions and results in good riding and handling. The strut, an inclined telescoping tube, takes the place of the upper control arm and upper ball joint in holding the top of the spindle assembly. In front suspension, the strut is free to turn for steering. In the rear it is fixed. The strut contains both a spring and a shock-damper, the spring on the outside and the damper on the inside. At its top, the strut mounts to the car body.

Hotchkiss Drive

The most common rear suspension is called the Hotchkiss drive. It uses two longitudinal semi-elliptical leaf springs, one on each end of a solid rear-axle housing. The front end of each spring mounts, through an eye and a bolt, to the car

frame. The rear ends of each are free to lengthen or shorten with spring flexing. These are carried with bolts and eyes on movable spring shackles. Somewhere forward of the mid-point of each spring, the rear axle is attached with U-bolts and spring pads.

Two drawbacks of the Hotchkiss drive are torque reaction during heavy acceleration and braking "winds up" the spring. Softly-sprung Hotchkiss-drive cars often have fore-aft links for torque control.

Coils for rear springs axle positioning are not as handy. For this, an A-frame may be attached to the car with a rubber connection at the center of the axle housing. The axle is kept at right angles to the car axis by adding a pair of fore-aft links.

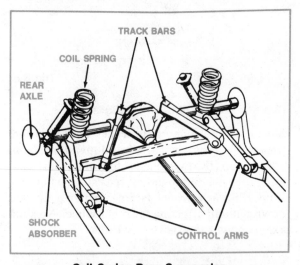

Coil-Spring Rear Suspension

Shock Absorbers

The ideal automotive spring would react to a jounce or rebound rapidly, then return *slowly* to its original position. Soft springs that give a smooth ride do not do this. They react too far then return past their original position, and then back again like a pendulum. An untamed auto spring gives a ride like a boat heading into waves. The bouncing does not stop until the car stops. Also, the unchecked wheels bounce up and down along the pavement. Since wheels off the road make for unsafe handling, traction and braking, this cannot be permitted.

To tame down the raw spring action, matched shock absorbers are positioned at the wheels. Most shock absorbers are of the direct-acting telescoping type, because they are double-acting, they restrict spring motion in both directions, jounce and rebound. In most, the downstroke is made with more resistance than the up-stroke. This allows the car to pass over bumps without transmitting the shock to the car body, but dampens the action as the wheel recovers and rebounds. Tight control on rebound also helps to keep the wheels from slamming down into chuckholes.

To prevent squeaks, shocks are attached to the car by rubber mounts. One end of the shock mounts to the car body or a heavy cross-member. The other fastens to the axle, or a control arm.

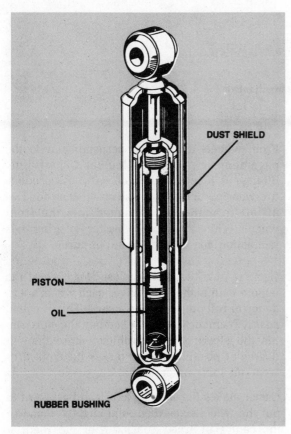

Shock Absorber Cross-Section

DUST SHIELD

PISTON

OIL

RUBBER BUSHING

A look inside a shock absorber shows how its function is accomplished. A piston attached to the car rides inside a cylinder filled with hydraulic fluid. A cylinder is attached to the suspension, so that up-and-down movement of the wheel causes a parallel action inside the shock. As the suspension moves up, the piston is forced down, forcing shock fluid through small valves or holes in the piston. These offer resistance to fluid passage, to create the desired effect.

Shock absorbers gradually lose their effectiveness as internal parts wear, and can cause problems ranging from a bouncy or rough ride to tires that wear excessively and show signs of cupping.

Stabilizer Bars

To minimize body roll during turns and over road irregularities, IFS cars often have stabilizer bars as integral suspension parts. The stabilizer bar (sway bar, or anti-roll bar) is a spring steel rod mounted in rubber across the front end of the car between the right and left IFS parts. Arms at each end connect it in rubber to the control arms. Control-arm motion that affects both sides equally simply rotates the stabilizer bar in its rubber mounts. But when one arm lifts while the other is stationary or moving down, the bar resists. The resistance helps to keep the car level on turns.

Car Structure

A car body may travel over rough roads during its lifetime yet it must not become twisted, bent or broken. Engine, doors, seats and suspension all need sturdy attachments. To provide this, for many years cars have been built on the body-frame design. Heavy box or channel steel frame members run most of the car's length. Cross-members are welded between the frame rails. Engine and body mount to them separately in rubber.

More recently the *unit body* car has caught on, especially for building compacts and subcompacts. In it, the car body is joined into one solid piece and reinforced at heavy-load points, such as engine and suspension attachments. It has no frame. Even the roof is an important structural part.

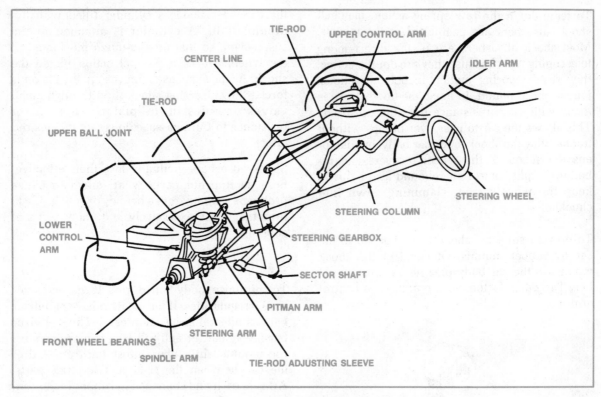

The Steering Mechanism

Increasing attention to occupant safety is creating car bodies that enclose the passengers inside a rigid box. Up front of the box is a *controlled collapse* front end that brings the car to a gradual stop in a head-on collision, keeping the passenger compartment intact.

Steering

Wagon steering in which the rigid front axle was pivoted at its center to turn worked well only with horses pulling. It is unworkable for automobiles. The Ackerman system of steering was adopted for cars and it has survived the test of time. With it, the two front wheels steer independently of each other, but they are turned in unison by connecting them with linkage. Thus, when one wheel is steered to the right, the other steers right, also.

The front wheel on the inside of a turn follows a shorter arc. To make it steer more sharply, the steering arms on each spindle slant toward the center of the rear axle. Called toe-out-on-turns this prevents tire resistance when turning.

Alignment Angles

Front wheels are not set perpendicular to the pavement or parallel to the car's centerline. Strange as it seems, squareness would produce tire-wearing and unsure steering. Instead, five different angles are designed into the front wheels. They are camber, caster, steering axis inclination, toe-in, and toe-out-on-turns.

Camber puts the wheels closer together at the bottom than at the top. It gives each wheel a tendency to roll outward, like a cone. This is called positive camber. The more camber, the more stable the steering. One problem: more than $1/2$ degree of positive camber makes the front tires wear on their outer edges.

Caster makes the steering axis lean backward to put the wheel's steering point slightly ahead of the center of tread contact with the road. It makes front wheels tend to follow along like those on a grocery cart. This is called positive caster. Some cars use negative caster with the steering point behind the center of tread contact.

This eases steering and minimizes road shock through the steering system.

Steering axis inclination slopes the car's steering axis out at the bottom to center it under where the tire centerlines meet the road. It makes the tires steer around a point rather than scrubbing around an arc each time you turn.

Toe-in is a necessary evil. The rapid tire-wearing alignment angle, some toe-in is necessary so that the wheels rest slightly "pigeon-toed" to offset their tendency to toe out when the car is traveling at road speed. The goal is to achieve *zero running toe*. Toe-in also gives a positive tendency to the wheels, keeping them from "hunting" between toed-in and toed-out.

Averages in wheel alignment mean little. Each car's wheels should be set to the car maker's alignment specifications. Three of the five alignment angles — camber, caster, and toe-in — are adjustable. Steering axis inclination and toe-out-on-turns angles are built into the wheel spindles.

Wheel Alignment

An alignment mechanic can bring the wheel angles to the car manufacturer's specifications. The specifications have tolerances so that the angles can be tailored to the kind of driving you do. When you go for a wheel alignment, you should tell the mechanic what your use of the car is. Empty or full? Fast or slow? City or freeway? If he knows what he is doing, he can then give you a custom wheel alignment. He should also be advised of any handling or steering problems you have noticed. This allows him to check for and correct them during the alignment.

Steering Gear

Steering gears reduce much rotary movement of the steering wheel to a little lateral movement of the steering linkage. This gives you power over steering. Most steering gears use worm-and-follower gears. When you turn the steering wheel, a worm gear rotates on the steering shaft. A sector, roller or lever follower is pushed or pulled, depending on which direction you turn. This moves a Pitman (steering) arm coming out of the steering gearbox. Some steering gears use

recirculating ball bearings between the worm and its follower for a more friction-free action.

The wheels are steered by linkage and a system of rods and levers connecting their steering arms to the Pitman arm. Rubber-cushioned or grease-lubed ball-and-socket joints in the linkage ends, called tie-rod ends, permit up-down and turning movements. Steering gear ratio is about 20 to 1.

Power steering adds a hydraulic pump to the engine. It connects to the steering gearbox by pressure hoses. Inside the gearbox, a hydraulic cylinder is pushed or pulled by fluid pressure. Valves sensitive to your turning actions route pressurized fluid to one side of the piston or the other.

Rack-and-pinion steering is more direct than the worm-and-follower method. A small, round pinion gear moves a long, flat rack gear left or right as you turn the steering wheel.

Manual steering gear needs checks of gear lube level in the gearbox. Power steering needs frequent fluid-level checks, plus keeping the power-steering pump belt properly tensioned. Troubles other than this call for immediate and expert diagnosis.

TIRES

Next to gasoline, the greatest cost of driving your car is for tires. Much is to be gained by selecting the right replacement tires for your car and caring for them properly. Buying new tires for the family car may seem complex, but it really is not. Three types are available: bias-ply, belted bias-ply and radial-ply. Choosing among them is easy. Most are the tubeless type for passenger-car use.

Bias-ply tires contain core layers, called plies, running in a criss-cross pattern across the tire at about a 35 degree angle to the tread. Least expensive, the bias-ply tire delivers a relatively soft ride because it is less rigid than the other types.

Belted bias-ply tires contain, in addition to the bias-cord plies, belts of steel, rayon or fiberglass. These stretch-free belts run directly beneath the external tread to reduce side-to-side squirm.

They prolong tire life and provide greater road-holding power. They also increase tire cost.

Radial-ply tires are like belted bias-ply ones but with their plies arranged at a 90 degree angle to the tread. Right-angle plies, along with the circumferential belts, create a firmer tread that runs flatter to the road. Radial-ply tires have flexible sidewalls that give on corners and allow the car to glide through turns with a minimum of squeal, side-slip and tread wear. Radial tires are far superior in their handling and cornering characteristics. Higher initial cost is more than made up for because they wear so well that the cost per mile for radials is lower than for either of the other types. What is more, radial tires offer lower rolling resistance than other types, and this saves fuel.

Replacement tires should be matched as closely as possible to size and type with the original or worn out tires. Bias-ply and bias-belted tires may be combined on the same car but should be equal across the axles. It is not a good idea to mix radials with other tire types on the same car.

Warranties

Just about all tires are sold with warranties. These vary by dealers and brands more than the tires do. Since the warranty follow-up depends on the dealer, choose a dealer carefully. Also, consider how the warranty would work if you needed replacement while away from home. Nationally sold tire brands allow any of their dealers to make good on warranties.

Many tire warranties go for the life of the tire and cover any failure except tread wear. How much of an adjustment you get depends on how much tread has worn off.

Making Sense of Sizes

Designations of tire size may seem confusing but they are not. The first number or letter-number combination in the size always refers to wheel rim diameter. Thus a 7.35-14 tire is about 7.35 inches wide from sidewall to sidewall and it fits on a 14 inch diameter rim.

The letter R in a designation means that the tire is a radial-ply tire. A 175 R13 tire is a metric-size radial that measures some 175mm wide (6.9 inches) and fits a 13 inch rim (that measurement is not metric).

The letters A to M preceding a number, such as 60, 70, 78, may take the place of the width designation. The letter stands for tire width. A is the narrowest, being some 6 inches wide; M is the widest, being some 9.25 inches wide.

In L78-15, for example, the letter L means that the tire is about 9.15 inches wide. The 78 means simply that the tire cross-section is 78 per cent as high as it is wide. Therefore, the tire is 7.2 inches high (9.25 x 78%   7.2).

Tread Wear Traction & Speed

Recently a new tire grading system was instituted. It rates new tires on their tread wear, their traction with the pavement and their ability to take high speeds. This information, too, is printed on the tire sidewall.

Snow Tires

In snow-and-ice driving, a special kind of tire is necessary. Snow tires give the increased traction that keeps you going through snow, mud and slush. On glare ice you need another type of tire called a studded tire. This contains hard-steel pins protruding slightly from the tread to give traction on ice.

Both kinds of winter tires should be installed only in season. The heat generated by friction between dry pavement and the larger snow or studded snow tires can bring on internal damage and cause tire failure in hot weather.

Retreaded Tires

When the tread is worn away on old tires, it is often possible to give them new life by fusing on a new tread. The finished product is called a retread. Retreaded tires are usually about half the cost of new ones. They give satisfactory service.

Tire Inflation

Some 25 per cent of all tire replacements are brought on prematurely by improper tire inflation pressures. The best way to get maximum life from your tires is to keep them properly inflated. The best way to be sure your tires are at the right inflation pressure is to purchase a tire-pressure gauge. Check tire pressures at least once a month and maintain them according to owner's manual specifications.

Valve Stems

Tubeless tires use valve stems that are mounted in holes in the wheel. These should be checked periodically for rubber deterioration.

Wheel Rotation

In order for a complete set of tires to wear out at approximately the same time or for a new spare tire to be utilized, tires should be rotated at about 6000-mile (10,000-k) intervals. However, the cost of having the rotation done can surpass any saving in tread wear.

Wheel Balance

Nearly all tires, when manufactured, contain "heavy" spots in the tread or sidewalls that make them unbalanced. Imbalance causes abnormal tire wear as well as instability at high speeds and can become a safety hazard.

Two kinds of imbalance affects tires: *static* and *dynamic*. Static imbalance is the unequal distribution of weight around the axle. A freely turning wheel that is out of static balance, when jacked off the ground, will rotate until its heavy spot comes to rest at the bottom. Static imbalance causes the wheels to bounce up and down (*tramp*) as the car moves forward. It is noticeable in the hood or seat cushion.

Dynamic imbalance has the weight of the wheel assembly unequally distributed across its vertical centerline. Front wheel wobble at high speeds, called *shimmy,* points to dynamic imbalance. Shimmy increases as speed increases. Dynamic imbalance is most noticeable in the steering wheel.

Both kinds of imbalance can be cured by the correct placement of balance weights around the wheel rim. The lead weights, placed opposite heavy spots, counteract them to permit tramp-free, shimmy-free wheel rotation.

Repairing Tires

Competent tubeless tire repair requires specialized knowledge and equipment. For this reason most repairs should be left to a tire shop.

MAINTENANCE AND CARE

Although many of the repairs on an automobile are shop jobs, various maintenance and care jobs can be done at home, to save money and to see that your car gets the best possible care.

Start with checking fluid levels, even though the same checks are made by others at the service station, because no one else has as much concern as you in keeping them properly.

Most important is engine oil level. This is measured by a flexible steel dipstick that reaches down into the crankcase. Always check the oil level with the engine stopped and the car parked on a level spot.

Compare the level with the indicator marks on the dipstick. Most dipsticks have two marks; an upper and lower one. The upper mark indicates *full;* the lower mark *add oil.*

Add oil through the oil filler opening usually located in the valve rocker cover on top of the engine. On V-8 engines this is found to one side. Check the dip-stick again after adding oil.

Coolant Level

Next, remove the radiator pressure cap and check the coolant level. Never do it when the engine is hot. Pressurization released, coolant can boil over, even scald you. If you cannot hold your hand on the top of the radiator, wait until another time to check the coolant.

Cars with closed cooling systems have see-through plastic reservoirs to the side of the engine compartment that allow a check when the engine is hot. The level should be up to the full line with a warmed-up system.

Brake Fluid

To check the brake fluid level, locate the brake master cyclinder, usually located on the driver's side of the engine compartment, back close to the fire-wall. A wire bail holds the top tightly down. Lift the bail, swing it down and the cover may be lifted off. Some master cylinders have threaded access plugs that are removed with a wrench.

The brake fluid level should be within half an inch of the top in both reservoirs. If not, fill to that point.

Battery Water

About once a month, remove all six cell caps from the battery. Add iron-free water until the electrolyte in each cell level reaches the bottom of the fill gauge. If the battery cells lack fill gauges, fill about $1/2$ inch over the tops of the plates. Don't overfill. Replace the cell caps.

Tire Check

Every couple of weeks you should check the tire pressure. Get a tire-pressure gauge and do it while they are cold; before the car has been driven, as pressures specified by manufacturer are based on cold tires. Driving warms the air in the tires and raises the pressure. Another reason for having your own tire-pressure gauge is the general inaccuracy of service station gauges.

Air Cleaner

Another filter element that you can change to save money is your engine's air filter. It is located inside the large air cleaner chamber on top of the carburetor. To get at it, simply remove the wing-nut that secures the top of the air cleaner.

The element is either a pleated paper cartridge of an oil-wet piece of plastic foam. If either are allowed to fill with the dirt, it chokes off intake air flow, which is like running the engine with the choke partially closed. Too much gasoline is drawn into the engine and burned. A clogged filter increases emissions and can make your engine use 10 to 15 percent more fuel. So do not let the air cleaner get dirty.

Plastic-foam air cleaner elements need not be replaced. They can be washed clean in strong household detergent and reused. Rinse and squeeze dry without twisting or wringing. Coat the foam with SAE 10W engine oil and knead it gently into the foam. Squeeze out any excess oil and install it back in the air cleaner.

Fuel System Maintenace

The best thing you can do for your car's fuel system is to keep it clean. Buy clean, water-free gasoline, keep a locked gas cap on your car to prevent contamination and change the fuel filters as often as called for in the owner's manual.

Cleaning Your Car

If you wash your car at home, get one of those hose ends that let you turn on the water by bending. Its rubber nozzle will not mar the finish if they contact accidentally. Other equipment you may need: the garden hose; a large sponge; several soft cloths; a pail; and a vacuum cleaner or whisk broom.

Work in the shade. Now check your car. Be sure the windows are up and that drain holes at the bottom of doors and side panels are unclogged so that water can drain out. Mix four capfuls of car-wash detergent in a pail of water and work on the car in sections. Hose the section to loosen dirt, then wipe with your sponge in a light circular motion. Rinse off the section with the hose and proceed to the next one, working from the roof down. Do a portion of the car, then rinse with water. Whatever you do, do not leave any detergent film on the finish. On a cold day, it helps to use hot, soapy water. A shag car wash mitt makes the work easier, or you can use a large cellulose sponge and waterproof work gloves.

Choose one of the easy-do wax/polishes. Paste waxes once were best, but that is no longer true. Today some of the liquids will outlast the pastes. Contrary to what seems right, some of the combination pastewax/polishes are easier to use than some liquid combinations. New products are coming on the market all the time, so what was best yesterday is not necessarily best today. Try several and, when you find one you like, stick with it.

If the finish is not the least dull or oxidized, but is unprotected by wax, you need not use a combination wax/polish, only wax. Otherwise, you need both. The combination products save you going over the car twice.

After washing the car, clean the windows. Nothing works as well on windows as a chamois. Get one and take good care of it. Both natural and man-made materials do the job. Use them on chrome, too, to take off water spots. If you have your car wax-washed at a car wash, be sure to clean wax off the windows and windshield wipers with window-cleaner. Otherwise, the wax film may cause a dangerous loss of visibility in a rainstorm.

Be sure to wax the chrome heavily during the winter season if highway departments in your area are using road salt to melt ice. Some car owners apply paste wax thickly over the chrome and leave it without polishing. This dulls the chrome temporarily, but gives protection against corrosion. Some trim is aluminum and need not be protected, as with plastic trim materials. In the winter a few owners coat steel-backed chrome, such as bumpers and side mirrors, with fine machine oil to protect against road-salt corrosion.

While cleaning, do not forget to clean around the doors and door openings. That contributes greatly to a neat appearance. Chamois the insides of the windows, too.

Vinyl Top

If your car has a vinyl top, clean it with a special top cleaner. Some of these are made with dyes matching the top's color to help restore a faded top. No need to use a dyed product unless your car top is actually faded. Follow the directions with the product you use.

Safety Check

A 15-minute safety inspection of your car is a small price to pay where life and health are concerned. That is all the time it takes to complete a 15-step check-up that the Ford Motor Company recommends to drivers before starting out on a trip.

Brakes

Make certain that the brake pedal is firm and cannot be pressed down within 1-1/2 inches (38 mm) of the floor. From a speed of about 25 mph (40 kph) apply firm, steady pressure to the brake pedal. Your car should slow down in relation to applied pressure and stop completely if the brake is not released. The pedal should be firm.

Tires

Flat spots on the tire treads or vibrations while driving may indicate that wheels are out of balance. Excessive wear on one side of a tire means that front-end alignment may be needed.

Lights

Pull the headlight switch to its first stop. The following lights should be on: instrument panel, parking, front and rear side markers, taillights, and license plate light. These lights should stay on when the switch is pulled completely out to turn on the headlights. Make certain that headlight high beams operate.

With the ignition on, the following lights should flash when the turn signal lever is moved up or down: parking, instrument panel turn indicator, and brake lights.

With the ignition on and a friend to help, place the transmission in reverse and make certain that the back-up lights are on. Step on the brake pedal to be sure that all brake lights go on.

Turn on the hazard warning light switch and see if all the directional lights flash.

Horn

Test the horn. It can help you avoid an accident.

Door Locks

Make certain that all doors close easily, that the latches open and close easily and stay secure when closed.

Visibility

Inspect all car windows for cracks that might possibly spread to obscure vision during high-speed driving. Mirrors should be securely fastened and properly positioned. With the engine running, test the operation of the windshield wipers and washers.

As a final precaution, check your emergency equipment such as spare tire, jack, road flares, and first-aid kit.

Table Saw

The magic in a table saw is there for all to use. Anyone who has used a handsaw and then accomplished similar chores with power knows the value of this basic machine. The increase in production and the decrease in expended energy by no means cover its total usefulness. The gain in accuracy (because the machine is organized to minimize the possibility of human error) is more impressive.

Straight, square, and smooth cuts become automatic, allowing you to concentrate on the creative end. Anyone can flick the switch, and the tool will respond whether the operator is an amateur or a professional. The span between the novice and the expert is bridged by knowing the tool and its myriad practical applications and making fullest use of them.

General Characteristics

Types

All table saws have the same general characteristics. A saw blade is mounted on an arbor that is turned by a motor; the blade projects through a table on which the work is rested. The table is slotted to receive a miter gauge and is organized to accommodate a laterally adjustable rip fence. Blade projection, miter-gauge head and blade angularity are controllable.

More important with individual tools are capacity, power, and physical machine size. All the table saws available will accomplish all the necessary operations. For more power and bigger tables with larger blades, you naturally spend more money, and there is no doubt that the bigger units are nice to have.

Safety

To talk about safety in relation to the table saw would be to fill this book with "do's" and

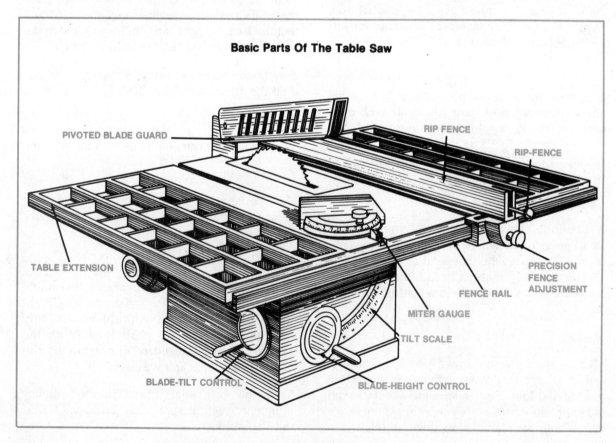

Basic Parts Of The Table Saw

PIVOTED BLADE GUARD

RIP FENCE

RIP-FENCE

TABLE EXTENSION

FENCE RAIL

PRECISION FENCE ADJUSTMENT

MITER GAUGE

TILT SCALE

BLADE-TILT CONTROL

BLADE-HEIGHT CONTROL

"don't's," and this approach would not reduce the responsibility of the operator. It's simply wise to accept the fact that any machine designed to cut wood can hurt you. Therefore, a constant respect for the machine is necessary to operate it safely. Become professional but never so confident that you become nonchalant. Use the guards and when they can't be used, know that you are exposed to a more dangerous situation and behave accordingly.

Correctly aligned tools, clean tools, sharp tools, and a clean shop are all important safety factors. Carefully follow the safety procedures outlined in your owner's manual and, most importantly, always keep your hands away from the cutting area.

Adjustments

A table saw consists of parts bolted and screwed together. If any part slips, even just a bit, you lose the precision that was built into the machine. Therefore, any table saw should be checked thoroughly when it is new, and regularly thereafter.

While methods of adjustment can vary from saw to saw, the correct relationship of components is the same. Doing the job is just a question of

carefully following the instructions that are in the owner's manual that comes with the tool. Three important alignment rules apply to any table saw: (1) The table slots, the rip fence and the saw blade must all be parallel. (2) The rip fence, the saw blade and the miter-gauge head must all be perpendicular to the table surface. (3) When the miter gauge is in the normal crosscut position, it must be at right angles to the blade and the rip fence.

Since the blade mounting, which is seated on the arbor, is the one thing over which you have no control, it's wise to start all alignment checks by determining whether the table slots are parallel to the saw blade. All other checks are made on the basis of this important relationship.

Distance between rip fence and blade at "A" and "B" should be equal unless a fraction is offset at "B" so "rear" teeth won't be rubbing the wood after the "front" teeth have made the cut,

Since eliminating human error is an important factor in doing accurate work, it's wise to equip yourself with gauge tools. These tools you can make yourself, but you must be most careful with the construction. The idea is to make them to perfection and to care for them so they will remain precise checking tools.

While blade projection is not an alignment factor, it's still a good idea to equip yourself with gauges that lead to accuracy, not so much for routine cutting where the blade projects through the work but for work like rabbeting, blind kerfing and dadoing.

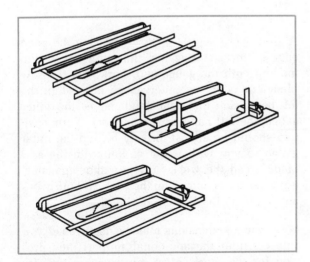

The three basic alignment rules for any table saw. Unless the handyman is aware of these and checks periodically to see that they are maintained, he will not function efficiently.

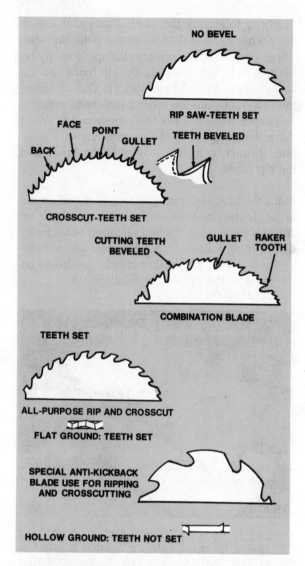

NO BEVEL

RIP SAW-TEETH SET

TEETH BEVELED

FACE
POINT
GULLET
BACK

CROSSCUT-TEETH SET

CUTTING TEETH
BEVELED
GULLET
RAKER
TOOTH

COMBINATION BLADE

TEETH SET

ALL-PURPOSE RIP AND CROSSCUT

FLAT GROUND: TEETH SET

**SPECIAL ANTI-KICKBACK
BLADE USE FOR RIPPING
AND CROSSCUTTING**

HOLLOW GROUND: TEETH NOT SET

Use this chart as a guide when trying to find the best blade to use for the job on hand.

Saw blades

The blade that comes with the machine will be a combination type, designed to do both crosscutting and ripping. It will be an efficient blade but not the very best blade you can get for either type of cut.

It would be expensive, and probably uncalled for, to equip yourself immediately with blades to meet all eventualities. It makes more sense to gradually increase your assortment of blades as you do more and more work and become more familiar with the table saw.

If you do a lot of work with plywood as most craftsmen do, you'll want to think immediately about getting a special plywood-cutting blade. This blade is designed to stand up under the abrasive action of the material while producing smooth cuts with minimum feathering.

Most blades have set teeth which produce a kerf that is wider than the blade gauge, and so provide clearance. The hollow-ground blade, which is very nice for miters and similar cuts, does not have set teeth. Kerf width at the points of the teeth is the same as the blade gauge. It gets clearance because the area of the blade buried in the work during the cut is ground thinner. That's why such a blade should get more projection. If it doesn't, it will burn itself and/or the work. Too little projection will most certainly dull it faster.

A 55 tooth carbide blade is often very popular. It's expensive, but it stays on the machine through countless hours of cutting materials including hardwoods, hardboards, plywood, laminates, plastics and even nonferrous metals.

No matter what blade you use, some attention to how fast you feed the work can result in better cuts. A slow feed is always better.

Cutting Procedures

Crosscutting

A simple crosscut is made by placing the good edge of the stock against the miter gauge and moving both the gauge and work past the saw blade. Usually, the miter gauge is used in the left-hand slot; the right hand moves the miter gauge, the left hand snugs the work. Your position should be almost directly behind the miter gauge so you will be out of line with the saw blade. Feed the work slowly, without pausing, until the cut is complete; then return both work and gauge to the starting position.

Miter-gauge extensions make sense even if you only consider the additional support they provide for the work. Most miter gauges are designed to accept extensions. The means of attachment may be wood screws or nuts and bolts through a set of holes or slots in the gauge head.

Cuts like this can result even with very good blades when the break through is too fast. Some of this feathering is inevitable but can certainly be minimized simply by slowing up.

Many times an extension is used when the work is long and calls for extra support. In such cases, don't use a hand to push against the free end of the work. This can close the kerf, bind the blade, and result in a kickback that can be dangerous.

Simple crosscut is accomplished by holding the work flat on the table and snug against the miter gauge head. The handyman should position himself out of line with the saw blade. (Blade is shown here far too high above work.)

When work is too wide to be handled conveniently in the normal miter gauge position, it can often be used backwards like this. Note use of the extension for more support.

Table Saw

Never pick the cutoff from the table while the blade is still running. Wait a few seconds for the blade to stop.

Crosscutting to length

Unless you are squaring off the end of a board, crosscutting is usually done to size a board to a certain length. Other times it's done to get duplicate pieces. In such cases, it's always wise to create some sort of mechanical setup so the length of the pieces will be gauged automatically. This may be done with commercial miter-gauge stop rods.

Never use the rip fence as a stop to gauge the cutoff length. The work will certainly be captured and twisted between the rip fence and the blade, and it can be tossed up or back and hit you.

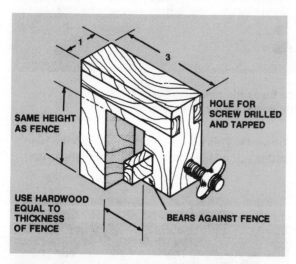

This stop block is made so it can be secured any place along the rip fence. It can be used to stop lengths of cuts, or to gauge lengths of cutoffs.

Using two miter gauges

As you learn more woodworking techniques, the addition of an extra gauge is something to consider. In crosscutting, for example, you could make an extension longer than the width of the saw table and back it up with a gauge in each slot. This can take care of two work extremes, the overly long piece that can use a great deal of support and the very small piece that can't be held safely without special consideration.

Better support, and greater control, are obtained with the use of two miter gauges to feed stock for angle cut.

Extra long work

Good work support is important for both accuracy and safety. For very long work, think in terms of more support than the table can provide. Rather than getting someone to hold up the free end, use a floor stand. Such stands are good for both crosscutting and ripping. In addition to providing support for extra long lumber work, you will find them useful in making initial sizing cuts on all sorts of panel materials.

For routine cuts, keep the left hand at the front of the table as the right hand continues to move the work past the blade. Keep the fingers hooked over the fence.

Ripping

A rip cut is made by passing the work between the rip fence and the saw blade. When the blade has set teeth, be sure to measure from a tooth that slants toward the fence. If you are using the offset fence alignment, measure from the front of the blade.

A simple rip cut is made by placing the work at the front edge of the table, snugly against the fence and flat down. Use your left hand to hold the work in position and your right hand, with fingers hooked over the fence, to feed the work forward. Keep your left hand in its original position, snugging the work throughout the pass.

Feed with your right hand until the work is well past the saw blade. There is no return on a rip cut. Feed until the overhang at the rear of the table causes the back end of the work to tilt up into

the palm of your hand. Then, grip tightly and lift it completely clear of the saw blade.

This process is standard as long as you have ample room between the fence and blade. On narrow cuts, when your hand gets about 6″ from the blade, substitute a push stick for your fingers.

A push stick often is nothing more than a narrow strip of wood salvaged from the scrap heap.

Often, multiple pieces can be produced by pre-shaping a wide board and then ripping off pieces. This is better than ripping the pieces and then shaping them.

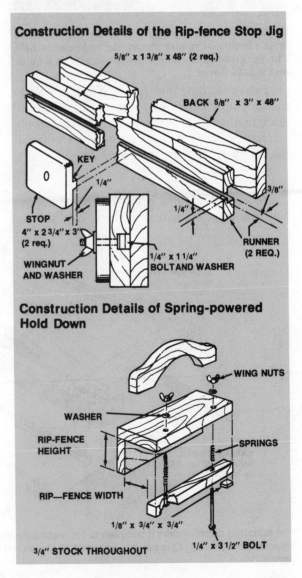

Construction Details of the Rip-fence Stop Jig

Construction Details of Spring-powered Hold Down

Simple pusher sticks or a combination pusher-hold down are easy to make and are a "must" for doing all jobs safely. The pusher-hold down may also be used for safety and convenience on the jointer.

Table Saw

Special setups are helpful on many jobs. Here, a large number of square pieces had to be cut in half. The jig, grooved to receive the stock, acts as a guide and a hold down.

On extremely long material, it might be wise to change your position about the middle of the cut. Start in the usual fashion, but approximately midway, move to the back of the saw and finish the cut by pulling the work through.

Squaring board

There are times when a piece of stock doesn't have an edge straight enough to ride the rip fence. Maybe it's left over from a jigsaw or band-saw job. The squaring board lets you mount it for cutting.

The jig is just a platform with a saw-table-slot guide fastened to its underside. The cleat, secured to the forward edge of the platform, is at right angles to the saw blade. You butt the work against the cleat and push the whole assembly past the saw blade. Of course, there is a size limit to work that can be handled on the jig.

Mitering

Few jobs in woodworking can be as frustrating as cutting a good miter joint. You can be a bit off in making the cut and the two parts will mate perfectly, but the angle formed by the two parts will not be 90°. This is discouraging on jobs that run from simple picture frames to the facing on case goods. The only solution to this problem is accuracy.

Make it a rule to make the cut line on the work. You'll know immediately whether you are getting the accuracy you want.

You can get help in holding the work against the gauge head by using a miter-gauge extension; even more helpful is facing the extension with sandpaper. Make the pass even more slowly

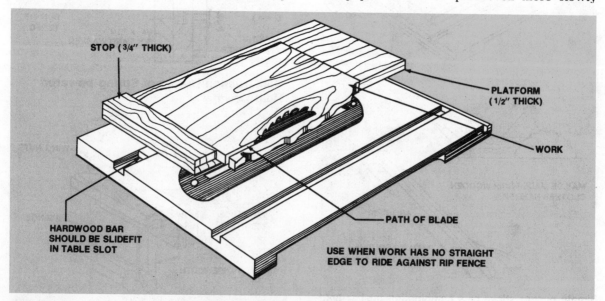

STOP (3/4" THICK)
PLATFORM (1/2" THICK)
WORK
HARDWOOD BAR SHOULD BE SLIDEFIT IN TABLE SLOT
PATH OF BLADE
USE WHEN WORK HAS NO STRAIGHT EDGE TO RIDE AGAINST RIP FENCE

The squaring board makes it possible to cut material lacking a straight edge for use against the rip fence. This can be the result of pieces left over from jigsaw or bandsaw operations.

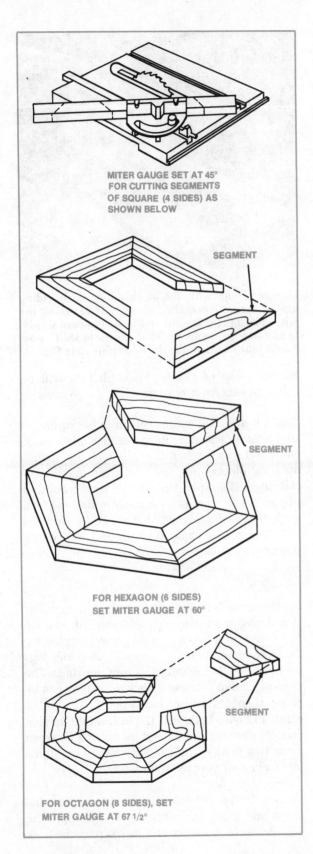

MITER GAUGE SET AT 45°
FOR CUTTING SEGMENTS
OF SQUARE (4 SIDES) AS
SHOWN BELOW

SEGMENT

SEGMENT

FOR HEXAGON (6 SIDES)
SET MITER GAUGE AT 60°

SEGMENT

FOR OCTAGON (8 SIDES), SET
MITER GAUGE AT 67 1/2°

Accuracy on miters can be spoiled simply because of the cut action. The work tends to pivot about the front edge of the miter gauge. It will also "creep." Firm work support is essential.

than you do normally. Needless to say, machine alignment has to be perfectly accurate.

Simple miter jigs

Part of the problem of cutting true miters is the difficulty of matching left and right-hand cuts. This is most critical when the work is shaped so that it can't be flipped because it means having to work on both sides of the blade. To do that, you also have to change the miter-gauge setting for

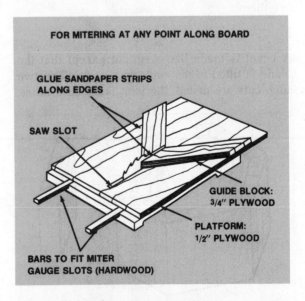

FOR MITERING AT ANY POINT ALONG BOARD

GLUE SANDPAPER STRIPS
ALONG EDGES

SAW SLOT

GUIDE BLOCK:
3/4" PLYWOOD

PLATFORM:
1/2" PLYWOOD

BARS TO FIT MITER
GAUGE SLOTS (HARDWOOD)

Construction detail of a sliding table for miter cuts, cutting consecutively from a single piece.

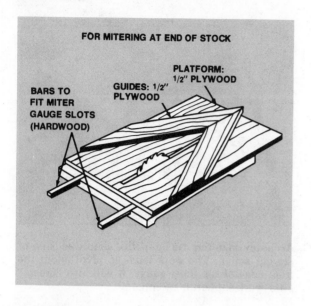

FOR MITERING AT END OF STOCK

PLATFORM: 1/2" PLYWOOD

GUIDES: 1/2" PLYWOOD

BARS TO FIT MITER GAUGE SLOTS (HARDWOOD)

This sliding table for miter cuts require the parts to be cut to length.

Beveling done with the stock on its edge, riding against the rip fence. Hold the work snug against the fence throughout the cut and make the pass slowly, to counter the tendency for the work to shift away. To do four edges, make the crossgrain cuts first.

mating cuts. You can avoid most of these problems by making some sliding tables.

These sliding tables are no more than platforms guided by twin bars that ride the slots in the saw table. Attached to the platforms are guides that position the work for the cut. If these sliding tables are made accurately and cared for, they will function in good style for as long as you care to use them.

Beveling

A bevel is made like a rip cut except that the blade is tilted to the angle required. When two such cuts are mated, the joint is called a miter.

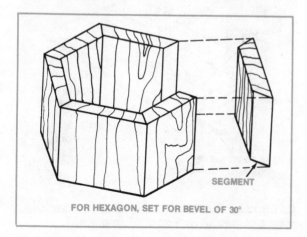

SEGMENT

FOR HEXAGON, SET FOR BEVEL OF 30°

For the sake of clarity, blade-tilt cuts will be called bevels from here on.

You can do bevel cutting on a number of pieces so that after assembly they will turn a corner. A circle is formed when the total included angles of all the pieces equal 360°. Determining the correct angle is simple. Divide 360° by the number of pieces you want in your circle to find the total angle that each piece will have. Then divide this in half to get the angle at which each side of the pieces should be cut.

Tapering

A taper-cutting jig is a good tool for you to make. It provides a straight side that can ride the rip fence and an adjustable side so you can set for the amount of taper you want. Keep the legs clamped together when you attach the hinge. The crosspiece that you use to lock the setting can be made of sheet metal or hardwood.

Mark a line on both legs 12" in from the hinged end. By opening the jig and measuring between these two marks, you can determine how much taper per foot you are setting for.

To use the jig, set the straight side against the fence and place the work against the opposite leg. Advance both jig and work past the saw

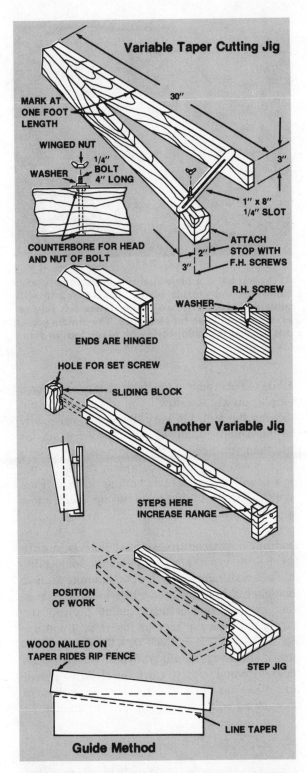

Variable Taper Cutting Jig

MARK AT ONE FOOT LENGTH

30"

3"

WINGED NUT

WASHER

1/4" BOLT 4" LONG

1" x 8" 1/4" SLOT

COUNTERBORE FOR HEAD AND NUT OF BOLT

2"

3"

ATTACH STOP WITH F.H. SCREWS

R.H. SCREW

WASHER

ENDS ARE HINGED

HOLE FOR SET SCREW

SLIDING BLOCK

Another Variable Jig

STEPS HERE INCREASE RANGE

POSITION OF WORK

WOOD NAILED ON TAPER RIDES RIP FENCE

STEP JIG

LINE TAPER

Guide Method

Construction details of various types of taper jigs. The variable one at the top left is the most useful for general work. At the lower right is a technique for cutting pieces too large to be handled any other way.

blade. If you require the same taper on both edges of the stock, open the jig up to twice the original setting before making the second cut.

There will be a tendency here for the work to move away from the jig as you cut, so be sure to set the work correctly at the beginning and keep it in place throughout the pass.

It's also possible to use notched jigs to accomplish taper cuts. These are pieces of wood with parallel sides. To do this, recess one side to match the shape and size of what you wish to remove from the work. You nestle the work in the notch and do the job like a rip cut. Notched jigs are good to use when the job calls for a setting that might be too extreme for the variable jig and for very small pieces. Notched jigs are also good for production runs since they eliminate resetting, thus reducing the possibility of error.

Compound angles

Some cuts require a miter-gauge setting, others a blade tilt. The compound angle requires both at the same time. Accuracy is essential. Settings must be done carefully and checked out on scrap before the good stock is cut.

In any event, use a blade that will produce a smooth cut, and be sure that it is sharp. Make all passes very slowly, and keep a firm grip on the work throughout.

Compound taper and bevel cut involves tilting the blade to correct angle. When the cut is repeated on the opposite edge, the jig is opened to twice the original angle to compensate for the first taper cut.

Table Saw

Dadoing

If you set a regular saw blade to less than the stock thickness and make repeat passes to widen the normal kerf, you get a U-shaped cut that is a dado when done across the grain, a groove when done with the grain. You may even hear the word "ploughing," but this is the same as grooving.

Dadoing tools

The dado assembly is a set of outside blades with a number of chippers. Cut width is determined by how many chippers you use. Most can be used for cuts that run from $1/4''$ to better than $3/4''$ wide.

"Wobblers" can be self-contained units or merely a set of washers that you use with a regular saw blade. In essence, the blade is set slightly vertical to the saw arbor. As the blade spins, the teeth move from side to side, so they cut a wide slot instead of a narrow kerf. The offset of the blade is adjustable. Since the lateral movement of the blade forms an arc at the tips of the teeth, the bottom of the dado will be slightly rounded instead of dead flat.

At the top left is a high-quality dado assembly with hollow-ground outside blades. Besides it is a self-contained wobbler. Two at the lower left rely on beveled or set teeth for clearance. The molding head can be used for dado work with blank knives doing the cutting.

All dado cuts remove much more material than a simple saw cut, so slow up on the feed to avoid choking the tool. On very deep cuts, especially on those wider than $3/8''$, set the projection for less than you need on the first pass and raise it for the second pass to complete the cut. Tool power will also affect this cutting process; if the work chatters or if the tool slows up, you'll know you are cutting too deeply.

Dadoing tools require special inserts simply because they make wider cuts. On some jobs, this can result in too much of an opening around the cutter. When this seems like an unsafe situation, make a special insert using plywood or hardboard. Use the regular insert as a pattern. Put the new insert in place with the dado at zero projection. Then, holding down the insert with a block of wood, slowly raise the dado so it will form its own slot. In this manner, you will have no opening whatever around the cutting tool.

Tenoning jig

It is not good practice to do dado work across the end of narrow stock without taking precautions to make the job accurate and safe. The tenoning jig is basically a U-shaped affair, so it can strad-

A wood facing for the rip fence is a good idea because it permits more flexible work positions. Length of this workpiece is too small to be fed safely over open table insert.

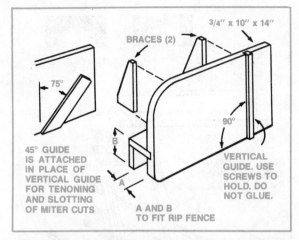

45° GUIDE IS ATTACHED IN PLACE OF VERTICAL GUIDE FOR TENONING AND SLOTTING OF MITER CUTS

75°

90°

BRACES (2)

3/4" x 10" x 14"

B

A

VERTICAL GUIDE. USE SCREWS TO HOLD. DO NOT GLUE.

A AND B TO FIT RIP FENCE

Construction details of a simple tenoning jig. Be sure that the vertical guide is exactly 90° to the saw table.

dle the rip fence and hold the work in relation to the cutter.

Slots

To form slots, you must lower the work over the turning dado and, of course, this calls for extra care. Whenever possible, use a stop block or a clamp on the rip fence to act as a gauge as well as to provide a brace point to help you do the job. To determine slot length, use two stop blocks.

Extensions

Miter-gauge extensions are useful for dado work, especially when you wish to automatically gauge the distance between cuts. In most cases, this can be accomplished by attaching a guide strip to the bottom edge of the extension.

A guide strip, nailed into a notch that is cut in a miter-gauge extension, automatically positions the work for equally spaced dadoes.

Round tenons

You can form tenons on round stock. Use the rip fence as a stop and the miter gauge to keep the work square. Keep the cutter projection to a minimum and use a hand position that pays maximum attention to safety. Advance the work and miter gauge to the depth of cut required, and then slowly turn the work against the direction of rotation of the cutter.

Molding heads

There are many kinds of molding heads on the market, but they all work the same way on a table saw. The knives, usually in sets of three, are locked into slots around the edge of the head. The head is mounted on the saw's arbor between washers in the same way as a blade or a dado tool.

You can start your collection of knives with a few basic types; then add new ones as you need them. Knives can be combination types that permit different cuts, depending on which part of the contour you use. Standard cutters are each designed to do a specific job and usually require using the full profile of the blade. Such items as

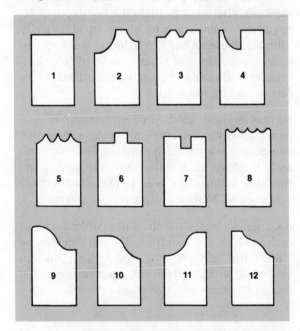

Typical molding knives: 1. blank; 2. combination 1/4", 1/2" quarter round; 3. glue joint; 4. cabinet-door lip; 5. V-flute; 6 & 7. tongue and groove set; 8. four-bead molding; 9. ogee; 10. ogee; 11. ogee; 12. reverse ogee;

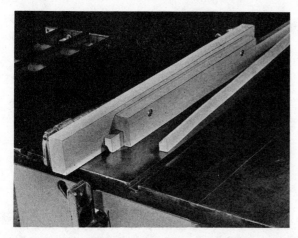

When slim moldings are needed, make a setup like this. Presized pieces are fed into one end of the fixture, pulled out the other, safely and surely.

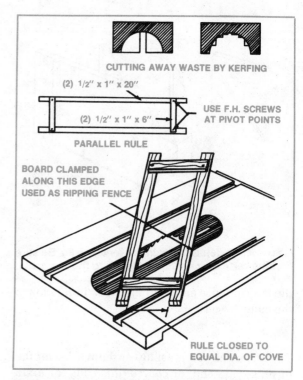

CUTTING AWAY WASTE BY KERFING

(2) 1/2" x 1" x 20"

USE F.H. SCREWS AT PIVOT POINTS

(2) 1/2" x 1" x 6"

PARALLEL RULE

BOARD CLAMPED ALONG THIS EDGE USED AS RIPPING FENCE

RULE CLOSED TO EQUAL DIA. OF COVE

How to make a parallel rule to be used to gauge cove cuts. Note that a good deal of stock may be removed by saw cuts before the coving is done.

window sash, glue joints, and panel door inserts fall in this category.

Much of what has been said about dado use applies to the molding head. Unlike a saw blade, which removes a minimum amount of material, the molding cutter takes a big bite. Never force the work or try to cut too deeply. On very deep cuts, make several passes, adjusting the height of the knife after each to attain the full depth of cut required. If the machine slows up drastically, vibrates, makes it hard to hold the work steady, throws out chunks of wood instead of fine shavings, or stalls, chances are you are feeding too fast or cutting too deeply.

No matter how good your equipment is, you won't get optimum cuts unless the setups that you make are accurate. So spend a few extra seconds to check such things as knife height and rip-fence settings. It's wise to make trial cuts in scrap wood before cutting actual parts.

It's a good idea to cut the full profile shape of each knife as you acquire it. The cut can then be "filed" for reference. By doing this, you can easily tell, without a trial cut, what knife or what part of the knife you need to do the job.

Coving

Oblique sawing makes it possible to get arched shapes with a regular saw blade. The basic procedure is to clamp a guide strip to the table at some angle to the saw blade. The blade is set at minimum projection, and the work is moved along the guide strip. Many passes are needed with the blade projected an additional $1/16''$ to $1/8''$ for each. How much you add to the blade projection for each pass will depend on the nature of the wood and the angle of the guide.

A parallel rule can be made, so you can predetermine the cove cut you will get. To use it, spread the legs so the inside measurement equals the diameter of the cove you want. Set the saw blade height to equal the radius of the cove. Set the parallel rule over the saw blade so the opposite inside edges of the legs just touch the front and rear teeth of the saw blade. This establishes the correct angle for the guide strip.

Notching jigs

There are times when a part can't be sawed accurately or safely using only the rip fence or the miter gauge. The part may be too small to be held safely or too oddly shaped to be done conventionally. A notched jig is often the solution.

This jig is a piece of wood with parallel sides. The notch can be the shape of the part you wish to keep, or it can be the shape of the waste piece. Usually, the jig will ride the rip fence and act as both carrier and gauge, allowing you to position the work precisely, even when unusual shapes are involved.

Notch on underside of this jig permits safe, easy cutting of similar pieces that might be needed.

Multi-blade work

Two or more saw blades turning on a single shaft speed the production on thousands of industrial duplicating jobs. In limited fashion, the same method can be employed by homecraftsmen. All you need are extra saw blades and some suitable washers.

The basic idea is to mount the extra saw blades on the arbor and use the washers to hold them

Cutting in double time, with a two-blade setup, to produce a number of similar parts. Washers or bushings determine spacing of blades. Feed the stock as for any rip cut.

the desired distance apart. With one pass of the stock through the blades, you have two or three accurately spaced cuts.

The limitations of this setup should also be mentioned. The spacing of the multiple cuts is restricted by the length of the saw's arbor and the width of the saw slot in the table. Fortunately, most circular saws have a fairly long shaft and a removable table insert.

Running off a large number of identical strips or slats is an obvious situation where extra blades mounted on the arbor can be very useful. With the rip fence spacing the first part, you'll get as many strips in one pass as there are saw blades on the arbor.

Two saw blades can be employed to make both cheek cuts for a tenon at the same time. Decoratively, multiple cutting can be used to saw parallel grooves or slots in panels or screens or to make multiple spiral grooves in doweling or spindles.

Wood bending

Bending wood with jigs and the use of steam is often impractical for the homecraftsman, especially when it is required on oversize pieces. For these, and any other wood-bending job where the full strength of the stock isn't needed, there is another and easier way. It's called "kerf curving".

The trick is to make a number of deep side-by-side cuts in the face of the stock. These cuts form

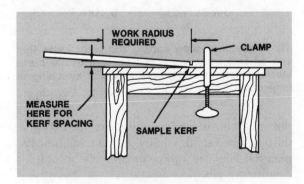

Guide to figuring kerf spacing. Type of wood, even variations in wood of the same species, requires consideration. It's wise to test in scrap stock first.

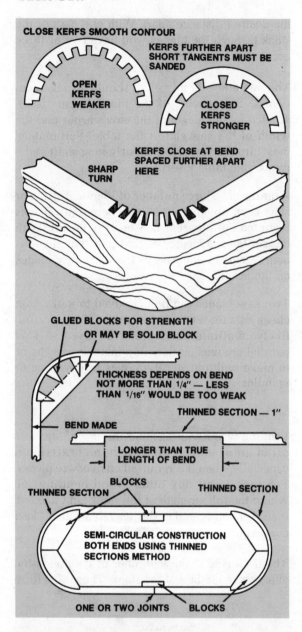

- CLOSE KERFS SMOOTH CONTOUR
- KERFS FURTHER APART SHORT TANGENTS MUST BE SANDED
- OPEN KERFS WEAKER
- CLOSED KERFS STRONGER
- KERFS CLOSE AT BEND SPACED FURTHER APART HERE
- SHARP TURN
- GLUED BLOCKS FOR STRENGTH OR MAY BE SOLID BLOCK
- THICKNESS DEPENDS ON BEND NOT MORE THAN 1/4" — LESS THAN 1/16" WOULD BE TOO WEAK
- THINNED SECTION — 1"
- BEND MADE
- LONGER THAN TRUE LENGTH OF BEND
- THINNED SECTION
- BLOCKS
- THINNED SECTION
- SEMI-CIRCULAR CONSTRUCTION BOTH ENDS USING THINNED SECTIONS METHOD
- ONE OR TWO JOINTS
- BLOCKS

These sketches show kerfing and other ideas that can be utilized so wood can be bent in the home workshop without having to resort to steaming or laminating.

the underside of the bend. In effect, the cuts give the opposite face flexibility. At the same time the material between each pair of kerfs becomes a reinforcing rib.

The closer you space the kerfs, the more sharply you can bend the wood.

When parts are to turn an outside corner and there is room to back them with glue blocks, you may find it easier to reduce the entire bend area to veneer thickness. When stock size permits, the job is best done on a jigsaw or band saw.

Cutting circles

Perfect circles can be cut on a table saw if you use a pivot-cutting technique. The trick is to remove the bulk of the waste stock by making tangent cuts first. This would be tedious with a miter gauge and unsafe to do freehand. But it can be done quickly and safely with a platform on which the work can ride.

Throughout the operation, the work is mounted on the platform by a nail pivot through the center of the work and into the platform.

For the tangent cuts, hold the work securely and make repeat, straight cuts. After the waste is removed, clamp the platform to the table so the center line of the work is near the front edge of the saw blade. Then, rotate the work slowly against the direction in which the blade is rotating.

First step in pivot cutting is to make tangent cuts to remove most of the waste stock. The pivot is a nail that goes through the work into a hardwood bar that rides the table slot. Make repeat passes, turning the work a bit after each.

Spirals

The table saw technique that will be discussed is used mostly to lay out a spiral pattern and to remove much of the waste stock that is ordinarily filed away. Of course, if square-shouldered spirals are acceptable, then the same technique can be used for a full job. A dado or a regular saw blade may be used to do the job.

To start the cut, hold the stock firmly against the miter-gauge head (or use an extension) and lower it slowly over the turning cutter. When the stock rests solidly on the table, turn it slowly toward the cutter. If you turn slowly and hold firmly, the work will automatically lead to the correct pitch.

First cut in making the finger lap joint is made by butting one piece against the guide block as the first pass is made.

Spirals may be formed by limiting the depth of cut and rotating the stock as it is held against a slanted guide. If stock is fed slowly, the cutting action will automatically hold the "pitch" established by the angle of the guide.

Special Joint Techniques

The finger lap

Finger lap joints are often found on old works of enduring excellence. These joints are exposed in some areas to denote a good degree of craftsmanship and are used in some hidden areas because of their strength. Structurally, the appeal of a finger-lap joint lies in the unusual amount of gluing surface it provides.

A ³/₈" finger looks quite good on stock that ranges from ³/₈" to ³/₄" thick. A ¹/₄" finger is effective on stock that ranges from ¹/₄" to ¹/₂" thick. If you ever work on material that is less than ¹/₄" thick, match the cut to the thickness of the material or just a bit less.

Place the first cut over the guide block and butt the second piece against it. Advance everything to make the second cut.

Cuts made are placed over the guide block to position the work for cuts that follow. Throughout the job, be sure that pieces are held firmly together and that passes are made slowly.

Table Saw

In making the sequence of cuts, precision is fine, but don't work toward making the tongue and groove so snug that you must mate them with a mallet. A slip fit is more practical.

Rabbet-miter joints

Aside from picture-frame moldings and those few other cases where it is the only suitable connection, the classic miter is still a popular joint for one reason: it enables you to join pieces along an edge or an end without exposing unsightly, hard-to-conceal edge or end grain.

To greatly improve the miter joint, you can incorporate a rabbet in the miter so you will end up with the good looks of the miter joint as well as considerable additional strength. The design also makes for more convenient assembly.

Three designs, the "simple," the "locked," and the "housed," are not difficult to make, but accuracy is very important. Work with a sharp blade that will produce smooth cuts, and be sure your table saw components are in correct alignment.

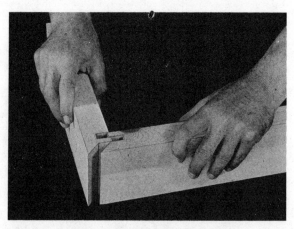

The locked rabbet miter fits together like so.

Splines and feathers

Splines are reinforcing, slim strips of wood set into grooves that are cut in the edges of mating pieces. One good rule is to cut the strips so the grain of the wood runs across the narrow dimension; then they can't be broken easily. It's often possible to cut splines from thin plywood if the thickness of what you have available is suitable for the job.

The "feather" is also a spline, but it's used most often across the edge of miter joints, in picture frames, for example. This calls for a triangular shape. In most cases, they are cut oversize and then sanded flush to the assembly after the glue has dried.

The dovetail

Making dovetails is not really a table saw operation, but the need for the application could arise

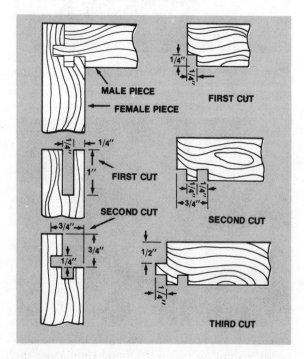

MALE PIECE

FEMALE PIECE

FIRST CUT

1/4" 1/4"

FIRST CUT

1/4" 1/4"

1"

SECOND CUT

SECOND CUT

1/4" 3/4"

3/4"

3/4"

1/4"

1/2"

1/4"

THIRD CUT

How to do a corner-lock joint. It is merely a series of straight cuts with 1/4" dadoes.

Splines are slim strips of wood that fit into grooves cut in the edges of mating pieces. Their basic purpose is to reinforce but on many types of joints they also help in assembly.

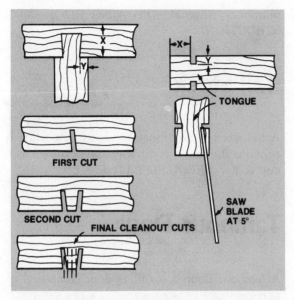

FIRST CUT

SECOND CUT

FINAL CLEANOUT CUTS

TONGUE

SAW BLADE AT 5°

How to cut a dovetail slot and tongue on the table saw. It can be done but the job is much easier to do on other tools.

for some special purpose such as a dovetail slot too large to be handled by more conventional means.

The idea is to make outline cuts with the saw blade slanted to the angle needed. Then, with the blade vertical, clean out the stock between. Blade slant, accuracy of cut, and good depth-of-cut settings are all very important. *SEE ALSO BAND SAW; BENCH GRINDER; DRILL PRESS; JIGSAW; JOINTER; LATHE; RADIAL ARM SAW; SHAPER; STATIONARY BELT & DISC SANDER.*

Table of Wattages

The following table provides the approximate consumption of each article in watts. This table may help to estimate operating cost or power required for the appliances listed.

Appliances	Watts
Air Conditioner, room type	800 to 1500
Blanket	150 to 200

Appliances	Watts
Clock	2 to 3
Coffeemaker (percolator)	500 to 1000
Dish washer	600 to 1000
Dryer, clothes	4000 to 5000
Fan, portable	50 to 200
Food mixer	120 to 250
Freezer, household	300 to 500
Fryer, deep-fat	1200 to 1650
Frying pan	1000 to 1200
Garbage disposal unit	200 to 400
Heater, portable	1000 to 1500
Heater, walltype, permanently installed	1000 to 2300
Heating pad	50 to 75
Heat lamp (infrared)	250
Hot plate, per burner	600 to 1000
Iron, hand (steam or dry)	660 to 1100
Lamps, fluorescent	15 to 60
Lamps, incandescent	10 and up
Motors: 1/4 horse power	300 to 400
1/2 horse power	450 to 600
over 1/2 h. p. per h. p.	950 to 1000
Radio	40 to 150
Range (all burners and oven on)	8000 to 14,000
Range oven (separate)	4000 to 5000
Range top (separate)	4000 to 6000
Razor	8 to 12
Refrigerator, household	150 to 300
Roaster	1200 to 1650
Rotisserie (broiler)	1200 to 1650
Sewing machine	60 to 90
Sunlamp (ultra-violet)	275 to 400
Television	200 to 400
Toaster	500 to 1200
Waffle iron	600 to 1000
Washer, automatic	600 to 800
Washing machine	350 to 550
Water heaters	2000 to 5000
Vacuum cleaner	250 to 800

Tacker

A tacker or stapling hammer is a stapling tool that is used like a hammer. The staple is released when the tacker makes contact with the surface. It is not designed for accuracy and is used on jobs such as tacking building paper and vapor barriers where accuracy is not needed. *SEE ALSO STAPLING TOOLS.*

Tack Rag

A tack rag is a cloth, preferably cheesecloth, permeated with varnish so that it becomes tacky. It is excellent for dust removal before applying a finish. Keep the tack rag in a closed container so that it does not dry out. *SEE ALSO WOOD FINISHING.*

Tacks

Tacks are small, sharp pointed nails used on light fastening jobs. They are usually used to attach fabric or carpet to wood. Tacks are made in a round or cut form. *SEE ALSO FASTENERS.*

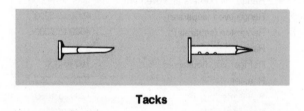

Tacks

Tail

A tail, also called an overhang, is an extension of a rafter. Tails may be found on hip jacks and common rafters. *SEE ALSO ROOF CONSTRUCTION.*

Tail Cut

A tail cut is the end cut of a rafter which is opposite the plumb cut. This cut is parallel to the

plumb or ridgecut. *SEE ALSO ROOF CONSTRUCTION.*

Tail Stock

A tail stock is an adjustable head of a lathe. It contains the dead center sometimes known as a cup center. *SEE ALSO LATHE.*

Tambour Door

A tambour door is a rolling door composed of narrow strips of wood glued to a flexible backing. Tambour doors are found on the top or front of cabinets and rolltop desks and do not need any swing space.

Tang Chisel

A tang chisel is one of the three kinds of wood chisels. The projecting end of the chisel, which is inserted in the handle to keep the two parts of the tool together, is the tang. This type of chisel is primarily used to smooth and finish cuts on wood. When fine work, such as paring stock, is to be done, driving pressure can be applied with the hand or lightly with a mallet. While employing the tang chisel, it should always be held with the backside of the chisel against the work. *SEE ALSO HAND TOOLS.*

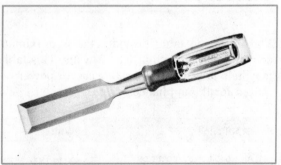

Courtesy of Stanley Works

Tang Chisel

Tape Measure

A tape measure should be the handyman's first choice for most measuring jobs. Most compact of all types of rules, the tape measure is generally available in lengths from 6' to 50'. One marked both in inches and in feet-and-inches is the most convenient. For easy inside measuring, major manufacturers make the tape container exactly 2" across the base. Because of its flexibility, this tape measures round as well as straight objects.

An important feature of quality tape measures is the end hook, which always appears to be loosely rivetted. Actually, it is mounted to slide a distance equal to its own thickness so both inside and outside measurements will be accurate. The average steel tape rule can be extended unsupported for a distance of about 3'. Where the tape is to be laid along a surface to permit marking at several points along the run, a lock-button type is best. In locked position the tape is held extended and will not roll up automatically, so both your hands are left free. Release the button and the tape rolls back into the container. *SEE ALSO HAND TOOLS.*

Tape Recording Equipment

The oldest form of magnetic tape is *open reel*, or reel-to-reel which was the only available format until the mid 1960's, when cartridge systems began to appear. There is a basic difference between the cartridge and the cassette — the cartridge is a continuous tape; the cassette is a reel-to-reel tape. The difference is pressure and tension on the tape. Much greater tension and therefore, greater wear is imposed upon the cartridge tape. To alleviate some of this, cartridges use lubricated tape.

Cartridge tape is wider than cassette tape — about twice as wide. But since cartridge tape has

twice the number of tracks on it, the tracks, cartridge or cassette, are about the same width and therefore have about the same audio characteristics.

The eight-track cartridge (a plastic box about the size of a paperback book containing an endless loop of tape) was introduced by Lear Jet in the mid-1960's. The eight-track cartridge is merely inserted in the player and begins to play. It plays over and over again with only brief interruptions while it switches automatically from one pair of tracks to the next.

Cartridges play continuously because the tape forms an endless loop. The quarter-inch tape, travelling at $3^3/_4$ inches per second, goes into a kind of a whirlpool to get from the inside of the storage spool to the outside. The frantic twisting and turning of the tape that this entails puts a heavy strain on a film of plastic only 1.5 thousandths of an inch thick. Because the endless loop design involves constant tape-against-tape movement eight-track tapes are graphite-lubricated to assure continued smooth operation.

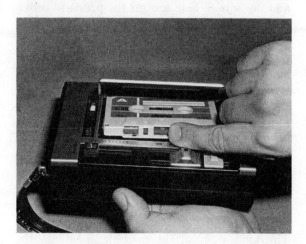

Cassette tape recorders, developed by Philips of Holland, were first available in monaural battery-operated portable models for voice recording. The first stereo cassette systems were sold in 1967. The cassette itself is a miniature tape handling system, with supply and take-up hubs, tape and the necessary guide rollers and pressure pads housed in a molded plastic case about 4" x $2^1/_2$" x $^3/_8$". The tape is only 0.15 inch wide, (compared to 0.25 inch for open reel tape)

and moves at 1$^7/_8$ ips or half the speed of the cartridge. It uses a length of tape shuttling between two tiny reels (instead of the continuous loop in a cartridge). The reel hubs have sprocket teeth so the reels can be driven without slippage.

At the front, three large square openings give access to the tape. The opening in the middle is where the record/playback head presses against the tape. There is a small felt pressure pad behind the tape.

The other two large square holes exchange functions when the cartridge is turned over. The one at the left gives access to the erase head, the other accepts the pressure roller that holds the tape against the drive capstan. There are four small round holes near the front edge. The two center ones are positioning guides. The capstan shaft fits up through whichever of the outer holes is behind the opening into which the pressure roller fits. That places the capstan shaft behind the tape, so it can be pinched between capstan and pressure roller. Flip the cartridge over and the other outer hole takes the capstan, and the square hole accepts the pressure roller.

A typical cassette deck resembles a basic open-reel tape recorder. Instead of placing a reel of tape on the supply hub, treading it across the heads (and sometimes around one or more tension rollers) and wrapping it around a take-up reel hub, the tiny cassette is merely snapped into a recess on the deck, much like an instant load camera, and is ready for playing (or recording). Removal is equally simple (and can be done at any time), since merely pressing an eject button or letter pops the cassette out of the machine.

The back edge of the cassette goes into the machine first. It has to push against a spring at the rear of the cassette-wall which holds the cassette forward firmly against the guide pins. The spring also keeps the cassette firm when the heads are brought forward against the tape.

The cassette lift mechanism is activated by depressing the cassette eject button. This action moves a metal slide which works a lever that raises a lifter bar that pushes up the front edge of

the cassette and literally flips the cassette out of the well.

The motor of the drive system is DC operated and power is usually applied through a locking button switch. Beneath the deck, a rubber drive belt fits around a pulley on the motor shaft and goes around a large heavy flywheel. The drive belt also passes over a plastic pulley wheel. When the button is pressed, this idler tightens the drive belt.

The heavy flywheel has a shaft extending through the deck to the top. That is the capstan. The headassembly plate moves back in the *Stop* position.

The pressure roller is mounted on the plate so it is away from the capstan shaft.

The capstan fits up through a hole in the cartridge, so that the tape fits between the capstan and the pressure roller. When the play button is pushed down, the head-assembly plate moves the pressure roller out against the capstan. With the motor running, the tape is then pulled along.

A unique feature of the cassette is its ability to safeguard against accidental erasure of a recording through built-in *lockout holes* (sometimes called anti-record notches) along the rear edge. When a blank cassette which has the lockout hole closed by a small plastic tab is in position, a little spring-loaded lever is pushed back. With the hole open, as it is on prerecorded cassettes or when the lock-out tapes are removed by the user, *nothing* pushes the lever back; it fits into the open hole, the lockout mechanism stays down, and the *Record* button cannot be pushed in. So, you cannot accidently ruin a prerecorded tape.

MAINTENANCE TIPS

Cleanliness is one of the most important factors in keeping your machine's sound crisp and interference-free. A good investment is an all-in-one clean-up kit, containing volatile cleaner, lubricant, and brushes. Put these to use in the following ways: The constant friction of tape against the magnetic record/playback head will transfer a bit of the brownish tape oxide to the head surface. It is easily removed by careful brushing with cleaner fluid. Similarly, cleaner can be used to remove oxides and grease from the drive wheel and capstan for better speed regulation.

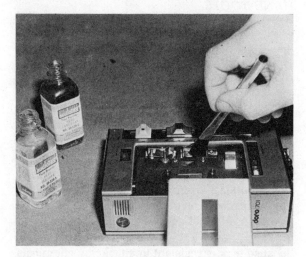

Apply a dab of head lubricant to a cleaned head to minimize friction and oxide build-up. (*Never* apply lubricant to drive components or rubber parts.).

A dry brush can be used to clean lint and dust from crevices around microphone parts.

Wrinkles or twists in a thin drive belt can destroy speed regulation in a cassette recorder. Straightening is a simple operation. Loose screws on motor pulley or mount can be

tightened in seconds and correct *flutter* and *wow* problems.

If your recorder is battery-powered, be sure you are using the right battery type. The alkaline type is a better, longer-life choice for running a tape motor than a flashlight battery.

Poor wire connections at battery compartment and speaker terminals can cause intermittent operation. Check these weak spots before taking your machine in for repairs.

"Scratchy" volume controls are fixed instantly with an aerosol spray cleaner/lubricant that has a thin extension tube designed to deposit cleaner in tight spots. The cleaner is inexpensive and available at any electronics distributor.

A final tip—make a regular check on the condition of plugs, wires and connectors used with your tape machine. A break in one of these may cause you to blame the machine when a stereo channel goes dead or the unit will not play.

Taper File

The taper file, also called a saw file, is commonly used for sharpening saws, axes and other tools that require a sharp edge. The taper file should have a cross section at least twice the depth of the saw's tooth, and be long to insure steady, efficient strokes. *SEE ALSO HAND TOOLS.*

Taps
[SEE DIES & TAPS]

Tap Splice

The tap splice is used when it is necessary to "tap" the current in an existing circuit. Strip about one inch of insulation from the circuit wire and approximately three inches from the tap wire. The splice is made by twisting the tap wire around the circuit wire until it is covered. Start the twisting at the ends nearest the insulation of the tap wire and at a point from which the twisting may be continued from left to right on the circuit wire. Solder and tape the splice. *SEE ALSO ELECTRICAL WIRING.*

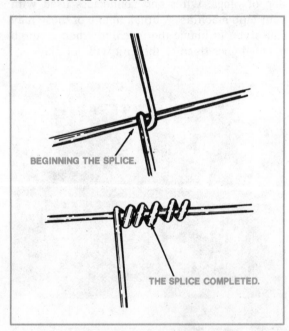

BEGINNING THE SPLICE.

THE SPLICE COMPLETED.

Making a tap splice.

T-Bevel Square

The sliding T-bevel is similar to a try square. However, it has a blade that is adjustable to any angle. The slotted blade can be extended to either side of the handle or centered to form the T that accounts for the name. While it can be used to measure an angle and then transfer it to another area, the T-bevel and to check the accuracy of a bevel being planed. *SEE ALSO HAND TOOLS.*

Teak

Teak is an exotic hardwood found in Thailand, India, Burma and Java. It is brown with olive-green or gold tints and has an unusual scent. The best finishing results are obtained with a penetrating stain. Teak is strong, hard and resistant to attacks from insects and fungus decay. The wood contains minerals and silicates which give it an oily feel and which dulls tools.

Because teak is resistant to attacks by chemicals such as acids or alkalis, it can be used for vats and laboratory benches. Teak is used in fine furniture and paneling. Because of its durability, it has become increasingly popular in shipbuilding. *SEE ALSO WOOD IDENTIFICATION.*

Tee-Nuts

Tee-nuts are screws used to fasten wood when steel threads are advantageous. They can attach permanent or temporary assemblies together. Tee-nuts can mount a speaker in a stereo cabinet or make a carport roof a temporary structure. *SEE ALSO NUTS & BOLTS.*

Telephone Answering Machines & Accessories

Countless telephone calls are now being handled by marvelously efficient secretaries like the highly sophisticated Doro 320 Automatic Telephone Answering/Recording machine.

Simply connect one to any telephone jack of your (unattended) phone line and right after the very first ring an amazing sequence of events takes place automatically in this unobtrusive electronic automation.

To get the machine ready for use, a 20 second message is recorded on an endless loop cassette which is then put into the Outgoing Message Compartment. Another cassette is placed in the incoming Message Compartment. The machine is then set up to record, the Ready button is pressed, the Ready light goes on and it is ready.

An incoming call activates the answering mechanism which plays back to the caller, the previously recorded message along the lines of "Mr. Jones is away, Please leave a message and he will call you back. Start talking when you hear the tone." Then it "beeps" the caller leaves a message (as long as he keeps talking the machine stays on) and hangs up - and so does the machine.

The owner may play back his message when he returns to the machine or he gets them remotely by phone. To do so, he calls his own number, waits for the beep and then places a unique transistorized remote control tone transmitter near the phone. By pressing the correct sequence of buttons he produces a group of tones that allow him to: retrieve messages and backspace as often as needed for "repeats" or record on the incoming message tape to leave his own

message. If he should so choose he can remotely change the outgoing message.

Many answering machines have a message waiting light so you can see immediately if anyone called. Most machines also allow you to listen in as messages are being left by callers. This allows you to screen calls and pick up your phone (the answering machines do not interfere with the normal use of the phone) only for those calls you wish to accept personally.

AUTOMATIC DIALER

An automatic magnetic memory dialer like the *dial-mate* shown, can store up to 40 phone numbers previously dialed into it and dial them for you on command simply at the touch of the button.

Courtesy of Phone Mate

To place selected phone numbers into the memory they are "dialed in" (area code and all) one at a time, as the selector button is successively moved from one position to the next. Write the name for the appropriate number on the index sheet and then each time the button is next to the selected name, the proper number is dialed every time you push the button.

The instrument is battery operated and easily installed. For a standard telephone with a four prong plug and socket, the dial-mate comes equipped with an adapter that is sandwiched between the plug and the socket. If your telephone has a row of push buttons and more than one phone line, another special 50 pin sandwich plug adapter is provided.

The self dialer function has been combined with a conferencer. This unit can connect together two or three different lines so they can converse together or as with the conference caller, can be used to transfer a call to another phone.

CALL DIVERTER

Telephone accessories have reached such a level of sophication that you can now obtain an instrument that will automatically and silently switch incoming telephone calls to any other number you select; local or long distance.

You simply set the outgoing number dials on the machine the number to which you want your incoming calls transferred and, without the calling party's being aware of the diversion, calls are directed to the number of your choice. You can change the forwarding number in just a few seconds by simply resetting the numbers on the dials.

TELEPHONE AMPLIFIER

A Speakerphone is a battery operated telephone accessory which plugs into any standard four-prong telephone outlet. It lets you write, work or

walk around the room while carrying on a telephone conversation. The Speakerphone broadcasts incoming calls over a loudspeaker, while the outgoing conversation is picked up through a separate microphone.

To use this instrument you simply dial the telephone (or answer it) in the normal manner then turn the Speakerphone on and hang up the telephone. A volume control adjusts the caller's voice to a suitable level. Then to terminate the call, simply turn the Speakerphone off.

The unit may also be used to receive incoming calls only without use of a telephone instrument. This is useful in such areas as playrooms, stockrooms or conference rooms where outside dialing capability is not needed.

TELEPHONE CONFERENCER

An inconspicuous little instrument called a Phone Sentry Conference caller can join together as many as five phone lines so they can all talk to each other. If you receive a call and want a three way conversation, simply call out on another line and when you get your party, put the switches of the two lines you are using on and the two parties can join you in a three way dialogue.

If you want to transfer an incoming call, put it on hold, get your number, and then put both switches on, and so you can talk to 2, 3, or more people at the same time. How many hook-ups you can make is only limited by the number of phone lines you have.

Courtesy of Phone Mate

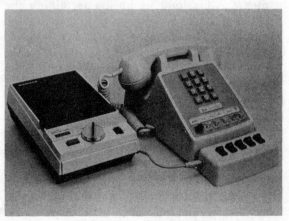

Courtesy of Phone Mate

Some models are equipped with a small jack that can connect to a tape recorder to make a permanent record of a fleeting, but important, conversation. The same jack can also be used to pipe in music or any other previously recorded information to any and all lines connected to the conference caller.

Installation is simple and all that is needed is a small plate attached to the front of the phone. A special two-way connector is attached to the multi-wire cable that comes from the conference caller.

This connector is sandwiched between the connector which now couples your phone to the one at the end of the cable from the phone lines. The whole assembly is held together with two screws as illustrated.

The connector on the phone cable slips into the female side of the Phone-Sentry Conference Caller's connector. The other side of the Phone Sentry Conference Caller's connector fits into the other half of the phone's connector. The assembly is secured with only two screws.

WIRELESS EXTENSION PHONE

No matter how many extension telephones you have they never seem to be in those hard-to-reach places like patios, gardens, bathrooms or basement laundry or workshop just when someone calls or you want to use the phone. A new "tag-along" telephone called a Rovafone operates like a standard extension telephone and is powered by rechargeable batteries. You dial

out and receive calls in the usual way, but you can carry the phone with you, and there are no cords to plug in or tag along.

The Rovafone contains a built-in transmitter and receiver that communicate over a distance no greater than 100 yards with a transponder unit connected to any standard telephone jack. The transponder relays the conversation from the Rovafone to the phone line.

A TELEPHONE WITH A MEMORY

The Star-Touch is a desk-type push-button telephone whose electronic memory stores the last complete number "touched in" on the push buttons — up to 20 digits — and redials that number automatically, as often as desired, simply by touching the star (☆) button. If you get a busy signal or just want to call back the party you talked to, simply pickup the hand set, listen for dial tone, touch the star (☆) button and the number will be dialed again. If it is still busy, hang up and try again as often as you wish.

For security you can touch in the number of the police, or fire departments before you retire. Or, if you want to leave a number with the baby sitter, just dial it in and hang up. A single brief touch on the Star and the complete number is dialed automatically. If while talking to a friend or information he gives you a number to call, simply dial it in *while you are still talking* and the Star-Touch will dial it for you next time you are ready to dial out.

Courtesy of Fonetron, Inc.

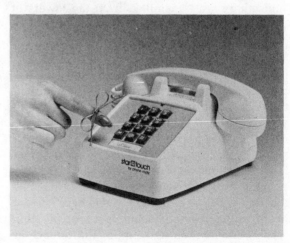

Courtesy of Phone Mate

Television Repairs & Troubleshooting

Experts estimate that up to 30 percent of all service calls made by television service technicians are not due to any problem within the set itself. If you include the problems that can arise with antenna and signal difficulties, the percentage rises even higher.

Other than checking these external causes, make no attempt to repair a receiver while it is still under warranty. To do so may invalidate the warranty. Refer these calls to an authorized servicing agency. Be sure that you have checked the external causes listed here, however; otherwise, you may be charged for the call.

If you have one of the newer solid state sets, there is very little internal work that you will be able to do even if you have the know-how. A lot of specialized equipment is required for this work. The trend to solid state components will hopefully serve to increase the reliability of the receiver.

To know what to do when a television set (receiver) fails to operate, it's important that you understand the fundamentals of its operation. To begin with, the air and atmosphere around us are filled with radio signals. Some are natural and others are transmitted from the towers of radio and television stations.

The antenna system serves to collect these signals out of the air and direct them to the appropriate terminals on your receiver. In addition to the ability of taking a signal and sending it to your set without outside interference, the antenna should also be capable of rejecting unwanted signals, primarily those striking the antenna from directions other than that from which the primary signal is being transmitted. Antennas that do a good job of this are said to have narrow beam width. Where ghosting is a problem, this type of antenna can make quite a difference in the picture that eventually gets to your screen.

Once the signal reaches the set it must be decoded before the set can put the appropriate picture on your screen and synchronize (or sync) each segment of the signal. To do this, it goes through a number of circuits within the set that electronically separate various portions of the signal, sending it to the proper point to do the job for which it is intended. Some of these signals go to sound circuits, similar to those found in an FM radio. Other portions go to provide such aspects of the picture as brightness, color, etc. The video portion provides the proper horizontal and vertical sweep and the image. Color carriers are directed to the appropriate "guns" within the picture tube which causes red, green, and blue phosphor dots on the screen to glow at a particular intensity to provide the correct color hue. These small dots, which in most standard color picture tubes are arranged in triads or triangles, combine when they reach your eye only a short distance from the screen. By varying the intensity of these primary colors, practically any shading desired can be obtained. Electrons emitted from the "guns" electronically "sweep" the face of the picture tube 30 times each second.

With these basics in mind, we can take a closer look at some of the more common problems that can arise with television receivers. To follow all of the procedures here, it will be *unnecessary* to remove the service panel from the set. Later on, information will be given about procedures that do involve service inside the set. These must be done with extreme caution, following all the precautions given. But even if you're working only with an antenna system, for instance, be sure to *unplug the receiver* and *disconnect the antenna lead from the set before preceding with service.* Under all circumstances avoid touching any terminal or component that may carry electrical current. This is important, since extremely high voltages (up to 25,000 volts) exist within television receivers.

HOW TO USE THE TELEVISION TROUBLE-SHOOTING CHARTS

The first thing that you should do when your television receiver fails to operate is to consult the information supplied by the manufacturer. These instructions will pertain to the particular make and model that you own, and should list any specific checks. Next, check the normal controls that might affect the portion of the set that the symptoms identify; both the charts and text of this entry will help you do this. Finally, if you elect to proceed further, the charts will give you an idea of the area and tubes which might likely cause the problem.

Read all of the safety precautions contained here and in your manufacturer's instructions before removing the service panel of a television receiver and proceed with utmost caution. Disconnect the set from the receptacle, discharge the picture tube or the high voltage to the main chassis of the set only, and move the set away

from any grounded objects. Use care to prevent injury from broken glass. When working around the picture tube, wear safety goggles.

When testing television receiving tubes on tube-testing equipment, check any new tubes that you purchase as well as any old ones. This helps to verify the results indicated by the tester.

Many retail stores which sell television sets also sell tubes. You can obtain a complete line of electronic parts by mail as well. Switches, knobs, and parts made for a particular set should be obtained from an authorized parts agency or ordered from the manufacturer.

NOTE: Disconnect all power to receiver, discharge high voltage, move receiver from grounded objects and observe all safety precautions when removing service panel from receiver. Use extreme caution.

TV CHART

Symptom	Possible Cause	Remedy
1. No picture, no sound screen dark	No voltage to TV receiver	Be sure that set is plugged in.
		Check receptacle with table lamp to see if voltage is reaching receptacle. Replace fuse or circuit breaker in house circuit. Check interlock at back of set.
	Circuit breaker in receiver kicked out.	Reset circuit breaker by depressing red button on rear of set. If set has electronic fuse, turn set off for two minutes, then turn back on.
	Tube burned out (series tube type set)	Look through vent openings to see if tube filaments are lit. If tubes have elements in series any open filaments would prevent all from operating. If tube designations begin with various and assorted numbers, chances are it's a series type system. If tubes begin with 6 or 12 you can assume that they are wired in parallel and this problem would not occur.
	Defective on/off switch, circuit breaker or fused wire. Open power supply or rectifiers.	Refer to service technician.
2. No picture, no sound screen lights.	Decoding or detector circuits inoperative.	Check mixer oscillator tubes, IF tubes and video detector tubes.
3. Has picture, no sound.	Station experiencing temporary difficulty.	Turn to another channel to check.
	No power to speaker	Check to see that speaker is connected. Turn volume control full or listen closely for "hiss" at speaker. If present, check audio output and audio amplifier tubes. If intelligible sound can be heard but at low level, check audio detector and audio IF tubes. If speaker is out altogether, check audio output tubes.
	Defective speaker.	Check by substituting another speaker of same impedance. If sound comes on, replace speaker.

TV CHART		
Symptom	**Possible Cause**	**Remedy**
4. Sound, no picture	Brightness control turned down	Adjust brightness correctly
	No high voltage to picture tube.	Check tubes marked high-voltage regulator, high-voltage rectifier, horizontal output, horizontal oscillator, damper, video output tubes. Note: if you find a bad high-voltage rectifier or horizontal oscillator tube change the horizontal output tube as well.
	Bad picture tube	Refer to service technician.
5. Has sound, picture poor	Weak signal reaching TV set receiver.	Check antenna connections at back of set, check antenna connections at antenna, check condition of antenna cable, check condition of antenna head.
	Picture out of focus	
	Bad focus rectifier tube.	Check and replace tube if necessary. Note: focus rectifier might also be a small selenium rectifier soldered into circuit.
	Insufficient high voltage.	Check high-voltage rectifier, voltage regulator, horizontal output tube.
	Defective picture tube or yoke.	Refer to service technician.
6. Horizontal tear.	Horizontal hold control out of adjustment.	Adjust horizontal hold.
	Problem in horizontal circuit	Check all tubes with horizontal pertaining to their name: oscillator, output, phase detector, sync separator.
	Problem with yoke.	Refer to service technician.
7. Vertical roll	Vertical hold set incorrectly.	Adjust vertical hold control.
	Problem in vertical circuit.	Check vertical oscillator, output, and check the sync tubes.
	Vertical adjustments out.	Adjust from rear when test pattern is being broadcast.
8. No contrast.	Contrast control adjusted incorrectly.	Adjust control.
	Problem in IF circuit, tuner, or video detectors.	Check video amplifier, video output, video detector and audio output tubes.
	Defective picture tube.	Refer to service technician.
9. Interference	External cause — ignition noise, amateur radio, etc.	Try to pinpoint source of interference by time observations, sounds, etc. Sometimes amateur radio voice or code transmission is audible through speaker of set. Ignition noise sounds like engine running and changes frequency with speed of engine. Consider installing coaxal or shielded lead-in cable.
	Loose antenna connections.	Check both internal and external connections and tighten.
	Power line interference	Install filter on line or eliminate source of interference.
10. Snow, no color, ghosts.	Usually antenna problems.	Check antenna, reorient it, replace wiring, or repair connections if necessary.
	Tuner contacts dirty.	Clean tuner with approved type of cleaner.

TV CHART		
Symptom	**Possible Cause**	**Remedy**
11. Sound bars in picture.	Fine tuning adjusted incorrectly	Readjust fine tuning with automatic control defeated.
	Tuner needs cleaning.	Clean tuner as necessary.
	Defective output tubes.	Check vertical, horizontal, and audio output tubes.
12. No color, black and white picture okay.	Weak signals reaching set.	Check antenna leads at back of set and antenna. Check for damaged antenna. Be sure that antenna is oriented correctly.
	Temporary difficulty at station.	Check other channels.
12. No color, black and white picture okay.	Dirty tuner contacts.	Clean tuner as required.
	Color intensity control incorrectly adjusted.	Adjust intensity control.
	Color killer out of adjustment.	Adjust color killer as described in text.
	Problem in color circuitry.	Check burst emplifier, bandpass amplifier, 3.58 oscillator, burst keyer, and color killer tubes.
13. Color outlines around black and white picture.	Color out of convergence	Requires dot-bar generator to adjust convergence. Refer to service technician.
14. Weak color	Color intensity control incorrectly set.	Adjust control.
	Problem in color circuitry.	Check IF tubes, RF amplifiers, bandpass amplifier, mixer oscillator, video amplifier.
15. Color-shading on black and white programs.	Picture tube needs demagnetizing (degaussing).	Obtain degaussing coil from radio supply or TV service center. Rotate around face of picture tube.
	Color intensity control set too high.	Adjust color intensity control correctly.
	Color triads not mixing properly.	Flip service switch and adjust screen controls as described in text.
	Purity incorrectly set.	Adjust purity at yoke of set. Usually calls for technician.

Tempering

Tempering is a process for giving steel toughness by removing a small degree of hardness and brittleness. The process is accomplished by heating the steel to a certain temperature that is determined by what function the tool is to serve.

Since color is the best guide for indication of the temperature, polish the area to be tempered so that the color can easily be seen. Polishing can be done with steel wool, sandpaper or by grinding. The color is caused by a coating of oxide that forms when the steel is polished, and this color

changes as the temperature increases. Use a small flame and turn the tool so that all sides are heated. Do not apply flame directly to the edge since this section may anneal very quickly. After the required color appears, plunge the metal into water and move it in a circular motion until it is completely cool.

Guide for Tempering			
TOOL	**TEMPERATURE**		**COLOR**
	Fahrenheit	Centigrade	
Hammers and knives	420°	215.34°	Yellow, faint
Scrapers, lathe tools	430°	220.89°	Yellow, light

Guide for Tempering			
TOOL	**TEMPERATURE**		**COLOR**
	FAHRENHEIT	**CENTIGRADE**	
Punches, reamers, dies, bits	460°	237.54°	Straw
Taps, twist drills	480°	248.64°	Brown, light
Drifts, axes, wood chisels	500°	259.74°	Brown, dark
Center punches, cold chisels	540°	281.94°	Purple
Gears, springs, screwdrivers	560°	293.04°	Blue
Spokeshaves, scrapers	600°	315.24°	Blue, dark

Template

A template is a pattern or stencil made of a thin material to be used as an outline for marking or cutting holes in walls or doors or when cutting lumber into special shapes.

Template also refers to a piece of wood placed horizontally under a girder to add extra strength and distribute weight and pressure.

Tenon

A tenon is a tongue or projection cut on the end of a piece of wood that fits into a corresponding hole or slot (mortise) in another piece of wood to make a joint. *SEE ALSO MORTISE & TENON JOINT; WOOD JOINTS.*

Tent Trailers

[SEE RECREATIONAL VEHICLES.]

Termites

[SEE INSECT & PEST CONTROL.]

Termite Shield

A termite shield is a piece of metal placed over the foundation to help protect the structure against the movement of termites. The metal is placed flush with the inside of the foundation and it extends about one inch beyond the outside. Bend the extensions downward. *SEE ALSO FLOOR CONSTRUCTION.*

Terra Cotta Water Pipes
[SEE PLUMBING MATERIALS]

Test Tee

A test tee is a cast-iron soil pipe fitting. Used to join a straight run, the test tee has a plug on its side. *SEE ALSO PIPE FITTINGS.*

Thermocouple

A thermocouple is a device in a gas burning furnace which converts the heat from the pilot light into a small electric current. This current holds open an electrical valve in the gas supply line to the main burner. If the pilot light should ever go out, the thermocouple cools and ceases to produce the electric current and the gas supply valve closes. In this way, gas is not allowed to escape unless the pilot light is lit.

On the other hand, if the pilot light should continually go out, the thermocouple may be defective and should be replaced. *SEE ALSO HOME HEATING SYSTEMS.*

Thermostat

A thermostat is an instrument which regulates temperature, in particular one which controls the operation of a heating or cooling unit. Thermostats may be activated manually or automatically by temperature change. The principle of unequal expansion or contraction of metals under different temperatures is used on most thermostats. The mechanism used is a bimetal strip of two different metals which bend with changes of temperature. This action causes an electrical circuit to open or close, thereby turning on the necessary unit. *SEE ALSO HOME HEATING SYSTEMS.*

Thermostat Lag

Thermostat lag is a condition which results when a room gets warmer than the temperature set on the thermostat. Because it takes time for the thermostat to react and activate the heating unit, the room temperature may continue to drop before the unit begins operating. Then when the set temperature is finally reached in the room, it takes time for the thermostat to respond and cut off the unit. Even after the burner is shut off, the blower will still distribute hot air. The room temperature may then be higher than the temperature set on the thermostat. *SEE ALSO HOME HEATING SYSTEMS.*

Thinner

A thinner is one or a mixture of several materials or solvents used to reduce the viscosity of a finishing substance. Thinners are primarily used for diluting and cleaning.

Thinners are excellent for cleaning painting equipment, removing accidental spots and spills and cleaning paint from hands and other parts of the body except the eyes and mouth. The main purpose is to dilute finishing materials for easier use and better results. Turpentine is used to thin varnish, denatured alcohol is used for shellac and lacquer thinner is used for lacquer. Although not used in latex paint, thinners are used in some paints to achieve the correct con-

sistency before use. Thinners also help lower the amount of solids occurring in some paints. *SEE ALSO PAINTS & PAINTING.*

Thin-Wall Conduit

Thin-wall conduit is a rigid pipe that forms the path for house wiring. Unlike cable, conduit must be wired after the pipe is installed. This type of wire protection is especially helpful under an old house or in northern areas, as conduit will help insulate the wires against cold. Although conduit is harder to install than flexible cable, some areas require it over other types of wiring (especially nonmetallic sheathed cable) because it forms its own grounding system.

Conduit requires a special tool for bending and special clamps and couplers for joining the unthreaded conduit lengths. After sliding the nut-like clamps over the pipe, its ends are inserted into a coupling joint. The clamps are then tightened onto this joint and the conduit is attached to metal boxes with a connector whose unthreaded end is slipped over the conduit. With the end tightly attached to the conduit, the connector is then inserted into the box through a knockout hole and held there with its own locknut. When cutting this particular type of pipe, use a hacksaw and a pipe reamer for smoothing the burrs made by the saw. This will eliminate the possibility of damage to wire insulation. *SEE ALSO ELECTRICAL WIRING.*

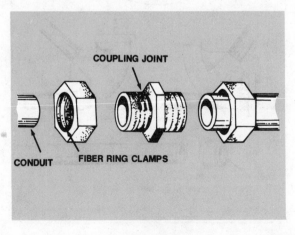

COUPLING JOINT

CONDUIT   FIBER RING CLAMPS

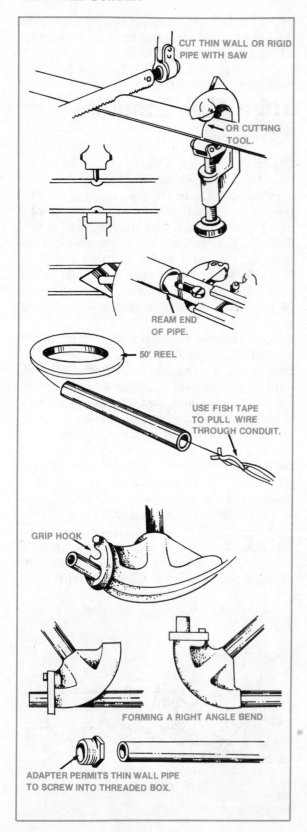

CUT THIN WALL OR RIGID PIPE WITH SAW

OR CUTTING TOOL.

REAM END OF PIPE.

50' REEL

USE FISH TAPE TO PULL WIRE THROUGH CONDUIT.

GRIP HOOK

FORMING A RIGHT ANGLE BEND

ADAPTER PERMITS THIN WALL PIPE TO SCREW INTO THREADED BOX.

Threading Bits

Two major types of threading bits are used in lathe work to form threads of precision accuracy: those which form external threads, as on a bolt, and those which form internal threads, as on a nut. Examples of the external type of threading bits are the pointed 60° tool and the Acme thread tool. The boring bar tool will form internal threads. These bits should all be used in conjunction with a cutting oil such as lard oil.

To sharpen a threading bit, grind only the top. *SEE ALSO LATHE.*

Three-Opening Despard

A three-opening Despard or Despard fixture is a wall plate with three openings that can accommodate a combination of devices such as individual outlets, switches, pilot lights or night lights. The wall plate comes with a metal strap with three openings on which the devices are mounted. The three devices can then be installed in an ordinary switch or outlet box. *SEE ALSO SWITCHES & OUTLETS.*

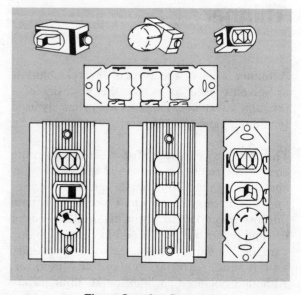

Three-Opening Despard

Three-Prong Grounded Plug

The three-prong grounded plug is a safety feature of many electrical appliances. The plug includes a third prong that serves to continue the grounding system through the appliance to the house ground and to assure that the plug is inserted into the receptacle correctly, avoiding a short circuit. A three-prong grounded plug and its receptacle should be installed in workshop and basement areas where the floor is frequently damp and in other areas where 240-volt appliances are located. *SEE ALSO PLUGS & CORDS.*

Three-Prong Plug Receptacle

A three-prong plug receptacle is an electrical outlet made to receive three-prong plugs. Two of the slots in the outlet and two of the plug prongs carry current. The third slot and prong provide a ground for the appliance because the third outlet slot is connected to ground and the third plug prong is connected to the frame or motor of the appliance or power tool. Two-prong plugs will also fit into this receptacle, but will not be grounded.

Three-Prong Plug Receptacles

In the past, this grounding type of receptacle was only required in workshops, garages or where there was a concrete or earthen floor. However, in 1962 the National Electrical Code required that three-prong plug receptacles be used in all household locations. *SEE ALSO SWITCHES & OUTLETS.*

Three-Square File

The three-square file, which is generally used for sharpening saws, is triangular-shaped at one end and tapered at the other. The triangular file and the three-square file are identical except for the fact that the three-square is doublecut and the triangular is singlecut. Because of its shape, the three-square file can also be used for filing angular notches and sharp corners in wood and metal work. *SEE ALSO HAND TOOLS.*

Three-Way Switch

Three-way switches are switches used in pairs to control one light from two different locations. For example, a light can be turned on from a switch at one location and turned off from a switch at another location regardless of the "on-

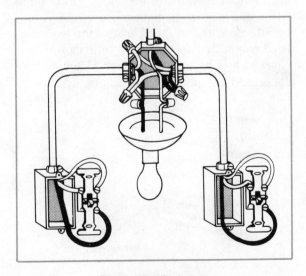

Three-Way Switches

off" position of the first switch. A three-way switch looks like an ordinary wall switch except that it has three terminals and the words "on" and "off" do not appear on the switch lever. *SEE ALSO SWITCHES & OUTLETS.*

Three-Wire Adapter

The three-wire adapter is a two-prong plug with three slotted face that continues the ground of an electrical appliance from its grounding system through a pigtail or neutral wire to the house grounding system. To install a three-wire adapter, connect the lug of the pigtail wire to the ground terminal of the receptacle or to the receptacle cover plate screw and insert the plug into the outlet receptacle. Then, plug the three-prong plug of an appliance into it. This will insure a grounding connection in the case that any live parts of the appliance become loose and touch the metal housing. *SEE ALSO PLUGS & CORDS.*

Three-Wire Cable

Three-wire cable, or service entrance cable, is used to bring power from outside lines to the main entrance switch of the house. Of its three wires, one is not insulated but consists of a number of fine wires wrapped around the two insulated wires. Over this is a flat steel armor further encased in a heavy fabric cover. When wiring,

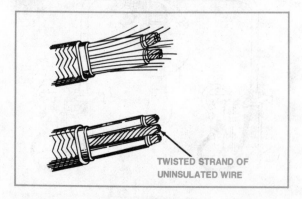

TWISTED STRAND OF
UNINSULATED WIRE

Three-Wire Cable

the fine uninsulated wires are twisted together to form a larger wire which can be used only as the grounded neutral. Besides its indoor and outdoor use, three-wire cable can also be used to wire large appliances such as stoves or water heaters. *SEE ALSO WIRE SIZES & TYPES.*

Three-Wire Circuits

Three-wire circuits increase the volt capacity of house wiring or allow for split circuits. There are two hot wires and a ground in a three-wire circuit. Both hot wires carry 120 volts each or may be combined to the same outlet, switch, etc. for 240 volts. In setting up split circuits, one hot wire is connected to one set of terminal screws of an outlet while the other hot wire is connected to another set of terminal screws on the same outlet. The only ground wire is connected to both sets of ground screws. Some receptacles in the house wiring system need to be wired for 240 volts by connecting both hot wires to the same terminal screws. An example of a receptacle with this requirement is the outlet for a small air conditioner. *SEE ALSO ELECTRICAL WIRING.*

Three-Wire Connections

Three-wire connections are made the same as the standard types with only a few exceptions.

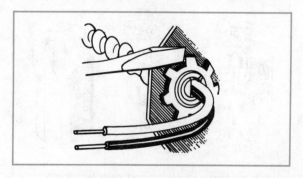

BX Cable to Receptacle Box

For example, in connecting BX or armored cable, a special connecting device is used. Making three-wire connections is shown below. *SEE ALSO ELECTRICAL WIRING.*

Conduit to Receptacle Box

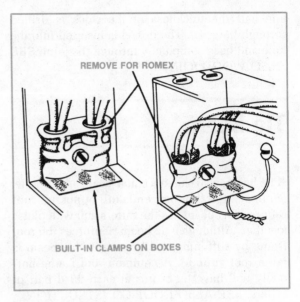

REMOVE FOR ROMEX

BUILT-IN CLAMPS ON BOXES

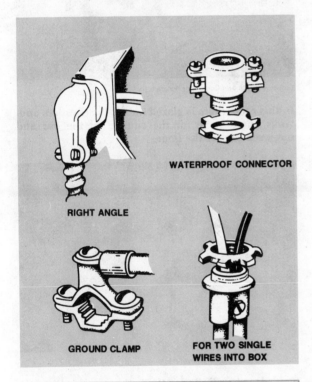

WATERPROOF CONNECTOR

RIGHT ANGLE

GROUND CLAMP

FOR TWO SINGLE WIRES INTO BOX

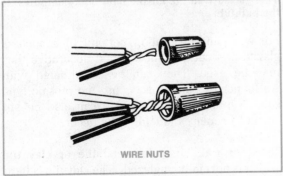

WIRE NUTS

Threshold

A threshold is a wood or aluminum trim piece that is beveled on each edge. Thresholds, sometimes called saddles, are used under outside doors to seal the space between the finished floor and the bottom of the door. *SEE ALSO MOLDING & TRIM.*

Through Dowel

A through dowel is used to lock a finger-lap joint. A hole whose diameter is not greater than

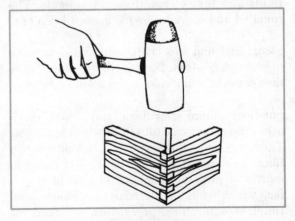

Through Dowel

one half the thickness of the stock is drilled through the joint. The dowel is inserted into the hole and goes completely through the joint. *SEE ALSO WOOD JOINTS.*

Tie Beam

A tie beam, also called a collar beam or rafter tie, connects the bottom ends of opposite roof rafters. This beam ties the rafters and wall plates together. Although a tie beam reinforces the roof frame by stiffening and bracing it, this beam is not a roof support. A common roof frame normally will have tie beams at each third pair of rafters. *SEE ALSO ROOF CONSTRUCTION.*

Tile

Tile is a thin piece of fired clay which may be either flat, or in round tubes or curved halves. Tile is sometimes left in its rough form or is glazed by chemical treatment to give it a smooth, polished surface. Tile can be used throughout the home and other buildings for floors, walls, roof, pipes and decoration.

The rough form of clay tile is used for making tile pipe. These tile pipes, such as concrete tile and vitrified tile pipes, are used in drainage fields and for sewage-disposal systems. The rounded and curved-type tile is used for pipes.

Floor, roof and especially wall and decorative tiles are made from finer grades of clay. These tiles come in many colors, sizes and textures.

For floors, there are rubber, cork, vinyl, vinyl-asbestos and ceramic tiles from which to choose. They may be laid on concrete, brick or wooden floors or over tile. Ceramic tile should be set in mortar or preferably bonded to a wooden surface which would be perfectly flat. Floors need rough-wearing tiles, preferably unglazed for safety purposes.

Courtesy of the Tile Council of America Inc.

In this room there is glazed tile for the counters and walls, mosaic tile for the counter of the bar and unglazed tile for the floor.

Courtesy of Sikes Corporation

This glazed wall tile for the bathroom compliments the bathtub.

For walls and decoration, ceramic tiles, such as glazed and ceramic mosaic and decorative tiles may be used. They can be coordinated with wallpaper or paint colors, and the mosaic type can be hung like a picture. It can also be put around fireplaces to add to the decor.

Tiles for roofs include metal tile or clay tile which is normally unglazed . The clay tile is hard and durable and is available in many shapes and textures to compliment different styles of buildings. *SEE ALSO FINISH FLOORING; REMODELING; SUSPENDED CEILINGS.*

Courtesy of Automated Building Components, Inc.

The blue roof tile adds to the oriental style home.

Tile, Acoustical
[SEE ACOUSTICS & SOUND CONTROL.]

Tile Floor Construction

Tile floor construction should be considered for any area that has constant heavy traffic. Tile floors are a wise investment because they can be easily cleaned, are resilient, and since tiles are available in a number of materials, styles and colors, they can be used in almost every room of the house. However, tile floors are most often found in basement recreation rooms, foyers and entrance halls and bathrooms.

Types of floor tile include cork, vinyl cork, solid vinyl, asphalt, vinyl-asbestos, and a variety of ceramic designs and colors. The most popular is vinyl-asbestos because it is inexpensive, and will adhere to any type of subflooring. In addition, a minimum of tools are needed when laying vinyl asbestos, because it can be cut with scissors.

The basic tools needed to lay tile are a chalk line, a pair of scissors or a ceramic cutter, a ruler and pencil, a marking awl, a paintbrush, a carpenter's square and perhaps a mastic spreader for some jobs. Consult a tile dealer for tools recommended for the particular choice of tile.

SELECTING THE TILE

Most tile comes in boxes of 80; however most dealers will split a box if asked. Remember to add a certain percentage for waste allowance and a few more to save for repairs in the future. The following chart will help when computing the number of tiles needed:

Square Feet	Number of Tiles Needed		
	6" x 6"	9" x 9"	12" x 12"
1	4	2	1
2	8	4	2
3	12	6	3
4	16	8	4
5	20	9	5
6	24	11	6
7	28	13	7
8	32	15	8
9	36	16	9
10	40	18	10
20	80	36	20
30	120	54	30
40	160	72	40
50	200	89	50
60	240	107	60
70	280	125	70
80	320	143	80
90	360	160	90
100	400	178	100
200	800	356	200
300	1200	534	300
400	1600	712	400
500	2000	890	500
600	2400	1068	600
700	2800	1246	700
800	3200	1424	800
900	3600	1602	900
1000	4000	1780	1000

Tile Waste Allowances

1 to 50 sq. ft.	14%
50 to 100 sq. ft.	10%
100 to 200 sq. ft.	8%
200 to 300 sq. ft.	7%
300 to 1000 sq. ft.	5%
over 1000 sq. ft.	3%

Use the chart like this: Suppose you are trying to compute the number of tiles needed for an area 629 sq. ft. First, find the size tile needed (given are the sizes most frequently used) and then find the number needed for 600 sq. ft. Add to that the number needed for 20 sq. ft. and then add that needed for 9 sq. ft. When these three numbers are combined, find the percentage for waste allowance and the total results.

PREPARING THE SUBFLOORING

Once the tile has been decided on, the subflooring must be inspected. Unless a tile is used that is hard like ceramic, the soft surface will mold to every bump and crack to produce an unsightly appearance. If the floor is concrete, fill in small holes and cracks with spackling compound. File level when dry. If the floor is wood, plane down any rough places and fill cracks with wood putty. Like concrete, it can be filed level when dry. If the floor is in poor condition, consider covering it with felt and applying a finish with plywood or underlayment. Both these materials cost about the same, although underlayment might be a better choice because it comes in 4′ x 4′, and 3′ x 4′ sizes that can make installation easier. Some underlayment is marked for nailing, which can be a great help. When laying either plywood or underlayment, never butt the edges. Leave a small space for natural expansion.

Once the floor is ready to receive the tile, there are several steps that should be followed. First mark the floor. To do this find the center of one of the walls and mark it with a tack. Attach a string to the wall that has been rubbed in chalk. Extend the string to the center line at the opposite wall and spring the chalk line to make a chalk line on the floor. Repeat this process on the adjacent walls. Tiles must be laid from the center to the edge and make sure the last tile laid is at least three-fourths of the tile to be used. If it is not move the chalk line a few inches left or right to allow for this. Spreading the adhesive is next.

APPLYING THE ADHESIVE

There are two types of adhesives. The best is clear because when it is spread on the floor, the small amounts that seep through the tile joints will be transparent. The second choice is black mastic. Note whether the adhesive chosen is combustible. If it is, use common sense about

lighting matches and cigarettes around the job site.

Brush a *thin* coat of the mastic over one fourth of the floor. When it is spread, give it time to set up before applying the tile. The adhesive is ready to accept the tile when the clear adhesive looses its color and the black adhesive no longer sticks to the fingers.

LAYING THE TILE

When laying the tile, start at the chalk lines and keep feet off the mastic. Work from the center of the room laying the first row along the chalk line. Work outward towards the walls. When cutting the border tiles, lay a second tile over the last tile and a second one over that, butted against the wall. Using the top tile as a straightedge, mark off a line where the overlap is on the tile under it. Now cut the tile and that will be the border tile.

Repeat the process over the remaining three-fourths of the floor.

TILE HINTS

For exterior use there is a selection of resilient tiles from which to choose. Made to cover concrete that is exposed to extreme weather conditions, these are easily cleaned by sweeping or hosing down with water. Never use an oil based product on this type of flooring.

Ceramic or clay tile is the oldest type of tile and provides a greater choice in combinations and designs than the other types of tile. Installation is similar to that of other types of tile except special types of cutters are used. *SEE ALSO FINISH FLOORING.*

Timber Saw

The timber saw is designed for cutting down trees. Its long blade, generally between five-and eight-feet long, has coarse teeth and wooden handles at each end to be used by two men working together. *SEE ALSO HAND TOOLS.*

Timers

[SEE AUTOMATION.]

Timing, Automobile

[SEE SYSTEMS, AUTOMOTIVE.]

Tires

[SEE SYSTEMS, AUTOMOTIVE.]

Toasters

[SEE ELECTRIC TOASTER REPAIR.]

Toenailing

Toenailing is a method of nailing in which the nail is driven in at an angle through the end or edge of one piece of lumber into another piece. Toenailing is the most effective way to nail wall studs to other framing. SEE ALSO NAILING.

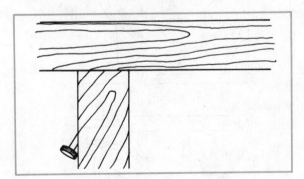

Toenailing

Toe Space

A toe space is located at the base of a cabinet and the floor. It is a recess that allows a person to stand close to a vertical surface without striking it with his toes. SEE ALSO CABINETMAKING.

Toggle Bolt

A toggle bolt is a fastener used on hollow walls. A hole must be drilled in the wall that is large enough for the spring-loaded wings to pass through. As the head is screwed, the wings spread and bear against the wall. SEE ALSO NUTS & BOLTS.

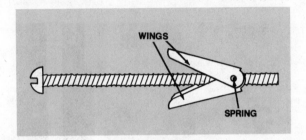

Toggle Bolt

Toilet

A toilet is a bowl-shaped bathroom plumbing fixture designed with devices to flush out waste.

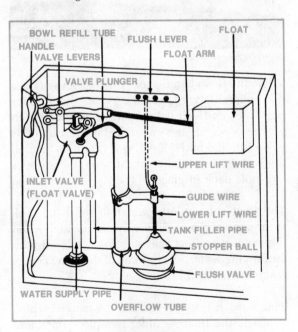

Parts of Toilet

Its main working mechanisms are found inside the holding tank which has a handle located on the outside. Pushing down the handle starts a series of movements which flush out the toilet bowl and refill it with fresh water.

A standard toilet tank includes these parts — the handle, upper and lower lift wires, guide wire, overflow and bowl refill tubes, stopper ball, flush valve, valve seat, float, float arm, ball cock valve or float valve, valve plunger and flush and valve levers.

Courtesy of American Standard

When the flush handle goes down, a lever raises the upper lift wire which elevates the stopper ball from its flush valve seat. From four to ten gallons of water goes out of the tank through this valve into the bowl, flushing it rapidly. Once all the water has gone out of the tank, the stopper ball falls back in place.

The float valve allows water to refill the tank from supply pipes. This valve is opened when the connecting float arm and float go down with outflowing water. Water to refill the bowl comes from another refill tube.

There are different types of toilet models which attach to the floor — older two-piece ones and newer tank-bowl combinations which don't

overflow. For modern decor, some toilets attach to the bathroom wall without touching the floor.

There are three major types of toilets: the siphon washdown, the reverse trap and the siphon jet. The siphon jet is the most recently developed of the three.

Water action through toilet bowls is basically the same in all models. When water goes into the bowl, it goes through little holes located around the bowl's circumference. This incoming water builds up pressure and goes over to the rear of the trap near the base of the bowl. The inlet in the trap is larger than its outlet. The trap design also allows water to come in faster than it goes out.

Trap passages become filled with water which is forced out by a siphoning vacuum-like action and air pressure. When the water level falls, air is sucked into the trap. The tank's refill tube then brings in more bowl water.

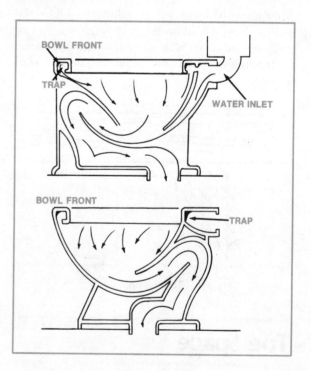

An inexpensive type toilet, the siphon washdown, has a trap in front of the bowl. Besides using more water in flushing than other types, this toilet is slower and louder. The water level inside the bowl is lower also, making cleaning difficult.

The reverse trap toilet has a back trap to let in more water, but otherwise is very similar to the washdown.

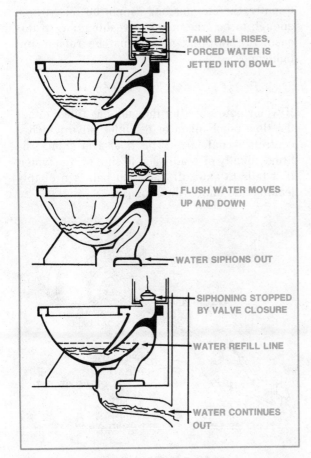

TANK BALL RISES, FORCED WATER IS JETTED INTO BOWL

FLUSH WATER MOVES UP AND DOWN

WATER SIPHONS OUT

SIPHONING STOPPED BY VALVE CLOSURE

WATER REFILL LINE

WATER CONTINUES OUT

The more efficient siphon-jet toilet has a rear trap like the reverse trap. Its jet-like action brings water into the trap quickly for quieter, more effective flushing. *SEE ALSO PLUMBING FIXTURES.*

Toilet Repair

Toilet repair can be quite simple since most toilets operate basically the same way. They are usually controlled by two valves which are opened and closed by levers and other connecting parts.

IMPROPER FILLING

One common problem is improper filling of the toilet tank. When water continues to run into the bowl after flushing, it may be accompanied by a singing noise or low whistling. This is caused by a worn rubber flush ball valve failing to fit into the flush valve seat.

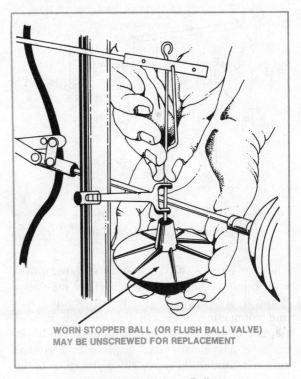

WORN STOPPER BALL (OR FLUSH BALL VALVE) MAY BE UNSCREWED FOR REPLACEMENT

Removal of Stopper Ball

STOPPER BALL REPLACEMENT

To replace a flush ball valve or stopper, first shut off the water supply to the toilet tank or tie the float ball arm up high to an overhead object. Both methods prevent the tank's refilling. Flush the tank to empty it and unscrew the stopper ball from its lower end. Check the valve seat and clean it before screwing on the new attachment.

CYLINDER REPLACEMENT

Some modern toilets have a flange instead of the stopper ball valve. This flange rests in the valve and rocks upward when the flush handle is activated. A cylinder attached to the flange has small holes in it to draw in water after flushing. When the water goes out, it drains through the bottom hole in the cylinder. As the cylinder empties, it loses its weight and repositions itself in the valve seat. The cylinder can be unscrewed to be replaced although it rarely goes bad.

FLUSH-VALVE UNIT REPLACEMENT

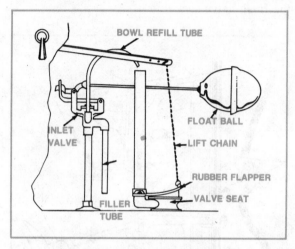

Flapper Flush Valve Tank

The new flapper valve type of flush valve unit is all rubber and slips over the overflow pipe after removal of the stopper guide, old stopper ball and connecting wires. In this more advanced flapper valve, a chain links the valve to the flushing arm. The unit is held in place by a rubber ring grip around the pipe. The distance from the old unit's overflow pipe surface to the center of its flush valve should match the distance from the friction ring grip of the new flapper valve unit to the center of its valve stopper ball. If distances do not match, the new flapper valve will not seat properly.

GUIDE AND STOPPER-STEM ALIGNMENT

The guide is an attachment on the overflow pipe which is connected to the stopper stem. If this stem, to which the flush ball valve connects, needs alignment, loosen the screw which holds it in place. Jiggle the guide to find the position required for the flush ball to drop into place correctly, then tighten the screw permanently.

When the stopper ball does not drop to the valve seat as the tank drains, it is sticking to the guide. This can be caused by a bent wire or other

linkage that is out of line. If wire in the linkage has become worn, it can be replaced with another wire or sometimes twine.

If the toilet handle has to be held down to flush the bowl completely, the stopper guide might be mounted too low on the overflow pipe. Consequently, the stopper ball cannot be raised high enough to be free of water rushing out. In this case, the stopper guide must be raised and tightened.

FAULTY FLOAT MECHANISMS

If water pours in after the tank has filled, either the float mechanism or the inlet valve which it controls is defective. The float arm should be lifted slightly or readjusted to shut off the water. If it fails to shut off, the float ball is probably leaking and should be replaced.

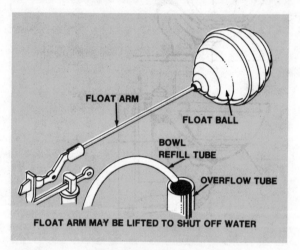

Float Mechanism

Another cause for continuous running water after the tank has filled is a faulty float valve. This is the water inlet valve, which is raised when the handle is turned down and the float arm lifted. This valve also shuts off water once the tank is filled. If the valve cannot be matched for replacement, an entire valve unit may be needed. To replace the unit, turn off the water and flush the tank to empty it. To replace the valve, disconnect the outer pipe supply leading to it by removing the rubber slip joint and nut connected. Remove the valve nut under the tank. To prevent any turning of the valve, make certain it is securely on the hex nut inside the tank. The complete valve unit will lift out. Worn washers should be replaced at the same time as the rubber gasket at the base of the valve pipe, if one is not included in the new unit. Position the valve so that the float arm is in the right place.

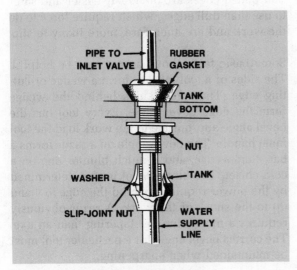

Float Valve Mounting

PARTIAL FLUSHING

If the toilet tank partially flushes, it is because the tank ball does not rise high enough. Shortening the upper lift wire and rehooking it to its lever alleviates this problem.

TANK SWEATING

Should water droplets form on the tank cover, a towel-type cloth cover will soak them up or the tank may be lined with foam sheets. Foam sheets come in packaged kits. The best solution for stopping tank sweating is to install a tempering valve in the cold-water line leading to the inlet. After the valve is in place in the cold-water line, the hot-water line should be connected to it. This valve allows warm water to enter the tank.

TOILET BOWL LEAKAGE

A tank or toilet bowl which is cracked may be repaired with silicone tub caulk. To apply it, first shut off water to the fixture and clean the damaged area. After making sure the room is warm enough, apply the sealant according to enclosed directions. Allow it plenty of time to set, especially in a break that goes all the way through the tank, before turning on the water.

A one-piece toilet which leaks at its base requires new seals. To repair this, shut off the water supply and disconnect the toilet by unscrewing the hold-down bolts. Lift the seat and remove the old seals. New floor-flange seals may be bought for replacement.

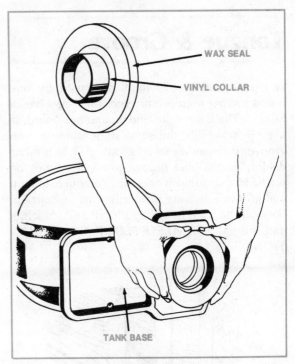

Replacement of Floor-flange Seal

REPAIR AND REPLACEMENT OF LOOSE BOWL PARTS

A loose toilet bowl may be repaired by removing the porcelain caps which connect it to the floor. If they are lined with caulking, gentle tapping will loosen them. The nuts underneath should be tightened to make the bowl secure.

To tighten a loose toilet seat, resulting from worn rubber washers or bumpers, the water should be shut off. Remove the tank cover and flush. Loosen the nuts; remove the seat and bolts. Then put the washers back on the shaft. Insert the bolts and apply the washers and nuts.

To replace the entire seat, find the distance in inches between the back hold-down bolts. Purchase a toilet seat the same size. Check to see if seat bolts go through the tank and make sure the new bolts will fit. It is a good idea when working on a toilet to always turn off the water and flush the tank. Then put the replacement seat in its proper position. Check for rust in old nuts holding the bolts in place. *SEE ALSO PLUMBING REPAIRS.*

Tongue & Groove

A tongue and groove joint is formed by one board having a groove or recess that receives a tongue. The tongue, located on another board, is a projection with the same dimensions as the groove. Because it can be supplied by a lumber dealer, tongue and groove joints need not be made in the home workshop. Although tongue and groove joints are primarily used in flooring, they can be used in ceiling tiles, furniture joints and siding. *SEE ALSO FLOOR CONSTRUCTION.*

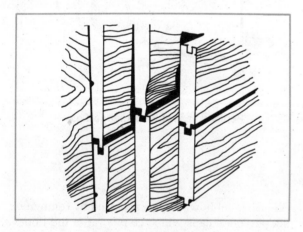

Tongue & Groove Joints

Tool Sharpening

Tool sharpening is a time and money-saving effort, as well as a very fulfilling process for the person who takes pride and interest in his tools.

Even the sharpest and most expensive tools become dull after prolonged use, and a power tool, such as an electric drill, can become steadily duller without being noticed, because the major effort required to push the tool is supplied by a motor instead of by muscle power. Sharpened edges are obviously easier and safer to use than dull edges, which require force to do the work and are, therefore, more likely to slip.

Some basic facts about cutting may be helpful. The sides of a tool meet to form a wedge or cutting edge. These two sides behind the wedge form the edge bevel angle. Every tool has the bevel angle appropriate to the work load the tool must handle. The bevel angle on a razor forms a hair-thin wedge, and a much blunter one on a cold chisel. The blade bevel is also determined by the power required behind the edge to stand up to the shock of the work. A razor obviously requires a much slimmer tapering than an axe. The correct bevel angle for a particular tool must be maintained when sharpening.

Every cutting edge consists of a line of ragged notches. In some tools, such as razors, these notches can be seen only under a microscope. But a dull edge has much deeper notches, causing a ragged edge contour which must be remedied by sharpening, so that the edge will cut instead of tear. In sharpening a dull-edged tool, metal is grooved or whetted down to the base of the deepest notch.

Removing metal from the correct place on the tool is very important. For example, when an edge has become dull or rounded, metal must be removed so that the rounding would be remedied, but the bevel angle would not be

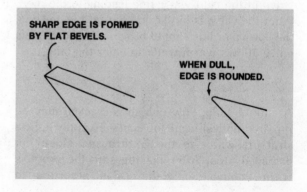

SHARP EDGE IS FORMED BY FLAT BEVELS.

WHEN DULL, EDGE IS ROUNDED.

altered. Also the least possible amount of metal should be taken off to prolong the working life of the tool.

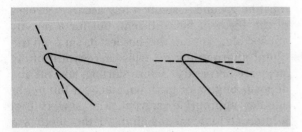

Dull edge is rounded, but incorrect sharpening changes bevel.

Grinding wheels, abrasive paper and handstones are the common tools used for sharpening. The abrasives are composed of a multiple of tiny natural or synthetic cutting particles. Emery, garnet and quartz are natural materials commonly used, but are surpassed in hardness, excepting diamond, by man-made grains, marketed under various tradenames. Hand and bench stones are hard, dense, produce very keen edges and are economical. A slipstone has rounded edges with a thicker edge on one side for sharpening concave surfaces. The flat surface is used for straight edge sharpening. Files are abrasive stones in stick form. They are available in triangular, square, round, flat and oval shapes. Stones should be soaked overnight in oil when purchased and lubricated during use to help rid the stone of metal and abrasive dust. Most grinding wheels are made of synthetic grains, which must constantly break away when worn, so that sharp ones can continue the work. The grinder may come with straight wheels, which use only the edge for grinding, or shaft-mounted wheels, which may be used in electric drills or hand grinders. Grinders are operated by a built-in motor or a separate motor driving a belt. Wheels should be free of cracks, and should produce a clear metallic ring when hit with a mallet or the wooden handle of a small tool. Bushings are provided to reduce the size of a wheel hole if it is larger than the spindle. Goggles are an extremely important safety precaution when using grinders, and the speed at which a wheel is driven should never exceed the maximum speed for which the wheel is marked.

YARD TOOLS

Hoes and spades are easily sharpened with a ten inch mill bastard file or a hard stone. A spade or shovel edge should also be filed for better working results. Scythes are stood on the handle with the blade almost horizontal, and a scythestone is moved downward and forward against the blade's flat surface, lifting the stone after each stroke so that the strokes overlap. The stone travels from the handle end of the blade out to the point, and both sides are sharpened.

Garden shears, such as grass snips and curved-blade pruning shears, can be filed or sharpened on a fine-belt ribbon sander, using a wood block with the sander for blade support and clearance for the handle. Straight-blade shears, like scissors, can be sharpened on a wheel, bench stone or belt sander since the blades can be opened wide. Hatchets, axes and adzes should have a short blade bevel and plenty of strength behind the edge for splitting; a longer bevel and more tapered blade for peeling, trimming or cutting, and should be sharpened accordingly. A wet or dry grinding wheel may be used. Axes should be whetted after grinding with circular strokes of a lubricated oilstone for a sharp edge. Long-bladed hedge clippers are sharpened with a file, wheel or belt sander or a sharpening disc in an electric drill. The disc may be mounted in a chuck or on an adapter. Aluminum-oxide papered sanding discs may also be used on electric drills.

HOUSEHOLD TOOLS

Smooth or grooved steels are used to reset a turned up knife edge, and may be used several times before grinding or whetting is needed. Stoning is also effective for knife sharpening. To sharpen a carving knife, the steel is held in the right or left hand, depending on the person. The end of the blade nearest the handle is under the tip of the steel, tilted at a downward angle. The knife is moved against the steel, edge first downward and to the right, so that at the completion of the stroke the tip of the blade is near the steel guard. To whet the other bevel, the blade is moved to the top of the steel end instead of under it, and stroked with the blade tilt up.

Whetting or stoning a razor blade will usually restore it to working condition. The double-edged blade is pushed back and forth over a concave stone, then turned over and honed on the other side.

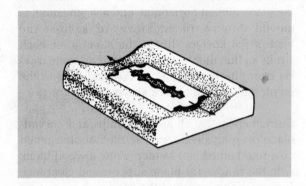

Honing a razor blade.

Moderately worn scissors are sharpened on a stone or ground on a belt sander or grinding wheel. When stoning, the blades are opened, and the shear face is turned up and moved several times across the stone at the correct bevel angle, edge first. The scissors are turned over and the other blade is whetted. For wheel grinding, the tool rest or table is set at the proper angle. The scissors are opened and one blade is placed on the table, shear face up. The wheel should be moving toward the edge as the blade is passed lightly over the abrasive from right to left. The whole edge should be ground evenly. The shears are then turned upside down for grinding the other blade edge.

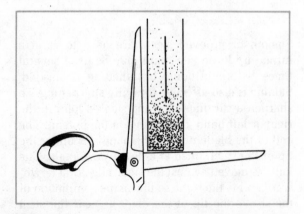

When using a grinding wheel on scissors, the shear face of the blade is turned up and the wheel turns toward the edge of the blade.

SAWS

All saw blades can be sharpened by filing, with the exception of carbide-tipped blades, which must be ground. Usually a few accurate strokes of the file will be sufficient, but for a heavily abused blade, or one that has lost its set from frequent sharpening, a series of reconditioning steps are necessary. Before starting, take off any deposits of gum or pitch with lacquer thinner or another appropriate solvent. The saw is first jointed, which means that all the teeth are ground, stoned or filed to the exact height. The next step is shaping, or filing the teeth to their original size and contour. The set of a blade is the alternating right and left bends of the tooth tips. This provides for free cutting and also allows a wider cut than the blade thickness. Saws may be set with a saw set, a tool made especially for this purpose.

Another method of saw setting involves a special anvil and a hammer to strike each tooth sharply to set it. This method, however, is more difficult and involves a great amount of skill. Setting is not necessary after every sharpening, but must be done after shaping. Filing, the final step, is used to restore edges and bevels of teeth that have been reshaped. The saw is held in a saw vise for filing.

Saw sharpening demands precision, and there are special jigs or aids which provide assistance. One type of hand setter fits into a groove of a table saw and the saw is set with a few taps of a hammer. An accessory for jointing circular saws has an arbor mount that provides for concentricity and acts as a guide to determine correct filing depth. These features make possible the jointing of all teeth to an equal length. Another accessory provides a jig fitted with a jigsaw for quicker shaping and filing of circular saw blades.

Handsaw reconditioning is a rather time-consuming process, but a useful skill to acquire. The saw is held in a saw clamp or vise and the teeth are jointed with a commercial handsaw jointer or a file. Next, the teeth are set, using one of the above methods. Then shape the teeth with a three-sided file, starting at the point of the saw and moving to the handle, filing alternate teeth against the teeth's front edge. The saw is reversed and the intervening teeth are filed. Finally, the saw is laid on its side and the sides of the teeth are brushed lightly with a file or oilstone to insure an even set and to dislodge any wire edge.

Chain saws are best sharpened if the chain of cutters is removed from the machine. The round-hooded cutters, the most common type, are mounted in a vise at waist height. Using a round file, the tip and side plates of the cutters are sharpened simultaneously, the top plate at a 35 degree angle and the side plate at a 90 degree angle. All the teeth are filed to the same length, using a forward stroke from the inside of the tooth to the outside.

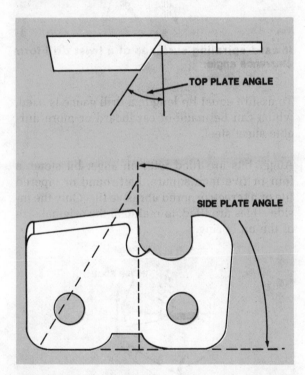

Side plate and top plate of chain saw cutters are sharpened simultaneously at 90 degree and 35 degree angles.

WOODWORKING TOOLS

Keen edges are also necessary for satisfactory woodworking results. An oiled whetstone or a file can be used on most chisels and scrapers, but for very dull edges a grinding wheel is preferred for reconditioning. A wet grindstone is

best to use, to minimize the possibility of losing the steel temper from burning.

Wood chisels are clamped in a vise and filed horizontally across the edge bevel.

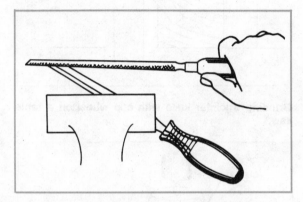

Sharpening a Wood Chisel.

When grinding a chisel or plane iron, the edge is held lightly against the wheel on the grind rest at a 19 degree angle. It is cooled in water between strokes.

Cabinet scrapers are first filed horizontally at a 45 degree angle, left to right. Then they are draw-filed at a 19 degree angle across the edge until a fine wire edge is removed by whetting the blade flat on a bench stone. Finally the edge is oiled and turned first to a 10 degree angle and then a 15 degree angle with a steel burnisher on both sides. Wood-turning chisels are ground with a flat bevel at the correct angle for the strength needed for lathe work.

The flat bevel edges of drawknives can be whetted with a fine stone, and jointer knives may be whetted while on the jointer, or on a grinding wheel. During grinding, the blade is held in a slotted piece of hardwood. The guide block is attached to the tool rest for grinding a hollow bevel.

A flat-ground bevel may be formed by grinding the knife on the side of a cup wheel on a table saw.

A horizontal bevel is produced by turning the slotted knife holder horizontally against a cup wheel attached to a drill.

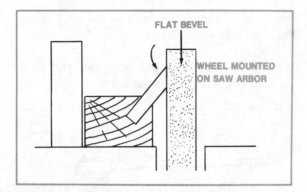

Grinding a jointer knife with cup wheel on a table saw.

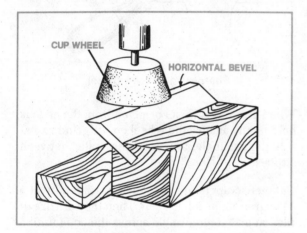

Grinding a horizontal bevel on a jointer knife.

The four cutting edges of mortising chisels, with inside bevels, are easily sharpened on a conical wheel in a drill press. Gouges and other carving tools have keen edges and should be whetted with a fine-grained stone or wheel.

TWIST DRILL AND DRILL BITS

Only the cutting lips of a twist drill, which do most of the work and wear the fastest, must

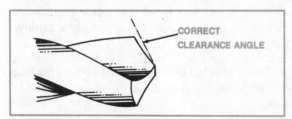

Grinding surfaces of a twist drill. The surfaces should be slightly whetted so that only the lip touches the working surface.

come in contact with the work surface. Slight grinding down of the point surfaces accomplishes the needed clearance.

As the surface is ground from lip to heel, the angle of grinding is changed, producing inward-spiraling surfaces. This is the clearance angle.

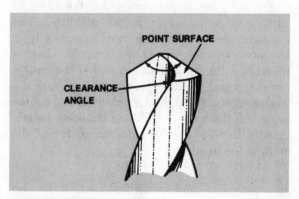

Inward-spiraling surfaces of a twist drill form clearance angle.

To assure equal lip length, a drill gauge is used, which can be made of cardboard or more durable sheet steel.

Auger bits are filed with an auger-bit stone, a four or five inch square, half-round or tapered file or a three-cornered abrasive file. Only the inside edges are filed, to maintain the original size of the bit boring.

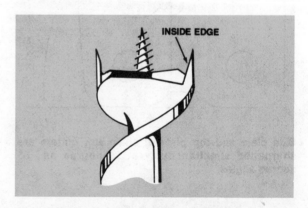

File only inside edges of auger bit.

The bevels of fly-cutter bits are ground or whetted flat. This bit also must have a clearance angle to operate. The bit may be turned inside out and may be beveled on one end and squared on the other for making discs with a square edge.

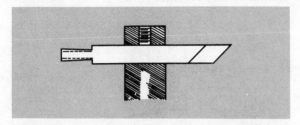

Fly-cutter bit with square nose and beveled end.

MISCELLANEOUS TOOLS

Reconditioning a screwdriver adds to its gripping power. Screwdriver blade tips can be ground on a wheel to produce a more tapered bit, a flatter bit or a hollow ground bit.

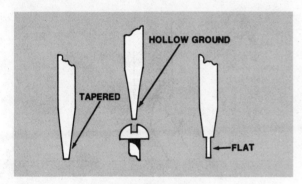

Screwdriver tips

The sides near the tip of the screwdriver should be ground parallel to prevent slipping. A belt-sander may also be used to hollow-grind the bits.

Deformed or nicked flats of a Phillips screwdriver are hand-stoned on a fine wheel, removing the least possible amount of metal.

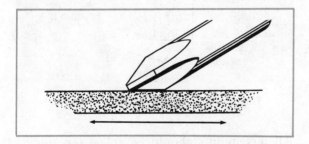

Sharpening Phillips screwdriver flats.

Punches, scribers or icepicks and other pointed tools can be easily sharpened on a bench or pocket stone. A fine-grit wheel is also a quick means of sharpening these tools. Be careful to keep the correct point angle.

Cold chisels with dulled edges or mushroomed or split heads are restored on a good grinding wheel. Chisels less abused can be handstoned.

Tin snips are sharpened on a wheel, belt sander or handstoned with a 20-25 degree bevel angle.

Countersinks are handstoned with a hard stone on the flat faces that are on a radius.

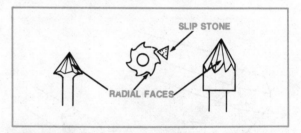

Use a triangular slip stone to whet the radial faces of a countersink.

When sharpening reamers, only the leading faces of the tooth crest should be whetted with a hard stone. Stoning the tooth tops would alter the tool's diameter.

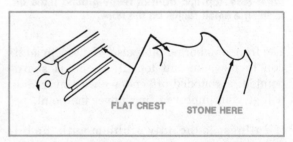

Whet only in groove of the reamer, keeping the tooth crests flat.

To sharpen ice skate blades, the skates are clamped in a vise and the concave face blade is honed with a fine round file. The stone is lubricated and turned after each stroke for equalization of wear. Then the blade is laid flat on the bench border and the side is whetted with a flat stone. Then turn the skate over and whet the other side.

GRINDING LATHE BITS

Lathe bits used for metal work must obviously be precisely shaped to bear the shock of the work and to perform accurately. These bits are mass-produced. Therefore, many times when they have just come directly from the manufacturer, new bits will need reconditioning to assure full strength cutting, to improve the finish on the work and to assure a longer-lasting bit. Also, the bits are in a holder in the lathe when cutting, and the grinding or sharpening must accomodate the bit size to the holder size. The top and side surfaces forming the cutting edge are whetted with a hard fine-grit stone.

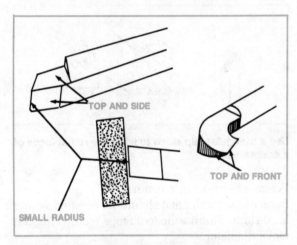

Whet side, top and front of ready-ground lathe bit, forming a small radius on the nose.

The front of a boring bit is also whetted, in addition to the side and top. If the bit is sharp-pointed, a rounded-off end with a tiny radius will give an improved finish over the point.

If dullness is the only problem with the bit, simply grind the side and top surfaces at the proper angle to restore the cutting edge.

Shaping of a cutter bit should be done with a 36-grit wheel. A finer grit wheel may be used for finish grinding to reduce the number of grinding marks prior to whetting.

Clearance angle for cutter bits may be formed with a minimum amount of grinding since the bits' blank ends are beveled, and grinding may be done on the wheel's surface. For side grinding, the tool rest or the bit is held at a tilt for formation of the side clearance.

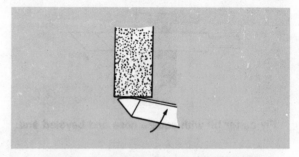

Correct tilt for side clearance formation.

To round the point, swing the bit in an arc against the face of the wheel.

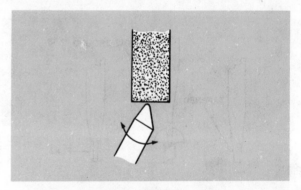

Rounding off point of bit.

The side and top rake or angle are ground simultaneously by tilting the bit at the correct angle.

This tilt on bit grinds back and side rake.

All bits' points should be set at the correct height, even with the center height of the lathe.

Top Coat

A top coat is applied over another coat of paint or other finishing material. It usually refers to the final coat. Any material, however, may be called a top coat when it is applied over a substrate. *SEE ALSO PAINTS & PAINTING.*

Top Plate

The top plate ties the studding together at the top and forms a finish for the walls. It is a connecting link between the wall and roof and furnishes a support for the lower ends of the rafters. One or two pieces of timber the same size as the studs make up the plate. *SEE ALSO ROOF CONSTRUCTION; WALL & CEILING CONSTRUCTION.*

Torches

A torch is any of the portable devices used for producing a hot flame. The two most popular torches for the home owner are propane gas torches and blowtorches. Although closely related, they work on different principles and vary in job capabilities.

Propane torches are used for a variety of tasks. They can be used to remove paint when the flame spreader attachment is connected but consider the fire hazard before employing it. They also can be used to soften the adhesive on the backs of tiles when replacement is necessary. If bad weather forms ice patches on stairs and sidewalks, a propane torch can be used to melt it away. In addition, it can thaw plumbing pipe and with the solder attachment, repair pipe that is broken. Propane torches are filled with propane gas that is under pressure. They are easy to ignite and handy in their simplicity. Follow the manufacturer's direction very carefully.

Blow torches are different from propane torches in that they are filled with unleaded or white gas and, on occasion, with alcohol. They dispense greater heat than propane gas torches and are used mainly for solder work. A few rules are applicable for this torch: never fill in a closed room; if stored for any length of time, empty the fuel; never fill the container more than three-fourths full. Also wipe the body dry after filling with fuel before igniting. *SEE ALSO BLOWTORCH; PROPANE GAS TORCH.*

Torpedo Level

The torpedo level has a lean, nine-inch body, from which it acquires its name. The average torpedo level has a plumb, level and 45° miter vial, but due to its size, it is usually difficult to achieve an accurate reading. *SEE ALSO HAND TOOLS.*

Total Run

The entire sum of treads in stair construction is called the total run. This can be applied to split-level, straight-run or circular design. *SEE ALSO STAIR CONSTRUCTION.*

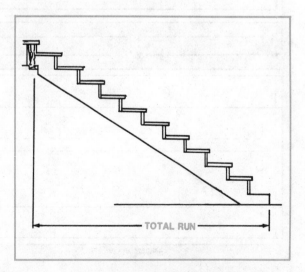

Total Run in Stair Construction

Toy Storage Chest

This chest features a box-type lid and will measure 3 feet long, 18³/₄″ deep and a little over 20¹/₄″ high. Due to a small loss of wood in the milling process, the width of the side pieces actually will come to about 17¹/₄″. Therefore the stock should be carefully laid out and measured as the chest is built.

The bottom, top, sides and ends all can be made from one length of board 12″ wide and two pieces 4″ wide. Start with the chest ends first, using a piece of 4″ board as the bottom piece and the 12″ board above it. The other piece of 4″ board forms a part of the lid.

Next build the front and back and put these into place. Use medium size finishing nails, counter-sinking them for a finished job. Do not fill the holes with plastic wood until after the chest has been stained. Smearing plastic wood on un-finished boards will prevent the stain from penetrating.

After attaching the sides to the front and back, nail a 1 x 2″ upright brace from top to bottom in each corner for strength. Next put the bottom on the chest. The cover is built in the same manner. With the 4″ boards build the frame, then add the top.

Drill holes in the chest-ends for rope handles. Tie knots in the rope ends inside the box and tack down the loose ends.

Next, stain the chest, then fill the nail holes with plastic wood. Attach hinges, corner hardware and lock or closure.

The box tray, measuring 17¹/₈″ by 13″, slides on two more 1″ x 2″ strips nailed across the front

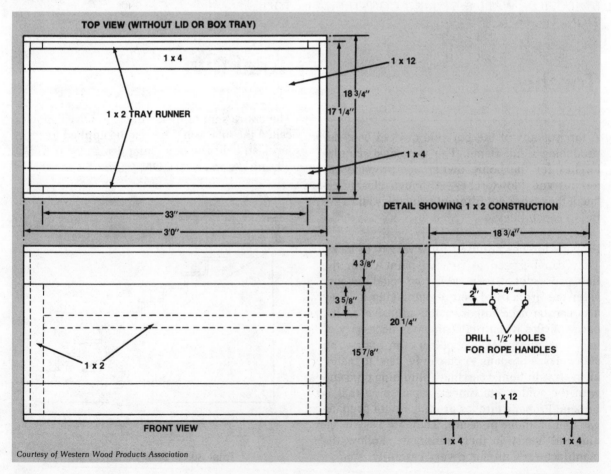

TOP VIEW (WITHOUT LID OR BOX TRAY)

1 x 4

1 x 12

1 x 2 TRAY RUNNER

18 3/4″

17 1/4″

1 x 4

33″

3'0″

FRONT VIEW

1 x 2

4 3/8″

3 5/8″

20 1/4″

15 7/8″

DETAIL SHOWING 1 x 2 CONSTRUCTION

18 3/4″

2″

4″

DRILL 1/2″ HOLES FOR ROPE HANDLES

1 x 12

1 x 4   1 x 4

Courtesy of Western Wood Products Association

and back of the chest. Place these strips at a height that will allow the top of the tray to meet flush with the top of the chest sides. This will permit some clearance for the lid to close down, even when items stored in the tray are heaped.

Dress up the inside top of the lid with a dime store map, or any other decorations to your liking. *SEE ALSO PROJECTS.*

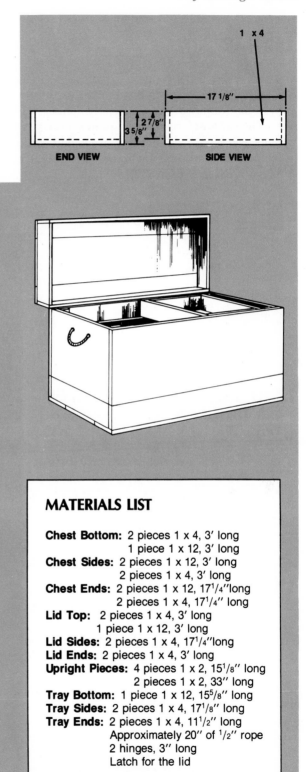

END VIEW   **SIDE VIEW**

FACE NAIL
TOENAIL
TRAY RUNNER

TRAY RUNNER
BOX TRAY
1 x 12
13"

MATERIALS LIST

Chest Bottom: 2 pieces 1 x 4, 3' long
1 piece 1 x 12, 3' long
Chest Sides: 2 pieces 1 x 12, 3' long
2 pieces 1 x 4, 3' long
Chest Ends: 2 pieces 1 x 12, 17$\frac{1}{4}$"long
2 pieces 1 x 4, 17$\frac{1}{4}$" long
Lid Top: 2 pieces 1 x 4, 3' long
1 piece 1 x 12, 3' long
Lid Sides: 2 pieces 1 x 4, 17$\frac{1}{4}$"long
Lid Ends: 2 pieces 1 x 4, 3' long
Upright Pieces: 4 pieces 1 x 2, 15$\frac{1}{8}$" long
2 pieces 1 x 2, 33" long
Tray Bottom: 1 piece 1 x 12, 15$\frac{5}{8}$" long
Tray Sides: 2 pieces 1 x 4, 17$\frac{1}{8}$" long
Tray Ends: 2 pieces 1 x 4, 11$\frac{1}{2}$" long
Approximately 20" of $\frac{1}{2}$" rope
2 hinges, 3" long
Latch for the lid

Courtesy of Western Wood Products Association

T-Plate

A T-plate is a metal plate that is attached at the joint in the framework of a structure. This gives the joint greater strength. T-plates come in various sizes and are usually predrilled with holes for conventional fasteners. *SEE ALSO WALL & CEILING CONSTRUCTION.*

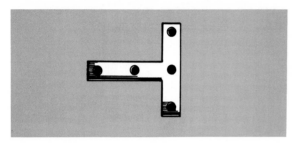

T-Plate

Trail Bikes & Minibikes
[SEE MOTORCYCLES, MINIBIKES, & TRAIL BIKES.]

Trailer, House
[SEE MOBILE HOME CONSTRUCTION.]

Trammel Points

Trammel points are sharp steel pins used to draw circles and curves over areas too large to be measured by a compass. To use the trammel points, clamp them onto a piece of wood — tips pointing downward to the surface to be marked — and use them as you would a compass. One point will be in the center of the curve or circle, and the other point will be extended to the desired radius. By moving the piece of wood around the center trammel point, the second trammel point will draw the circle or curve. *SEE ALSO HAND TOOLS.*

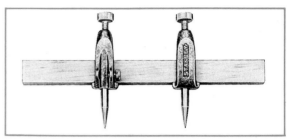

Courtesy of The Stanley Works

Trammel Points

Transformer

A transformer is a device which transfers electrical energy from one circuit to another using the principle of electromagnetic induction rather than a direct connection. The transformer's purpose is to convert this energy from the power source to a form that can be used at the load, in other words a change in voltage.

The inductor connected to the power source is called the primary winding, while the inductor connected to the load is the secondary winding. These two separate coils are wrapped around the same core, and the ratio of the primary winding to the secondary winding determines the ratio of the change of voltage. For example, a ratio of 1:2 (or a secondary winding with twice the turns of the primary winding) would convert 110 volts at the source to 220 volts at the load. This is called a *step-up* transformer. The transformer commonly seen on utility poles is a *step-down* transformer because it converts the several thousand volts in the main power lines to 240 volts in the power lines to a residence.

The transformer in a doorbell is a small unit which converts regular house current of 120 volts to anywhere from 6 to 20 volts, as required by the size of the chime. This reduction in voltage permits the use of a small gauge wire rather than cable from the chime to the door button. It also eliminates the danger of shock from regular house wiring. *SEE ALSO ELECTRICAL WIRING.*

Transit

Transits are tools used by professional surveyors, who must receive months of training, for measuring distances and checking alignments before construction of a building. Two of the more common transits are the level transit and the builders' level transit. *SEE ALSO HAND TOOLS.*

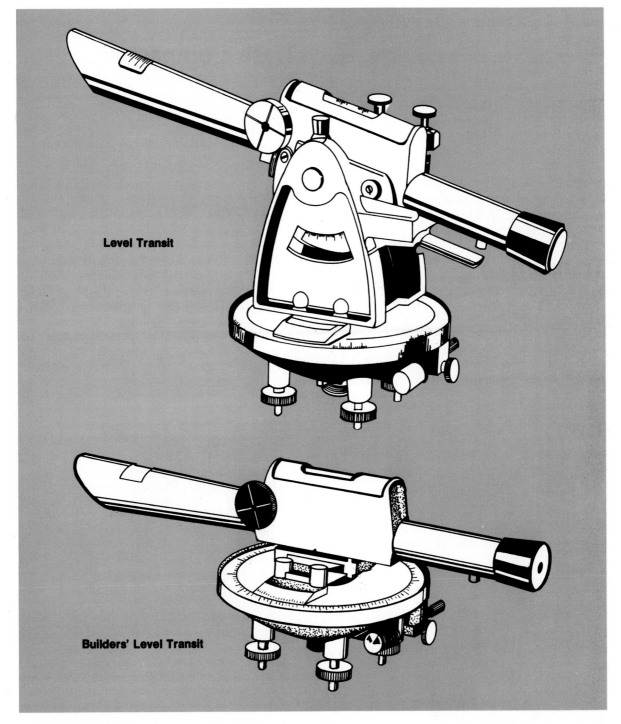

Level Transit

Builders' Level Transit

Transit Mix

Transit mix, also called you-haul concrete, is a type of concrete used for middle-sized concrete jobs requiring from a quarter of a yard to a yard. The transit mix comes in three versions: trailer haul, trailer-mixer and pick-up mixer. Trailer haul involves concrete, with additional ingredients to keep it from setting in transit, loaded into a trailer, which is attached to your car. A "cannon," also called a trailer-mixer, is a device which revolves to keep the concrete from setting in transit and is hooked directly to your car. A pick-up mixer includes a mixer cannon mounted on a truck. Instructions on using the various means of hauling concrete are available from the dealer. Additional tools may usually be rented at the same place. *SEE ALSO CONCRETE.*

Transom

A transom is the horizontal crossbar over a door, in a window or between a window and a door. It may also be used to name the small opening, such as a window or louvered panel, hinged above a door or window for added ventilation.

Trap

A trap is an S-shaped or a U-shaped bend of pipe that is attached to every plumbing fixture. The purpose of the trap is to retain water, making a seal against sewer gas, rodents, vermin and various types of bacteria. Conversely, it also keeps foreign objects such as silverware and jewelry that is accidently dropped into the drain from passing through the entire plumbing system. *SEE ALSO PIPE FITTINGS.*

Trash Compactors

The trash compactor is one of the newest major convenience appliances. It doesn't change the weight of the garbage, but decreases the volume so that it only has to be removed about once a week. Used in conjunction with a garbage disposal, this schedule is entirely possible for an average family.

There are both top-loading and front-loading compactors. The design depends upon the manufacturer's provisions for loading the unit. Basically, the garbage goes into a container which may be a paper, plastic or plastic-lined bag. Some units use standard grocery bags. A sleeve is usually inserted which fills the circumference of the bag. Before the trash is emptied, the sleeve is removed. Some compactors also have a container with which you can carry out the trash when the bag is emptied. Once it's

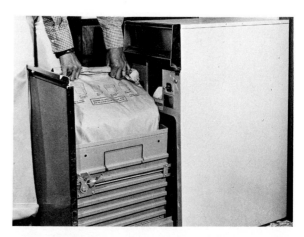

Some compactors use a carrying container to empty bag. Do not handle bags themselves. Often sharp pieces of broken glass can stick through paper liner. Use a container to carry it to the garbage can.

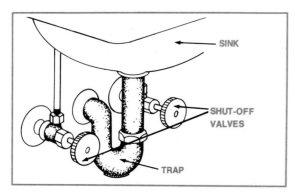

A Typical Trap System

placed in the garbage can, the garbage remains in the bag that was originally inserted.

Compactors work best if the cycle is initiated each time that trash is placed into the container. When the start button is pressed and the key lock is turned to the "on" position, a ram travels down into the container, compacting the trash in the bottom of the container. It's not uncommon for a unit to exert 2,000 pounds of pressure upon the trash. This is sufficient in most cases to flatten cans and often break bottles. Don't use this as a gauge for its operation, however. Whether or not it happens to break a bottle or compact a can fully depends upon the design and strength of the bottle or can and the compaction of the material that is under it at the time. To obtain some idea as to the efficiency of the compactor, you can place a couple of bricks or other hard material in the botton of an empty bag within the compactor. Be sure that this extends a minimum of four inches off the bottom of the floor of the container. Then place a couple of empty cans upon the brick. When the ram comes down it will compress the cans against the bricks and they will come out quite flat if the proper force is being exerted.

It's a good idea to place a newspaper, cardboard, or other scrap paper at the bottom of a new bag. This serves to absorb juices from any wet garbage that may find its way into the compactor and it also reduces the possibility of glass from broken bottles piercing the bottom of the bag. Be wary of broken glass when emptying a compactor bag. The bags are heavy, usually weighing 20 pounds or more, and sharp edges of glass can penetrate the edges of the bags that contain the garbage. It is a good idea to use a stronger container such as a rather large garbage can or one of the containers especially made for the purpose to transport the compactor bags to the garbage can. Always handle a full bag by the top only, never by the bottom sides, to prevent the possibility of injury.

Like any other appliance, be sure to unplug a compactor before inspection or when carrying out any repair work. Little maintenance is required, however, since the compactor is a new breed of appliance and requires a minimum of

service, there is little lubrication that is necessary unless the compactor is serviced.

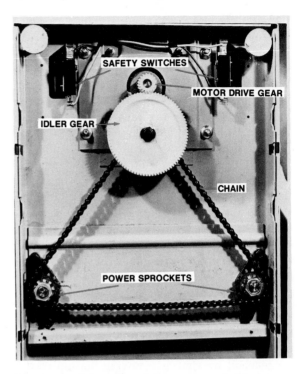

Motor speed is reduced by means of drive gear. Chain turns power sprockets which in turn cause power shafts to rotate.

The compactor is driven by a chain, much like a sprocket chain on a bicycle, or by a cogged belt. This passes across to a couple of sprockets, usually located at the bottom of the equipment, that turns two large threaded shafts that pass vertically up each side of the container. At the top of each shaft the ram is fitted with threaded nuts on either side. These nuts run up and down the threaded shafts as the shafts turn. When the start switch is turned on, the motor begins to run and turns the threaded shafts. These in turn tend to pull the nuts and the attached ram downward and into the container. The ram is usually set to compact to within four inches of the bottom of the container. The first garbage that is put into the container won't compress to a large extent until it begins to exceed this depth.

As the ram proceeds downward, it begins to be met with more and more resistance as the trash is compacted. Finally, it reaches a point where the motor can no longer drive the threaded shaft and the motor stalls. Just after the motor went into operation, a reversing switch transferred but it could have no effect upon the motor rotation until the motor was stopped. This is because the reversing switch operates through the relationship of the running and starting windings, and the starting windings were removed from the circuit before the transfer occured. However, when the motor does stop for any reason the rotation is automatically reversed as soon at it restarts. This causes the ram to travel back up. The pitch of the threads on the shafts and the respective sizes of the motor sprockets and the two drive sprockets are designed to provide the desired pressure on the ram at the point that the motor stalls. Never attempt to replace a compactor motor with a motor designed for another appliance since the motor is sized to provide the correct amount of force for the equipment.

If for any reason it is necessary to replace the drive nuts on the ram, they should be lubricated with the manufacturer's extreme-pressure lubricant after they are reassembled. These nuts can be reached by simply removing the top of the compactor. This also gives access to the reversing switch and the limit switch which stops the ram's travel upwards by turning the motor off when the ram is in correct position. These switches usually have elongated slots which allow adjustment. The ram should be able to travel approximately one-half inch downwards before the limit switch transfers. The reversing

The key switch and pushbutton start switch are part of the safety features found on compactors.

switch transfers when the motor has proceeded roughly a quarter-inch downwards.

If a compactor fails to operate at all, first check the fuse or circuit by plugging in a table lamp at the same receptacle. If this checks all right review the operating procedure and be sure that the key switch is turned on and that the start button is depressed. If the drawer is tilted to one side it is likely that the drawer switch has been opened. This is a safety switch which prevents the machine from operating when the door is in a tilted position. Usually it can be lifted and moved enough to start the compactor if this is the case. As soon as the compactor motor begins to run, the ram will travel upwards and shut off. Then open the door and rearrange the trash which has caused the door to tilt to one side.

The drive mechanism is usually serviced from the bottom of the compactor. If a chain should break, replace or repair the chain as recommended by the manufacturer. Be sure that all sprockets are tight on their shafts and at the motor.

Most compactors have removable ram covers, the lower portion that comes in contact with the garbage. Remove this and clean it about once each month. Be sure that the seal and lock is in position when reinstalling it. Never place aerosol cans or any containers that previously contained flammable or poisonous contents within the compactor. Empty containers of paint, varnishes, oils, or insect repellents should be placed outside in the regular garbage container.

Travel Trailers
[SEE MOBILE HOME CONSTRUCTION.]

Tread

A tread is the part of a stair step that is horizontal and takes the initial weight of the foot. A tread needs to be broad enough to allow sure footing. Check the local building code for specifications.

The tread is supported by the stringer or carriage, and one tread makes up a unit run. The entire sum of the treads make up the total run of stairs. *SEE ALSO STAIR CONSTRUCTION.*

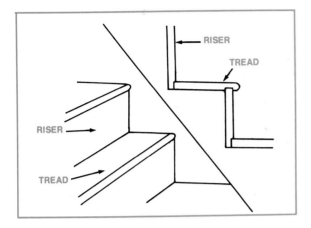

Tree House

A tree house can be constructed with a minimum of materials. Any sturdy tree with spreading branches is an ideal place to construct a platform tree house. The ideal height for a tree house is six to eight feet above the ground.

Begin construction by making the frame from 2 x 4 stock and $^1/_2$ inch plywood. Dimensions for the example platform are 4 feet x 5 feet, but the dimensions can vary depending on the tree. To form the frame, butt joint two 5' length of 2 x 4 pine to two 3 foot 8 inch length of 2 x 4. Fasten a 3 foot 8 inch brace down the center of the frame. If a limb is near the center of the frame, add shorter lengths as braces. Fasten the $^1/_2$ inch plywood to the top of the frame using $1^1/_2'$ galvanized nails spaced about 6 inches apart. To avoid nailing the tree, in each corner drill holes $^3/_8$ inches in diameter 6 inches from the outside edge to allow for lashing the frame to the tree. Drill two mounting holes for a rope ladder making them $^3/_8$ inch in diameter and 12 inches apart. The posts for the back railing are made from 2 x 4 x 2 foot pieces of pine which are fastened to the platform with four No. 9 flathead screws. Fasten the 2 x 4 x 3 foot 8 inch railing pieces to the posts with $3^1/_2$ inches galvanized nails. Predrill the holes to prevent splitting the ends of the lumber. Screw four 1 inch eye bolts at 12 inch intervals along the top of the back railing.

Meanwhile, sew a 4 foot long piece of 1 inch fringe on one end of a brightly colored piece of canvas, and four 12 inch pieces of rope, folded double, at 12 inch intervals onto the opposite end. Weatherproof the material if desired by applying one of the clear weatherproofing solvents available at most hardware stores.

Paint the entire platform with either weather-resistant paint or clear polyurethane varnish. Then, lash the platform to the tree using $^1/_2$ inch nylon rope. The rope is run through the holes in the sides of the platform securing the platform to the tree without driving nails into the bark. Be sure the ladder is attached before securing the platform in the tree. *SEE ALSO PROJECTS.*

MATERIALS LIST

LUMBER
$^1/_2''$ x 4' x 5' piece of plywood
two 2" x 4" five feet long
two 2" x 4" three feet eight inches long

NAILS AND SCREWS
$3^1/_2''$ galvanized nails
$1^1/_2''$ galvanized nails
3-4 inch flat head screws

OTHER
Canvas 4' x $9^1/_2'$
1" fabric fringe 4' long
paint or clear polyurethane varnish
two 1" dowels 4' long
six 1" dowels 1' long
two optional 1" dowels 1' long
two optional 1" dowels 5' long
nylon rope ($^1/_2''$)
four 1" eyebolts

Tree Saw

The tree saw, usually shaped like a bow saw, is for pruning tree limbs. *SEE ALSO HAND TOOLS.*

Tree Stump Removal

Tree stumps are easily removed by burning or by letting them rot in moist soil. Use kindling wood to start the fire, and then add charcoal or coal. A metal container with the top and bottom removed will restrict the fire. Punch some holes near the bottom of the container. If the stump is larger than the container, it will have to be moved to other parts of the stump to complete the job.

To speed the burning process, apply chemicals in early summer to allow time for them to reach the entire root system by fall. Burning should not begin until early fall. One excellent mixture is of 4.5 parts sodium dichromate, 1.5 parts cupric chloride, 1 part manganese dichloride and 1 part lead acetate. Cut the stump as nearly even with the ground as possible. Holes six inches deep should be bored about six inches apart and then treated with the chemicals. The chemicals will be in powder form and will need to be mixed with water. One fourth cup should be poured into each hole.

Start the fire after the stump has been covered with a waterproof material during the summer. The stump will smolder for one to three weeks before removal is complete. A reflector shield of aluminum foil on a frame will speed the burning.

A slower way of removing a tree stump is to cover it with soil, allowing it to rot away. Cut the stump even with the ground. Bore holes in the stump and bury it in soil. Keep the soil moist and the stump will eventually rot away.

Trellises
[SEE ARBOR & TRELLIS.]

Trellis Slats

A trellis is made like lattice work and is usually attached to a wall. The size and design of a trellis is subject to individual tastes as are the trellis slats. Most trellises are made from 1 x 2 strips of wood, although other materials can be used such as rope, plastic or metal. To construct a trellis, the upright slats are placed first and the diagonal or horizontal slats are fastened to criss-cross or form a diamond pattern. When choosing the material and design, select material that can support the weight of heavy, climbing plants, and can withstand the environment. Paint the slats with weatherproof paint and fasten with non-rusting fasteners. *SEE ALSO ARBOR & TRELLIS.*

Trench Details in Septic Tank Installation

A large amount of trench digging is involved when installing a septic tank. When digging the trenches, a backhoe will probably be the best tool to use.

The first trench to dig ranges from five to ten feet long and may contain a cast-iron, clay tile, plastic, fiber or cement-asbestos pipe. This trench connects the sewer line, which leads from the house, to the septic tank. This pipeline must be enclosed to keep the sewage in and any roots out. Its diameter should measure at least four inches, sloping from $1/8''$ to $1/4''$ per foot from the house. For efficient performance, sewer lines should be placed on the solid trench bottom. However, if the trench is dug too deeply, it must be filled with crushed gravel or stone and leveled.

The next trench, leading from the septic tank to the distribution box, which regulates the flow of waste material, should be only deep enough to make the sealed-joint pipe connection between these two areas not more than three feet.

This network of pipe lines, leading from the distribution box, is known as the drainage or disposal field. These drainage pipes are laid on about six inches of gravel which may be level or sloping away from the box not more than six inches for every 100 feet. They may consist of four inch concrete or clay tiles or plastic or fiber pipes which are perforated. Perforated pipes, usually in lengths of ten feet, have holes which permit seepage. Because those drainage pipes should not be watertight, the tiles which are one-foot in length should be laid with spacing from $1/4''$ to $1/2''$ between them. To prevent earth from sifting into the tiles, tar paper or lightweight roofing may be used to cover the gap.

When the drainage tiles are set, cover them with about two inches of gravel. Over this, place a layer of newspaper or a two inch layer of straw to keep the earth which is shoveled in, out of the gravel or crushed stone. By the time the straw or paper has decayed, the earth will be packed firmly around the gravel to prevent any soil infiltration. After being inspected, the system may be covered with soil and graded. Grass may be planted to absorb some of the soil's moisture.

To prevent large amounts of end seepage, the ends of the tile runs may be closed with a masonry block or filled in about six inches with gravel or crushed stone. Generally, runs should be no longer than 100 feet and at least six feet or three times the width of the trench apart. Location of the field should not be in an area where automobiles will drive. Planting a few small perennial flowers for identification at the pump-out opening and distribution box location is helpful. This reduces the amount of exploratory digging needed to repair and pump out the tank.

Dry wells or seepage pits may be used instead of a disposal field if there is little land space or on steep slopes where the contours of the terrain make it impractical. These wells must be placed near trees or wooded areas. It is best to use a stone pit or the kind of well which is filled with crushed stone and rocks so that the tree roots can help in disposing of the water. *SEE ALSO SEPTIC SYSTEMS.*

Trestles, Scaffolding

Trestles, or trestle jacks, are a type of scaffold used mainly for interior work. The jack is attached to a ledger which supports a low platform. A safe ledger must be strong and stable, and the jack must be the correct weight and size to support the scaffold. *SEE ALSO SCAFFOLDS & LADDERS.*

Triangular File

The triangular file is usually single cut to provide a smooth finish. Shaped like a triangle, the slip-tapered triangular can be used for sharpening bandsaw blades, while the regular triangular files, because they are not tapered as much as slim-tapered files, are useful in filing angular notches, as in handsaws. *SEE ALSO HAND TOOLS.*

Trim
[SEE MOLDING & TRIM.]

Trimmer

A trimmer is used in framing to add support to the side of an opening, such as a window or door. It is the extra stud or joist to which a header is connected. *SEE ALSO FLOOR CONSTRUCTION; WALL & CEILING CONSTRUCTION.*

Tripod
[SEE PHOTOGRAPHY.]

Trowels

Trowels are tools used in masonry work to spread and smooth mortar, concrete, mastic, grout and plaster. The brick trowel has a wooden handle at one end of a spade-shaped blade which is used for laying mortar, trimming cut brick, tapping bricks into place, forming brick work joints and smoothing mortar or concrete around posts. Notched and small-area trowels are used for spreading thin layers of mastic in ceramic tile work. They are rectangular with handles and notched edges to prevent the mastic from building up. This assures that the tiles can be laid evenly. The rubber-surfaced trowel is also used for applying grout in ceramic tile installation. This trowel is also rectangular-shaped. It has a handle on one side and a rubber surface on the other. The steel finishing trowel is one of the most common tools in concrete and masonry work. It is used to spread and smooth concrete on patios, driveways, sidewalks, along block or brick walls and for smoothing plaster in wall repair. *SEE ALSO CONCRETE & MASONRY TOOLS.*

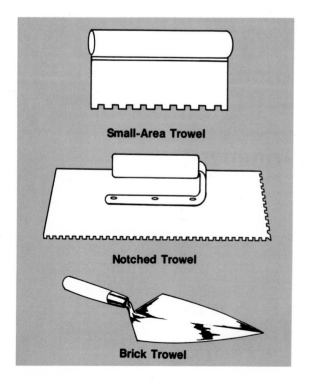

Small-Area Trowel

Notched Trowel

Brick Trowel

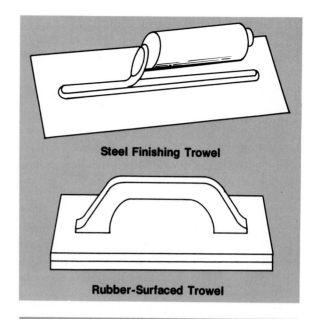

Steel Finishing Trowel

Rubber-Surfaced Trowel

Truck Campers
[SEE RECREATIONAL VEHICLES.]

Truss

A truss is the triangular brace to which a roof is attached. Truss construction varies, but generally they must be well braced and the joints immobilized by special connectors. Once the connectors are attached, a metal or plywood gusset or truss plate is secured to the joint. This keeps any part of the truss from moving or shifting thus giving the truss maximum support. *SEE ALSO ROOF CONSTRUCTION; WALL & CEILING CONSTRUCTION.*

Truss Connector

When constructing trusses, joint separation must be minimal. To keep the joints from slipping special connectors must be part of the project. There are a variety of types available. They must be applied after all the joints are fastened together. Since some require the boring of preliminary holes for the fasteners, make sure of the specifictions of your connector. Some may be glued or bolted for a temporary bondage. The main rule to remember is that truss connectors do just what the name implies: they connect. Make sure the joints match up correctly before they are applied. *SEE ALSO ROOF CONSTRUCTION.*

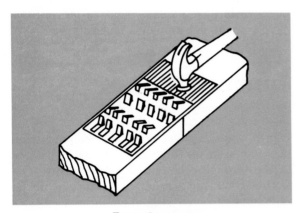

Truss Connector

Truss, Prefabricated

A prefabricated truss is a supporting member of a roof that is measured, cut and assembled at a factory rather than at the construction site. *SEE ALSO ROOF CONSTRUCTION.*

Truss Plate

Truss plates hold all joints together in truss construction. They are available in various sizes,

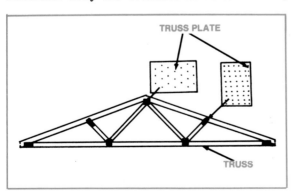

shapes and types. Most truss plates are pre-drilled for nails, screws or other fasteners. In other plates the metal has been serrated so the grate-like protrusions of metal bite into the wood when they are attached. This gives greater adhesion to the wood. Occasionally truss plates have nails already attached to the plate. *SEE ALSO ROOF CONSTRUCTION.*

Try Square

The try square has a thin metal blade four- to 12-inches long joined at a right angle with a thick, short handle. This square is generally used for drawing straight lines in making even saw cuts, but can also be utilized to test the "squareness" of corners and joints. To do this, hold the handle firmly against one surface with the blade touching the other surface. Any light appearing between the blade edge and the surface shows the areas where it is not square. *SEE ALSO HAND TOOLS.*

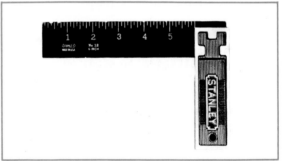

Courtesy of The Stanley Works

Try Square

T-Sill Construction

A T-sill is a type of framing member that sits on the foundation and supports the uprights. In T-sill construction, the wooden sill is fastened to the concrete foundation with anchor bolts, the sole secured parallel to the sill and the studs placed perpendicular to the sole and joists. *SEE ALSO FLOOR CONSTRUCTION.*

Tube Tester

The tube tester is an apparatus for testing components of electronic equipment such as radios. Some of the types most often used are filament testers, emission-type testers and conductance-type testers.

The filament tester is the simplest device, yet the least used. Because few modern tubes are faulty as a result of burned-out or disconnected filaments, this instrument is unreliable.

The emission-type tester is often found in drug stores. It can be used to check the power potential of tubes by short circuiting the grids of the plate electrode.

The conductance-type testers duplicate the conditions particular to circuit when electricity is flowing through it. For this reason, the conductance-type tester is the most reliable in checking faulty tubes. *SEE ALSO ELECTRICIAN'S TOOLS & EQUIPMENT.*

Tuck Pointer's Rake

Tuck pointer's rakes are for smoothing out and filling in mortar around brick joints to provide a neat surface. One style of tuck pointer's rake has a wooden handle that slopes down at an angle to a flat, slender, steel blade. Another variety has a shorter blade that widens slightly as it curves into a round handle making this tuck pointer's rake one solid piece of steel. *SEE ALSO CONCRETE & MASONRY TOOLS.*

Tuck Pointing

Tuck pointing is the process of smoothing and filling mortar joints in brick or stone work, using a tuck pointer's rake. *SEE ALSO BRICK & STONE WORK.*

Tungsten Carbide

Tungsten carbide is a corrosion-resistent alloy which is used to cover steel bodies and shanks of tools, surgical instruments, electric knives, power drill bits and saw blades to prevent rust development and provide a tough finish.

Turnbuckle

A turnbuckle is a type of nut and bolt combination that is made of two screw eyes that are driven through each end of a steel sleeve. The sleeve is rectangular but curves in slightly at each end on each side. The screw eyes are threaded differently so they must be turned in opposite directions to drive them in or out of the sleeve.

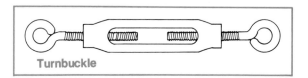

Turnbuckle

Turned Tenon

A turned tenon is a round tenon that is formed on a lathe and may act as a dowel. With this type tenon, furniture legs may be joined to wood slabs by driving the tenon into predrilled holes in the slab. *SEE ALSO WOOD JOINTS.*

Turning Chisels

The five main kinds of turning chisels are the skew, gouge, spear-point, round-nose and parting tool. These tools are used in lathe work to cut stock. When cutting, the chisels are braced on a tool rest that slides on the lathe bed. *SEE ALSO HAND TOOLS; LATHE.*

Turn Screw

The turn screw, a tool made specially for driving wood screws, has either an oval or eggshaped handle and a flat upper blade to accommodate a wrench.

Turpentine

Turpentine is a semifluid oleoresin which is yellow to brown in color and may be used to clean paint brushes, rollers and pads, to thin paint, paste-type wood fillers and to remove paint from furniture and other wood objects. Turpentine may also act as a wetting agent for pigmented wiping stains. *SEE ALSO PAINTS & PAINTING.*

Tweezers

Tweezers are small, pincher-shaped tools used for plucking, holding or manipulating. Referred to as pickup tools, these instruments may have other functions and can be referred to by various names, such as needlenose pliers. Cosmetic tweezers are helpful aids in the workshop because of their tight grip and small size. *SEE ALSO HAND TOOLS.*

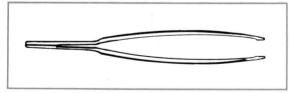

Cosmetic Tweezers

Twist Drill

Twist drills or drill bits are available for boring holes in metal, wood or both wood and metal.

Those intended primarily for use in metal work have the cutting edges ground to an angle of 59 degrees, while those intended exclusively for wood have a much sharper point. The most popular type of twist drill is made to drill both metal and wood and comes in sizes $1/16$- to $1/2$-inch. *SEE ALSO HAND TOOLS.*

Two Pipe Heating System
[SEE HEATING SYSTEMS.]

Two-Way Cable

Two-way cable (or two-wire cable) can contain two or three wires, a black wire (hot), a white wire (neutral), and an optional third wire (ground). This type of wire is available in several kinds of coverings, depending upon whether it is used above or below ground, or in wet or dry locations. *SEE ALSO WIRE SIZES & TYPES.*

Two-Wire Entrance

The two-wire entrance was once used to lead power from the utility pole to the house and carried a 120-volt hot wire and a ground wire. Two-wire entrances have become nearly obsolete because they do not supply enough power for modern appliances such as dishwashers, ranges and air conditioners. If the homeowner is experiencing frequently blown fuses, he should examine the service entrance. If the entrance is equipped with only two wires (a hot and a ground wire), he should replace it with a three-wire entrance for safer, more effective wiring. Frequently blown fuses may indicate inadequate wiring, so the homeowner may also have to replace the circuit with either a 240-volt three wire circuit or three-wire split circuit wiring. *SEE ALSO ELECTRICAL WIRING.*

Underground Cable

Underground cable is coated with a tough, water-resistant outer layer and is classified in the National Electrical Code as Type USE (Underground Service Entrance) and Type UF (Underground Fused). Both of these cables can be buried in the ground without further protection. Type USE and Type UF are available with single or multiple conductors and can be used in the same way, but Type UF must be protected by fuses or circuit breaker.

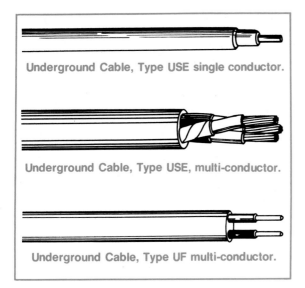

Underground Cable, Type USE single conductor.

Underground Cable, Type USE, multi-conductor.

Underground Cable, Type UF multi-conductor.

Lay undergrond cable at least 12 to 18 inches deep. In areas where underground cable might be disturbed by cultivation or digging, it should be buried even deeper and a protective shield placed on top of it before refilling the dirt. Underground cable must *never* be spliced. *SEE ALSO WIRE SIZES & TYPES.*

Underlayment

Underlayment is a rigid sheet material — hardboard, plywood or particleboard — used in covering a rough subfloor to provide a smooth base for application of the finished floor.

You'll most often need underlayment where you are going to lay resilient flooring, such as vinyl or vinyl-asbestos tile or roll flooring. With a very rough subfloor it is worthwhile to use underlayment before carpeting as well, so that the carpet will last longer. Nearly all subfloors will require use of underlayment before installation of "seamless" flooring (see entry), the kind that comes in liquid form and is poured on.

For most purposes, underlayment of approximately $1/4''$ or $3/8''$ thickness is suitable. But if your subfloor is thin plywood, such as $1/2''$, or is made tongue-and-groove boards more than $3''$ wide (or of ordinary boards of any width) you will usually do better to use thicker underlayment. You'll also want the thicker material when it is necessary to build up the thickness of the floor to match another floor. It is customary to use $5/8''$ underlayment, for example, where the resilient floor must produce the same level as a neighboring $3/4''$ wood floor.

PLYWOOD UNDERLAYMENT

Softwood plywood underlayment lays easily, stays flat, and is strong and rigid. It resists shrinkage, swelling, warping and buckling. The large panels cut installation time.

It is available in interior grade for installations where moisture is not a problem and in intermediate and exterior grades for uses where moisture conditions exist. It is manufactured with a "C" plugged face sanded for smoothness. The veneer under the face is "C" or "C" plugged for strength and economy. The other three plies are "D" veneer.

When installing plywood underlayment, you can follow in general the instructions given in detail below for the particleboard type.

HARDBOARD UNDERLAYMENT

This kind of panel is dense, grainless, strong, durable and moisture-resistant. It shrugs off scrapes and hammer blows and offers superior internal bond strength. Some brands are precision-sanded to exactly .215 inch. The coarse sanded surface has increased adhesive bonding properties. Usual dimensions are 4' wide by 3', 4' and 8' long.

Small panels of underlayment 3' by 4', are easy to handle, especially in small rooms. Open packages and let panels stand against walls for 24 hours.

Hardboard underlayment may be used under vinyl tile, linoleum and parquet floorings of all kinds not less than $1/16''$ thick. For best results, hardboard underlayment should be applied to structurally sound, properly nailed, clean, dry, level sub-flooring. It is not recommended for installation directly over on-grade or sub-grade concrete slabs.

Before installing hardboard underlayment, a few preliminary steps should be taken: (1) Check the existing floor for tightness and also for protruding nails. Re-nail if necessary. (2) The hardboard underlayment will bridge minor surface irregularities, but if the existing floor is too uneven, it should be sanded or filled. (3) In new construction or remodeling, wait until the enclosed area reaches normal moisture conditions and then stand individual sheets on edge for 24 hours or more to enable them to adjust to the surrounding air.

Installation Tips

Use normal woodworking tools and procedures when cutting. Allow your factory square edges to butt together, if possible. Stagger the joints in bricklayer's fashion, taking care that the underlayment joints do not coincide with sub-

floor joints. Panels should be spaced approximately $1/20''$ or the equivalent of a dime coin on all sides of the board. However, the panels should be spaced $1/8''$ from any structural member at the perimeter of the room.

Ordinary power or hand woodworking tools are suitable for any type of underlayment. Try to use original factory-cut edges where panels butt together within room.

Remember to lay panels rough side up to provide a superior bonding surface for the floor covering. Space nails at 3'' intervals around edges and 6'' intervals throughout the panel. Do not nail closer than $3/8''$ along the edge. Use special hardboard underlayment nails, or annular ring or ring-groove type 4-D cement-coated sinker nails.

Maintain recommended spacing when nailing panels down, nailing in center first and then around the edges. Drive nails fully flush with the surface of the underlayment.

Underlayment

Mastic and Adhesives

Water-based emulsion type adhesives are not recommended. Follow the manufacturer's application instructions for adhesive spread.

PARTICLEBOARD UNDERLAYMENT

Particleboard underlayment is composed of wood particles mat-formed, then compressed to uniform density and bonded under heat and pressure with urea adhesives. It is flat, free of voids, knots, grain and core defects. It will not split, crack, warp or delaminate. Particleboard underlayment has good thermal and acoustical insulation values for warmer floors and quieter rooms. This kind of underlayment is likely to be found at a lumber yard in a variety of thicknesses — $1/4''$, $3/8''$, $1/2''$ and $5/8''$. It is made in 4' widths, usually 4', 6', 8', 12' and sometimes 14' long.

It is well to store particleboard panels flat on skids in a dry place. On new construction, try not to bring the panels to the job site before they are needed. They should not be installed before concrete, plaster and lumber are dried to the approximate conditions that will be found in the structure during occupancy. Underlayment should be installed just before the floor covering, and after other interior finishing work is completed. The subfloor should be of wood construction, dry, level, securely nailed and free of all foreign matter and projections. Ground level in *basementless* spaces should be at least 18 inches below bottoms of floor joists. It is unwise to apply particleboard underlayment over concrete or below grade. Plywood subfloors must be at least $1/2''$ thick. If $1/2''$ plywood is used, $5/8''$ or thicker particleboard underlayment must be glue-nailed to the plywood subfloor. Face grain should be perpendicular to joist span. Board subfloors must be at least 1'' nominal thickness and not over 8'' wide. A vapor barrier with a maximum rating of 1.0 perm should be used over subfloors (except when underlayment is glue nailed) and as a ground cover in all basementless spaces. Areas over furnaces should be insulated to prevent localized drying and shrinkage of floor components. If radiant-electric-heat panels are used in the floor, insulation should be installed to prevent localized drying of the floor system.

If the underlayment has been subjected to high humidity conditions before application, separate the panels with sticks so that air can circulate, and use furnace heat to dry them.

Start laying the panels at a corner of the room. Leave a $3/8''$ gap between underlayment and walls. Arrange panels so that four panel corners do not meet at one point. Butt all panel edges and ends to a light contact. With plywood subfloor, offset the underlayment panel joints, and plywood panel joints that are at right angles to the joists, at least 2''. Offset underlayment panel joints and plywood panel joints that are parallel to the joists at least one joist. When $3/8''$ or thinner particleboard underlayment is used, the floor thickness (subfloor plus underlayment) must not be less than 1''. With board or decking subfloors installed perpendicular to the joists, apply underlayment panels with edges over the joists, and with ends offset at least 2'' from a subfloor joint. Use a minimum particleboard thickness of $3/8''$. With board or decking subfloors applied at an angle to the joists, apply the underlayment panels perpendicular to the joists with end joints parallel to and over a joist. Use a minimum particleboard thickness of $3/8''$.

Fastening

Nailing

Use ring-grooved underlayment nails if possible, although cement-coated box nails are often used. Start nailing in center of panel and work toward edges. Drive nails perpendicular to the surface and set flush. It's best to drive nails no closer than $1/2''$ or farther than $3/4''$ from the panel edges. Nail each panel completely before starting the next. For panels thinner than $3/8''$, use 6d nails spaced 3'' apart around the perimeter of the panel and 6'' on centers each way throughout the body of the panel. For panels $3/8''$ to $5/8''$ thick, use 6d nails spaced 6'' apart around the perimeter of the panel and 10'' each way throughout the body of the panel. Nail to joists wherever possible.

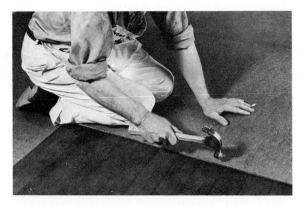

Start the application of the panels in one corner of the room, allowing ¹/₈″ of space at the wall. Try to keep underlayment joints from falling along those in the subfloor.

Stapling

Galvanized divergent-chisel-point, power-driven staples may be used. They should be a minimum of ⁷/₈″ long, 18-gauge and ³/₁₆″ crown for ¹/₄″ thick underlayment; 1-¹/₈″ long, 16-gauge and ³/₈″ crown for ³/₈″ underlayment; 1-⁵/₈″ 16-gauge and ³/₈″ crown for ¹/₂″ and ⁵/₈″ underlayment. Staples should be spaced no further apart than 3″ around the perimeter of the panel, ¹/₂″ from the edge and 6″ each way throughout the body of the panel. Countersink staples no more than ¹/₁₆″.

A nailing or stapling machine, often available from tool rental companies, will speed the job. You can use ⁷/₈″ staples spaced 3″ around edges, 6″ throughout body of panel.

Glue-Nailing

For a superior floor system, use the glue-nailing method of applying underlayment. Make sure the subfloor is free of all dust, dirt and debris. Apply adhesive such as a hard-setting casein glue or a polyvinyl acetate floor underlayment glue to the subfloor in a pattern providing a 2″ wide strip along each underlayment-panel end, a 3″ wide strip along each panel edge, and a 6″ wide strip down the center of the panel parallel to the edges. Spread the glue with a roller, notched trowel or brush. When glue-nailing over board subfloors, use particle-board underlayment at least ¹/₂″ thick. Don't use water-emulsion asphalt adhesives, brush-on or roll-on adhesives on particle-board underlayment. Nailing should be done as described previously, except that the spacing can be increased to 16″ centers both around the perimeter and throughout the body of the panel.

Resilient flooring should be at least ¹/₁₆″ thick, and ¹/₈″ is a safer minimum. Again, joints should not be allowed to coincide with those in previous layer.

Filling and Sanding

Fill gouges, gaps and any chipped edges with a hard-setting patching compound. Allow patches to dry thoroughly and then sand flush. Sand any uneven joints between panels, too, since panel joints must be perfectly matched to prevent show-through. When putting down resilient flooring, avoid using anything thinner than ¹/₁₆″.

1805

Underwriter's Knot

A simple knot to insure a sturdier connection between the wires of a cord and the plug terminal screws is the Underwriter's Knot. Forming an Underwriter's Knot is a simple task. Make a loop in one of the two wires of a cord, then slip the second wire into this loop, forming a loop in the second wire simultaneously. Slip the end of the first wire through the second loop and pull the ends of both wires. This should form a tight knot in the recess between the terminal screws, causing the wires to point in opposite directions of their respective screws. Wrap one wire at a time along the inside of the plug until it reaches its correct terminal screw, then tighten the screws. The Underwriter's Knot is used in lamp cords or wherever there is a possibility of the cord being accidentally jerked from the outlet, loosening the connection. *SEE ALSO PLUGS & CORDS.*

Underwriter's Laboratories
[SEE NATIONAL ELECTRICAL CODE.]

Union

A union is a galvanized steel or copper tube fitting. Divided by an outer rim with the appearance of a large hex nut, the union is screwed on to the ends of the pipes and is then tightened by screwing the hex nut divider. *SEE ALSO PIPE FITTINGS.*

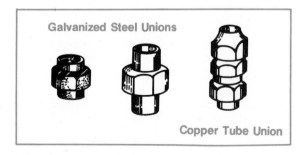

Galvanized Steel Unions

Copper Tube Union

Upholstery

Removal of the upholstery fabric was the first step. Since it was old and worn, it ripped away with little effort, but left behind a host of rusty tacks. These can be removed with a tack lifter, but this is a slow process. Professionals use an offset cold chisel, or a ripping chisel when confronted with a long line of tacks. The chisel is tapped along the row of tacks with a wooden mallet, and the tacks pop out of the wood. Be sure to wear glasses when doing this. With the fabric removed, the old padding was pulled away.

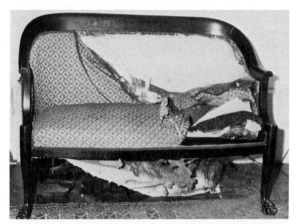

CHOOSING THE FABRIC

Measure for the upholstery fabric with economy as well as beauty in mind. Some fabrics have a soft surface that is quick to pick up soil; some are treated to resist and release soil with the usual home care. Some, like the plastics, require practice before a good-looking job results. Look for a firm tight-weaved fabric in a desirable color.

SELECTING THE FOAM

Choosing the foam is best done if there is an outlet in the area where the foam can actually be seen and felt as it is available in many thicknesses and in varying degrees of firmness. The firmest is still comfortable, and will stand up better in the long run than the softer types.

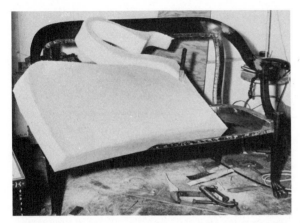

Foam cushioning, available through mail-order or from suppliers of upholstery materials, and $1/4$ inch plywood as the support was chosen for the job.

THE UPHOLSTERING PROCESS

First, lay the chair on its back and place the foam that has been cut to fit on the inside back. It will stay there as the piece of fabric which is to cover it is fitted over the foam. Adjust it so the fabric pattern looks right. Use a staple gun to anchor the center of the back top frame. Smooth the material across the back and anchor it at the two top corners. Fill in the gaps between with staple *stitches* for a smooth line. Then staple the material down the two sides toward the seat. Ease the fabric as you go. When the back rail of the seat is reached, pull the fabric taut and smooth. Working again from the center towards the outer edges (the sides), pull and staple for a nice fit.

If the fabric was cut in one continuous length for the back and seat, all that has to be done is to flip the remaining material over the back, while the seat cushioning material is put in place. Then pull the fabric toward the front of the seat, smoothing as you go, and place a staple at the center of the front seat rail. Follow the same procedure as at the top of the back — smooth and staple until a neat fit is made. Now turn the chair face down and do a similar job on the outside of the back.

Trim closely all around the edges of the staple *stitches,* so there is an even line for applying the trim, which will conceal any minor flaws in handiwork.

Trim comes in so many styles and varieties that there is bound to be one to suit one's situation and taste. It ranges from fringe, the narrow type known as *moss fringe,* guimpe, braid and cording.

Corners can present a problem to the novice upholsterer, but if time is taken to *work* the fabric with the fingers, a smooth professional result can be achieved. Three small folded pleats, or a simple single pleat facing toward the back of the seat can take care of this. When fitting fabric on a round seat by the staple or tack method described (tacks can be substituted for staples, but staples are easier by far), always pull the fabric straight down all around the curve of the seat. Angling simply distorts the fabric and the results are disappointing.

PARTIAL UPHOLSTERY REPAIR

When repairing a piece that is only partially in bad shape, it pays to revert to the old fashioned method. If there are only a few strips of webbing that need replacing, or a spring or two that requires re-tying, it would be foolish to strip the piece down and re-do it. If the piece is turned upside down, old webbing can be replaced easily and quickly. A webbing stretcher and strip webbing will be needed to do this properly. If springs are tipped over, new cord is also required to re-tie them so they will maintain their original upright position. To do the job on the springs, it is necessary to work from the top. Remove old fabric carefully, if it is reusable, and the padding, unless it is so badly compressed it needs replacing. Take a good look at the insides, making a few notes or a simple diagram of the tying pattern, so replacement parts can be refastened easily. Mail-order houses have kits containing a good range of materials for this type of repair, but in most cases the old coil springs are not too readily available. Instead, no-sag wire spring material with clips to anchor the wire type springing is offered. Tool kits are also offered mail-order, to facilitate the job. When the old springs are beyond repair, replacement with the no-sag wire spring type or the plywood-base-foam method is the only way. Weigh the work involved, the tool supply and the time taken for the work. When cushions for an older sofa or overstuffed type chair are needed, the foam units come in sizes that can replace most standard ones.

Upholstery Tools & Equipment

There are many tools designed specifically for upholstering. Both the upholsterer and the home carpenter should know these tools so that they will not be misused in either field.

The magnetic tack hammer weighs between six and nine ounces and has a five-and-one-half inch curved head that fits into a hickory handle, usually 11 or 12 inches long. The head of the hammer is split at one end and is magnetized to hold the tack until it has been started and can be driven with the other end. For removing old fabric from a chair or sofa, a ripping hammer is best. It is slightly heavier than the magnetic tack

hammer and has a five-inch head that also fits in a hickory handle.

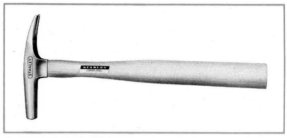

Courtesy of The Stanley Works

Magnetic Tack Hammer

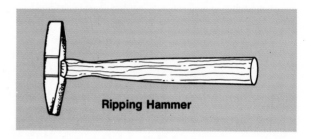

Ripping Hammer

Upholstering shears should be 10 to 12 inches long and have a bent handle so the material will not lift and distort during cutting.

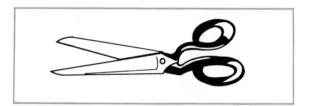

Upholstering Shears

Webbing stretchers are blocks of hard wood slightly curved in on each side for an easy grasp while stretching webbing. Webbing stretchers have steel points at one end for holding the webbing and the other end should be padded with rubber to prevent scarring the wood.

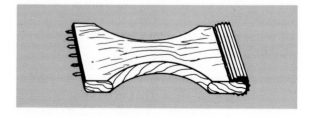

Webbing Stretchers

To remove tacks before replacing old covers, upholsterers use either a ripping tool or claw tool. The claw tool has a rectangular notch in the center of its blade and impedes quick removal of tacks, since the tackheads often stick in the notch. The ripping tool has an unnotched blade and is used more by professionals than the claw tool.

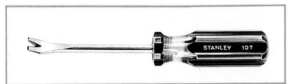

Courtesy of The Stanley Works

Claw Tool

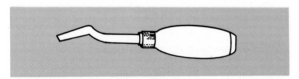

Ripping Tool

A rubber mallet weighing 16 or 32 ounces is sometimes used to drive the ripping or claw tool when removing tacks or upholstery nails from a frame. Rubber or rolled rawhide mallets will not mar the wood surface.

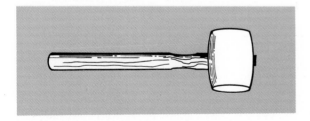

Rubber Mallet

When tacks or nail heads are driven too deeply in wood for easy removal with a ripping or claw tool, use a pair of nail pliers. They grip the head of the tack and pull it either far enough out (if not completely out) for final removal with a claw or ripping tool.

Spring-clip pliers are a useful item designed especially for setting edge wire or spring clips.

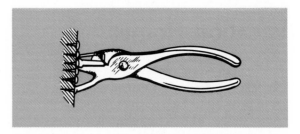

Nail Pliers

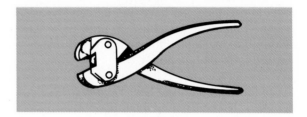

Spring Clip Pliers

Straight, curved and packing needles are for sewing material onto the furniture frame. Straight needles come in lengths from 4 to 20 inches and are available in either single point or double point styles. The double-pointed type is better because the upholsterer can push the needle back through the fabric without reversing. Curved needles are 2 to 10 inches long and come in extra light, light and heavy grades for different fabric weights. The curved needle does not require the upholsterer to reach behind the work each time and push the needle through, as must be done with straight needles. Packing needles come in straight or curved styles and are the heaviest grade used for coarse material.

The stuffing rod is usually 1½ feet long and is used for punching the stuffing into difficult areas such as the end of armrests.

Although some upholsterers prefer to use tacks and upholstery nails, both manually-operated and pneumatic staple guns can be used for tacking down webbing and fabric. *SEE ALSO HAND TOOLS.*

Stuffing Rod

Vacation Homes

The family planning a vacation home has a variety of possibilities to consider. They can build a home using plans developed by building materials companies; they can assemble a home using modular, panelized or pre-cut factory-built home; they can have an architect design a home; they can purchase a unit in a condominium development; or they can purchase a factory built mobile home.

All of these possibilities have validity for various families. To determine which possibility is best for the family, a few selection considerations must be made.

SELECTION CONSIDERATIONS

All selection considerations are basically attempts to determine if a particular sort of vacation home will meet the needs of a family.

Does the family enjoy the site area? Most families have definite preferences for vacation activities. The house or site being considered should provide easy access to such activities.

Is the design easy to maintain? Since a vacation home is a place to relax and enjoy a break from everyday chores, a vacation home should demand a minimum of upkeep.

Is the design large enough for family and guests? People particularly with vacation homes in the mountains or at a beach will probably have

Courtesy of Spacemakers, Inc.

A snug cabin amid snow banks and pine trees is the dream of many prospective vacation home owners.

houseguests. The bunk rooms, lofts, or other sleeping areas will need to be large enough to accommodate them, particularly for possible several-day stays. Similarly, the kitchen of the design should be able to handle possible entertaining chores without overloading either itself or the cook.

Does the design fit the climate? If the vacation area is in a hot, humid area, a design must have provisions for good ventilation or air conditioning (or both). A ski lodge needs good insulation, good heating and a "snow room," for changing skiis, parkas, and boots.

Can the site handle the necessary utilities? Space will be needed for a septic tank drain field, if public utilities are not available. Will building codes accept alternate systems than a septic tank, if space is limited? Does the well provide sufficient water? Is there space for a storage tank, if needed? What electricity is available? How reliable is the service?

These and similar considerations must be made before finally deciding upon a vacation home.

VACATION HOME DESIGNS

Many companies have designed vacation home plans. These plans are available to the prospective buyer at reasonable cost. The designs provide a variety of imaginative solutions to the choice of a vacation home.

Courtesy of Western Wood Products Association

This light-filled design encircles a fireplace and conversation pit capped with clerestory windows.

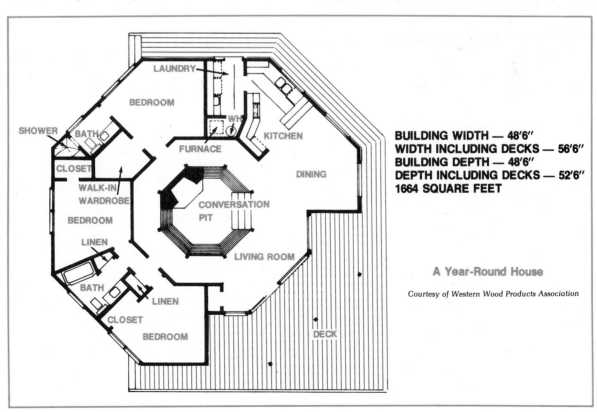

BUILDING WIDTH — 48'6"
WIDTH INCLUDING DECKS — 56'6"
BUILDING DEPTH — 48'6"
DEPTH INCLUDING DECKS — 52'6"
1664 SQUARE FEET

A Year-Round House

Courtesy of Western Wood Products Association

Courtesy of Western Wood Products Association

The skiier has a warm base to return to in this chalet. The two-story design features a large fireplace, three bedrooms and wide decks. The decks can be used as an area to shed boots and parkas.

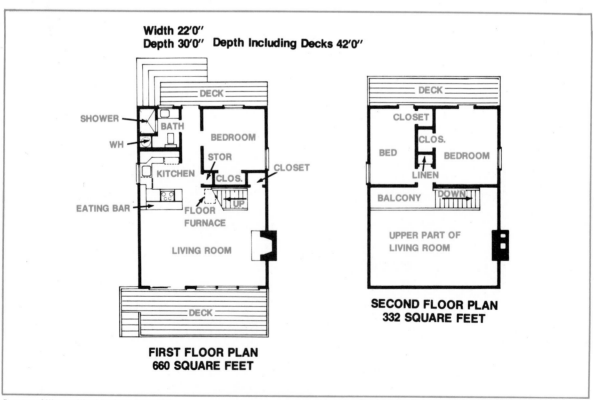

Width 22'0''
Depth 30'0'' Depth Including Decks 42'0''

DECK

SHOWER

BATH

WH

BEDROOM

STOR

KITCHEN

CLOS.

CLOSET

EATING BAR

FLOOR FURNACE

UP

LIVING ROOM

DECK

**FIRST FLOOR PLAN
660 SQUARE FEET**

DECK

CLOSET

CLOS.

BED

BEDROOM

LINEN

BALCONY

DOWN

UPPER PART OF
LIVING ROOM

**SECOND FLOOR PLAN
332 SQUARE FEET**

Courtesy of Western Wood Products Association

A Chalet for Skiiers

Courtesy of Western Wood Products Association

Open planning plus a window — all that makes the spacious deck a part of the living area contribute to the indoor-outdoor feeling of this plan. A balcony sleeping area adds to the openness of the plan.

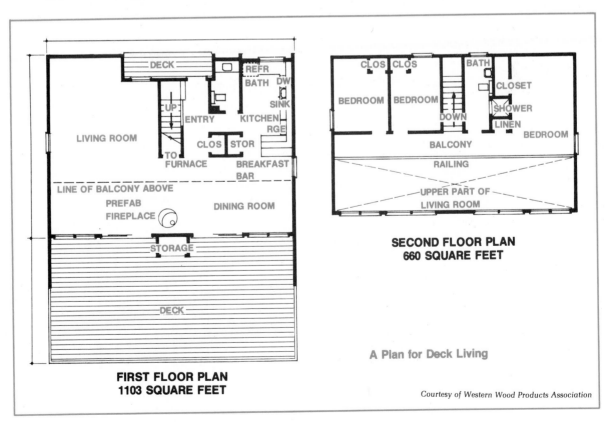

**FIRST FLOOR PLAN
1103 SQUARE FEET**

**SECOND FLOOR PLAN
660 SQUARE FEET**

A Plan for Deck Living

Courtesy of Western Wood Products Association

Courtesy of Home Building Plan Service, for The American Plywood Association

A raised hearth and a open fireplace provide a warm welcome in the living area of this mountain chalet. With three bedrooms and a garage, this plan could be developed into a year-round retirement home.

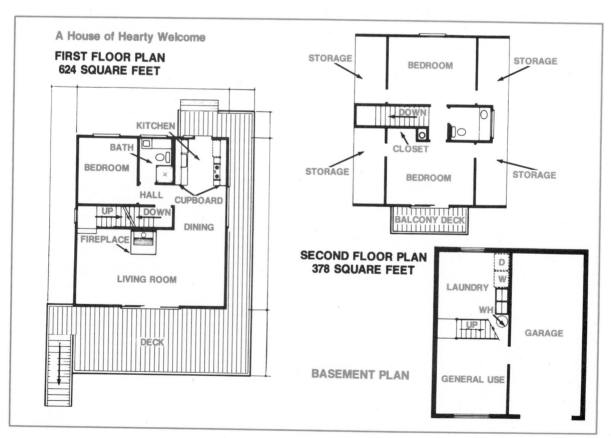

A House of Hearty Welcome

FIRST FLOOR PLAN
624 SQUARE FEET

KITCHEN

BATH

BEDROOM

HALL

CUPBOARD

UP   DOWN

DINING

FIREPLACE

LIVING ROOM

DECK

STORAGE   BEDROOM   STORAGE

DOWN

CLOSET

STORAGE   BEDROOM   STORAGE

BALCONY DECK

SECOND FLOOR PLAN
378 SQUARE FEET

D
W

LAUNDRY

WH

UP   GARAGE

BASEMENT PLAN

GENERAL USE

Courtesy of Home Building Plan Service for American Plywood Association

This design incorporates the most desirable features developed for the A-frame house. Perimeter walls are 5 feet high for adequate furniture placement. Front and rear doors are both protected and have adequate deck space. Stairs are not too steep and have a full landing area.

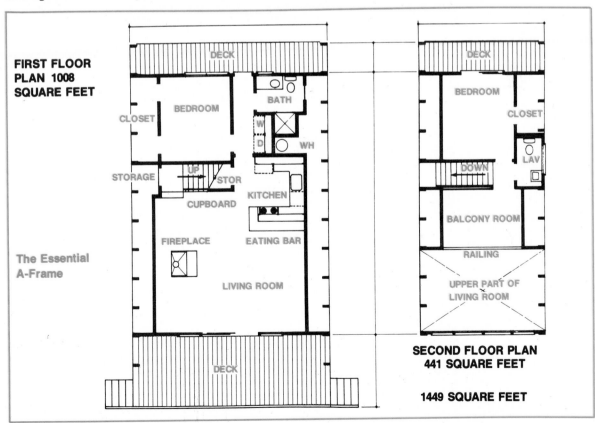

FIRST FLOOR PLAN 1008 SQUARE FEET

The Essential A-Frame

DECK

CLOSET
BEDROOM
BATH
W
D
WH
STORAGE
UP
STOR
CUPBOARD
KITCHEN
FIREPLACE
EATING BAR
LIVING ROOM
DECK

DECK
BEDROOM
CLOSET
DOWN
LAV
BALCONY ROOM
RAILING
UPPER PART OF LIVING ROOM

SECOND FLOOR PLAN 441 SQUARE FEET

1449 SQUARE FEET

Courtesy of the American Plywood Association

Here the A-frame concept has been worked out for maximum convenience on a minimum budget. An insulating glass window wall provides a dramatic view from both levels. Texture One-Eleven siding is applied to the roof grooved-side-in for an unusual ceiling design.

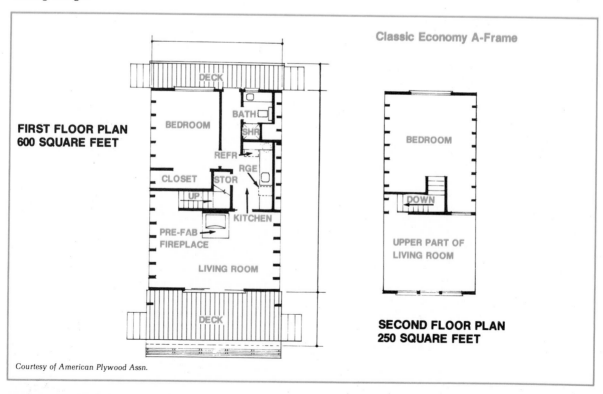

Classic Economy A-Frame

FIRST FLOOR PLAN 600 SQUARE FEET

DECK

BEDROOM

BATH

SHR

REFR

RGE

CLOSET — STOR

UP

KITCHEN

PRE-FAB FIREPLACE

LIVING ROOM

DECK

BEDROOM

DOWN

UPPER PART OF LIVING ROOM

SECOND FLOOR PLAN 250 SQUARE FEET

Courtesy of American Plywood Assn.

MANUFACTURED HOMES

The vacation home purchaser will find that factory-built homes are available in an almost infinite variety of designs, construction methods or states of assembly. Three general classifications of manufactured homes are modular, panelized and pre-cut.

Modular Home

The modular home is built within a factory and shipped to a site as one or more units to be positioned on a prepared foundation. A modular home can be bought in several stages of completion, ranging from a completely finished and equipped "turn key" package to a completed shell.

Courtesy of Designaire

This modular vacation home is a completely equipped unit with wiring, plumbing, installed kitchen, electric baseboard heat, and carpeting. Each wing is delivered to the site on a special trailer, and it is there lifted onto the prepared foundation.

Courtesy of Designaire

This home can be erected and made ready for occupancy by a four man crew in two days. (Note: Site preparation may take a bit longer.)

Panelized Home

Construction of a panelized home is a relatively quick process also. Large panelized homes can be assembled and made weather-tight in two working days.

Courtesy of Techbuilt, Inc.

The panelized home package has been delivered to the site.

Courtesy of Techbuilt Inc.

The first wall section is removed from the package.

Courtesy of Techbuilt Inc.

Two carpenters brace a 20 foot wall panel.

Courtesy of Techbuilt, Inc.

With first floor walls in place at end of first day, living room roof beams are set in place.

Courtesy of Techbuilt Inc.

At the beginning of the second day, the second floor flooring panels are installed.

Courtesy of Techbuilt, Inc.

At the end of the second day, the roof panels are installed.

Courtesy of Techbuilt, Inc.

At the end of two days, the house is weather-tight. Construction took place in cold, snowy weather.

Pre-Cut Homes

Several manufacturers make pre-cut all-wood vacation homes. These designs range from the rustic warmth of the traditional log cabin to natural appeal of dressed lumber. All of the designs are based upon some form of interlocking joint system.

Courtesy of Justis Homes

After initial site and foundation preparation, the construction of a solid wood pre-cut home is relatively straightforward. The first wall timber of this design is the only one needing nailing.

Courtesy of Justis Homes

The walls are driven together without sealant for an airtight fit. Note the use of a nailing block to protect the tongues on the timber.

Courtesy of Justis Homes

The solidity of the interlocking timber walls is seen here. Note nailing blocks in position to protect joints.

Courtesy of Justis Homes

The walls are assembled like fine cabinetwork, yet can be constructed by a relatively inexperienced craftsman. The timbers are double tongue and grooved, machined to a zero tolerance fit and joined at all corners with dovetail joints, locking the structure into one solid unit.

Courtesy of Justis Homes

Roof beams are fitted into pre-cut notches in wall timbers.

Courtesy of Justis Homes

Natural wood home in a forested area blends well with its environment.

Courtesy of POLYARCH Homes

The fiberglass units and wooden end panels for a 680 square foot vacation home arrive at the site on one flat bed truck.

Courtesy of POLYARCH Homes

The completed 680 square foot fiberglass unit. The temporary supports will be replaced with interior partitions of normal frame construction.

Courtesy of POLYARCH Homes

A fiberglass building segment is easily carried to position by 3 men. If a hoist is available for handling the building units, the work crew may be reduced from 6 to 2.

Courtesy of POLYARCH Homes

This mountainside vacation home uses the basic fiberglass structure supplemented with native stone and wood construction.

Courtesy of POLYARCH Homes

One man holds up the open end of a building segment while a temporary support is placed in position.

Courtesy of Acorn Structures, Inc.

This attractive lakefront home presents an exterior of relatively conventional design.

1820

Courtesy of Acorn Structures, Inc.

The interior, however is flooded with natural light from the dramatic central skylight.

Man-Made Materials

An imaginative use of man-made materials can be found in some manufactured homes. Fiberglass, more often found in home draperies, has been used to develop a home construction package that may be easily adapted to the needs of a vacation home buyer.

Individualized Design

A number of manufacturers of factory-built homes provide extensive individualized design service. When a prospective home buyer is interested in a basic design, a wide variety of options and changes can be made within the bounds of the module (substituting windows for doors, reversing room layouts, etc.) for minimal cost. With some companies, rather extensive changes can be worked out with their architectural design staffs. With such changes, a builders basic design can be completely individualized to meet a family's vacation home needs.

Courtesy of Boise Cascade Corporation (Kingsberry Homes)

A sweeping deck and towering cedar shake roof help this vacation home design blend with its wooded location. The sleeping loft provides space for overnight guests.

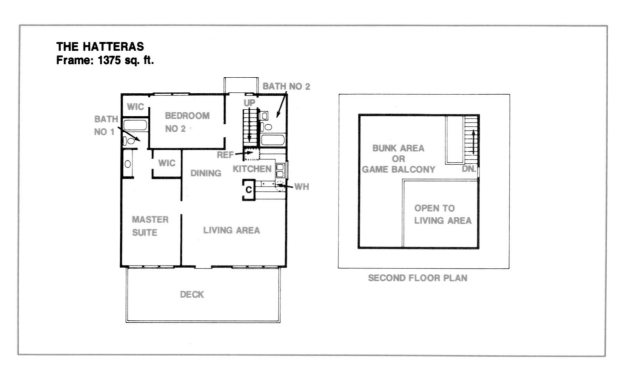

THE HATTERAS
Frame: 1375 sq. ft.

BATH NO 2

WIC

BEDROOM NO 2

UP

BATH NO 1

WIC

REF

DINING

KITCHEN

C

WH

MASTER SUITE

LIVING AREA

DECK

BUNK AREA OR GAME BALCONY

DN.

OPEN TO LIVING AREA

SECOND FLOOR PLAN

Courtesy of Boise Cascade Corporation (Kingsberry Homes)

This house with its wide deck and natural siding is roomy enough to serve as a year-round home.

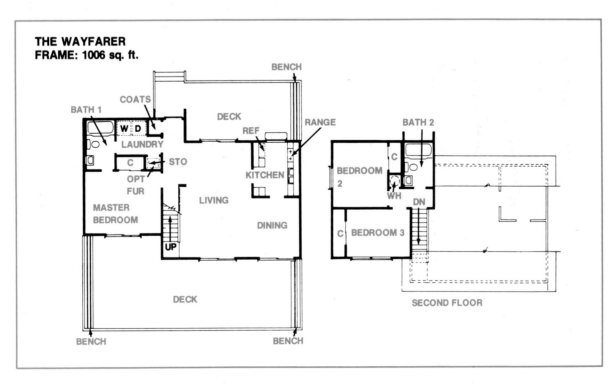

THE WAYFARER
FRAME: 1006 sq. ft.

BENCH

COATS

BATH 1

DECK

RANGE

BATH 2

W D

REF

LAUNDRY

C

C STO

OPT FUR

KITCHEN

BEDROOM 2

WH

MASTER BEDROOM

LIVING

DN

UP

DINING

C BEDROOM 3

DECK

SECOND FLOOR

BENCH

BENCH

Courtesy of Spacemakers

The spaciousness of the upper level of the mansard design is seen in this interior view. The upper level has much more usable space than would the ordinary A-frame design.

Energy-Saving Design

Many manufactured homes are designed for minimum energy use, and maximum use of natural heating and cooling. Such attention to these design features is helpful. Since many vacation homes are located far from any public utility company, design features that lessen reliance on electricity or LPG make the vacation home more usable at less expense.

Courtesy of Spacemakers

Usable floor space near the walls is gained on the lower level of the mansard design. The window wall across the end of the house provides a dramatic view of the surrounding countryside.

Courtesy of Spacemakers

This mansard design retains the advantages of the A-frame, while eliminating one of its problems. The sloping side walls retain the low cost of roof construction, while the lowered top both provides more additional usable second floor living space, and eliminates the heat trap of the upper A-frame area.

Courtesy of Spacemakers

Gable vents and high windows, plus sliding doors in the end wall provide for the rapid removal of hot air during the summer months. Conversely, the smaller windows, plus the closed vents, in winter eliminate a major source of heat loss.

Pole Houses

The pole house, which is possibly the logical completion of the concept of post-and-beam construction, has gained favor with some manufacturers. One advantage of pole house construction is that it provides for the economical construction of vacation homes on previously unusable or inacessible land. The foundation of a pole house is a series of pilings which extend upward to become the supporting posts for the house walls. The pole foundation can be adapted to extremely irregular terrain at far less cost than the traditional poured concrete foundation. In addition, the pole foundation disturbs the site far less than a traditional foundation.

Courtesy of The Koppers Company

The pole house is constructed entirely of wood. The supporting poles and beams are pressure-treated to prevent decay. Walls are of textured redwood. Ceilings, roof, and closet doors are cedar. Custom designed and fitted cabinets are mahogany.

Courtesy of The Koppers Company

The houses are designed to bring the outdoors in. Wide verandas surround the house, and each room opens on a deck. The wide eaves keep off the hot sun, and protect the windows from sudden rains. Combined with the ceiling vents, the design keeps the home cool and dry.

This pole house design built in Hawaii makes use of ceiling vents to eliminate the need for mechanical air conditioning.

Courtesy of The Koppers Company

INDIVIDUALLY DESIGNED HOMES

Families with unique needs or desires for a vacation home, that cannot seem to satisfy their requirements with manufactured homes, can turn to an architect for the solution to their problem.

Courtesy of The California Redwood Association

Sweeping ocean views are gained from the deck of this seaside house. The redwood siding has weathered to a natural gray color.

Courtesy of The California Redwood Association

Warm redwood siding stands out against the white snow and blue sky. This architect-designed vacation home takes full advantage of its location.

Courtesy of The California Redwood Association

The roof lines of this beach house provide sheltered areas for outside activities. The naturally weathered color of the redwood siding helps the house fit into the landscape.

The family that uses an architect to solve their vacation home problem will achieve a unique solution to their vacation problems.

OTHER SOLUTIONS

Two other solutions to the problem of the vacation home exist: the condominium unit and the mobile home.

The condominium unit is a relatively new addition to the vacation home scene. With a condominium unit, the vacation home buyer purchases one of a series of housing units. The management firm that supervises the condominium will maintain the unit, and, if the owner desires, rent the condominium to other vacationers when the owner is not using it. Condominiums have been most successful in areas with high tourist turnover, such as beach areas or ski areas.

Courtesy of The Sikes Corporation

Attractive condominium units in an oceanfront area will help pay for themselves with off-season rental. The ceramic tile floor is typical of the low-care surfaces any vacation home should have.

The mobile home is also a solution for the vacation home. Such manufactured units may be set up on the owner's site, or established as part of a mobile home community. A far cry from yesterday's "trailer park," contemporary mobile home communities are laid out with the care and concern for the amenities of siting and landscaping found in many modern subdivisions.

A mobile home may be further tied into the landscape with the addition of carport and terrace structures.

Courtesy of Western Wood Products

Carport and terrace additions to a standard mobile home help tie it into the landscape.

Mobile homes, condominiums, architect designs, pre-cut, panelized, or modular factory-built homes, or building company designs, all provide ways for a family to obtain a vacation home that meets their needs. *SEE ALSO MOBILE HOME CONSTRUCTION.*

Vacuum Cleaner Repair

A vacuum cleaner contains a motor, usually the universal type, that drives a large blower which forces the air through a filtering bag and back into the room. As air passes through the bag, any lint or dust particles that it contains are deposited within the bag. The high-powered motor used on many types of vacuums is the multi-stage type with multiple impellers (fans) stacked one on top of the other for maximum suction.

The vacuum cleaner is a simple appliance, consisting primarily of an electrical switch, the motor and the fan assembly. But it is critical if hoses or tubes become blocked with a foreign object. Lint quickly builds up and completes the blockage. For this reason, it is much easier to take care of these problems at first indication.

Preventive maintenance is important for a vacuum. If bags are allowed to overfill, some lint escapes and must pass through the vacuum motor. If this condition lasts long enough, it can create wear within the blowers and damage the motor itself.

To prevent this, a special motor filter is used on most vacuums. It's located behind the bag directly over the opening for air to flow into the blower assembly. Filters should be removed and cleaned at least every six months and replaced each year. If the filter becomes torn or can no longer be cleaned easily, it should be replaced more often.

A clogged hose is first indicated by a lack of suction power. If it becomes a complete blockage, there will be no suction at all. This condition is usually caused by an article such as a match stick or toothpick becoming lodged within the hose itself. As lint builds up, the blockage becomes more severe. Remove the hose from the vacuum and run a garden hose through it from the vacuum side toward the end of the hose where the tool attaches. The garden hose is usually sufficient to dislodge any blockage within the vacuum hose.

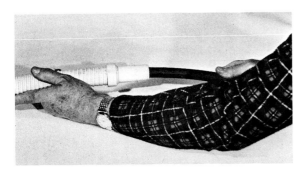

Obstruction in vacuum hose can be removed by forcing garden hose through it. Plastic tape, stretched tightly over break or cut, can make temporary repair of plastic or fabric hose.

The tools can also become blocked. When they do, it is usually simple to use a long sharp object such as a screwdriver to remove a blockage. If brush areas of the tool become worn, parts are

available for many models. Replacement of the entire tool such as a floor brush is not necessary.

Floor tools can often be repaired simply by prying brush and holder apart. Obtain replacement brush from dealer.

The motor unit on both upright and canister type vacuums is similar, except on the canister type a power takeoff is used to drive a revolving brush.

On-off switch is often at fault when cleaner fails to operate. Check or replace it (after unplugging vacuum) by removing attaching screws or snapping switch up from housing.

This is usually done by a means of an O-ring or flat belt driven from a pulley off the motor.

To repair a canister vacuum, first unplug it from the receptacle and then open the housing. Look for screws under rubber bumpers and along the back part of the housing. Also look for them beneath the vacuum. Sometimes it is necessary to remove a trim plate or the wheel assembly to get at these screws. With the housing apart, the motor windings are usually visible.

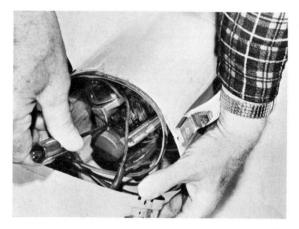

Motor brushes can wear after long periods of use. Brush position in this vacuum is indicated by screwdriver. Obtain exact replacements and be sure that commutator is cleaned.

After long usage it may be necessary to replace the motor brushes on a vacuum cleaner. If their length is less than one-third of an inch, it's time for them to be replaced. Take the old brushes with you when purchasing replacement parts to be certain to obtain the correct size. If the copper bars on the end of the motor armature (called the commutator) are discolored or burned, polish them with a hardwood stick before putting new brushes in place. Brush away all lint and dust before reassembling the housing.

A noisy vacuum is sometimes due to a loose fan. Some of these motor units are sealed and are not serviceable. If a fan should become loose, it would be necessary to replace the entire unit. On others the fan is held in place with a nut. Be sure that the nut is tightened thoroughly and the fan seated properly when reinstalling the motor.

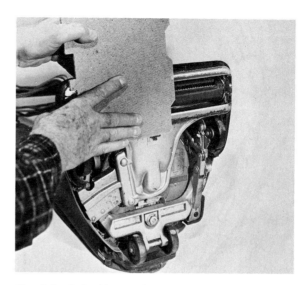

Check for belt slippage by using hardboard pressed against revolving brush. Slippage here indicates faulty brush. Be sure and keep fingers away from moving parts.

If belts are a constant problem on an upright type vacuum, it's possible that the bearings on the end of the rotary brush may have filled with lint and are binding. Before installing a new belt, give the rotor a spin by hand and be sure that it turns freely. If not, remove the rotary brush by pulling forward. It is often held in place with a clip. Remove the bearings in each end of the brush and check them carefully. Soaking in light oil should solve the problem. It may be

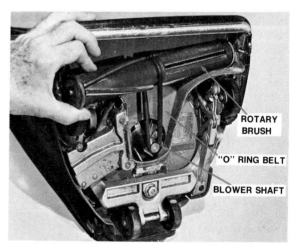

ROTARY BRUSH

"O" RING BELT

BLOWER SHAFT

If belt on upright vacuum or motor-driven brush attachment breaks, be sure to check conditions of bearings at end of brush when replacing belt. Lubricate with drop of oil.

necessary to use an old toothbrush to clean them carefully. Be sure that any seals or shields at the end of the rotary brush bearings are in place before it is put back into position. *SEE ALSO APPLIANCE REPAIR, SMALL.*

Valley Flashing

Valley flashing is necessary to make roofs water tight where two slopes intersect causing a valley. Flashing material may be galvanized metal, lead, tin-coated metal, roll roofing, asphalt shingles, aluminum or copper. Roll roofing is used most frequently with asphalt shingles.

Flashing is done by first centering a strip of roll roofing no less than 18 inches wide over the area to be flashed, mineral surface down. Nail the strip down and then nail another strip 36 inches wide over the first with the mineral side up. If joining is necessary with any strips, lap them at least 12 inches and secure with plastic asphalt cement. Nailing should be done so that before the second edge of material is secured it is pressed into the valley so that it follows the valley shape. Fasten the second edge of roll roofing, and finish applying the shingles. *SEE ALSO ROOF CONSTRUCTION.*

Valley Jack

A valley jack is a type of rafter that resembles the upper portion of a common rafter but, rather than intersecting a plate, it crosses a valley rafter. *SEE ALSO ROOF CONSTRUCTION.*

Valley Rafter

A valley rafter is a rafter that extends diagonally from ridge to plate in the area where two roof sections intersect. *SEE ALSO ROOF CONSTRUCTION.*

Vaporizers & Bottle Warmer Repair

Many vaporizers and bottle warmers heat the water without a heating element. They use the water itself as a resistance. They work like this: two conductors are suspended within the water, usually inside a Bakelite or plastic housing to prevent the user from coming into contact with them. When the vaporizer is plugged in, these two electrodes are energized with current directly from the line. Current flows between the electrodes through the water within the housing. The water becomes heated and boils away.

The housing serves another purpose also. It has a small hole at the bottom to allow water to flow in and out. If the electrodes were suspended in the entire jar of water at once, heating would be slow and eventually all the water would tend to heat. The orifice admits cold water as the water in the housing boils away.

If you use your vaporizer and bottle warmer carefully, chances are that you will never have to perform any service other than an occasional cleaning. Do this by removing the screws that hold the housing in place over the electrodes. With the electrodes exposed, mineral deposits can be brushed or chipped away. Be careful not

Handle a vaporizer only when it's unplugged. To reach electrodes, remove screws holding electrode housing to cover plate.

to bend the electrodes, and be sure to observe the proper gap when reassembling them as this distance is critical. If the electrodes become coated badly enough with minerals from the water, they may fail to heat at all.

Other reasons for a non-heating condition include a lack of voltage to the receptacle, easily checked with a table lamp, or a defective cord or connection. Check carefully around the strain relief where it enters the top of the vaporizer and around the plug.

Electrodes are cleaned using a knife, file, or light sandpaper. Scrape heavy mineral deposits first. Use care to prevent alteration of spacing.

With cover plate removed, electrodes are easily accessible for service. This will consist primarily of cleaning.

Since the condition of the water used in a vaporizer will vary, so will the resistance of this "heating element". If water has a high mineral content it will have a low resistance and will conduct readily. It can easily blow a fuse — particularly if another heating element is being used on the line. On the other hand, if there is little mineral content in the water, it will fail to conduct and produce heat. In areas where soft water prevails, additives such as baking soda or salt are often used in small amounts to increase the conductivity of the water. But consider that this can also damage the electrodes in time. If the water is high in mineral content, it can conduct so swiftly it can tend to "spit" water from the top of the vaporizer. If this occurs, mix some distilled water or rain water with the water in the reservoir to eliminate the problem.

If the unit heats slowly or only partially, it is time to clean the electrodes. This problem can also result from a plugged orifice in the bottom of the housing which can be opened with a toothpick. Be sure that all gaskets are back in place when reassembling and that the air gap space is correct on the electrode. Never allow the electrodes to touch — this would result in a short circuit that would blow the fuse as soon as the vaporizer is plugged in. A 50 per cent solution of water and vinegar can be helpful in cleaning the electrodes.

Another vaporizer, one that does not use heat, uses a small shaded pole motor to drive an impeller or disc which acts as a pump of sorts. This pulls water from the bottom of the reservoir and whirls it away from the disc at high speed. Since the disc also acts as a fan, the resulting vapor flows into the room area.

Problems which could arise with this type vaporizer include foreign matter entering and blocking the fan or pump or a problem within the motor itself, causing it to turn slowly or not at all. Even though no heat is used, mineral build-up could still occur over a period of time in hard water areas. If this happens it will be necessary to disassemble the machine and remove mineral deposits. Often this can be removed by soaking the components in a 50 per cent solution of water and white vinegar for a short period of time or by using a cleaning agent as specified by the manufacturer. *SEE ALSO APPLIANCE REPAIR, SMALL.*

Varnishes & Varnishing

A varnish is an oleoresinous clear finish that leaves resins which harden by chemical curing or oxidation. The resins used most often in varnishes are alkyds, which come in glossy and satin, the phenolic types, used more often externally and urethanes, which resist abuse and chemicals. Some varnishes also contain a vinyl formula which produces a quick-drying, lustrous, flexible finish that resists water and alcohol. The quality of a varnish is measured largely in its resistance to yellowing. Urethane varnishes, unlike yellow phenolic varieties, are clear and produce little color change. Alkyds differ somewhat so the only guarantee of a good alkyd varnish is to purchase one from a reputable manufacturer.

SURFACE PREPARATION

If varnish is to be applied to bare wood, check the surface thoroughly for blemishes, finger marks and dirt and, if necessary, clean it with either lacquer thinner, mineral spirits or a multisolvent product. Use fine sandpaper if sanding is required and run over the entire blemished area to insure uniform coloration.

On stained wood pieces, make sure that the surface is totally dry and is the desired color before applying varnish. In areas that are too dark, lighten them with fine steel wool and pigmented wiping stains. Test the stain and varnish combination on scrap wood before applying varnish to the piece.

An old finish that needs a new coat of varnish should be cleaned of oil, grease, wax and dirt with water and detergent and mineral spirits or lacquer thinner. Glossy surfaces should be roughened with fine sandpaper to provide good adhesion.

Dust can make a varnish finish rough by settling onto it. To avoid this, varnish the piece in an isolated area. If the job must be done in a workshop, sweep, dust and wait one hour before placing the project in the room. Then, dust the project with a clean paintbrush and spray it with air from a tire pump or other compressor. Use a tack rag for final dusting and work in lint-free clothing to prevent the accumulation of more dust.

VARNISH APPLICATION

Bare wood or wood tinted with non-grain-raising or water stains should have a first coat of one part turpentine to four parts varnish to act as a sealer. Pigmented wiping stains require no sealing coat. All following coats should be brushed on without thinners unless the varnish becomes too thick for a smooth application. Then, a small amount of turpentine may be added and slowly stirred in with the varnish.

Work on horizontal surfaces to prevent runs and place the object in front of a white wall to check the glare made by the level of varnish. Begin application at the far edge of the work and make two or three brush-wide stripes with a brush width between them. Brush the varnish crosswise to smooth it out, and use the bristle tips to provide a smooth finish. Continue these three steps until the entire surface is covered. Varnish should be spread slowly and smoothly to avoid the formation of air bubbles. Allow each coat to dry separately and sand between each one with fine sandpaper to insure good adhesion.

VARNISHING CURVED SURFACES

Irregularities in wood surfaces tend to scrape varnish off the brush in large amounts, causing puddles. In these areas, use a moderately dry brush.

On turnings and rounds such as spindles, stretchers and round legs, brush the varnish back and forth across the round. Level the strokes lengthwise and use smaller brushes on small spindles.

Ogee, head, cove and similar moldings are easily varnished with lengthwise strokes. However, carvings require dabbing the varnish into the crevices and then gently stroking the varnish out with a brush to alleviate puddled areas.

Panels on a paneled door are varnished first at the inner edge of the frame. Put the bristle tips on the cracks, pull out any excess varnish and then coat the frame edges.

To prevent build up on edges of vertical or horizontal surfaces, lift the brush up so that the bristles leave the edge before running over it and depositing extra varnish. On inside corners, pull out the varnish as described previously. *SEE ALSO WOOD FINISHING.*

Venetian Blind Repairs

Venetian blind repairs usually involve replacing worn tapes and defective lift and tilt cords. Replacement parts can be purchased in hardware and variety stores and should be the same size as the old parts. Begin by removing blinds from the window; if they are metal, lift up lock lever on the front ends of the headbox and slide blinds out; and if wooden, remove face board and lift out blinds.

To replace worn tapes, stretch out the blinds on a flat surface and remove the bottom bar either by detaching the metal bar clamp on metal blinds or removing staples that attach tape to the bottom slat of wooden blinds. Both lift cords should be unknotted and pulled through the slats. This action releases the slats so that they can be pulled out of the old tapes and cleaned. Remove old tapes from headbox clamps and install new

tapes at the top and bottom exactly as the old ones were. Insert the slats into the new tapes.

While the blinds are still disassembled, the lift cords can be replaced. The length of the new lift cord should equal the length of the blind multiplied by two plus the blind width plus six more feet for the pull loop. First remove the equalizer clip from the old lift cord pull loop. Since the lift cords have already been pulled through the slats, disengage them from the pulleys in the headbox and discard them. Double the new cord forming the pull loop and thread the two loose ends through the pulleys in the headbox. Rethread the new lift cords through the slats making sure they pass on alternate sides of the tape cross straps. Make a knot in the end of both cords after they pass through the bottom bar and replace metal clamps.

To replace lift cords when tapes do not need to be replaced, untie the cord under the bottom slat on the tilt cord side. Join the new cord to the old cord with tape, thread, or a staple. Pull on the other end of the old cord and gently thread the new cord through the path of the old cord until the knot on the other end of the old cord is

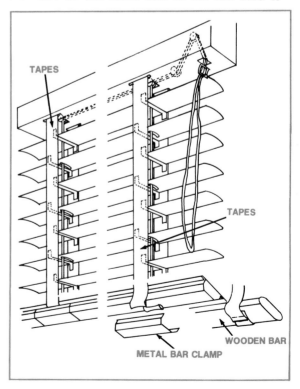

reached. Tie off the new lift cord under the bottom bar and replace metal slat or clamp.

The tilt cord can be replaced at the same time. Merely untie knot on one end of old tilt cord pulling on the other end until the cord is released from its pulley. Loop the new cord over the pulley, thread the plastic cones over the cord and tie a knot in both ends.

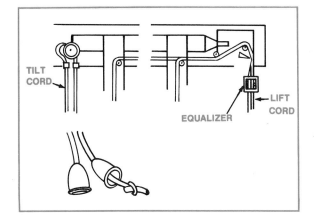

Vent

A vent is a pipe or opening which supplies air to drainage lines, allows gas or liquid to escape or relieves pressure.

By admitting air to the pipes in the plumbing system, drainage downflow is not slowed down by a vacuum and the build-up of sewer gas is prevented. Every fixture must have a vent located near it.

Several vents may be attached to one large vent or stack, extending up through the roof to the air, or one vent may be extended individually. The main vent pipe is the upper section of the soil stack which extends up through the roof. A vent increaser, which is a cast-iron soil pipe fitting, joins different sized pipes, thus increasing the diameter of the vent pipe at roof level. If the vent increaser extends far enough out of the roof, it may be used as a vent pipe also. To prevent freeze-ups in the vent pipe, its diameter should be at least three inches.

There are other kinds of vents used in construction. Button vents, which are small openings having a diameter of one to four inches, release moisture that is trapped in the walls. Ridge, roof, triangle, square and soffit vents release heat and moisture found in attics. The ridge vent is installed over a gap in the sheathing at the ridge. Roof vents are placed over cut openings between rafters. Triangle vents are found under the roof gable, making large vents at the gable end's highest point. Soffit vents take the place of some of the soffit material, providing steady ventilation along it. Brick and cement block vents, which are 8 by 16 inches, are placed in foundation walls to help release dampness from a crawl space. To vent crawl space, at least four block vents should be used.

In the heating system there are vents, such as the chimney and air vents. The chimney is normally referred to as a vent in gas heating systems. For a fireplace, the chimney vent, which is extended through the roof, releases the smoke from the fire. Air vents are located on the side of radiators to release air or steam. In electric boilers, automatic air vents slowly release trapped air. *SEE ALSO PLUMBING SYSTEMS.*

Ventilation, Home

With electric rates going up because of inflation and the energy crisis — an almost 90 percent increase in some areas — keeping a house comfortable can become a budgeting problem. Unfortunately, too, one energy-saving method — thoroughly caulking and weatherstripping a house — has added a problem. The more nearly airtight the house, the harder it is to get rid not only of warm air but water vapor, smoke and fumes from household chemicals.

There is a way of ridding the home of many such hazards. Install the right ventilation system to reduce the load on your air conditioner and provide house ventilation at times when the air conditioner is unnecessary. In some regions where the year-around climate is normally comfortable, a good ventilating system is all that is necessary.

JUDGING A VENTILATING FAN

Different size rooms require different air movement. Help in choosing the right size is made available by the Home Ventilating Institute, and independent testing bureau at Texas A&M University which issues a guide (write Home Ventilating Institute, 230 Michigan Ave., Chicago, Ill. 60601) telling how much capacity is needed for each room's ventilating task. Most manufacturers who sell ventilating equipment use HVI standards and so label their products. If you look at a ventilating fan, or range hood containing a fan, in a store, you will find a tag or label (sometimes on the container) listing CFM (cubic feet per minute) air delivery, the amount of air the unit will move.

Not long ago the sone or sound level of the unit was added. A sone is merely an internationally accepted unit of loudness. It is a less difficult term to understand than the decibel which is figured on a logorithmic scale. In number form (called sound level on the model or its container) it is an easy way of judging the amount of noise produced by that unit compared to other similar units. One sone is just about as much noise as your refrigerator produces when it is running. A multiple-speed fan is usually rated for its top sone level. Look also for figures which give noise level at other speeds.

Portable Fans — How Well Do They Ventilate?

A window fan will exhaust some of the inside air and do a fair job of bringing cool air into the house once outdoor temperature has dropped. However, a table, floor, or personal desk fan will not do much more than stir a breeze. It neither cools the air nor gets rid of smoke and vapor. Recently there has been a revival of the old fashioned ceiling fan.

WHERE ARE VENTILATING FANS NEEDED?

Kitchen. Twelve or more pounds of water vapor, smoke and grease build up each day in the average kitchen. Unless exhausted mechanically, these contaminants can endanger the structure of your home. Vapor gets into the

walls and causes paint and wallpaper to peel. Eventually moisture will start rot in wood.

The chief offenders are the sink and range. However, the problem has been increased in recent years by the heavy use of small appliances such as fry pan, toaster-oven, electric tea kettle, egg cooker and rice steamer.

Bathroom. The shower and tub produce steam and heat; cosmetics leave a residue of chemical fumes; and odors linger even though there may be a window which can be opened.

Garage, shop basement. Power saws, grinders, welding torches, paint sprayers all produce air pollution. Automobile fumes cannot escape once the door is closed, and may penetrate the house.

Laundry. It is especially important to have exhaust ventilation if the washer and dryer are in an enclosed utility area with no outdoor ventilation.

Family room. A large party produces a lot of heat, moisture and often smoke. Odors from a barbeque or a fireplace may penetrate the room in spite of a chimney.

Attic. All moist warm household air rises and is trapped here unless vented through roof or eaves.

SELECTING THE RIGHT VENTILATION

The kitchen range should have a ventilating hood mounted 21 to 24 inches above the cooking surface, never more than 30 inches. Choose a type with a ducted fan which will exhaust air outdoors. The best duct system is short and straight, with no reduction in size at any point. If size reduction is essential, and there are one or more elbow bends to get outside, it is better to go to a larger duct size.

Non-ducted range hoods often come in the same styles and shape as the ducted types. However, they cannot rid a room of moisture or heat but merely filter the contaminants through a mesh or screen system and return the air to the room. If you use one (and it may be the only solution on a remodeling job) install an additional wall or ceiling fan in some other part of the room.

An increasingly popular and useful exhaust fan (suitable for any small room) is one which combines heat and light with ventilation, or one with just light-ventilation. In the bath it is a quick source of comfort in early morning or during the night when central heating may not be operating. Some models have a timer switch, a safety and energy saving factor, especially in a family with youngsters.

Fan Capacity

You can match specific ventilation requirements to any ventilating fan by using the following charts recommended by the U. S. Department of Housing and the Home Ventilating Institute. It is desirable to select a fan with more than required capacity needed and then control its effectiveness with a multiple-speed switch.

TABLE TO MATCH CFM TO ROOMS

CFM-to-Room Area for HVI Standard Ventilation

Recommended CFM	Kitchen Sq. Ft.	Laundry, Family or Recreation Room Sq. ft.	Bathroom CFM	Sq. ft.
40	—	50	40	35
60	—	75	50	45
80	—	100	60	55
100		125	70	65
120	60	150	80	75
140	70	175	90	85
160	80	200	100	95
180	90	225	110	105
200	100	250		
250	125	310		
300	150	375		
350	175	435		
400	200	500		
450	225	560		
500	250	625		
550	275	685		

Typical CFM ratings (not every one) are shown above. Ceiling height of 8 feet is assumed.

* Cubic-Feet-Minute

**Home Ventilating Institute

Wall and Ceiling Fans	Recommended Air Changes/ Hour	Formula (8 ft. ceiling)
Kitchen	15	Sq. ft. of floor x 2 = CFM Example: 100 sq. ft. x 2 = 200 CFM
Bathroom	8	Sq. ft. of floor x 1.07 = CFM Example: 55 sq. ft. x 1.07 = 60 CFM (rounded)
Recreation Room, Utility Room, Laundry Room Basements, Other Rooms	6	Sq. ft. of floor x 0.8 = CFM Example: 150 sq. ft. x 0.8 = 120 CFM

ATTIC VENTILATION

Without ventilation, an attic can turn into an inferno on an average summer day. Outdoor temperature may be in the mid-nineties, but the trapped air in the attic may reach over 130 degrees. This heat not only adds considerably to the discomfort of the downstairs area, but if the house is air-conditioned, it also puts an extremely heavy load on the cooling system.

The ordinary attic fan exhausts hot air through an attic vent, drawing in cool air from below, and setting up air circulation throughout the house. To ventilate an entire house, or just a few rooms at a time, you will need a fan of the right size; this means a fan which can change the air about once a minute, if you live in the South, and about once every 1$^1/_2$ to 2 minutes in the North.

All you need do is figure the volume of space to be ventilated. Determine the amount of square feet of floor area of all areas to be ventilated. (Don't count closets, storage wall area, cabinet space, or the attic.) Divide the amount by 1$^1/_2$ to get the cubic-foot-per minute (CFM) rate of the fan you'll need. Your figures probably will not match the exact capacity of any one fan, so go to the next larger size to be safe. A small fan will not do the job.

Consider also, the "blade type" of the fan. A squirrel cage model is better than the ordinary propeller blade fan. A two-speed fan, at somewhat higher cost than a one-speed, is worth the money, because it permits you to adjust the speed according to the weather and degree of ventilation you want.

Where and How to Place the Attic Fan

A ventilating fan can be placed in one of several ways: The most effective method is to mount it horizontally on the attic floor, directly over an air intake. If there are already existing vents at either end of the attic, hot air will be exhausted effectively through them. Or, secondly, the fan could be mounted in a perpendicular position close to the intake vent in the floor. With this set-up you should have a plenum chamber, a device which sucks the air through the opening in the floor. Third, the fan could be placed vertically just behind an exhaust opening at the end of the attic just under the eaves. This is probably the most effective and quietest arrangement and does provide daytime ventilation of the attic itself, something which cannot be done with the first method.

Exhaust Intakes

Air openings to the outdoors must be twice the area of the fan orifice. Since this opening is usually covered by louvers and screening, which cut down on fan efficiency, the opening may have to be enlarged to several times the area of the fan orifice. An exhaust opening should face away from the prevailing wind. Move any furniture, or storage which blocks air from the fan and exhaust area. The fan should have a 120-volt, 20-amp circuit.

Using the Fan

A fan can be used in several ways. It can lower attic temperature only. It can pull cool air through the whole house once you open an outside door or window. Or it can cool just one area, the bedrooms, for instance, if you open a window and a door in that area and close off other areas of the house.

VENTILATING WITHOUT USING ELECTRICAL ENERGY

Install a skylight that opens. This type of ventilation is especially useful in a bath or kitchen where the skylight will supply soft glareless illumination and you can open the dome and release steam and heat which rises naturally to the ceiling. A handyman can easily install a commercially manufactured skylight (available in kit form) or design a simple one of his own.

Ventilating with louvers is still another way of saving electrical energy. Louvers under windows, or even the old-fashioned louvered doors (installed outside a regular door) provide ventilation, shade, and privacy.

Commercially manufactured louvers come in many sizes and are made of plastic, wood, steel or aluminum. Louvers with small slits $1/8$ x $1''$ are preferable to those with large openings which usually need to be screened.

KEEPING THE VENTILATING SYSTEM RUNNING

More ventilation systems break down from lack of cleaning than from failure of mechanical parts. Don't wait until the unit stops. Range hood fans should be cleaned several times a year, because trapped grease is a fire hazard. Other units should be cleaned annually, or more often if yours is an area with a high degree of dust and pollen.

If something goes wrong during operation, check to see if the fan is still plugged in. Try cleaning it; maybe the fan is dirty. If a fuse has blown, check the wiring. If none of these seem to be the problem, you may need to call a repairman.

LOUVERS

Louvers are regaining popularity as they are a way of getting ventilation nature's way without using electricity to bring air and a breeze into the home.

Louvers are an easy add-on to a remodeling job, or an efficient and economical way of providing ventilation in a vacation cabin where you do not want a lot of expense or the safety hazard of movable windows.

Vent Increaser

A vent increaser is a cast-iron soil pipe fitting. It joins different sized pipe to increase the vent pipe diameter at the roof level. *SEE ALSO PIPE FITTINGS.*

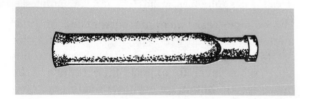

Vent Increaser

Venting of Sewer Gas

Venting of sewer gas in a drainage system is needed to let dangerous and unhealthy gases escape. When vents permit this gas to escape, sewer gas pressure, which can be explosive, does not build up in the system.

To operate effectively, vents must be located near every plumbing fixture. Several vents may be attached to one large vent or stack, extending up through the roof to the air or one vent may go directly up through the roof to the air. By supplying air to drains, vents stop vacuums from forming that would slow down the drainage flow. They also prevent the sewage downflow from sucking or siphoning air through the pipes. *SEE ALSO DRAINAGE SYSTEMS.*

Vent Stack Flashing

Vent stack flashing seals and waterproofs the joint where the sewage vent pipe projects through the roof. It is a skirt made from lead or plastic that is sealed to the roof with roofing cement. If a leak occurs around the flashing, apply a fresh coat of roofing cement all over the flashing and up the side of the pipe. *SEE ALSO FLASHING; ROOF CONSTRUCTION.*

Vermiculite

Vermiculite consists of granular minerals derived from mica which when heated expand to form a lightweight, very water-absorbent material with insulating properties. It is used in seedbeds and as a rooting medium, in plaster or concrete as a substitute for sand, and in walls, ceilings and floors as insulating material. *SEE ALSO WALL & CEILING INSULATION.*

Vinyl Flooring Materials
[SEE FINISH FLOORING; REMODELING; RESILIENT FLOORING.]

Vise, Plumbing

A pipe vise or machinist's vise is used to hold pipes for threading or cutting. The handiest one for the plumber can be clamped to a bench or a vertical support. It should be firmly mounted so that the vise jaws meet accurately to insure a tight grip. Excellent for fast work, this device will open and close smoothly.

Vises
[SEE CLAMPS & VISES.]

Vitrified Tile

Vitrified tile or glazed tile is reddish-brown with a shiny surface. Used to connect house drainage systems to the sewer or septic tank, it can be purchased in lengths of 21 feet with four inch diameters. Often seen stacked in building-supply yards, vitrified tile, like cast-iron pipe, is made with a hub at one end so that the other end will slip easily and securely into the hub portion.

To connect tile, construct a vitrified pipe joint, which is made like a cast-iron joint except cement is used instead of molten lead. *SEE ALSO PLUMBING MATERIALS.*

Volt-ohm-meter (VOM)

The volt-ohm-meter, or VOM as it is commonly known in the trade, is a precision instrument that is used to measure the voltages, resistances and small currents found in equipment used in home and industry. It is one of the basic tools of professional trouble-shooters. Since inexpensive instruments of good quality have become available in recent years, it is almost an indispensable tool for serious home repairs.

The front panel of a VOM appears complex and confusing at first glance. At the top is a dial or scale which corresponds to various settings of the meter. On most VOMS, voltage readings increase from left to right while resistance readings decrease similarly.

Below the scale, you will usually find a large switch with numbers marked around it. This is the range switch, which puts various values into

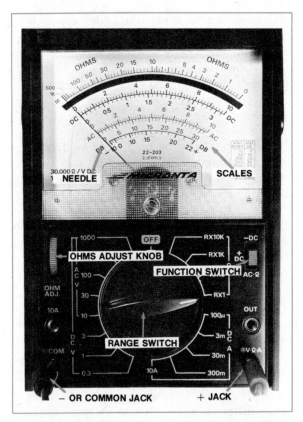

Typical panel front (this one from Micronta, model 22-203, $24.95 from Radio Shack) shows location of primary components used for testing electrical circuits in appliances, radio-TV's and automobiles.

the voltage, resistance and current fed into the meter. When you are selecting a range for the VOM, use the highest scale first if you are not sure what level to expect, then reduce it as necessary to obtain an accurate reading.

A third knob found on the front panel is the zero ohms adjustment. The resistance reading is obtained by passing a current from a small battery in the VOM through the unit you are testing. This shows the opposition that the current meets and registers the measurement in ohms. Since the battery condition can vary as the battery is used and since it varies with the several ranges of resistance scales that are found on a meter, there must be some way to calibrate this to obtain a precise reading. The zero ohms knob accomplishes this purpose.

Circuit jacks are also found on the front of the meter. These jacks are intended for the test probes that are used for the various electrical values of the circuit. Always put the red probe in the positive jack and the black probe in the *common* or negative one. In DC tests the polarity of these two probes is critical.

The test leads consist of two pieces of long or flexible wire two to three feet long. On one end is a probe which fits the jack of the meter tightly. On the opposite end is another probe or an alligator clip. Both probes have insulated handles.

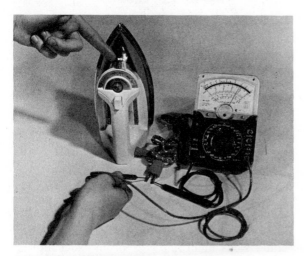

Resistance measurements tell you whether circuit has continuity (is unbroken) and what its resistance is, in ohms. Generally, you set the switch to RX 1 and read meter scale directly; that is, a reading of 15 on resistance scale means 15 ohms.

Heavy duty residential circuits such as those used for large air-conditioners, ranges, etc. should read 230 volts across the two outer terminals and 115 volts from the middle (neutral) terminals to the outer terminals. These circuits are comprised of three wires. One is grounded and the other two carry voltage. Actually the voltage will vary from 220 to 240 volts on a standard heavy duty circuit. However, 230 volts is the average and the figure that is used for practically all calculations.

115 volt circuits have only one fuse and two wires leading to the receptacle or appliance. This circuit is measured across the two wires, with one probe fastened to one and the other probe fastened to the other. Voltages on these circuits will vary from 110 to 120 volts, thus the 115 volt figure is used for the calculation.

Electron flow in a DC circuit is always from the negative terminal (which has an excess of electrons) to the positive terminal. The positive terminal attracts electrons, creating a one-way flow. Failure to get the positive (red) probe in your VOM on the positive terminal of a DC circuit will cause the meter needle to "peg" against the stop on the left instead of the right. If the voltage is high, it can damage the meter.

Remember that all the elements in an electrical circuit — both the components and the wiring that connects them — must be continuous for the circuit to function. Current will not flow across a gap. The circuit may be interrupted intentionally by opening a switch or by a failure such as a blown fuse or broken wire or a component which is open. Whenever this situation is encountered, we say that the circuit is open. When a component does not conduct the current from the battery in the VOM, we say that the component is open. When the component is functioning normally and registers the proper resistance or a resistance on the meter scale, we say that it has continuity. This is usually a good test to use when repairing household equipment and appliances. With the VOM, you can quickly test for resistance within the component to pin down a problem.

Volts

Volts are a unit of measure for designating electrical pressure, much like pounds per square inch designate water pressure. Most modern homes receive 240-volts of electrical power that enters a home by way of an electrical service entrance, travels through the meter and is then distributed throughout the house as it is needed. Home appliances, like toasters, electric skillets and blenders, usually operate on a 120-volt current, with ranges, hot water heaters and central air conditioning systems requiring at least 240 volts. *SEE ALSO ELECTRICITY.*

Waffle Iron Repair

A waffle iron is an appliance that heats a top and bottom casting with a resistance heater under each casting. These heaters are sometimes the ribbon type and sometimes the open coil type, supported by porcelain blocks. In either case there are two elements in waffle irons, one in the top and one in the bottom.

The thermostat, usually the bimetal type, is clamped to one of the housings to sense the temperature. When the waffle batter is poured in, the temperature will drop, then slowly rise until the correct level is reached when the waffle is done. The thermostat then turns the heating elements off and the waffle is then ready to take out.

A pilot light is often used on a waffle maker to tell when the batter is cooked. Often this is simply a jeweled indicator glass that allows the glow of the heating element to be seen.

If a waffle iron fails to heat at all, check the wall receptacle with a table lamp to see if voltage is reaching that point. If it is, unplug it and look closely around the cord and the place where the cord is connected to the waffle maker. Since the waffle maker is not heating at all, it is unlikely that both elements have failed simultaneously. It is more likely that either an electrical connection has loosened or the thermostat contacts are not closing.

Remove the housing or griddle that allows access to the heating element and thermostat. Often this is accomplished by unclipping the griddle from its mounting point. On other models it may be necessary to remove the screws on the bottom that hold the housing in place.

If the thermostat contacts appear to be burned and pitted, clean them with an automotive point file and polish them with a hardwood stick until they are bright and shiny. Check all connections carefully. Use high heat-resistant wiring and connections for any repairs that may be necessary to any of the wiring. Be sure that all

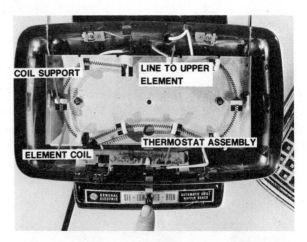

Lower element of this waffle iron is visible when griddle is removed. The thermostat is seen towards the bottom of the photograph. Failure in heating element will be obvious. Be sure that plug is removed from the receptacle before grids are removed on this type waffle iron.

terminals are polished and shiny before attaching a wire to them in case a burn-off is discovered.

If only one section of a waffle iron heats there is the possibility that an element has failed. The break will usually be visible. You can purchase either stock nichrome wire or an exact replacement of the type used in your equipment. There is another possibility that should not be overlooked. The wire connecting the upper and lower unit is often run through a spring assembly in the back, allowing it to flex more easily. Over a period of time, the wire may break. Check this carefully, and replace with new heat-

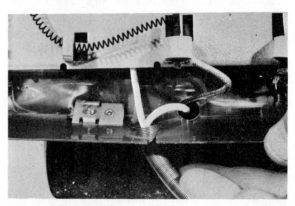

Look closely at point where wire passes from lower to upper element. Use only heat-resistant type wire for replacement purposes.

resistant wiring if this problem comes up. Don't attempt to splice such a wire outside the housing. Use a new wire to replace that section.

Many thermostats in waffle makers have a calibration screw provided that will raise and lower the temperature to some degree. If the waffle is not done, or overdone slightly, adjusting this screw may eliminate the problem. Since it is practically impossible to sense the griddle temperature with an ordinary thermometer (special thermocouples are used for this when testing in factories), this will still allow you to obtain optimum results. If the thermostat wanders far out of calibration, it should be replaced rather than adjusted.

If the waffle iron overheats greatly, it's almost a sure sign that the thermostat contacts are sticking. If the waffle iron shocks the user be sure to use a VOM to check for grounds before putting it back into use. Possible causes of this are sagging or broken elements or a broken wire inside a metallic housing or sleeve.

Wainscoting

Wainscoting, or dado, is the paneling or lining on the lower three or four feet of an interior wall. This method of wall finishing is used for its contrasting, decorative effect and for the protection it gives the wall from bumping furniture and smudgy fingers. The molding that separates the wainscoting from the rest of the wall is called variously *chair rail* or *wainscoting cap.*

Wainscoting Cap

Wainscoting cap or *cap molding* is used with wainscot paneling (paneling on just the lower part of the walls), or as a cap for baseboards. Defects in craftsmanship can be concealed by using wainscoting cap with a wraparound lip. *SEE ALSO MOLDING & TRIM.*

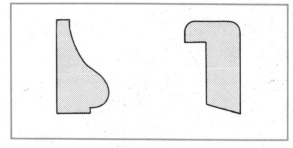

Wainscoting cap

Wall & Ceiling Construction

Wall and ceiling construction are two basic parts of the framing for a building. The wall framings provide a skeleton for the structure. The ceiling frame provides a support for the roof and ties the outside wall frames together.

WALLS

Wall framing includes the structuring of horizontal and vertical portions that compose both interior and exterior walls. Wall frames support ceilings, roofs and upper floors, if any.

Parts Of The Frame

One of the more basic items in wall framing is studding. Although they can be placed 24 inches off center, studs are more often positioned 16 inches off center. Additional studding is used at corners, sides of openings and where an interior wall joins an outside wall.

Wall framing lumber should have certain characteristics. It must be strong, free of warp and have good nail-holding abilities. Number 1 and 2 grades are preferred. Species such as yellow pine, spruce, douglas fir, hemlock and larch are generally recommended.

Wall Framing

The easiest method of framing a wall is to build it flat on the subfloor and tilt it up. The first step is to align the plate with the floor frame and

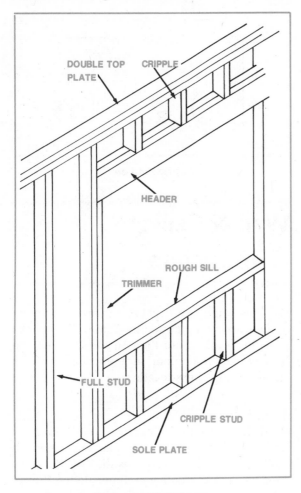

Parts of a Wall Frame

building plan the handyman will find the measurements for rough openings listed with width first and then height.

Trussed Headers

mark the positions of the regular stud spacing. The center lines for doors and windows are to be marked. Measure one half the width of the opening from the center line and mark for trimmer studs. On the outside of the trimmer stud, mark for a full length stud. Mark the spaces between trimmer studs for cripple studs. The positions should be marked with a *C* for cripple stud, *T* for trimmer stud and *X* for full length stud.

Since most constructions for rough openings use headers, they can be assembled ahead of time. A header is made by nailing two members together with ³/₈ inch plywood spacers inserted to make the pieces equal to the thickness of the wall. The length of the header is equal to the rough opening plus two trimmer studs. If the load to be carried by the header is especially heavy or the span is wide, a truss should be used. On the

The next step is to move the top plate a stud length away from the sole plate and turn both on edge with layouts marks inward. At specified positions, place the full length studs and then nail the top plate and sole plate to the studs using two 16d nails at each end. The next step is positioning the trimmer studs and nailing them to the full length studs. The header is set so that it is tight against the end of the trimmer. To nail, use 16d nails and drive them through the full length stud. The upper cripple can be positioned and nailed like a full length stud after the header is in place. By following the markings that are transferred from the sole plate to the rough sill, the lower cripple studs can be nailed using 16d nails.

Studs and blocking where partitions will join walls are to be added. Any special bracing should now be done. Remember: The inside surface of the frame is turned face down.

Because the wall frame is heavy and awkward, it is preferred that at least two people erect the frame. Before raising the wall, be sure that it is in the right place and that bracing is easily available. Once the wall is in a vertical position, it should be secured with braces near the top and bottom.

Make final adjustments to the sole plate before nailing it to the floor frame with 20d nails that are driven through the subfloor and into the joists. Remove braces one at a time. Plumb at corners and midpoint of the wall. Now that the wall is in place, the handyman can proceed to the next section. Although there is no specific sequence, most builders find it easier to erect all main side walls and then handle end walls and smaller projections.

Corners

Outside corners can be completed by either of three methods. The method most commonly used is to install a second stud in the side wall frame. It is spaced from the end stud with three or four blocks. Then when the wall is raised, the corner is complete. Another method is to turn the position of the extra stud so that it faces the end stud of the other section. The third method is simply erecting the frames so that when the sections of a side wall and end wall are together they will form a corner. Corners are made up separately and installed as an individual unit in balloon construction. Be sure only straight studs are used for corners. Use 10d nails staggered

from one edge to the other approximately 12 inches apart.

Partitions

Once the outside wall frames are completed and erected, the partitions can be started. As a general rule, only those partitions that support the ceiling or roof are installed. Nonload-bearing wall installation usually comes later. If roof trusses which are supported completely by the outside walls are used, partition work usually is not started until the roof is complete. When the appropriate time for construction of partitions arrives, a study of the building plans is made to determine the center lines of the partitions. The lines are then marked on the floor with chalk lines.

Sole plates and top plates are laid out while studs and headers are cut and assembled. The partitions are constructed and erected in the same manner as outside walls. However, there can be a reduction in the size and amount of blocking, especially in nonload-bearing partitions. Nailing surfaces at the inside and outside corners for attaching wall coverings is the prime concern.

Headers are not needed on nonload-bearing partitions. The sole plate is included at the bottom of the opening for door openings and after the frame work is erected, the sole plate is cut out

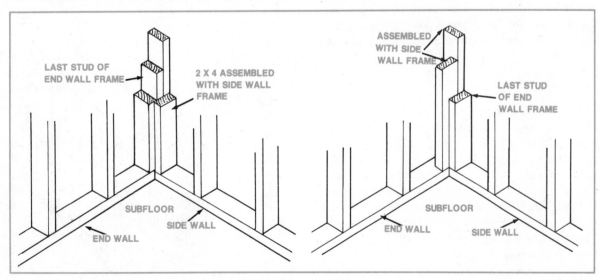

Outside Corner Designs

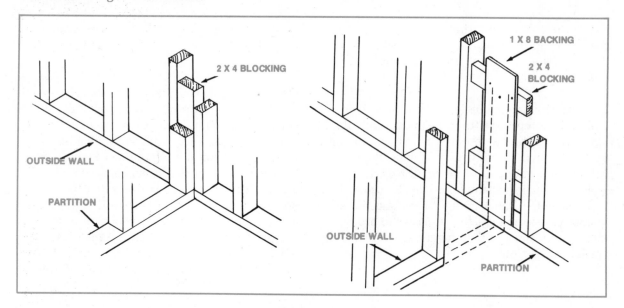

Partition Intersections

with a hand saw. Around bathrooms, partitions containing plumbing pipes need to be thicker. This thickness can be obtained by fastening strips on the edge of the regular frame. Other areas such as wardrobes, partitions in closets and small alcoves do not need to be as thick and can be framed with 2 x 2 material or by turning a 2 x 4 sideways.

Small but important details can be added during wall partition framing. Extra support for plumbing fixtures, framing for recessed cabinets, corner blocks for nailing baseboards and openings for ventilation ducts are among many details that can be accomplished at this stage of construction.

Partition Intersections

The single most important feature of partition intersection with outside walls is solid anchorage. Frame design of inside corners is like that of outside corners; it should produce a corner to which wall-covering materials can be attached. There are two basic methods used for partition intersection. The first method uses an additional stud in the outside frame that is turned sideways. This provides a solid surface to attach the partition. The second method uses the regular stud spacing. Blocking and a backing or nailer are inserted between the studs to provide for attaching

to the partition. The blocking is two feet off center.

Bracing

Bracing is needed to give exterior walls added resistance to lateral stresses. Check local codes for bracing requirements. Materials such as plywood when applied can give enough rigidity so that bracing can be eliminated.

Braces are made from solid 1 x 4 lumber. After cutting to the proper length and angling the bot-

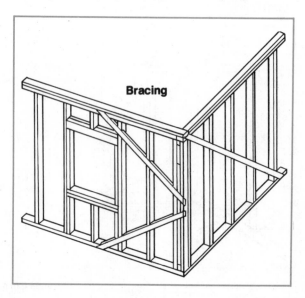

Bracing

tom end, temporarily nail the brace in position. Mark the intersection of the stud and the brace onto the stud. Remove the brace, estimate the depth of the cut to be made and make side cuts with a saw. After removing the wood between the cuts with a chisel, nail the brace in place. Two 8d nails should be used at each stud. Lastly, trim off the top end.

For additional support under rafters and joists as well as further tying the wall frame together, a double top plate can be used. The double plate should be installed with 10d nails with 2 nails near the end and others staggered 16 inches apart. Joints should be at least 4 feet from those in the first top plate.

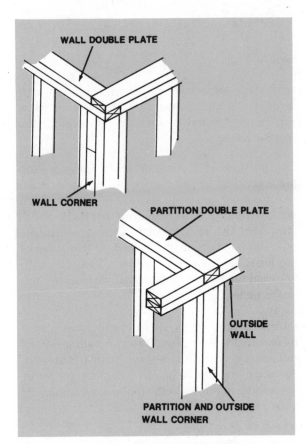

Double Plate Intersections

CEILINGS

A ceiling frame is located below the roof and it supports a ceiling-covering material. The construction of ceiling framing is very similar to

floor framing. The major difference is that lighter weight materials are used for ceiling frames. After the wall studding is complete, ceiling joists are positioned and nailed together. Without ceiling joists, the weight and push of the rafters would push the exterior walls out.

The ceiling joists are the main members of the ceiling frame. Their size is determined by the spacing and the length of the span to be covered. A spacing of 12 or 16 inches off center is most commonly used. Local codes will list requirements on size and quality. Ceiling coverings are also determiners of the size and quality.

Ceiling joists run from outside walls to interior walls or partitions. Usually spanning the narrower dimension of the structure, ceiling joists are toenailed to the top plate of the outside wall with two 10d nails. At the center partition, the ceiling joists are lapped and nailed on each side with two 10d nails. Some ceiling joists may run in one direction while others run at a right angle to them. This arrangement can reduce the length of span.

In large rooms a beam may be needed to support the midpoint of the joists. This beam is either flush with or just below the joists. In attic areas, the beam may be installed above the joists and tied together with metal straps.

The upper corner of the joists must be trimmed at the outer end to match the slope of the roof. A

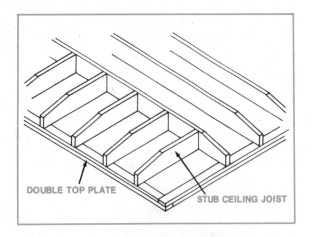

Stub Ceiling Joists

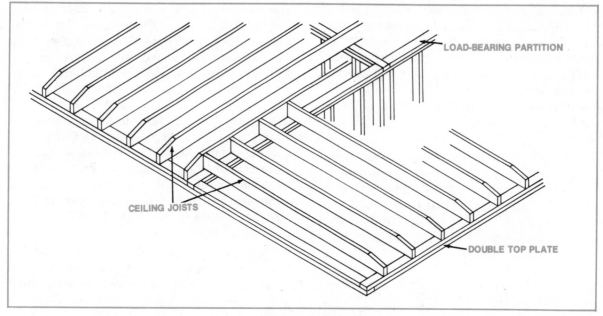

Ceiling Frame

framing square can be used or when the amount of wood to be removed is small, the cutting may be done with a small saw or hatchet after the joists and rafters are in place.

If ceiling joists are running parallel to the roof edge, the outside member will interfere with the

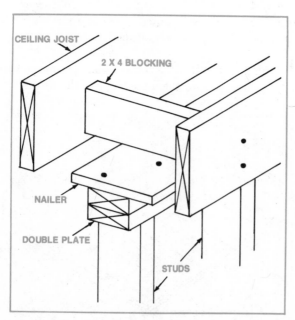

Ceiling joists anchored to partition that is running parallel to it.

roof slope especially in low-pitched hip roof designs. To eliminate this problem, stub joists can be constructed to run at a right angle to the regular joists.

The position of the ceiling joists along the top plate is layed in position by using a rod much like for floor joists. Joists do not have to align with studs if a double top plate is used. However, the ceiling joists should coordinate with the position of roof rafters so that some of the joists can be nailed to them. Two 10d nails are used on each side to toenail the ceiling joists to the plate.

Partitions running parallel to ceiling joists must be fastened to the ceiling frame. A nailing strip is necessary to handle the ceiling material. Although this can be handled in many ways, the main thing to remember is that adequate support must be provided for.

Attic area entrances are provided for in the ceiling frame. Specific requirements can be obtained from local codes and fire regulations. The opening is framed by using the same method as for a floor opening. When openings are not much larger than two to three square feet, joists and header do not need to be doubled.

Wall & Ceiling Fixtures

[SEE LIGHTS & LIGHTING.]

Wall & Ceiling Insulation

Insulation keeps a home warmer in cold weather, cooler in hot weather and, after paying for itself in a few years of reduced energy bills, begins to put money back into the homeowner's pocket.

There are several specific gains to aim for when insulating:

Winter comfort. No amount of heat consumption can produce warmth in the presence of chilly walls and other surfaces.

Summer comfort. A naturally cool house feels better than one heavily air-conditioned.

Smaller furnace and air-conditioner. Whether you are dealing with new heating or cooling equipment in a new or old home or with an existing unit that is straining to keep up with demand, better insulation can help. The dollars that can be saved by not buying the bigger unit are a fine start toward paying for insulation. Air ducts can often be smaller too, for a further saving.

Fuel economy. A properly insulated house means that heating and cooling equipment runs fewer hours in extreme weather, possibly not at all on mild days. Money is saved twelve months a year while the world's energy supply is conserved and its pollution lessened.

Quiet and safety. Although thermal insulation is not the most effective sound-deadening treatment, it does help substantially to reduce noise transmission from outside. Mineral wool that fills wall cavities also serves to discourage the vertical spread of fire.

HOW INSULATION WORKS

There are two ways that insulation works to stop the movement of heat. One is by providing air spaces that reduce conduction. The other is by providing reflective surfaces, usually aluminum foil, that reduce radiation.

The most common kind of insulation, called *bulk* or *mass* type, consists of an extremely large number of tiny airspaces. The fiber glass, or other fiber, of which the insulation is made surrounds these spaces while adding a minimum of conductive material.

The insulating efficiency of such a material can be measured by its conductivity; the less conductive it is, the better it insulates.

Since the cost of insulating is remaining moderate while fuel prices escalate, it is worth while to provide full insulation.

KINDS OF INSULATION

The varieties of insulation on the market break down into a limited number of basic types. Some are suitable only for a few special uses. Others work well almost anywhere, yet may be highly efficient for one job and only moderately so for another.

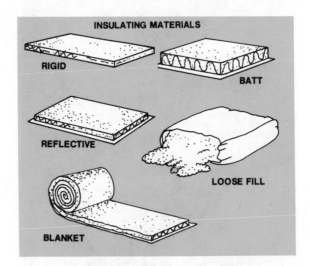

INSULATING MATERIALS

RIGID

BATT

REFLECTIVE

LOOSE FILL

BLANKET

A shortcut calculation of quantity when buying insulating materials is to take the gross area of wall, floor, or ceiling, then subtract 10% if framing members are on 16-inch centers. With 24-inch-centers framing, subtract only 6%.

Blanket insulations come in long rolls to be cut to length and placed in a wall, ceiling or floor. They are most often made of mineral wool (glass or rock).

Many blanket insulations have a vapor barrier paper on one side. This is always placed toward the inside of the building. Blankets, commonly used in insulating a house during construction, also are excellent to insulate the floor of an attic having no finished floor already in place.

Loose fill is one of the most familiar and versatile forms of insulation. It usually comes in sacks from which it is poured or blown into a wall or ceiling. It offers almost the only feasible means of insulating the walls of a completed house unless extensive remodeling is being done.

Most often loose fill is one of three forms of mineral wool: rock wool, slag wool or glass wool. In each case it is made by passing steam through a molten mass of material and then forming the hair-like threads into nodules.

Batts today are usually fiber glass and are interchangeable with blanket insulation for most applications. They are less handy than blankets

Strips of cardboard cut from old cartons are useful for reinforcing stapling or tacking of insulation wherever there's no adequate flange.

for long uninterrupted openings or for areas of odd shape or size.

Batts are commonly made to fit between framing that is on 16 or 24 inch centers. They are usually 48 inches long. Some types are just insulation, with no backing or wrapping paper. Most, however, have a backing that forms a vapor barrier and acts as a flange for nailing.

Reflective insulation, depending entirely upon their surface characteristics, work by reflecting the radiant heat.

There are three main types. One is aluminum foil on one or both sides of a roll of kraft paper; a less expensive variation is made by applying aluminum pigment rather than foil to a heavy building paper. The pigment type usually reflects only about 80 percent of the radiant heat striking it, while the foil type reflects 95 percent.

The second type in common use is multiple foil. It consists of two or more layers of foil. It comes in a tight roll and expands in accordion fashion when stretched into place, creating air space between the layers.

The efficiency of foil insulation depends very much on the position in which it is used. Foil is extremely efficient when used in a roof to reflect the heat of the summer sun.

This same foil, on the other hand, is relatively ineffective against heat loss through the roof in winter. It is only moderately effective in sidewall use.

The third variety of reflective insulation is foil used in combination with mass insulation. Much of the bulk insulation sold has a layer of foil on one side to add reflective insulation and a good vapor barrier.

Insulating board is a dual-purpose product. It has structural value as well as insulating value. Naturally, it gives less insulation for the money than regular insulations do; its other qualities compensate for this.

The sheathing type of insulating board is a waterproofed sheet material that provides a substantial amount of insulation in a wall and, at the same time, takes the place of both sheathing and building paper. It usually comes in sheets four feet wide and eight to twelve feet long, with square edges, or in 2 x 8 foot planks with tongued-and-grooved edges. It is ordinarily used only in new construction, being nailed to the studs from the outside, then covered by siding.

One of the newest kinds of insulations is a plywood-styrofoam panel which combines underlayment with insulation. It provides an excellent remodeling material for a concrete floor in a basement or garage being converted to living space.

Styrene foam panels for insulation jobs can be bought above or below grade, inside or out. Only a knife and caulking gun is needed to put them over the inside of a masonry wall, where they form a good basis for decorative paneling. There are ³/₄ inch panels that are flame retardant and the equivalent of two inches of fiber glass insulation. This material in tongue-and-groove type can be used in either new construction or remodeling to wrap a house in insulating sheathing. For this purpose it is nailed to the framing on the outside, usually three nails through each piece of insulation at each stud.

WHERE TO INSULATE

It is best to completely insulate a house. Wrap the whole house, or at least all of it that is heated in winter, in a heat-stopping barrier. If the whole job cannot be tackled at once, overhead is an ideal place to begin. Insulating the ceiling or roof will give the biggest dollar saving in fuel for each dollar that is spent for insulation. Thoroughly insulating the ceiling of a one-story house, for example, may cut one-third off the fuel bill.

Most houses offer two possibilities in choosing where to insulate overhead. If the attic has no floor and one is not going to be put in, the place for insulation is between the joists. Then heat will not be leaking through the ceiling into an unheated attic.

If the attic is already floored or if it may be heated at some later time, the roof and the gable

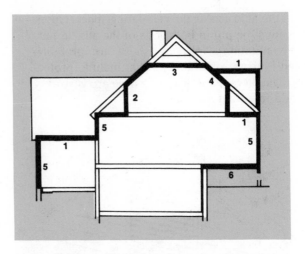

Here's where to insulate. Numbers are keyed to the diagram:
1. Ceilings. Don't overlook dormer ceilings.
2. "Knee" walls of a finished attic.
3. Between attic "collar" beams.
4. The sloping portion of the roof in a finished attic. Leave an air space between insulation and roof.
5. Exterior walls.
6. Floors above cold crawl spaces. Floors above a porch or an unheated garage.

ends should be insulated. This insures that the attic is included within the heat-stopping blanket. If the attic has already been made into living space with sidewalls, floor and ceiling, put the insulation above the ceiling and behind the walls.

In a frame house, the sidewall insulation goes between the studs. It should extend from the floor to the ceiling. What can be done with a masonry house depends upon its construction. It often is possible to insulate hollow block walls by dumping loose fill insulation, such as vermiculite, into the hollows from the top.

VENTILATION AND VAPOR BARRIER

Whenever walls, ceilings and floors are insulated, they must be ventilated. This applies particularly to roof jobs, where an air space above the insulation will permit the accumulated heat from the sun to be carried off.

When the insulation goes into the floor of an attic or the ceiling of a one-story house with a low roof, the attic acts as the ventilating space. Openings must be put in both ends of the attic to permit ventilation. Normally, these are prefabricated louvers of some type that include protection against rain and insects. These are very easy to add in an older home.

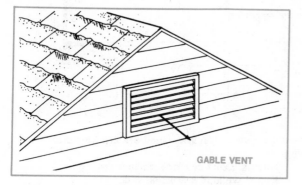

GABLE VENT

Louvered, screened ventilators can be put in, allowing one square foot of ventilator for each 100 to 120 square feet of attic floor space.

If the roof is being insulated, do not carry the insulation all the way to the peak. Bring it up the rafters to the height required for the attic ceiling and across collar beams. Then vent the space above it as described.

Ventilation serves a second purpose. It helps to carry off moisture that comes from cooking, bathing, breathing, etc. One symptom and result of condensation, produced by not having a vapor barrier where it is needed, is peeling of the outside house paint.

Because of this moisture, which is an increased problem in today's insulated and tightly-sealed houses, a vaporseal usually must be included in an insulating job. It is an FHA requirement, particularly in colder parts of the country. This barrier can be provided by using batt or blanket insulation that has it built in, or by installing a vaporseal paper on the *room* side of the insulation.

Wallcoverings

Modern wallcoverings are *prepasted* and come in vinyls, foils, cloths, plastic-coated and flocks as well as paper, offering a variety of colors, patterns and materials to work with.

GETTING READY

You have chosen the pattern and have the right number of rolls. Chances are you also have the few simple tools needed to do the job, such as a *yardstick* and *pencil* for measuring and marking, *string* and a *weight* to make a plumb-line, *scissors, razor knife, broad putty knife* for cutting and trimming, and a *bucket, water box* and *sponge* for application.

Getting the wall ready is the most important step to the successful application and removal of wallcovering.

If the wall has been previously painted with latex paint, it will be porous and should first be sealed with inexpensive *wall sizing*. This acts as a filler and produces better adhesion qualities.

Wallboard and other paper-faced surfaces must be sealed with a coat of oil-based enamel undercoat. This should be followed with a coat of wall sizing. Cracks and holes should be filled with a patching compound, allowed to dry, then sanded smooth. If your walls have been previously papered, they should be stripped before new wallcoverings are applied.

APPLYING THE WALLCOVERING

If you have not already done so, check all the rolls to make sure that they are all of the right pattern and the same lot number. Slight color variations can occur in the best wallcoverings from different mill runs.

Now, carefully climb the ladder and with your yardstick, mark off 19¹/₂ inches from a corner. This is one inch less than the width of a roll and allows for the inevitable irregularities found in walls. (No home has perfectly straight walls.)

Next, put a thumbtack into the mark you have made and hang a plumb-line from it. Any piece of string that measures just short of the ceiling-to-baseboard height, with a weight tied to it, (like a heavy key or a pair of scissors) will do nicely. This is the simple way to make sure that the wallcovering is applied straight. When the plumb-line is hanging perfectly still, follow it down with your yardstick and pencil, drawing a straight line from ceiling to floor. You can now remove the plumb-line.

Measure the length of your first strip on the wall, allowing two to three inches extra at the top and bottom.

Place the water box at the baseboard, directly under the area where you will be applying the first strip. Fill it to the level mark with lukewarm water. Place your first rolled strip into the water and let it soak evenly for about 15 seconds. Then, feed it under the guide-wire and pull it slowly up the wall. Try to keep it clear of the wall as you take it up to the ceiling.

Line up the right-hand edge of the paper with the pencil line on the wall. Do not be afraid to handle the wet wallcovering. It is surprisingly tough and you can slide it around on the wall, even lift it and replace it, until you have the edge lined up. Smooth out the strip with a wet sponge, working down the center and out to the sides to remove wrinkles and large bubbles. The smaller bubbles will dry out smooth. Do not overwork the edges.

Now that the first strip is in place, trim the excess off at the top and bottom. Use the blunt edge of the scissors to crease the paper where the wall

and ceiling meet. Peel the paper back from the wall slightly and cut the surplus off along the marked line with the scissors. Smooth the paper back into place.

To fit the paper around window sills, cut it diagonally, up to the edge of the sill. Then fold it back, and mark the excess and cut it off. The same procedure is used around curves in molding.

The first step in putting up the second strip is to match the pattern with the strip you have just applied. You may have to waste several inches at the top, but do not be concerned as there is an extra six square feet in each roll to allow for pattern matching.

Measure the second strip just as you did the first one; remembering to allow an extra two or three inches at top and bottom for trimming purposes. Follow the same steps to apply this strip to the wall, starting from the ceiling. This time, line-up the left edge of the new strip with the right edge of the previous strip, matching the pattern as you go. Butt the edges, do not overlap them and remember not to overwork the seams.

Keep matching, measuring, cutting and hanging successive strips until you come to the end of the wall, and of course, a corner. The last strip is sure to be less than the width of a roll. So, measure the distance between the righthand edge of your last strip and the corner, then add one inch. The extra inch will extend around the corner and take care of any unevenness in the wall. After measuring the length of this last strip, lay it out on a table or floor. Mark and cut it lengthwise to the width required. Then, apply it in the usual manner. Keep the balance of this strip; you will be applying it on the adjoining wall.

The next step is to measure and mark on the wall the width of the piece cut from the last strip. So, measure, put in your thumbtack and use the plumb-line again. Apply this narrow strip of paper, lining up the right hand edge with the vertical plumb-line. Although only a short piece was needed above the door, the plumb-line method should be followed every time you go around a corner to guard against starting off at a slant.

HELPFUL HINTS

Switchplates, thermostat covers and light fixtures are usually easy to remove and it makes a neater and much more professional-looking job if you remove and paper under them. (So that you will remember where the light switches and electrical outlets are, mark or punch a small hole in the paper when you cover them. Then you can trim out the holes and put the parts you have removed back again.)

Do not try to cut wallpaper to fit around doors and windows before you put it up. When you come to an obstruction, paper right over the edge. Then, before you trim at ceiling and baseboard, trim around the window or door by making diagonal cuts up to and slightly beyond the corners, which you mark with your finger. Fold the extra piece back, score it to mark the edge, peel it back slightly and cut it off with your scissors. Do the same down the side.

The professionals trim off edges by using a broad putty knife, at least three inches wide, to push the paper into the edge and hold it there while you cut off the waste with a sharp single-edge razor blade or knife.

Clean up is simple *if* as you have been working you have folded your scraps, glued sides together and put them into one centrally located newspaper. All you need do then is toss this neat package into the garbage.

Wall-Hanging Desk

This wall-hanging desk is used in conjunction with a six-peg coat rack and adjustable shelves

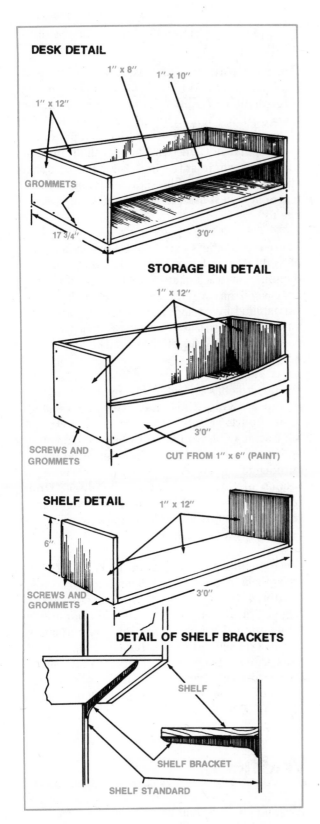

DESK DETAIL

1" x 12"

1" x 8"

1" x 10"

GROMMETS

17 3/4"

3'0"

STORAGE BIN DETAIL

1" x 12"

SCREWS AND
GROMMETS

3'0"

CUT FROM 1" x 6" (PAINT)

SHELF DETAIL

1" x 12"

6"

SCREWS AND
GROMMETS

3'0"

DETAIL OF SHELF BRACKETS

SHELF

SHELF BRACKET

SHELF STANDARD

Courtesy of Western Wood Products Association

on metal standards. It looks particularly handsome when attached to a paneled wall. Although the plans call for a bulletin board, a mirror can easily be substituted if desired. The following are suggested bottom-of-desk to floor clearances: children 5 to 12 years, 18" to 24"; adults, 26" to 28".

Attach this unit to the wall with No. 10 round head wood screws. When fastening the unit to either a plaster or gypsum board wall, 2¹/₂" toggle bolts are recommended.

MATERIALS LIST

Shelves:
　　3 pieces 1 x 12, 34¹/₂" long (bottoms)
　　6 pieces 1 x 12, 6" high (sides)

Desk:
　　1 piece 1 x 12, 34¹/₂" long (back)
　　2 pieces 1 x 12, 17³/₄" long (sides)
　　1 piece 1 x 8, 34¹/₂" long (top)
　　1 piece 1 x 10, 34¹/₂" long (top)
　　1 piece 1 x 8, 34¹/₂" long (bottom)
　　1 piece 1 x 10, 34¹/₂" long (bottom)

Bin:
　　1 piece 1 x 6, 36" long (front)
　　1 piece 1 x 12, 34¹/₂" long (bottom)
　　2 pieces 1 x 12, 12¹/₄" long (sides)
　　1 piece 1 x 12, 34¹/₂" long (back)

Coat Rack:
　　1 piece 1 x 12, 36" long
　　Dowels: 6 pieces ³/₄" x 6"

Formica for Desk Top — 1 piece 17" x 34¹/₄"

Shelf Hardware:
　　shelf standards — 2 pieces 6' long
　　shelf brackets — 8

Bulletin Board:
　　cork or fiber board 24" x 36"

Bulletin Board:
　　cork or fiber board 24" x 36"

Screws & Grommets
　　3 dozen No. 10 round head wood screws
　　　　(bright finish)
　　3 dozen grommets

Wall Joint Sealer

Wall joint sealer is a wallboard joint paste used to seal and disguise the vertical inside and outside corners and horizontal joints between panels after the wallboard has been attached to the framing studs. It is available premixed or in a powdered form to be mixed with water. *SEE ALSO DRYWALL.*

Wall Tie

A wall tie is a metal strap or wire reinforcement used to bond layers of masonry to each other, intersecting partition walls to masonry walls, and brick veneer to a wood frame wall. *SEE ALSO BRICK & STONE WORK; WALL & CEILING CONSTRUCTION.*

Walnut

Walnut, a warm-colored, smoothly textured hardwood, comes from a broadleafed deciduous tree and is used more today for furniture than any other wood. Though more costly than softwoods, it is strong, fine-textured, does not warp or shrink and is easy to work with and to finish.

It is sometimes called American walnut or black walnut because of the color of the nut shells. The heartwood varies in color and ranges from light to dark chocolate brown. The sapwood of walnut is usually pale brown but is sometimes darkened artificially by steaming to give it the appearance of heartwood. The original Persian walnut or Circassian walnut is rare today. It is used for highly dramatic figuring and is good for inlay work with its varied black and brown streaks.

Walnut has sufficient hardness and strength for general use. It has a rich color, luster and distinct figure. It is used extensively for building both solid and veneered furniture and for more costly types of interior trim, millwork and fine cabinetwork.

The popularity of walnut has been enduring. It was used for William and Mary chests throughout the American colonial period, for the Queen Anne shell-knee ball-foot chairs and for elaborately carved tables for Victorian parlors. It was popular in Civil War days for the frames of black horsehair sofas and for carved, dark-stained chests and tables. For contemporary furniture, it is best used in its most natural-grained beauty.

There is an endless variety of figures in the grain of walnut, about two dozen different types of dapplings,swirls and stripes. One type of walnut heartwood has a dark center section of board surrounded by irregular oblong bands of lighter tone. There are three types of heartwood in walnut: narrow-hearted, broad-hearted and wild-hearted.

Walnut crotches are cut just below tree branches where growing fibers have become twisted. Walnut burls or cuts from wart-like growths on the tree, may be wall hung. A burl contains tiny buds produced by the tree in an effort to repair an outside injury. When it is cut crossways, a section of tiny circles appears. Veneer from wood at the stump of the walnut tree comes in a great variety of dark and light tones to provide a different-looking pattern.

When buying walnut furniture, be careful to read labels to make sure it is not imitation. Most furniture that is solid or walnut-veneered is tagged *The American Walnut Manufacturer's Association.* Tags indicating *solid walnut* show that all exposed parts are solid. *Genuine walnut* indicates that exposed parts are walnut veneer over hardwood plywood containing solid walnut in structural parts. *SEE ALSO WOOD IDENTIFICATION.*

Washers

Washers are thin rings or discs of metal, leather, rubber or some similar material, available in a variety of types. Washers act as a rest for a bolt or nut head to secure the nut in place. They also serve as packing, eliminate leakage, reduce friction and bear or support a pivoting mechanism.

Types of washers include flat, spring lock or tooth washers, usually used in furniture construction between the wood and the nut in bolt fastening. Seat washers are used at the valve seat of a washer-type faucet. A rubber spud washer is located at the base of a toilet tank, providing a base for the outgoing piping.

Washing Machine Repair

Many appliance industry experts say that the majority of calls made by service technicians on automatic washers involve very simple repairs or adjustments. If you understand how the equipment operates, you can often take care of a problem without calling in a technician. Remember to unplug the machine whenever you are working on or inspecting an automatic washer. Keep away from any moving part and watch out for sharp edges on the sheet metal.

One of the best ways to tell if your washer is overloaded or not is to watch the clothing in the water after the machine is running. If the clothing moves and circulates freely in the water, you can be sure that you don't have an overloaded condition. If the agitator is turning in the middle of a pile of clothing which appears to be standing still, some of the clothing should be removed or more water added for proper washing results.

A timer controls the functions of a washer. It triggers the water inlet valve, also known as the mixing valve. This is the point where hot and cold water are mixed and where they are turned on and off. On this valve are two or three electromagnetic coils. Each of them has a plunger which is pulled up inside the coil when the coil is energized. When the plunger is raised,

a diaphragm pops open to allow water to enter the machine. When the power supply is removed from the coil by the timer, the plunger drops back and water flow is shut off.

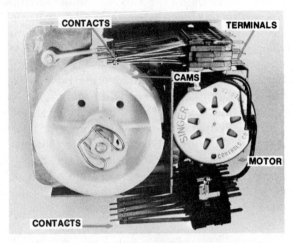

The washer timer can be a fairly complex mechanism, having as many as 30 separate contacts and switches built into it.

If a valve has two of these coils (which may be identified by the two wires going into each of the coils), it is called a two-port mixing valve. This usually gives three water temperatures; hot — when the hot port is open —, cold — when the cold port is open —, and warm — when both are open. A three-port valve can have as many as five temperatures. The third port gives a predetermined mixture of hot and warm water. Therefore, when hot and warm is mixed a

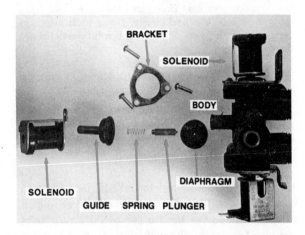

Component parts of an inlet valve are visible in this photograph. The diaphragm should be cleaned under running water using a soft brush.

medium temperature is gained and when warm and cold are mixed a cool temperature is gained.

Inside the valve is a neoprene diaphragm for each of the solenoids on the valves. The diaphragm has several tiny *bleed* holes which allow water to flow through and equalize pressure on both sides. A tiny grain of sand or any foreign particle that may get into the valve and to this point can block the bleed holes and keep the valve from closing when the solenoid is de-energized. To prevent this, manufacturers place at least one and usually two tiny screens in the water lines that enter the washer. One of these is located just within the valve itself, where the hose attaches at the back of the washer. The other one is located in the hose, usually as part of the washer at the faucet end.

Small mesh strainers that enter the valve and hose inlet should be cleaned yearly. Use a toothbrush to be sure that all traces of algae and solid particles are removed.

If water fails to enter the machine and you hear a low buzzing sound, the noise tells you that the solenoids are being energized by the timer. You now know that the problem is not electrical. This means that it is a good idea to check the screens; they may be completely clogged.

If the water should fail to cut off, it is time to have a look at the inlet valve itself. Be sure and turn off all power before removing any access panels. To get to the valve, look at the point where the hose enters the machine. They will be attached directly to the body of the inlet valve.

There are usually one or two screws that hold this entire assembly in place. From the inside of the machine (after loosening and raising the top) the valve can now be pulled forward. At this point it is now necessary to remove the smaller hose that carries the water to the inlet at the top of the tub and to remove the wires from each solenoid. Make a sketch noting the color-coding or mark the wires in some manner so that you will be sure to get them back on the same terminal when reinstalling the valve.

With the valve removed, take the entire valve to the sink and remove the two or three retaining screws at each solenoid. The solenoid coil, plunger and diaphragm can now be lifted from the valve. Flush the body of the valve, the diaphragm and the inside of the plunger guide, along with all parts that come into direct contact with the water.

If the diaphragm appears to be deteriorating it should be replaced. Appliance parts distributors will usually carry these in stock as a component part for most standard valves.

You will need a continuity tester or VOM to test the condition of the electrical coils. However, if one should fail the symptom would be that water would not enter the machine. If you hear a low buzzing sound you can be certain that the coil is okay, since it is the source of the buzzing sound.

After the machine is filled with water it will begin to agitate. The agitator is driven by a fractional-horsepower electrical motor, usually the split-phase or capacitor-start type. A belt drive from the motor turns a gear case (transmission) which in turn gives the agitator its moving action to force the water through the clothing.

There are two primary methods of controlling the agitation cycle. In one instance the timer gives a command to a solenoid which is energized to engage the gear box and turn the agitator. The other method is to reverse the direction of the motor, using one direction for spinning and an opposite direction for agitation. Internal *torque springs* act as a clutch to grip a shaft or release the force of the motor from that shaft.

If a washer fails to agitate, listen for any unusual noise. It could be a simple matter like a loose agitator cap which holds the agitator in place. If not, take a look at the motor by removing either the rear access panel or by removing the front of the machine. The sound that the machine makes will direct you to the problem, if the motor is running. No sound at all will indicate a possible lack of power to the machine.

If the motor runs but does not turn the gear case, look for a broken or loose drive belt. Often drive belt tension is adjusted by loosening the motor mounts and sliding the motor away from the gear case to increase tension on the belt. Belt tension is ample when a half inch of deflection is noted between the motor, pulley and drive pulley of the gear case. Only special belts made for the purpose should be used for belt replacement on automatic washers. The belts are often reinforced with special material such as fiberglass and are formed specifically for the job that they are intended to do on the washer. If the

belt seems to be turning the transmission but it is not driving the agitator, and the solenoid that controls the transmission shifting seems to be operating, the problem probably lies within the transmission itself. If this is the case, an expert should be called in to take care of the problem.

After the wash period it is necessary to get rid of the water. This is accomplished by a mechanical pump, usually of the centrifugal type, that forces the water up through the line into the house drain line (standpipe) which carries it away.

One cause of pump problems in an automatic washer is a foreign object, often a nail or a chain or bobbypin, that has passed through the basket and into the pump. There it can become lodged under the impeller and stop the pump from turning. When you encounter this, the first problem is getting rid of the water.

If your machine has a front panel, turn off the power or unplug the machine and remove the panel. Grasp the pump pulley and turn it backwards, possibly dislodging the object. If the pump seems to free itself, replace the panel and start it up momentarily. If the machine pumps the water out, well and good. If not, the problem is still with you. When the hose exits at the bottom of the washer it is often possible to lay it down into a drain or pan and allow the water to drain in this manner. If it comes from the top of the machine, the only choices left are to take a small plastic pail or bucket and start dipping, or take a section of hose and siphon it into a bucket.

Unless absolutely necessary, do not attempt to move a machine that is full of water. It weighs some 150 pounds more than when it is empty.

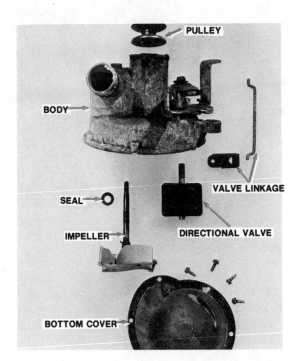

The washer pump must usually be disassembled to remove foreign objects. Take the cover off and note the position of all seals and gaskets. If the shaft which extends through pump housing is worn to a large degree, the pump should be replaced.

You can recognize the pump on the automatic washer because the drain line is attached to it on one side and the drain from the tub is attached to it on the other side. Some pumps are fastened directly to the bottom of the tub, allowing free access to the water at that point. Be sure that the machine is unplugged and loosen the screws that hold the pump in place. If spring-type clamps are used on the hoses that connect to the pump on your washer, you will have to remove them using a pair of hose clamp pliers. You can obtain these at an automotive supply store. They are indispensable for this type of job and for repairs to your automobile as well. Slide each hose clamp away from the pump and pull the hoses off one at a time. When the first hose is removed, it is likely that some water left in the machine will drain out. If it is necessary to lay the machine over during this operation, be sure and place it on a pad or quilt to protect the finish and the floor. When the hoses are removed from the pump loosen the screws or clamps that hold it together and separate the sections. If there is a foreign object in the pump it will usually be visible. Grasp the pump by the pulley and turn it to be sure that it is free. If the pump seems to be binding but no foreign object is apparent, the problem is probably due to bearing failure.

To check this condition remove the pump pulley, which may be held in place by a setscrew or which may be threaded onto the shaft. With the pulley off or loose, tap the impeller shaft out with a block of wood. Check the bearings by sight. If the opening in which the impeller shaft is inserted is oval in shape, make no attempt to use the old bearings. For many new pumps, bearing assemblies are available as a component part. If not, it is necessary to replace the housing or the entire pump.

As you might imagine, quite a bit of force is required to start the basket spinning. In most washers some sort of clutch device is employed to take up this load and bring it gradually up to speed (around 525 to 600 rpm in most models).

On models employing a centrifugal type, the clutch may be removed after first turning off the power and removing the access panel. The clutch is usually held directly to the motor shaft with setscrews and can be taken apart. Most centrifugal clutches are of the internal expanding type and parts for the clutches are available from servicing dealers and appliance parts distributors. A failing clutch will usually disclose itself by a slow spin speed long before it fails altogether.

Clutches of the dry-disk type are usually raised and lowered by the operation of a solenoid or a bar which is solenoid-operated. This type of

clutch has an adjusting nut which can be used to compensate for wear over a period of time. If the spin speed seems slower than normal but there is no indication of water being left in the basket or of excessive use of detergent, lowering this nut to increase clutch contact can solve the problem, particularly if the machine is an old one.

In addition to the basic mechanism which creates the required functions of the washer, there are often a variety of accessories as well. These include shut-off switches to stop the machine if the basket should get out of balance and dispensers to add bleach, detergent and rinse additives at the proper times. These dispensers should be flushed with clear water about once a month. This removes any residue and prevents the blockage of the tubes from the dispenser that can occur in some machines after several years of usage. Be sure and follow the manufacturer's instructions regularly for cleaning.

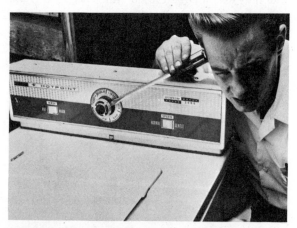

Noises can be tracked down fairly easy by using a screwdriver as a stethoscope, allowing it to touch cabinet at various points.

Noises and vibrations can often be tracked down by using a small screw driver or even by ordering an inexpensive stethoscope. By placing this at various points on the outside of the cabinet while the machine is in operation (be sure not to remove any access panels while it is in operation), you can get a general idea of the area where the noise originates.

When it is necessary to wash a large or heavy object such as a throw rug, try to put some smaller articles in with it. This will help balance the load dynamically when the basket starts to spin and eliminate extreme vibrations that occur with such a load when the heavy wet garment naturally becomes positioned to one side when the basket enters the spin cycle.

Look for detergent stains when you suspect a water leak. They can often lead to the source of the problem even after the water has dried.

Waste Stack

A waste stack is a $1^1/_2$ inch vertical pipe which collects wastes from plumbing fixtures other than a toilet, such as sinks and washtubs. It connects to the basement sewer and runs up through the roof where its top is left open for venting. The soil stack is not located near this pipe. Fixtures are connected to the waste stack by branch drains. *SEE ALSO DRAINAGE SYSTEMS.*

Water Hammer

Water hammer is a loud banging noise which occurs when water pipes are shaken by an abrupt shut-off of water running at a high volume per minute.

The volume per minute depends on the length and width of the pipes and the height of the outlet from which the water comes.

Since many pounds of water are put through pipes in just a few seconds, approximately four pounds a second, it is easy to see why a sudden stoppage causes the pipes to shake.

Air cushions, or devices called air chambers in the water system, can prevent water hammer. They are airtight pipes, each about one foot in length, which are put in the water system close to the faucet. Air chambers are connected to the regular water pipes. When the water is quickly turned off, the water compresses the cushions of air, eliminating the noise. *SEE ALSO PLUMBING NOISES.*

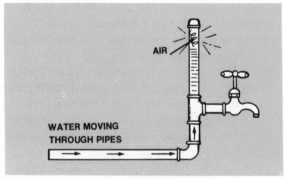

Air Chamber

Water Heater Repair

A water heater is one of the simplest of the major appliances. However, it can be one of the hardest to diagnose when service problems arise. In addition, there are certain safety devices which must be installed and operating properly to insure the safety of the unit. This is one of the most important aspects of servicing this particular appliance.

The water heater is basically a tank to contain water which is heated by electrical heating elements or by a gas burner. The tank has ample insulation around it to retain the heat. A cabinet surrounds the tank, insulation and any wiring.

Other things enter into the operation of the water heater that are not so apparent. One of these is a

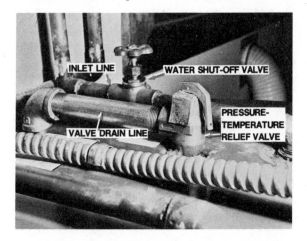

INLET LINE WATER SHUT-OFF VALVE

VALVE DRAIN LINE

PRESSURE-
TEMPERATURE
RELIEF VALVE

device for separating the cold water in the tank from the hot water as it becomes heated. To an extent this will occur automatically, since heated water tends to rise while the colder water will remain in the bottom. One way of achieving this efficiently is to bring the cold water line into the side of the tank near the bottom. In recent years, some models bring both lines into the top of the tank. In many areas where space is at a premium, this aids installation of the heater.

When installing, an internal tube runs from the point where the cold water line enters the tank to a point just a few inches above the bottom of the tank. This tube is called a dip tube. It is accessible at the connection of the cold water line at the top of the tank.

A dip tube is important for several reasons. One is if any internal leakage occurs near the top of it, a bypass situation is set up which will allow cold water to flow directly over to the nearby hot water outlet which is always located in the top of the water tank. This results in a mixture of hot and cold water flowing from the faucet when the hot water is turned on. A large volume of warm water may flow but it will not be very hot. The mixing occurs throughout the tank when this situation exists. Another reason for being aware of dip tubes is that when they were first used in water heaters, problems arose when some of them melted while they were exposed to situations where the water heater had overheated. These tubes, which were made of a plastic substance, formed a collodial suspension in the water. When a safety valve opened in the line,

the molten plastic flowed out with the water. Immediately coming in contact with cool air at the safety valve outlet, the plastic hardened and blocked the valve.

Dip tubes in modern water heaters are immune to this problem. Even though some are still made of plastic, the tubes are tested to a point well above that which the heater would reach when protected by the proper type of valve. In most cases a sticker or decal is attached to the outside of the heater cabinet which states something like this: "the water-ways of this tank are tested to 400 degrees Fahrenheit". If there are any doubts about the type of dip tube used in your heater, first be sure that it has one.

Most water heaters today are of the *glass-lined* type. The term *glass-lined* means that the inside of the tank surfaces have been sprayed with a coating of porcelain which is intended to protect the tank against corrosion. It works very well. The life of a glass-lined tank is normally several times longer than that of a standard galvanized steel tank.

However, there is a potential problem associated with these tanks as well. It's not possible to be absolutely certain that every section of bare metal within the water heater tank is completely covered. Invariably there is one or more little *pin-hole* where the porcelain did not bond or where the spray or dip missed.

One of the chief causes of corrosion within this appliance is due to electrolytic action between dissimilar metals that are in the same water system. The water, with the impurities which it invariably contains even under the best conditions, forms a solution that will conduct an electrical current. Within the water system in the home there are a number of metals which have unlike properties. In this situation, electrical flow is set up between the metallic electrodes.

Most manufacturers have discovered the means to combat this problem is to place a sacrificial anode within the tank itself. This anode extends from a plug in the top of the tank, usually close to the point where the dip tube enters. The anode itself looks very much like a dip tube except that it is a solid metallic rod rather than being a hollow tube. The anode used in most water heaters is made of magnesium. The properties of magnesium are such that if there is a pin-hole in the porcelain coating within the tank, the magnesium will flow through electrolysis to that particular point and attach itself to the steel, rather than having the steel eaten away by some other metal in the system. In this manner the magnesium becomes a protective coating for the steel of the tank.

One of the most important components found on a water heater is not really part of the water heater.

It is a group of safety devices, the primary one being a pressure-temperature relief valve that will protect the heater if it overheats. It is *imperative* that these valves are connected into the system at the water heater and that they are installed in the correct places. If you discover that they are not, turn the water heater off.

A residential water system is a *closed* system in most municipalities because a check valve is placed at the water meter. This prevents contaminated water from re-entering the main system. When water is heated within a closed system, as it is in a heater tank, it expands and causes a pressure buildup at the rate of ten pounds per degree.

This in itself is a good reason to install a valve. The main reason however, is to protect the heater and the dwelling in case a situation arises which would cause the water heater to overheat

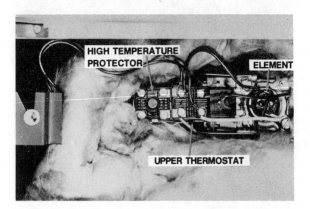

to abnormal temperatures, even possibly to a point where steam was created.

There is another device that can be installed on a water heater that will add further to protection. This is a high-limit protector. It is used in conjunction with many electric water heaters to shut off both sides of the 230 volt line if overheating should occur. With the protector in place, a manual reset button must be pushed to put the heater back into operation.

Equipped with the proper safety devices, a water heater is probably one of the safest and most trouble-free appliances that one can own, even though it is on duty 24 hours a day. Without proper protection, however, it can be like living with a bomb in your home. The force of an exploding water heater has been compared to the equivalent of ten sticks of dynamite.

COMPLAINTS (PROBLEMS)

One of the most common complaints about water heaters is that there is not enough hot water. This may be due to one of several external reasons as well as a fault within the water heater. If water runs out after a period of time, the first thing to consider is whether your demands for hot water have increased.

Often during winter months there is a pronounced drop in the temperature of the water entering the house. This increases the load on the heater and also reduces the recovery rate, since it takes longer for the colder water to heat up.

Another cause of insufficient hot water is found primarily in dual element electric heaters where the lower element is failing to operate. This could be due to a defective element, a defective thermostat or a break in the wiring. If you suspect that this is the problem, the wiring can be inspected after first turning off the power and removing the access panel. However, a continuity tester or VOM is needed to test the thermostat and element unless visual indication shows that a terminal is burned or that the element is leaking at the terminals.

If the thermostat is defective, it can be replaced by pulling the thermostat from behind the spring-loaded clip that holds it tightly in place against the clamp. In most cases the new thermostat can be inserted into the mount, the wires removed from the old one one at a time and put into place in the new one. This avoids any possibility of mis-wiring.

If a heating element must be removed, all power must be turned off and the tank drained. To do this turn the water supply to the heater off by turning the shut-off valve on the cold water line. Fasten a hose to the drain outlet at the bottom of the tank. This usually extends through to the outside of the cabinet. Open the drain valve.

When the tank has drained, remove the access panel and remove the two wires that are connected to the faulty element. The terminals to which each of these is connected is not important in this case, so there is no need to mark it. When the wires are loosened, loosen the four bolts that hold the element flanges to the heater. After these are removed it may be necessary to pry gently between the tank flange and the element flange in the area of the gasket.

Before installing a new element be sure and clean any rust or old gasket material from the

tank flange to provide a clean seating surface for the new element. When reinstalling a new element, follow any special instructions that may have been packed with it. When tightening the bolts, adjust them snugly and then crisscross the final tightening sequence. Reconnect the wiring, reinstall the access panels and the job should be complete.

If for any reason the thermostat is removed from a gas water heater, be sure that the sensing tube is recessed back into the well as it was originally positioned. The pilots on gas water heaters sometimes become linted, especially if they are located in a laundry room. If this happens, the lint can usually be cleaned away with a brush such as an old toothbrush. Look closely around the area where the pilot is located for this condition in the event of pilot failure. Also, remove the vent pipe from a gas water heater after a year or so of operation and clean away any soot or carbon which may have been deposited on the vent pipe or the flue liner. A gas water heater located within a small utility room should have outside combustion air provided or a grill within the door. Be sure that gas is turned off before attempting to service any gas water heater.

Overheating or shocking at any point on the plumbing are conditions that require immediate attention. If a volt-ohm-meter is not available to

check for the causes of these problems, call in an expert. Turn the power off to the heater and do not use it until it has been checked and approved for operation. A common cause of both of these problems could be a grounded element or thermostat.

Sometimes after a long period of usage, water heaters may begin to make noise. This is usually caused by mineral deposits or a buildup of sediment in the bottom of the tank. If a garden hose is attached to the drain outlet and the tank flushed yearly, after turning off the power this situation is not likely to occur. In very severe cases it is sometimes necessary to completely remove the drain and run an iron rod into the bottom of the tank to brush away the scaling that may have built up. *SEE ALSO APPLIANCE REPAIR, MAJOR.*

Water Softeners

Water softeners are manual or automatic appliances which may be purchased or rented. The number of grains of calcium carbonate per gallon of water usually determines the degree of hardness. Water is soft if the grains number less than one, but if the water contains over 3.5 calcium carbonate grains per gallon, it is hard. Most suppliers of water softening equipment will test the water.

Water may be too hard if laundry is dingy, pipes are easily clogged, bathtub rings are difficult to remove or if more soap or detergent has to be used than should be necessary.

Most water softeners have one tank with a bed of synthetic resin and one tank that stores salt and dissolves it to form brine. When hard water is sent through the resin, the hard calcium and magnesium ions are exchanged for soft sodium ions. The softener goes through a regeneration process when hard ions saturate the bed.

Since hot water systems are more noticeably affected by hard water, softening the cold water may not be desirable. In that case, an opening should be made in the line carrying cold water to the water heater.

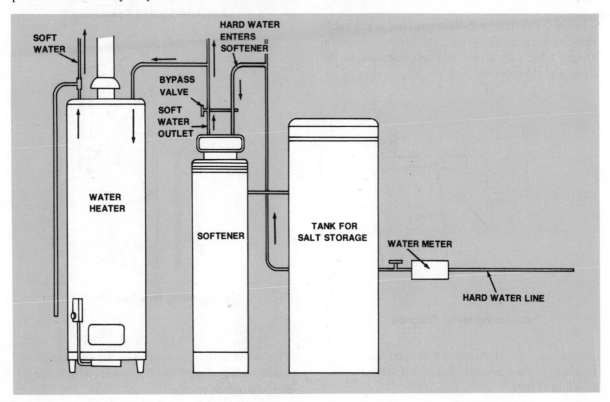

Watts

Watts are a unit of measuring electrical power that is obtained by multiplying the number of amperes (amps) an item uses by the volts in the power line. For example, a lamp drawing 20 amps from a six-volt battery uses 120 watts. Because watts are such a small amount of power, electricity is measured in kilowatts which is 1,000 watts. *SEE ALSO ELECTRICITY.*

Weatherstripping

Weatherstripping is a thin strip of metal, plastic, felt or wood. It is used to cover the joint between a door or window sash and the jamb, casing or sill to keep out rain, drafts, sound and dirt. If weatherstripping is efficient, it will help retain indoor temperature by keeping out air and moisture. This may result in a 15 to 25 per cent fuel saving.

The most common weatherstripping is probably interlocking jamb weatherstripping or metal strips, which interlock and are fastened to the door and door jamb.

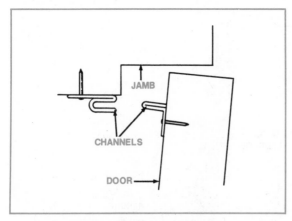

Interlocking Metal Channels

Spring-type metal strips are shaped to provide an air-tight cushion either with a U-shaped fold or slight crimp.

WEATHERSTRIPPING WINDOWS

There are several basic types of weatherstripping for double-hung windows which do not require special tools for installation: thin spring-metal strips; vinyl, available in tubular form and as a covering over a sponge core, and adhesive-backed foam rubber. All attach to molding and fit snugly against the sash.

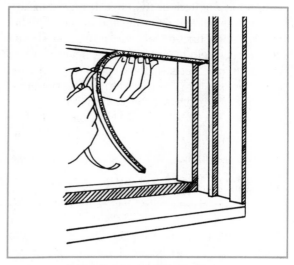

Adhesive-backed Foam Strip

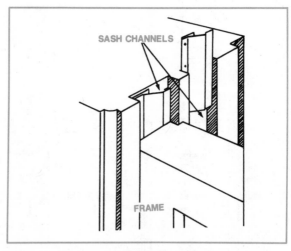

Spring-metal Weatherstripping

WEATHERSTRIPPING DOORS

The most efficient door weatherstrippings are interlocking aluminum channels, which are fitted around door edges.

There are three basic types of weatherstrips which fit outside door jambs: adhesive-backed foam strips, wood strips with foam backing and aluminum channels with vinyl backing. All make tight seals when the door is closed.

An aluminum channel may be applied between the bottom of a door and its threshold. It should be fitted down on the threshold snugly against both sides of the door jamb with screws. The vinyl backing or flap should face the outside.

Other aluminum channel weatherstripping may be fitted to the bottom of the door. Vinyl fits inside the channel.

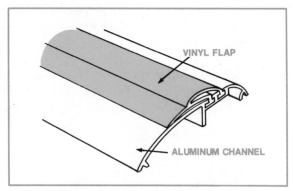

Aluminum Channel with Vinyl Flap

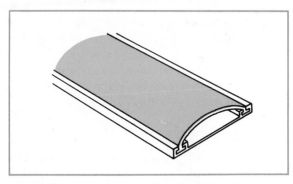

Aluminum/Vinyl Channel Fits to Bottom of Door.

Web Clamp

To simplify the assembly of round or irregular shapes, a web or band clamp is utilized. This device is made of fabric bands fastened securely by a crank or ratchet mechanism. When tighten-

ing and loosening the crank, a wrench is used. The web clamp is placed around the object, pulled firmly in place at the clamp and tightened by applying tension with the crank. *SEE ALSO HAND TOOLS.*

Courtesy of The Stanley Works

Web Clamp

Weed Killers

Weed killers or herbicides sold today are usually mixed with fertilizers. They can be obtained in granular form and can be applied with a fertilizer spreader.

It is recommended, in most instances, for the average home owner whose lawn has some weeds and other turfed areas where size is not a factor, that a chemically prepared herbicide fertilizer mix be purchased and used.

Herbicides are applied as dry granules, wettable powder suspension or liquid solutions. Excessive amounts of any herbicide will damage lawn grasses. A herbicide may kill one weed and not affect others. Controlling some weeds may result in permanent damage to other grasses.

Herbicides are sold in liquid, powder and granular forms, most having common names which have been assigned to their chemical names.

PRECAUTIONS

Always follow instructions for applying herbicides, being careful not to use overdoses. Apply weed-killer sprays only when temperature is between 70 degrees and 85 degrees Farenheit, when there is little wind blowing and when no rain is expected for at least several hours.

Store herbicides in their original containers out of the reach of children and pets and away from foods.

Apply weed killers selectively, out of the danger of drifts. Be fully clothed when applying herbicides and avoid prolonged inhalation of a spray or dust.

After handling herbicides do not eat, drink or smoke until you have washed. If a weed-killer gets in the eyes, follow label directions for first aid and get medical attention promptly.

Dispose of empty herbicide containers in newspaper and place them in a trash can. To prevent injury to desirable plants, do not use the same equipment for insecticides and fungicides that has been used for herbicides.

The following table is a listing for springtime preemergence crabgrass control and reseeding with bluegrasses and fescues. The herbicides listed are usually sold prepackaged for a specific lawn area shown on the label.

Herbicide	Dose, Relative to time of treatment
DCPA	3.7 oz./1,000 sq. ft., Reseed fall before or 60 days after.
Bensulide	5.5 oz./1,000 sq. ft., Reseed fall after spring treatment.
Siduron	2.2 oz./1,000 sq. ft., Reseed any time — before, at or after.
Benefin	0.7 oz./1,000 sq. ft., Reseed fall after spring treatment.
Terbutol	3.7 oz./1,000 sq. ft., Reseed fall after spring treatment.

SPRAYERS

It is best to use a sprayer that can be adjusted to make a coarse spray at low pressure. A garden sprinkling can may be used on small areas where even distribution is not difficult. When using a pressure sprayer on a large area, avoid leaving wide gaps or making overlaps by setting stakes or placing objects on the ground and walking toward them while applying the spray. Guide rings may be stretched across the lawn also.

Clean sprayers after each use. Washing with water and detergent is sufficient if the herbicide was a dalapon, DSMA, metham, dazomet or DCPA.

When a sprayer has contained 2,4-D or silvex and might be used for spraying fungicide or desirable plants, clean it with activated charcoal or household ammonia.

Use charcoal together with one or two ounces of household detergent in 2½ gallons of water. Use two tablespoons of ammonia to one quart of water. With either solution, fill the sprayer and operate to clean it. Let part of the ammonia solution stand overnight. Rinse with clean water.

WEED GRASSES

Lawn weeds are classified as weed grasses or broadleaf weeds.

Crabgrass

Crabgrass may be treated two ways: by preemergence treatment or applying the herbicide in the spring before seeds germinate; by postemergence treatment or applying the herbicide after crabgrass emerges.

Preemergence herbicides for crabgrass include DCPA, benefin, bensulids, terbutol and siduron.

All except siduron should be applied only on established lawns. Sprinkle the lawn with water after preemergence herbicide application to let it seep into the soil.

DSMA gives good postemergence control. It should be applied three times in seven to ten day intervals soon after the crabgrass emerges. Make sure the soil is moist and, if not, water it down a few days before and after each application. Do not use DSMA on St. Augustine grass.

If broadleaf weeds are present, they may be controlled by adding 2, 4-D or silex to the DSMA solution in the first application. Afterwards use DSMA full-strength at normal intervals.

BROADLEAF WEEDS

Control broadleaf weeds such as chickweed, henbit, knotweed, ground ivy and oxalis with silvex alone or added to an equal amount of 2,4-D, both mixed half-strength.

Dicamba and 2,4-D are useful for controlling knotweed, ground ivy, clover, red sorrel and speedwell species.

If bentgrass and clover are to be maintained on lawns, apply 2,4-D or MCPA at 0.1 to 1.2 ounce per 1,000 square feet. Silvex destroys white clover and dichondra, which are also sensitive to 2,4-D.

Apply herbicides in spring or fall on 60-degree F. days when the wind is still. Lawn grasses will fill in bare spots after fall treatment, but crabgrass is more likely to fill them in after spring treatment.

It is best to wait four to six weeks after seedlings emerge to apply herbicide on new lawns. If broadleaf weeds are an acute problem in a new seedling, use 2,4-D, and silvex or MCPA at 0.01 ounce per 1,000 square feet.

Wild onion or wild garlic may be controlled with low volatile ester formulations of 2,4-D. It should be applied at 0.07 ounce per 1,000 square feet or according to directions on the label. Make the

treatment in March or April of every year and in October or November until control is achieved.

Treat scattered stands of dandelions or other broadleaf weeds with a 2,4-D mixture with a small sponge attached to the end of a stick or another similar applicator designed for spot treatments. Press the sponge against the base of each weed. *SEE ALSO LAWNS & GARDENS.*

Courtesy for Control and Dosage Charts and other information contained in Weed Killers: U.S. Department of Agriculture

Welding & Welding Equipment

The word *welding* means heating two pieces of metal to their melting points and allowing them to flow together or coalesce, until they form one mass. It differs somewhat from *brazing* which is the joining of metals with the aid of a filler metal of a different composition and a melting point above 800 degrees Fahrenheit. Below this temperature the operation is called *soldering*.

GAS WELDING

Oxyacetylene welding is a gas-welding process wherein coalescence is produced by an oxyacetylene gas flame. Pressure can be used, but in some cases, is not necessary. In oxyacetylene welding the edges to be welded are first properly prepared, then correctly spaced and aligned for welding. Next the edges are melted down with the oxyacetylene flame produced at the tip of the welding torch.

Fusion and penetration through the entire thickness of the metal is, of course, essential. Where the metal is too thick to secure complete penetration with a square butt joint, the edges are beveled

The equipment required for oxyacetylene welding consists, as a rule, of a cylinder of oxygen, a cylinder of acetylene, an oxygen regulator, an acetylene regulator, a length of oxygen hose, a length of acetylene hose, and a welding torch. Accessories needed are a welding rod (usually), flux (if necessary), goggles or spectacles, a sparklighter, and gloves.

TYPES OF FLAMES

The chemical characteristics of the oxyacetylene flame and, consequently, its action on molten metal can be varied over a wide range by changing slightly the proportions of oxygen and acetylene in the mixture. The neutral, or balanced, flame is produced with a mixing ratio of approximately 1 volume of oxygen to 1 volume of acetylene. It is a clearly defined flame, readily obtained with a little practice. When the flame is of the carburizing type, whitish streamers of unburned acetylene are seen leaving the blue inner cone and entering the sheath flame. As the acetylene supply is decreased, these streamers decrease in length until there remains only the sharply defined blue cone and the sheath flame forming the neutral oxyacetylene flame. The carburizing flame is produced with a mixing ratio of slightly less than 1 volume of oxygen to 1 of acetylene.

The oxidizing flame is produced with a mixing ratio of slightly more than 1 volume of oxygen to 1 of acetylene. It is more difficult to adjust to a definite oxidizing degree than it is to adjust to a neutral or carburizing flame. The oxidizing flame is used for welding copper and brasses.

FLAME ADJUSTMENT

First, both oxygen and acetylene lines must be purged. Then in lighting the torch, only the acetylene valve is opened. As soon as the torch has been lighted, the oxygen valve is opened and the flame adjusted to neutral.

WELDING METHODS

There are several different methods of oxyacetylene welding which produce good results. Right-handed welders usually hold the torch in the right hand and welding rod in the left hand. Some welders prefer to weld from left to right, while others prefer to weld from the opposite direction. The most suitable method to employ depends largely upon the type of work. However, the various methods, are based upon the same general principles, some of which are: (a) a pool of molten metal should be maintained which progresses evenly down the seam as the weld is made, (b) the end of the welding rod should be melted by immersing in the puddle; it should not be held above the puddle and allowed to drip into it; (c) the inner flame cone should not be permitted to come in contact with the welding rod or the molten metal of the puddle or base metal; (d) the flame should bring the edges of the weld to the fusion point ahead of the puddle, as it is advanced along the seam; (e) most important of all, the penetration of molten metal should be all the way down to the bottom surface of the weld, but without permitting the molten metal to drip in beads from the bottom.

Backhand Welding

A later welding technique is known as backhand welding. In this method, the torch tip precedes the rod in the direction of welding. The torch flame is pointed back at the molten puddle and completed weld. The end of the rod is in the flame between the tip and the weld. These positions of torch and welding rod requires less manipulation than forehand welding. The motion of the welding rod may be a rotating one (using the rod unbent), with the end rolling from side to side in the puddle; or the rod may be bent and moved back and forth across the puddle. Again, the rod end may be made to describe full circles within the puddle, or semi-circles partway around the puddle and back again. The torch is usually held with the flame quite still, with practically no motion to and fro across the weld, but advancing slowly and evenly along the seam in the direction of welding.

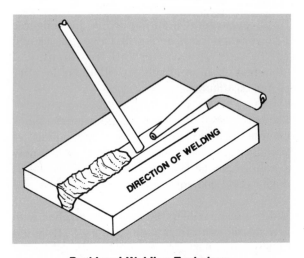

Backhand Welding Technique

Forehand, Puddle or Ripple Welding

In the forehand method of welding the rod precedes the tip in the direction in which the weld is being made. The flame is also pointed in the direction of the welding and at the same time is directed at an angle downward, so that it will preheat the edges of the joint. The torch tip and welding rod are manipulated to give opposite movements in semi-circular paths, to uniformly distribute the heat and the molten metal.

This is an older method of welding and has some disadvantages for greater thicknesses, in that the walls of the required vee have to be deeply melted to obtain good fusion of the added metal with the base metal.

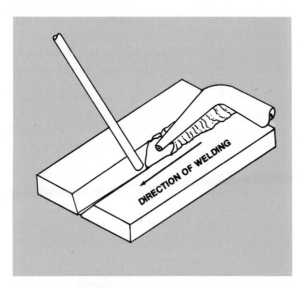

Forehand, Puddle or Ripple Welding Technique

Multi-Layer Welding

In making heavy welds in a single layer it is necessary to carry a large puddle, which is difficult to handle. The side walls of the vee are apt to be melted excessively as you endeavor to secure proper penetration, and the surface of the weld will widen too much as you attempt to avoid overlapping.

With multi-layer welding, these difficulties are avoided by cutting down the cross-section of the weld to the point where it can be controlled easily.

OXYGEN-PROPANE TORCHES

Designed for the do-it-yourselfer who has only occasional, light welding needs, these compact torches have heating power of up to 5000°F. That is hot enough to weld a broken garden tool or mower, repair a car body, or work wrought-iron projects at home.

While not quite equal to the oxyacetylene torch, the oxypropane torch is a very capable performer in braze welding. Rods up to $1/2$ inch diameter and flat material up to $3/16$ inch thick are easily joined. A $5/8$ inch bolt or $1/4$ inch flat steel can be cut through readily. Silver soldering also lies within the oxypropane torch's capabilities (working temperature of silver is in the range of 1100-1400°F). Nickel, silver, bronze, aluminum and steel can be brazed with appropriate rods.

Technique of oxypropane torch use is similar to that of the oxyacetylene torch, though made simpler by the light weight and portability of the setup.

Standard protective equipment must be used (gloves, goggles, etc.). *Always wear colored goggles when welding and don't let bystanders watch unless they, too, wear goggles!* The dazzling radiance of the torch flame contains ultraviolet radiation that can permanently damage eye tissues. Eye protection is mandatory.

SAFETY PRECAUTIONS IN GAS WELDING

The fierce high temperatures used in gas welding should inspire great caution in your working habits. Gas torches of any type, even the simple propane torch, have the capacity to inflict major injury or property damage. Regard these precautions as general in nature and be sure you have all the detailed information and protective equipment you need before tackling any *gas* welding job.

Never work in a poorly ventilated area. Combustion gases are irritating, smoke dangerously obscures what you are doing and the potential exists that a leak may occur, allowing gases to accumulate to explosive levels.

Check your equipment thoroughly before use. Leaks can occur in valves, hoses, fittings and tanks. Be sure that gas feeds are under your control at all times.

Never weld without proper eye protection. Radiant energy from the torch can damage the retina. Wear safety goggles to block this energy and to keep sparks, flying slag, fumes, and smoke out of your eyes. (Low-temperature brazing operations do not produce harmful radiation. Nevertheless, safety goggles, even if the clear variety, should be worn to physically protect the eyes).

Wear leather welding gloves when using a high-temperature torch. Severe burns may result from accidental skin contact with the torch or hot workpieces. Unexpected hot metal sparks can also cause reflex reactions that turn the torch on you. Gloves are a sensible precaution in high-temperature work.

Avoid direct contact with the workpiece or brazing rod. Use tongs or pliers to move parts. Place a hot rod so that you will not touch the end just used in joining. Move finished pieces to an out-of-the way cooldown area where they can return to safe handling temperature.

Use fireproof materials around the torch. Asbestos sheet or firebrick makes a good work surface, especially if placed over a metal sheet to absorb and radiate heat that slowly filters through.

Do not operate a torch in the presence of flammable fuels or solvents.

Use a sparklighter to light torch. Use of matches may result in severe hand burns.

Point the torch tip away from yourself and others when lighting and using.

ELECTRIC WELDING

The major electrical welding process is arc welding, where heat is generated by an electric arc struck between a welding electrode, or rod, and the workpiece. The arc is quite hot, and melting and subsequent solidification of the weld metal occur very rapidly. Largely because of this speed, arc welding has become the favorite of industry.

An AC or DC power source, fitted with whatever controls may be needed, is connected by a ground cable to the workpiece and by a "hot" cable to an electrode holder of some type, which makes electrical contact with the welding electrode. When the circuit is energized and the electrode tip touched to the grounded workpiece, and then withdrawn and held close to the spot of contact, an arc is created across the gap. The arc produces a temperature of about 6500°F at the tip of the electrode, a temperature more than adequate for melting most metals. The heat produced melts the base metal in the vicinity of the arc and any filler metal supplied by the electrode or by a separately introduced rod or wire. A common pool of molten metal is produced, called a *crater*. This crater solidifies behind the electrode as it is moved along the joint being welded. The result is a fusion bond.

Use of the heat of an electric arc to join metals, however, requires more than the moving of the electrode in respect to the weld joint. Metals at high temperatures are reactive chemically with the main constituents of air—oxygen and nitrogen. Should the metal in the molten pool come in contact with air, oxides and nitrides will be formed, which upon solidification of the molten pool can destroy the strength properties of the weld joint. For this reason, the various arc-welding processes provide some means for covering the arc and the molten pool with a protective sheild of gas, vapor, or slag. This referred to as *arc shielding*.

Any arc-welding system in which the electrode is melted off to become part of the weld is described as "metal-arc". If the electrode is refractory—carbon or tungsten—there are no molten droplets to be forced across the gap and onto the work. Filler metal is melted into the joint from a separate rod or wire.

Since there must be an ionized path to conduct electricity across a gap, the mere switching on of the welding current with a cold electrode poised over the work will not start the arc. The arc must first be ignited. This is accomplished either by supplying an initial voltage high enough to cause a discharge or by touching the electrode to the work and then slowly withdrawing it as the contact area becomes heated.

Arc welding may be done with either AC or DC current and with the electrode either positive or negative. The choice of current and polarity depends on the process, the type of electrode, the arc atmosphere, and the metal being welded.

The exact current selected for a job depends upon the size of the pieces to be welded and the position of welding. Generally a lower current will be sufficient for welding on a small part than would be necessary to weld on a large piece of the same thickness. Similarly with a given size of electrode a lower current should be used on thin metals than on the heavier sections.

STRIKING THE ARC-RUNNING BEADS

In learning to weld there are certain fundamental steps which must be mastered before you can attempt to weld on actual work. Preparatory to the actual striking of an arc, carefully insert the electrode in the holder. To strike an arc, use what is commonly known as the "scratching technique". In this method the striking end of the electrode is dragged across the work in a manner much the same as striking a match. When the electrode touches the work, the welding current starts. If held in this position, the electrode would freeze or weld itself to the work. To overcome this problem, the electrode is withdrawn from the work immediately after contact has been made. The amount that the electrode is withdrawn is small and depends upon the diameter; this distance is known as the *arc*

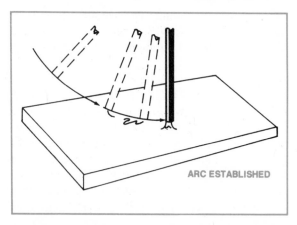

ARC ESTABLISHED

length. If in striking an arc, the electrode freezes, it may be freed by a quick twist of the wrist.

Determination of the correct arc length is difficult since there is no ready means of measuring it. As a preliminary guide, use about $1/16$ inch arc length on $1/16$ and $3/32$ inch electrodes; for $1/18$ and $1/32$ inch electrodes use about $1/8$ inch arc length. When skill is acquired, the sound of the arc will be a good guide. A short arc with correct current will give a sharp, crackling sound.

Once the knack of starting and holding an arc has been learned, turn next to depositing weld metal. In the beginning it is best to run beads of weld metal on flat plates using a full electrode. Practice moving from left to right and from right to left. The electrode should be held more or less perpendicular to the work, except that tilting it ahead, in the direction of travel will prove helpful. To produce these results it is necessary to hold a short arc, travel at a uniform speed, and feed the electrode downward at a constant rate as it melts.

ELECTRIC ARC WELDING SAFETY PRECAUTIONS

Don't Get Burned. The Welding Arc is intense and visibly bright. Its radiation can damage eyes, penetrate lightweight clothing, reflect from light-colored surfaces, and burn the skin and eyes.

Wear long-sleeve clothing (particularly for gas-shielded arc) in addition to gloves, hat, and shoes. As necessary, use additional protective clothing such as leather jacket or sleeves, flame-proof apron, and fire-resistant leggings. Avoid outer garments of untreated cotton. Wear dark, substantial clothing. Button collar to protect chest and neck and button pockets to prevent entry of sparks.

Protect Eyes from Exposure to Arc. Never look at an electric arc without protection. A welding helmet or shield containing a filter plate must be used when welding. Place over face *before striking arc.* Looking at an arc momentarily with unprotected eyes (particularly a high intensity gas-shielded arc) can cause a retinal burn that may leave a permanent dark area in the field of vision.

Exposed hot conductors or other bare metal in the welding circuit, or ungrounded electrically-HOT equipment can fatally shock a person whose body becomes a conductor. Do not stand, sit, lie, lean on, or touch a wet surface when welding, without suitable protection.

Connect the frames of each unit such as power source, control and work table to the building ground. Conductors must be adequate to carry currents safely.

Frequently inspect cables for wear, cracks and damage. *Immediately replace* those with excessively worn or damaged insulation to avoid possibly-lethal shock from bared cable.

Before installation, inspection of service of equipment, shut *off* all power and remove line fuses (or lock or red-tag switches) to prevent accidental turning ON of power. Disconnect all cables from welding power source, and pull all 115 volt line-cord plugs.

Do not open power circuit or change polarity while welding. If, in an emergency, it must be disconnected, guard against shock, burns, or flash from switch arcing.

Well Pump Systems

Well pump systems refer to the type of pump and method used to draw water from a well to the surface. They consist of three types of pumps: suction, lift and jet.

SUCTION

A suction pump operates with the aid of atmospheric pressure. Even though pressure is lowered in a pipe, the surrounding fluid still has normal atmospheric pressure exerted on it. Since this normal pressure is actually higher than the pressure in the pipe, the heavier pressure forces water to flow into the area having the lower pressure.

Pressure is lowered by drawing air from the pipe much like drawing air from a straw. After the air is drawn out, a low pressure area exists. Because atmospheric pressure is still exerting the normal 15 pounds per square inch on the surrounding water, the well water is forced through the intake and up the pipe to the water-supply tank.

LIFT

A lift pump uses the principle of *lifting* water up the pipe. Most lift pumps use a piston to force water up the pipe. As the piston falls in the pipe, a small valve opens and allows water to lodge above the piston. As the piston rises, the valve closes, and the trapped water is carried up the pipe and flows through an outlet near the top.

JET

The jet pump uses two pipes. The first contains a Venturi tube in the hairpin curve that is below water level. The second pipe, a straight run coming from the well to the surface, connects with the first pipe.

A jet pump uses the principle of the Venturi tube along with Bernoulli's law. A Venturi tube is simply a tube with a restriction or narrow area in the pipe. The fluid flowing through the tube must increase its velocity to move through the passage. Bernoulli's law states that as velocity increases the pressure decreases. The fluid under higher pressure will be pushed into the fast-moving stream of water. Since well water is under normal atmospheric pressure, the water is forced into the fast-moving pump stream.

Because more water is delivered than is sent, the excess is diverted into a water-supply tank.

Well & Septic Tank Systems

If a well and septic tank system are included in your home building plans, major problems can be avoided by designing before constructing. Besides being on the higher part of the property, the well should be at least 50 feet from the septic tank and about 100 feet from distribution boxes and disposal lines. Before deciding on the size of the disposal field, soil absorption tests need to be made. Allow for an extended field in case it is needed later. This pre-planning will help to specify the location of the house which should be in compliance with building and plumbing codes.

If a municipal water supply system is not available, water may be received from your own well. Either a shallow or a deep well may be used, depending upon the area.

A shallow or dug well can provide water in open country. This well may be dug by hand. It consists of a hole between 15 and 30 feet deep which is lined with uncemented stones. Rain water and other water from surface sources filter through the soil and into the well.

Areas which are more densely populated or have little surface water can be serviced by a deep well. A deep well, drilled by machine, may have a depth ranging from 100 to several hundred feet, depending on the level of the water source. Water is usually found beneath a buried rock layer which prevents surface water and other contamination from directly entering it. Surface water is suitable for feeding a deep well after undergoing extensive natural filtration.

Have the local health department test the water for potability before using it. Bacteria and other contamination may be present even in clear water. Check the water source periodically for surface water infiltration. *SEE ALSO SEPTIC SYSTEMS.*

Western Union Splice

The Western Union splice is used to make a wire connection when two wires will be under pressure or tension. Three inches of insulation are cleaned from two individual wire ends. About half an inch from the remaining insulation, bend the bared wires and hook them together. While holding the hook with a pair of pliers, twist the wires one by one around each other. Soldering and taping will insure good contact, so that the wire splice will stand a considerable amount of tension. *SEE ALSO ELECTRICAL WIRING.*

Whimble Brace

The whimble brace is a hand tool used for drilling holes in wood. It has the advantage of the head position being to one side of the sweep of the handle, rather than above the bit chuck as in most standard drills. This serves as a second crank handle and allows the operator to apply turning force with both hands. *SEE ALSO HAND TOOLS.*

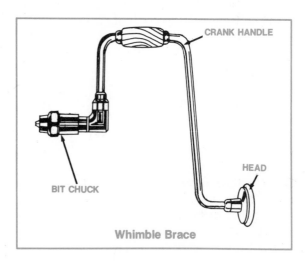

Whimble Brace

White Fir
[SEE FIR.]

White Oak

The two distinct groups of American oak are Red Oak and White Oak. The leading North American species is White Oak. The leaf lobes of White Oak are rounded and the acorns mature in one season. Its annual rings are compact and pores in the summer wood are very small.

The heartwood of White Oak is a brownish color and is more durable than Red Oak heartwood. When White Oak has been freshly cut, it will have a distinctive odor.

This oak works best with power tools, and is used for carvings, interior finish, furniture and boat structure. *SEE ALSO OAK.*

Willow

The willow tree that is used for lumber grows on sand bars and other low, wet land close to the Mississippi River. The black willow, which reaches 130 feet in height and 3 feet in diameter, is the only species used commercially.

In North America, the willow is the softest hardwood and working with willow is easy. It is the best wood to use when gluing and is very strong considering its weight. It is used extensively for wall paneling and in furniture. Willow also goes into packing cases, beverage boxes, crates and other shipping containers.

Some willow furniture may be called by the name "Salix" because many people know only of the small Northern willow trees, not of the strong Southern variety used for lumber. *SEE ALSO WOOD IDENTIFICATION.*

Windows & Window Hardware

Windows allow light and air to enter a room but may also provide privacy. They are usually factory-produced and shipped to the work site in completed units. In choosing the correct window type, consider the window's location, purpose, design and necessary clearance.

TYPES

Windows may be divided into three basic types, sliding, swinging and fixed. Sliding windows include double-hung and horizontal windows. Casement and awning windows are typical swinging windows hinged on their sides or ends. Fixed windows are used to permit daylight and a view and are often used in combination with the other types. Consider how much clearance, both inside and out, the window will need before choosing a particular window, as a casement window which opens out may block passage, as on a porch.

MATERIALS

Window frames may be made of aluminum, steel or wood. Wood frames, although requiring preservatives or paint, are most often used

Courtesy of the Andersen Corp. (Perma-Shield Narroline Windows)

A fixed picture window may be used in combination with smaller side windows.

Courtesy of Marvin Windows

Muntins may be permanently attached or designed to be removed for easy cleaning.

Courtesy of Marvin Windows

A variety of window styles may be used on a residential dwelling.

because they usually do not condense moisture vapor. Glass is manufactured in standard qualities and thicknesses and may be used in single or double layers, such as in storm panels. In large spans, tempered glass should be used for safety. Muntins were originally used to join small panes of glass to make a large window, but often today they are made of plastic or wood and are simply placed over large sheets of plate glass for decoration.

PARTS & HARDWARE

The basic parts of a window include the head, or top of the window, the jamb, or side, and the sill, or bottom. Sash locks and pulleys are used to open and secure windows. Hinges and cranks are usually placed on windows which open in or out, such as casement or awning windows. Locks may be used on windows for added security.

SIZES & POSITION

In most residences, windows are a standard height of 6'8'' from the window head to the finished floor. The dimensions of a window usually include glass and sash size, rough frame opening size and masonry or unit opening size. Most manufacturers provide dimensions for standard units.

INSTALLATION

Following manufacturer's directions, install windows in a rough opening with 1/2 inch clearance on each side and 3/4 inch clearance above the head. After checking the size and level of the rough opening, place the window in the opening and temporarily nail in place. Wedge blocks may be used to help level the window. After leveling the sill, nail through the side casing in the bottom of the frame. Level the side jambs, and square the corners before nailing the top side casing. Open any ventilating sashes to be sure they work before permanent nailing is done.

REPAIRS

Stuck or jammed windows can usually be repaired by breaking the paint seal with a spatula or putty knife. If the window is warped, the stop moldings may have to be adjusted. Rattling windows can be cured also by moving the stop moldings. Sash cords may need replacement, a time-consuming task but not a difficult one.

Window glass panes may often need to be replaced, and weather stripping may be needed if a window lets air in.

Wing Divider

The wing divider resembles and is used like a compass. It has two steel legs and a quadrant-shaped wing running from one leg through a slot in the other that can be locked in position with a screw. To use the wing divider, set and lock the approximate spacing, then use it like a compass for dividing lines and arcs, scribing circles and finding the center of a circle. *SEE ALSO HAND TOOLS.*

Wire Brush

Wire brushes have fine, medium or coarse wire bristles and may have a wooden handle for hand use or be circular for use with an electric drill, drill press or a sanding machine. They are a useful tool when painting the exterior of a house, to scrape off loose paint, debris and dirt. Wire brushes are also used to remove paint from metal surfaces, rust on tools, and even for metal polishing. These brushes should be stored in a dry place in greaseproof paper. A rust preventive compound should be applied to the bristles.

Wire Connections
[SEE ELECTRICAL WIRING.]

Wire, Copper

Copper wire, the most common type of wire used in electrical wiring, is one of the best conductors of electricity. Its thinness insures flexibility and permits easy twisting and bending. Whether grouped into cables and cords or used individually, copper wire transmits the electric current in homes and other buildings. *SEE ALSO WIRE SIZES & TYPES.*

Wire Cutters

Wire cutters are a type of pliers designed to cut wire and strip insulating material without damaging the wire. They may be used much the same as diagonal-cutting and end-cutting pliers. Wire cutters may have functions other than cutting wire and may not be identified exclusively with this function. *SEE ALSO HAND TOOLS.*

Wire Edge

A wire edge, or feather edge, is the turned up section of a blade which forms during whetting, indicating sufficient sharpening. The wire edge is too unstable to be of use, and tends to dull the working edge. It should be broken off by rubbing a small piece of hardwood across the edge, followed by a light honing. *SEE ALSO TOOL SHARPENING.*

Wire Glass

Wire glass, also known as safety glass, contains a netting of wire mesh located in or near the center of the sheet. This wire is incorporated in the glass during the manufacturing process. The netting minimizes the probability of shattering when shock or heat causes the glass to crack. Wire glass is often used in public buildings as a safety precaution against vandalism.

Wireless Intercoms

Installing intercoms usually calls for snaking wires inside walls and under floors to get from room to room. This doesn't have to be so. The *wireless* intercom, eliminates all the trouble of stringing wires.

Units can be unplugged and moved from room to room as desired, or even used outdoors. They can also be used to communicate between adjoining houses — so long as both homes are supplied from the same side of the main power transformer in that area.

Wireless intercoms transmit their signals over the existing 115 volt wiring in your house, using a form of transmission called *carrier current*. Low-frequency radio waves are sent over the wires from one unit and are received by another unit in a different part of the house. The process is like radio transmission except that the signals go through the wires instead of the air.

In addition to easy installation, wireless intercoms have other advantages. In a typical wired system, there is usually one *master* station and several *slave* or *satellite* stations. Slave stations can only call the master, not each other. Adding units tends to complicate the wiring, especially if there is need for more than one master station. In a wireless system, any station can call any other station since all units are on the same line. Adding stations is simple because you just plug them in, as many as you want, wherever you have wall outlets. You can move them around as needs change and take them with you if you move — not easily done with a permanently wired system. By the same token, any response will be heard in all other stations which are turned on at that time.

Wireless intercoms do have a potential disadvantage over wired ones that are connected directly one to the other with their own set of wires. The wireless units are subject to background electrical noise, such as interference caused by various appliances, fluorescent lights or other electrical equipment operated nearby, in particular, light dimmers. These can cause an almost unbearable hum unless there are built-in noise filters that are specifically designed to suppress this type of interference. If your circuits are badly overloaded, or if wiring is inadequate (a problem in many older houses), then reception may also prove poor at times.

Wireless intercoms are ideal for temporary communication. For example: to keep in touch with

someone inside the house while you're working outside; to hear outside the house when the phone rings inside; as a temporary voice link between the sickroom, darkroom, kitchen, garage, workshop; or as a baby sitter while visiting next door neighbors.

You can keep one station of either set locked into the "talk" position and use an intercom that way to monitor a sleeping baby. Put one station next to the crib and lock it into the talk position. Then you can listen for the baby's cry over the other station plugged in at the kitchen counter, or whatever.

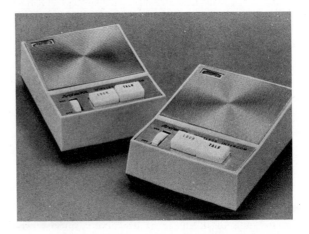

There should be no difficulty in communicating over a distance of 500 feet. Thus it is quite possible to set up an intercom system between your home and a neighbor's. An intercom won't work between houses served by different power-line distribution transformers, but chances are pretty good that any given pair of adjoining houses are being served by the same transformer.

WIRELESS REMOTE CONTROL

Your appliances, TV, radio Hi-Fi, lamps or any other AC powered equipment can be turned on and off from any convenient location with a wireless remote control system which consists of a sender and a receiver. When the sender is on, it directs a control signal into the powerline. When this signal reaches the receiver, it activates a relay circuit within the unit and this makes line voltage available at the receiver's AC socket. Turn the transmitter off and the receiver's relay circuit removes AC power from it's socket.

Wire Sizes & Types

Electricity flows from its point of origin to its destination (outlet receptacle, switch, fuse box, etc.) through wires of different sizes and types. Copper wire is used most often, but the greater availability of aluminum has resulted in an increase in the use of aluminum wire.

WIRE SIZES

In the United States, wire size is indicated by number using the Brown and Sharpe Gauge (B&S), also called the American Wire Gauge (AWG); the larger the number, the smaller the wire size. Wire sizes range from 60 (AWG) up to 0000. Number 50 is about the diameter of a human hair and weighs about one pound per sixty miles. Wire of this type is used in intricate electrical and electronic work. Number 14 has been the most commonly used for house wiring and the smallest wire size permitted for this purpose, although No. 12 is becoming the most common. Number 1 is the heaviest size usually used in household and farm wiring. Numbers 8 and 6 are used in either solid or stranded form as service leads to homes and for heavy power circuits.

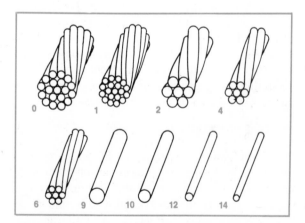

Cables (multiple-stranded wires) are used for supplying much of the electricity in the home (to operate large appliances or light fixtures) or for carrying heavy loads of electricity from the service entrance to the distribution panel and then to the various outlets as individual strands of wire are inadequate. Cables consist of two or three separately insulated wires wrapped with a protective covering. A stranded wire heavier than No. 0000 is known as a "cable".

TYPES OF CABLE

There are three basic types of multi-strand wire or cable: flexible armored cable, nonmetallic sheathed cable and plastic-covered cable.

Flexible armored cable has a spiraled steel armor which permits flexibility and makes the cable a grounding conductor. Flexible armored cable can be used for both concealed and exposed interior wiring but only in permanently dry locations.

Nonmetallic sheathed cable is encased in a moisture- and fire-resistant braided fabric covering. It is used extensively for ordinary house wiring, but only in permanently dry locations, since moisture would rot its covering.

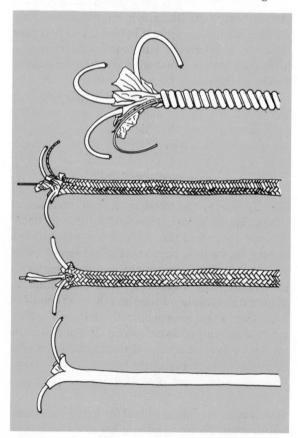

Plastic-covered cable is coated with a tough waterproof plastic so that it can be used underground without further protection. Plastic-covered or underground cable is used in damp locations, out of doors, underground and also indoors.

COLOR CODING

The individual wires in a cable are color coded for identification to prevent wiring mistakes. Of the possible three wires plus the uninsulated ground wire in each cable, the black wire is hot, the white wire is neutral and the red wire is hot. Black wires always connect to black wires or to brass-colored terminals; white wires always connect to white wires or the silver-colored terminals. *SEE ALSO PLUGS & CORDS.*

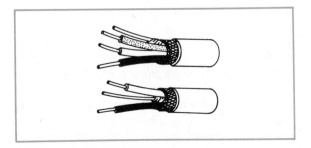

Wire Strippers

Wire strippers are a handy tool for the home craftsman in wire splicing or in making other connections to terminal screws. This instrument cleans insulation from wire ends so that a good contact can be made. *SEE ALSO ELECTRICIAN'S TOOLS & EQUIPMENT.*

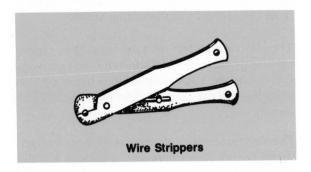

Wire Strippers

Wiring Systems, Electrical

The electrical wiring in a house serves the important function of distributing the electric current supplied by the local power company to the many different electrical appliances, heating and air conditioning, lights, power tools, motors, and tv's, radios and stereos installed in the house.

BASIC TERMINOLOGY OF ELECTRICITY

An *electric current* is the flow of minute electrically-charged particles called *electrons* through a *conductor*. Technically speaking, a conductor is any material which readily permits the flow of electricity, while an *insulator* is any material which blocks (or, more accurately, does not permit) the movement of electrons. Most metals are excellent conductors.

In wiring terminology, the word "conductor" specifically refers to wire designed to conduct electricity. In common usage, a conductor is a single wire, while a *cable* consists of two or more wires (conductors) enclosed in an outer sheath or jacket.

The flow of an electric current through a conducting wire is somewhat analogous to the flow of water through a pipe. The *rate* of electric current flow, a quantity similar to gallons-per-minute of water flow, is called *amperage*. A current of one *ampere* (abbreviated *amp*) is equivalent to the movement of 6,280,000,000,000,000,000 electrons through a conductor in one second.

As with water, a source of "pressure" is a necessary to push electrons through the conductor. In technical language, this is called *electromotive force* (or EMF), and is measured in *volts*. Actually, the term EMF is almost never used to talk about electrical wiring; it has been universally replaced by the word *voltage*.

Even the best conductors offer some opposition to the flow of electric current. This opposition is called *resistance,* and it is measured in *ohms.* The lower the resistance, the greater the current flow (the greater the amperage) that will move through a conductor for a given applied voltage. The resistance of a conductor is one of the factors that determines the maximum current it can safely carry; excessive current causes the conductor to heat up. Broadly speaking, the resistance of electrical wire is determined by its physical diameter. In turn, this factor determines the *ampacity* (or maximum amperage) of a given conductor. The following table lists the ampacities of wires in conduits, or in armored or sheathed cables:

WIRE SIZE	AMPACITY
No. 14	15-amps
No. 12	20-amps
No.10	3o-amps
No. 8	40-amps
No. 6	55-amps
No. 4	70-amps

It is important that ampacity limitations be observed: at best, incorrect (too small) wire size can affect appliance performance; at worst, it can pose a fire hazard due to overheating.

An electrical circuit, in the most basic sense of the term, is simply a path through which an electric current can flow. A practical household electrical circuit consists of one or more wiring devices (switches, receptacles, fuses, etc.) linked together with appropriate cables or conductors.

Broadly speaking, electrical circuits can be grouped into two categories: series and parallel circuits. A series circuit has all of its elements wired together in a single loop; current must flow through all of the circuit elements on its way through the circuit. By contrast, a parallel circuit has its elements in separate circuit "legs"; current flows in each leg independent of current flow in other legs.

Nearly a century ago, the series circuit was proposed for household lighting. However, its two most serious deficiencies made its use impractical: Because current flows simultaneously through all parts of a series circuit, it is impossible to turn on or turn off individual lights independently. And, a single burned-out light bulb will interrupt circuit current flow and extinguish the other bulbs.

Thus, all modern house wiring schemes are based on the parallel circuit, with each outlet and lighting fixture being an independent circuit leg. This arrangement permits individual control of each appliance, lamp, power tool, etc.

There is one exception to the parallel circuit concept: all overcurrent protection devices (fuses and circuit breakers) are wired in series with the circuit they protect. Thus, a "blown" fuse or "open" circuit breaker will interrupt current flow in the entire circuit.

BASIC WIRING SYSTEM ELEMENTS

The four major parts of a modern household electrical wiring system are: incoming service conductors, electric meter, electric service entrance panel (which includes fuses and circuit breakers) and the branch circuits. The incoming service conductors of a modern installation consist of three wires: two *hot* (or electrically live) wires and a single *neutral* wire. The neutral wire is connected to the ground and to electrically grounded objects (such as water piping).

Typically, the voltage measured between the two hot wires is 240-volts AC; the voltage measured between either hot wire and the neutral (or ground) is 120-volts AC. Thus, 240-volts is available for high-wattage major appliances (clothes dryer, range, etc.), and 120-volts AC is available for other appliances. Note that the neutral wire carries current (even though it may be uninsulated leading from the power line) and is an integral part of the wiring system.

The electric meter records the quantity of electrical energy (measured in kilowatt-hours) flowing into the house; your electric bill is based on total electrical energy consumption per month or bi-month.

The electric service entrance panel is the link between the incoming service conductors and the house branch circuits. The panel holds the set of fuses or circuit breakers that protect the individual circuits; all circuit wiring leads into the panel housing.

The service capacity of a wiring installation is defined by the ratings of the two master fuses or circuit breakers — one for each incoming hot wire — installed in the service panel. The service capacity represents the total quantity of electrical power that can be supplied to all the branch circuits. For example, "100-amp service" means that a total of 100 amperes of current can be supplied to the individual appliances, lights, and electrical devices throughout the house. Note that service capacity is ultimately determined by the size of the incoming service conductors; capacity cannot safely be increased simply by upping the master fuse or circuit breaker rating.

Although 60-amp service is still an acceptable minimum capacity for small homes, 100-amp service is recommended for most homes up to 3000-square feet internal floor area. When a home will be centrally air-conditioned or electrically heated, even greater service capacity (150 or 200-amps) is recommended.

The branch circuits distribute current to individual receptacles, lighting fixtures, and major appliances. Each circuit is protected by an individual fuse or circuit breaker in the service panel.

Branch circuits for household wiring are rated at 15-amp or 20-amp capacity, depending on the size of the wire used (No. 12 wire provides 20-amp service; No. 14 wire gives 15-amp service).

HOUSEHOLD WIRING RECOMMENDATIONS

The National Electric Code specifies that at least two 20-amp branch circuits serve the kitchen, dining room and laundry (independent of circuits serving lighting fixtures). This is a fairly conservative recommendation; additional circuits will be required in most situations, as well as individual branches.

Additional circuits to serve the rest of the house (as well as lighting in the kitchen, dining room, and laundry) are recommended on the basis of one 20-amp branch circuit per 500 square feet of floor space (or one 15-amp branch circuit per 375 square feet).

Wall-mount receptacles must be installed to take maximum advantage of the branch circuit capacity. There are two very good rules to follow that have Code Endorsement: In kitchens, one receptacle should be installed for every four linear feet of counter work space. Throughout the house, one receptacle should be installed for every twelve feet of wall dimension.

FUSES AND CIRCUIT BREAKERS

Overcurrent limiting devices, specifically fuses and circuit breakers, protect incoming service conductors and branch circuit wiring from excessive current flow (such as a short circuit). Left unchecked, excessive current can overheat wiring and start fires.

The heart of a fuse is a carefully shaped piece of metal of low melting point. Excessive current flow through the fuse rapidly heats and melts the metal segment, interrupting current flow.

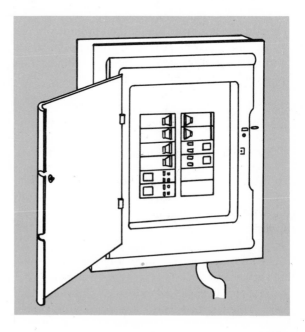

Most home circuit breakers work magnetically; excessive current flowing through an internal coil produces sufficient magnetic attraction to "trip" the mechanism and open the overloaded circuit.

Note that only the *hot side* of a branch circuit, the side leading to one of the two incoming hot service conductors, is protected by a fuse or breaker. An overcurrent device is never installed in the neutral side of any branch circuit; this insures that the connection to ground is never broken.

THREE-WIRE GROUNDING RECEPTACLES

By National Electrical Code mandate, wiring in new construction utilizes grounding-type receptacles that are equipped with *three* openings: the usual two parallel slots for the twin blades of a power plug, plus a third round or "U" shaped hole. The third hole accepts a matching pin found on the power plug of many appliances and all metal-cased hand-held power tools. The function of the pin and corresponding hole is to ground the housing of the appliance or tool when it is plugged in.

Grounding is a valuable safety measure: the ground connection protects the user of the appliance or tool from the potential shock hazard of an internal insulation failure. In certain circumstances, such a failure might "connect" the hot side of the power line to the appliance housing so that anyone touching the appliance or holding the tool would be subject to a dangerous (possibly lethal) electric shock.

Note: The term "three wire" is also used to describe the method of wiring split circuits.

COLOR CODING

To insure accurate and fast identification of hot, neutral and ground wires, a standard color coding scheme for wiring insulation has been developed:

BLACK colored wires connect to the hot incoming service conductors (via the service panel and meter) and become the hot sides of branch circuits. When *split circuits* are wired, the three-conductor cable used contains black and red wires; both become hot sides of their respective branch circuits.

WHITE colored wires lead to the neutral incoming service conductor and become the neutral sides of branch circuits.

GREEN colored wires are ground connections (often, ground wires in cables will be bare).

The terminals of sockets, receptacles and other wiring devices are also color coded. Natural brass color means that the terminal must be connected to the hot side or black wire of the branch circuit; white metal or silver color identifies the terminal to be connected to the neutral side (white wire); green metal identifies the ground connection.

Note that all the terminals of a switch will be brass colored. This is because the switch is wired into the hot side of the circuit feeding a light fixture. Thus, both switch terminals are considered to be hot.

NONMETALLIC AND METAL-PROTECTED CABLE

An adequately planned household wiring system can last the lifetime of the structure it serves if the various conductors are well protected. This is the job of nonmetallic sheathing and/or steel armor and conduit. There are three distinct types of wiring in widespread use:

Nonmetallic sheathed cable: the conductors are individually insulated, then encased in a tough, flexible outer jacket (typically made of plastic). Older types of nonmetallic cable surround the wires with a paper wrapper and jute cords, then an outer layer of waxed and impregnated fabric. Nonmetallic sheathed cable is easy to "snake" or "fish" through existing walls, and so is often used, if permitted by local codes, for wiring additions or modifications. Perhaps its major shortcoming is its susceptability to mechanical damage, by nails accidentally driven through its sheathing, for example. In some places, this type of cable is called "Romex", the trade name of a specific brand.

Common sense (and the national Electric Code) dictates that nonmetallic sheathed cable should be adequately protected when installed. In most cases, this requirement is met by supporting cable with clamps, running it *through* rather than around stud work, using wood "running boards" to support cable traversing under ceiling joists, and by using wooden guard strips on either side of cable running over attic floor joists.

Flexible armored cable: the insulated conductors are wrapped in stiff paper then surrounded by a spiral-like steel armor sleeve. The sleeve's design makes it flexible. In some places, armored cable is called "BX", the trademark of a specific brand.

Armored cable cannot be used outdoors or in damp or wet indoor locations because of corrosion problems.

Steel conduit: this is, quite literally, "plumbing" for electrical wiring. Conduit is installed empty, then insulated conductors are snaked into place to complete the wiring.

There are two types of conduit: *rigid* and *thin wall.* Rigid conduit looks much like water pipe; it is joined to wiring boxes with threaded connectors. Thinwall conduit is lighter; in fact, too thin to thread (it is joined with compression-type couplings). Obviously, neither type of conduit can be snaked through existing construction; thus, conduit is best suited for new construction (and, in fact, is specified by many local codes). Conduit can be installed indoors or out, in damp or dry locations, with one major exception: it cannot be installed inside cinder block or cinder concrete due to corrosion.

NATIONAL ELECTRIC CODE

The National Electric Code is a complex mass of wiring rules and recommendations published by the National Fire Protection Association (60 Batterymarch St., Boston 02110). The code is revised every three years; the latest revision is dated 1975. The National Electric Code (or NEC) is the basis of good wiring practice. By itself, the NEC does not carry the weight of law. However, the NEC is usually the basis of local codes which are enforced by village, township, city and county electrical inspectors. Often, local codes are stricter than the NEC.

The intent of the NEC is to promote safety. Consequently it details specific methods and techniques of safe wiring practice (using "shall" and "shall not" language) that covers an extremely broad range of electrical installations, electrical wiring devices, and wiring systems. Note, though, that the code is not a how-to wiring guide.

UNDERWRITERS' LABORATORY

When a wiring device, cable, receptacle or other piece of equipment carries a label or tag that says *Underwriters' Laboratory Listed* (or, occasionally, just *UL*), it signifies that the product has been tested and found to meet *minimum safety standards* by Underwriters' Laboratory, Inc., an independent testing organization.

UL listing is not an endorsement of quality. It simply affirms that the product is safe when used for its intended purpose.

Wood Block Floors

The new parquets are easy enough to install to permit a householder with no previous wood-flooring experience to do a small room in an afternoon, a really big one in a single day. There's no nailing, sanding, staining or varnishing involved, except possibly in applying trim. Once the blocks are laid, the floor is finished.

One thing that gives the modern parquets great appeal to the do-it-yourself homeowner is their versatility. They can be laid in almost any room in any existing house no matter what the floor.

HOW TO DO IT

With either self-stick or liquid-adhesive parquet floor tiles, there are preliminary operations, of course, as well as some cut-and-fit stages. The steps that follow are specifically for the more usual tiles that do not have self-stick backing. But with a few obvious changes, they apply equally to the foam-backed tiles.

Tools and supplies you'll want to have at hand, in addition to the flooring and the special mastic adhesive, are the following: a trowel; a sponge and a bucket of water; a broom and if possible a vacuum cleaner; and a small hand or power saw.

Remove the baseboards and molding, to be put back later or replaced by new trim. Make sure your floor is clean, level and dry. Renail old wood floor where necessary. If you're working over old tiles, make sure they are securely bonded — or remove them. If only a few places are loose you can fill as shown in the photographs. Rough-sand if necessary to remove wax from old tiles. Sweep and vacuum for a thorough clean-up.

Before spreading mastic, test-lay a row of blocks each way to avoid if possible coming out along any wall with a very narrow gap to fill. The classical method of laying any tile begins with lines drawn across the center of the room at right angles to each other, but you may find it simpler to begin along one wall, especially if you are using mastic rather than self-stick methods.

Bear down as you spread the adhesive, making it as thin as possible between the notches. Adhesive too thickly applied can squeeze up between blocks and require messy clean-up.

For a typical parquet adhesive you'll want one to two notches to the inch, making them "V"

shaped and about $3/16$ inch wide and $1/4$-inch deep. To remove any adhesive that sneaks onto the surface of a block, use the solvent suggested on the adhesive label — sponge with water in case of most modern adhesives, although you will require paint thinner or mineral spirits once the adhesive has hardened.

Lay first row of blocks, the second, preferably working from center toward ends. Watch out for slipping of blocks while adhesive is setting.

Tight fit is obtainable also by use of wedge, to be removed later. Slight expansion space is a good idea, though with this type of tile it is needed only with a big room. Make it narrow enough to be covered by trim.

Except for finishing up with waxing and buffing, if the instructions with your flooring say you should, there's no more to do except replace the molding.

Wood Chisel

Wood chisels are used to remove chips or sections of wood. These kinds of chisels have steel blades with flat cutting edges and plastic or wooden handles which fit over the blades' tangs. The width of the blades range from $1/8''$ to $1\frac{1}{2}''$ with their total length ranging from $7\frac{3}{4}''$ to $10''$. *SEE ALSO HAND TOOLS.*

Wood Decks

If your house seems cramped, especially during leisure hours or while entertaining, a deck may be the answer. Building one is a way to add outdoor living space at one-tenth the cost of indoor space. Compared with adding interior space, building a deck has other attractions. It causes little household disruption. Since the carpentry can be rough, it is a do-it-yourself project for even the most inexperienced householder. Everyone in the family can help, just as everyone in the family will benefit from the deck. The deck is also a first-class investment, since one that is well-planned will add far more than its

cost to the resale value of a home. Meanwhile, it pays dividends in comfort and convenience to the homeowner.

In planning a deck, as in planning a house, location may well be your first consideration. This is true since location will be a major factor in determining both how you will use the deck and how you will go about building it.

Since the most useful deck is one designed and built to fit the special requirements of the site and the house on it, it is necessary to examine a variety of solutions, each of which will be effective in one situation but quite out of place in others.

LIVING AND ENTRY DECKS

Living decks are for the whole family, for guests, for entertaining and when they serve as entries, for visitors too. When this kind of deck is placed to serve as an entrance to the home, it gives an added feeling of hospitality and functions much

Courtesy of Western Wood Products Association

as the old front porch did, although usually placed for more privacy.

KITCHEN & FAMILY ROOM DECKS

An all-purpose deck to be used for lounging, dining, play and perhaps outdoor cooking is most useful if its access is from kitchen, dining room or family room.

BEDROOM DECKS

Unbeatable for privacy is a deck that can be reached only from a bedroom, or possible from two. Such a deck will ordinarily be a simple one, as the designs here suggest, and building it could well be a one-day or single-weekend chore.

WHERE TO PUT A DECK

From the point of view of construction, decks come in four location-types: low, high, hillside and rooftop.

Low-level decks are usually the easiest to construct and give the most utility for the cost and effort of building them. They can be supported simply on concrete piers or short posts closely spaced, so they do not need heavy girders or timbers to give them stiffness.

Their only special problem is drainage, if they are on low or dead-level ground. Provision to drain off water should be made before the deck is built, to keep the ground firm for adequate support of the deck and to avoid dampness that could encourage decay.

Courtesy of Western Wood Products, Association

High-level decks are for upstairs rooms and for houses with living quarters high above ground. Ordinarily they will require long posts spaced far apart, with girders or joists heavy enough for comparatively long spans. If the deck is narrow and is planned as part of the construction of the house, the support problem can be simplified by cantilevering the decks, which may be narrow enough to be called a balcony, from the house.

Hillside decks are usually partly high-and partly low-level decks. Typically such a deck is low-level where it is attached to the house and needs only simple supports. As it reaches away from the house, and the ground slopes away under it, it comes to need tall posts and stout framing like any high-level deck.

Rooftop decks save space and solve special problems. Such a deck will be quite simple to build where there is a flat roof, most often over a garage, and a little more complicated where the roof slopes.

KINDS OF LUMBER

While any lumber species used in construction can make a good deck, an attractive and durable one with low maintenance requires lumber with these characteristics: high decay resistance, non-splintering, wear resistance, good stiffness and strength and freedom from warping. Woods that combine these requirements to a high degree include California redwood, Douglas fir, white oak, western larch, cedar and southern pine.

If redwood is selected for its freedom from decay, grades containing sapwood should be avoided. These creamy-white streaks are as subject as any other lumber to decay. Construction heart is a comparatively economical grade of redwood that is free of sapwood.

Whatever the lumber, a surfaced grade is ordinarily required for the decking and for any bench that is part of the railing. Posts, beams, joists and possibly railings may be rough lumber. Advantages of using rough lumber are the rustic appearance with potential for weathering attractively and the greater strength it affords. Since a rough 4 x 4, for example, will average a full 4 inches and a surfaced one only about 3¹/₂, the rough timber will contain about one-third more lumber and will be stronger in the same proportion.

Where a solid deck is required, plywood is commonly used. It should be exterior type; interior type, even when made with exterior glue, is not recommended where any surface or edge is permanently exposed to the weather. Plywood marked C-C Plugged Exterior or Underlayment Exterior (C-C Plugged) is acceptable, but a higher grade such as B-C or even A-C Exterior is more often used for residential decks.

HOW TO PREVENT DECAY

The most economical way to fight off decay is to build your deck so that it drains well and does not trap moisture. A well-ventilated and well-maintained high-level deck, for example, may be as durable as the house to which it is attached — even though constructed of ordinary lumber — if it does not have shapes or joints that absorb or trap water.

Add to good design the choice of a naturally decay-resistant wood (redwood, cedar, cypress) and no initial treatment or later maintenance may be needed to avoid danger or decay.

Most effective decay-preventive of all is use of lumber that has been pressure-treated with a preservative. It is sensible to compare the cost of this kind of lumber with that of the naturally resistant species available when choosing material for deck construction.

PREPARING THE SITE

For a high-level deck, which normally means one held up by visible posts, very little site preparation may be needed. Often the ideal is to disturb the natural terrain as little as possible, while grading just enough to insure adequate rain water drainage.

When decks are made in the usual way with spaced boards, most of the water that falls on them will be absorbed by the soil underneath. Solid decks, however, behave more like roofs and may require gutters and downspouts and some kind of artificial drainage at ground level.

Courtesy of California Redwood Association

With a low-level deck, some control of weed growth may be needed, and this should be taken care of before the deck boards are laid. The objection to weeds under the deck, aside from the possibility of their growing through the cracks, is that they can lead to a high moisture content in the supporting members with danger of decay. A weed killer may be used, or the ground may be covered by a membrane of 4- or 6-mil polythylene or 30-pound asphalt-saturated felt.

MAKING FOOTINGS

Deck construction usually begins with placing of footings to support the posts that will hold up the beams or joists. The simplest approach is no footing at all: a pressure-treated pole embedded to a depth of several feet, with soil or gravel tamped around it.

JOISTS & BEAMS

If your decking is to be supported on 2-inch joists, you will want to space them from 16 to 32 inches on center, since otherwise they will handle only very short spans. The table below shows the maximum spans usually allowed, but in use should be checked against any local building code that is in force. These figures assume that the joist is placed on edge. They allow 10 pounds of dead load (meaning the weight of the decking and the joists themselves) and 40 pounds of live load (furniture and people) per square foot. This latter figure is the one usually employed in designing any part of a house. It is

MAXIMUM ALLOWABLE SPANS FOR DECK JOISTS

Species	Joist size (in.)	Joist spacing (in.) 16	24	32
Douglas fir	2 x 6	9'-9"	7'-11"	6'-2"
Larch	2 x 8	12'-10"	10'-6"	8'-1"
Southern pine	2 x 10	16'-5"	13'-4"	10'-4"
Hemlock	2 x 6	8'-7"	7'-0"	5'-8"
Fir	2 x 8	11'-4"	9'-3"	7'-6"
Douglas fir south	2 x 10	14'-6"	11'-10"	9'-6"
Redwood Cedar Spruce	2 x 6	7'-9"	6'-2"	5'-0"
	2 x 8	10'-2"	8'-1"	6'-8"
Western pine	2 x 10	13'-0"	10'-4"	8'-6"

also assumed that lumber of No. 2 grade is being used.

POST SIZES

Your final bit of engineering is the simplest. It is determining what diameter posts you will need to hold up your deck, assuming it is sufficiently high-level to need posts. It will be a question of whether you can get by safely with 4 x 4s or will have to go to 4 x 6s or 6 x 6s.

Before bothering to figure, you may want to consider the esthetic side. With a rather high deck placed so that its posts are easily seen, 4 x 4s may look so spindly, even though fully adequate to do their job, that you may prefer to go to the more expensive 6 x 6s for their appearance alone.

MINIMUM BEAM SIZES AND SPANS

Species group	Beam size (in.)	4	5	6	7	8	9	10	11	12
Douglas fir, Larch, Southern pine	4x6	Up to 6-ft. spans →								
	3x8	Up to 8-ft. →		Up to 7' →	Up to 6-ft. spans →					
	4x8	Up to 10'	Up to 9' →	Up to 8' →	Up to 7' →		Up to 6-ft. spans →			
	3x10	Up to 11'	Up to 10' →	Up to 9' →	Up to 8' →		Up to 7'. →		Up to 6-ft. →	
	4x10	Up to 12'	Up to 11' →	Up to 10' →	Up to 9-ft. →		Up to 8'. →		Up to 7'. →	
	3x12		Up to 12' →	Up to 11' →	Up to 10' →	Up to 9-ft. →	Up to 8-ft. spans →			
	4x12			Up to 12-ft. →		Up to 11' →	Up to 10-ft. →		Up to 9-ft. →	
	6x10					Up to 12' →	Up to 11' →	Up to 10-ft. spans →		
	6x12						Up to 12-ft. spans →			
Hemlock, Fir, Douglas fir south	4x6	Up to 6-ft. →								
	3x8	Up to 7-ft. →		Up to 6-ft. →						
	4x8	Up to 9'	Up to 8' →	Up to 7-ft. →		Up to 6-ft. →				
	3x10	Up to 10'	Up to 9' →	Up to 8' →	Up to 7-ft. →		Up to 6-ft. spans →			
	4x10	Up to 11'	Up to 10' →	Up to 9' →	Up to 8-ft. →		Up to 7-ft. spans →			Up to 6'
	3x12	Up to 12'	Up to 11' →	Up to 10' →	Up to 9' →	Up to 8-ft. →		Up to 7-ft. spans →		Up to 6'
	4x12		Up to 12' →	Up to 11' →	Up to 10-ft. →		Up to 9-ft. →		Up to 8-ft. →	
	6x10			Up to 12' →	Up to 11' →	Up to 10-ft. →		Up to 9-ft. spans →		Up to 8-ft. →
	6x12				Up to 12-ft. spans →			Up to 11-ft. →		Up to 10'
Redwood, Cedar, Spruce, Western pine	4x6	Up to 6'								
	3x8	Up to 7'	Up to 6' →							
	4x8	Up to 8'	Up to 7' →	Up to 6-ft. →						
	3x10	Up to 9'	Up to 8' →	Up to 7' →	Up to 6-ft. spans →					
	4x10	Up to 10'	Up to 9' →	Up to 8-ft. →		Up to 7-ft. →		Up to 6-ft. spans →		
	3x12	Up to 11'	Up to 10' →	Up to 9' →	Up to 8' →	Up to 7-ft. spans →			Up to 6-ft. →	
	4x12	Up to 12'	Up to 11' →	Up to 10' →	Up to 9-ft. →		Up to 8-ft. →		Up to 7-ft. →	
	6x10		Up to 12' →	Up to 11' →	Up to 10' →	Up to 9-ft. →		Up to 8-ft. spans →		
	6x12			Up to 12-ft. →		Up to 11-ft. →		Up to 10-ft. →		Up to 8'

For a post calculation, begin by figuring how many square feet each post will be supporting. In general, you can find this by multiplying the center-to-center spacing of the beams (or whatever timbers the posts are to hold up) by the center-to-center spacing of the posts.

When your post is Douglas fir and not over 8 feet tall, a 4 x 4 will support as much as 144 square feet of deck; for a post 8 to 10 feet tall the limit is 108 square feet; and for one 10 to 12 feet tall, 72 square feet.

A 4 x 6 Douglas fir post can be as long as 12 feet and support 120 square feet, as long as 10 feet and support 144 square feet. A 6 x 6 can be 12 feet high and still easily handle an area of as much as 144 square feet.

If your posts are western pine, cedar, spruce or redwood, they can handle 144 square feet each if they are 4 x 4s no more than 6 feet long or 4 x 6s no longer than 8 feet. They can support up to 96 square feet if they are 4 x 4s up to 8 feet long or 4 x 6s up to 10 feet. They can support 60 square feet if they are 10-foot 3 x 6s or 12-foot 4x 6s. A 12-foot-high 4 x 4 post of these species should not be asked to support more than 36 square feet of deck. If you use 6 x 6s posts they can be as tall as 12 feet and still support deck areas up to 144 square feet.

Wood Finishing

Wood is still the most common building material, but it is much more than that. It is, in a very real sense, valuable raw material. In the hands of a skilled furniture maker, wood is a "diamond" in the rough. Some pieces of furniture are not only valuable antiques, but are also true works of art.

REVIVING AND REAMALGAMATING

Beginning wood finishers assume that any old finish must be removed before the wood can look like anything at all. This is not necessarily true. Before committing yourself to the time-con-

suming job of stripping and refinishing, take a few minutes to try out a cleaner-conditioner. You can buy effective cleaner-conditioners at hardwood stores, or you can make one yourself with a mixture of 3 parts boiled linseed oil to 1 part turpentine.

A cleaner-conditioner will not only remove dirt, but clean up haziness, disguise imperfections and restore natural grain and color. For badly soiled areas, apply it hot. Grease spots or other stains may respond to simple "green soap," available at most drug stores. You may even find that a piece not in too bad condition to begin with will look like new after an old-fashioned application of white soap and water. (Use water sparingly, however, on shellac.)

There is another technique which is halfway between cleaning and complete refinishing. It's called reamalgamation, a process which more or less dissolves and re-uses the old finish. To do this, the refinisher must determine what the old finish is and use the appropriate solvent. (In all of these techniques be sure to use a spanking clean brush.)

Shellac — the solvent for shellac is alcohol. Odds are that the old finish will be shellac, and it is the easiest material to dissolve, so start with alcohol when testing. Rub a bit of denatured alcohol (shellac thinner) in an inconspicious spot. If the finish starts to fall apart, you are dealing with shellac. To reamalgamate, rub alcohol over the whole surface and spread the residue around with a rag. Let it dry and see how it looks. If this works, you may find that the new surface makes the rest of the piece look worse, and that you'll have to reamalgamate the whole thing. Even so, it's considerably less trouble than complete refinishing.

Lacquer — the solvent for lacquer is *lacquer thinner,* which is available at paint and hardware stores. The thinner will make lacquer look scuffed-up where it is applied, but the highly volatile thinner will soon evaporate, leaving the surface a little smoother and glossier than before. To reamalgamate with this, use the same technique as with shellac, but work a little faster because of rapid evaporation of the thinner.

Varnish — this finish cannot really be amalgamated, although there are several compounds on the market (mostly acetone) which claim to be able to do so. The only real solvent is paint and varnish remover, but paint and varnish remover will work on any kind of finish. That is why alcohol and lacquer thinner should be used first. If neither touches the finish, it is presumed to be varnish. As above, the "reamalgamator" is the solvent and the solvent here will remove, rather than restore, the finish.

Removing the Old Finish

The only intelligent way to remove old paint and varnish is with paint and varnish remover. You can, if you wish, save time and money by using lye or a blowtorch, but each of these other methods is too dangerous. Sandpaper is too time-consuming, particularly on curved or carved surfaces.

The best remover is the semi-paste kind which does not need a water bath when finished. It is applied from a can with a rag or brush in heavy layers, and let stand for 15 minutes or so. It is then scraped off with a wide-bladed putty knife

After the surface is scraped, it is rubbed with coarse steel wool and then washed off with a damp rag.

Usually, two, three or more applications are necessary to remove several coats of old finish. Grooves, carvings, etc., are scrubbed with an old toothbrush to get rid of all traces of old varnish or paint.

Paint and varnish remover will remove both shellac and lacquer. But if you know that the finish is not varnish, it is sometimes easier and usually cheaper to use a solvent to remove the finish.

Some shellac is a "tough" variety used on some furniture from roughly the time of the Civil War until just after World War I. It was a mixture of shellac and a primitive lacquer. Just in case you run into this type of finish, mix one part of lacquer thinner with four parts of denatured alcohol or shellac thinner. This combination will take off the toughest shellac. If you know that the finish was applied during the past 50 years, you don't have to bother with the lacquer thinner, but the mixture is good for just plain shellac, too, so many people use it routinely.

Lacquer is, of course, removed with lacquer thinner. Actually, though, lacquer thinner works smoother and faster with the addition of a little alcohol. The formula is just the opposite of the above — one part alcohol to four parts lacquer thinner. Both shellac and lacquer are removed by the same techniques as varnish remover. The job is a little less messy, though, with alcohol and lacquer thinner.

You should, by the way, be prepared for a wax coating on top of the finish, and the wax must be removed before using any remover or solvent. Remove wax by rubbing hard with a little turpentine.

Bleaching

When it looks like the job is completely done, go over it all with alcohol to remove the remover — plus dirt, grime, bits of paint, varnish, steel wool, etc. If the remover has darkened the surface, or if the color of the natural wood is just too dark for you, you may want to bleach the dark areas with a half-and-half mixture of oxalic acid and water, but regular household bleach is handier and will do almost as good a job. Don't worry about a gray or whitish cast to the wood after bleaching. It will go away once the finish is applied (unless you are working with softwood, in which case rub with 2/0-grade steel wool after bleaching).

Two-step bleaches are the best materials to use if you are trying to lighten or "lime" a dark wood. There are two bottles, labeled #1 and #2, usually, and they are applied in that order with a brush. Waiting time between the two bottles is usually 20 minutes. Here, as with any of the chemicals discussed, read and follow manufacturer's instructions carefully.

Stains

Before staining, the wood must be free of all finishing materials. At this point, a refinished piece is in the same condition as unfinished wood. The comments from here on apply equally well to either type of furniture.

Before starting staining, however, consider carefully whether or not the wood needs staining. Not every wood is improved by staining; rather, the reverse is true, that the best woods look better unstained. Included in this group, at the very least, are: butternut, cedar, cherry, chestnut, mahogany, oak, rosewood, teak and walnut. At one other end of the spectrum are woods which should be stained, because the color and grain of the neutral wood are somewhat dull. These are ash, basswood, beech, gumwood, pine and poplar. All others are in the optional category. Stain them if you think you must, but think about it, and experiment with a little finish in an inconspicuous spot to see what it might look like unstained. You may like it that way.

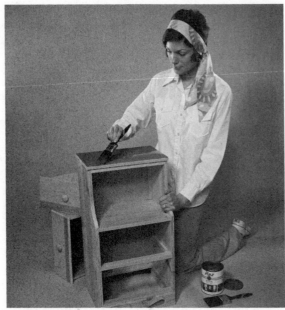

Courtesy of Pittsburg Plate Glass Industries

Although many types of stain are available, most people have the best luck with pigmented wiping stains. Most of the stains you buy at the hardware or paint store are of this type. They are easy to use and do a very creditable job. The stain is brushed on and stands for a few minutes, then is wiped off with a rag. The pigments in the stain, meanwhile, are absorbed by the softer fibers of the wood and bring out the beauty of the grain. You will not have much success with wiping stains on dense woods such as hard-rock maple. There are so few soft fibers that no stain gets absorbed. Ask your paint dealer for directions on some of the other stain types that will do for this type of wood to give it a natural finish.

SEALER COATS AND FILLERS

It is general practice to coat the stained wood with a sealer coat. Note this is not the same as penetrating sealer or a sealer finish. The term is used only to imply that this coat seals in the stain, so that it is not affected by subsequent coats of varnish or other finishes.

On the other hand, it is good to know that the "sanding sealers" sold in most paint houses are quick and effective (although more costly), so use them instead if you wish. For the purists, here are the sealer coats recommended for the various finishes:

Shellac: half shellac, half alcohol

Lacquer: half lacquer, half lacquer thinner. Two coats are required.

Varnish: half natural varnishes (no synthetics for this) and half turpentine.

After the sealer is completely dry, go over the entire wood surface thoroughly with either 4/0 (fine) sandpaper or 7/0 (very fine) steel wool. "Thoroughly" does not mean "harshly." On the contrary, the touch should be very light, and be especially careful on edges and corners so as not to cut through the thin sealer coat.

Do *not* sand at this time if you are going to use a wood filler. Whether you use a wood filler or not is a matter of taste more than necessity. Some people like the smooth, mirror-like surface that a filler gives to wood; others prefer the more natural look.

Sometimes a filler causes poor adhesion of the finish, and it is wise not to use them except when necessary. It is almost a necessity for certain coarse-grained woods to be filled. Oak and some others are so open-grained that finishes will not take (but consider penetrating sealers, instead).

Paste fillers are the most common type, although liquid fillers are available for use on fine-grained woods. Fillers come either transparent, wood-colored or pigmented. You may want to try the brightly pigmented fillers on paneling and trim, or even furniture, but the typical filler is the same shade as, or slightly darker than, the wood itself. If you wish, you can buy neutral filling material and mix in your own pigments, but the beginner should stick with the pre-mixed types.

After the mixture stands for a half hour, wipe up with a piece of cloth, followed by another cleaning with cloth or burlap. Work across the grain until all traces of filler are gone. Then take another clean piece of cloth and wipe slowly and carefully one last time, this time with the grain. When dry, touch up lightly with used 7/0 (very fine) sandpaper.

Preparing for the Finish

A refinished surface can be ready for finishing just as soon as the old finish is removed and the surface is given a final sanding. Staining, sealing and filling are optional steps. If you haven't done so before, go over the entire surface of the wood lightly with 7/0 paper before applying the finish. Don't use regular sandpaper if you can help it, but garnet or silicon carbide papers, which last longer and deposit less grit. Even if you stain, seal and fill the surface, this final once-over sanding is important for a smooth surface. Actually, worn or used paper is best, since it is even less abrasive than new paper.

The raw wood used in unfinished furniture requires careful and thorough sanding, starting with a medium grit and working down to very fine or superfine grades of the better sandpapers. Wrap strips around a sanding block (a piece of 2 x 4 will do) and you will work faster and better on flat surfaces.

No matter what finish you use, make sure that the surface is extremely smooth, clean and dust-free before application. Wipe the surface with a tack-cloth, available at paint stores, before finishing. The tack cloth picks up even minute pieces of dirt and dust embedded in the finish as it dries. You will be surprised at how noticeable a speck of dirt is on a newly finished surface.

Which Finish

There are lots of furniture finishes available, but there is little reason to use anything other than quick-drying varnish. Varnishes, particularly the modern synthetics, offer ease of application, relatively fast drying time, a fine-looking warm glow and—best of all—a hard surface that is impervious to water, alcohol, dirt, grit and the blows of children.

Shellac, though it provides a beautiful finish after a number of coats, simply will not hold up to liquids. If you like it (and most people do), use it in places where it will get little wear like picture and mirror frames and hatracks. Shellac is easy to apply and gives a nicer look to pine and other light woods than varnish. Do not use it, though, if there is any chance of contact with liquids.

Lacquer, on the other hand, stands up beautifully to liquids, is very fast-drying, and imparts a lovely clear finish. It is quite difficult to apply except with expensive spray equipment.

Linseed oil makes a nice finish if it is applied correctly but it can take up to a year of applications and is often unsuccessful with beginners. If you like the natural look, a penetrating resin sealer is easy to use and wears quite well. Many people do not like the neutrality of penetrating sealers, but they certainly are a boon to those who want a quick, tough finish.

Wax is often considered to be a finish, but it isn't. It can be a protective coating over a sealer or some other finish. *Never use wax on bare wood as it gets gummy and grimy.*

Using Shellac

Shellac is made from an insect secretion called "lac" combined with alcohol. The degree of dilution with alcohol is called a "cut." The novice should start with a "thin" cut, one pound or so. Buy three- and four-pound cuts and cut them with half as much (50 percent) alcohol. As you get better at the job, use less and less alcohol, but remember that all shellac must be cut with *some* alcohol. Use white shellac unless you want the dark coloring of orange shellac.

Since even quick-drying varnish takes longer to dry than shellac, many finishers use a coat or two of shellac first, then follow it with another coat of varnish. Another professional trick is to give the entire piece a couple of coats of shellac and then just use varnish on the top or other vulnerable places.

Apply shellac with a perfectly clean brush, using long, even strokes and slightly lapping each time.

When the first coat has dried completely, rub it down with a piece of 3/0 steel wool, then wipe with a dry cloth to remove dust and steel frag-

ments. Apply at least one more coat in the same manner, then perhaps a third or even more. The more the better, but three are usually enough, and two will suffice under varnish or in areas that are not subject to hard wear.

When you have applied the final coat, examine the gloss. If you like it (somewhat shiny), rub down the final coat with the finest grade of steel wool you can find, 5/0, 6/0 or even finer. A duller, "satin" finish is more popular today. For this, use 3/0 steel wool. When finished, rub thoroughly with a clean, dry cloth and put on an application of wax.

Varnish

Although dust specks are somewhat of a problem with shellac, they become a real headache when using varnish. It is imperative to work in as dust-free environment as possible.

There are many kinds of varnish available, and the best guide for applying them are on the labels of the various containers. A few general rules apply such as, the varnish should be quick-drying. Polyurethane is considered the best all-around varnish. It is a plastic varnish, however,

Courtesy of Armstrong Cork Company

and should not be applied over shellac unless the label says it is all right.

The one kind of varnish you must not use is spar varnish. As the name implies, it is meant for boats and other outdoor uses. The formula contains virtually no drying agent, so that the sun does not dry it out, which means that it stays tacky for days.

Varnish is best applied with a good quality, two-inch bristle brush. Again, the brush must be clean. Although there are a few types of varnish, like certain satin urethanes, which should be stirred, the vast majority of varnishes should be disturbed only as necessary. Do not stir them, do not rub the brush along the rim and do not dip the brush too far into the container. Any action that causes bubbles should be avoided.

When applying varnish, hold the brush almost straight, bending the bristles just a little. *Flow* the varnish on parallel with the grain, then brush at right angles. Finish by *tipping off* (stroking lightly) with just the tips of an almost dry brush. Work with the grain only during this step.

As you work, try to pick off any settled dust with a cotton swab. Let the surface dry thoroughly,

One coat of varnish is enough over shellac, and two should be enough for any other surface.

Between coats, varnish should be rubbed down with a very fine grade of sandpaper or steel wool. Always work with the grain when sanding, and work lightly. Dust thoroughly and go over with a tack rag before applying another coat.

The final step in varnishing should be another rub-down with very fine steel wool or pumice and oil after the varnish has cured for a week. Rub the pumice and machine-oil mix into the surface in the direction of the grain with a folded pad of heavy, lint-free cloth. Wipe off with another clean, dry cloth. If the surface is too dull for your taste, give it yet another rub-down with rottenstone and oil for a smooth sheen. Both pumice and rottenstone are available at paint and hardware dealers.

Using Penetrating Sealers

Probably the most convenient of all finishes, penetrating sealers, are often neglected by the home wood finisher and by the paint store, too. Sealers dry very quickly and are thus not subject to annoying dust on the surface while drying. They are resistant to moisture, alcohol, acids, alkalis, heat, cold, grease and scuffing. However, the invisible look of penetrating sealers makes them unsuitable for those woods that do not have a natural sheen.

When buying sealers, read the labels carefully. Make sure that you are getting a thin penetrating resin sealer, one that contains varnish, not wax. Exceptions are Early American styles of furniture, which look better with wax added; and open-pored woods, which take a thick sealer.

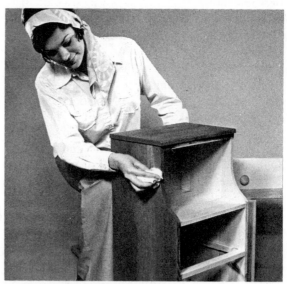

Courtesy of Pittsburg Plate Glass Industries

The sealer is applied with a piece of clean, lint-free cloth used in a circular motion, working mainly across the grain. Let it sit for about 10 minutes, then wipe off with a similar piece of cloth.

The next step is hand rubbing. This is done immediately after the excess sealer is wiped off. Simply rub your hands over the just-finished surface, warming the sealer and helping its absorption into the pores of the wood.

After waiting 24 hours, smooth the surface gently with a piece of 3/0 steel wool. Wipe with a clean cloth, then a tack cloth. After this step, you can go to a wax coating, or some varnish. Sealer purists, however, will simply go to another coat of the same material. On the second and subsequent coats, many finishers use "crocus cloth" instead of the clean, lintless cloths used for the first coat. Crocus cloth is impregnated with iron oxide and imparts a reddish tint to the wood as well as an extra smoothness. It should be used only on darker shades of wood, and once the color is imparted, it cannot be removed. It is best to use crocus cloth first in an inconspicuous corner where you can observe the effect.

At least three coats of sealer are required, and probably more. The only reliable rule is to stop when you like the way the finish looks. When you do reach this stage, give the piece a good final rubdown with 4/0 or 5/0 steel wool and/or the pumice/oil mixture discussed above.

Linseed Oil

Whenever linseed oil is discussed in furniture work, *boiled* linseed oil is meant. And it isn't really boiled at all. Drying agents have been added, and that's the only real difference. "Raw" linseed oil does not contain dryers and is used in spar varnish and some house paint.

The surface to be worked on must be perfectly smooth, wiped with a dry cloth and a tack rag. Mix the boiled linseed oil two-to-one with mineral spirits or turpentine, then heat in a double boiler (never directly over the heat because of the fire hazard).

Apply the mixture with a lint-free cloth, working on the flat surface first, then the carved or grooved parts after the mix has cooled. Keep rubbing for five to 20 minutes or until the wood can absorb no more. Wipe away the excess, changing cloths as soon as they become saturated. Be particularly careful to remove the oil from all crevices, or it will harden and become sticky. (Actually, if the piece contains many cracks and grooves where oil will get trapped, a linseed finish should not be used.) After all the excess oil is removed, polish each section for 10 to 20 minutes. A piece of flannel can be used for this, but a firmly woven, hard cloth is best. Keep rubbing until you can put your hand down and pick up no trace of oil. Four coats at the very least must be applied with a week's drying time in between. For a truly fine finish, however, between eight and 12 coats should be used. It is not unknown to keep applying coats for up to a year. To keep the finish looking nice, a "booster" coat should be given every six months.

Wax and Polish

Wax and polish are used to preserve and protect wood. Neither should be used on bare wood, although both can be used on any finished surface. There is a bewildering array of polishes on the market and it is difficult to know what is really in any of them (oils and waxes, most likely). Tung oil is one of the best old polishes, but it is hard to find.

A true wax "finish" is beautiful when it is done well, but it is a lot of work. The important thing to remember is to use paste wax, as hard a variety as possible, and lots of rubbing. The best paste wax contains a high proportion of carnauba wax, the hardest kind, or candelilla wax, second hardest. Many people use an automotive wax like Simonize.

Wax must always be applied as thinly as possible. This doesn't mean to skimp, but to apply it thoroughly without any thick build-up. The more you rub each coat, the better it looks.

A penetrating sealer finish requires several coats of wax, but varnish requires just one, or none, if you prefer. Occasional polishing is all that new furniture, with a factory sprayed lacquer finish, requires. Shellac wears better with a coat or two of wax, and most other finishes benefit from a little wax. No matter what the type of finish, the coats should always be very thin.

After six months or so, wax needs rebuffing and perhaps another coat. Just so many coats can be applied, however, before the finish starts to look gummy or overshiny. When that happens, remove all the wax with turpentine or mineral spirits and start over.

"Woodgraining" is a technique similar to antiquing, and can be used on metal or any other material. A base coat (A) is laid down, then a stain is applied, let dry for 20 minutes, and wavy lines are drawn with a dry brush (B). To complete the effect, use special tool to remove enough stain to allow the base coat to show through (C).

PAINT

All the finishes mentioned so far are designed to bring out the natural wood grain, to enhance the appearance of the fine wood. Paint is designed to *cover* the grain and hide the wood. It seems clear, then, that paint should be used only when the wood surface is so badly damaged, or poorly grained, that it would look better covered up.

One of the virtues of paint is that stripping of the old finish is unnecessary. The surface should, however, be sanded to remove rough spots and peeling finish.

Enamel, which is really just varnish with a pigment, is the type of paint ordinarily used on furniture, but semi-gloss is sometimes used for a more satin look. Never use latex or other water-soluble paints for furniture.

Antiquing

Antiquing has become very popular over the past few years, and it is a clever way to give furniture an older look without going through the rather involved steps in true refinishing. Ready-made kits, with all materials and tools inside, have made antiquing an easy job for the beginning finisher.

What the kits contain, in addition to cheap brushes, cheesecloth, etc., are enamel and glaze or "toner." You can mix your own toner if you like, using the following formula:

> 3 tablespoons gum turpentine
> 1 tablespoon varnish
> 1 teaspoon of desired oil color(s)

The most commonly used oil colors are the earth colors, like raw or burnt umber and the siennas, although you can add any color that suits your fancy. Mix the ingredients thoroughly and remember that a little bit of oil color goes a long way. For the "base coat" use ordinary enamel in an appropriate color.

When applying the base coat, use the same techniques as with enamel or varnish. The glaze is put on with a flat, wide brush in long, even strokes with the grain. Do the carved surfaces first, to allow more absorption of the glaze.

Work on one surface at a time, allowing the glaze to set for 10 to 20 minutes before wiping. Then wipe away with a soft, clean cloth. Use a circular motion, starting at the center of flat surfaces and working toward the edges. Turn your cloth to a fresh surface after each wiping. Leave the center lightest, with the color darkening gradually toward the edges. Remember that the glaze is supposed to replace the patina of age, and that the areas which would ordinarily receive more wear (like the center) are to be wiped cleanest and left with just a little glaze.

Blend by patting the surface with a clean piece of cheesecloth, then go over very lightly with a dry paint brush. This last step is barely perceptible, yet it is the most important step in achieving an authentic look. To achieve a woodgrain effect, make the lines slightly wavy. The glazed surface, when completely dry, should be protected with a coat of varnish. This last coat can be given a pumice oil treatment

Wood Float

A wood float is a piece of wood with a handle used to smooth concrete surfaces. A wood float smoothes, levels and gives the concrete a rough surface. *SEE ALSO CONCRETE & MASONRY TOOLS.*

Wood Identification

The structure of wood is basically uniform for every kind of tree, which makes identification of the different types easier. There are several keys to follow in identifying wood, and it is wise to consider more than one of these characteristics to be accurate.

The first key is based on color. Wood is either whitish, yellowish, purplish or crimson, reddish or pinkish, brownish, or blackish or grayish.

Secondary color is the shade of the heartwood of the timber. Some woods have a combination of colors on their surface.

The annual growth rings are another important characteristic. The rings are usually distinct, except for some species which are classified as *rings obscure.*

The grain, which is the pattern or appearance of the pores and rings together, is also either distinct or obscure, as are the rays, cells extending radially within the tree.

The smell of the wood comes from the volatile chemicals contained in the timber, so freshly cut or felled timber smells strongest. Smell decreases as the wood gets older, but exposure of a fresh surface to an open space restores the scent.

Wood Joints

The important factors to consider when choosing a type of wood joint are appearance, strength, the tools available to work with, and the materials involved.

Appearance depends upon the project. For example, utility shelves in the basement or the garage do not have to be as pretty as a piece of furniture. Although the joints must be strong, the application will tolerate exposed end grain, visible nails, screws or reinforcement hardware and even uncovered plywood edges.

Strength is a common factor but it is not dependent entirely on the design of the joint. Reinforcements and modern adhesives can compensate for minimum contact surfaces in the joint.

The kind of tools that are available to work with can be a consideration. *Any* joint can be made with hand tools, but designs like the dovetail, the mortise-tenon and the fingerlap are much easier to do when the handyman has equipment like a stationary saw, a drill press or a router.

The material plays a major role in joint selection. The prime example is plywood because, when working with this material, a joint that conceals edges is usually chosen.

GLUE AREA

The amount of glue area, which has a bearing on strength, depends on the shape of the joint. The miter joint is very common, yet it really does not have much more strength than a simple butt joint. The slant-cut of the miter does provide a little more gluing surface, but the main reason for its choice is that it conceals end or edge grain. The strongest miter is one that is reinforced with a spline or with concealed glue blocks.

In all cases, it will be evident that more glue area can be obtained by cutting fancier joints. Check for this by comparing a fingerlap with a miter, or a dado with a butt or a plain edge-to-edge joint with one that is splined. Of course, the fancier joints also have some degree of interlock which contributes to strength. The great feature of the dovetail, for example, is that the parts will hold together even if the glue fails.

JOINT STRESS

Try to visualize the stress that will be applied to a joint. A drawer, especially one that must hold heavy contents, takes much punishment where the side of the drawer is connected to the front. The dovetail is often used here but similar strength characteristics can be achieved by forming a rabbet in the drawer-front and connecting the side with glue and dowels or screws.

Such factors as stress causing compression, twisting or components pulling apart are guides for joint selection and the amount of reinforcement or modification of a joint.

BUTT JOINTS

The basic objection to a butt joint when used at a corner is that the end grain of one of the components is exposed. Yet, when the end grain is sealed, sanded and finished, it is not really objectionable and can even be a detail of the overall design.

EDGE-TO-EDGE JOINTS

An edge-to-edge joint is actually a butt joint used mostly to form slabs from narrow pieces. It is done often with solid lumber but chances of success with better grades of plywood are also good. Modern adhesives make it feasible to do such joints without reinforcement, especially when the material is $3/4$ inches thick and up. Extra attention to the mating edges provides a safety factor. When constructing a large slab, edge treatments such as dowels, splines, tongue and groove, etc., do much to keep the parts in alignment.

Warpage is more likely to result when wide boards are used to make a slab. It is better to rip the boards into narrow pieces about four inches and glue them back together after inverting alternate ones. This establishes a grain pattern that counteracts the cumulative warpage that might otherwise result.

DADOES AND GROOVES

U-shaped cuts are *dadoes* when formed *across* the grain and *grooves* when formed *with* the grain. Typical applications are shelves, vertical dividers in case goods, letting in of drawer bottoms and backs, etc. In the case of shelves, these

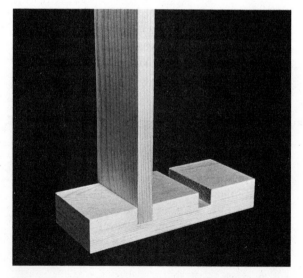

The dado is a U-shaped cut that is made *across* the grain of the wood. It can be done by using a dado assembly on a power saw or by working with a handsaw and a chisel.

joints are much stronger than a butt joint because of the extra gluing area and because the shelf actually sits on a ledge.

MORTISE-TENON

The mortise-tenon is one of the joints which demonstrates dedicated craftsmanship. It takes some time to do, especially when working with hand tools, but it does pay off in terms of strength and durability. Typical applications are joining rails to legs for chairs, tables or benches, stretcher assemblies, T joints, etc.

The joint consists of a square or round-end cavity or *mortise* in one part and a mating projection or *tenon* on the other part. The tenon is easy to cut on a table saw by making multiple cuts with a regular saw blade or by working with a dado assembly. The mortise becomes relatively easy if special equipment is used on a drill press.

Another way to form the mortise is to drill a series of overlapping holes on a drill press or by hand and then clean out the waste stock with a sharp chisel. When done in this manner the ends of the slot can be left round and the tenon is about $1/_{32}$ inch less than the depth of the mortise. This will provide room for excess glue.

RABBETS

The rabbet is an L-shaped cut that runs along ends or edges of stock. Like a dado, it can be cut on a table saw with a regular saw blade or by using a dado assembly or with a portable router. It is an improvement from a butt joint when used on corners, but only because the extra glue area provides more strength and the shoulder helps fight some stresses. When viewed from the front edge of the assembly, its appearance is as objectionable as the dado's. Typical applications are letting in the back on a piece of case goods, shelves, drawer fronts, etc. Often, it is used in combination with a dado where it does much the same job as a tongue and groove assembly.

Generally, the width of a rabbet equals the thickness of the stock to be inserted. Its depth should be about three fourths that thickness. The same types of reinforcements used for the butt joint may be used with the rabbet joint.

MITERS

Miters are popular joints simply because they hide end-grain. However, they are not much stronger than butt joints. Splines are the best type of reinforcement to use. A bonus feature of splines is that they maintain alignment of the parts when gluing or clamping.

Be especially careful when making the angle cuts for miter joints. A tiny error multiplied eight times is a sizable gap at assembly time. The compound miter, often seen on picture frames, requires very precise cutting. When done on a table saw, for example, the cut requires both a blade tilt and a miter gauge setting.

The compound angle joint involves a combination miter and bevel cut. It is often called a "hopper" joint and is seen frequently on picture frames.

LAP JOINTS

Joints of this type are strongest when they are *full laps* or *half laps*. In both cases, the interlocking feature of the designs adds strength and an antitwist feature that a simple overlap cannot provide. For both the full and the half, the width of the cut equals the width of the insert piece. Depth of cut for the full lap equals the thickness of the insert. For the half lap, cut-depth is one-half the thickness.

Courtesy American Plywood Association

Wood Paneling

PANELING WITH BOARDS

Plain boards butted together and firmly fastened are the most elementary form of paneling,

These may be merely butted together, or battens can cover the joints. This is a logical treatment when the house has a board-and-batten exterior; it is particularly effective when continued past a window wall so that both exterior and interior board-and-batten walls are seen at the same time.

Before You Panel

Most paneling is done with lumber that has been thoroughly kiln-dried at the mill but it may not be as dry as it looks by the time you get it. That is

why it's best to buy far enough ahead so that you can *stick* the lumber for at least a week, to let it assume a moisture content similar to that of the house in which it is being used. Very dry lumber put up in a room that becomes humid could bulge and cup; moist lumber that dries after being installed will show cracks between pieces. The sticking method is also useful if you buy green lumber for reasons of availability or economy and want to let it air-dry before turning it into paneling.

Any finish that changes the color of the wood at all should be applied before the paneling is put up—and not only because it's easier then. Getting finish onto the tongues or laps of matched boards means cracks will be less noticeable as boards move with changes in humidity.

How to Put up Paneling

Correct nail selection is the most important part of proper application procedures. Choice of size

Courtesy of Western Wood Products Association

and type of nail will depend upon what is being nailed and where.

Tongue and Groove

This pattern should be nailed directly to the framing members in both horizontal and vertical applications. Vertical applications require furring strips 48 inches O.C.

Blind Nailing. Narrow widths (4, 5, 6 inches) of T&G are normally blind nailed. This eliminates the need for counter-sinking and filling, and results in a smooth blemish-free surface. For this reason, blind nailing is of particular importance when a natural, bleach or varnish is applied. In the narrower widths, standard 6d finish nails are recommended for interior work.

Face Nailing. It is important to countersink nails slightly and fill depression with a wood putty or filler when treating interior walls. Oil putty will leave oil rings unless a linseed oil stain is planned for use. Face nail panels 6 inches or less with one nail per bearing. For 8 inches or wider use two nails per bearing.

Board and Batten

Fasten the under board with one 8d nail per bearing driven through the center of the board. Underboards should be spaced approximately $1/2$ inch apart. One 10d nail per bearing is driven through the center of the batten strip, so that the shank passes between the edges of the underboards.

PANELING WITH PREFINISHED OR TEXTURED PLYWOOD

There is probably no other single home improvement that will do as much for the appearance of your home while demanding so little in time, money and skill as a wall or more of prefinished plywood paneling.

In choosing your paneling you can select today from actually hundreds of grains, groove patterns and extremely durable factory-applied finishes. This type of paneling, by far the most popular for the purpose, can be used only indoors. It is usually $1/4$ inch thick, or slightly less.

American Plywood Association

1904

Courtesy of American Plywood Association

Its face veneer has been toned with a stain or other nonopaque finishing material and then given some sort of protective coating; less often, it has been printed with a woodgrain or a graphic design or, in one particular type, given an enamel-like surface in a bright color. In most instances the surface will contain a series of parallel V-grooves and the long edges will be eased in such a way that when two panels have their edges butted together a joint is formed that closely resembles the grooves and so is not noticeable. Whatever the spacing of the grooves, whether regular or apparently random, there will normally be a groove at 16 inches from each side of the panel, at the point where the center of a 2 x 4 stud will fall in the most usual kind of frame wall construction.

Paneling with Exterior Siding

The other answer to the problem of getting an attractive finish when using softwood or other inexpensive kinds of plywood is the use of textured exterior siding. This, too, has grooves of one type or another, matched by eased or shiplap edges to make it difficult for the eye to see where one panel ends and the next begins. The texture on most types of siding makes the grain much less prominent and makes finishing easier.

Most usual of the textured sidings are those made of softwoods with faces grooved and textured, but not finished. Easiest way to use these for interior paneling is by prefinishing them with brush or roller with the panels placed conveniently face up on a bench or table or across saw horses.

Measuring

Having determined the kind of plywood you are going to use and on which walls, you will want to start by measuring to see how many panels to buy, allowing doors, windows and fireplaces. Begin by determining the perimeter. This is merely the total of the widths of all the walls in the room. Use the conversion table below to figure how many panels you will need.

Perimeter	No. of 4 x 8 Panels Needed
36 feet	9
40 feet	10
44 feet	11
48 feet	12
52 feet	13
56 feet	14
60 feet	15
64 feet	16
68 feet	17
72 feet	18
92 feet	23

For example, if your room walls measured 14 feet ± 14 feet ± 16 feet ± 16 feet, this would equal 60 feet or 15 panels required. To allow for areas such as windows, doors, fireplaces, etc., use these deductions listed below:

Deductions	
Door	½ panel (A)
Window	¼ panel (B)
Fireplace	½ panel (C)

Thus, the actual number of panels for this room would be 13 pieces (15 pieces minus 2 total deductions). If the perimeter of the room falls in between the figures in the above table, use the next highest number to determine panels required. These figures are for rooms with 8 inch ceiling heights or less.

Methods of Fastening

No matter whether the application is direct to studs or over backer board or over an old wall, panel edges should join over a stud. For application direct to studs, use 1 to $1\frac{1}{4}$ inch (3d) finishing nails. You can set the nails $\frac{1}{32}$ inch and fill the holes with matching putty stick or other wood dough or filler or eliminate this chore by using colored nails.

For application over furring, the recommendation is for use of the same nails but spaced 8 inches along the edges of the panels and 16 inches (going into the horizontal furring) elsewhere.

Courtesy of Western Wood Products Association

Courtesy of Georgia Pacific

Panel adhesives or other construction adhesives in tubes to fit squeeze guns may be used, as may wallboard mastics applied from a can. Contact-bond cement is also effective, although somewhat slower to use since it must be applied to the studs or furring, or in stripes on an existing wall, and then in matching stripes on the backs of the panels.

Installing Molding

The secret of a good, professional-looking molding job is to start with accurate measurements. Measure along the ceiling line for the cove or crown molding, along the floor for the exact length of base and shoe molding. It is not safe to assume that the floor and the ceiling are the same length.

The basic operation in working with molding is mitering joints. Unless a table saw or radial saw is close at hand, use a miter box with a fine-tooth saw for accuracy. Most cuts will be either at right angles, where a piece of molding stops, or at 45 degrees. Make 45-degree cuts in pairs not only for both inside and outside corners but also, for neatness where a splice is required. Such a cut takes no longer than 90-degree ones and makes for a much neater fit.

Courtesy of Western Wood Products Association

Fasten the molding in place with 3d finish nails, countersunk and filled (or not, just as with the paneling) or use colored nails to match. You can also use panel or construction adhesive, an especially good idea in tight corners and where there is no satisfactory surface to nail to.

Prefinished Moldings

Prefinished moldings available today include not only wood but also vinyl (polyvinyl chloride), which is tough in use and easy to work with because it is not delicate. Prefinished moldings are, frankly, expensive but will match many prefinished panelings.

Special Problems

Plywood paneling should generally not be put directly over a masonry wall, even one that is sound and level. Furring in the pattern should be applied, along with a layer of polyethylene sheeting if there is any possibility of dampness. With the ordinary load-bearing stud wall with double top plate, the paneling may be applied over studs placed on 24 inch centers with satisfactory solidity only if it is thicker than the usual prefinished types.

One problem, is making cut-outs for electric outlet and switch boxes, and getting them in the right places the first time so that you don't wind up with a damaged panel to salvage. The errors to which this method is prone can be eliminated by use of a special measuring device you may find in your hardware store or where panels are sold. Another approach is to make a little device of sheet metal that will fit onto the box and, with small prongs, mark the back of the panel when you press the panel temporarily into place to check for fit. Even simpler, if the electric box protrudes slightly above the old wall surface, is to rub chalk over it and transfer this to the back of the panel by tapping the plywood.

In some paneling situations it will be necessary to move electric boxes outward by the amount of

Courtesy of Western Wood Products Association

1908

thickness added to the wall by furring strips and paneling.

This job can be avoided when only a small change is required, as when installing the paneling right onto an old wall surface, by putting one or two little washers under the screws by which the switch or outlet is mounted in its box. To get just the right thickness automatically, instead of washers you can shim the switch or outlet with a scrap of the paneling material you are using wedged under each mounting ear beside the screw.

Wood Preservatives

Wood preservatives are substances which are applied to wood to protect against deterioration resulting from insect or fungus attack, especially where the wood is exposed to moisture. The most commonly used wood preservatives are oil-based creosote, and the modern preservatives pentachlorophenol and zinc and copper napthenates in a petroleum solution, and water-soluble salts, such as copper sulfate. A sufficient amount of the chemical must penetrate the wood as deeply as possible for effective results.

The commercial preservatives, prepared for on-the-job use, are applied by brushing, spraying or soaking, the latter being the recommended method. Paint may be applied after the preservative has completely dried. *SEE ALSO PRESERVATIVES.*

Wood Rasps

Wood rasps have slightly coarser teeth than files and are used primarily for removing general wood stock before smoothing with a file. Wood rasps, similar in shape to some files, are available in flat, round and half-round styles, with the most common being the half-round. *SEE ALSO HAND TOOLS.*

Wood Siding

Wood siding is one of the most popular, attractive and economical exterior coverings used in building construction. Types of wood siding include board and batten, shiplap, bevel siding, vertical boards and many types of hardwood and plywood coverings. Wood siding is very sturdy, providing for decreased maintenance and repair costs. It may be painted, stained or simply left to weather, and the beauty of real wood is increased with age. Wood provides natural insulation, cutting down on heating and air conditioning expenses and it is very versatile in terms of architectural styles. *SEE ALSO SIDING.*

Courtesy of California Redwood Association

Natural redwood siding forms a pleasing background for massed flowers. Saved trees provide shade.

1909

Courtesy of Western Wood Products Association

Hardboard siding can be made to resemble shake or shingle installations.

Wood siding provides a warm-toned background for a dramatic fire pit. Courtesy of Western Wood Products Association

Woodworker's Vise

A woodworker's vise is used only with wood and, unlike most vises, is mounted below the bench so that the jaws are flush with the bench surface. Most models have a stop in the outer jaws that can be raised above the bench, and a few are equipped with a half thread that allows the jaws to slide against the work without much handle turning. The jaws of the woodworker's vise should have a 12 inch capacity and open and close rapidly. Some jaws will already be padded with wood to protect the wood surface, but if not, scrap wood can be used. Woodworker's vises are used for holding wood tightly during sawing, planing, filing and gluing. *SEE ALSO HAND TOOLS.*

Workbenches

Workbenches are an essential part of any workshop. They should be selected and designed according to the amount and type of work to be done and the space available. Kits which have materials for a workbench can be purchased and the workbench assembled at home. For an inexpensive workbench, an old chest or desk will provide drawer space, and a larger and sturdier top may be attached. A multi-purpose bench may also be adapted for workbench use.

The size of a workbench will depend on individual preference. Most workbenches are from 24 to 30 inches wide and four feet or more long. The height should be anywhere from 30 to 36 inches, with the top about even with the handyman's hip joint to avoid stooping. There should be at least 18 inches clearance at each end to provide room for working.

A workbench is usually placed against one wall, but it is up to the individual handyman where it will be placed. If the workshop is small, try a fold-down workbench, which may be folded against the wall and out of the way. If space is not a problem, the workbench may be placed in the middle of the room and all four sides will be clear for working.

The top of the workbench is usually plywood, hardboard or composition board. Some carpet scraps may be attached to form a surface where easily scratched objects can be repaired. Carpet also keeps tools and materials from rolling off the workbench top. A yardstick is handy if attached along the top edge of the workbench. Containers or built-in shelves or holders are necessary to hold tools so that the workbench does not become a catch-all for tools. Drawers and shelf space underneath the workbench also provide needed storage space. Good lighting is essential, and electrical outlets should be placed near the workbench for use with power tools.

Workshops

In the literal sense a workshop is a room or a building where work is done.

The location of the shop is not important but it should be as large as possible, well designed for maximum storage, and should contain a full complement of hand and power tools. The expense and effort of the organization is justified by the interest.

There is a *minimal* shop, an *average* shop, and an *advanced* shop. The first one is usually a few hand tools or stored tool chest. The second one

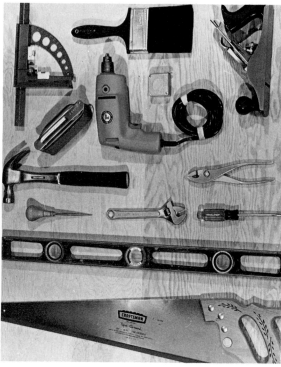

Here is a set of tools that should be in every homeowner's shop. Much home maintenance and many small projects can be accomplished with this basic assortment. Shop space requirements are minimal.

The hobbyist who does woodworking strictly for fun will use:		As a craftsman interested mostly in home maintenance chores, you will need:	
STATIONARY	**PORTABLE**	**STATIONARY**	**PORTABLE**
Jigsaw	Pad sander	Table saw	1/4" drill (w/variable speed)
Lathe	1/4" drill (w/variable speed)		Belt sander
Drill press			Pad sander (optional)
Disc-belt sander			
If you are a dedicated craftsman but with tastes that run to simplicity in style such as modern furniture and built-ins, then you will need the following:		The dedicated craftsman who wants everything he needs to produce fine pieces of furniture will need:	
STATIONARY	**PORTABLE**	**STATIONARY**	**PORTABLE**
Table saw	Pad sander	Table saw	Pad sander
Drill press	Sabre saw	Drill press	Router
Disc-belt sander	1/4" drill (w/variable speed)	Disc-belt sander	1/4" drill (w/variable speed)
Jointer	Belt sander router	Lathe	Belt sander
		Jigsaw	
		Jointer	
		Band saw	

must be viewed in terms of work scope. The third speaks for itself. In all cases, what you plan to do bears much on tool choice and the number of tools you should have. The more tools, the bigger the shop.

Workshop Safety

Safety rules are as applicable to the experienced handyman as they are to the beginner. Statistics show that people familiar with tools have more accidents than amateurs. They use the tools more often, no longer have the beginner's fear of them, and therefore get careless.

SAFETY TIPS FOR USING TOOLS

As a general procedure, inspect a tool before using it. Make sure that it is clean and in good condition. Grease or oil on the handle is an invitation to injury. Look for those parts or other defects that might cause malfunctions.

Hand Tools

1. Make sure wood handles are sound and free of splinters. Check hammer and hatchet heads to be sure they are securely attached.

2. Keep the blades of cutting tools sharp and properly beveled. Working with a sharp tool is more efficient and presents less danger of injury resulting from the blade slipping or sticking.

3. Use tools only as they were designed to be used. The use of a screwdriver as a pry bar is dangerous.

4. Don't brace lumber with a knee when sawing; clamp it.

5. Hold a nail near the head when first driving it. This avoids smashing fingers between the hammer and another unyielding surface.

6. When using a wrench, either pull the handle toward you or push with your hand open. If the wrench slips, there is less chance of smashing or skinning knuckles.

7. Keep the sharp points and edges of tools pointing down when not in use. Never carry sharp tools in pockets.

Power Tools

1. Always unplug tools before changing bits or blades.

2. Set table saw blades so that only two or three teeth appear above the material being sawed.

3. Use a push stick to guide narrow pieces of wood through a table saw.

4. Do not stand directly in line with an operating saw blade.

5. Wait until the action of a portable power tool stops before laying it down. Never turn a power tool on until it is firmly in hand.

6. Do not force tools. Find out what is causing the problem if a tool refuses to work.

7. Stop work before becoming too tired. Remaining alert is a most important safety precaution.

8. Do not be distracted while working. Stop work to chat. Do not try to eat or drink, especially alcoholic beverages, while working.

9. Do not leave a power tool while it is in operation.

10. Never use a power tool around inflammable liquids or gases. A spark from the motor can cause an explosion.

11. Before using any power tool, roll shirt sleeves above the elbow, and remove all jewelry.

Wrecking Bar

A wrecking bar has one slightly offset chisel end for prying. The other end has a gooseneck shape and is specially designed for pulling up tough nails and spikes. Most wrecking bars are 18 to 30 inches long. *SEE ALSO HAND TOOLS.*

Wrenches

Wrenches are used in both wood and metal-work, plumbing and auto maintenance mainly for adjusting nuts and bolts. Open-end, socket, box and adjustable are among the more common wrench types. *SEE ALSO HAND TOOLS.*

Yankee® Push Drill

A Yankee® push drill is designed to drill small holes quickly. The ratchet action of the spirally threaded shaft allows the bit to revolve several times with a single push stroke of the drill. Yankee® push drills are used many times to drill pilot holes for nails and screws or to drill a starting hole for a larger drill. *SEE ALSO HAND TOOLS.*

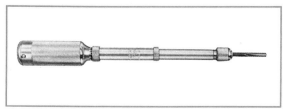

Courtesy of The Stanley Works
Yankee® Push Drill

Yankee® Screwdriver

Yankee® is a trademark of Stanley Works, Inc., that is used in connection with a variety of screwdrivers such as the offset ratchet, cabinet and standard, but is most commonly associated with the spiral-ratchet screwdriver. *SEE ALSO HAND TOOLS.*

Yardstick

The yardstick is a piece of wood or metal three feet long, one to one and one half inches wide and $1/8$ to $1/4$ inch thick. It has marked graduations on both sides that usually run as small as $1/16$ inch. A yardstick nailed to the surface of a workshop bench is good for measuring and marking lumber in rough cutting. Placed on one end, it can measure vertical distance and, when held horizontally on a surface, it can serve as a straightedge for making even lines. If a yardstick is going to be used often as a straightedge, the metal ones are best since they don't chip or break as easily as the wooden variety. There are many uses for a yardstick and its only drawback is that most are only three feet long and cannot precisely measure long distances. *SEE ALSO HAND TOOLS.*

Y-Branch

A Y-branch is a copper, fiber, steel or cast-iron pipe fitting. It joins straight run pipe with a branch that is entering at an angle. *SEE ALSO PIPE FITTINGS.*

You-Haul Concrete
[SEE TRANSIT MIX.]

Zebrawood

Zebrawood is a small tree that grows in the equatorial region of Western Africa. It reaches a height of about 65 feet and is no larger than 8 feet round.

Zebrawood has alternating yellow and brown stripes which give it its name. The sapwood does not have stripes. The leaves are compound, having 16 leaflets. The wood is heavy and hard. Zebrawood, because it is so colorful, must be used skillfully to achieve a tasteful effect. It is often used decoratively in shops and restaurants and on large furniture pieces. *SEE ALSO WOOD IDENTIFICATION.*

Zero Clearance Fireplaces

A little-known, essentially one-manufacturer product only a few years ago, the zero-clearance fireplace has come into its own during the decade of the 1970s.

The reason is simple: it installs like a stove yet looks the way a fireplace traditionally should. A zero-clearance fireplace is generally indistinguishable from a masonry fireplace built by the time-consuming methods developed over the centuries. It can be faced with brick, block, stone, tile, metal—or with plasterboard, hardboard or wood paneling as long as 6 inches of incombustible trim is used around the edge of the firebox.

Being so simple to install, a zero-clearance-unit fireplace naturally is economical to use; and it permits total flexibility in room arrangement since there are no foundation requirements to consider. It is about as easy to locate such a fireplace upstairs as down, in the center of a house as on an outer wall.

Yet a zero-clearance fireplace is a true wood-burner, handling all kinds of logs in the same way a masonry fireplace does. With its floor and back wall of fire proof ceramic material, it is not subject to possible burn-out, as a metal fireplace is. Most units come with firescreens of the familiar kind, and accessory grates, baskets and andirons work with them in the usual way. Although it used to be necessary to cut a hole through a sidewall of the unit if the owner desired to install a gas-fired kindler, units now commonly come with knockouts for this use.

Of course, trim materials will add something to the cost, whether obtained in kit form from the maker of the unit or chosen from among ordinary supplies. As with any wood-burning fireplace, there must be a fireproof hearth. Chimney sections in addition to those furnished with the unit will have to be bought if the house has an unusually high roofline or if the fireplace is to be installed downstairs in a two-story building.

The "zero-clearance" designation of these units means that they are so designed and insulated that they may be placed near combustible materials without requiring any clearance from them. In practice this means that you can place the unit directly onto a wooden floor or subfloor or onto a wooden raised platform if you wish to have a raised fireplace.

Wood framing to support the wall in front of the unit or to its sides can touch the metal unit with no fire danger, vastly simplifying the carpentry. Any clearance from combustibles required for the starter section of chimney is guaranteed by built-in metal flanges or fins; and the chimney sections themselves are held the necessary 1 inch from ceiling or roof by firestop spacers that are part of the package you buy.

The light weight of these units means that they are suitable for all types of room location. Since the whole fireplace, including chimney, weighs no more than an occupied sofa, there is no need of supporting it with reinforced framing or some kind of masonry foundation.

When it comes to placing your fireplace, you may—even with this unlimited freedom—prefer the traditional placement in the center of a wall. To do this push the unit against the wall, then cut out the ceiling (or ceilings) and roof to fit the spacers and chimney. When boxed in, the fireplace then becomes a rectangular wooden column with the room.

In some rooms, a fireplace in a corner may be the only feasible location. With this kind of location in mind, manufacturers make most zero-clearance units with back corners cut off or sides tapered so that they will fit closely into a corner. For a fireplace located on a corner that juts into a room, a special unit that is open on right or left side—you must specify which in ordering—is now made.

A final basic decision you will want to make before ordering a zero-clearance unit is how high you want to place it. A raised fireplace, commonly a foot or a foot and a half above the floor is easier to tend.

Choosing and using facing, trim and hearth material can be done either of two ways. You can do the whole job with masonry or synthetic masonry units of any type light enough in weight to be supported by the framing available. Assuming you are not using one of the types that can burn, you will have no further problems.

If you choose facing-plus-trim treatment (also shown in some of the illustrations) you will need only enough noncombustible material to make a hearth and trim. Trim kits of marble, black glass, noncombustible imitation masonry and the like are available from dealers selling the fireplace units or you can use such ordinary building materials as brick or stone or ceramic tile.

Instructions with your unit will tell you precisely what is permitted, but the usual safety requirement for trim around the firebox is that it must be at least 5 inches wide at the sides and 6 inches wide above the opening. Ordinary ceramic tile, cemented on, is an easy and decorative way to

Courtesy of Martin Industries

One of the easiest ways to design a fireplace with modern zero-clearance units is to place it within the room, surround it with masonry and use space at the sides for built-in desk and buffet.

satisfy this requirement. The same material can form a hearth, for which a common specification is that it should be at least 16 inches wide and extend at least 8 inches on each side of the opening. Making it a little bigger (using three rows of 6-inch tiles, for example) adds a margin of safety and usually improves the appearance as well. For a full facing job with the appearance of traditional heavy masonry, cast masonry units resembling stone have come into widespread use.

Zig-Zag Rule

Actually a trademark of Stanley Tools, zig-zag rule is a term often applied to spring-joint folding rules in general. Introduced in the United States about 1899, this rule gets its name from the manner in which it is opened and closed. It is, in its simplest form, about 7 ½'' long folded, 6' long extended, with all section corners except the shorter ones rounded to reduce wear on work clothes pockets. *SEE ALSO HAND TOOLS.*

Zone Heating Systems

A zone heating system provides heat only where it is needed. If one section of the house is warm enough, the heat will be blocked from that zone.

This type of heating system is possible in forced-air or hydronic systems. A thermostat is placed in each zone. No matter how many zones a house has, different temperatures may be maintained in each. Supply pipe valves that are electrically operated control the heat flow in a hydronic system. If the house has a forced warm air system, heat is blocked or released by shutters in the ducts. The shutters are electrically operated.

Split-level homes often require a zone system. The heat drifts upward, causing more heat to be needed only on the lower level. A zone system can provide this heat while not causing the temperature of the top level to increase. *SEE ALSO HEATING SYSTEMS.*